SOCIAL MOVEMENTS

Perspectives and Issues

Steven M. Buechler
Mankato State University

F. Kurt Cylke, Jr.
State University of New York at Geneseo

MAYFIELD PUBLISHING COMPANY
Mountain View, California
London • Toronto

Library of Congress Cataloging-in-Publication Data
Social movements : perspectives and issues / [edited by] Steven M.
  Buechler, F. Kurt Cylke, Jr.
      p.   cm.
  Includes bibliographical references.
  ISBN 1-55934-569-1
  1. Social movements.   2. Social change.   3. Group identity.
  I. Buechler, Steven M.   II. Cylke, F. Kurt.
  HM131.S5883   1996
  303.48′4—dc20   96-7995
                                                                                               CIP

Manufactured in the United States of America

10   9   8   7   6   5   4   3   2   1

Mayfield Publishing Company
1280 Villa Street
Mountain View, California 94041

Sponsoring editor, Serina Beauparlant; production, Publication Services; copyeditor, Jim Evans; art director and cover designer, Jeanne M. Schreiber; text designers, Linda M. Robertson and Dorothy Evans; manufacturing manager, Randy Hurst. The text was set in 10/12 Book Antiqua by Publication Services and printed on 45# Ecolocote by Malloy Lithographing, Inc.

Cover image: Wassily Kandinsky. *Accent en rose.* 1926. Paris, Musée National d'Art Moderne. Giraudon/Art Resource, NY. By permission.

 This book is printed on acid-free, recycled paper.

Preface

The master's tools will never dismantle the master's house

—Audre Lorde

One of the most exciting classes offered at most colleges is the course on social movements. The study of social movements is the study of dreams fulfilled and unfulfilled. In the context of social movements almost anything is possible or at the very least worth considering. There are no formal rules or binding legal constraints on social movements. Movements are about changing the rules, frequently by breaking the rules. In a world in which large bureaucratic structures and forces of international capital increasingly dominate virtually every aspect of our lives, it is refreshing and exciting to explore the processes by which many of our fellow citizens step outside their daily routines and demand change, refusing to take "no" for an answer. Social movements are filled with the emotions of life. Movements are filled with great tension and anxiety as activists engage in acts of civil disobedience. There are moments of joy and happiness when small victories are won. As in other aspects of life, there are often moments of intense sorrow when activists are assaulted, killed, or jailed. This volume seeks to make sense out of a seemingly chaotic process of demands for change. To this end, the best of what sociology has to offer has been compiled.

Many have contributed to the production of this book. In particular, we are indebted to Serina Beauparlant of Mayfield Publishing without whose vision and encouragement this book never would have materialized. We were fortunate to have the assistance of a number of people in compiling this volume, and we wish to pay special thanks to them now. In addition to Sarah Harrington, Case Cullen, Nicole Montanga, and Anna Kowalchuk, we are indebted to the reviewers of early drafts whose many suggestions and criticisms helped us construct the final version. These colleagues are Gary Brock, Southwest Missouri State University; Charles Hunt, University of Utah; Valerie Jenness, Washington State University; Robert Kleidman, Cleveland State University; Clarence Lo, University of Missouri at Columbia; John McCarthy, Catholic University of America; Suzanne Staggenborg, McGill University; Randy Stoecker, University of Toledo; Verta Taylor, Ohio State University; and Carol Wharton, University of Richmond.

Social movements represent hope for a better future. Because this book is fundamentally about people passionately fighting for social change, it is appropriate to thank the millions of activists who, despite great personal risk, continue to fight for their beliefs.

Contents

CONTEMPORARY APPROACHES: RESOURCE MOBILIZATION

CONTEMPORARY APPROACHES: SOCIAL CONSTRUCTIONISM

CONTEMPORARY APPROACHES: NEW SOCIAL MOVEMENTS

Part III   Movement Issues   320

MOBILIZATION OBSTACLES

ORGANIZATIONAL DYNAMICS

CONTINUITY AND CYCLES

CULTURE AND COLLECTIVE IDENTITY

FUTURE SCENARIOS

About the Contributors

Robert D. Benford (Readings #14 and #28) is an associate professor at the University of Nebraska at Lincoln. He established a chapter of Nebraskans for Peace on the UNL campus and co-founded a gun-free zone movement there as well. He attributes his initial interest in social movement "framing" to Ronald Reagan's election, an election that confirmed that style was more important than substance.

Steven M. Buechler (Readings #13 and #19) is a professor of sociology at Mankato State University. He is the author of numerous books and articles, including *Women's Movements in the United States: Woman Suffrage, Equal Rights and Beyond* (Rutgers, 1990) and *The Transformation of the Woman Suffrage Movement: The Case of Illinois, 1850–1920* (Rutgers, 1986).

Herbert Blumer (Reading #5) spent most of his professional career at the University of Chicago and the University of California at Berkeley. Blumer established symbolic interactionism as a major sociological perspective in American sociology.

Richard A. Cloward (Reading #20) is an internationally known author/activist. He has long been associated with grassroots movements of the poor.

Randall Collins (Reading #1) became a sociologist during the civil rights and anti-war movements of the 1960s. He switched from psychology to sociology because it seemed more relevant and more interesting. Since that time he has worked on topics in social conflict (such as the downfall of the Soviet Union) and on long-term social change (such as the rise of capitalism in Japan and the downfall of education in the United States).

Friedrich Engels (1820–1895) (Reading #4) was born in Barmen, Germany. He and Karl Marx co-authored numerous works, including *The Manifesto of the Communist Party* (1848), from which an excerpt is included in this volume.

Ron Eyerman (Reading #16) is a lecturer in the department of sociology at the University of Lund. He is the co-author of *Social Movements: A Cognitive Approach* and co-author of *The Making of the New Environmental Consciousness*, with Andrew Jamison and Jacqeline Cramer.

Richard Flacks (Reading #3) is a professor of sociology at the University of California at Santa Barbara. As a graduate student, he participated in the founding of Students for a Democratic Society—the leading organization of the white new left. He did path-breaking research on the family backgrounds and socialization of student activists; among his many writings on the student movement of the sixties is the book, *Youth and Social Change*. His study, with Jack Whalen, of the political fate of the sixties generation is described in their book, *Beyond the Barricades*. The article reprinted here continues his long-term effort to understand the potentials for radical democratic movement in the United States (an effort discussed in his book, *Making History: The American Left and the American Mind*).

William A. Gamson (Readings #15 and #30) co-directs the Media Research and Action Project (MRAP) at Boston College. MRAP works with social movement activists, running workshops and consulting with them on the best way to get access to the mass media and the best way of getting their message across when they talk to journalists.

James A. Geschwender (Reading #7) is a professor of sociology at State University of New York at Binghamton. He has served as both a scholar and an artist. In addition to having written a great deal about racial/ethnic stratification and movements for change, he was an active participant in change-oriented movements in locations as diverse as Tallahassee, Florida; London, Ontario; and Honolulu, Hawaii.

Joseph R. Gusfield (Reading #18) is a long-time member of the faculty of the University of California at San Diego. His research on the temperance movement is embodied in his classic work, *Symbolic Crusade*.

Andrew Jamison (Reading #16) is a lecturer in the department of sociology at the University of Lund. He is the co-author of *Social Movements: A Cognitive Approach* and co-author of *The Making of the New Environmental Consciousness* with Ron Eyerman and Jacqueline Cramer.

Hank Johnston (Reading #18) teaches at San Diego State University. He was a Peace Corps volunteer in Venezuela for two years and traveled extensively in Colombia, Equador, Peru, and Bolivia, and all through Central America. Professor Johnston has studied social movements in Catalonia and the Basque region in Spain and most recently in Estonia. He is the founding editor of *Mobilization: An International Journal*, a journal of research and theory about social movement protest and collective behavior.

Bert Klandermans (Reading #21) is a professor of Applied Social Psychology at the Free University, Amsterdam, The Netherlands. He has devoted much of his academic work to the study of participation in social movements such as the labor movement, the women's movement, and the peace movement. Currently he is involved in research on farmers' protest in the Netherlands and Spain, political protest in South Africa, and right-wing activism in Europe.

Lewis M. Killian (Reading #9) is professor emeritus at the University of Massachusetts at Amherst and faculty associate at the University of West Florida. His research interests include race, ethnic, and minority relations and collective behavior. He has authored numerous books and articles including the classic textbook, *Collective Behavior* (with Ralph H. Turner).

William Kornhauser (Reading #6) spent most of his professional career as a professor at the University of California at Berkeley. He is the author of numerous books, including *The Politics of Mass Society*.

Enrique Laraña (Reading #18) is a professor of sociology at the University of Madrid. He is the co-editor (with H. Johnston and J. Gusfield) of *New Social Movements*.

Seymour Martin Lipset (Reading #23) is a Senior Fellow at the Hoover Institution and the Hazel Professor of Public Policy at the Institute of Public Policy at George Mason University. His major work is in the fields of political sociology, trade union organization, social stratification, public opinion, and the sociology of intellectual life. He has also written extensively about the conditions for democracy in comparative perspective. His two most recent books are (with Earl Raab) *Jews and the New American Scene* (1995) and *American Exceptionalism: A Double-Edged Sword* (1996).

Gary T. Marx (Reading #22) is the author of *Undercover: Police Surveillance in America* and other works. He became interested in the topic of his article as a result of his experience as an activist in a civil rights group.

Karl Marx (1818–1883) (Reading #4) was born in Trier in the Prussian Rhineland. He was a prodigy, receiving his doctorate in philosophy from the University of Jena at the age of 23. He and Friedrich Engels co-authored numerous works, including *The Manifesto of the Communist Party* (1848), from which an excerpt is included in this volume.

Doug McAdam (Readings #10, #12, and #29) teaches sociology at the University of Arizona in Tucson. His research on the civil rights movement includes *Political Process and the Development of Black Insurgency* (1982) and *Freedom Summer* (1988). When he is not "pushing back the frontiers of science," he enjoys playing basketball, exploring Anasazi ruins, and backpacking with his wife and two daughters.

John D. McCarthy (Reading #11) continues his study of collective action that began with his undergraduate involvement in the Student Peace Union's campaign against nuclear testing. His projects have included how both the movement against drunk driving and community organizations mobilize citizens, the dynamics of public protest in Washington, D.C. in the post-Vietnam War era, and a comparison of the dynamics of public protest in Germany and the United States in the post-WWII period. He is presently Ordinary Professor of Sociology and Member of the Life Cycle Institute at the Catholic University of America in Washington, D.C.

Alberto Melucci (Reading #17) is a professor of cultural sociology at Milan University. He has authored more than ten books and numerous articles on social movements, cultural change, and collective identity. Among his many books available in English is *Nomads of the Present: Social Movements and Individual Needs in Contemporary Society*.

Aldon D. Morris (Reading #24), professor and chair of the department of sociology at Northwestern University, states: "Sociologists study and generate knowledge about the human condition. Which aspect of the human condition a sociologist studies is crucially influenced by that person's own life experiences. It is not by happenstance that I study social movements generally and the American Civil Rights Movement (CRM) in particular. Even as a young African-American, I realized that social inequality had devastating consequences for members of my community. The CRM caught my attention instantly because I recognized it as a force capable of transforming American race relations. I continue to study social movements because they are intricately linked to the possibility of democracy throughout the world."

Tahi L. Mottl (Reading #25) is author of the classic statement on counter movements, *The Analysis of Countermovements*. His research interests include race, ethnicity, collective behavior, and social movements.

Frances Fox Piven (Reading #20) has been a political activist since the 1960s, when she worked with the welfare rights movement. More recently, she has been a major actor in the effort to reduce barriers to voter registration that culminated in the "motor voter" act. She is also a professor at the Graduate School of the City University of New York, where she teaches political science and sociology. She is the author of many books on social movements, electoral politics, and welfare policy, including *Regulating the Poor* and *Poor Peoples' Movements*, both co-authored with Richard A. Cloward.

Dirk Oegema (Reading #21) teaches in the department of political science of the Free University in Amsterdam. His current research includes an analysis of the conflict between

Greenpeace and Shell about the Brent Spar as presented in the Dutch, German, and English Media. He is also studying the effects of daily media content (television and newspapers, text and images) on party preferences in the 1994 elections in the Netherlands and Germany.

E. Burke Rochford, Jr., (Reading #14) is a professor of sociology and anthropology at Middlebury College in Vermont. For the past twenty years he has conducted research on the Hare Krishna movement in North America and worldwide. In addition to his book *Hare Krishna in America* (Rutgers University Press, 1985), he has written numerous articles on the movement. He is presently writing a book on the family, the second generation, and the cultural development of the movement. Professor Rochford serves on the movement's North American Board of Education and is working on various projects to help improve educational opportunities for Krishna young people.

Neil J. Smelser (Reading #8) received his Ph.D. in sociology from Harvard University and was professor of sociology at the University of California at Berkeley. In 1994 he retired to take up the directorship of the Center for Advanced Study in the Behavioral Sciences. His main areas of research are social theory, economic sociology, social movements, social change, and the sociology of education. His ambition in writing *Theory of Collective Behavior* was to develop a general theory of collective behavior and social movements that included both the social-psychological and social-structural approaches to the subject matter.

Jackie Smith (Reading #33) is a researcher at the Kroc Institute for International Peace Studies at the University of Notre Dame. Her interest in international social movements was inspired through her participation in the peace movement during the 1980s and through her experience as an exchange student in China during the 1989 pro-democracy movement. Her current research focuses on transnational efforts to influence international environmental and human rights policy and the factors that influence social movement effectiveness.

David A. Snow (Readings #14 and #28) is professor and chair of the department of sociology at the University of Arizona in Tucson. He is the author or co-author of more than 50 articles and chapters on a range of topics, including homelessness, social movements, religious cults and conversion, and qualitative methods. He also is the author of a number of books, including *Down on Their Luck: A Study of Homeless Street People*, which was co-written with Leon Anderson and has received several scholarly achievement awards.

Sidney Tarrow (Readings #27 and #34) teaches government and sociology at Cornell University. His first movement experiences were as part of the Berkeley student movement and the peasant movement in Southern Italy. He has studied contentious politics in Italy and France, cycles of protest, and democratization movements. He is currently a member of the Mellon Foundation Research Group on Contentious Politics.

Verta Taylor (Readings #26 and #31) teaches sociology at the Ohio State University, where she has won numerous teaching awards. She is co-author (with Leila J. Rupp) of *Survival in the Doldrums: The American Women's Rights Movement, 1945 to the 1960's*, and co-editor (with Laurel Richardson) of *Feminist Frontiers* (now in its fifth edition). She has published numerous articles and chapters on women's movements, lesbian feminism, and social movement theory. She has recently completed a book on gender, women's self-help movements, and the meaning of modern feminism entitled *Rock-a-by Baby: Gender, Self-Help, and Postpartum Depression*.

Ralph H. Turner (Reading #9) is a professor of sociology at the University of California at Los Angeles. He has written numerous books on social psychology and collective behavior including the classic textbook, *Collective Behavior* (with Lewis M. Killian).

Nancy E. Whittier (Reading #31) is an assistant professor of sociology at Smith College. Her research has focused on the women's movement and the gay and lesbian rights movement. Her most recent book is *Feminist Generation: The Persistance of the Radical Women's Movement* (Temple, 1995).

Steven K. Worden (Reading #14) is an associate professor at the University of Arkansas. His main research interest is in applying symbolic interaction theory to the ethnographic study of unfashionable social worlds, including those of pigeon racing, cockfighting, and small-town Salvation Army rescue missions.

Mayer N. Zald (Readings #11 and #32) is a professor of sociology, social work, and business administration at the University of Michigan. He has written widely on social movements, organizational theory, and the relationship of social science to the humanities. Most recently, he led a year-long seminar dealing with social movements and social change in a globalizing world.

Howard Zinn (Reading #2) is a historian and playwright. He is the author of numerous books, including *A People's History of the United States*. During his active teaching career he taught at Spelman College in Atlanta, Georgia. He is a long-time member of the faculty at Boston University.

Introduction
Social Movements and Social Change

. . . while there is a lower class, I am in it;
while there is a criminal element, I am of it;
while there is a soul in prison, I am not
free.

—EUGENE DEBS

Social movements are one of the most exciting topics for sociological inquiry. By their
nature, social movements challenge various
aspects of society and are frequently on the
fringes of what many people view as acceptable political and social behavior. Despite
the vital role of social movements in shaping
our society, many Americans have limited
knowledge and many prejudices about
social movements and their participants. We
often hear reporters, politicians, and even
our friends dismiss social activists as cra-
zies, fanatics, or extremists. It is also not
uncommon to hear activists derisively
referred to as throwbacks to the 1960s,
implying that the social movements of the
1960s were somehow foolish. To engage in
acts of civil disobedience or to be arrested in
the name of a cause is often seen as being
somehow un-American. Such interpretations imply that no sane, responsible citizen
would engage in certain types of social
protests. Unfortunately, such statements
allow us to dismiss the goals of social
activists, deny the legitimate grievances of
many movements, and obscure the impact
of activism in shaping our present society.

To truly understand social movements,
we need to suspend our personal beliefs
about the rightness or wrongness of specific
movements. While we may not agree with
the goals and actions of right-wing citizen
militias, environmentalists, animal rights

advocates, feminists, or any of the dozens of
other social movements found in the contemporary United States, dismissing them
as morally objectionable, wrongheaded, or
bizarre precludes a sociological understanding of their multifaceted impacts on
American life.

Developing such an understanding of
individuals working together to change
society (while oftentimes breaking laws or
other social norms) requires a variety of
sociological tools. First and foremost, understanding movements necessitates coming to
terms with power relations in society.
Modern industrial societies are characterized by significant levels of political and
economic inequality, violence, and corruption. Class-, race-, and gender-based discrimination are among the more prominent
manifestations of power relations but are by
no means the only source of structured
inequality found in contemporary society.
Acknowledging these problems gives rise to
numerous sociological questions. Whose
interests are being served by the status quo?
What are people doing about these problems? Why do some people participate in
movements and others do not? Why do
some movements become violent? Why are
some movements successful and others less
so? The number of questions about social
movements is limited only by one's sociological imagination.

Fortunately, sociologists who study
social movements have made significant
advances in understanding many aspects of
movements. In addition to documenting
specific movements, some of the best minds
in the discipline are actively researching

social movements. Indeed, theoretical advances have occurred with increasing frequency over the past two decades. As the twentieth century draws to a close, sociology is uniquely equipped to explain many of the complexities of social movements. There has probably never been a more exciting time in the sociology of social movements.

This reader is designed to be used in sociology courses on social movements. As such, this reader breaks with the tradition of merging collective behavior (fads, panics, rumors, etc.) and social movements. Our emphasis reflects trends in the discipline. At one time, social movements were studied alongside more traditional forms of collective behavior. However, since the early 1970s, the sociological analysis of social movements has rapidly developed its own theoretical orientation and literature. To do justice to this ever growing literature, the emphasis here is almost exclusively on social movements.

We recognize that most students have little exposure to the rich history of social movement activity in the United States. Most public education has done students, and our society, a grave disservice by failing to fully expose them to the rich drama of social conflict, which spans the entire course of human history in North America. Numerous observers of public education have commented that history and social studies books tend to gloss over conflict, favoring a generic narrative in which our great nation (i.e., the federal government) has overcome a series of unfortunate challenges only to become an even greater nation. Such a simplistic notion of progress does not equip students to understand contemporary movements, and it robs them of knowledge about the hard work, sorrow, and loss of life experienced by activists who believed they were struggling to make America a more humane and decent society. America has a long and proud history of

average citizens who were genuinely committed to the belief that the goals of various social movements were worth fighting and dying for.

One of the primary purposes of this reader is to demonstrate that social movements continue to represent central mechanisms for social change (see Table 1). Additionally, this book provides students with the sociological tools necessary to critically evaluate contemporary movements and movement activity. To this end, thirty-four articles have been selected and organized into three parts.

The first part, "The Significance of Social Movements," analyzes both the centrality of social movements in shaping American society and the importance of political and economic structures in understanding social relations. The readings in this section focus on three themes: (1) the normative nature and principle sources of social conflict, (2) the role of social movements in the foundation of the American Republic, and (3) trends in American movements since the 1960s. Taken as a whole, these readings underscore the dialectical relationship between ongoing structural inequality, social movements, and the shape of contemporary society.

The second part, "Theoretical Foundations," presents the sociological tools (theory) applicable to the analysis of social movements. This section is divided into traditional and contemporary approaches. The traditional approaches treat social movements as one of a variety of forms of collective behavior. With a few exceptions, collective behavior approaches share a stereotypical view of movement participants as dangerous and irrational individuals responding to a variety of social stresses. Contemporary approaches, emerging in the 1970s and early 1980s, break with the tradition of viewing movements and participants as pathological by emphasizing the rational

TABLE 1.   A Partial List of Modern American Social Movements

Civil Rights movement	Black Power movement
Women's movement	Anti-Bussing movement
Anti-Apartheid movement	Women's Health movement
Zero Population Growth movement	Women's Suffrage movement
American Indian movement	Pro-Choice (Abortion) movement
Anti-Abortion movement	Labor movement
Equal Rights Amendment movement	Anti-ERA movement
Men's Liberation movement	Homosexual Rights movement
New Right movement	Environmental movement
Anti-Nuclear Weapons movement	Peace movement
Anti-War movement	Anti-Nuclear Power movement
Animal Rights movement	Temperance movement
Anti-Drug movement	Anti-Drinking and Driving movement
Anti-Smoking movement	Marijuana Legalization movement
Anti-Pornography movement	Farm Workers movement
Student movement	Free Speech movement
Draft Resistance movement	Welfare Rights movement
Sanctuary movement	Tenants Rights movement
Utopian movements (e.g., Oneida)	Religious movements (e.g., Moral Majority)
White Supremacy movements	Community Organization movement
Consumer's movement	Puerto Rico Liberation movement
Anti-Environmental movement	Prostitute's Rights movement

aspects of movements. More recently, theorists have focused attention on the social construction of grievances and the collective identities of movement participants.

The third part, "Movement Issues," offers insight into more specific issues confronting social movements. The readings in Part Three focus on important concerns about mobilization obstacles, organizational dynamics, culture and collective identity, and issues of continuity and cycles. We thereby hope to show the usefulness of sociological theory for understanding and explaining events in the "real world." Part Three ends with a speculative section on the future of social movements in modern society.

In C. Wright Mill's classic formulation, the sociological imagination involves seeing the connections between broad social structures, emerging historical moments, and prevailing individual biographies. This prescription for understanding the social world has a particular relevance in the case of collective action. Social movements provide some of sociology's most exciting dramas, in which individuals come together at a certain historical moment to change the structure of society. Such dramas have profoundly shaped our present world, and they will play an increasingly important role in shaping our future world. A broader sociological understanding of these dramas holds the promise of a more informed citizenry, a more active democracy, and a more equitable society. We hope this volume can contribute to these ends.

PART I
The Significance of Social Movements

That to secure these rights, Governments are instituted among men, deriving their just powers from the consent of the governed, that whenever any form of Government becomes destructive of these ends, it is the right of the people to alter or abolish it and to institute a new government.

—DECLARATION OF INDEPENDENCE, 1776

The history of the United States contains some of the most fascinating stories in human history. Since the first humans settled North America, a continuous series of intense moral, political, and economic struggles to determine the nature of society have occurred. There are no "good old days" in which life was simple and free of serious conflict. There is no era in our past in which universal consensus dominated public life. That conflict has always been a part of American society does not necessarily imply a pathological component of American culture. All societies contain conflict. Moreover, all societies are inevitably in a constant state of change. The forces driving social change are complex and fascinating. Often social change is preceded by a technological innovation such as the invention of the steam engine, airplane, or telephone. It is also not uncommon for politicians and leaders of industry to initiate change. The magnitude of the changes that have occurred in the United States only begins to hint at the dramatic transformations that our society will experience in the twenty-first century.

For many Americans, social change seems beyond the control of the individual. Surely, most people have little influence over which technologies industry selects for development and production. Nor do most individuals exercise control over wars, trade deficits, real wages, inflation, or the unemployment rate. Yet, American society has been substantially shaped by ordinary individuals. Slavery did not just end, blacks were not simply "given" voting rights, and polluted rivers have not miraculously become clean. People made these changes happen through social conflict with others who opposed them. Such examples demonstrate that people are not merely passive bystanders in social life. Rather, individuals actively participate in re-creating and changing society. Indeed, individuals from humble working- and middle-class origins have profoundly influenced American society by forming and participating in social movements.

Like many other modern industrial societies, our federal and state governments are, to varying degrees of success, structured around democratic principles. The Constitution and its amendments provide formal access to public debate for a variety of Americans. One result of such access is that much of the political and social conflict that defines us as a society occurs within the context of normal political processes. However, formal democracy has not provided most Americans with substantive input into political decision making or protection from economic injustices. Hence, many citizens with moral, political, and economic grievances find themselves politically and economically disenfranchised. Although such disenfranchisement can lead to passive disengagement, it has also stimulated active participation in social movements. In the latter case, such participation has included everything from riots, bombings, strikes, and protest marches to direct action, civil disobedience, and letter writing campaigns.

The readings in Part One provide a foundation for understanding social conflict and the role social movements have played in shaping American society. In the first selection, Randall Collins provides an overview of the major theoretical approaches for understanding conflict in society. The general principles he draws from leading theorists offer useful insights into the relationship between conflict and social change.

In the second section, Howard Zinn focuses attention on political and economic discontent in eighteenth century America. This broad historical perspective allows us to compare present-day conflicts to those of the past and to detect patterns of conflict and change. Dismissing popular beliefs about a unified effort on the part of American colonists to overthrow British rule, Zinn explores the complex nature of class- and race-based conflict in colonial America. Rather than representing the formation of a democratic republic in which all citizens would have equal opportunity, Zinn reveals how the American Revolution provided political and economic advantages to an elite class. The exclusion of Indians, blacks, slaves, and women from political life laid the foundations for future grievances, ensuring that social conflict would emerge from this new social order.

The final reading provides an overview of the state of contemporary social movements and the political system in which they operate. Richard Flacks assesses major trends in social movements and American society and speculates about future possibilities. Flacks's central argument is that social movements arise and are revitalized when normal political processes fail. In light of current social trends, he concludes that social movements are situated to play an increasingly responsible role for the social future.

1

CONFLICT AND SOCIAL CHANGE

RANDALL COLLINS

Conflict theory began as a development from the Marxian tradition. On one side, there was an effort on the part of non-Marxists to develop a non-Marxian theory of conflict; on the other, revisions within Marxism led to the point where certain fundamental assumptions about the primacy of economics were replaced. Ultimately, both sides of conflict theory cut themselves adrift from the Marxian political program as well; modern conflict theory is "agnostic" on the question of socialism vs. capitalism, as it is on the desirability or necessity of revolution. It moves to a more detached level of analysis and a search for the general laws of society. Such principles, in turn, might be applied in support of various political ends, though there is a tendency for conflict theorists to support the liberal or left side of the political spectrum and to be critical of the abuses of power and property in modern society. But the basic thrust is toward understanding society as a system of conflicting interests, rather than taking sides with a particular economic class or promoting a particular kind of economic revolution.

Intellectually, this has proven to be a fruitful approach. The original strength of conflict theory is as a theory of social change, stratification, and large-scale organization. Moreover, conflict theory is per-

haps the prime area in sociological theory where general theoretical principles are fairly well buttressed by empirical research. Current conflict theory is able to make contact with micro theories and micro research on interaction, cognition, and emotion in everyday life. It has a detailed program for establishing the micro-macro connection and has a branch showing how conflicting interests also operate on the level of micro interaction.

As conflict theory has broadened, its name has become somewhat misleading. Initially it began as a theory of conflict itself, considering the causes and consequences of conflict and engaging in a polemic with functionalist theory over the question of which has primacy, conflict or social order. But conflict theory is not merely about the occasions when conflict breaks out, nor merely about social change. It is also concerned with explaining social stability because it aims to be a general theory of society. Where it differs from the traditional functionalist concerns is that it sees social order as the product of contending interests and the resources groups have for dominating one another and negotiating alliances and coalitions. Its basic focus has become not overt conflict, but (in Dahrendorf's terms) *latent conflict*; it deals with social order as domination and negotiation. For this reason, conflict theory is not surprised by sudden upheavals and changes in times of war or revolution. It expects this pattern of movement, because it sees social order as maintained by forces of domination which cling to the status quo and attempt to legitimate it by traditional ideals; but this leaves tremendous stores of social energy locked up in latent opposition, capable of being suddenly released by a catalytic event.

This is not to say that everyone is in conflict with everyone else all the time. Society may be something of an ongoing war, but it is not a war of all against all. One reason, as we shall see, is that conflict tends to limit itself. Conflict is a form of social organization, mainly carried out by groups rather than by individuals. How then are groups organized? How do they maintain the internal solidarity which is a crucial weapon in imposing their interests on one another? The answer to this takes us into certain aspects of micro theory, and especially into the Durkheimian/Goffmanian tradition of social rituals which produce solidarity, moral sentiments and ideas. As we have seen, aspects of this Durkheimian tradition have been used by Parsons to bolster his argument for the primacy of values in society as a whole. I believe Parsons was correct to a certain extent, but that he was mistaken about the level of analysis at which the argument applies. Values are crucial for social integration, but this applies at the level of particular groups, rather than to the social system as a whole. Furthermore, value integration is a variable which can range empirically from low to high. Seen in this light, we can move forward to a stronger explanatory theory which shows the conditions and resources that actually produce moral sentiments and group symbols or ideologies.

Conflict thus becomes an *analytical* rather than a concrete category. It is part of a set of concepts, some of which come from theories for analyzing social order. The question is, how do they mesh together? Modern, multidimensional conflict theory is a strategy for building a complete and general sociological science. At the fundamental level, it does not ask whether something is good for society (which is what functionalism does) or bad for the members of society (which is the ultimate thrust of Marxism); but it asks the more fundamental questions, why are things as they are, what conditions produce them, and what conditions change them into something else? If we have such a theory, we will at last be in a position to know what we really *can* do about the shape of our society.

General Principles of Conflict

Simmel and Coser: Conflict and Social Integration

Modern conflict theory began early in the twentieth century with the work of Georg Simmel (1908), which was revived and systematized 50 years later by Lewis Coser (1956). Simmel's concern was to deal with conflict in abstract terms and, specifically, to show that conflict operates on a much more general level than the particular instance of Marxian class conflict. In fact, both Simmel and Coser (especially the former) were more conservative than the Marxists. They wished to show that conflict does not always (or even usually) lead to social change and that it can be the basis of social order. Coser even couched his argument in functionalist terms (the title of his book is *The Functions of Social Conflict*), as if to show that there is a functional need for conflict to support society. Let us see how much validity there is in these arguments.

Simmel's basic point is that conflict is not the opposite of social order. The opposite of order would be indifference or isolation; there would be no society only if people were in a condition of having nothing to do with one another. In other words, society does not automatically disappear because of conflicts among opposing interests. There are two alternatives, "fight or flight," and society ceases to exist only if the latter alternative is taken.

Conflict, in fact, is a rather intense form of interaction. Even in sheer physical terms, it is likely to bring people more closely together than normal nonconflictual social order. Think of an excited crowd in the streets or a riot or revolution, or the way in which a quarrel between two persons locks them together into matching each other's gestures and angry tone of voice as they trade insult for insult. It is only because we tend to put a value judgment upon peaceful interaction that we let it monopolize the term "social order." In fact, conflict is itself a very strong form of order in the structural and behavioral sense.

Nor does the conflict have to be overt for it to constitute a social structure. The Hindu caste system, Simmel observes, is a structure based precisely on a strong principle of repulsion among members of groups. Conflicting interests thus can shape people into the repetitive, enforced behaviors that make up a structure. By implication, any stratified social order will be largely structured by conflict.

Conflict Promotes Social Integration The Simmel/Coser theory offers a series of principles by which conflict leads to the integration of society. Such conflict can be either with external groups or within the group itself. Let us illustrate first with external conflict.

1. Conflict sharpens the sense of group boundaries and contributes to a feeling of group identity. Members of a nation never feel more clearly that they are Germans, French, Americans, Russians, (or whatever) as when they are at war with someone else. This holds for conflicts or contests of any sort between groups. For this reason, high school and college sports are so important as a source of community identification.

2. Conflict leads to a centralization of the internal structure of the group. In times of war, for example, the power of the government increases as people feel more willing to subordinate everything to the common effort. In smaller groups, the more external conflict there is, the more the group gathers around and gives power to a strong leader.

3. Conflict leads to a search for allies. Modern warfare between two states immediately sets both of them on the path to bringing other countries in as their allies. In primitive tribal societies, warfare was of great importance in this respect. Since these groups were usually geographically isolated and economically self-subsistent, it was only because of conflicts that they established bonds with their neighbours, usually in the form of exchanges of marriages. Conflict thus divides two groups, but on either side of the divide it results in an extension of the network of social ties, thus promoting more social organization than had existed in times of peace.

Simmel adds the curious point that one group even has an interest in maintaining the social existence of their enemy. For if external conflict is the only thing that holds one's own group together—say it is a tribe whose centralized leadership emerges only in times of war—then a complete victory and the destruction of the enemy means the destruction of one's own group as well. The implication seems to be that group leaders might try covertly to maintain their enemies. Certainly it is true in modern times that there is a covert alliance between the most militaristic factions in enemy countries: the huge arms budgets of both the United States and the [former] USSR depend[ed] upon both sides keeping up the conflict.

Do the same principles hold in internal conflict? Simmel and Coser do not systematically treat this as a separate question, but many of their examples refer to internal conflicts. Internally, conflict is between the group and some of its own members who serve as a scapegoat. In highly religious societies, such as those of late medieval Europe (or the American colonies), internal enemies were heretics or witches, and these societies gained a strong sense of their community identity and a reinforcement of defining values by gathering in the village square to watch a few lone individuals tortured or burned to death (Erikson, 1966; K. Thomas, 1971). In modern societies, the scapegoats tend to be ethnic and racial groups: the Jews who presumably contributed to the group identification of the anti-Semitic majority, and the blacks who held together the group boundaries of whites. Similarly, criminals and moral deviants—homosexuals, drug users, pornographers, gamblers—are functionally useful internal enemies, the struggle against whom contributes to the self-identity and moral solidarity of the "moral" majority. Empirical support of this relationship is found in our own time; for example, the scapegoating of women who have abortions is strongest among those who most closely identify themselves with society and its moral order in the traditional sense (Luker, 1983; Cavanaugh, 1986).

Thus, there does seem to be some truth in the principle that internal as well as external conflict contributes to group boundaries and social identity. In the case of internal conflict, however, the other two principles are dubious. It does not seem to be true that internal conflict necessarily leads to a centralization of social organization; much of the persecution of minorities and scapegoats is carried out at the "grass-roots" level, especially in small communities and by the lower-middle classes and below. Nor does the principle necessarily hold that internal conflict leads to an extension of networks through a search for allies. Moreover, there is a major flaw in the first principle. Simmel and Coser use examples only of small or even tiny minorities: a single old woman being burned as a witch, a handful of homosexuals, small minorities of Jews or blacks. Here we have got a one-sided persecution rather than a fully fledged conflict between two well-mobilized sides. Simmel and Coser avoid mention of class conflict, precisely because it is a more equal conflict among major groups. When both groups are large, it is less possible for one to monopolize the official definition of reality and to label the other as merely deviant. Empirically, too, it is doubtful whether two-sided internal conflict promotes social integration of the larger group in which it takes place. In fact, it would seem to be doing just the opposite. On this point the theory fails.[1]

The Self-Limitation of Conflict   Simmel and Coser argue on the more general level that conflict is not inherently destructive because it tends to limit itself. If both sides are aiming at the same object (say, control of the state or the economy), they nevertheless have an interest in limiting the conflict so that their mutual object is not destroyed (Simmel, 1908/1955: 27). In consequence, standards arise to restrict conflict so that it is reduced to a regular competition following rules of the contest: medieval warriors develop a code of honor, economic struggle becomes politically regulated, and the struggle for power turns into peaceful elections. Simmel even comments that a conflict group has an interest in maintaining the unity of its enemy; otherwise it would be hard to get a decisive victory. For instance, an army can win a war if it captures the enemy's capital city, but has a much harder time if it has to deal with disunified guerrillas spread out all over the countryside. The point gains some credence when we observe that business associations (such as in the auto industry) prefer to negotiate with a single union rather than deal separately with the less controllable mass of unruly local unions.

These examples show that there is some truth to the suggestion that conflicts tend to limit themselves. But it is only a partial truth. Simmel himself pointed out elsewhere in his works that a major way of winning is to "divide and conquer," to break the enemy's force by breaking his organization into mutually contending parts. Similarly, there are plenty of instances in which a conflict has gotten out of hand, and armies have ended up destroying the territory they were fighting to control. All-out nuclear war would clearly be an example of this sort. Again, the Simmel/Coser theory is not strong enough to state the conditions under which one or the other result might occur.

Subsequent research on the escalation and de-escalation of conflict helps clarify the issue (Kriesberg, 1982). Conflict escalates when the use of force or other sanctions by one side provokes a reprisal from the other, resulting in a continuously reinforcing spiral. The original issue widens to include grievances about subsequent reprisals; attitudes polarize and conflict grows. This is the opposite of the self-limitation of conflict. However, we may add that conflict does not always escalate, nor does the use of repressive force against a conflict group always lead to counterattacks. The empirical examples usually given (Kriesberg, 1982) refer to such cases as the use of violence by police against protesters in a civilian context, usually in a democracy; the result is to further outrage the protesters and to bring in allies who are similarly outraged. But extreme uses of repressive violence—for example, in an authoritarian state with a strong military—can end escalation by destroying opposition. The proper generalization would seem to be that counterforce leads to

an escalation of conflict when both sides have sufficient resources for continuing to mobilize. Bombing attacks on an enemy do not usually end a war as long as the enemy still has governmental control and the resources to fight on. Similarly, merely "punitive" strikes, such as those used against terrorists, do not sufficiently destroy resources and probably enhance group solidarity in the side under attack (as follows from the principles stated above).

But even when escalating processes do occur, conflicts always come to an end. De-escalating processes often set in after a passage of time. De-escalation involves the contraction of goals from demands for all-out (but usually symbolic) destruction of the enemy to realistic compromises; the fragmentation of issues, separating out points which can be settled piecemeal; and, as the result of these steps, a reduction in polarization (Kriesberg, 1982). The emotional arousal of intense conflict mobilization eventually becomes exhausted. Behind these processes, I would suggest, is a resource factor: the material costs of conflict eventually reduce the capacity for mobilization, and it becomes less and less possible to carry on conflict. A missing part of a comprehensive sociological theory is the time-laws which are involved in this process. In the case of wars, the time limit may be several years, depending on the level of destructiveness. (This refers to all-out modern wars, which usually last four years or less; lower levels of mobilization, as in guerrilla wars, can go on much longer.) In general, I would propose, the less expensive the conflict (that is, the less violent it is, and the more it depends on regular organizational resources rather than requiring the creation of special *ad hoc* conflict organizations), the longer it is possible for conflict to go on without de-escalation. At the opposite extreme, very destructive war ends itself even without de-escalation, simply by destroying the population or social organization. Thus, a modified version of the principle of the self-limitation of conflict says that conflict must stay at moderate levels beyond which it exhausts itself increasingly rapidly.[2]

Cross-Cutting Conflicts   The major principle of self-limiting conflict is known as the *pluralist theory,* of which Coser (1956) is principal advocate. If there is more than one conflict going on at the same time, and the groups involved have cross-cutting, overlapping boundaries, then conflict on one dimension will reduce conflict on other dimensions. For example, there is a division between workers and capitalists in modern society; but if this is cross-cut by racial divisions (some workers and some capitalists are both black and white), ethnic divisions (some of each are Anglo, Italian-American, Mexican, and so forth), religious divisions (Protestant, Catholic, Jewish), or gender division (male, female), then conflict will be reduced. We might call this the "grid-lock" model of social conflict: there is conflict in so many directions that no one dimension can become very intense. The reason is that any one individual is a member of several different conflict groups. If he is a white, Italian-American, Protestant worker, his class conflict with capitalists will be diminished by his conflict with blacks (many of whom are also workers), Catholics, women, and so forth.

The pluralistic model has given rise to a great deal of controversy. This is largely because it has been taken as a political doctrine, denying that any serious class conflict is possible in the United States. However, an important distinction must be made. The *theoretical* statement is that *if* there are cross-cutting group memberships, *then* conflict will be gridlocked into a low level of intensity. Most of the controversy has centered on a second question, the *empirical* issue of whether in fact *there really are such cross-cutting groups in the modern United States.* It is pointed out, for example, that the majority of blacks are members of the working class, and that religion may reinforce class, so that really there are only a few significant divisions, and pluralism *as a fact* may not be true.

The theoretical question is what is at issue here, however. Is the if–then relationship between cross-cutting groups and low intensity of conflict a reality? There is little research of a sufficiently comparative sort to bear on this theoretical question. But I think it can be said that the theory suffers from being framed mainly in order to show why class conflict is relatively slight in the United States. Class conflict is only one form of conflict; the if–then relationship posited in the theory says that cross-cutting groups should reduce conflict on *all* dimensions. If we look at the recent history of the United States (certainly, ethnically and religiously one of the most heterogeneous of modern societies), it is true that class conflict has been low. But the 1960s—not long after the pluralist theory was put forward—began with a period of intense and violent conflict between blacks and whites, followed by equally intense conflict between college-age youth and their elders over the Viet Nam war, followed by a very militant phase of conflict between females and males over women's rights. At a minimum, we would have to say that the pluralist theory is no use at all in predicting when and why such conflicts should break out. More abstractly, there must be a logical flaw in the theory, since it predicts a low intensity of conflict on *all* dimensions, not just in class conflict. It is also damaging to the theory that the various conflicts of the 1960s and 1970s not only did not diminish each other, but were actually linked together. The antiwar movement developed out of white activism in the Civil Rights (racial equality) movement, and the militant feminists organized out of participation in the antiwar movement. The pluralist model has not only empirical but theoretical problems, and needs considerable revision. (This is why pluralist theory has given way to resource mobilization theory and other newer models.)[3]

Dahrendorf: Power Groups and Conflict Mobilization

The German sociologist Ralf Dahrendorf writing at about the same time as Coser, made a further move toward generalizing a theory of conflict. Unlike Simmel and Coser, his aim was not to downplay Marxian class conflict, but to develop a theory which would revise Marx to account for the shape of modern society. Hence the title of his major book: *Class and Class Conflict in Industrial Society* (1959). The problem is the familiar one, which gave rise to other modern revisionist versions of Marxism. Dahrendorf's work marks the break from Marxism into conflict theory, however, since he went over the dividing line and became a true heretic of the Marxist tradition. The central concept in Marxian sociology is *property,* and the ownership of the means of production is seen as the basis of social class. Thus, conflicts are over property; they are structured into the economic system around the capitalists' search for profit to enhance and protect their property against the workers. In turn, the workers are subject to the labor market in order to stay alive. Dahrendorf took the fatal plunge and redefined class and class conflict so that it was no longer based on property but on *power.*

Class Divisions As Power Divisions   The main empirical problem confronting Marxism in the twentieth century, in Dahrendorf's view, is not that class conflict disappears, but that it appears where it should not be

and does not appear where it should. Strictly speaking, if we divide classes into property owners vs. non-property owners, then most white-collar employees would be members of the working class.[4] But in their voting patterns, social behavior, and personal identification, they act not as workers but as if they were members of the dominant class. Marxian theory has tended to treat this as the question of "false consciousness"; in empirical sociology, on the other hand, researchers have simply redefined class as if it were synonymous with manual vs. nonmanual employees. Empirically, this does seem to identify a main dividing line (Halle, 1984), but it is definitively contradictory to the Marxian definition of class. For that matter, even the top level managers, in so far as they do not own their companies but merely work as employees of the stockholders, should also count as workers. Why, then, do they act as if they were loyal capitalists?[5]

A related issue, especially important to a West German like Dahrendorf, is the fact that the socialist countries of Eastern Europe (such as East Germany) were themselves stratified. There have even been severe outbreaks of what looks like class conflict in these nations: a violent revolt in East Berlin in 1953, another in Hungary in 1956, the Russian invasion of Czechoslovakia to put down an insurrection in 1968, and the struggles of Polish labor unions against the socialist government in the early 1980s. It is difficult even to conceptualize such conflicts in Marxist terms, since socialist societies have no property, and hence, by definition, no classes.

Dahrendorf solves both problems regarding stratification in modern capitalist and socialist societies by redefining class. Wherever there is any organization in which some people have power, there is a division between those who give orders and those who have to take orders. Giving orders is pleasurable, and it is also the major means to acquiring wealth, prestige, material goods, and almost all other desirables. Taking orders is intrinsically unpleasurable, and the lack of power means that one will be less well off on other dimensions. Hence, power divides people into classes, order givers vs. order takers, and creates class conflict.

Marx is thus subsumed into a broader theory rather than disproven. In his day—the early 1800s—property was indeed the most visible form of power. Government agencies were virtually nonexistent, and businesses were run by their owners, who personally gave orders to their employees. Marx did not live long enough to see the bureaucratic corporation or the massive growth of government bureaucracy. Modern socialism is essentially rule by government bureaucracy, so that its classes and class conflicts become entirely those of sheer organizational power.

This aspect of Dahrendorf's theory is surely correct. It brings a mass of empirical evidence back into agreement with conflict theory. The research which shows the strongest divisions between manual and white-collar workers, and between particular sectors among them, shows that these divisions take place between those who take orders and those who give orders.[6] Goffmanian micro theory provides a solid foundation for these divisions in the processes of everyday life, and explains why order giving and order taking have very different cultural and behavioral effects. On the macro level, there is good evidence that power is a strong predictor of many other things, including the distribution of economic wealth. And in analyzing the current world scene, Dahrendorf's model is essential for understanding why there are conflicts such as those in Poland, which [are] no doubt latent in the USSR and other socialist states. For the Marxists, history comes to an end once socialism appears, since their theoretical apparatus, based on property classes, no longer applies. Dahrendorf reopens that large part of the world to theoretical analysis and enables us to ask such questions as, under what conditions would a revolution actually be possible in the Soviet Union?

The weakness in Dahrendorf's redefinition of class as power is that he tends to see all modern societies as being essentially the same. Organizationally, insofar as socialist and capitalist societies are both ruled by bureaucracies, the class structure and conflicts are analytically similar in both. However, Dahrendorf fails to pay enough attention to subtypes of power. Property remains a kind of power resource different from sheer bureaucratic or political party power; for one thing, it connects property holders through banks, stock markets, the monetary system, and hence market relationships, which are quite a different sort from the organizations found among the elite in a socialist society. In a sense, the ways in which power is organized under modern capitalism are more complex than under socialism; capitalism has both the bureaucratic power form and an additional form based on property. A theory of capitalism is still necessary, even in the modern era.

Overt Conflict Is Always Two-Sided If order givers vs. order takers is the basis of social conflict, how many social classes are there? Potentially, there could be a very large number. For one thing, there may be several different kinds of organizations in a society, so there can be power conflicts within government and its various agencies, the military, business corporations, philanthropic organizations, clubs, sports, churches—even within the home. Furthermore, in any large-scale organization, there are several levels of hierarchy: not only are there persons at the top who give orders and those at the bottom who take them, but there are levels in between which both give and take orders. Dahrendorf's model suggests that conflict might be very complex indeed.[7]

Dahrendorf's is a realistic view, leading to an organizational analysis in which society is made up of multiple lines of power conflict. It fits a multidimensional theory of class cultures, grounded both in micro theory and empirical evidence. But the identification of multiple lines of conflict does lead to a question about social change, and indeed whether conflict can actually break out. For as Simmel and Coser have argued, multiple lines of conflict may negate each other, draining off energy from one conflict into one dimension after another, and thus resulting in conflict gridlock and social stability rather than change. Dahrendorf also accepts that multiple cross-cutting conflicts may have this effect. But he does not see this as the main point of a theory of conflict, but only a particular arrangement of variables.

His more generalized point is that conflict may be latent or mobilized. *Quasi-groups,* in his terminology, are persons who share a similar position in one of the many possible lines of power conflict in a society. But they only become real *conflict groups* if they are mobilized into action. This overt conflict is always two-sided. Middle managers, say, might be latently in conflict with their superiors, who give them orders, as well as with their subordinates, who take orders from them. But they cannot overtly be in conflict with both at the same time. Conflict always boils down to two sides. Once it breaks out between two parties, the other parties must either stand aside as neutrals or join one side or the other.

This appears to be a structural necessity. Wars, for example, always take this two-sided pattern, even though they often involve more than two parties. Some conflicts, however, get put aside until one conflict is over. (For instance, in World War II, Japan, the Chinese nationalists and their allies, and the Chinese communists were mutual antagonists, but the latter pair made a tacit alliance until the Japanese were defeated, whereupon their own war started again.) Sports, which are controlled forms of conflict, virtually always have this two-sided structure; to understand why, imagine the chaos that would ensue if there were three basketball teams, or three football teams, playing at once.[8]

Dahrendorf's main deduction is that if conflict is two-sided, one side (the order takers) favors change and the other side (the order givers) favors stability. This leads to his conflict-based theory of social change. He neglects the fact that changes may be imposed "from the top," as has often been the case in "modernization," which Reinhard Bendix (1967, 1978) describes as a chain of emulation of more powerful states in the world arena by less powerful ones. Further, change does not happen merely because it is intended by some group; the process of conflict itself may result in a change in the structure, different from what either side intended.

Of greater theoretical importance is Dahrendorf's focus on the structure of relationships among latent and overt conflict groups. It is implicit in some of the classic analyses of the maneuvering among factions in revolutions (for instance, Marx's *Eighteenth Brumaire of Louis Bonaparte;* see my analysis in Collins, 1985: 76–78), and is central to theories of coalitions in parliamentary and electoral politics. To work out a fully explicit structural theory of overt conflict along these lines remains a major goal for sociology.

Conditions of Conflict Group Mobilization

Dahrendorf prefers to concentrate on the conditions that turn latent quasi-groups into mobilized conflict groups. There are three kinds of conditions:

1. *Technical conditions:* the presence of a leader and an ideology.
2. *Political conditions:* sufficient political freedom in the surrounding society to allow groups to organize themselves.
3. *Social conditions:* communication among group members, geographical concentration, and similar culture.

This third category of conditions is analytically identical to the conditions of political mobilization in the Marx-Engels model. The theory here has been elaborated under the rubric of "means of mental production" and "material means of mobilization," and leads to the *resource mobilization theory.*

The first and second conditions, however, are more dubious, or at least incomplete, as a general theory. In the second Dahrendorf is making the point that there will be more overt conflict in a democracy than in an authoritarian regime because political freedom allows it. But this begs a crucial question that a conflict theory must be able to face: what determines the amount of political freedom or authoritarianism in a state. A crucial type of conflict is precisely that which allows democratic revolutions to break through authoritarianism. Thus, although democracy may facilitate the mobilization of conflict groups, it cannot be necessary for any mobilization at all to occur. Marx's model seems more accurate here, stressing social conditions as more fundamental.

Similarly, technical conditions seem to be only an additional, incidental factor. I am inclined to believe, along with Marx, that leaders are produced by circumstances, not vice versa, and that sufficient social conditions for mobilization will produce both leaders and ideology.

Consequences of Conflict: Intensity, Violence, and Social Change Dahrendorf proposes two sets of principles about the nature and consequences of conflict, once it occurs. He distinguishes between first the *violence* of conflict—how much actual physical destruction there is (and relatedly, how much emotional hatred)—and second the *intensity* of conflict—how strongly rooted it is, how long it goes on. One of his major points is that conflict may be intense without being violent, as well as vice versa. A democracy, in his view, fosters a good deal of conflict, but it is not generally very violent conflict; in addition, he believes that it *may* not even be very intense. The former judgment may be more accurate than the latter.

(1a) *The better organized the conflict groups, the less violent the conflict;* (1b) *absolute deprivation* (physical abuse, starvation, poverty) *leads to more violent conflict, whereas relative deprivation* (having less than the higher classes) *leads to less violent conflict* (1c) *but the more violent the conflict, the more rapid the social change.* This is summarized in Figure 1.1.

Principle (1a) is probably correct. Dahrendorf draws his evidence from the history of labor unions, which began as violent, revolutionary movements when they were illegal, underground associations; but as they achieved recognition, acquired bureaucratic organization and a full-time staff of their own, they became part of the normal condition of society. Robert Michels (1911), writing about the transformation of the German socialist labor unions from Marxist revolutionaries into part of the Establishment, enunciated the so-called "Iron Law of Oligarchy" to refer to this conservatizing of leadership by its own bureaucratization. But it should be borne in mind that this process affects the violence of conflict and the desire for a radical social change. It does not affect the intensity of conflict, since labor unions exist precisely in order to carry on their demands over wages, working conditions, and so forth.

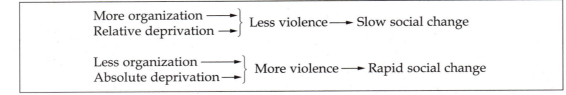

More organization ——→ ⎱
Relative deprivation ——→ ⎰ Less violence ——→ Slow social change

Less organization ——→ ⎱
Absolute deprivation ——→ ⎰ More violence ——→ Rapid social change

FIGURE 1.1

Institutionalizing conflict does not make it go away, but it does make it less violent and revolutionary. That, in fact, is Dahrendorf's advice about the extent to which conflict can be limited.

Principle (1b) does not appear to be correct. Dahrendorf offers no evidence for it, and it would seem from studies of revolutionary movements and riots (Tilly, 1978) that violent conflict does not break out where the lowest class is most oppressed, but where it has the resources to mobilize itself (compare my theory on the conditions of extreme violence, "Three Faces of Cruelty" in Collins, 1981).

Principle (1c) is also dubious. Dahrendorf appears to be thinking that a violent revolution is the fastest form of social change. But many violent transfers of political power (for example, South American revolutions, or the numerous changes of emperors in the later Roman Empire) produced no real social change at all. Violent riots also may be totally without effect, especially if the rioters are severely repressed. The Paris commune of 1871 was put down with over 20,000 dead; however, it did not result in a rapid change toward a socialist France but the opposite, the reimposition of bourgeois society. Violence, in fact, may be connected not with rapid, revolutionary change so much as with what Georges Sorel in his *Reflections on Violence* (1906) called a "myth"—the belief among the conflict group that they are fighting for a very high ideal. Sorel argued that violent conflict and its accompanying belief exist not

mainly for the social changes that are actually produced, but because of the solidarity they produce within the conflict group itself.[9]

(2a) *Where membership lines among contending power groups are superimposed, conflict is more intense;* however, *where such dividing lines are dissociated or cross-cutting, conflict is less intense.* Here Dahrendorf adopts the Simmel-Coser "pluralist" or "gridlock" theory, except that he makes explicit that these conditions refer to the intensity of conflict rather than its violence. The same criticisms of the validity of this theory (page 12) apply here. (2b) *The more intense the conflict, the more radical the social change:* that is to say, where groups are mobilized for a long, hard struggle, the end result is that society will be pervasively changed. Again, the principle of social change seems dubious. Dahrendorf offers no evidence for it, but seems to be deducing logically that stronger conflict forces will change society more than weak forces.

What Dahrendorf leaves out of both his principles of social change, (1c) and (2b), is any consideration of *who wins.* He baldly states that more intense or more violent conflict will produce social change of a pervasive or rapid sort. But if the conservative side wins, there may be no change at all, or possibly a change in the direction of building more repressive structures to preserve other structures (for example, to protect the property system, or the religious Establishment). There is also the possibility that neither side will win, but that conflict will go on at great length. This is a formula in which intense conflict leads to a complete blockage of any movement in the society. I would suggest that this is a major problem of democracies, since it mobilizes classes and other power groups, but enables them to neutralize each other. In short, Dahrendorf is probably correct that conflict has, at least potentially, something to do with social change, but the process is much more complex than his principles allow. On the face of it, only principle (1a) appears to be generally correct (and even that has exceptions, such as the fact that well-organized armies can produce more violence than less-organized ones; though it may well be true that well-organized groups have to overcome more inertia to get themselves into action). Dahrendorf opened the way to a conflict theory of social change, but the theory itself has to be built from elements found elsewhere.

Conflict Theory of Social Change

The conflict approach to social change analyzes social process in terms of the actors pursuing their interests and the resources they have relative to each other. This is a generalization of the Marx-Engels theory of class interests and the material conditions of political mobilization. However, interests are now broadened to include any kinds of interests and groups; and resources are broadened to include the social and symbolic resources that allow individuals to form into groups, both formal organizations and informal communities of consciousness. The theory, in other words, has become multidimensional. Ultimately, there can be a conflict theory of change in any aspect of society: economy, technology, demography, religion, intellectual life, or anything else. For

brevity, we will focus here on political change.

Weber's Theory of Politics

What should a theory of political change explain? A comprehensive theory should explain (1) the conditions under which various kinds of state structures (democracy, dictatorship, feudalism, centralized empires, and so forth) will emerge; (2) who the actors in the political drama will be—the lineup of groups who fight over power at any given time; (3) the kind of political events that will take place; and (4) who will win what in these struggles. A truly comprehensive theory of this sort has not been built, although some pieces of it exist. Notice that explaining changes in all these features is the same thing as explaining what structures, groups, and so forth will exist statically, at any given time; the static-comparative theory is just an outcome of the dynamic theory, since it is the dynamic processes that produce the "snapshots" that we may see if we stop the action at some point in time. We should notice, too, that a full theory of politics will overlap into many areas of sociology, the kinds of groups that take part, and the way they see the world, are the subject of stratification theory and class culture theory; while the organizational structure of the state will lead us to organization theory, and the processes of politics will lead into some versions of network theory. In a sense, the intellectual strategy of conflict theory is to look for the "political" side of everything—"organizational politics" in organizations, "family politics" in families, and so on.

The main focus of a theory of politics is the state. Weber (1922/1968) defined the state as an organization claiming a monopoly over the legitimate use of violence upon a given territory. There are three crucial elements in his definition: violence, legitimacy, and territory.

Violence   The state has a military foundation. Most states throughout history were formed by a military coalition, by military conquest or diplomatic annexation of other territories, or by revolution or splits within an already existing state.[10] Up until 1800 in Western Europe, states consisted of little more than an army (or even just a network for raising troops), and military expenses were by far the largest part of government expenses (Mann, 1986: 416–99). The bureaucratic apparatus of the state has developed, largely in the last few centuries, to collect taxes and supply the military. Once this bureaucracy was in existence, its uses could be extended to other forms of regulation—support for the economy, the supply of welfare, the provision of education, or the regulation of civilian life. But as Mann (1986) has shown, the modern state expanded from a military core, and it exercises control, ultimately, by backing up its commands with the threat of force. What makes something legally binding, rather than merely a private understanding, is the assumption that it will be enforced by the courts, the police, and other government officials; and the fact that their authority, if challenged, is ultimately backed up by the army. The power—and indeed the very existence—of a state depends on its military organization; for when a state loses all military power, it ceases to be a real state. The disintegration or defection of an army is always the final and decisive element in any revolution.

At the core of any state, then, is its military apparatus. Weber says that a state claims a monopoly over force; that is, it attempts to be the sole military organization for that area. This is an ideal type definition, which recognizes that states do not always succeed in this monopolization. Feudalism, for example, is a coalition of self-armed lords; the official coalition, based on the loyalty of lower lords to higher ones in a hierarchy culminating with the king, is theoretically a single military unit, but in practice it tends to undermine the monopoly of the means of violence. In a sense, feudalism is only a quasi-state. This definitional problem should not mislead us into believing that a Weberian approach cannot be used for feudalism. Politics is a dynamic struggle to build or maintain states; the full-fledged, force-monopolizing state is the goal of the centralizing faction, and the theory gives the conditions under which it succeeds or fails.

Legitimacy   Weber adds that the state aims not just at monopolizing force, but monopolizing legitimate force. Criminal violence may exist within a state, but the state is not challenged as long as that violence is regarded as illegitimate. Legitimacy is a claim that the use of force is proper, that it is procedurally and morally justified. Weber points out that a legitimate state can rule more easily than one relying on sheer terroristic coercion. People are more likely to obey orders willingly, or at least without resistance, if the state is regarded as legal or otherwise legitimate.[11]

This introduces a cultural element into Weber's multidimensional theory. However, we should not conclude that culture is a static or transcendental intrusion into the theory. The state is not simply determined by ideals. Legitimacy is caused by social conditions and rises and falls with changes in those conditions. In a little-known part of his theory, Weber (1922/1968: 901–10; also Collins, 1986: 145–66) points out that, historically, the state acquired legitimacy by forging a coalition to fight wars. The ideal of defense against external enemies (or in early conquest states, the ideal of conquering a new land for the people) is the crucial element in state legitimacy. As long as a state is able to carry out this successfully, it will be legitimate; when it ceases to have enough military power, its legitimacy disappears. Originally, this legitimacy was felt only by the warriors themselves; in a feudal society or patrimonial empire, the conquered peasants generally did not regard the state as legitimate, but as alien oppressors (Eberhard, 1965: 1–17). But since the peasants were unmobilized, their opinions did not count; the only feelings of legitimacy that were important were those among the nobility themselves. (And these feelings could shift from one ruling house to another in the interminable dynastic intrigues and wars of feudal-patrimonial states.) Weber traces the rise of modern mass legitimacy of the state to the creation of mass conscript armies, beginning in the 1700s and 1800s in Europe; only when all adult males were subject to fighting in their state's armies did the state acquire the modern "nationalist" sense of legitimacy.[12]

It is consistent with this theory that modern states began to create compulsory public education systems at the same time that they created modern mass armies (Collins, 1977; Ramirez and Boli–Bennett, 1982). Often it was the threat from military rivals which provided the immediate impulse to institute school reforms. Durkheim (1961), who was himself involved in building the French school system after the French had been defeated in the Franco-Prussian war of 1870–71, theorized that it would provide a secular basis for national solidarity; empirical studies on the effects of schools on childrens' political attitudes have proved him correct (Hess and Torney, 1967).

Weber's theory thus makes legitimacy into a dynamic process, rather than a static quality which all states possess. We might, in fact, define politics as the struggle for legitimacy. Politicians attempt to attach the feelings of state legitimacy to themselves while undermining the legitimacy of their opponents. There are several elements in such a theory. Weber gives us only the starting point. He argues that the legitimacy of a state (and hence of its leaders at a particular time) depends on its international power prestige. Populations of states which are strong vis-à-vis their neighbors have intense feelings of legitimacy (that is, in whatever population is actually politically mobilized). States which are weak, defeated in wars, or dramatically humiliated by their enemies lose legitimacy. There are several consequences of this. One is the importance of foreign affairs for the success or failure of politicians;[13] as a result, politicians are strongly motivated to make face-saving or prestige-enhancing gestures in foreign affairs (which is one of the dynamics producing international crises). Failure in foreign affairs reduces legitimacy; at an extreme, it is a major cause of revolution.[14]

International power prestige is the first and most important element in a state's legitimacy. Other sources of legitimacy can be added onto this. A state may gain or lose legitimacy, depending on how well its domestic economy is doing; ancient Chinese emperors could lose "the Mandate of Heaven" if the people were devastated by famine or flood, and modern politicians can lose office during an economic depression. Although the relative weights of these factors have not been measured, I would judge this a weaker determinant of legitimacy than sheer military strength. Traditional empires never fell merely because of natural disasters, but only if there was also a military crisis. Some types of states are more vulnerable to economic legitimacy processes than others; feudal states, which took no economic responsibility at all, were oblivious to them; the modern welfare state, in which a large proportion of the population is employed by the state itself, seems to be most vulnerable. But even in modern states, the most extreme shifts of legitimacy—revolutionary downfalls of the state—have never happened as the result of economic depressions, even severe ones, but have frequently occurred as the result of military strains or defeats.[15]

Finally, we should add that feelings of legitimacy persist for some time. A military defeat does not immediately destroy the legitimacy of the government. It may even increase it temporarily by motivating people to rally around their leaders (by actual participation in political rituals, or by an increase in the ritual density of the society. This is an application of the Simmel-Sorel principle that conflict produces solidarity, although it also adds limitations to it.) Even a conquest by alien forces may leave feelings of resistance alive, attached to the ideal of the no-longer-existing state. Though we have not measured this precisely, it appears that such lingering feelings of legitimacy for a particular state can survive for a few years, but not usually for more than a generation.[16] Eventually, success does breed legitimacy; whatever state maintains itself in power long enough will generate its own feelings of legitimacy, especially if it makes use of secondary ritual procedures (such as the indoctrination of a school system and the mass media).

Territory   The third element in the Weberian definition is that the state controls a given territory. This may seem obvious, but it suggests a crucial line for the development of explanatory theory. A successful state is usually one that controls a lot of territory, especially territory rich in population and resources. States lose power by losing territory. The history of states is to a large extent the history of wars in which territory is gained or lost. Organizationally, the form of the state was initially laid down by the structures for controlling and supplying an army, including raising taxes for its support.

Because power prestige is crucial for legitimacy, this same process has also determined the sense of national identity and the fate of politicians in the state. Wars account for much of the suddenness of change, for the jerky rather than smooth and evolutionary nature of human history.

Putting these three factors together, we can see that a basic theory of politics must include an explanation of the power of military organizations, of the territories they can defend, conquer, or lose, and hence of the resulting ups and downs of legitimacy of politicians inside a state.

Geopolitical Theory of the State

The following are some geopolitical principles of state power (from Collins, 1978, 1981; Stinchcombe, 1968: 218–30). They are based on an examination of historical evidence, including historical atlases, for the territories of Europe and China over the past 3,000 years.

1.0 Territorial Resource Advantage. States based upon the largest and wealthiest heartlands tend to dominate the smaller and poorer ones.

> **1.01** Larger and wealthier territories have greater population and production for a given territory. Hence they have larger armies, and defeat smaller states and expand at their expense.

2.0 Marchland Advantage. States with enemies on fewer sides are stronger than comparably sized states with enemies on more sides.

> **2.01** Therefore peripheral ("marchland") states are stronger than centrally located states. Peripheral states tend to capture territory over time, while centrally located states tend to lose territory. In a milder form, weak central states lose control of their military forces by becoming dependent "allies" of the stronger states.

3.0 Stable Balances of Power. Large, strong states meeting on opposite sides of a natural land barrier foster a stable buffer state on the barrier.

3.1 Unstable Balances of Power. Multisided balance of power among numerous states results in the long-term fragmentation of the middle states.

> **3.11** The militarily weaker position of interior states (because of 2.0) results in their loss of territory [and hence, from Weber's theory of legitimacy, internal circulation of elites].

> **3.12** Alliances with neighboring states split different internal factions within the interior states, fostering political fragmentation, internal struggle, or the tendency to break away and form separate, smaller states. Principles 3.1–3.12 then repeat.

4.0 Cumulative Resource Advantage. Larger, wealthier, and geographically peripheral states grow cumulatively larger over time, while their neighbors progressively diminish. This may also occur through the development of informal empires, in which weaker states are made to be allies of the stronger ones.

5.0 Cumulative Turning Points. Peripheral states (or alliance networks) grow cumulatively larger and wealthier, while their central neighbors become progressively smaller (from 4.0). Eventually all central states are swallowed up, and the large peripheral empires (or alliances) confront each other in a showdown war [unless a natural barrier exists, within which a buffer state is fostered, as in 3.0].

> **5.01** Major wars occur at cumulative turning points, characterized by an unusually high degree of military mobilization, ferociousness, expenses, and casualties.

> **5.02** The outcome of a showdown war is either destruction of one state and the establishment of a universal empire; or the mutual military and economic exhaustion of both sides, leading to the decline of both empires and the revival of smaller states.

6.0 Overexpansion and Disintegration. States disintegrate militarily when they attempt to conquer territories more than one natural heartland away from their own economic-territorial base.

> **6.01** Organizational and economic strain of transporting military forces increases beyond each ecologically unified heartland economy according to Stinchcombe's (1968: 221) principle:

$$V_{OA} = \sum_i (1 - cd)\, kIp_i$$

> where V is the military vulnerability of any point A to state O; k is a constant; I is average per capita income; p is the population of area i; d is the distance in kilometers from area i to point A; and c is the proportion of military resources used up in transporting it one kilometer. That is, vulnerability goes down the farther a point is from the home territory on which an army draws its economic resources and manpower, and as more of its resources are used up in transporting them to distant places.

> **6.02** Legitimacy strain increases exponentially as military conquest is extended further from home ethnic territory. [Ethnic identity is determined by the number of generations of politically and economically connected community lives on a given territory.] The strain of administering a state across two or more ethnically distinct territories is militarily very high; breakdown in control results relatively quickly.

The geopolitical approach is unusual in sociology, but it is becoming increasingly important. It is a world-system model in which causal conditions work from the outside inward. It differs from the neo-Marxian world system of Wallerstein in that it regards military-political conditions rather than economic conditions as central. But the two are connected. Wallerstein's model makes military hegemony a crucial factor in a state's ability to create an empire over the world periphery, and hence to acquire the cheap materials and labor which build its economic position. The geopolitical model fills in a crucial blank in Wallerstein's theory: namely, which state will become hegemonic and which will win the showdown wars which Wallerstein sees as occurring in periods of long-term cyclical transition from the B_2 phase to a new A phase. In the geopolitical theory, too, possession of economic resources is one of the factors influencing military strength, which in turn can bring acquisition of new territories and hence a further growth in economic resources. But the geopolitical theory adds further factors: even economic resources do not bring expansion if they are matched by an unfavorable geographical position, whereas a "marchland" position with enemies on few sides aids a state militarily. There is also a danger of too much success: an overextension of conquests too far from home base strains a state's resources and makes it vulnerable to sudden disintegration of its military apparatus. A similar process of strain can occur if a state is engaged in a deadlock war with an equally matched rival (or coalition of rivals). These weaknesses caused by wars, as we shall see, are crucial in revolutions.[17]

Resource Mobilization Theory

Resource mobilization theory proposes that conflict and power are functions of the resources that particular interest groups can draw upon in order to mobilize themselves for struggle. Geopolitical theory, in a sense, is a resource mobilization theory at the level of the state vis-à-vis other states. The better known version was formulated to explain internal conflict within states. It began as a theory of social movements, especially revolutionary protest movements (Tilly, 1978; Oberschall, 1973). *Resource mobilization theory may be seen as an elaboration of Dahrendorf's point regarding the social conditions for conflict group formation (pages 15–16).*

Tilly (1978) developed the resource mobilization model in reaction to theories which held that revolutionary protest is the result of deprivation and oppression. These may be factors, but they are not a sufficient explanation. Historically, most revolutionary or dissident movements have arisen not at the worst periods of deprivation, but at times of comparatively mild distress. Classically, the deprivation theory was reformulated to account for this by the hypothesis of rising expectations: protest breaks out not when things are absolutely at their lowest but when conditions are improving, and then receive a setback (Davies, 1962). However, Tilly points out that even this is not a sufficient condition for a protest movement, still less a successful one. The merely psychological conditions of discomfort are not enough to get a movement organized; there must also be actual organizational resources available. Examining peasant uprisings in agrarian societies and workers' movements in early industrialized societies, Tilly finds that the strongest movements occur where certain organizational conditions are present—for example, where peasants are settled on land in such a way that they habitually communicate with one another in their own villages—whereas mobilization is low—even with equal or worse conditions of deprivation—where the peasants are split up geographically or where the villages are controlled by government agents and priests.

In the same vein, we may add that exposure to the capitalist market is itself mobilizing. For example, Calhoun (1982) shows that the radical protest movements in England during the early industrial period (the early 1800s) were primarily among independent craftsworkers rather than machine operators in the new factories. The craftsworkers were most immediately threatened by the market, since they were being driven out of business by competition from the new factories; hence their struggle developed against the capitalist system itself. The factory workers, on the other hand, were shielded from the direct effects of the market by their employers; their struggle was less revolutionary and was directed toward a local effort to build trade union strength in their own factories. We will see again the importance of markets as a mobilizing factor when we come to Barrington Moore's theory of revolutions.

Resource mobilization theory has been criticized (Skocpol, 1979) as inadequate to explain revolutions. No matter how mobilized a peasants' or workers' movement is, it does not produce a revolution unless the state itself crumbles. A revolution thus requires a crisis or breakdown of state power. Nevertheless, this objection may be reformulated as an extension of resource mobilization theory. The weakness of the current theory is that it focuses on only one side of the conflict, the protest movement from below. But the dominant elite or class also has organizational resources; because the rulers are more mobilized, they are able to hold power. A crisis or breakdown is important because it reduces the resource mobilization of the elite to a point below the level of the mobilization of their opponents.

There is evidence that the dominant class is better mobilized (Mann, 1970). Its resources include those which produce greater class consciousness and greater awareness of its own interests and of itself as a group. Thus, the higher social class is usually more politically interested and active than subordinate classes. One of the factors which produce this mobilization in a capitalist society is the market, just as exposure to the market tends to mobilize workers. But capitalists are themselves active in attempting to manipulate markets, rather than merely being subject to the market after the fashion of the workers and small producers; and they have some unity already through the role of financial institutions. Businesses mutually monitor one another. All this increases the mobilization and the class consciousness of capitalists and makes them better able to push their interests politically.

A full theory of political power would take into account the resources which mobilize all factions, both dominant, subordinate, and intermediate, as well as the various particular interests among them. The general hypothesis is that the most mobilized interest group wins the most power (for a version of this applied to the democratic politics of modern Sweden, see Korpi, 1983).[18]

Revolutions

Barrington Moore's seminal theory (1966) stresses the importance of revolutions in shaping the nature of the modern state. Moore rejects the evolutionary model which claims that all societies proceed through the same stages and that the "modern" is characterized by democracy. Instead, there are at least three different types of modern state: democracy, as found in capitalist states such as Britain and the United States; state socialism of the Soviet type; and authoritarianism, of which the most extreme examples were the Fascist governments of Germany, Italy, and Japan.

The preconditions for these structures were laid down in the previous period, the beginning of commercialization and industrialization within agrarian societies. The first wave of commercialization, and hence of capitalism, occurred in the rural sector, in agricultural production. The class conflicts around this development produced various kinds of revolutions and hence modern states. Moore examines a series of case studies: England, France, the United States, China, Japan (and drawing on earlier material, Prussia and Russia). His theoretical model must be extracted from these accounts. In general form, it proposes that social groups act politically to favor their economic interests. In this sense, it is a neo-Marxian conflict theory. But it is a sophisticated interest-group model; the government that each group prefers is that which best matches its own interests, but that depends on who the opposing forces are. Thus the overall *structure* of contending interests (we might say, the relative resource mobilization of different sides) determines what a group will do. Each group has its first choice for type of government, and a second choice which it will turn to if its first choice is not possible.

According to Moore, there are five main actors in this drama: the bourgeoisie, the landowners, the government bureaucrats, the peasants, and the workers.

The *bourgeoisie* prefers democracy if possible. This is because they are best able to influence this type of government in favor of their interests. We may gloss this point by saying that if economic conditions are not interfered with, the capitalists will dominate a market system because of their superior mobilization (as indicated above). However, if capitalism itself is threatened by a strong workers' movement, or by a government bureaucracy as a form of socialism, the bourgeoisie will fall back on their second choice, authoritarian government. Usually this is done through an alliance with conservative land-owning and military classes.

The *landowners* prefer authoritarian government, to maintain their aristocratic privileges against the bourgeoisie, peasants, and workers. If these classes are weak, however, and the main threat to the landowners is the central bureaucracy itself, the landowners will favor a mild form of democracy, that is, a decentralized sharing of power among the aristocratic class. (This point was stressed not by Moore but in Montesquieu's (1748/1949) and Tocqueville's (1852/1955) classic theories, pointing to the parliamentary institutions and assemblies of nobles which balanced the power of medieval kings in Europe.)

The *government bureaucrats* favor traditional authoritarian rule as a means of keeping up their elite privileges. They are especially likely to make this choice if they are recruited from the landed aristocracy. Their second choice, perhaps surprisingly, is socialism, since it keeps the bureaucracy in power, instead of rendering it subservient to the bourgeoisie (whom the aristocracy traditionally held in contempt). This second alternative is especially likely when there is a conflict between the central bureaucracy and the landowners, or when the bureaucrats are recruited from a competitive educational system rather than via hereditary position. (Hence the number of revolutionary leaders who came from careers in the lower bureaucracy: Lenin, Mao, Robespierre.)

The *peasants* are generally unmobilized. Though they are sometimes capable of protest, they cannot take over the state themselves and are always pawn for other forces. Their revolts against absentee landlords can provide the revolutionary forces which bring down a traditional authoritarian regime and produce either democracy or socialism. But the end result of a revolution is often that the peasants expropriate the land, and thus turn themselves into small commercial farmers. This makes them the weakest members of the capitalist class and those most subject to economic pressures if the prices for agricultural products decline. Hence post-revolutionary peasants tend to turn into a conservative force and are likely to join an authoritarian (especially Fascist) movement against what they perceive as the threat of socialism in the urban sector.[19]

The *workers* are the strongest opponents of authoritarian government because of its threat of direct coercion in their own working conditions (these are better formulated by Bendix, 1956, than in Moore). If the bourgeoisie allies with the state and the landowners in order to get control of labor (as happened in Germany during the Bismarck era or in Russia during industrialization under the czars), the workers favor socialism. If the bourgeoisie remains liberal and allows the formation of trade unions, the workers' struggle is confined to limited issues of wages and working conditions instead of establishing a "workers' state," and hence their political aim is to acquire the franchise within a democracy. (This was the path followed in England.)

The fulcrum of this system is the landowners. Which way they move depends on how they carry out the commercialization of agriculture. The landowners may go directly into the market by driving the peasants off their traditional plots, enclosing their lands to produce wool or establishing mines or factories on them, and using hired wage labor. In this case, the landowners actually eliminate themselves as a traditional aristocracy by becoming rural capitalists. Henceforward, their interests are those of capitalists, and their first choice of government is democracy. This was the English route; the English revolutions of the 1600s where those of the commercial aristocracy (led by Cromwell) with the urban bourgeoisie as a junior partner, defeating a coalition of the traditional aristocracy and the king. The process also removed the peasants from the land, which eliminated a potential

source of authoritarian political support. England thus became the classic case of democratic capitalism, in which the major antidemocratic forces were weakened or eliminated.[20]

A second possibility is that the landowners become rentiers, retiring to the city and collecting rents from their peasants, who are allowed to go into the market themselves. This reduces the power of the landowners, since they are no longer directly involved in production or in controlling their peasants. It also tends to mobilize the peasants, since they are directly subject to the vicissitudes of the market. (This follows from the principle that markets mobilize, as noted above.) When prices fall due to a market glut, or when weather conditions cause hardships and reduce crops, the peasants nevertheless continue to owe rents to the landowners. This increases resentment against the landowning class, who become viewed as worthless parasites (and who are no longer capable of dominating the situation of ritual deference, due to their absence from the countryside). The weakness of the aristocracy and the mobilization of the peasants tends to result in a revolution. This was the scenario of the French Revolution of 1789, and the Chinese Revolution of 1949. The structural outcomes of these revolutions differed because of the other class actors who remained on the scene. In China, the bourgeoisie was weak, and the revolution was organized into socialism by state bureaucrats. In France, the end result was a rough balance between class forces, which resulted in long-term political instability. France thus had a series of revolutionary conflicts—1830, 1848–51, 1871, the 1930s, and after World War II that tended at different times toward all three structural alternatives—authoritarian government, democracy, and state socialism.

The third possibility is that the landowners produce crops for the market, but do this by keeping the peasants on the land and attempting to squeeze more productivity out of them by tightening traditional labor controls. The aristocrats remain tied to the state since they need its support to enforce control over the peasantry, while the peasants remain unmobilized, since they are subject to traditional deference conditions and are not directly exposed to the market. This is the route followed in the commercialization of agriculture in Prussia and in the "revolution from above" by which Japan modernized after the Meiji Restoration in 1867. This was the political formula for Fascism.

Moore's theory has been extended to a number of other cases. Paige (1975) shows that the various types of commercialization of agriculture explain the kinds of politics and revolutions experienced by many twentieth-century states in Asia, Latin America, and elsewhere.

Moore's theory focuses on the political results of revolutions. One of his former students, Theda Skocpol (1979), develops the prior question of when and why revolutions break out in the first place. Skocpol takes issue with the traditional theory of revolutions, shared by both Marxists and non-Marxists, that revolutions are caused by rising social classes "bursting the bonds of the old social order." The bourgeoisie, she points out, was not historically strong before the French Revolution or the English Revolution, but developed its power after those revolutions, and largely as the result of them. Revolutions pave the way for economic transformations as much as they are caused by them, and hence revolutions give rise to new social classes. The most basic factor in the revolution, rather, is a breakdown in the military power of the state. The state is no longer able to enforce control, which in turn allows rebellious forces to mobilize. Skocpol concentrates on the three great revolutions of modern times: the French Revolution (1789–99), the Russian revolution (1917), and the Chinese Revolution (1911–49). In each case the state was weakened by war: either because of direct military defeat of its armies (Russia in World War I, and China by Western colonial incursions and then the Japanese invasion of the 1930s) or because military expenses had built up to a point where state bankruptcy threatened (as in France before 1789).

Skocpol's theory thus far resembles the geopolitical theory, which predicts state breakdown or revolution as the result of military defeat or geopolitical overextension. Skocpol adds a distinction between types of revolutions. One type is *political revolution*, which changes mainly the type of government (examples include the English revolutions of 1640 and 1688, the American Revolution of 1776–83, the Prussian reform movement of 1807–14, the Meiji Restoration in Japan in 1867, as well as numerous revolutionary coups in Latin America, Africa, and elsewhere). A second type is *social revolution*, which includes not only a political change but a transformation in the class structure of society. These are much less frequent; Skocpol confines the instances to the French, Russian, and Chinese cases.

Skocpol argues that social revolutions always involve a three-sided struggle: the state class versus the property-owning class versus the producing class. In her historical cases, these were the king (or emperor) and his bureaucracy, the rural landowners, and the peasants. These are the major classes of Moore's theory (with the workers and bourgeoisie reduced to minor roles). Notice the implication that the state itself is now treated as a social class. The bureaucrats do not merely carry out the interests of other classes, as in classic Marxian theory, nor mediate between them as in structuralist Marxism, but have economic interests of their own. The bureaucrats are interested in increasing state revenue, while the landowners attempt to exempt themselves from taxation. Since the landowners are the wealthiest class, the power of the state is curtailed unless it can win concessions or gain control over the landowners. The major class struggle within the feudal-agrarian state, then, is between the two different ruling classes. A paralyzing struggle between state officials and the landed aristocracy weakens the power of the state; then a peasant rebellion sets in motion the revolution.

Skocpol's model is a version of Moore's. She adds to it an explanation of why the struggle between state bureaucracy and landowners becomes acute: it is because the state has been involved in wars which have been militarily disastrous or which have strained the resources of the state treasury. Hence, the state has been weakened vis-à-vis its principal domestic opponent, the aristocracy, and has had to make concessions to them in order to extract more wealth to support its armies. This was the pattern of France, following its long series of expensive wars in the 1700s (and just before the 1789 crisis, the costly support of the American colonies in their fight against England), as well as of the military strains of Russia and China, which resulted in a series of inconclusive reform efforts prior to their revolutions. In these cases, the reforms just enhanced the deadlock between opposing elites. This created a vacuum, into which revolutionary forces could move, especially when the army actually disintegrated because of defeat in war or lack of pay.

Skocpol, however, has focused on a limited set of Moore's conditions. All three of her revolutions are cases in which the landowners had commercialized agriculture by becoming absentee rentiers. This is the formula, as we have seen, for a weak aristocracy, as well as for a militant and rebellious peasantry. Skocpol's France, Russia, and China thus had not only a weak state (by military strain) and a weak aristocracy, but as a result, the revolutionary forces were able to get the upper hand. The English

Revolution, which Skocpol does not treat because she regards it merely as a "political" rather than "social" revolution, may also be explained by extending the model. Here, too, the government was locked in a struggle over revenues with the landowners and had to make concessions to parliament. The situation grew acute because of expenditures that built up in England's foreign wars, both with Spain in the previous century and before 1640 with Scotland. This was the formula for state breakdown and revolution; but the peasant rebellion was missing because of the way English agriculture had commercialized in a capitalist direction. This is not to say that England had no social transformation; but the social change occurred separately from the political revolution, as the landowners peacefully transformed themselves into capitalists and their peasants into workers, while the revolution shifted the form of government power.

The chain of causes in Skocpol's theory can be better understood by invoking geopolitical theory: why does a state get in the position where its government is militarily strained? Notice that this is not simply a matter of being defeated in a war, since this has happened to numerous states throughout history without creating revolution. Small states are usually just swallowed up by their conquerors or become client states with puppet governments propped up from outside. Skocpol's great revolutions all occurred in large, resource-rich states; they were too large to be directly swallowed up, so that a weakened but autonomous government was left to undergo a revolution. Various conditions can contribute to this outcome: in England, the protection of being an island; in China, the fact that the Japanese invaders were themselves being driven out by defeat at the hands of the United States on another front; in Russia, the fact that victorious Germany was still occupied on the western front.

In terms of geopolitical theory, these prerevolutionary states had mixed ratings in the different geopolitical factors: all were strong in territorial resource advantages, but they were weak on the marchland position (that is, they fought in too many directions at once) or were militarily overextended by the range of their former wars. Their size and resource advantage kept them from being directly taken over by their conquerors after their defeat (in the case of Russia and China), thus allowing a revolution to take place. Putting the various parts of the theory together: revolutions tend to happen when a state has considerable size and resource advantages which have tempted it to expand too far from home base or take on too many enemies at once; when these geopolitical advantages result in military defeat or severe budget crisis; and when the government thereby becomes paralyzed in a struggle between revenue-seeking bureaucrats and property-owners whom they seek to tax. In this situation, efforts at reform often serve to mobilize oppositional interests, creating a liberalizing expectation which is frustrated by the continuing deadlock of opposing elites. This is a formula for political revolution. In addition, if the situation in the rural sector involves absentee rentier landlords and a commercialized peasantry, there will be a revolutionary peasant movement, resulting in a destruction of the aristocracy and the old absolutist state and its replacement with a socially revolutionary state. From the most macro perspective, we may say that revolutions are likely in a world system in which the major states are well balanced, and hence subject to a continuous probability that they will become temporarily overextended and subject to abrupt military crises.

Because Skocpol emphasizes the role of the peasants in producing a social revolution, she concludes that there will be no more great social revolutions. The peasant class is gone in the late twentieth century, and the great revolutions are merely historical events of the past. Any further great social changes, she proposes, will happen by peaceful parliamentary politics. However, this conclusion is overdrawn. It may be true that peasant revolutions are becoming increasingly unlikely, but there are parts of the world (Algeria in the 1950s and 1960s, Iran in the 1970s, and so forth) where similar conditions still exit. And more generally, the model of revolutions which stresses geopolitical conditions resulting in the breakdown or fiscal strain of the state, paralysis between different elite factions, and the mobilization of an oppositional underclass should continue to be valid. Wars, unfortunately, are still with us, and the potential for state breakdown via defeat or the strains of overextension continues. Government officials and the military, as well as capitalist interests in some societies, are capable of deadlocking among themselves in a time of budgetary crisis or military defeat; and other oppositional classes (for example, an upsurge of unemployed white-collar workers displaced by robotization and artificial intelligence; or less remotely, an urban underclass of the chronically unemployed, which has already contributed to numerous black ghetto uprisings in the 1960s) could take the place of the peasants. One state that may well experience a revolution in the next century is the USSR; its overextended geopolitical position and resulting fiscal strains provide some of the basic ingredients[21] (see Collins, 1986: 186–209).

Most work on the theory of revolutions has focused on the famous revolutions of the last few centuries. When seen more abstractly, the theory of revolutions summarized here may explain revolutions in a variety of contexts. Although "social revolutions" of the sort Skocpol focuses upon may be particularly interesting—especially for someone coming from the Marxian tradition and looking for the sources of "bourgeois" or "socialist" eras—it should be recognized that there are many other social and political outcomes that can be produced by other arrangements of conditions. It is often of interest to understand the conditions for merely political revolutions, as well as for various social outcomes (like the "revolution from above" which followed the purely political Meiji restoration in Japan after power prestige was dashed by the incursion of U.S. warships). Revolutions are not characteristic merely of modern or early modernizing times; they also occurred in the city-states of ancient Greece, in Rome, and in the cities of medieval Europe. All of these involved multisided class struggles, as well as geopolitical conditions. A truly general theory, based on the elements that we now have, can be built by further comparisons.

Summary

1. Simmel and Coser's theory proposes that conflict leads to social integration. Conflict sharpens the sense of boundaries and contributes to group identity. Conflict leads to centralization of the group, and to a search for allies. A conflict group has an interest in maintaining the existence of its enemy. Some of these principles apply to internal conflicts within a group as well as to external conflicts, but only if one side is much more powerful than the other, especially a majority attacking weak scapegoats. Where there is conflict between equally powerful factions inside a social group, the result is not integration but disintegration.

2. Simmel and Coser theorize that conflict tends to be self-limiting for three reasons: opponents have an interest in not destroying the object they are fighting over, norms develop which regulate conflict, and the victorious side has an interest in maintaining the unity of its enemy. But there are instances in which conflict does escalate beyond these limits, such as when there is a mutually reinforcing spiral of attacks and reprisals. Yet, even these escalations eventually lead to de-escalation as the goals of the conflict are reduced and issues are fragmented and settled piecemeal. How long it takes for a conflict to de-escalate depends on how expensive it is; the less expensive the conflict, the longer it can continue.

3. Coser proposed the "pluralist" theory that cross-cutting lines of group division keep conflict from becoming intense on any single dimension. There is an empirical issue, however, of whether such cross-cutting groups exist in a given case or whether different lines of group cleavage (for instance, class, race, religion) are superimposed.

4. Dahrendorf revised Marxian theory to take account of the fact that major differences among stratified groups exist not merely between property owners and non–property owners, but between white-collar and manual workers, and between similar groups, even in socialist societies. The fundamental class division is in the organization of power, between persons who give orders and those who take orders.

5. Although there may be many potential factions and conflicts, overt conflict can take place between only two sides at once. Hence, the existence of some overt conflicts inhibits other conflicts. Latent *quasi-groups* consist of persons who share similar positions within the organization of power. They can become mobilized into overt *conflict groups*, especially under social conditions of communication among group members, geographical concentration, and similar culture.

6. Dahrendorf theorized that the better organized the conflict groups, the less *violent* (physically destructive and emotionally aroused) the conflict will be. This appears to be true, but two other of his principles may not be empirically accurate: that absolute deprivation increases violent conflict, while relative deprivation lowers it; and the more violent the conflict, the more rapid the social change.

7. According to Dahrendorf's theory, conflict is most *intense* (continues for the longest time) when membership lines among power groups are superimposed rather than cross-cutting. The more intense the conflict, the more radical the social change. Dahrendorf's propositions about social change are weakened because they leave out any consideration of who wins. The victory of conservative forces, for example, or a stalemate between the sides would be very unlikely to affect the rate of change.

8. A theory of politics should explain the conditions for various kinds of state structures, the lineup of groups who contend for power, the political events that take place, and who wins what in these struggles. Weber's theory defines the state as an organization claiming a monopoly over the legitimate use of violence within a given territory. The legitimacy of a state rises or falls depending on its level of international power prestige; one consequence is that politicians rise and fall depending on the prestige of their state in foreign affairs. There are also domestic factors which determine the legitimacy of the political leaders in office, including economic conditions and natural disasters. But the most extreme shifts in legitimacy, revolutionary downfall of the state, have been due primarily to military defeats or strains caused by military expenses.

9. Geopolitical theory proposes that the power of a state is determined by its size and wealth, and whether it has enemies on few or many sides. States in an interior position between enemies tend to fragment over long periods of time, which makes them progressively weaker; peripheral states tend to grow cumulatively larger and more powerful by acquiring formal or informal empires of weaker states. Showdown wars between major powers occur when rival empires have acquired control of the intervening territory between them; the outcome of these major wars is either the establishment of a universal empire or mutual exhaustion of both sides and the decline of both empires. States also disintegrate rapidly or undergo revolutions, when they strain themselves militarily in attempting to rule territories too far from their home economic and social base.

10. Resource mobilization theory argues that social movements of revolt do not occur when deprivation is at its worst; nor are merely psychological feelings of discomfort due to rising expectations a sufficient explanation. Organizational conditions for mobilization are necessary for a movement to arise. These include geographical patterns of residence and work which permit communication within the group and freedom from surveillance by government agents. The capitalist market itself mobilizes those groups which are nost directly in contact with it. Resource mobilization theory has been criticized as inadequate to explain revolutions, because the breakdown of the state is also required. More generally, however, it can be seen that the resource mobilization of all the opposing sides determines the outcome of conflict.

11. Barrington Moore theorizes that the nature of the modern state is determined by revolutions which took place during the period when agriculture became commercialized. The outcome depended on the structural lineup among the contending classes. The *bourgeoisie* prefers democracy if it can control it, but falls back on authoritarian government if capitalism is threatened by other social classes. *Landowners* prefer authoritarian government to protect their aristocratic privileges, but will favor democracy if their main threat is from the power of government bureaucracy. *Government bureaucrats* favor traditional authoritarian rule, but will support socialism in a situation of class conflict. *Peasants* are only weakly mobilized as a class and can join revolutionary forces, but they typically attempt to expropriate their own land and become small commercial farmers, which turns them into weak members of the capitalist class. *Industrial workers* oppose authoritarian government and hence favor either democracy or socialism.

12. The landowners were the crucial determinant of political change. Where landowners established capitalist agriculture by driving the peasants off the land, the landowners themselves became a capitalist class and other prodemocratic classes were strengthened; the result was democracy (the English route). Where the landowners became absentee rentiers, the peasants were squeezed between the market and the landlords, and became revolutionary; the result is state socialism (the Chinese route). Where the landowners produced crops for the market by tightening traditional controls over the peasantry, the aristocrats remained tied to the authoritarian state, and the result was Fascism (The German and Japanese route).

13. Skocpol's theory proposes that full-scale social revolutions involve a three-sided struggle between the state bureaucracy, the property-owning class, and the producing class. Military defeat or expenses weaken the state and set it at odds with the property-owners, from whom it attempts to extract more resources; when this deadlock between the two dominant classes coincides with a revolt from below by the peasantry, the result is a major revolution. This theory combines Moore's model of the commercialization of agriculture with a geopolitical theory of state power. A more general theory of revolutions (and other transfers of state power) can be developed by extending these two types of conditions.

NOTES

1. In their effort to play down class conflict, Simmel and Coser tend to go to the extreme of asserting nothing but functional interpretations of conflict. Thus, persecuting minorities and scapegoats emerges as a kind of normal function of society, a useful thing to keep society together. But surely this is displaying society at its most despicable. In addition to the empirical inadequacies noted above, it is worth pointing out that a more adequate theory would not merely carry the implication that this kind of persecution is an inevitable, functionally useful part of social integration, but would show the conditions under which this kind of persecution is most and least likely to happen. I would suggest that it depends on the level of resources different groups have to defend themselves, to turn one-sided domination into two-sided conflict. Groups which are small but nevertheless begin to make gains or challenge a majority's domination are probably those which are most subject to persecution. But we must also explain why it is that particular groups are disliked in the first place. A hypothesis is that this derives from differences in cultural style which offend ritually central symbols of the dominant group.

2. There are other specific arenas in which the principle of the self-limitation of conflict

does seem to hold. Goffman (1969) shows that on the micro level, games of mutual deception (such as espionage) cannot be carried very far, because of the difficulties of carrying out sustained deception or living at an extremely high level of suspicion and self-reflectiveness. Another instance is in intellectual competition where I have proposed that the number of intellectual factions always tends to reduce itself over a period of years to between three and six factions; larger numbers of contenders than this tend to self-destruct (Collins, 1987).

3. I would even suggest that class conflict is likely to return to the forefront in the 1990s. If current trends continue towards displacing workers with robots and white-collar employees with computers, there will undoubtedly develop increasing conflict over economic issues of employment and the distribution of wealth, and quite possibly, a full-scale Marxian-style underconsumption crisis in capitalism.

4. This is using the Marxian criterion of ownership of the *means of production*. Home ownership does not make one a member of the capitalist class. It does, however, have a conservatizing effect on political attitudes (Halle, 1984).

5. It should be pointed out that there is an empirical, as opposed to a theoretical, controversy over this issue. Considering the economy as a whole instead of individual organizations, top managers tend to be stockholders of other companies and hence are members of the capitalist class in that regard (Useem, 1986).

6. The neo-Marxian empiricism of Erik Olin Wright (1978, 1979) actually uses a Dahrendorfian definition of class.

7. By contrast the Marxian model reduces conflict analytically to the dividing line of property owners versus non–property owners, which allows for greater simplicity in prediction. In practice, though there are different modes of property (land owners, manufacturers, finance capitalists, petty bourgeois worker/owners); and conflicts for domination can go on within a class (for instance, in business competition) as well as among these classes. Hence, even a Marxist economic model faces the Dahrendorfian problem of explaining the effects of multiple conflicts.

8. There are a few sports, like golf, in which there are multiple competitors. But these are more properly "contests" rather than "conflicts," since each player is trying to get the best score, without impeding the other players. In short, there is no defense in golf, and logically speaking, no offense either. It is not a zero-sum game, whereas power, the prototype of conflict, is zero-sum: whatever one side gains the other side loses.

9. Sorel was a contemporary of Simmel but connected with the French Left. His theory of conflict producing solidarity within the group is similar to Simmel's theory, except that Sorel adds that violence is especially likely to produce solidarity. He also points out that this solidarity consists of a feeling that the group is defending morality. In this respect, Sorel's theory is really a conflict version of the Durkheimian theory of rituals. One might reconstruct Sorel's theory as saying conflict produces a "natural ritual" through a high focus of attention and social density, in which the build-up of emotion is based on anger and hatred.

10. There is a controversy, however, about how the very earliest states first emerged (see Mann, 1986: 34–178). The early Mesopotamian and Egyptian states, *ca.* 2000–3000 B.C., grew up around temple storehouses; they were both economic producers and suppliers of welfare—in a sense, something like primitive socialism under a religious guise. Economic coordination seems to have come first in these instances (and perhaps others, as in the networks of economic exchange which were seen in complex tribal societies in Africa, the Pacific, and elsewhere). The military state seems to have emerged out of temporary defensive armies, whose leaders made themselves permanent and embarked on conquest abroad and despotism at home. But it appears that even the early "coordinating" aspect of the state was felt to be coercive by much of its population; Mann (1986) points out that until people became "caged" by ecological constraints and dependence on the state centers, they usually escaped from state power whenever they could, by migration or resistance. After the full military-centered state emerged, some of these ancient and medieval states continued to regulate the economy (as in the Chinese empire after about 200 B.C., which controlled public works in the form of irrigation systems and

canals). But they performed this regulation by coercion, forcing peasants to contribute to the state storehouses and carrying out public works projects by coerced labor.

11. Legal legitimacy is characteristic of bureaucratic states, but there are other types of legitimacy. Traditional legitimacy, as found in feudal or patrimonial states, can be based on family loyalty or the prestige of a ruling house, or on religious beliefs in the sanctity of existing authorities. Charismatic legitimacy is based on the emotional appeals and the ideals enunciated by the leader of a social movement.

12. This theory would not account for feelings of state legitimacy among women. However, women did not acquire the vote in most places until the twentieth century. When they did, they were brought into a political system already characterized by the emotional dynamics of mass legitimacy. We may thus broaden the model to a chain-linked set of causes: military participation provides the core of the original state and its legitimacy; mass armies then broaden legitimacy feelings by extending them to the adult male population; and finally, additional processes of incorporation and "emotional production"— such as public schools set up by the state— extend the legitimacy feelings throughout the rest of the population.

13. The ups and downs of American presidents, in the wake of various foreign crises, are readily accessible illustrations of this process: the Viet Nam war, the Iranian hostage crisis in 1980, the Grenada invasion in 1984, the Libya bombing raid in 1986 (and no doubt whatever else has happened by the time one reads this book).

14. It is sometimes argued that if a world-system perspective is adopted, it is not permissible to refer to states as a unit of analysis, nor to "foreign affairs," since this would be from the perspective of a particular state. However, a world system nevertheless does have states in it, and it would put unnecessary blinders on oneself to avoid ever looking at how the world system appears from the point of view of one of these states.

15. A current example: [The USSR] has a level of economic production and a dearth of civilian consumer goods that would be fatal for any politician's career in the United States; but [its] military strength keeps the state not only strong but highly legitimate.

16. The long-lived Polish nationalism of the nineteenth century, after the Polish state itself had disappeared as a result of German and Russian conquests, is an exception. A comparative study of the survival of national identity under different conditions would help refine the theory of legitimacy. See A. Smith (1986).

17. Wallerstein (1974: 133–45) argues that a state can enter a cycle of military expenditure and income. It is a vicious cycle when the state expands its military commitments faster than it conquers economic resources (including the ability to coerce more taxation out of its own domestic population). The cycle is positive when the military successes are easy or cheap, and revenues get ahead of expenditures, thus allowing further successful expansion, further revenue, and so on. Whether a state will get into a vicious or a positive cycle is left unexplained in Wallerstein's model. It appears to be the result of geopolitical advantages or disadvantages, which determine whether a state will fight easy enemies or face extensive (and hence expensive) opposition, and whether it will strain its resources by becoming geopolitically overextended.

18. A related theory (Andreski, 1968; Weber, 1923/1961: 237) explains the degree to which a state is democratic by its military participation ratio. Where the weapons used by a state foster mass military participation, it tends to be democratic. Instances of this are ancient Athenian democracy, which depends on maximizing the number of citizens to row in its war fleet, and the spread of the voting franchise with the creation of mass conscript infantries, beginning at the time of the Napoleonic wars and reaching its culmination with the massive armies of the twentieth century. Where weapons are restricted to a small fighting elite, such as armored knights, participation in state power is restricted to an aristocracy.

19. Lipset (1950) has shown that under special conditions there are rural populist movements favoring agrarian socialism. Wiley (1967) analyzes such movements in the late nineteenth-century United States as a class conflict on the credit market.

20. Moore classifies the United States as a similar case. The American states lacked peasants or hereditary land-owning aristocracy and

had little central government; U.S. agriculture was largely commercial from the outset, and its policies pro-capitalist and pro-democratic. The only threat to democracy came from the slave-owning states of the South, where the slave-owners were the closest equivalent to a conservative aristocracy, relying upon the power of the state to control their slaves. The Civil War, by eliminating slavery, was the equivalent of the English revolution, removing the last threat to democracy.

21. Recent revolutions demonstrate that the military breakdown of the state can take yet other forms. The inability of the U.S. forces to win in Viet Nam and the economic strains of fighting a long distance war, which resulted in the pullout in 1975, not only allowed a victory of the communist forces there, but also undermined the power of other dictatorial military regimes supported by the United States. This, in turn, led to the revolutions in Iran (1979) and Nicaragua (1979). The administration of President Carter, which took office on a liberal platform after the Viet Nam defeat (which had occurred during a conservative administration), contributed to these revolutions by its own reform efforts, vacillating though they were, in withdrawing or threatening to withdraw support from dictatorial regimes. This is not an accidental feature: the replacement of a conservative by a liberal government in the United States was itself a result of the defeat in Viet Nam, illustrating the principle that the domestic legitimacy of a party declines when it is in office during a drop in international power prestige. Similarly, President Carter was defeated in his bid for reelection as the result of the Iranian hostage crisis in 1980.

REFERENCES

Andreski, Stanislav. 1968. *Military Organization and Society.* London: Routledge and Kegan Paul.

Bendix, Reinhard. 1956. *Work and Authority in Industry.* New York: Wiley.

———. 1978. *Kings or People: Power and the Mandate to Rule.* Berkeley: Univ. of California Press.

Calhoun, Craig. 1982. *The Question of Class Struggle.* Chicago: Univ. of Chicago Press.

Cavanaugh, Michael A. 1986. "Secularization and the Politics of Tradition: The Case of the Right-to-Life Movement." *Sociological Forum* 1: 251–83.

Collins, Randall. 1977. "Some Comparative Principles of Educational Stratification." *Harvard Educational Review* 47: 1–27.

———. 1981. *Sociology Since Midcentury: Essays in Theory Cumulation.* New York: Academic Press.

———. 1985. *Three Sociological Traditions.* New York: Oxford Univ. Press.

———. 1986. *Weberian Sociological Theory.* Cambridge and New York: Cambridge Univ. Press.

Coser, Lewis A. 1956. *The Functions of Social Conflict.* New York: Free Press.

Dahrendorf, Ralf. 1959. *Class and Class Conflict in Industrial Society.* Stanford: Stanford Univ. Press.

Davies, James C. 1962. "Toward a Theory of Revolution." *American Sociological Review* 27: 5–18.

Durkheim, Émile. 1903/1961. *Moral Education.* New York: Free Press.

Eberhard, Wolfram. 1965. *Conquerors and Rulers.* Leiden: Brill.

Erikson, Kai. 1966. *Wayward Puritans.* New York: Wiley.

Halle, David. 1984. *America's Working Man.* Chicago: Univ. of Chicago Press.

Hess, R. D., and J. Torney. 1967. *The Development of Political Attitudes in Children.* Chicago: Aldine.

Korpi, Walter. 1983. *The Democratic Class Struggle.* London: Routledge and Kegan Paul.

Kriesberg, Louis. 1982. *Social Conflicts.* Englewood Cliffs, N.J.: Prentice-Hall.

Lipset, Seymour Martin. 1950. *Agrarian Socialism.* Berkeley: Univ. of California Press.

Luker, Kristin. 1983. *Abortion and the Politics of Motherhood.* Berkeley: Univ. of California Press.

Mann, Michael. 1970. "The Social Cohesion of Liberal Democracy." *American Sociological Review* 35: 423–39.

———. 1986. *The Sources of Social Power.* Vol. 1. New York: Cambridge Univ. Press.

Michels, Robert. 1911/1949. *Political Parties.* Glencoe, Ill.: Free Press.

Montesquieu, Charles, Baron de. 1748/1949. *The Spirit of the Laws.* New York: Hafner.

Moore, Barrington, Jr. 1966. *Social Origins of Dictatorship and Democracy.* Boston: Beacon Press.

Oberschall, Anthony. 1973. *Social Conflicts and Social Movements.* Englewood Cliffs, N.J.: Prentice-Hall.

Paige, Jeffery. 1975. *Agrarian Revolution.* New York: Free Press.

Ramirez, Francisco O., and John Boli-Bennett. 1982. "Global Patterns of Educational Institutionalization." In Philip Altbach, Robert Arnove, and Gail Kelley, eds., *Comparative Education.* New York: Macmillan.

Simmel, Georg. 1908/1955. *Conflict and The Web of Group-Affiliations.* New York: Free Press.

Skocpol, Theda. 1979. *States and Social Revolutions.* New York: Cambridge Univ. Press.

Smith, Anthony D. 1986. *The Ethnic Origins of Nations.* New York: Blackwell.

Stinchcombe, Arthur L. 1968. *Constructing Social Theories.* New York: Harcourt.

Thomas, Keith. 1971. *Religion and the Decline of Magic.* New York: Scribner.

Tilly, Charles. 1978. *From Mobilization to Revolution.* Reading, Mass.: Addison-Wesley.

Tocqueville, Alex de. 1852/1955. *The Old Regime and the French Revolution.* New York: Doubleday.

Useem, Michael. 1986. *The Inner Circle: Large Corporations and the Rise of Business Political Activity in the U.S. and U.K.* New York: Oxford Univ. Press.

Wallerstein, Immanuel. 1974, 1980. *The Modern World System.* Vols. 1 and 2. New York: Academic Press.

Weber, Max. 1922/1947. *The Theory of Social and Economic Organization.* New York: Oxford Univ. Press.

———. 1922/1968. *Economy and Society.* New York: Bedminster Press.

Wright, Erik Olin. 1978. *Class, Crisis, and the State.* London: New Left Books.

———. 1979. *Class Structure and Income Determination.* New York: Academic Press.

2

TYRANNY IS TYRANNY

HOWARD ZINN

Around 1776, certain important people in the English colonies made a discovery that would prove enormously useful for the next two hundred years. They found that by creating a nation, a symbol, a legal unity called the United States, they could take over land, profits, and political power from favorites of the British Empire. In the process, they could hold back a number of potential rebellions and create a consensus of popular support for the rule of a new, privileged leadership.

When we look at the American Revolution this way, it was a work of genius, and the Founding Fathers deserve the awed tribute they have received over the centuries. They created the most effective system of national control devised in modern times, and showed future generations of leaders the advantages of combining paternalism with command.

Starting with Bacon's Rebellion in Virginia, by 1760, there had been eighteen uprisings aimed at overthrowing colonial governments. There had also been six black rebellions, from South Carolina to New York, and forty riots of various origins.

By this time also, there emerged, according to Jack Greene, "stable, coherent, effective and acknowledged local political and social elites." And by the 1760s, this local leadership saw the possibility of directing much of the rebellious energy against England and her local officials. It was not a conscious conspiracy, but an accumulation of tactical responses.

After 1763, with England victorious over France in the Seven Years' War (known in America as the French and Indian War), expelling them from North America, ambitious colonial leaders were no longer threatened by the French. They now had only two rivals left: the English and the Indians. The British, wooing the Indians, had declared Indian lands beyond the Appalachians out of bounds to whites (the Proclamation of 1763). Perhaps once the British were out of the way, the Indians could be dealt with. Again, no conscious forethought strategy by the colonial elite, but a growing awareness as events developed.

With the French defeated, the British government could turn its attention to tightening control over the colonies. It needed revenues to pay for the war, and looked to the colonies for that. Also, the colonial trade had become more and more important to the British economy, and more profitable: it had amounted to about 500,000 pounds in 1700 but by 1770 was worth 2,800,000 pounds.

So, the American leadership was less in need of English rule, the English more in need of the colonists' wealth. The elements were there for conflict.

The war had brought glory for the generals, death to the privates, wealth for the merchants, unemployment for the poor. There were 25,000 people living in New York (there had been 7,000 in 1720) when the French and Indian War ended. A newspaper editor wrote about the growing "Number of Beggers and wandering Poor" in the streets of the city. Letters in the papers questioned the distribution of wealth: "How often have our Streets been covered with Thousands of Barrels of Flour for trade, while our near Neighbors can hardly procure enough to make a Dumplin to satisfy hunger?"

Gary Nash's study of city tax lists shows that by the early 1770s, the top 5 percent of Boston's taxpayers controlled 49% of the city's taxable assets. In Philadelphia and New York too, wealth was more and more concentrated. Court-recorded wills showed that by 1750 the wealthiest people in the cities were leaving 20,000 pounds (equivalent to about $2.5 million today).

In Boston, the lower classes began to use the town meeting to vent their grievances. The governor of Massachusetts had written that in these town meetings "the meanest Inhabitants . . . by their constant Attendance there generally are the majority and outvote the Gentlemen, Merchants, Substantial Traders and all the better part of the Inhabitants."

What seems to have happened in Boston is that certain lawyers, editors, and merchants of the upper classes, but excluded from the ruling circles close to England—men like James Otis and Samuel Adams—organized a "Boston Caucus" and through their oratory and their writing "molded laboring-class opinion, called the 'mob' into action, and shaped its behaviour." This is Gary Nash's description of Otis, who, he says, "keenly aware of the declining fortunes and the resentment of ordinary townspeople, was mirroring as well as molding popular opinion."

We have here a forecast of the long history of American politics, the mobilization of lower-class energy by upper-class politicians, for their own purposes. This was not purely deception; it involved, in part, a genuine recognition of lower-class grievances, which helps to account for its effectiveness as a tactic over the centuries. As Nash puts it:

> James Otis, Samuel Adams, Royall Tyler, Oxenbridge Thacher, and a host of other Bostonians, linked to the artisans and laborers through a network of neighborhood taverns, fire companies, and the Caucus, espoused a vision of politics that gave credence to laboring-class views and regarded as entirely legitimate the participation of artisans and even laborers in the political process.

In 1762, Otis, speaking against the conservative rulers of the Massachusetts colony represented by Thomas Hutchinson, gave an example of the kind of rhetoric that a lawyer could use in mobilizing city mechanics and artisans:

> I am forced to get my living by the labour of my hand; and the sweat of my brow, as most of you are and obliged to go thro' good report and evil report, for bitter bread, earned under the frowns of some who have no natural or divine right to be above me, and entirely owe their grandeur and honor to grinding the faces of the poor. . . .

Boston seems to have been full of class anger in those days. In 1763, in the Boston *Gazette*, someone wrote that "a few persons in power" were promoting political projects "for keeping the people poor in order to make them humble."

This accumulated sense of grievance against the rich in Boston may account for the explosiveness of mob action after the Stamp Act of 1765. Through this Act, the British were taxing the colonial population to pay for the French war, in which colonists had suffered to expand the British Empire. That summer, a shoemaker named Ebenezer MacIntosh led a mob in destroying the house of a rich Boston merchant named Andrew Oliver. Two weeks later, the crowd turned to the home of Thomas Hutchinson, symbol of the rich elite who ruled the colonies in the name of England. They smashed up his house with axes, drank the wine in his wine cellar, and looted the house of its furniture and other objects. A report by colony officials to England said that this was part of a larger scheme in which the houses of fifteen rich people were to be destroyed, as part of "a War of Plunder, of general levelling and taking away the Distinction of rich and poor."

It was one of those moments in which fury against the rich went further than leaders like Otis wanted. Could class hatred be focused against the pro-British elite, and deflected from the nationalist elite? In New York, that same year of the Boston house

attacks, someone wrote to the New York *Gazette*, "Is it equitable that 99, rather 999, should suffer for the Extravagance or Grandeur of one, especially when it is considered that men frequently owe their Wealth to the impoverishment of their Neighbors?" The leaders of the Revolution would worry about keeping such sentiments within limits.

Mechanics were demanding political democracy in the colonial cities: open meetings of representative assemblies, public galleries in the legislative halls, and the publishing of roll-call votes, so that constituents could check on representatives. They wanted open-air meetings where the population could participate in making policy, more equitable taxes, price controls, and the election of mechanics and other ordinary people to government posts.

Especially in Philadelphia, according to Nash, the consciousness of the lower middle classes grew to the point where it must have caused some hard thinking, not just among the conservative Loyalists sympathetic to England, but even among leaders of the Revolution. "By mid-1776, laborers, artisans, and small tradesmen, employing extralegal measures when electoral politics failed, were in clear command in Philadelphia." Helped by some middle-class leaders (Thomas Paine, Thomas Young, and others), they "launched a full-scale attack on wealth and even on the right to acquire unlimited private property."

During elections for the 1776 convention to frame a constitution for Pennsylvania, a Privates Committee urged voters to oppose "great and overgrown rich men . . . they will be too apt to be framing distinctions in society." The Privates Committee drew up a bill of rights for the convention, including the statement that "an enormous proportion of property vested in a few individuals is dangerous to the rights, and destructive of the common happiness, of mankind; and therefore every free state hath a right by its laws to discourage the possession of such property."

In the countryside, where most people lived, there was a similar conflict of poor against rich, one which political leaders would use to mobilize the population against England, granting some benefits for the rebellious poor, and many more for themselves in the process. The tenant riots in New Jersey in the 1740s, the New York tenant uprisings of the 1750s and 1760s in the Hudson Valley, and the rebellion in northeastern New York that led to the carving of Vermont out of New York State were all more than sporadic rioting. They were long-lasting social movements, highly organized, involving the creation of countergovernments. They were aimed at a handful of rich landlords, but with the landlords far away, they often had to direct their anger against farmers who had leased the disputed land from the owners. (See Edward Countryman's pioneering work on rural rebellion.)

Just as the Jersey rebels had broken into jails to free their friends, rioters in the Hudson Valley rescued prisoners from the sheriff and one time took the sheriff himself as prisoner. The tenants were seen as "chiefly the dregs of the People," and the posse that the sheriff of Albany County led to Bennington in 1771 included the privileged top of the local power structure.

The land rioters saw their battle as poor against rich. A witness at a rebel leader's trial in New York in 1766 said that the farmers evicted by the landlords "had an equitable Title but could not be defended in a Course of Law because they were poor and . . . poor men were always oppressed by the rich." Ethan Allen's Green Mountain rebels in Vermont described themselves as "a poor people . . . fatigued in settling a wilderness country," and their opponents as "a number of Attorneys and other gentlemen, with all their tackle of ornaments, and compliments, and French finesse."

Land-hungry farmers in the Hudson Valley turned to the British for support against the American landlords; the Green Mountain rebels did the same. But as the conflict with Britain intensified, the colonial leaders of the movement for independence, aware of the tendency of poor tenants to side with the British in their anger against the rich, adopted policies to win over people in the countryside.

In North Carolina, a powerful movement of white farmers was organized against wealthy and corrupt officials in the period from 1766 to 1771, exactly those years when, in the cities of the Northeast, agitation was growing against the British, crowding out class issues. The movement in North Carolina was called the Regulator movement, and it consisted, says Marvin L. Michael Kay, a specialist in the history of that movement, of "class-conscious white farmers in the west who attempted to democratize local government in their respective counties." The Regulators referred to themselves as "poor Industrious peasants," as "labourers," "the wretched poor," "oppressed" by "rich and powerful . . . designing Monsters."

The Regulators saw that a combination of wealth and political power ruled North Carolina, and denounced those officials "whose highest Study is the promotion of their wealth." They resented the tax system, which was especially burdensome on the poor, and the combination of merchants and lawyers who worked in the courts to collect debts from the harassed farmers. In the western counties where the movement developed, only a small percentage of the households had slaves, and 41 percent of these were concentrated, to take one sample western county, in less than 2 percent of the households. The Regulators did not represent servants or slaves, but they did speak for small owners, squatters, and tenants.

A contemporary account of the Regulator movement in Orange County describes the situation:

> Thus were the people of Orange insulted by The sheriff, robbed and plundered . . . neglected and condemned by the Representatives and abused by the Magistracy; obliged to pay Fees regulated only by the Avarice of the officer; obliged to pay a Tax which they believed went to inrich and aggrandise a few, who lorded it over them continually; and from all these Evils they saw no way to escape; for the Men in Power, and Legislation, were the Men whose interest it was to oppress, and make gain of the Labourer.

In that county in the 1760s, the Regulators organized to prevent the collection of taxes, or the confiscation of the property of tax delinquents. Officials said "an absolute Insurrection of a dangerous tendency has broke out in Orange County," and made military plans to suppress it. At one point seven hundred armed farmers forced the release of two arrested Regulator leaders. The Regulators petitioned the government on their grievances in 1768, citing "the unequal chances the poor and the weak have in contentions with the rich and powerful."

In another county, Anson, a local militia colonel complained of "the unparalleled tumults, Insurrections, and Commotions which at present distract this County." At one point a hundred men broke up the proceedings at a county court. But they also tried to elect farmers to the assembly, asserting "that a majority of our assembly is composed of Lawyers, Clerks, and others in Connection with them. . . ." In 1770 there was a large-scale riot in Hillsborough, North Carolina, in which they disrupted a court, forced the judge to flee, beat three lawyers and two merchants, and looted stores.

The result of all this was that the assembly passed some mild reform legislation, but also an act "to prevent riots and tumults," and the governor prepared to crush them militarily. In May of 1771 there was a decisive battle in which several thousand Regulators were defeated by a disciplined army using cannons. Six Regulators were hanged. Kay says that in the three western counties of Orange, Anson, and Rowan, where the Regulator movement was concentrated, it had the support of six thousand to seven thousand men out of a total white taxable population of about eight thousand.

One consequence of this bitter conflict is that only a minority of the people in the Regulator counties seem to have participated as patriots in the Revolutionary War. Most of them probably remained neutral.

Fortunately for the Revolutionary movement, the key battles were being fought in the North, and here, in the cities, the colonial leaders had a divided white population; they could win over the mechanics, who were a kind of middle class, who had a stake in the fight against England, who faced competition from English manufacturers. The biggest problem was to keep the propertyless people, who were unemployed and hungry in the crisis following the French war, under control.

In Boston, the economic grievances of the lowest classes mingled with anger against the British and exploded in mob violence. The leaders of the Independence movement wanted to use that mob energy against England, but also to contain it so that it would not demand too much from them.

When riots against the Stamp Act swept Boston in 1767, they were analyzed by the commander of the British forces in North America, General Thomas Gage, as follows:

> The Boston Mob, raised first by the Instigation of Many of the Principal Inhabitants, Allured by Plunder, rose shortly after of their own Accord,

attacked, robbed, and destroyed several Houses, and amongst others, that of the Lieutenant Governor. . . . People then began to be terrified at the Spirit they had raised, to perceive that popular Fury was not to be guided, and each individual feared he might be the next Victim to their Rapacity. The same Fears spread thro' the other Provinces, and there has been as much Pains taken since, to prevent Insurrections, of the People, as before to excite them.

Gage's comment suggests that leaders of the movement against the Stamp Act had instigated crowd action, but then became frightened by the thought that it might be directed against their wealth, too. At this time, the top 10 percent of Boston's taxpayers held about 66 percent of Boston's taxable wealth, while the lowest 30 percent of the taxpaying population had no taxable property at all. The propertyless could not vote and so (like blacks, women, Indians) could not participate in town meetings. This included sailors, journeymen, apprentices, servants.

Dirk Hoerder, a student of Boston mob actions in the Revolutionary period, calls the Revolutionary leadership "the Sons of Liberty type drawn from the middling interest and well-to-do merchants . . . a hesitant leadership," waiting to spur action against Great Britain, yet worrying about maintaining control over the crowds at home.

It took the Stamp Act crisis to make this leadership aware of its dilemma. A political group in Boston called the Loyal Nine— merchants, distillers, shipowners, and master craftsmen who opposed the Stamp Act— organized a procession in August 1765 to protest it. They put fifty master craftsmen at the head, but needed to mobilize shipworkers from the North End and mechanics and apprentices from the South End. Two or three thousand were in the procession (Negroes were excluded). They marched to the home of the stampmaster and burned his effigy. But after the "gentlemen" who organized the demonstration left, the crowd went further and destroyed some of the stampmaster's property. These were, as one of the Loyal Nine said, "amazingly inflamed people." The Loyal Nine seemed taken aback by the direct assault on the wealthy furnishings of the stampmaster.

The rich set up armed patrols. Now a town meeting was called and the same leaders who had planned the demonstration denounced the violence and disavowed the actions of the crowd. As more demonstrations were planned for November 1, 1765, when the Stamp Act was to go into effect, and for Pope's Day, November 5, steps were taken to keep things under control; a dinner was given for certain leaders of the rioters to win them over. And when the Stamp Act was repealed, due to overwhelming resistance, the conservative leaders severed their connections with the rioters. They held annual celebrations of the first anti-Stamp Act demonstration, to which they invited, according to Hoerder, not the rioters but "mainly upper and middle-class Bostonians, who traveled in coaches and carriages to Roxbury or Dorchester for opulent feasts."

When the British Parliament turned to its next attempt to tax the colonies, this time by a set of taxes which it hoped would not excite as much opposition, the colonial leaders organized boycotts. But, they stressed, "No Mobs or Tumults, let the Persons and Properties of your most inveterate Enemies be safe." Samuel Adams advised: "No Mobs—No Confusions—No Tumult." And James Otis said that "no possible circumstances, though ever so oppressive, could be supposed sufficient to justify private tumults and disorders. . . ."

Impressment and the quartering of troops by the British were directly hurtful to the sailors and other working people. After 1768, two thousand soldiers were quartered in Boston, and friction grew between the crowds and the soldiers. The soldiers began to take the jobs of working people when jobs were scarce. Mechanics and shopkeepers lost work or business because of the colonists' boycott of British goods. In 1769, Boston set up a committee "to Consider of some Suitable Methods of employing the Poor of the Town, whose Numbers and distresses are dayly increasing by the loss of its Trade and Commerce."

On March 5, 1770, grievances of ropemakers against British soldiers taking their jobs led to a fight. A crowd gathered in front of the customhouse and began provoking the soldiers, who fired and killed first Crispus Attucks, a mulatto worker, then others. This became known as the Boston Massacre. Feelings against the British mounted quickly. There was anger at the acquittal of six of the British soldiers (two were punished by having their thumbs branded and were discharged from the army). The crowd at the Massacre was described by John Adams, defense attorney for the British soldiers, as "a motley rabble of saucy boys, negroes, and mulattoes, Irish teagues and outlandish jack tarrs." Perhaps ten thousand people marched in the funeral procession for the victims of the Massacre, out of a total Boston population of sixteen thousand. This led England to remove the troops from Boston and try to quiet the situation.

Impressment was the background of the Massacre. There had been impressment riots through the 1760s in New York and in Newport, Rhode Island, where five hundred seamen, boys, and Negroes rioted after five weeks of impressment by the British. Six weeks before the Boston Massacre, there was a battle in New York of seamen against British soldiers taking their jobs, and one seaman was killed.

In the Boston Tea Party of December 1773, the Boston Committee of Correspondence, formed a year before to organize anti-British actions, "controlled crowd action against the tea from the start," Dirk Hoerder says. The Tea Party led to the Coercive Acts by Parliament, virtually establishing martial law in Massachusetts, dissolving the colonial government, closing the port in Boston, and sending in troops. Still, town meetings and mass meetings rose in opposition. The seizure of a powder store by the British led four thousand men from all around Boston to assemble in Cambridge, where some of the wealthy officials had their sumptuous homes. The crowd forced the officials to resign. The Committees of Correspondence of Boston and other towns welcomed this gathering, but warned against destroying private property.

Pauline Maier, who studied the development of opposition to Britain in the decade before 1776 in her book *From Resistance to Revolution*, emphasizes the moderation of the leadership and, despite their desire for resistance, their "emphasis on order and restraint." She notes: "The officers and committee members of the Sons of Liberty were drawn almost entirely from the middle and upper classes of colonial society." In Newport, Rhode Island, for instance, the Sons of Liberty, according to a contemporary writer, "contained some Gentlemen of the First Figure in Town for Opulence, Sense and Politeness." In North Carolina "one of the wealthiest of the gentlemen and freeholders" led the Sons of Liberty. Similarly in Virginia and South Carolina. And "New York's leaders, too, were involved in small but respectable independent business ventures." Their aim, however, was to broaden their organization, to develop a mass base of wage earners.

Many of the Sons of Liberty groups declared, as in Milford, Connecticut, their "greatest abhorrence" of lawlessness, or as in Annapolis, opposed "all riots or unlawful assemblies tending to the disturbance of the public tranquility." John Adams expressed the same fears: "These tarrings and featherings, this breaking open Houses by rude and insolent Rabbles, in Resentment for private Wrongs or in pursuing of private Prejudices and Passions, must be discountenanced."

In Virginia, it seemed clear to the educated gentry that something needed to be done to persuade the lower orders to join the revolutionary cause, to deflect their anger against England. One Virginian wrote in his diary in the spring of 1774: "The lower Class of People here are in tumult on account of Reports from Boston, many of them expect to be press'd & compell'd to go and fight the Britains!" Around the time of the Stamp Act, a Virginia orator addressed the poor: "Are not the gentlemen made of the same materials as the lowest and poorest among you? . . . Listen to no doctrines which may tend to divide us, but let us go hand in hand, as brothers. . . ."

It was a problem for which the rhetorical talents of Patrick Henry were superbly fitted. He was, as Rhys Isaac puts it, "firmly attached to the world of the gentry," but he spoke in words that the poorer whites of Virginia could understand. Henry's fellow Virginian Edmund Randolph recalled his style as "simplicity and even carelessness. . . . His pauses, which for their length might sometimes be feared to dispell the attention, rivited it the more by raising the expectation."

Patrick Henry's oratory in Virginia pointed a way to relieve class tension between upper and lower classes and form a bond against the British. This was to find language inspiring to all classes, specific enough in its listing of grievances to charge people with anger against the British, vague enough to avoid class conflict among the rebels, and stirring enough to build patriotic feeling for the resistance movement.

Tom Paine's *Common Sense*, which appeared in early 1776 and became the most popular pamphlet in the American colonies, did this. It made the first bold argument for independence, in words that any fairly literate person could understand: "Society in every state is a blessing, but Government even its best state is but a necessary evil. . . ."

Paine disposed of the idea of the divine right of kings by a pungent history of the British monarchy, going back to the Norman conquest of 1066, when William the Conqueror came over from France to set himself on the British throne: "A French bastard landing with an armed Banditti and establishing himself king of England against the consent of the natives, is in plain terms a very paltry rascally original. It certainly hath no divinity in it."

Paine dealt with the practical advantages of sticking to England or being separated; he knew the importance of economics:

> I challenge the warmest advocate for reconciliation to show a single advantage that this continent can reap by being connected with Great Britain. I repeat the challenge; not a single advantage is derived. Our corn will fetch its price in any market in Europe, and our imported goods must be paid for by them where we will. . . .

As for the bad effects of the connection with England, Paine appealed to the colonists' memory of all the wars in which England had involved them, wars costly in lives and money:

> But the injuries and disadvantages which we sustain by that connection are without number. . . . any submission to, or dependence on, Great Britain, tends directly to involve this Continent in European wars and quarrels, and set us at variance with nations who would otherwise seek our friendship. . . .

He built slowly to an emotional pitch:

> Everything that is right or reasonable pleads for separation. The blood of the

slain, the weeping voice of nature cries, 'TIS TIME TO PART.

Common Sense went through twenty-five editions in 1776 and sold hundreds of thousands of copies. It is probable that almost every literate colonist either read it or knew about its contents. Pamphleteering had become by this time the chief theater of debate about relations with England. From 1750 to 1776 four hundred pamphlets had appeared arguing one or another side of the Stamp Act or the Boston Massacre or the Tea Party or the general questions of disobedience to law, loyalty to government, rights and obligations.

Paine's pamphlet appealed to a wide range of colonial opinion angered by England. But it caused some tremors in aristocrats like John Adams, who were with the patriot cause but wanted to make sure it didn't go too far in the direction of democracy. Paine had denounced the so-called balanced government of Lords and Commons as a deception, and called for single-chamber representative bodies where the people could be represented. Adams denounced Paine's plan as "so democratical, without any restraint or even an attempt at any equilibrium or counter-poise, that it must produce confusion and every evil work." Popular assemblies needed to be checked, Adams thought, because they were "productive of hasty results and absurd judgements."

Paine himself came out of "the lower orders" of England—a stay-maker, tax official, teacher, poor emigrant to America. He arrived in Philadelphia in 1774, when agitation against England was already strong in the colonies. The artisan mechanics of Philadelphia, along with journeymen, apprentices, and ordinary laborers, were forming into a politically conscious militia, "in general damn'd riff-raff—dirty, mutinous, and disaffected," as local aristocrats described them. By speaking plainly and strongly, he could represent those politically conscious lower-class people (he opposed property qualifications for voting in Pennsylvania). But his great concern seems to have been to speak for a middle group. "There is an extent of riches, as well as an extreme of poverty, which, by harrowing the circles of a man's acquaintance, lessens his opportunities of general knowledge."

Once the Revolution was under way, Paine more and more made it clear that he was not for the crowd action of lower-class people—like those militia who in 1779 attacked the house of James Wilson. Wilson was a Revolutionary leader who opposed price controls and wanted a more conservative government than was given by the Pennsylvania Constitution of 1776. Paine became an associate of one of the wealthiest men in Pennsylvania, Robert Morris, and a supporter of Morris's creation, the Bank of North America.

Later, during the controversy over adopting the Constitution, Paine would once again represent urban artisans, who favored a strong central government. He seemed to believe that such a government could represent some great common interest. In this sense, he lent himself perfectly to the myth of the Revolution—that it was on behalf of a united people.

The Declaration of Independence brought that myth to its peak of eloquence. Each harsher measure of British control—the Proclamation of 1763 not allowing colonists to settle beyond the Appalachians, the Stamp Tax, the Townshend taxes, including the one on tea, the stationing of troops and the Boston Massacre, the closing of the port of Boston and the dissolution of the Massachusetts legislature—escalated colonial rebellion to the point of revolution. The colonists had responded with the Stamp Act Congress, the Sons of Liberty, the Committees of Correspondence, the Boston Tea Party, and finally, in 1774, the setting up of a

Continental Congress—an illegal body, forerunner of a future independent government. It was after the military clash at Lexington and Concord in April 1775, between colonial Minutemen and British troops, that the Continental Congress decided on separation. They organized a small committee to draw up the Declaration of Independence, which Thomas Jefferson wrote. It was adopted by the Congress on July 2, and officially proclaimed July 4, 1776.

By this time there was already a powerful sentiment for independence. Resolutions adopted in North Carolina in May of 1776, and sent to the Continental Congress, declared independence of England, asserted that all British law was null and void, and urged military preparations. About the same time, the town of Malden, Massachusetts, responding to a request from the Massachusetts House of Representatives that all towns in the state declare their views on independence, had met in town meeting and unanimously called for independence: ". . . we therefore renounce with disdain our connexion with a kingdom of slaves; we bid a final adieu to Britain."

"When in the Course of human events, it becomes necessary for one people to dissolve the political bands . . . they should declare the causes. . . ." This was the opening of the Declaration of Independence. Then, in its second paragraph, came the powerful philosophical statement:

We hold these truths to be self-evident, that all men are created equal, that they are endowed by their Creator with certain unalienable Rights, that among these are Life, Liberty and the pursuit of Happiness. That to secure these rights, Governments are instituted among Men, deriving their just powers from the consent of the governed, that whenever any Form of Government becomes

destructive of these ends, it is the Right of the People to alter or to abolish it, and to institute new Government. . . .

It then went on to list grievances against the king, "a history of repeated injuries and usurpations, all having in direct object the establishment of an absolute Tyranny over these States." The list accused the king of dissolving colonial governments, controlling judges, sending "swarms of Officers to harass our people," sending in armies of occupation, cutting off colonial trade with other parts of the world, taxing the colonists without their consent, and waging war against them, "transporting large Armies of foreign Mercenaries to compleat the works of death, desolation and tyranny."

All this, the language of popular control over governments, the right of rebellion and revolution, indignation at political tyranny, economic burdens, and military attacks, was language well suited to unite large numbers of colonists, and persuade even those who had grievances against one another to turn against England.

Some Americans were clearly omitted from this circle of united interest drawn by the Declaration of Independence: Indians, black slaves, women. Indeed, one paragraph of the Declaration charged the King with inciting slave rebellions and Indian attacks:

He has excited domestic insurrections amongst us, and has endeavoured to bring on the inhabitants of our frontiers, the merciless Indian Savages, whose known rule of warfare is an undistinguished destruction of all ages, sexes and conditions.

Twenty years before the Declaration, a proclamation of the legislature of Massachusetts of November 3, 1755, declared the Penobscot Indians "rebels, enemies and traitors" and provided a bounty: "For every scalp of a male Indian brought in . . . forty pounds. For every scalp of such female Indian or male Indian under the age of twelve years that shall be killed . . . twenty pounds. . . ."

Thomas Jefferson had written a paragraph of the Declaration accusing the King of transporting slaves from Africa to the colonies and "suppressing every legislative attempt to prohibit or to restrain this execrable commerce." This seemed to express moral indignation against slavery and the slave trade (Jefferson's personal distaste for slavery must be put alongside the fact that he owned hundreds of slaves to the day he died). Behind it was the growing fear among Virginians and some other southerners about the growing number of black slaves in the colonies (20 percent of the total population) and the threat of slave revolts as the number of slaves increased. Jefferson's paragraph was removed by the Continental Congress, because slaveholders themselves disagreed about the desirability of ending the slave trade. So even that gesture toward the black slave was omitted in the great manifesto of freedom of the American Revolution.

The use of the phrase "all men are created equal" was probably not a deliberate attempt to make a statement about women. It was just that women were beyond consideration as worthy of inclusion. They were politically invisible. Though practical needs gave women a certain authority in the home, on the farm, or in occupations like midwifery, they were simply overlooked in any consideration of political rights, any notions of civic equality.

To say that the Declaration of Independence, even by its own language, was limited to life, liberty, and happiness for white males is not to denounce the makers and signers of the Declaration for holding the ideas expected of privileged males of the eighteenth century. Reformers and radicals, looking discontentedly at history, are often accused of expecting too much from a past political epoch—and sometimes they do. But the point of noting those outside the arc of human rights in the Declaration is not, centuries late and pointlessly, to lay impossible moral burdens on that time. It is to try to understand the way in which the Declaration functioned to mobilize certain groups of Americans, ignoring others. Surely, inspirational language to create a secure consensus is still used, in our time, to cover up serious conflicts of interest in that consensus, and to cover up, also, the omission of large parts of the human race.

The philosophy of the Declaration, that government is set up by the people to secure their life, liberty, and happiness, and is to be overthrown when it no longer does that, is often traced to the ideas of John Locke, in his *Second Treatise on Government*. That was published in England in 1689, when the English were rebelling against tyrannical kings and setting up parliamentary government. The Declaration, like Locke's *Second Treatise*, talked about government and political rights, but ignored the existing inequalities in property. And how could people truly have equal rights, with stark differences in wealth?

Locke himself was a wealthy man, with investments in the silk trade and slave trade, income from loans and mortgages. He invested heavily in the first issue of the stock of the Bank of England, just a few years after he had written his *Second Treatise* as the classic statement of liberal democracy. As adviser to the Carolinas, he had suggested a government of slaveowners run by forty wealthy land barons.

Locke's statement of people's government was in support of a revolution in England for the free development of mercantile capitalism at home and abroad. Locke himself regretted that the labor of poor children "is generally lost to the public till they are twelve or fourteen years old" and suggested that all children over three, of families on relief, should attend "working schools" so they would be "from infancy . . . inured to work."

The English revolutions of the seventeenth century brought representative government and opened up discussions of democracy. But, as the English historian Christopher Hill wrote in *The Puritan Revolution:* "The establishment of parliamentary supremacy, of the rule of law, no doubt mainly benefited the men of property." The kind of arbitrary taxation that threatened the security of property was overthrown, monopolies were ended to give more free reign to business, and sea power began to be used for an imperial policy abroad, including the conquest of Ireland. The Levellers and the Diggers, two political movements which wanted to carry equality into the economic sphere, were put down by the Revolution.

One can see the reality of Locke's nice phrases about representative government in the class divisions and conflicts in England that followed the Revolution that Locke supported. At the very time the American scene was becoming tense, in 1768, England was racked by riots and strikes—of coal heavers, saw mill workers, hatters, weavers, sailors—because of the high price of bread and the miserable wages. The *Annual Register* reviewed the events of the spring and summer of 1768:

A general dissatisfaction unhappily prevailed among several of the lower orders of the people. This ill temper, which was partly occasioned by the high price of provisions, and partly proceeded from other causes, too frequently manifested itself in acts of tumult and riot, which were productive of the most melancholy consequences.

"The people" who were, supposedly, at the heart of Locke's theory of people's sovereignty were defined by a British member of Parliament: "I don't mean the mob. . . . I mean the middling people of England, the manufacturer, the yeoman, the merchant, the country gentleman. . . ."

In America, too, the reality behind the words of the Declaration of Independence (issued in the same year as Adam Smith's capitalist manifesto, *The Wealth of Nations*) was that a rising class of important people needed to enlist on their side enough Americans to defeat England, without disturbing too much the relations of wealth and power that had developed over 150 years of colonial history. Indeed, 69 percent of the signers of the Declaration of Independence had held colonial office under England.

When the Declaration of Independence was read, with all its flaming radical language, from the town hall balcony in Boston, it was read by Thomas Crafts, a member of the Loyal Nine group, conservatives who had opposed militant action against the British. Four days after the reading, the Boston Committee of Correspondence ordered the townsmen to show up on the Common for a military draft. The rich, it turned out, could avoid the draft by paying for substitutes; the poor had to serve. This led to rioting, and shouting: "Tyranny is Tyranny let it come from whom it may."

3

THINK GLOBALLY, ACT POLITICALLY
Some Notes toward New Movement Strategy

RICHARD FLACKS

Social movements arise when normal politics fail. The great American movements of labor, women, and blacks expressed the exclusion of their constituencies from the central political processes. Workers had no rights in their workplace to defend their life interests; at the same time, they could not find adequate political representation. Women and blacks could not vote at all, nor did they have institutional power to protect themselves.

The primary victories of these movements were political: the right to vote, the right to organize and strike, the development of electoral constituencies with leverage, the achievement of legislative and judicial acknowledgement of and protection for rights, the establishment of organizational infrastructures that formulate public policies and lobby for them, the achievement of some veto power in the political arena, the capacity to elect representatives in localities where the movement has been strong. In the course of decades of struggle by these movements, the American definition of citizenship rights became more inclusive. Groups previously denied full citizenship achieved legal recognition. Areas of life previously excluded from government intervention became subject to it.

From *Cultural Politics and Social Movements*, edited by Darnovsky, Epstein and Flack. Reprinted by permission of Temple University Press.

Movements and Electoral Politics after the Sixties

By the end of the 1960s, movement activists came to see that the achievement of political inclusion and citizenship as defined by the Constitution and mainstream political culture had been accomplished. This achievement, however, was insufficient: Millions of workers—black and white—remained poor and insecure, women remained subordinated, major social needs remained unfulfilled, the quality of urban life was deteriorating, militarism and war remained the first priority of the state.

In short, despite movement gains, normal politics were still not a framework in which the pressing needs and interests of movement constituencies could be fulfilled. Indeed, some groups who had previously felt represented (especially members of the growing intellectual/professional strata) were experiencing the established political framework as irrational and closed. Elite domination of the state and of the political parties frequently thwarted the popular will; at the same time, racial, ethnic, and other organized minorities were necessarily disadvantaged within the electoral process.

A number of movement projects were initiated in that period whose purpose was to restructure electoral and governmental processes:

The Reform of the Democratic Party

Labor activists had sought representation in the Democratic Party since the New Deal days and during the 1940s and 1950s had taken considerable control of particular state and local Democratic Party organizations. Similar representation was one of the main goals of the southern civil rights movement; by the late sixties, black voting blocs in the South became the basis for considerable party realignment. By the early 1970s, a wide range of movement-based activists pressed for party reform that would undermine the power of traditional machine politicians and compel the recognition of women and minorities. The McGovern candidacy in 1972 offered hope that a new national Democratic Party could be created that would be rooted in the mass constituencies mobilized for change in the sixties, combined with the working-class base that formed during the New Deal. It turned out, of course, to be impossible to forge such a coalition, given the racial and cultural barriers among the constituencies and, indeed, among the activist leaderships as well.

Twenty years later, many activists still hope for a progressive national political party as the key to an effective political strategy for change. Each movement has some capacity to advance a particular agenda to protect certain interests and to veto certain threats. But no movement on its own has the potential to achieve the redistribution of wealth, power, and social priorities that would significantly improve the life chances of their constituents or sustain their deepest aspirations. A political party representing the common ground of progressive movements would seem to be the obvious framework for mobilizing the political resources and formulating the programmatic agenda for change. And yet, no leadership has emerged in the last twenty years to work systematically to create such a party. Movements continue to act as pressure groups within the Democratic Party. The Jesse Jackson campaigns created moments in which a "common ground" politics seemed to promise results. Experiments

in the creation of third parties have had some local success. But in the climate of the last fifteen years, as mainstream politics moved rightward and movement gains came under attack, prospects for a progressive national force seemed always receding.

Single-Issue Coalitions

Although systematic efforts to create a national electoral coalition did not eventuate, single-issue, ad hoc coalition projects became increasingly evident and effective in the 1980s and 1990s. Some examples: the campaign against Robert Bork's Supreme Court nomination; the campaigns against aid to the contras in Nicaragua; the anti-apartheid disinvestment efforts; the anti-NAFTA campaign; the campaign for national health care reform. In all of these, national and local organizations and activists from diverse movements were able to collaborate on common projects focused on a particular well-defined and short-term objective. Seemingly insurmountable barriers—for example, those between labor unions and the peace movement—were in some cases overcome. New institutional sources for activist energy came into being—for example, liberal religious communities. The ad hoc nature of these efforts meant that they did not seem to build on one another; still, they offered evidence that, despite the fragmentation of the left and the rise of a politics of identity, coalescence, at least under immediate conditions of practical necessity and opportunity, was possible.

Localism

Since the sixties, movement activists have had substantial success in influencing electoral politics and governmental policy at city and state levels. Considerable numbers of New Left activists came to see that the student movement as such was a limited vehicle for advancing far-reaching social change. The university campus, despite its significance in postindustrial society, remained too isolated from the political and cultural mainstream; students, despite their capacity for dramatic and effective disruption, could not achieve their goals without substantial links to potential majorities. And, from a biographical perspective, students had to graduate into a wider world and find new arenas in which to fulfill their political commitments.

Many student activists, accordingly, sought to overcome their political and cultural isolation and searched for activist vocations by settling into particular local communities. What we mean by "new social movements" has much to do with these post-sixties organizing efforts, for it is out of these that feminism, environmentalism, gay liberation, and the antinuclear movements emerged.

The localist emphasis of post-sixties activism resulted in part from the limited resources available to the left; most particularly the absence of any central organizational authority that could have directed a national strategy. But localism derived also from the ideological perspectives that dominated the New Left—the emphasis on participatory democracy, on decentralization, on human scale. The feminist critique of patriarchal leadership reinforced these perspectives by encouraging both male and female activists to work in nonhierarchical, face-to-face ways—rather than in the self-promoting, top-down manner that seems required by efforts to assert national leadership.

The new movements developed, accordingly, in highly decentralized ways. Although each of them contained national organizational structures, these had relatively little to do with directing the manifold movement activities that emerged out of issues arising in particular regions, communities, neighborhoods, and workplaces.

The environmental movement is a prototypical case. Environmentalism did not become a mass movement because of the initiatives of national organizations; rather, the movement was constructed out of a host of seemingly disparate local protests and projects: struggles over land use, urban development, population growth, toxic waste disposal, nuclear power, neighborhood preservation, defense of traditional culture, occupational hazards, and so forth. Typically, members of a local community came together and acted in response to a locally experienced threat—at times, using the resources (language, know-how, material support) made available by the formal organizations of the national movement. In the midst of such local struggles there were often some veteran activists—people whose identities were shaped in the Old or New Left. Over the course of time, the influence of experienced activists was no longer a necessary ingredient for enabling local protest to take off. After twenty-five years, many who don't consider themselves to be activists have acquired the consciousness and skills to act effectively in local protest.

The local creativity of the new social movements was an important, if largely hidden, feature of American social history during the last quarter century. Local protests often succeeded in deflecting the particular threats that initially sparked them, or won certain concessions and accommodations from the corporate and state bureaucracies that encroached on community life. Moreover, locally based movement activity rather quickly developed a certain strategic thrust that went beyond the merely reactive. The political aim of grassroots activism was to win a degree of direct voice in the decisions and policies that determine the community's future. This implicit strategy was implemented in a variety of political projects.

Beginning in the early seventies, new social movement activists, especially in towns with sizable university populations, began competing directly for local office. In the eighties this effort widened with the development of local "rainbow" coalition politics in a number of cities, whereby black community activists made electoral alliance with feminist, environmentalist, gay, and peace constituencies. Eventually progressive coalitions came to local power in a variety of places rather different from the progressive university town. Indeed, there is probably no major city in the country whose politics has not been affected by the separate and combined efforts of movement activists to win at least a piece of local power.[1]

In addition to seeking electoral office, locally based movements have pressed for structural reform at the local and state level—reform that would provide movement constituencies with legal bases for intervening in the decision-making process and holding government directly accountable. Decisions previously reserved for specialized or elite arenas were now subject to public scrutiny and voice.

A major example of movement initiatives in this regard is with the Environmental Quality Act in California (CEQA), which requires that all local development be subject to environmental impact review. The EIR process compels a public weighing of social costs and provides an arena for public testimony and an opportunity for public negotiation of "mitigations" with respect to all changes of land use. Governmental procedures such as mandatory public hearings provide community movements with significant opportunities for mobilization, public education, the development of expertise, and the exercise of community leadership. From the perspective of public authority, the process was agreed to in an effort to get community residents "off the streets" and into the bureaucratic structure; in practice, however, it has provided a degree of information and opportunity for public participation not previously available.

In general, in the last twenty-five years, a variety of mechanisms embodying principles of public review and participatory planning have emerged in American community and institutional life. Public mechanisms similar to those provided by the EIR exist in some locales with respect to job hiring and promotion policies, police practices, health service provision, provision of services for the aged, and public education (where local control has, of course, a long tradition in the United States). The development of these mechanisms has meant considerable change in the structure of power at the local level.

But the local democracy achieved during this past quarter century is a limited one: American communities are now places where social movements have some ability to veto or modify unwanted decisions. Largely missing at the community level are institutional mechanisms for promoting economic redistribution, for effectively controlling the flow of capital, or for effectively determining the planning processes that shape their futures. These processes are determined beyond the locality.

Having learned to "act locally while thinking globally," movement activists discovered that the innovative post-sixties political strategies had effective limits: They could not provide a significant way to protect local communities from the incursions of globalized megacorporations nor from the globalizing cultural frameworks provided by the megamedia.

The Failure of Normal Politics

In general, movement activists hope that the outcome of mass protest will be the democratizing of normal politics. Normalcy is necessary in the aftermath of protest. Grassroots movement participants need eventually to go home to raise their families and live in the freer space that their protests have helped open. Meanwhile, committed activists hope to find long-term careers within stable political institutions, representing the grassroots, serving the people as professionals, administrators, politicians.

The sixties generation's hopes for the establishment of a liveable normal politics were exercised through the strategies I have enumerated above. These were, I have suggested, not unsuccessful. The most egregious denials of human rights characteristic of American society prior to the sixties have been removed. Avenues for democratic participation for a variety of previously excluded groups have been opened; arenas of life previously subject to authoritarian control are now less so; daily life and human relations are in many ways more free and cultural expression far less repressed and homogenized.

We do not, however, now have a normal politics in which the relatively disadvantaged groups in society believe that their interests and needs and aspirations can be effectively expressed and addressed. Indeed, the evidence is that millions of Americans who formerly thought themselves to be represented politically are increasingly alienated. Few constituencies feel adequately represented by political leadership; populist mistrust of politicians is pervasive; government is perceived largely as a burden rather than a resource.

Normal politics worked in the aftermath of the thirties. The labor movement and radical ferment of the Depression years helped solidify the Keynesian–welfare-state model for sustaining political stability and steady economic growth. After World War II, mass parties, claiming to represent workers and other mobilized constituencies, effectively determined national policies in many countries.

These mass parties established their dominance not only by being a voice for dis-advantaged mass constituencies but by maintaining the *silence* of some of these (women, ethnic minorities, the least skilled, for example). The upsurges of the sixties were in large part due to the prior under-representation or exclusion of such groups from the normal politics that the labor movement of the thirties had helped create.

Sixties activists in Europe and the United States assumed initially that the established mass parties could be made more inclusive. As we have seen, one of the key strategic projects of activists in the United States in the early seventies was the reform of the Democratic Party so that it could effectively represent the claims of previously marginalized constituencies and thereby establish a new majority coalition. Hopes for a revitalization of the European social democratic parties were also prevalent in the seventies.

Efforts to broaden the mass parties as effective vehicles of economic redistribution and democratization were largely frustrated. Much discussion in Europe and the United States in the seventies envisioned a new social democratic program "beyond the welfare state"—that is, reasserting efforts to promote popular democratic control of planning and investment, workplace democracy, environmentalism, and women's liberation. Programmatic change in these directions did occur in some of the European parties. Once in power, however, European social democratic parties (for example, in France and Spain) reverted to versions of neoliberalism, abandoning even their prior commitment to preserving the welfare state. A similar shift to the right has been evident during the brief periods when the Democratic Party has controlled the White House.

Why did this eminently rational hope for the revitalization of social democracy remain unfulfilled? Part of the problem the mass parties faced was the splintering of their traditional base. The very success of the post–World War II social contract in raising living standards of industrial workers and promoting economic growth meant that large numbers of workers sought to protect their relative advantage, resented taxation that supported the welfare state, and hoped for more opportunity to own things. Against this, traditional party rhetoric about solidarity and equality and the common good seemed stultifying. Just when parts of the working class "bourgeoisified," these parties were, at the same time, compelled to respond to the rising demands of ethnic minorities, women, and the less skilled for recognition, justice, and voice. Class identity, which had undergirded the political strength of these parties, broke into many fragments. No single leadership could claim to speak for these diverse and conflicting parts. Indeed, white male working- and middle-class voters resonated far more to Reaganite and Thatcherite political appeals than to the increasingly hollow rhetoric of their putative party leaderships.

The heart of the problem is that the mass parties no longer can muster the resources within the scope of their domestic political economies to sustain the programs and policies required by Keynesian and welfare-state logics. The globalization of the world economy weakens the capacity of mass parties to use the state as an instrument for allocating resources to benefit their constituencies. Welfare states face intensifying fiscal crisis, capital flow is beyond state control, and Keynesian policies supporting high wages seem to conflict with the need to revitalize national competitiveness. The social-democratic/welfare-state program no longer seems sustainable, and promises made in its name lose credibility.

As a result, the parties find themselves paralyzed, no longer able to offer a credible majoritarian program that meets the needs of both the relatively advantaged and the newly emergent groups that constitute their base. Limited on the one hand by the conservatism of their more advantaged constituents and on the other hand by the fiscal constraints resulting from dependency on global capital flows, these once-dominant parties appear mired in compromise and contradiction. Because state-based strategies of social reform—whether called socialist, capitalist, corporatist, or something else— appear to be politically and economically unviable, the parties whose programs were based on such strategies seem to have had their day as embodiments of popular hope.

The United States has, of course, always lacked a European-style social-democratic party. But after the 1960s the Democratic Party's dilemmas were quite similar to those experienced by mass parties elsewhere. Many movement activists, either explicitly or implicitly, imagined that a movement coalition on the national level would revitalize the Democratic Party and usher in a scenario of the following sort: A progressive Democrat would enter the White House with the promise of completing the welfare state agenda of the New Deal and the Great Society. The bloated military budget would be redistributed to domestic investment that would create full employment by rebuilding the inner cities, constructing affordable housing, expanding education and other human services, and so on. The social wage would be expanded by providing universal health care, reforming welfare, and establishing entitlements for child care, lifelong education, and the like. In such a climate, the social movements would be institutionalized as frameworks for the advancement of constituencies' rights and interests within the electoral and judicial process. Movement activists would find fruitful vocations as advocates, representatives, and professionals in service to their constituencies.

There was, of course, no such new New Deal in the postwar America of the

1970s and the 1980s. Public policy was moved sharply rightward, and so the hope of a normal politics into which the pursuit of equality and social justice could be incorporated never materialized. The movements did become institutionalized: in the seventies a host of lobbying organizations emerged out of the civil rights, women's, peace, and environmental movements; a vast industry of direct-mail solicitation for such causes largely replaced street-level protest; large numbers of activists entered electoral politics, public service, and academic and professional roles with some continuing commitment to their movement identities guiding their work.

In the eighties, the movements lost much of their will and capacity to mobilize direct-action and anti-institutional protest. But it would be quite wrong to describe the seventies and eighties as a period of popular demobilization. As we have seen, at the level of town and neighborhood and local institution, within workplaces and families, the "abnormal" politics of new social movements continued. It was in this period that environmentalism and feminism became integral to the practices of daily life of millions and were incorporated into the political and social life of communities and institutions. This was the era of gay liberation, of collective action by the disabled, and of the cultural politics of racial identity.

Indeed, in the last few years, there has been a tendency among movement-oriented intellectuals and academics to want to redefine the historical meaning of social movements. Rather than measure movements' impacts in terms of political reform, we increasingly stress their impact on culture, consciousness, and identity. A number of recent efforts to theorize movements are very much in this vein.[2]

This interpretation of social movements is paralleled by the apparently interminable debate within academia about "multiculturalism" and "political correctness." The so-called "culture wars" in higher education derive from the effort by academically rooted movement activists, begun in the 1960s, to make higher education more demographically and intellectually inclusive and from counter-efforts to block or dilute this thrust.

The cultural turn, from one angle, represents an important advance in the theory and practice of democratic social action. A new complex of understandings about social power and about the institutional sources of social change is embedded in efforts consciously to reconstruct identity, redefine the boundaries of social knowledge, and reform education. But certainly there is a dark side to this emphasis: the turn to culture is a turn away from efforts to analyze and strategize economic and state power on the part of movement activists and intellectuals. And the emphasis on "new" social movements focused on racial, ethnic, sexual, and other status-based identities has seemed to invalidate class as a basis for collective action.

The political vacuum left by the decline of socialist organizations and social-demo-cratic parties cannot adequately be filled by the politics of culture and identity. Cultural projects are inherently nonstrategic; they don't redistribute wealth or address state power, they don't require the mobilization of grassroots collective action to challenge institutionalized power structures. Societal reconstruction requires that people organize in their shared interest while also defending and fulfilling their collective identities. Movements must embody material goals and debate strategies for achieving them, even as members engage in re-envisionings of the terms and meanings of their lives.

Elements of a New Movement Strategy

The parties and organizations of the left, for a century, provided the primary space within which questions of strategy, program, and class interest were thrashed out. Such space is now largely gone. Where does such discussion now take place? Primarily in the periodicals and journals of leftward orientation and in the forums provided by the university. Accordingly, public discourse about movement strategy and program is largely the province of intellectuals, whose life situation is likely to be at least somewhat removed from that experienced by movement constituencies. Political discussion under university auspices, moreover, is constrained in a number of ways by canons of academic discourse. Until some organizational format is created to permit university-based intellectuals to connect with movement-based activists and intellectuals, efforts to reconstitute a political strategy and program will be hampered.

Despite the absence of such an organizational format, I think those who are concerned about sustaining democratic action—whether we are housed in universities or in movements—need to carry on strategic discussion where we can and perhaps by so doing begin to open the social space a new politics requires. So, for the sake of discussion, I would like to suggest some possible lines along which movement strategy might develop in the coming period. Such strategy must begin with the fact that the capacities of states to do economic steering, allocate capital, and redistribute income have been largely superseded by global capital flow, transnational corporate organization, and the dynamic of the world market.

The globalization dynamic has ravaging effects on the daily lives of many who once believed themselves to be secure, provoking widening ripples of anxiety in the great majority of people in the apparently affluent regions of the world. The most evident expressions of popular insecurity and grievance take the form of protectionism, ex-pressed in varying degrees of virulence. Alongside resistance to "free trade" policies are demands to exclude immigrants, violent "ethnic cleansing" projects, tax revolts, popular support for xenophobic and demagogic politicians, a general disgust with the political mainstream (a disgust endlessly reinforced by the discovery and mongering of political and personal scandal). The one remaining power clearly controlled by national states—the power to police—becomes, increasingly, the defining political issue.

In this situation, it seems to me, there are several strategic imperatives shared by democratic movements—lines of action required for their common defense that, at the same time, have the potential of advancing the possibilities for democratic alternatives to protectionism. The following strategic directions are applicable, at least, to the American movements:

A New Internationalism

Protectionism resists economic changes that threaten the wages and well-being of relatively well-off sectors of the working class. The alternative is to support improved living standards for workers in the poor countries. How? The most obvious way would be for American unions and labor organizers to provide direct assistance to labor struggles in those countries to which industrial jobs and capital have been and are being exported. Concerted action by Americans in support of such struggles—sympathetic demonstrations, political action, and job action—is necessary. Environmental internationalism (already evident in growing international networks of environmental activists and global environmental conferences) provides a second, equally important, track for strategic internationalism.

Americans have not been averse to mass action that either directly or indirectly expresses cross-national solidarity. Such action was integral to the anti-war and anti-interventionist activity during the Vietnam War, and of course manifested by strong grassroots opposition to U.S. policy in Central America. The most effective and relevant solidarity movement was the anti-apartheid struggle, which made extensive use of economic leverage. The campaign against NAFTA, although labeled as protectionist, undoubtedly raised popular awareness about the plight of Mexican workers and peasants and may well have stimulated movement networks that could be activated for longer-term internationalist projects.

Such projects are made more likely by a fundamentally new social reality: Americans increasingly are in the same boat as the rest of the world. If, historically, American living standards were enhanced by imperialism, today the American population is increasingly being colonized by the same supranational forces that are at work in the rest of the planet. American elites can no longer credibly promise Americans that they will be advantaged in the global economy. The increasing congruence of interests between the peoples of the northern and southern hemispheres provides a material basis for a new internationalist consciousness. The growing popularity of "world music" is a cultural manifestation of this potential.

Community Empowerment

As the nation state declines, the local community becomes the focus of hope for collective power to maintain everyday life.

Whenever corporate decisions threaten economic loss and social dislocation, community-based mobilization has been an increasingly frequent—and often surprisingly effective—response. Struggles to prevent or mitigate plant closings and relocations, to oppose corporate pollution or destructive development—or force the mitigation of these—are integral to local scenes everywhere. Increasingly, communities seem to have developed considerable expertise about means of resistance; the need for "outside" organizers seems less than in the past as indigenous leadership grows in sophistication and creativity.

In the United States, as we have seen, a growing body of law has provided some legal foundation for community empowerment. State and national environmental legislation adopted over the last twenty-five years provides rights previously unavailable for local movements to challenge proposed developments because of their environmental impacts. Efforts to win similar legal protection for communities that are threatened with economic disruption—as, for example, the effort to pass plant-closing legislation—have been less successful.

In addition to legal support for community voices in corporate decisions, communities need access to capital for local investment, capital not now available from conventional private sources of finance. Community economic development grounded in democratic planning may be a fundamental strategy for protecting living standards against the ravages of the global market. I refer here not to the commonplace and often disastrous efforts by communities to invite their own rape by corporations and developers, but to efforts to develop community investment and ownership of enterprises that might be job creating and locally beneficial. Moreover, the provision of life necessities—including food, housing, recreation, child care—through community-directed, nonmarket mechanisms can provide social wage substitutions for declining or insecure private wages.

A promising strategic direction for community-based movement activists, therefore, would be to formulate an agenda for national legislation to empower localities. Such an agenda would include establishing national rules requiring the inclusion of community voices in corporate decisions that affect localities, and providing major national resources to support community planning, development, ownership, and control aimed at sustainable local and regional economies.

Participatory Democracy

The global market and the decline of the state compel the restructuring of private and public institutions. Corporate and bureaucratic downsizing, when carried out from above, is designed to protect the incomes and perquisites of those at the top while imposing the costs of economic realism on those with the least leverage. Within each institution, fear, demoralization, and resentment are the result. In the larger society, increasing economic insecurity and dislocation for previously comfortable middle layers accompany the further degradation of the poorest. In the name of efficiency, environmental protections are threatened, previously taken-for-granted fringe benefits are liquidated, all of the institutional "frills" that make up a reasonably varied daily life are abolished. Rearguard resistance to such changes often proves frustratingly ineffective.

The alternative is to enable—and indeed compel—all of the constituencies of a given institution (workplace, school, government bureaucracy) to participate in the planning of institutional change. This means, of course, open books, the diffusion of expert knowledge, the development of institu-

tional mechanisms of representation, voice, and accountability.

There is considerable evidence that demands for participation are a typical response to the threat of retrenchment and downsizing. Cuts are often administered so quickly that the opportunity to mobilize a response from below is short-circuited. But in instances, such as in universities, where retrenchment warnings have happened in advance of implementation, the mobilization of energy and the capacity of affected groups to grasp technical issues and to bargain about these is evident.

Instead of simple resistance to such threats (which often does not materialize because people see cuts as necessary or inevitable, or otherwise become hopeless) movement strategy might focus on demands for the democratic restructuring of institutional life. Such demands are not for self-interested or privileged protection of particular groups. They are in fact quite the opposite: The aspiration to exercise institutional voice is integrally connected with the need to take institutional responsibility.

To conclude: Social movements arise and are revitalized when normal politics fail. We seem to have entered an epoch in which normal politics not only are failing but cannot be restored in the traditional ways. Government based on representation through political parties and capable of steering national economies is now obsolete. Social polarization, tribalistic fragmentation, and cultural despair are looming dangers. Social movements—the semi-spontaneous upsurges of grassroots initiative—have until now been understood as spasmodic moments in which popular intervention revitalized and reformed institutions. Now that the parties are over, the fate of democracy and the chances for social justice will depend on the movements' capacity to take ongoing responsibility for the social future.

NOTES

1. The rise of progressive electoral coalitions has been described in Pierre Clavel, *The Progressive City* (New Brunswick, N.J.: Rutgers University Press, 1986). Studies of two key cases include Mark Kann, *Middle Class Radicalism in Santa Monica* (Philadelphia: Temple University Press, 1986); W. J. Conroy, *Challenging the Boundaries of Reform: Socialism in Burlington* (Philadelphia: Temple University Press, 1990); J. M. Berry et al., *The Rebirth of Urban Democracy* (Washington: Brookings Institution, 1993); R. E. DeLeon, *Left Coast City* (Lawrence: University of Kansas Press, 1992). See also J. M. Kling and P. S. Posner, *Dilemmas of Activism* (Philadelphia: Temple University Press, 1990).

2. Important discussion of the impact of movements on culture and consciousness may be found in Alberto Melucci, *Nomads of the Present* (Philadelphia; Temple University Press, 1989); Ron Eyerman and Andrew Jamison, *Social Movements* (University Park: Pennsylvania State University Press, 1991); and Barbara Epstein, *Political Protest and Cultural Revolution* (Berkeley: University of California Press, 1991).

PART II
Theoretical Foundations

Sit Down and Read. Educate yourself for the coming conflicts.

—MARY HARRIS "MOTHER" JONES

The discipline of sociology emerged during a period of massive social change in Western European societies in the early nineteenth century. By the end of that century, a distinctively sociological approach to studying the social world had crystallized, and that approach has matured throughout the twentieth century. From the beginning, this sociological approach has included questions about social change as well as social order. Questions about social change, in turn, have included inquiries into the relationship between social change and social movements.

There is a rough consensus within sociology that the relationship between social change and social movements is dialectical. That is, social change often provides opportunities for a social movement to appear where none existed before. Conversely, social movements often cause important social changes, though rarely as much change as social movement activists might like. Social movements are thus one side of a dialectical relationship between collective action and social change. Social change, in turn, is part of a larger dialectic with social order that constitutes the foundation of ongoing social life.

Alongside broad investigations into the relationship between social movements and social change, there are a number of more specific questions that can be asked about social movements. Why do movements appear in some times and places but not others? Why do some individuals partici-

pate as leaders or followers while others do not? Why do some movements persist over time while others seem to disappear quickly? What motivates some people to assume the substantial risks of collective action when the potential gains are so uncertain? Why do movements seem to cluster together in time and space? Who is most likely to join a social movement? Is collective behavior fundamentally similar to or different from behavior in other settings? Are social movements a rational response to social problems or simply another kind of social problem? Why do some movements succeed while others fail (and most fall somewhere between these extremes)? In attempting to answer such questions, sociologists have developed a number of theories of social movements to explain one of the most dramatic forms of human action.

The readings in this section illustrate the range of answers sociologists have offered to the many questions about social movements. The selections are loosely divided between "traditional" and "contemporary" approaches. Although there are significant differences between these approaches, there is also great variation within each of these categories. One lesson to draw from the variety of these readings is that sociologists have not arrived at a single theoretical approach that can answer all the different questions about social movements. Even so, the study of social movements has undergone a revival over the last two decades, and we now have more answers—and better answers—than ever before to the myriad questions about social movements.

Most traditional approaches to social movements have subsumed them in a broader category known as collective behavior. Although this term includes movements, it also includes gatherings, crowds, panics, crazes, and riots. Collective behavior theorists argue that although much of social life is routine, patterned, and institutional, collective behavior tends to be more spontaneous, unformed, and unpatterned. Theorists of collective behavior fall into two subgroups. Those affiliated with the tradition of symbolic interaction (for example, Herbert Blumer, Ralph Turner, and Lewis Killian) view collective behavior as a prime example of the fluid, socially constructed nature of social life, and they focus on how processes of social interaction and cultural interpretation produce episodes of collective behavior. The other wing of collective behavior theory is affiliated with structural-functionalist theory (for example, Neil Smelser) and views collective behavior as an irrational and "short-circuited" response to social strains and deprivations. Despite important differences, both versions of the theory imply that social movements are better seen as spontaneous and unpatterned forms of collective behavior than as patterned and institutionalized modes of social action.

The readings in the "traditional approaches" section include several representatives of the collective behavior tradition as well as one earlier statement. The lead selection, by Karl Marx and Friedrich Engels, stands apart from the collective behavior tradition because it offers a structural theory of the origins of collective action. Taken from *The Communist Manifesto,* this reading presents their classic statement of why class exploitation in capitalist society can be expected to produce revolutionary social movement activity. In the next reading, Herbert Blumer introduces the collective behavior tradition by summarizing the symbolic interactionist perspective on collective behavior and illustrating how this perspective looks at many different forms of behav-

ior through the same conceptual lenses. William Kornhauser describes mass society theory and its distinctive claim that the most isolated and alienated members of a society are the most likely recruits to collective behavior. James Geschwender summarizes the perspective of relative deprivation, with its emphasis on subjectively perceived inequalities as the root of collective action. Neil Smelser analyzes norm-oriented movements through a multistage theory of the emergence of collective behavior in response to structural strain and ambiguities. Ralph H. Turner and Lewis M. Killian provide a more recent statement of the collective behavior tradition with a specific focus on the role of emergent norms in the genesis of social movements. Finally, the closing selection, by Doug McAdam, offers some important criticisms of what he calls the "classical model" of collective behavior.

By the 1970s, many sociologists had become dissatisfied with traditional approaches to social movements and with collective behavior theory in particular. This dissatisfaction had both intellectual and political roots. On intellectual grounds, as McAdam's critique suggests, the image of collective behavior as a psychological response to social strains seemed increasingly inadequate to explain many social movements. More broadly, the assumption that movements are short-lived, unpatterned, and spontaneous phenomena seemed too restrictive for analyzing a number of organized and ongoing social movements. On political grounds, many sociologists rejected the collective behavior tradition because of its implicit (and sometimes explicit) characterization of social movement participants as dangerous, extremist, and irrational. These assumptions originated with theories of mobs and crowd behavior, and they could still be found in Kornhauser's mass society theory and Smelser's structural-functionalist approach.

These stereotypes were contradicted by the movement experiences of many social activists of the 1960s who became sociologists in the 1970s and who increasingly rejected the simplistic caricatures of collective behavior theory. For all these reasons, the 1970s represents a major divide in social movement theory between traditional and contemporary approaches to the field.

Contemporary approaches treat social movements as an analytical category in their own right rather than as a subcategory of collective behavior. This makes it easier to recognize aspects of social movements that had been obscured by collective behavior theory: their organizational dimensions, their long-term persistence, their patterned nature, and their rational qualities. These features define the focus of the resource mobilization perspective, which broke most sharply with the collective behavior tradition and which remains the most prominent contemporary perspective in the study of social movements. Resource mobilization approaches claim that resources and opportunities are more important than grievances and deprivation in causing movements to emerge. This helps explain why many groups with grievances do not give rise to social movements: because the resources and opportunities to do so are not available. This perspective also argues that movements tend to emerge out of preexisting social networks among people that serve as channels of mobilization. Thus, in contrast to mass society theory, resource mobilization theory holds that the most "connected" individuals—not the most alienated—are likely to become active in social movements. Finally, resource mobilization approaches propose that both individuals and organizations are best understood as "rational actors" who calculate the costs and benefits of engaging in certain lines of action and make strategic decisions accordingly.

Building on these core assumptions, several variations of the resource mobiliza-

tion perspective have become prominent. The entrepreneurial version is especially likely to downplay grievances as explanations for social movement activity. Indeed, this version sometimes argues that grievances are manufactured by opportunistic leaders seeking to create a movement. This version thus sees social movement activism as akin to economic activity or organizational behavior, with enterprising leaders mobilizing resources and seizing opportunities to create new movements to occupy an available niche in the market of the social movement industry. In this view, social movement activism has become a highly professionalized, businesslike activity.

The other major version of the resource mobilization approach is the political process model. Unlike the "top-down" view of the entrepreneurial version, the political process model is more likely to take a "bottom-up" view in which the mobilization and organization of masses of people with long-held grievances are crucial components in movement emergence. This version also emphasizes the "external" variable of opportunity by studying how changing opportunity structures influence whether movements will appear. This version thus sees movement activity as akin to political struggle, while recognizing the potential for collective action to become more unruly and to operate outside the conventional political system. Both versions have thrived because they tend to focus on different types of movements, with the entrepreneurial approach typically analyzing middle-class, single-issue reform movements and the political process approach studying larger mobilizations of less privileged groups. Thus the resource mobilization perspective is not a unified theory as much as a common core of assumptions that supports differing versions of the perspective.

For a brief period in the late 1970s and early 1980s, resource mobilization approaches enjoyed an almost unchallenged dominance in the field of social movements. Shortly thereafter, two theoretical challengers appeared on the scene. One is social constructionism, which analyzes cultural processes of how activists use symbols and define meanings in the course of movement activity. In keeping with the premises of symbolic interactionism, this perspective views movements as ongoing and fluid processes rather than as rigid structures or unified actors. Central questions involve how individuals interact with one another, negotiate meanings, manipulate symbols, and construct their activity as a social movement. These questions have called attention to the process of "framing" or sense-making in social movements. *Framing* refers to how movements identify and interpret certain ideas and beliefs as grievances that can motivate people to act in a collective fashion. Doing so requires "frame alignment" whereby movements articulate grievances in ways that correspond to the worldviews of actual and potential movement participants, and thus retain existing members and recruit new members. Since the mass media are important sources of such frames, some theorists in this tradition have been especially attentive to the positive and negative impact of mass media frames on social movement outcomes.

Social constructionism may be "located" theoretically in several ways. On the one hand, it is a revival of the symbolic interactionist wing of the collective behavior tradition of Blumer, Turner, and Killian. On the other hand, it represents a critical alternative to the contemporary paradigm of resource mobilization. The role of grievances in social movements provides one good example. Whereas resource mobilization approaches downplayed the explanatory importance of grievances (by seeing them as constant or even as manufactured), social constructionism has insisted that grievances must be created through sym-

bolic framing processes and cannot be taken for granted. In other words, grievances are socially constructed and interactively negotiated meanings that diagnose a problem, identify an enemy, suggest a strategy, and motivate a movement. For all these reasons, grievances cannot be assumed to be constant, background features of social activism; they are variables that may well be central to the success or failure of efforts to mobilize people for collective action.

Another example of social constructionism as an alternate paradigm is provided by the concept of resources. Resource mobilization approaches assume that though the availability of resources may be a problem for movements, the definition of what constitutes a resource is straightforward. Social constructionists challenge this assumption by suggesting that resources are themselves socially constructed and interactively framed through ongoing negotiations among movement participants and sympathizers. Thus, whether one sees one's money, time, or skills as a potential movement resource depends on how these items are framed and interpreted. The same could be said of the whole process of calculating "costs and benefits," which is central to the logic of resource mobilization approaches. Whether people see participation in collective action as a cost or a benefit will depend on how that participation is framed, that is, on what cultural meanings are associated with such activity. On these and related issues, social constructionism has provided an important corrective to resource mobilization approaches by underscoring the centrality of cultural processes of meaning, symbols, and interaction in the conduct of social movements.

The other challenger to the resource mobilization perspective is new social movement theory. This perspective emerged out of a critical encounter with the Marxist tradition. Marx expected that capitalism would produce its own gravediggers in the form of a revolutionary working class that would overthrow capitalism. New social movement theorists argue that contemporary society has changed in important ways that have eclipsed the "old" social movement of the working class with a variety of "new" social movements that do not derive from class exploitation or invoke working-class identities. These new social movements are rooted in other identities like race, gender, sexuality, and age, and they give rise to other kinds of movements like the civil rights, women's, gay and lesbian, and youth movements. New social movements may also be issue oriented, focusing on themes of peace, justice, and ecology. In any case, these movements are typically analyzed as responses to advanced capitalist society in which profit-seeking corporations and power-hungry bureaucracies threaten to dominate all aspects of social life. New social movements are also thought to rest upon collective identities and group memberships that are somewhat fragile and temporary in nature. This helps account for the episodic quality of much contemporary collective action, as it alternates between brief periods of overt conflict and longer periods of relative dormancy.

New social movement theory complements and extends our understanding of social movements in several ways. Whereas resource mobilization approaches are better at describing how movements operate than why, new social movement theory is better at analyzing why they emerge than how they operate. The explanations point to the structure of advanced capitalist societies in which centralized economic and political power fosters forms of domination that are felt by many different groups of people in many ways. The multiple and diverse forms taken by new social movements are thus interpreted as logical responses to the multiple and diverse forms of social control and manipulation that have become available in contemporary society.

New social movement theory also complements social constructionist approaches. The latter tend to focus on micro-level processes of interpersonal interaction and group dynamics and to ignore macro-level social structure and organization. New social movement theory tends to focus precisely on the larger social structures that are often the ultimate causes of the grievances expressed by social movements. At the same time, new social movement theorists would agree with social constructionists that cultural processes of meaning and interpretation are critical in movement activism. This is especially evident in new social movement theory's focus on the construction of collective identity, that is, the creation of a meaningful "we" who comprise the social movement in opposition to a "they" who are defined as the opponents or enemies of the movement. New social movement theory thus adds a third distinctive voice to contemporary theoretical understandings of social movement activism.

For the last ten years, sociological analysis of social movements has largely consisted of a three-way conversation between resource mobilization, social constructionism, and new social movement theory. The conversation has been productive because, although each perspective has its disagreements with the other two, they also have a complementary character. Thus, new social movement theory focuses on the macro-level of structure and context, resource mobilization addresses the meso-level of resources and organization, and social constructionism analyzes the micro-level of framing and interaction. By focusing on different levels, each perspective adds something distinctive to our understanding of social movements.

The readings in the "contemporary approaches" section convey some of this conversation, and they are organized around the three theoretical paradigms just discussed. In the resource mobilization section, the lead article, by John D. McCarthy and Mayer N. Zald, is the classic statement of this perspective, with some good illustrations of the entrepreneurial version of the theory. The next article, by Doug McAdam, presents a partial criticism of the McCarthy and Zald version of the theory and spells out the political-process version of resource mobilization theory. The closing article, by Steve Buechler, summarizes the criticisms of the resource mobilization perspective as a whole and suggests the need for complementary perspectives.

In the social constructionist section, the lead article, by David Snow and his associates, is the classic statement of how framing processes operate in social movement mobilization and participation. The next article, by Bill Gamson, extends this analysis to look specifically at the role of mass media in the framing process and analyzes how this both helps and hinders the process of movement mobilization. The closing article, by Ron Eyerman and Andrew Jamison, offers yet another view of the symbolic role of social movements as knowledge creators in society.

In the new social movement section, the lead article, by Alberto Melucci, is a seminal statement of the issues addressed by new social movement theory. The next reading, by Hank Johnston and his associates, is a more recent assessment of this approach, with a particular focus on the differing dimensions of identity in new social movements. The closing article, by Steve Buechler, offers a more structural assessment of new social movement theory and identifies two partially separate versions of the theory.

As we hope these readings suggest, the past two decades have been an exciting and invigorating period in the development of social movement theory. Critically building on traditional approaches, there are now several insightful, contemporary theories of collective action that can begin to answer many questions about social movements. Although the nature of collective action is certain to change in the future, sociology has a solid foundation for analyzing those changes and for further developing our theoretical understanding of social movements.

4

BOURGEOIS AND PROLETARIANS[1]

KARL MARX • FRIEDRICH ENGELS

The history of all hitherto existing society[2] is the history of class struggles. Freeman and slave, patrician and plebeian, lord and serf, guild-master[3] and journeyman, in a word, oppressor and oppressed, stood in constant opposition to one another, carried on an uninterrupted, now hidden, now open fight, a fight that each time ended, either in a revolutionary reconstitution of society at large, or in the common ruin of the contending classes.

In the earlier epochs of history, we find almost everywhere a complicated arrangement of society into various orders, a manifold gradation of social rank. In ancient Rome we have patricians, knights, plebeians, slaves; in the Middle Ages, feudal lords, vassals, guild-masters, journeymen, apprentices, serfs; in almost all of these classes, again, subordinate gradations.

The modern bourgeois society that has sprouted from the ruins of feudal society has not done away with class antagonisms. It has but established new classes, new conditions of oppression, new forms of struggle in place of the old ones.

Our epoch, the epoch of the bourgeoisie, possesses, however, this distinctive feature: it has simplified the class antagonisms. Society as a whole is more and more splitting up into two great hostile camps, into two great classes directly facing each other: Bourgeoisie and Proletariat.

From the serfs of the Middle Ages sprang the chartered burghers of the earliest towns. From these burgesses the first elements of the bourgeoisie were developed.

The discovery of America, the rounding of the Cape, opened up fresh ground for the rising bourgeoisie. The East-Indian and Chinese markets, the colonization of America, trade with the colonies, the increase in the means of exchange and in commodities generally, gave to commerce, to navigation, to industry, an impulse never before known, and thereby, to the revolutionary element in the tottering feudal society, a rapid development.

The feudal system of industry, under which industrial production was monopolized by closed guilds, now no longer sufficed for the growing wants of the new markets. The manufacturing system took its place. The guild-masters were pushed on one side by the manufacturing middle class; division of labour between the different corporate guilds vanished in the face of division of labour in each single workshop.

Meantime the markets kept ever growing, the demand ever rising. Even manufacture no longer sufficed. Thereupon, steam and machinery revolutionized industrial production. The place of manufacture was taken by the giant, Modern Industry, the place of the industrial middle class, by industrial millionaires, the leaders of whole industrial armies, the modern bourgeois.

Modern industry has established the world market, for which the discovery of America paved the way. This market has

Reprinted from *The Communist Manifesto* by Karl Marx and Friedrich Engels.

given an immense development to commerce, to navigation, to communication by land. This development has, in its turn, reacted on the extension of industry; and in proportion as industry, commerce, navigation, railways extended, in the same proportion the bourgeoisie developed, increased its capital, and pushed into the background every class handed down from the Middle Ages.

We see, therefore, how the modern bourgeoisie is itself the product of a long course of development, of a series of revolutions in the modes of production and of exchange.

Each step in the development of the bourgeoisie was accompanied by a corresponding political advance of that class. An oppressed class under the sway of the feudal nobility, an armed and self-governing association in the medieval commune;[4] here independent urban republic (as in Italy and Germany), there taxable 'third estate' of the monarchy (as in France), afterwards, in the period of manufacture proper, serving either the semi-feudal or the absolute monarchy as a counterpoise against the nobility, and, in fact, corner-stone of the great monarchies in general, the bourgeoisie has at last, since the establishment of Modern Industry and of the world market, conquered for itself, in the modern representative State, exclusive political sway. The executive of the modern State is but a committee for managing the common affairs of the whole bourgeoisie.

The bourgeoisie, historically, has played a most revolutionary part.

The bourgeoisie, wherever it has got the upper hand, has put an end to all feudal, patriarchal, idyllic relations. It has pitilessly torn asunder the motley feudal ties that bound man to his 'natural superiors', and has left remaining no other nexus between man and man than naked self-interest, than callous 'cash payment'. It has drowned the most heavenly ecstasies of religious fervour, of chivalrous enthusiasm, of philistine sentimentalism, in the icy water of egotistical calculation. It has resolved personal worth into

exchange value, and in place of the numberless indefeasible chartered freedoms, has set up that single, unconscionable freedom—Free Trade. In one word, for exploitation, veiled by religious and political illusions, it has substituted naked, shameless, direct, brutal exploitation.

The bourgeoisie has stripped of its halo every occupation hitherto honoured and looked up to with reverent awe. It has converted the physician, the lawyer, the priest, the poet, the man of science, into its paid wage-labourers.

The bourgeoisie has torn away from the family its sentimental veil, and has reduced the family relation to a mere money relation.

The bourgeoisie has disclosed how it came to pass that the brutal display of vigour in the Middle Ages, which Reactionists so much admire, found its fitting complement in the most slothful indolence. It has been the first to show what man's activity can bring about. It has accomplished wonders far surpassing Egyptian pyramids, Roman aqueducts, and Gothic cathedrals; it has conducted expeditions that put in the shade all former Exoduses of nations and crusades.

The bourgeoisie cannot exist without constantly revolutionizing the instruments of production, and thereby the relations of production, and with them the whole relations of society. Conservation of the old modes of production in unaltered form, was, on the contrary, the first condition of existence for all earlier industrial classes. Constant revolutionizing of production, uninterrupted disturbance of all social conditions, everlasting uncertainty and agitation distinguish the bourgeois epoch from all earlier ones. All fixed, fast-frozen relations, with their train of ancient and venerable prejudices and opinions are swept away, all newformed ones become antiquated before they can ossify. All that is solid melts into air, all that is holy is profaned, and man is at last compelled to face with sober senses, his real conditions of life, and his relations with his kind.

The need of a constantly expanding market for its products chases the bourgeoisie over the whole surface of the globe. It must nestle everywhere, settle everywhere, establish connexions everywhere.

The bourgeoisie has through its exploitation of the world market given a cosmopolitan character to production and consumption in every country. To the great chagrin of Reactionists, it has drawn form under the feet of industry the national ground on which it stood. All old-established national industries have been destroyed or are daily being destroyed. They are dislodged by new industries, whose introduction becomes a life and death question for all civilized nations, by industries that no longer work up indigenous raw material, but raw material drawn from the remotest zones; industries whose products are consumed, not only at home, but in every quarter of the globe. In place of the old wants, satisfied by the productions of the country, we find new wants, requiring for their satisfaction the products of distant lands and climes. In place of the old local and national seclusion and self-sufficiency, we have intercourse in every direction, universal inter-dependence of nations. And as in material, so also in intellectual production. The intellectual creations of individual nations become common property. National one-sidedness and narrow-mindedness become more and more impossible, and from the numerous national and local literatures, there arises a world literature.

The bourgeoisie, by the rapid improvement of all instruments of production, by the immensely facilitated means of communication, draws all, even the most barbarian, nations into civilization. The cheap prices of its commodities are the heavy artillery with which it batters down all Chinese walls, with which it forces the barbarians' intensely obstinate hatred of foreigners to capitulate. It compels all nations, on pain of extinction, to adopt the bourgeois mode of production; it compels them to introduce what it calls civilization into their midst, i.e., to become bourgeois themselves. In one word, it creates a world after its own image.

The bourgeoisie has subjected the country to the rule of the towns. It has created enormous cities, has greatly increased the urban population as compared with the rural, and has thus rescued a considerable part of the population from the idiocy of rural life. Just as it has made the country dependent on the towns, so it has made barbarian and semi-barbarian countries dependent on the civilized ones, nations of peasants on nations of bourgeois, the East on the West.

The bourgeoisie keeps more and more doing away with the scattered state of the population, of the means of production, and of property. It has agglomerated population, centralized means of production, and has concentrated property in a few hands. The necessary consequence of this was political centralization. Independent, or but loosely connected, provinces with separate interests, laws, governments and systems of taxation, became lumped together into one nation, with one government, one code of laws, one national class-interest, one frontier and one customs-tariff.

The bourgeoisie, during its rule of scarce one hundred years, has created more massive and more colossal productive forces than have all preceding generations together. Subjection of Nature's forces to man, machinery, application of chemistry to industry and agriculture, steam-navigation, railways, electric telegraphs, clearing of whole continents for cultivation, canalization of rivers, whole populations conjured out of the ground—what earlier century had even a presentiment that such productive forces slumbered in the lap of social labour?

We see then: the means of production and of exchange, on whose foundation the bourgeoisie built itself up, were generated in feudal society. At a certain stage in the development of these means of production and of exchange, the conditions under which feudal society produced and exchanged, the feudal organization of agriculture and manufacturing industry, in one word, the feudal relations of property become no longer compatible with the already developed productive forces; they became so many fetters. They had to be burst asunder; they were burst asunder.

Into their place stepped free competition, accompanied by a social and political constitution adapted to it, and by the economical and political sway of the bourgeois class.

A similar movement is going on before our own eyes. Modern bourgeois society with its relations of production, of exchange and of property, a society that has conjured up such gigantic means of production and of exchange, is like the sorcerer, who is no longer able to control the powers of the nether world whom he has called up by his spells. For many a decade past the history of industry and commerce is but the history of the revolt of modern productive forces against modern conditions of production, against the property relations that are the conditions for the existence of the bourgeoisie and of its rule. It is enough to mention the commercial crises that by their periodical return put on its trial, each time more threateningly, the existence of the entire bourgeois society. In these crises a great part not only of the existing products, but also of the previously created productive forces, are periodically destroyed. In these crises there breaks out an epidemic that, in all earlier epochs, would have seemed an absurdity—the epidemic of over-production. Society suddenly finds itself put back into a state of momentary barbarism; it appears as if a famine, a universal war of devastation had cut off the supply of every means of subsistence; industry and commerce seem to be destroyed; and why? Because there is too much civilization, too much means of subsistence, too much industry, too much commerce. The productive forces at the disposal of society no longer tend to further the development of the conditions of bourgeois property; on the contrary, they have become too powerful for these conditions, by which they are fettered, and so soon as they overcome these fetters, they bring disorder into the whole of bourgeois society, endanger the existence of bourgeois property. The conditions of bourgeois society are too narrow to comprise the wealth created by them. And how does the bourgeoisie get over these crises? On the one hand by enforced destruction of a mass of productive forces; on the other, by the conquest of new markets, and by the more thorough exploitation of the old ones. That is to say, by paving the way for more extensive and more destructive crises, and by diminishing the means whereby crises are prevented.

The weapons with which the bourgeoisie felled feudalism to the ground are now turned against the bourgeoisie itself.

But not only has the bourgeoisie forged the weapons that bring death to itself; it has also called into existence the men who are to wield those weapons—the modern working class—the proletarians.

In proportion as the bourgeoisie, i.e., capital, is developed, in the same proportion is the proletariat, the modern working class, developed—a class of labourers, who live only so long as they find work, and who find work only so long as their labour increases capital. These labourers, who must sell themselves piecemeal, are a commodity, like every other article of commerce, and are consequently exposed to all the vicissitudes of competition, to all the fluctuations of the market.

Owing to the extensive use of machinery and to division of labour, the work of the proletarians has lost all individual character, and, consequently, all charm for the workman. He becomes an appendage of the machine, and it is only the most simple, most monotonous, and most easily acquired knack, that is required of him. Hence, the cost of production of a workman is restricted, almost entirely, to the means of subsistence that he requires for his maintenance, and for the propagation of his race. But the price of a commodity, and therefore also of labour, is equal to its cost of production. In proportion, therefore, as the repulsiveness of the work increases, the wage decreases. Nay more, in proportion as the use of machinery and division of labour increases, in the same proportion the burden of toil also increases, whether by prolongation of the working hours, by increase of the work exacted in a given time or by increased speed of the machinery, etc.

Modern industry has converted the little workshop of the patriarchal master into the great factory of the industrial capitalist. Masses of labourers, crowded into the factory, are organized like soldiers. As privates of the industrial army they are placed under the command of a perfect hierarchy of officers and sergeants. Not only are they slaves of the bourgeois class, and of the bourgeois State; they are daily and hourly enslaved by the machine, by the overlooker, and, above all, by the individual bourgeois manufacturer himself. The more openly this despotism proclaims gain to be its end and aim, the more petty, the more hateful and the more embittering it is.

The less the skill and exertion of strength implied in manual labour, in other words, the more modern industry becomes developed, the more is the labour of men superseded by that of women. Differences of age and sex have no longer any distinctive social validity for the working class. All are instruments of labour, more or less expensive to use, according to their age and sex.

No sooner is the exploitation of the labourer by the manufacturer, so far, at an end, that he receives his wages in cash, than he is set upon by the other portions of the bourgeoisie, the landlord, the shopkeeper, the pawnbroker, etc.

The lower strata of the middle class—the small tradespeople, shopkeepers, and retired tradesmen generally, the handicraftsmen and peasants—all these sink gradually into the proletariat, partly because their diminutive capital does not suffice for the scale on which Modern Industry is carried on, and is swamped in the competition with the large capitalists, partly because their specialized skill is rendered worthless by new methods of production. Thus the proletariat is recruited from all classes of the population.

The proletariat goes through various stages of development. With its birth begins its struggle with the bourgeoisie. At first the contest is carried on by individual labourers, then by the work-people of a factory, then by the operatives of one trade, in one locality, against the individual bourgeois who directly exploits them. They direct their attacks not against the bourgeois conditions of production, but against the instruments of production themselves; they destroy imported wares that compete with their labour, they smash to pieces machinery, they set factories ablaze, they seek to restore by force the vanished status of the workman of the Middle Ages.

At this stage the labourers still form an incoherent mass scattered over the whole country, and broken up by their mutual competition. If anywhere they unite to form more compact bodies, this is not yet the consequence of their own active union, but of the union of the bourgeoisie, which class, in order to attain its own political ends, is compelled to set the whole proletariat in motion, and is moreover yet, for a time, able to do so. At this stage, therefore, the proletarians do not fight their enemies, but the enemies of their enemies, the remnants of absolute monarchy, the landowners, the non-industrial bourgeois, the petty bourgeoisie. Thus the whole historical movement is concentrated in the hands of the bourgeoisie; every victory so obtained is a victory for the bourgeoisie.

But with the development of industry the proletariat not only increases in number; it becomes concentrated in greater masses, its strength grows, and it feels that strength more. The various interests and conditions of life within the ranks of the proletariat are more and more equalized, in proportion as machinery obliterates all distinctions of labour, and nearly everywhere reduces wages to the same low level. The growing competition among the bourgeois, and the resulting commercial crises, make the wages of the workers ever more fluctuating. The unceasing improvement of machinery, ever more rapidly developing, makes their livelihood more and more precarious; the collisions between individual workmen and individual bourgeois take more and more the character of collisions between two classes. Thereupon the workers begin to form combinations (Trades Unions) against the bourgeois; they club together in order to keep up the rate of wages; they found permanent associations in order to make provision beforehand for these occasional revolts. Here and there the contest breaks out into riots.

Now and then the workers are victorious, but only for a time. The real fruit of their battles lies, not in the immediate result, but in the ever-expanding union of the workers. This union is helped on by the improved means of communication that are created by modern industry and that place the workers of different localities in contact with one another. It was just this contact that was needed to centralize the numerous local struggles, all of the same character, into one national struggle between classes. But every class struggle is a political struggle. And that union, to attain which the burghers of the Middle Ages, with their miserable highways, required centuries, the modern proletarians, thanks to railways, achieve in a few years.

This organization of the proletarians into a class, and consequently into a political party, is continually being upset again by the competition between the workers themselves. But it ever rises up again, stronger, firmer, mightier. It compels legislative recognition of particular interests of the workers, by taking advantage of the divisions among the bourgeoisie itself. Thus the Ten Hours bill in England was carried.

Altogether collisions between the classes of the old society further, in many ways, the course of development of the proletariat. The bourgeoisie finds itself involved in a constant battle. At first with the aristocracy; later on, with those portions of the bourgeoisie itself, whose interests have become antagonistic to the progress of industry; at all times, with the bourgeoisie of foreign countries. In all these battles it sees itself compelled to appeal to the proletariat, to ask for its help, and thus, to drag it into the political arena. The bourgeoisie itself, therefore, supplies the proletariat with its own elements of political and general education, in other words, it furnishes the proletariat with weapons for fighting the bourgeoisie.

Further, as we have already seen, entire sections of the ruling classes are, by the advance of industry, precipitated into the proletariat, or are at least threatened in their conditions of existence. These also supply the proletariat with fresh elements of enlightenment and progress.

Finally, in times when the class struggle nears the decisive hour, the process of dissolution going on within the ruling class, in fact within the whole range of old society, assumes such a violent, glaring character, that a small section of the ruling class cuts itself adrift, and joins the revolutionary class, the class that holds the future in its hands. Just as, therefore, at an earlier period, a section of the nobility went over to the bourgeoisie, so now a portion of the bourgeoisie goes over to the proletariat, and in particular, a portion of the bourgeois ideologists, who have raised themselves to the level of comprehending theoretically the historical movement as a whole.

Of all the classes that stand face to face with the bourgeoisie today, the proletariat alone is a really revolutionary class. The other classes decay and finally disappear in the face of modern industry; the proletariat is its special and essential product.

The lower middle class, the small manufacturer, the shopkeeper, the artisan, the peasant, all these fight against the bourgeoisie, to save from extinction their existence as fractions of the middle class. They are therefore not revolutionary, but conservative. Nay more, they are reactionary, for they try to roll back the wheel of history. If by chance they are revolutionary, they are so only in view of their impending transfer into the proletariat, they thus defend not their present, but their future interests, they desert their own standpoint to place themselves at that of the proletariat.

The 'dangerous class', the social scum, that passively rotting mass thrown off by the lowest layers of old society, may, here and there, be swept into the movement by a proletarian revolution; its conditions of life, however, prepare it far more for the part of a bribed tool of reactionary intrigue.

In the conditions of the proletariat, those of old society at large are already virtually swamped. The proletarian is without property; his relation to his wife and children has no longer anything in common

with the bourgeois family relations; modern industrial labour, modern subjection to capital, the same in England as in France, in America as in Germany, has stripped him of every trace of national character. Law, morality, religion, are to him so many bourgeois prejudices, behind which lurk in ambush just as many bourgeois interests.

All the preceding classes that got the upper hand sought to fortify their already acquired status by subjecting society at large to their conditions of appropriation. The proletarians cannot become masters of the productive forces of society, except by abolishing their own previous mode of appropriation, and thereby also every other previous mode of appropriation. They have nothing of their own to secure and to fortify; their mission is to destroy all previous securities for, and insurances of, individual property.

All previous historical movements were movements of minorities, or in the interest of minorities. The proletarian movement is the self-conscious, independent movement of the immense majority, in the interest of the immense majority. The proletariat, the lowest stratum of our present society, cannot stir, cannot raise itself up, without the whole superincumbent strata of official society being sprung into the air.

Though not in substance, yet in form, the struggle of the proletariat with the bourgeoisie is at first a national struggle. The proletariat of each country must, of course, first of all settle matters with its own bourgeoisie.

In depicting the most general phases of the development of the proletariat, we traced the more or less veiled civil war, raging within existing society, up to the point where that war breaks out into open revolution, and where the violent overthrow of the bourgeoisie lays the foundation for the sway of the proletariat.

Hitherto, every form of society has been based, as we have already seen, on the antagonism of oppressing and oppressed classes. But in order to oppress a class, certain conditions must be assured to it under which it can, at least, continue its slavish existence. The serf, in the period of serfdom, raised himself to membership in the commune, just as the petty bourgeois, under the yoke of feudal absolutism, managed to develop into a bourgeois. The modern labourer, on the contrary, instead of rising with the progress of industry, sinks deeper and deeper below the conditions of existence of his own class. He becomes a pauper, and pauperism develops more rapidly than population and wealth. And here it becomes evident, that the bourgeoisie is unfit any longer to be the ruling class in society, and to impose its conditions of existence upon society as an overriding law. It is unfit to rule because it is incompetent to assure an existence to its slave within his slavery, because it cannot help letting him sink into such a state, that it has to feed him, instead of being fed by him. Society can no longer live under this bourgeoisie, in other words, its existence is no longer compatible with society.

The essential condition for the existence, and for the sway of the bourgeois class, is the formation and augmentation of capital; the condition for capital is wage labour. Wage labour rests exclusively on competition between the labourers. The advance of industry, whose involuntary promoter is the bourgeoisie, replaces the isolation of the labourers, due to competition, by their revolutionary combination, due to association. The development of Modern Industry, therefore, cuts from under its feet the very foundation on which the bourgeoisie produces and appropriates products. What the bourgeoisie, therefore, produces, above all, is its own grave-diggers. Its fall and the victory of the proletariat are equally inevitable.

NOTES

1. By bourgeoisie is meant the class of modern Capitalists, owners of the means of social production and employers of wage labour. By proletariat, the class of modern wage-labourers who, having no means of production of their own, are reduced to selling their labour power in order to live. [*Note by Engels to the English edition of 1888.*]

2. That is, all *written* history. In 1847, the pre-history of society, the social organization existing previous to recorded history, was all but unknown. Since then, Haxthausen discovered common ownership of land in Russia, Maurer proved it to be the social foundation from which all Teutonic races started in history, and by and by village communities were found to be, or to have been the primitive form of society everywhere from India to Ireland. The inner organization of this primitive Communistic society was laid bare, in its typical form, by Morgan's crowning discovery of the true nature of the *gens* and its relation to the *tribe*. With the dissolution of these primeval communities society begins to be differentiated into separate and finally antagonistic classes. I have attempted to retrace this process of dissolution in: *Der Ursprung der Familie, des Privateigenthums und des Staats* (*The Origin of the Family, Private Property and the State*), 2nd edition, Stuttgart 1886. [*Note by Engels to the English edition of 1888.*]

3. Guild-master, that is, a full member of a guild, a master within, not a head of a guild. [*Note by Engels to the English edition of 1888.*]

4. 'Commune' was the name taken, in France, by the nascent towns even before they had conquered from their feudal lords and masters local self-government and political rights as the 'Third Estate'. Generally speaking, for the economical development of the bourgeoisie, England is here taken as the typical country; for its political development, France. [*Note by Engels to the English edition of 1888.*]

    This was the name given their urban communities by the townsmen of Italy and France, after they had purchased or wrested their initial rights of self-government from their feudal lords. [*Note by Engels to the German edition of 1890.*]

5

ELEMENTARY COLLECTIVE GROUPINGS

HERBERT BLUMER

The Crowd

Much of the initial interest of sociologists in the field of collective behavior has centered on the study of the crowd. This interest was lively particularly towards the end of the last century, especially among French scholars. It gained its most vivid expression in the classical work, *The Crowd*, by Gustave LeBon. This work and others have provided us with much insight into the nature and behavior of the crowd, although much still remains unknown.

Types of Crowds

It is convenient to identify four types of crowds. The first can be called a *casual* crowd, as in the instance of a street crowd watching a performer in a store window. The casual crowd usually has a momentary existence; more important, it has a very loose organization and scarcely any unity. Its members come and go, giving but temporary attention to the object which has awakened the interest of the crowd, and entering into only feeble association with one another. While the chief mechanisms of crowd formation are present in the casual crowd, they are so reduced in scope and weak in operation, that we need not concern ourselves further with this type of crowd. A

second type may be designated as the *conventionalized* crowd, such as the spectators at an exciting baseball game. Their behavior is essentially like that of casual crowds, except that it is expressed in established and regularized ways. It is this regularized activity that marks off the conventional crowd as a distinct type. The third type of crowd is the *acting*, aggressive crowd, best represented by a revolutionary crowd or a lynching mob. The outstanding mark of this type of crowd is the presence of an aim or objective toward which the activity of the crowd is directed. It is this type of crowd which is the object of concern in practically all studies of the crowd. The remaining type is the *expressive* or "dancing" crowd, such as one sees in the case of carnivals or in the beginning stage of many religious sects. Its distinguishing trait is that excitement is expressed in physical movement primarily as a form of release instead of being directed toward some objective. We shall consider the acting crowd, and then the expressive crowd.

Formation of Crowds

The essential steps in the formation of a crowd seem to be quite clear. First is the occurrence of some exciting event which catches the attention and arouses the interest of people. In becoming preoccupied with this event and stirred by its excitatory character, an individual is already likely to lose some of his ordinary self-control and to be dominated by the exciting object. Further, this kind of experience, by arousing impulses and feelings, establishes a condition of tension which, in turn, presses the individual on to action. Thus, a number of people stimulated by the same exciting event are disposed by that very fact to behave like a crowd.

This becomes clear in the second step—the beginning of the milling process. The tension of individuals who are aroused by some stimulating event, leads them to move around and to talk to one another; in this milling the incipient excitement becomes greater. The excitement of each is conveyed to others, and, as we have indicated above, in being reflected back to each, is intensified. The most obvious effect of this milling is to disseminate a common mood, feeling, or emotional impulse, and also to increase its intensity. This leads to a state of marked rapport wherein individuals become sensitive and responsive to one another and where, consequently, all are more disposed to act together as a collective unit.

Another important result may come from the milling process, and may be regarded as the third important step in the formation of the acting crowd. This step is the emergence of a common object of attention on which the impulses, feelings, and imagery of the people become focused. Usually the common object is the exciting event which has aroused the people; much more frequently, however, it is an image which has been built up and fixed through the talking and acting of people as they mill. This image, or object, like the excitement, is common and shared. Its importance is that it gives a common orientation to the people, and so provides a common objective to their activity. With such a common objective, the crowd is in a position to act with unity, purpose, and consistency.

The last step may be thought of as the stimulation and fostering of the impulses that correspond to the crowd objective, up to the point where the members are ready to act on them. This nurturing and crystallizing of impulses is a result of the interstimulation that takes place in milling and in response to leadership. It occurs primarily as a result of images that are aroused through the process of suggestion and imitation, and reinforced through mutual acceptance. When the members of a crowd have a common impulse oriented toward a fixed image and supported by an intense collective feeling, they are ready to act in the aggressive fashion typical of the acting crowd.

The Acting Crowd

It should be noted, first, that such a group is spontaneous and lives in the momentary present. As such it is not a society or a cultural group. Its action is not preset by accepted conventions, established expectations, or rules. It lacks other important marks of a society such as an established social organization, an established division of labor, a structure of established roles, a recognized leadership, a set of norms, a set of moral regulations, an awareness of its own identity, or a recognized "we-consciousness." Instead of acting, then, on the basis of established rule, it acts on the basis of aroused impulse. Just as it is, in this sense, a noncultural group, so likewise it tends to be a nonmoral group. In the light of this fact it is not difficult to understand that crowd actions may be strange, forbidding, and at times atrocious. Not having a body of definitions or rules to guide its behavior and, instead, acting on the basis of impulse, the crowd is fickle, suggestible, and irresponsible.

This character of the crowd can be appreciated better by understanding the condition of the typical member. Such an individual loses ordinary critical understanding and self-control as he enters into rapport with other crowd members and becomes infused by the collective excitement which dominates them. He responds immediately and directly to the remarks and actions of others instead of interpreting these gestures, as he would do in ordinary conduct. His inability to survey the actions of others before responding to them carries over to his own tendencies to act. Consequently, the impulses aroused in him by his sympathetic sharing of the collective excitement are likely to gain immediate expression instead of being submitted to his own judgment. This explains why suggestion is so pronounced in the crowd. It should be noted, however, that this suggestibility exists only along the line of the aroused impulses; suggestions made contrary to them are ignored. This limiting of the area of suggestibility, but with an intensification of the suggestibility inside of these limits, is a point which is frequently overlooked by students of crowd behavior.

The loss of customary critical interpretation and the arousing of impulses and excited feelings explain the queer, vehement, and surprising behavior so frequent among members of a genuine crowd. Impulses which ordinarily would be subject to a severe check by the individual's judgment and control of himself now have a free passage to expression. That many of these impulses should have an atavistic character is not strange, nor, consequently, is it surprising that much of the actual behavior should be violent, cruel, and destructive. Further, the release of impulses and feelings which encounter no restraint, which come to possess the individual, and which acquire a quasi-sanction through the support of other people, gives the individual a sense of power, of ego-expansion, and of rectitude. Thus, he is likely to experience a sense of invincibility and of conviction in his actions.

It should be borne in mind that this state of the members of the crowd is due to their extreme rapport and mutual excitement; and, in turn, that this rapport in the acting crowd has become organized around a common objective of activity. Common focusing of attention, rapport, and individual sub-mergence—these exist as different phases of one another, and explain the unity of the crowd and the general character of its behavior. We should note that individuals may be physically present in a crowd yet not participate sympathetically in its process of shared excitement; such individuals are not true members of the crowd.

To prevent the formation of a mob or to break up a mob it is necessary to disrupt the milling process so that attention ceases to be focused collectively on one object. This is the theoretical principle underlying crowd control. Insofar as the attention of the members is directed toward different objects, they form an aggregation of individuals instead of a crowd united by intimate rapport. Thus, to throw people into a state of panic, or to get them interested in other objects, or to get them engaged in discussion or argumentation represents different ways in which a crowd can be broken up.

Our discussion of the crowd has presented the psychological bond of the crowd, or the spirit, that may be called "crowd-mindedness," to use a felicitous phrase of E. A. Ross.[1] If we think in terms of crowd-mindedness, it is clear that many groups may take on the character of a crowd without having to be as small in size as in the instance of a lynching mob. Under certain conditions, a nation may come to be like a crowd. If the people become preoccupied with the same stirring event or object, if they develop a high state of mutual excitement marked by no disagreement, and if they have strong impulses to act toward the object with which they are preoccupied, their action will be like that of the crowd. We are familiar with such behavior on a huge scale in the case of social contagion, like that of patriotic hysteria.

The Expressive Crowd

The distinguishing feature of the acting crowd, as we have seen, is the direction of the attention toward some common objective or goal; the action of the crowd is the behavior gone through to reach that objective. In contrast, the expressive crowd has no goal or objective—its impulses and feelings are spent in mere expressive actions, usually in unrestrained physical movements, which give release to tension without having any other purpose. We see such behavior in a marked form in the saturnalia, the carnival, and the dancing crowds of primitive sects.

Comparisons with the Acting Crowd   In explaining the nature of the expressive crowd we should note that in formation and fundamental character it is very much like the acting crowd. It consists of people who are excited, who mill, and who in doing so, spread and intensify the excitement. There develops among them the same condition of rapport marked by quick and unwitting mutual responsiveness. Individuals lose awareness of themselves. Impulses and feelings are aroused, and are no longer subject to the constraint and control which an individual usually exercises over them. In these respects the expressive crowd is essentially like the acting crowd.

The fundamental difference is that the expressive crowd does not develop any image of a goal or objective, and, consequently, suggestion does not operate to build up a plan of action. Without having an objective toward which it might act, the crowd can release its aroused tension and excitement only in physical movement. Stated tersely, the crowd has to act, but it has nothing toward which it can act, and so it merely engages in excited movements. The excitement of the crowd stimulates further excitement which does not, however, become organized around some purposive act which the crowd seeks to carry out. In such a situation the expression of excited feeling becomes an end in itself; the behavior, therefore, may take the form of laugh-

ing, weeping, shouting, leaping, and dancing. In a more extreme expression, it may be in the form of uttering gibberish or having violent physical spasms.

Rhythmic Expression   Perhaps the most interesting feature of this expressive behavior, as it is carried on collectively, is that it tends to become rhythmical; so that with sufficient repetition and with the existence of sufficient rapport, it takes on the form of people's acting in unison. In more advanced form it comes to be like a collective dance; it is this aspect that leads one to designate the expressive crowd as a dancing crowd. It may be said that just as an acting crowd develops its unity through the formation of a common objective, the expressive crowd forms its unity through the rhythmical expression of its tension.

This feature is of outstanding significance, for it throws considerable light on the interesting association between "dancing" behavior and primitive religious sentiment. To illustrate this point, let us consider the experience of the individual in such a crowd.

The Individual in the Expressive Crowd   The stimulation that the individual receives from those with whom he is in rapport lessens his ordinary self-control and evokes and incites impulsive feelings which take possession of him. He feels carried away by a spirit whose source is unknown, but whose effect is acutely appreciated. There are two conditions which are likely to make this experience one of ecstasy and exaltation, and to seal it with a sacred or divine stamp. The first is that the experience is cathartic in nature. The individual who has been in a state of tension, discomfort, and perhaps anxiety, suddenly gains full release and experiences the joy and fullness that come with such relief. This organic satisfaction unquestionably yields a pleasure and exhilaration that makes the experience momentous. The fact that this mood has such complete and unobstructed control over the individual easily leads him to feel that he is possessed or pervaded by a kind of transcendental spirit. The other condition which gives the experience a religious character is the approval and sanction implied in the support coming from those with whom he is in rapport. The fact that others are sharing the same experience rids it of suspicion and enables its unqualified acceptance. When an experience gives complete and full satisfaction, when it is socially stimulated, approved, and sustained, and when it comes in the form of a mysterious possession from the outside, it easily acquires a religious character.

The Development of Collective Ecstasy

When an expressive crowd reaches the height of such collective ecstasy, the tendency is for this feeling to be projected upon objects which are sensed as having some intimate connection with it. Thereupon such objects become sacred to the members of the crowd. These objects may vary; they may include persons (such as a religious prophet), the dance, a song, or physical objects which are felt to be linked with the ecstatic experience. The appearance of such sacred objects lays the basis for the formation of a cult, sect, or primitive religion.

Not all expressive crowds attain this stage of development. Most of them do not pass beyond the early milling or excited stage. But implicitly, they have the potentiality of doing so, and they have most of the characteristic features even though they be in a subdued form.

Like the acting crowd, the expressive crowd need not be confined to a small compact group whose members are in immediate physical proximity of one another. The behavior which is characteristic of it may be found on occasion in a large group, such as the nation-wide public.

Evaluation

A brief evaluation of the acting crowd and the expressive crowd can be made here. Both of them are spontaneous groupings. Both of them represent elementary collectivities. Their form and structure are not traceable to any body of culture or set of rules; instead, such structures as they have, arise indigenously out of the milling of excited individuals. The acting crowd focuses its tension on an objective and so becomes organized around a plan of action; the expressive crowd merely releases its tension in expressive movement which tends to become rhythmical and establishes unity in this fashion. In both crowds the individual is stripped of much of his conscious, ordinary behavior, and is rendered malleable by the crucible of collective excitement. With the breakdown of his previous personal organization, he is in a position to develop new forms of conduct and to crystallize a new personal organization along new and different lines. In this sense, crowd behavior is a means by which the breakup of the social organization and personal structure is brought about, and at the same time is a potential device for the emergence of new forms of conduct and personality. The acting crowd presents one of the alternative lines for such reorganization—the development of aggressive behavior in the direction of the purposive social change. We shall view this line of reorganization as giving rise to a political order. The expressive crowd stands for the other alternative—the release of inner tension in conduct which tends to become sacred and marked by deep sentiment. This might be regarded as giving rise to a religious order of behavior.

The Mass

We are selecting the term *mass* to denote another elementary and spontaneous collective grouping which, in some respects, is like the crowd but is fundamentally different from it in other ways. The mass is represented by people who participate in mass behavior, such as those who are excited by some national event, those who share in a land boom, those who are interested in a murder trial which is reported in the press, or those who participate in some large migration.

Distinguishable Features of the Mass

So conceived, the mass has a number of distinguishable features. *First,* its membership may come from all walks of life, and from all distinguishable social strata; it may include people of different class position, of different vocation, of different cultural attainment, and of different wealth. One can recognize this in the case of the mass of people who follow a murder trial. *Second,* the mass is an anonymous group, or more exactly, is composed of anonymous individuals. *Third,* there exists little interaction or exchange of experience between the members of the mass. They are usually physically separated from one another, and, being anonymous, do not have the opportunity to mill as do the members of the crowd. *Fourth,* the mass is very loosely organized and is not able to act with the concertedness or unity that marks the crowd.

The Role of Individuals in the Mass

The fact that the mass consists of individuals belonging to a wide variety of local groups and cultures is important. For it signifies that the object of interest which gains the attention of those who form the mass is something which lies on the outside of the local cultures and groups; and therefore, that this object of interest is not defined or explained in terms of the understandings or rules of these local groups. The object of mass interest can be thought of as attracting the attention of people away from their local cultures and spheres of life and turning it toward a wider universe, toward areas which are not defined or covered by rules, regulations, or expectations. In this sense the mass can be viewed as constituted by detached and alienated individuals who face objects or areas of life which are interesting, but which are also puzzling and not easy to understand and order. Consequently, before such objects, the members of the mass are likely to be confused and uncertain in their actions. Further, in not being able to communicate with one another, except in limited and imperfect ways, the members of the mass are forced to act separately, as individuals.

Society and the Mass

From this brief characterization it can be seen that the mass is devoid of the features of a society or a community. It has no social organization, no body of custom and tradition, no established set of rules or rituals, no organized group of sentiments, no structure of status roles, and no established leadership. It merely consists of an aggregation of individuals who are separate, detached, anonymous, and thus, homogeneous as far as mass behavior is concerned. It can be seen, further, that the behavior of the mass, just because it is not made by pre-established rule or expectation, is spontaneous, indigenous, and elementary. In these respects, the mass is a great deal like the crowd.

In other respects, there is an important difference. It has already been noted that the mass does not mill or interact as the crowd does. Instead, the individuals are separated from one another and unknown to one another. This fact means that the individual in the mass, instead of being stripped of his self-awareness is, on the other hand, apt to be rather acutely self-conscious. Instead of acting in response to the suggestions and excited stimulation of those with whom he is in rapport, he acts in response to the object that has gained his attention and on the basis of the impulses that are aroused by it.

Nature of Mass Behavior

This raises the question as to how the mass behaves. The answer is in terms of each individual's seeking to answer his own needs. The form of mass behavior, paradoxically, is laid down by individual lines of activity and not by concerted action. These individual activities are primarily in the form of selections—such as the selection of a new dentifrice, a book, a play, a party platform, a new fashion, a philosophy, or a gospel—selections which are made in response to the vague impulses and feelings which are awakened by the object of mass interest. Mass behavior, even though a congeries of individual lines of action, may become a momentous significance. If these lines converge, the influence of the mass may be enormous, as is shown by the far-reaching effects on institutions ensuing from shifts in the selective interest of the mass. A political party may be disorganized or a commercial institution wrecked by such shifts in interest or taste.

When mass behavior becomes organized, as into a movement, it ceases to be mass behavior, but becomes societal in nature. Its whole nature changes in acquiring a structure, a program, a defining culture, traditions, prescribed rules, an in-group attitude, and a we-consciousness. It is for this reason that we have appropriately limited it to the forms of behavior which have been described.

Increasing Importance of Mass Behavior

Under conditions of modern urban and industrial life, mass behavior has emerged in increasing magnitude and importance. This is due primarily to the operation of factors which have detached people from their local cultures and local group settings. Migration, changes of residence, newspapers, motion pictures, the radio, education—all have operated to detach individuals from customary moorings and thrust them into a new and wider world. In the face of this world, individuals have had to make adjustments on the basis of largely unaided selections. The convergence of their selections has made the mass a potent influence. At times, its behavior comes to approximate that of a crowd, especially under conditions of excitement. At such times it is likely to be influenced by excited appeals as these appear in the press or over the radio—appeals that play upon primitive impulses, antipathies, and traditional hatreds. This should not obscure the fact that the mass may behave without such crowdlike frenzy. It may be much more influenced by an artist or a writer who happens to sense the vague feelings of the mass and to give expression and articulation to them.

Instances of Mass Behavior

In order to make clearer the nature of the mass and of mass behavior, a brief consideration can be given to a few instances. Gold rushes and land rushes illustrate many of the features of mass behavior. The people who participate in them usually come from a wide variety of backgrounds; together they constitute a heterogeneous assemblage. Thus, those who engaged in the Klondike Rush or the Oklahoma Land Boom came from different localities and areas. In the rush, each individual (or at best, family) had his own goal or objective so that between the participants there was a minimum of cooperation and very little feeling of allegiance or loyalty. Each was trying to get ahead of the other, and each had to take care of himself. Once the rush is under way, there is little discipline, and no organization to enforce order. Under such conditions it is easy to see how a rush turns into a stampede or a panic.

Mass Advertising

Some further appreciation of the nature of mass behavior is yielded by a brief treatment of mass advertising. In such advertising, the appeal has to be addressed to the anonymous individual. The relation between the advertisement and the prospective purchaser is a direct one—there is no organization or leadership which can deliver, so to speak, the body of purchasers to the seller. Instead, each individual acts upon the basis of his own selection. The purchasers are a heterogeneous group coming from many communities and walks of life; as members of the mass, however, because of their anonymity, they are homogeneous or essentially alike.

Proletarian Masses

What are sometimes spoken of as the proletarian masses illustrate other features of the mass. They represent a large population with little organization or effective communication. Such people usually have been wrested loose from a stable group life. They are usually disturbed, even though it be only in the form of vague hopes or new tastes and interests. Consequently, there is a lot of groping in their behavior—an uncertain process of selection among objects and ideas that come to their attention.

The Public

We shall consider the public as the remaining elementary collective grouping. The term *public* is used to refer to a group of people (*a*) who are confronted by an issue, (*b*) who are divided in their ideas as to how to meet the issue, and (*c*) who engage in discussion over the issue. As such, it is to be distinguished from a public in the sense of a national people, as when one speaks of the public of the United States, and also from a *following*, as in the instance of the "public" of a motion-picture star. The presence of an issue, of discussion, and of a collective opinion is the mark of the public.

The Public as a Group

We refer to the public as an elementary and spontaneous collective grouping because it comes into existence not as a result of design, but as a natural response to a certain kind of situation. That the public does not exist as an established group and that its behavior is not prescribed by traditions or cultural patterns is indicated by the very fact that its existence centers on the presence of an issue. As issues vary, so do the corresponding publics. And the fact that an issue exists signifies the presence of a situation which cannot be met on the basis of a cultural rule but which must be met by a collective decision arrived at through a process of discussion. In this sense, the public is a grouping that is spontaneous and not pre-established.

Characteristic Features of the Public

This elementary and spontaneous character of the public can be better appreciated by noticing that the public, like the crowd and the mass, is lacking in the characteristic features of a society. The existence of an issue means that the group has to act; yet there are no understandings, definitions, or rules prescribing what that action should be. If there were, there would be, of course, no issue. It is in this sense that we can speak of the public as having no culture—no traditions to dictate what its action shall be. Further, since a public comes into existence only with an issue it does not have the form or organization of a society. In it, people do not have fixed status roles. Nor does the public have any we-feeling or consciousness of its identity. Instead, the public is a kind of amorphous group whose size and membership varies with the issue; instead of having its activity prescribed, it is engaged in an effort to arrive at an act, and therefore forced to *create* its action.

The peculiarity of the public is that it is marked by disagreement and hence by *discussion* as to what should be done. This fact has a number of implications. For one thing, it indicates that the interaction that occurs in the public is markedly different from that which takes place in the crowd. A crowd mills, develops rapport, and reaches a unanimity unmarred by disagreement. The public interacts on the basis of interpretation, enters into dispute, and consequently is characterized by conflict relations. Correspondingly, individuals in the public are likely to have their self-consciousness intensified and their critical powers heightened instead of losing self-awareness and critical ability as occurs in the crowd. In the public, arguments are advanced, are criticized, and are met by counterarguments. The interaction, therefore, makes for opposition instead of the mutual support and unanimity that mark the crowd.

Another point of interest is that this discussion, which is based on difference, places some premium on facts and makes for rational consideration. While, as we shall see, the interaction may fall short by far of realizing these characteristics, the tendency is in their direction. The crowd means that rumor and spectacular suggestion predominate; but the presence of opposition and disagreement in the public means that contentions are challenged and become subject to criticism. In the face of attack that threatens to undermine their character, such contentions have to be bolstered or revised in the face of criticisms that cannot be ignored. Since facts can maintain their validity, they come to be valued; and since the discussion is argumenta-

tive, rational considerations come to occupy a role of some importance.

Behavior Patterns of the Public

Now we can consider the question as to how a public acts. This question is interesting, particularly because the public does not act like a society, a crowd, or the mass. A society manages to act by following a prescribed rule or consensus; a crowd, by developing rapport; and the mass, by the convergence of individual selections. But the public faces, in a sense, the dilemma of how to become a unit when it is actually divided, of how to act concertedly when there is a disagreement as to what the action should be. The public acquires its particular type of unity and manages to act by arriving at a collective decision or by developing a collective opinion. It becomes necessary to consider now the nature of public opinion and the manner of its formation.

The Public, the Crowd, and the Mass

Before concluding the discussion of the public, it should be pointed out that under certain conditions the public may be changed into a crowd. Most propaganda tends to do this, anyway. When the people in the public are aroused by an appeal to a sentiment which is common to them, they begin to mill and to develop rapport. Then, their expression is in the form of public sentiment and not public opinion. In modern life, however, there seems to be less tendency for the public to become the crowd than for it to be displaced by the mass. The increasing detachment of people from local life, the multiplication of public issues, the expansion of agencies of mass communication, together with other factors, have led people to act increasingly by individual selection rather than by participating in public discussion. So true is this, that in many ways the public and the mass are likely to exist intermingled with one another. This fact adds confusion to the scene of contemporary collective behavior and renders analysis by the student difficult.

Collective Groupings and Social Change

In the discussion of elementary collective groupings we have considered the acting crowd, the expressive crowd, the mass, and the public. There are other primitive groupings which we can mention here only briefly, such as the panic, the stampede, the strike, the riot, the "popular justice" vigilante committee, the procession, the cult, the mutiny, and the revolt. Most of these groupings represent variations of the crowd; each of them operates through the primitive mechanisms of collective behavior which we have described. Like the four major types which we have considered, they are not societies, but operate outside of a governing framework of rules and culture. They are elementary, natural, and spontaneous, arising under certain fit circumstances.

The appearance of elementary collective groupings is indicative of a process of social change. They have the dual character of implying the disintegration of the old and the appearance of the new. They play an important part in the development of new collective behavior and of new forms of social life. More accurately the typical mechanisms of primitive association which they show have a significant role in the formation of a new social order.

It is to this problem of the formation of a new social order, that we shall now devote ourselves. Our task will be to consider primarily the social movements by which new kinds of collective behavior are built up and crystallized into fixed social forms.

Social movements can be viewed as collective enterprises seeking to establish a new order of life. They have their inception in a condition of unrest, and derive their motive power on one hand from dissatisfaction with the current form of life, and on the other hand, from wishes and hopes for a new scheme or system of living. The career of a social movement depicts the emergence of a new order of life. In its beginning, a social movement is amorphous, poorly organized, and without form; the collective behavior is on the primitive level that we have already discussed, and the mechanisms of interaction are the elementary, spontaneous mechanisms of which we have spoken. As a social movement develops, it takes on the character of a society. It acquires organization and form, a body of customs and traditions, established leadership, an enduring division of labor, social rules and social values—in short, a culture, a social organization, and a new scheme of life.

Our treatment of social movements will deal with three kinds—general social movements, specific social movements, and expressive social movements.[2]

General Social Movements

By general social movements we have in mind movements such as the labor movement, the youth movement, the women's movement, and the peace movement. Their background is constituted by gradual and pervasive changes in the values of people—changes which can be called cultural drifts. Such cultural drifts stand for a general shifting in the ideas of people, particularly along the line of the conceptions which people have of themselves, and of their rights and privileges. Over a period of time many people may develop a new view of what they believe they are entitled to—a view largely made up of desires and hopes. It signifies the emergence of a new set of values, which influence people in the way in which they look upon their own lives. Examples of such cultural drifts in our own recent history are the increased value of health, the belief in free education, the extension of the franchise, the emancipation of women, the increasing regard for children, and the increasing prestige of science.

Indefinite Images and Behavior

The development of the new values which such cultural drifts bring forth involves some interesting psychological changes which provide the motivation for general social movements. They mean, in a general sense, that people have come to form new conceptions of themselves which do not conform to the actual positions which they occupy in their life. They acquire new dispositions and interests and, accordingly, become sensitized in new directions; and, conversely, they come to experience dissatisfaction where before they had none. These new images of themselves, which people begin to develop in response to cultural drifts, are vague and indefinite; and correspondingly, the behavior in response to such images is uncertain and without definite aim. It is this feature which provides a clue for the understanding of general social movements.

Characteristics of General Social Movements

General social movements take the form of groping and uncoordinated efforts. They have only a general direction, toward which they move in a slow, halting, erratic yet persistent fashion. As movements they are unorganized, with neither established leadership nor recognized membership, and little guidance and control. Such a movement as the women's movement, which has the general and vague aim of the emancipation of women, suggests these features of a general social movement. The women's movement, like all general social movements, operates over a wide range—in the home, in marriage, in education, in industry, in politics, in travel—in each area of which it represents a search for an arrangement which will answer to the new idea of status being formed by women. Such a movement is episodic in its career, with very scattered manifestations of activity. It may show considerable enthusiasm at one point and reluctance and inertia at another; it may experience success in one area, and abortive effort in another. In general, it may be said that its progress is very uneven with setbacks, reverses, and frequent retreading of the same ground. At one time the impetus to the movement may come from people in one place, at another time in another place. On the whole the movement is likely to be carried on by many unknown and obscure people who struggle in different areas without their striving and achievements becoming generally known.

A general social movement usually is characterized by a literature, but the literature is as varied and ill-defined as is the movement itself. It is likely to be an expression of protest, with a general depiction of a kind of utopian existence. As such, it vaguely outlines a philosophy based on new values and self-conceptions. Such a literature is of great importance in spreading a message or view, however imprecise it may be, and so in implanting suggestions, awakening hopes, and arousing dissatisfactions. Similarly, the "leaders" of a general social movement play an important part—not in the sense of exercising directive control over the movement, but in the sense of being pace-makers. Such leaders are likely to be "voices in the wilderness," pioneers without any solid following, and frequently not very clear about their own goals. However, their example helps to develop sensitivities, arouse hopes, and break down resistances. From these traits one can easily realize that the general social movement develops primarily in an informal, inconspicuous, and largely subterranean fashion. Its media of interaction are primarily reading, conversations, talks, discussions, and the perception of examples. Its achievements and operations are likely to be made primarily in the realm of individual experience rather than by noticeable concerted action of groups. It seems evident that the general social movement is dominated to a large extent by the mechanisms of mass behavior, such as we have described in our treatment of the mass. Especially in its earlier stages, general social movements are likely to be merely an aggregation of individual lines of action based on individual decisions and selections. As is characteristic of the mass and of mass behavior, general social movements are rather formless in organization and inarticulate in expression.

The Basis for Specific Social Movements

Just as cultural drifts provide the background out of which emerge general social movements, so the general social movement constitutes the setting out of which develop specific social movements. Indeed, a specific social movement is usually a crystallization of much of the motivation of dissatisfaction, hope, and desire awakened by the general social movement and the focusing of this motivation on some specific objective. A convenient illustration is the antislavery movement, which was, to a considerable degree, an individual expression of the widespread humanitarian movement of the nineteenth century. With this recognition of the relation between general and specific social movements, we can turn to a consideration of the latter.

Specific Social Movements

The outstanding instances of this type of movement are reform movements and revolutionary movements. A specific social movement is one which has a well-defined objective or goal which it seeks to reach. In this effort it develops an organization and structure, making it essentially a society. It develops a recognized and accepted leadership and a definite membership characterized by a "we-consciousness." It forms a body of traditions, a guiding set of values, a philosophy, sets of rules, and a general body of expectations. Its members form allegiances and loyalties. Within it there develops a division of labor, particularly in the form of a social structure in which individuals occupy status positions. Thus, individuals develop personalities and conceptions of themselves, representing the individual counterpart of a social structure.

A social movement, of the specific sort, does not come into existence with such a structure and organization already established. Instead, its organization and its culture are developed in the course of its career. It is necessary to view social movements from this temporal and developmental perspective. In the beginning a social movement is loosely organized and characterized by impulsive behavior. It has no clear objective; its behavior and thinking are largely under the dominance of restlessness and collective excitement. As a social movement develops, however, its behavior, which was originally dispersed, tends to become organized, solidified, and persistent. It is possible to delineate stages roughly in the career of a social movement which represent this increasing organization. One scheme of four stages has been suggested by Dawson and Gettys.[3] These are the stage of social unrest, the stage of popular excitement, the stage of formalization, and the stage of institutionalization.

Stages of Development

In the first of these four stages people are restless, uneasy, and act in the random fashion that we have considered. They are susceptible to appeals and suggestions that tap their discontent, and hence, in this stage, the agitator is likely to play an important role. The random and erratic behavior is significant in sensitizing people to one another and so makes possible the focusing of their restlessness on certain objects. The stage of popular excitement is marked even more by milling, but it is not quite so random and aimless. More definite notions emerge as to the cause of their condition and as to what should be done in the way of social change. So there is a sharpening of objectives. In this stage the leader is likely to be a prophet or a reformer. In the stage of formalization the movement becomes more clearly organized with rules, policies, tactics, and discipline. Here the leader is likely to be in the nature of a statesman. In this institutional stage, the movement has crystallized into a fixed organization with a definite personnel and structure to carry into execution the purpose of the movement. Here the leader is likely to be an administrator. In considering the development of the specific social movement our interest is less in considering the stages through which it passes than in discussing the mechanisms and means through which such a movement is able to grow and become organized. It is convenient to group these mechanisms under five heads: (1) agitation (2) development of *esprit de corps*, (3) development of morale, (4) the formation of an ideology, and (5) the development of operating tactics.

The Role of Agitation   Agitation is of primary importance in a social movement. It plays its most significant role in the beginning and early stages of a movement, although it may persist in minor form in the later portions of the life-cycle of the movement. As the term suggests, agitation operates to arouse people and so make them possible recruits for the movement. It is essentially a means of exciting people and of awakening within them new impulses and ideas which make them restless and dissatisfied. Consequently, it acts to loosen the hold on them of their previous attachments, and to break down their previous ways of thinking and acting. For a movement to begin and gain impetus, it is necessary for people to be jarred loose from their customary ways of thinking and believing, and to have aroused within them new impulses and wishes. This is what agitation seeks to do. To be successful, it must first gain the attention of people; second, it must excite them, and arouse feelings and impulses; and third, it must give some direction to these impulses and feelings through ideas, suggestions, criticisms, and promises.

Agitation operates in two kinds of situations. One is a situation marked by abuse, unfair discrimination, and injustice, but a situation wherein people take this mode of life for granted and do not raise questions about it. Thus, while the situation is potentially fraught with suffering and protest, the people are marked by inertia. Their views of their situation incline them to accept it; hence the function of the agitation is to lead them to challenge and question their own modes of living. It is in such a situation that agitation may create social unrest where none existed previously. The other situation is one wherein people are already aroused, restless, and discontented, but where they either are too timid to act or else do not know what to do. In this situation the function of agitation is not so much to implant the seeds of unrest, as to intensify, release, and direct the tensions which people already have.

Agitators seem to fall into two types corresponding roughly to these two situations. One type of agitator is an excitable, restless, and aggressive individual. His dynamic and energetic behavior attracts the attention of people to him; and the excitement and restlessness of his behavior tends to infect them. He is likely to act with dramatic gesture and to talk in terms of spectacular imagery. His appearance and behavior foster the contagion of unrest and excitment. This type of agitator is likely to be most successful in the situation where people are already disturbed and unsettled; in such a situation his own excited and energetic activity can easily arouse other people who are sensitized to such behavior and already disposed to excitability.

The second type of agitator is more calm, quiet, and dignified. He stirs people not by what he does, but what he says. He is likely to be a man sparing in his words, but capable of saying very caustic, incisive, and biting things—things which get "under the skin" of people and force them to view things in new light. This type of agitator is more suited to the first of the social situations discussed—the situation where people endure hardships or discrimination without developing attitudes of resentment. In this situation, his function is to make people aware of their own position and of the inequalities, deficiencies, and injustices that seem to mark their lot. He leads them to raise questions about what they have previously taken for granted and to form new wishes, inclinations, and hopes.

The function of agitation, as stated above, is in part to dislodge and stir up people and so liberate them for movement in new directions. More specifically, it operates to change the conceptions which people have of themselves, and the notions which they have of their rights and dues. Such new conceptions involving beliefs that one is justly entitled to privileges from which he is excluded, provide the dominant motive force for the social movement. Agitation, as the means of implanting these new conceptions among people, becomes, in this way, of basic importance to the success of a social movement.

A brief remark relative to the tactics of agitation may be made here. It is sufficient to say that the tactics of agitation vary with the situation, the people, and the culture. A procedure which may be highly successful in one situation may turn out to be ludicrous in another situation. This suggests the problem of identifying different types of situations and correlating with each the appropriate form of agitation. Practically no study has been conducted on this problem. Here, one can merely state the truism that the agitator, to be successful, must sense the thoughts, interests, and values of his listeners.

The Development of Esprit de Corps

Agitation is merely the means of arousing the interest of people and thus getting them to participate in a movement. While it serves to recruit members, to give initial impetus, and to give some direction, by itself it could never organize or sustain a movement. Collective activities based on mere agitation would be sporadic, disconnected, and short-lived. Other mechanisms have to enter to give solidity and persistency to a social movement. One of these is the development of *esprit de corps*.

Esprit de corps might be thought of as the organizing of feelings on behalf of the movement. In itself, it is the sense which people have of belonging together and of being identified with one another in a common undertaking. Its basis is constituted by a condition of rapport. In developing feelings of intimacy and closeness, people have the sense of sharing a common experience and of forming a select group. In one another's presence they feel at ease and as comrades. Personal reserve breaks down and feelings of strangeness, difference, and alienation disappear. Under such conditions, relations tend to be of cooperation instead of personal competition. The behavior of one tends to facilitate the release of behavior on the part of others, instead of tending to inhibit or check that behavior; in this sense each person tends to inspire others. Such conditions of mutual sympathy and responsiveness obviously make for concerted behavior.

Esprit de corps is of importance to a social movement in other ways. Very significant is the fact that it serves to reinforce the new conception of himself that the individual has formed as a result of the movement and of his participation in it. His feeling of belonging with others, and they with him, yields him a sense of collective support. In this way his views of himself and of the aims of the movement are maintained and invigorated. It follows that the development of *esprit de corps* helps to foster an attachment of people to a movement. Each individual has his sentiments focused on, and intertwined with, the objectives of the movement. The resulting feeling of expansion which he experiences is in the direction of greater allegiance to the movement. It should be clear that *esprit de corps* is an important means of developing solidarity and so of giving solidity to a movement.

How is *esprit de corps* developed in a social movement? It would seem chiefly in three ways: the development of an in-group–out-group relation, the formation of informal fellowship association, and the participation in formal ceremonial behavior.

The In-Group–Out-Group Relation   The nature of the in-group–out-group relation should be familiar to the student. It exists when two groups come to identify each other as enemies. In such a situation each group regards itself as the upholder of virtue and develops among its members feelings of altruism, loyalty, and fidelity. The out-group is regarded as unscrupulous and vicious, and is felt to be attacking the values which the in-group holds dear. Before the out-group the members of the in-group not only feel that they are right and correct, but believe they have a common responsibility to defend and preserve their values.

The value of these in-group–out-group attitudes in developing solidarity in a social movement is quite clear. The belief on the part of its members that the movement is being opposed unjustly and unfairly by vicious and unscrupulous groups serves to rally the members around their aims and values. To have an enemy, in this sense, is very important for imparting solidarity to the movement. In addition, the "enemy" plays the important role of a scapegoat. It is advantageous to a movement to develop an enemy; this development is usually in itself spontaneous. Once made, it functions to establish *esprit de corps*.

Informal Fellowship   *Esprit de corps* is formed also in a very significant way by the development of informal association on the basis of fellowship. Where people can come together informally in this way they have the opportunity of coming to know one another as human beings instead of as institutional symbols. They are then in a much better position to take one another's roles and, unwittingly, to share one another's experience. It seems that in such a relationship, people unconsciously import and assimilate into themselves the gestures, attitudes, values, and philosophy of life of one another. The net result is to develop a common sympathy and sense of intimacy which contributes much to solidarity. Thus, we find in social movements the emergence and use of many kinds of informal and communal association. Singing, dancing, picnics, joking, having fun, and friendly informal conversation are important devices of this sort in a social movement. Through them, the individual gets a sense of status and a sense of social acceptance and support, in place of prior loneliness and personal alienation.

Ceremonial Behavior   The third important way in which social movements develop *esprit de corps* is through the use of formal ceremonial behavior and of ritual. The value of mass meetings, rallies, parades, huge demonstrations, and commemorative ceremonies has always been apparent to those entrusted with the development of a social movement; the value is one that comes from large assemblages, in the form of the sense of vast support that is experienced by the participant. The psychology that is involved here is the psychology of being on parade. The individual participant experiences the feeling of considerable personal expansion and therefore has the sense of being somebody distinctly important. Since this feeling of personal expansion comes to be identified with the movement as such, it makes for *esprit de corps.* Likewise, the paraphernalia of ritual possessed by every movement serves to foster feelings of common identity and sympathy. This paraphernalia consists of a set of sentimental symbols, such as slogans, songs, cheers, poems, hymns, expressive gestures, and uniforms. Every movement has some of these. Since they acquire a sentimental significance symbolizing the common feelings about the movement, their use serves as a constant reliving and re-enforcement of these mutual feelings.

Esprit de corps may be regarded, then, as an organization of group feeling and essentially as a form of group enthusiasm. It is what imparts life to a movement. Yet just as agitation is inadequate for the development of a movement, so is mere reliance on *esprit de corps* insufficient. A movement which depends entirely on *esprit de corps* is usually like a boom and is likely to collapse in the face of a serious crisis. Since the allegiance which it commands is based merely on heightened enthusiasm, it is likely to vanish with the collapse of such enthusiasm. Thus, to succeed, especially in the face of adversity, a movement must command a more persistent and fixed loyalty. This is yielded by the development of morale.

The Development of Morale As we have seen, *esprit de corps* is a collective feeling which gives life, enthusiasm, and vigor to a movement. Morale can be thought of as giving persistency and determination to a movement; its test is whether solidarity can be maintained in the face of adversity. In this sense, morale can be thought of as a group will or an enduring collective purpose.

Morale seems to be based on, and yielded by, a set of convictions. In the case of a social movement these seem to be of three kinds. First is a conviction of the rectitude of the purpose of the movement. This is accompanied by the belief that the attainment of the objectives of the movement will usher in something approaching a millennial state. What is evil, unjust, improper, and wrong will be eradicated with the success of the movement. In this sense, the goal is always overvalued. Yet these beliefs yield to the numbers of a movement a marked confidence in themselves. A second conviction closely identified with these beliefs is a faith in the ultimate attainment, by the movement, of its goal. There is believed to be a certain inevitability about this. Since the movement is felt to be a necessary agent for the regeneration of the world, it is regarded as being in line with the higher moral values of the universe, and in this sense as divinely favored. Hence, there arises the belief that success is inevitable, even though it be only after a hard struggle. Finally, as part of this complex of convictions, there is the belief that the movement is charged with a sacred mission. Together, these convictions serve to give an enduring and unchangeable character to the goal of a movement and a tenacity to its effort. Obstructions, checks, and reversals are occasions for renewed effort instead of for disheartenment and despair, since they do not seriously impair the faith in the rectitude of the movement nor in the inevitability of its success.

It is clear from this explanation that the development of morale in a movement is essentially a matter of developing a sectarian attitude and a religious faith. This provides a cue to the more prominent means by which morale is built up in a movement. One of these is found in the emergence of a saint cult which is to be discerned in every enduring and persisting social movement. There is usually a major saint and a series of minor saints, chosen from the popular leaders of the movement. Hitler, Lenin, Marx, Mary Baker Eddy, and Sun Yat-sen will serve as convenient examples of major saints. Such leaders become essentially deified and endowed with miraculous power. They are regarded as grossly superior, intelligent, and infallible. People develop toward them attitudes of reverence and awe, and resent efforts to depict them as ordinary human beings. The pictures or other mementos of such individuals come to have the character of religious idols. Allied with the saints of a movement are its heroes and its martyrs. They also come to be regarded as sacred figures. The development of this whole saint cult is an important means of imparting essentially a religious faith to the movement and of helping to build up the kind of convictions spoken of above.

Similar in function is the emergence in the movement of a creed and of a sacred literature. These, again, are to be found in all persisting social movements. Thus, as has been said frequently, *Das Kapital* and *Mein Kampf* have been the bibles respectively of the communist movement and of the National Socialist movement. The role of a creed and literature of this sort in imparting religious conviction to a movement should be clear.

Finally, great importance must be attached to myths in the development of morale in a social movement. Such myths may be varied. They may be myths of being a select group or a chosen people; myths of the inhumanity of one's opponents; myths about the destiny of the movement; myths depicting a glorious and millennial society to be realized by the movement. Such myths usually grow out of, and in response to, the desires and hopes of the people in the movement and acquire by virtue of their collective character a solidity, a permanency, and an unquestioned acceptance. It is primarily through them that the members of the movement achieve the dogmatic fixity of their convictions, and seek to justify their actions to the rest of the world.

The Development of Group Ideology   Without an ideology a social movement would grope along in an uncertain fashion and could scarcely maintain itself in the face of pointed opposition from outside groups. Hence, the ideology plays a significant role in the life of a movement; it is a mechanism essential to the persistency and development of a movement. The ideology of a movement consists of a body of doctrine, beliefs, and myths. More specifically, it seems to consist of the following: *first*, a statement of the objective, purpose, and premises of the movement; *second*, a body of criticism and condemnation of the existing structure which the movement is attacking and seeking to change; *third*, a body of defense doctrine which serves as a justification of the movement and of its objective; *fourth*, a body of belief dealing with policies, tactics, and practical operation of the movement; and, *fifth*, the myths of the movement.

This ideology is almost certain to be of a twofold character. In the first place, much of it is erudite and scholarly. This is the form in which it is developed by the intellectuals of the movement. It is likely to consist of elaborate treatises of an abstract and highly logical character. It grows up usually in response to the criticism of outside intellectuals, and seeks to gain for its tenets a respectable and defensible position in this world of higher learning and higher intellectual values. The ideology has another character, however—a popular character. In this guise, it seeks to appeal to the uneducated and to the masses. In its popular character, the ideology takes the form of emotional symbols, shibboleths, stereotypes, smooth and graphic phrases, and folk arguments. It deals, also, with the tenets of the movement, but presents them in a form that makes for their ready comprehension and consumption.

The ideology of a movement may be thought of as providing a movement with its philosophy and its psychology. It gives a set of values, a set of convictions, a set of criticisms, a set of arguments, and a set of defenses. As such, it furnishes to a movement (a) direction, (b) justification, (c) weapons of attack, (d) weapons of defense, and (e) inspiration and hope. To be effective in these respects, the ideology must carry respectability and prestige—a character that is provided primarily by the intelligentsia of the movement. More important than this, however, is the need of the ideology to answer to the distress, wishes, and hopes of the people. Unless it has this popular appeal, it will be of no value to the movement.

The Role of Tactics We have referred to tactics as the fifth major mechanism essential to the development of a social movement. Obviously the tactics are evolved along three lines: gaining adherents, holding adherents, and reaching objectives. Little more can be said than this, unless one deals with specific kinds of movements in specific kinds of situations. For, tactics are always dependent on the nature of the situation in which a movement is operating and always with reference to the cultural background of the movement. This functional dependency of tactics on the peculiarity of the situation helps to explain the ludicrous failures that frequently attend the applica-

tion of certain tactics to one situation even though they may have been successful in other situations. To attempt revolutionary tactics these days in terms of the tactics of two centuries ago would be palpably foolish. Similarly, to seek to develop a movement in this country in terms of tactics employed in a similar movement in some different cultural setting would probably bring very discouraging results. In general, it may be said that tactics are almost by definition flexible and variable, taking their form from the nature of the situation, the exigencies of the circumstances, and the ingenuity of the people.

We can conclude this discussion of the five mechanisms considered merely by reiterating that the successful development of a movement is dependent on them. It is these mechanisms which establish a program, set policies, develop and maintain discipline, and evoke allegiance.

Reform and Revolution

Mention has been made of the fact that specific social movements are primarily of two sorts: reform and revolutionary movements. Both seek to effect changes in the social order and in existing institutions. Their lifecycles are somewhat similar, and the development of both is dependent on the mechanisms which we have just discussed. However, noteworthy differences exist between the two; some of these differences will now be indicated.

The two movements differ in the *scope of their objectives*. A reform movement seeks to change some specific phase or limited area of the existing social order; it may seek, for example, to abolish child labor or to prohibit the consumption of alcohol. A revolutionary movement has a broader aim; it seeks to reconstruct the entire social order.

This difference in objective is linked with a *different vantage point of attack*. In endeavoring to change just a portion of the prevailing social order, the reform movement accepts the basic tenets of that social order. More precisely, the reform movement accepts the existing mores; indeed, it uses them to criticize the social defects which it is attacking. The reform movement starts with the prevailing code of ethics, and derives much of its support because it is so well grounded on the ethical side. This makes its position rather unassailable. It is difficult to attack a reform movement or reformers on the basis of their moral aims; the attack is usually more in the form of caricature and ridicule, and in characterizing reformers as visionary and impractical. By contrast, a revolutionary movement always challenges the existing mores and proposes a new scheme of moral values. Hence, it lays itself open to vigorous attack from the standpoint of existing mores.

A third difference between the two movements follows from the points which have been made. A reform movement has *respectability*. By virtue of accepting the existing social order and of orienting itself around the ideal code, it has a claim on existing institutions. Consequently, it makes use of these institutions such as the school, the church, the press, established clubs, and the government. Here again the revolutionary movement stands in marked contrast. In attacking the social order and in rejecting its mores, the revolutionary movement is blocked by existing institutions and its use of them is forbidden. Thus, the revolutionary movement is usually and finally driven underground; whatever use is made of existing institutions has to be carefully disguised. In general, whatever agitation, proselytizing, and maneuvers are carried on by revolutionary movements have to be done outside the fold of existing institutions. In the event that a reform movement is felt as challenging too seriously some powerful class or vested interests, it is likely to have closed to it the use of existing institutions.

This tends to change a reform movement into a revolutionary movement; its objectives broaden to include the reorganization of the institutions which are now blocking its progress.

The differences in position between reform and revolutionary movements bring in an important distinction in their *general procedure and tactics*. A reform movement endeavors to proceed by developing a public opinion favorable to its aims; consequently, it seeks to establish a public issue and to make use of the discussion process which we have already considered. The reform party can be viewed as a conflict group, opposed by interest groups and surrounded by a large inert population. The reform movement addresses its message to this indifferent or disinterested public in the effort to gain its support. In contradistinction, the revolutionary movement does not seek primarily to influence public opinion, but instead tries to make converts. In this sense it operates more like a religion.

This means some difference as to groups among which the two movements respectively conduct their agitation and seek their adherents. The reform movement, while usually existing on behalf of some distressed or exploited group, does little to establish its strength among them. Instead, it tries to enlist the allegiance of a middle-class public on the outside and to awaken within them a vicarious sympathy for the oppressed group. Hence, generally, it is infrequent that the leadership or membership of a reform movement comes from the group whose rights are being espoused. In this sense a revolutionary movement differs. Its agitation is carried on among those who are regarded as in a state of distress or exploitation. It endeavors to establish its strength by bringing these people inside of its ranks. Hence, the revolutionary movement is usually a lower-class movement operating among the underprivileged.

Finally, by virtue of these characteristic differences, the two movements diverge in their functions. The primary function of the reform movement is probably not so much the bringing about of social change, as it is to reaffirm the ideal values of a given society. In the case of a revolutionary movement, the tendency to dichotomize the world between those who have and those who have not, and to develop a strong, cohesive, and uncompromising group out of the latter, makes its function that of introducing a new set of essentially religious values.

A concluding remark may be made about specific social movements. They can be viewed as societies in miniature, and as such, represent the building up of organized and formalized collective behavior out of what was originally amorphous and undefined. In their growth a social organization is developed, new values are formed, and new personalities are organized. These,

indeed, constitute their residue. They leave behind an institutional structure and a body of functionaries, new objectives and views, and a new set of self-conceptions.

NOTES

1. E. A. Ross, *Social Psychology* (New York: Macmillan Co., 1908).
2. Attention is called, in passing, to spatial movements, such as nomadic movements, barbaric invasions, crusades, pilgrimages, colonization, and migrations. Such movements may be carried on as societies, as in the case of tribal migrations; as diverse peoples with a common goal, as in the case of the religious crusades of the Middle Ages; or as individuals with similar goals, as in most of the immigration into the United States. In themselves, such movements are too complicated and diversified to be dealt with adequately here.
3. C. A. Dawson and W. E. Gettys, *Introduction to Sociology* (Rev. ed.; New York: Ronald Press Co., 1935, chap. 19).

6

THE POLITICS OF MASS SOCIETY

WILLIAM KORNHAUSER

Mass society is a situation in which an aggregate of individuals are related to one another only by way of their relation to a common authority, especially the state. That is, individuals are not directly related to one another in a variety of independent groups. A population in this condition is not insulated in any way from the ruling

group, nor yet from elements within itself. For insulation requires a multiplicity of independent and often conflicting forms of association, each of which is strong enough to ward off threats to the autonomy of the individual. But it is precisely the weakness or absence of such social groups, *rather than their equality*, which distinguishes the mass society, according to these theorists. In their absence, people lack the resources to restrain their own behavior as well as that of others. Social atomization engenders strong feelings of alienation and anxiety, and therefore the disposition to engage in extreme behavior to escape from these tensions. In a mass society there is a heightened readiness to form hyper-attachments to symbols and leaders. "Such loyalty can be expected only from the completely isolated human being who, without any other social ties...derives his sense of having a place in the world only from his belonging to a movement" (Arendt, 1951, pp. 316–17). Total loyalty, in turn, is the psychological basis for total domination, i.e., totalitarianism.

There are three major terms implied in the democratic criticism of mass society growing: (a) growing atomization (loss of community); (b) widespread readiness to embrace new ideologies (quest for community); (c) totalitarianism (total domination by pseudo-community). In this universe of discourse, mass society is a condition in which elite domination replaces democratic rule. Mass society is objectively the *atomized* society, and subjectively the *alienated* population. Therefore, mass society is a system in which there is *high availability of a population for mobilization by elites.*

People become available for mobilization by elites when they lack or lose an independent group life. The term *masses* applies "only where we deal with people who...cannot be integrated into any organization based on common interest, into political parties or municipal governments or professional organizations or trade unions" (Arendt, 1951, p. 305). The lack of autonomous relations generates widespread social alienation. Alienation heightens responsiveness to the appeal of mass movements because they provide occasions for expressing resentment against what is, as well as promises of a totally different world. In short, *people who are atomized readily become mobilized.* Since totalitarianism is a state of total mobilization, mass society is highly vulnerable to totalitarian movements and regimes.

Mass behavior is a form of collective behavior exhibiting the following character-

istics.[1] (a) *The focus of attention is remote from personal experience and daily life.* Remote objects are national and international issues or events, abstract symbols, and whatever else is known only through the mass media. Of course, not *any* concern for remote objects is a manifestation of mass behavior. Only when that concern leads to direct and activist modes of response can we speak of mass behavior. However, merely by virtue of the fact that mass behavior always involves remote objects certain consequences are likely to follow. Concern for remote objects tends to lack the definiteness, independence, sense of reality, and responsibility to be found in concern for proximate objects. The sphere of proximate objects consists of things that directly concern the individual:

> his family, his business dealings, his hobbies, his friends and enemies, his township or ward, his class, church, trade union or any other social group of which he is an active member—the things under his personal observation, the things which are familiar to him independently of what his newspaper tells him, which he can directly influence or manage and for which he develops the kind of responsibility that is induced by a direct relation to the favorable or unfavorable effects of a course of action. (Schumpeter, 1947, pp. 258–9)

The sense of reality and responsibility declines as the object of concern becomes more remote:

> Now this comparative definiteness of volition and rationality of behavior does not suddenly vanish as we move away from those concerns of daily life in the home and in business which educate and discipline us. In the realm of public affairs there are sectors that are more within the reach of the citizen's mind than others. This is true, first, of local

affairs. Even there we find a reduced power of discerning facts, a reduced preparedness to act upon them, a reduced sense of responsibility. . . . Second, there are many national issues that concern individuals and groups so directly and unmistakably as to evoke volitions that are genuine and definite enough. The most important instance is afforded by issues involving immediate and personal pecuniary profit to individual voters and groups of voters. . . . However, when we move still farther away from the private concerns of the family and the business office into those regions of national and international affairs that lack a direct and unmistakable link with those private concerns, individual volition, command of facts and method of inference soon [decline]. (Schumpeter, 1947, pp. 260–1)

(b) *The mode of response to remote objects is direct.* The lessening of the sense of reality and responsibility and effective volition with the greater remoteness of the focus of attention has particularly marked consequences when the mode of response is direct, rather than being mediated by several intervening layers of social relations. People act directly when they do not engage in discussion on the matter at hand, and when they do not act through groups in which they are capable of persuading and being persuaded by their fellows.

At times, people may act directly by grasping those means of action which lie immediately to hand. They may employ various more or less coercive measures against those individuals and groups who resist them (Heberle, 1951, p. 378). For example, when large numbers of people feel that taxes are intolerably high, they may engage in quite different types of action. On the one hand, they may seek to change the tax laws by financing lobbyists, electing rep-

resentatives, persuading others of their views by means of discussion, and so forth. These types of action are mediated by institutional relations, and are therefore subject to rules concerning legitimate modes of political action. On the other hand, people may seek to prevent others from paying their taxes and forcibly impede officials from collecting taxes, as in the instance of the Poujadists in France. This is direct action.

Mass behavior is associated with activist interpretations of democracy and with increasing reliance on force to resolve social conflict. . . . The breakdown of normal restraints, including internalized standards of right conduct, and established channels of action . . . frees the mass to engage in direct, unmediated efforts to achieve its goals and to lay hands upon the most readily accessible instruments of action. Ordinarily, even in countries having democratic constitutional systems, the population is so structured as to inhibit direct access to the agencies of decision. The electorate participates at specified times and in defined ways; it is not free to create *ad hoc* methods of pressure. The citizen, even when organized in a pressure group supporting, say, a farm lobby, can vote, write letters, visit his congressman, withhold funds, and engage in similar respectable actions. Other forms of activity are strange to him. But when this code has lost its power over him, he will become available for activist modes of intervention. (Selznick, 1952, pp. 293–4)

Political activism tends to be undemocratic because it abrogates institutional procedures intended to guarantee both majority choice and minority rights, and denies respect for principles of free competition and public discussion as the bases for compromising conflicting interests. When political activism is taken to the extreme, it is expressed in violence against opposition. This violence may be restricted to sporadic riots and mob action; or it may become embodied in the very principles of a mass movement. A philosophy of direct action was developed by Sorel (1950) in his idea of the general strike, an idea which influenced such mass movements as revolutionary syndicalism in France, as well as many totalitarian movements, such as fascism in Italy, nazism in Germany, and communism in Russia (Heberle, 1951, pp. 382–6). Totalitarian movements carry their activism to extremes, as indicated by the widespread use of violence on the part of the Fascists in post-war Italy, the Nazis in the Weimar Republic, and the Communists in all countries in which they have developed organizations. Violence also characterizes certain mass movements, like the I.W.W. and the K.K.K. Violence in word and deed is the hallmark of the mass movement uncommitted to institutional means. Mass behavior, then, involves direct, activist modes of response to remote symbols.

(c) Mass behavior also tends to be highly unstable, readily shifting its focus of attention and intensity of response. Activist responses are likely to alternate with apathetic responses. *Mass apathy* as well as mass activism is widespread in mass society. Mass apathy, like mass activism, is unstable and unpredictable, since it, too, is born of social alienation; and as an expression of resentment against the social order it can be transformed into extremist attacks on that order in times of crisis. In these respects, mass apathy differs from that indifference to public matters that is based on traditional conceptions of appropriate spheres of participation (for example, the indifference of women who believe that politics is a man's affair).

(d) When mass behavior becomes organized around a program and acquires a certain continuity in purpose and effort, it takes on the character of a *mass movement* (Blumer, 1946, p. 187). Mass movements generally have the following characteristics: their objectives are remote and extreme; they favor activist modes of intervention in the social order; they mobilize uprooted and atomized sections of the population; they lack an internal structure of independent groups (such as regional or functional units with some freedom of action). Totalitarian movements also possess these characteristics, but mass movements need not become totalitarian. The distinctive character of totalitarian movements lies in their effort to gain total control over their followers and over the whole society. Totalitarian movements are highly organized by an elite bent on total power, whereas mass movements tend to be amorphous collectivities, often without any stable leadership. The difference between the Communist movement and the I.W.W. is an example of the difference between a totalitarian movement and a mass movement.

Mass movements are miniature mass societies; totalitarian movements are miniature totalitarian societies. This parallelism implies the major similarity and the major difference between the two types of social movements: they both are based on atomized masses rather than on independent social groups, as are mass societies and totalitarian societies; on the other hand, the amorphous structure of the mass movement corresponds to the ease of access to elites in mass society, while the cadre organization of the totalitarian movement corresponds to the inaccessibility of the elite in totalitarian society.

Mass movements offer excellent opportunities for penetration by totalitarian groups. The Communist party, for example, deliberately creates cadres for the purpose of capturing mass movements.

> The Communist membership functions as the cadre of a wider mass movement. Each member has special training and ideally should be able to lead nonparty groups as they may from time to time become accessible. . . . In sum, the cadre party is a highly manipulable skeleton organization of trained agents; it is sustained by political combat and is linked to the mass movement as its members become leaders of wider groups in the community. (Selznick, 1952, p. 18)

Examples of mass movements which have been penetrated by the Communist party with varying success include anarchist and syndicalist movements in France, Italy, and Spain.

Since totalitarian movements typically are mass movements which have been captured by totalitarian cadres, we shall refer to totalitarian movements as "mass movements" in the present study when we wish to emphasize the contention that totalitarian movements are organizations of masses. This is not a matter of definition, but requires theoretical and empirical support. For there is a widely-held theory that communism and fascism (the major cases of totalitarian movements) are essentially *class* movements, that is, expressions of specific class interests and forms of class organization bent on furthering these interests. It undoubtedly is true that not only some theorists but also many individual citizens (for example, in France) think in these class terms, and in the latter case express this belief by voting for a Communist (or Fascist) slate. The burden of the present study, however, is that large numbers of people do not respond to totalitarian movements primarily from the standpoint of economic calculus; but instead, they respond to the nihilistic tone of totalitarian movements, as an expression of their feelings of resentment against the present and

hope for something completely new in the future. Considerable evidence shows that the strongest response to the totalitarian appeal is *not* to be found among those who are involved in class organization and class struggle; on the contrary, the strongest response comes from people with the weakest attachment to class organizations, or any other kind of social group. A totalitarian movement attracts socially isolated members of all classes. Furthermore, whenever totalitarian groups gain power, they seek to smash all class organizations and to suppress all class interests. The inference is that movements which repeatedly have shown their contempt for class interests they are sometimes alleged to embody (and themselves sometimes claim to represent) can hardly be said to make their primary appeal to class interests.[2]

What class analysis does not help to explain is the *extremism* of totalitarian movements: their appeal to the most extreme dispositions of individuals and their readiness to go to any extreme in the pursuit of their objectives. But it is precisely this quality of extremism which makes these movements so threatening to democratic politics and individual liberty.

> The extremist must be deeply alienated from the complex of rules which keep the strivings for various values in restraint and balance. An extremist group is an alienated group. This means that it is fundamentally hostile to the political order. It cannot share that sense of affinity to persons or the attachment to the institutions which confine political conflicts to peaceful solutions. Its hostility is incompatible with that freedom from intense emotion which pluralistic politics needs for its prosperity. (Shils, 1956, p. 231)

The present study is concerned with the fate of democracy insofar as it is affected by the opportunities provided for the growth of mass movements and it seeks to analyze these opportunities with the aid of concepts of mass society.

Mass society is characterized by an abundance of mass movements. Other types of society are characterized by different kinds of social movements. Social movements which arise within communal society are characteristically traditional movements. For example, revival movements tend to be tradition-oriented, and manifest many of the features of the communal society within which they arise. Social movements which develop within pluralist societies are typically reform movements. For example, labor movements are reform movements when they seek to change only limited and specific aspects of working conditions, by developing a public opinion favorable to their aims in a constitutional manner. In totalitarian society, there is only one effective movement, and that is the totalitarian movement which supports the regime.

Mass movements may arise in non-mass societies, although they are not frequent in these societies. For example, millennial movements with mass characteristics arose at least as early as the Middle Ages. Mannheim has fixed the beginning of movements which combine the idea of a millennial kingdom on earth with the activism of large numbers of people in the "orgiastic chiliasm" of the Anabaptists: "the 'spiritualization of politics' . . . may be said to have begun at this turn in history" (1936, p. 191). The appearance of outbursts of social chiliasm in the Middle Ages should not obscure the fact that they were only sporadic occurrences which, though they may have engendered new sects, generally did not transform major institutions (Talmon, 1952, p. 9).

Mass behavior occurs at a low rate and in peripheral spheres in communal society, because the inaccessibility of elites inhibits mass behavior from above and the unavailability of non-elites inhibits it from below. In pluralist society, mass behavior also is located in peripheral areas, but the rate is higher because there are more remote symbols clamoring for attention (due to the accessibility of channels of communication). In totalitarian society, the great power of the elite suppresses spontaneous behavior of masses, but that mass behavior that does occur tends to impinge on the vital centers of society (witness the rarity but the explosiveness of spontaneous mass actions in totalitarian societies, such as those which took place in East Berlin, Potsdam, and Budapest). In mass society, mass behavior occurs at a high rate and in central spheres of society; mass behavior is inhibited neither from above nor from below because mass society possesses both accessible elites and available non-elites.

NOTES

1. Our conception of mass behavior borrows from Blumer (1946, pp. 185 ff.) and Selznick (1952, pp. 281–97). However, it departs from both in several respects. Reiwald (1949) provides an extensive review of the literature on mass behavior and related phenomena.

2. If we were trying to tell the whole story of why people support totalitarian movements, we would have to differentiate between leaders, active members, inactive members, voters, etc.—since reasons for adherence are associated with extent of involvement in a movement. Since the present study is primarily concerned with the *popular* response to totalitarian movements (as indicated, for example, by the number of votes totalitarian parties gain), differences like those which obtain between leaders and members of these movements are not very relevant. For a study which shows differences of this order, see Almond (1954).

REFERENCES

Arendt, Hannah. *The Origins of Totalitarianism.* New York: Harcourt Brace, 1951.

Blumer, Herbert. "Collective Behavior," in *New Outlines of the Principles of Sociology,* ed. A. M.

Lee, pp. 165–222. New York: Barnes and Noble, 1946.

Heberle, Rudolf. *Social Movements.* New York: Appleton-Century-Crofts, 1951.

Mannheim, Karl. *Ideology and Utopia.* London: Routledge and Kegan Paul, 1936.

Schumpeter, Joseph. *Capitalism, Socialism, and Democracy.* New York: Harper and Bros., 1947.

Selznick, Philip. *The Organizational Weapon.* New York: McGraw-Hill, 1952.

Shils, Edward A. *The Torment of Secrecy.* Glencoe: the Free Press, 1956.

Sorel, Georges. *Reflections on Violence.* Glencoe: The Free Press, 1950.

Talmon, J. L. *The Rise of Totalitarian Democracy.* Boston: Beacon Press, 1952.

7

EXPLORATIONS IN THE THEORY OF SOCIAL MOVEMENTS AND REVOLUTIONS

JAMES A. GESCHWENDER

James C. Davies made a first step toward formulating a theory of societal conditions which tend to produce revolutions.[1] His formulation is limited in two ways. First, Davies overly restricted himself by limiting his concern to "progressive" revolutions rather than analyzing the preconditions for revolutions of either a leftist or rightist direction. As a result, he formulated a statement of a set of preconditions which may be a special case of a more general set which would produce revolutions of either type.

The second limitation arises from his failure to distinguish between two separate but related problems. One may attempt to ascertain those factors which dispose specific individuals or types of individuals to take part in revolutionary activity or one may attempt to ascertain those factors which produce a revolution at a particular time and place. These two problems require different types of information. The former requires a theory of motivation which predicts that individuals experiencing certain specified conditions will manifest the behavioral response of revolutionary activity. It would further require the ability to document the existence of instantiations or examples of the classes of preconditions called for in the motivational theory.

The second problem requires an explanation in terms of conditions which disrupt the normal societal or institutional processes operating at a given time. One may tie the two problems together by assuming that revolutions occurring at a particular time and place are the final product of intra- and interindividual expressions of revolutionary activity of sufficient intensity. If one makes this assumption, it follows that *conditions which produce a revolution are no different in principle from those which produce a smaller or even an unsuccessful protest movement.* The major difference between the two would be

Reprinted from *Social Forces* 47(2), December 1968. "Explorations in the Theory of Social Movements and Revolutions" by James A. Geschwender. Copyright © The University of North Carolina Press.

in the numbers of individuals aroused to revolutionary activity and in those processes which develop after the protest movement has begun. The present analysis will parallel Davies as it will be limited to the initial conditions producing a movement.

The Rise and Drop Hypothesis

Let us examine the structure of the argument put forth by Davies. He explicitly focused on the problem of specification of conditions that produce a revolution at a particular time and place. But the structure of his reasoning is focused upon the manner in which specific sets of objective conditions impinge upon individuals or types of individuals and motivate them to take part in revolutionary activities. He states his reasoning as follows:

> Revolutions are most likely to occur when a prolonged period of objective economic and social development is followed by a short period of sharp reversal. The all-important effect on the minds of people in a particular society is to produce, during the former period, an expectation of continued ability to satisfy needs—which continue to rise—and, during the latter, a mental state of anxiety and frustration when manifest reality breaks away from anticipated reality. The actual state of socioeconomic development is less significant than the expectation that past progress, now blocked, can and must continue in the future.[2]

The conclusion that actual conditions of deprivation are less important than the development of a particular state of mind wherein one believes that he is unjustly deprived relative to another possible state of affairs is consistent with the earlier writings of L. P. Edwards[3] and Crane Brinton.[4] The suggestion that this state of mind may be produced by a period of progress followed by a sharp reversal is well documented in Davies' analysis of Dorr's Rebellion, the Russian Revolution, the Egyptian Revolution, and numerous other civil disorders. However, Davies' preoccupation with the point at which revolution begins led to overlooking the fact that his own data suggest the existence of other patterns which would also produce this state of mind.

Alternative Patterns: The Rising Expectations Hypothesis

Davies included a diagram of the period preceding Dorr's Rebellion.[5] This illustrates the fact that the rebellion broke out in 1842 after just such an improvement and decline in socioeconomic conditions as predicted. However, the earlier period is of considerable interest. Davies labeled the period from about 1812 to about 1838 as a period of increased agitation for suffrage. This period of increased agitation represents a period of protest—the beginning of a movement—which results from the same state of mind that produces revolutionary activity. The individuals who are engaged in protest and agitation are doing so because they perceive an intolerable gap between a state of affairs believed possible and desirable and a state of affairs actually existing. This perception of an intolerable gap did not result from the curve of economic development proposed by Davies but rather from a simple decline in the rate of social and economic progress. The diagram shows a continued increase in the level of need satisfaction from 1812 to 1835 but at a slower rate of increase than had occurred from 1790 to 1810. In short, the mere decline in the rate of improvement in the level of need satisfaction was sufficient to produce a gap between expectations and experience great enough to be considered intolerable by some.

This pattern of development of a gap between level of need satisfaction and expected level of need satisfaction appears to be a slight variant of the pattern suggested for the French Revolution by de Tocqueville,[6] and also suggested by Edwards,[7] and Crane Brinton[8] in their studies of commonalities in the Puritan, French, Russian, and American Revolutions. They stated that the experiencing of a period of improvement yields the expectation of, and desire for, further improvements. When these come too slowly, rebellion follows.

It seems that this scheme could be used to account for a portion of the protest activities on the part of Negroes in American society today. One could say that the improvement in general social conditions as evidenced by a certain amount of school integration, improved opportunities to vote, etc., have led many American Negroes to believe that progress is possible. They have experienced some acceptance into American life and expect to receive more. Once given this hope of full participation they become dissatisfied with the rather slow rate of change which may be observed. They see school integration, but only on a token basis; they see the loosening of many restrictions, but at such a slow rate that they become concerned that their shackles will never be completely thrown off. As they become increasingly impatient with the rate of improvement in social conditions, they begin to resort more and more to direct action, to sit-ins, wade-ins, etc.[9]

The Relative Deprivation Hypothesis

Marx suggested that workers become restless and eventually revolt after experiencing a similar improvement in the material conditions of their lives.[10] He suggested that workers develop the standards for their desired and expected level of need satisfac-

tion from the level that they see prevailing throughout society. Their desired level of need satisfaction rises at a pace equivalent to the rate of improved living standards for the rest of society so that, despite an improvement in the objective level of need satisfactions, there is an increasing gap between what the workers feel they should get and what they actually receive. This gap grows until the workers revolt. In this case, the level of expected need satisfaction derives from perception of the level of need satisfaction experienced by a reference group.

The current Negro revolt has been explained in terms of relative deprivation.[11] Many Negroes believe that Negroes are improving their objective position in American society but they are not gaining relative to whites. They use the metaphor of a train starting from New York to California and say that while they have reached Chicago they are still riding in the caboose and maybe the train has grown longer. In other words, the Negro today is better off than his grandfather but so is the white, and possibly the gap between Negro and white has increased. Thus, dissatisfaction results and leads to protest activities.

The Downward Mobility Hypothesis

While he did not study social revolutions, implications regarding the nature of the process of development of discrepancies between aspirations and need satisfactions may be drawn from Durkheim's classic study of suicide.[12] Durkheim's analysis of the development of anomie revolved around the relationship between needs (goals) and means of satisfying these needs. He assumed that satisfaction is a result of balance between needs and means of need satisfaction. Dissatisfaction results whenever needs exceed the means of need satisfaction. These needs may be dichotomized into organic and nonorganic needs. The former are limited in an absolute sense, while the latter are unlimited by nature. One's position in the stratification system places a limit upon aspirations and therefore maintains a balance between needs and need satisfactions.

Durkheim contended that the individual is in trouble whenever anything happens to disrupt this balance between needs and satisfactions. He will be frustrated whenever his desires exceed his achievements. A sudden improvement in wealth or power of the type that is expected to precede revolutions stimulates aspirations causing them to grow beyond means of satisfaction.

But improvements in status were not the only means envisioned by Durkheim whereby the balance between needs (aspirations) and means of satisfaction would be upset. He also stated that economic disasters upset the balance. Disasters declassify individuals, forcing them into a lower state than their previous one. This necessitates the painful process of reducing aspirations or needs to the level of possible need fulfillment. This is just as painful and disorienting a process as that which results from sudden improvement in one's position. It seems that this particular type of imbalance could also be brought about through downward social mobility in either an absolute or a relative sense.

Relative downward mobility refers to the felt loss of status experienced by a group which observes a previously inferior group closing the gap between them. Killian points out that southern whites who have migrated to Chicago feel a loss of status relative to Negroes despite the fact that they have experienced an objective improvement in economic conditions.[13] This type of imbalance between reality and desire is as likely to produce a social movement or revolution as the types discussed above.[14]

There are sufficient empirical data to support the notion that rebelliousness may grow out of a decline in one's objective material position. Lipset's analysis of the rise of the C.C.F. (an agrarian socialist political party) in Saskatchewan is a case in point.[15] Lipset interpreted the C.C.F. as the culmination of a class-conscious movement on the part of Canadian wheat farmers. He suggested that the C.C.F. received its earliest and most consistent support from those groups in the rural population who had the highest social and economic status. By this he meant that they had the largest farms and were least likely to be tenants. The poorer farmers were more difficult to organize during the Thirties. However, once they were organized they turned out to be the movements' staunchest supporters during the war years. The Thirties were times of severe depression, and the war years were prosperous times for the wheat farmers.

It is possible to reanalyze Lipset's findings with a view toward determining what happened during the Depression and how this led to the development of the movement. Historically, wheat farmers have an insecure income. They fluctuate between good and bad times depending upon the price of wheat. All farmers are not equally affected by economic fluctuations, as is especially revealed by the Depression. "In the first period, 1929–31, the small farms had a net cash income but increases in the size of the farm were accompanied by a declining income until at 500 acres no Net Cash Income and increasingly larger operating losses resulted for the larger farms."[16]

The wealthier farmers during the Depression experienced a rapid and sharp decline in their economic position in both absolute terms and relative to the poorer farmers. This decline relative to their previous high position (which we may assume they preferred) led to their organization and participation in the C.C.F. The poorer farmers did not become strong supporters until they experienced a rapid improvement in their objective economic status. They engaged in protest activity only after it had been demonstrated that this type of activity could bring about objective improvements. They were responding not only to the improvements, but also to the example set by the wealthier wheat farmers. The wealthier farmers protested in response to a deteriorating objective state and, in turn, acted as agitators in stimulating unrest and protest activities in others.

The American Populist Movement seems to have been produced by the same type of situation that gave rise to the C.C.F. Draper described the Populists as, "property-conscious farmers threatened with debt and bankruptcy."[17] Kornhauser suggests that the Italian Fascist and German Nazi movements drew heavily from individuals who had undergone a decline in their objective economic position. It is not unreasonable to assume that they looked back to their former positions as desirable and proper.[18] Therefore, they perceived themselves as experiencing an "intolerable gap" between their proper level of need satisfaction and their actual level. This experience led them to participate in a revolutionary protest movement.

The Status Inconsistency Hypothesis

All of the patterns of conditions likely to produce protest or revolution discussed above have had temporal change as an essential element. They all analyzed the manner in which changes in one's position over time give rise to a belief in the possibility and justice of an improvement in circumstances. The difference between desired and actual circumstances is what leads to revolutionary or protest activity. The concept of status consistency, developed by Lenski, makes possible the analysis of a nontemporal source of this discrepancy.[19]

Broom agreed that status inconsistents may make up the membership of a social movement and gives the concept special relevance for ethnic minorities.[20] He suggested that an aggregate with a low degree of stratum consistency, i.e., a number of persons having similar patterns of inconsistency, may develop ethnic-consciousness. He predicted that tension will be positively associated with low attribute consistency. This is based on the assumption that an erratic profile will reflect areas of blockage of mobility opportunities. If a group's mobility were strictly determined by the abilities and initiative of its individual members, it would be expected to move up in all status hierarchies at corresponding rates. If their mobility in one dimension lags behind others it indicates the existence of impediments to free mobility. These impediments tend to create tensions which could produce protest activity. Status inconsistent members of minority groups have been found to participate in social movements, such as the N.A.A.C.P., European Socialist parties, and the C.C.F. in Canada.[21]

Sorokin used the concept of "multibonded stratification" to analyze the relation between status inconsistency and revolutionary behavior.[22] He considered stratification in terms of a number of status dimensions that are bonded or welded together to form affine or disaffine strata. Affine strata are defined as those groups whose multiple bonds are mutually congenial and lead the members of such groups to the same type of behavior or mentality. Disaffine strata are those whose bonds are innerly contradictory. This would include groups who are high occupationally but low racially or ethnically, or high on the racial-ethnic dimension but low in economic status, as well as other combinations. Sorokin emphasized that these disaffine strata are not rare or exotic. They tend to appear quite frequently, though less frequently than affine strata. He further states that the disaffine strata are unstable and tend to decompose rapidly to be replaced by a new affine coalescence of the stratifying bonds.

The simultaneous appearance in a population of two double disaffine groups is a symptom which portends revolutionary change. Sorokin stated that the French Revolution was a perfect example of this. The nobility was a politically powerful group which had little economic wealth, while the third estate was a wealthy group virtually powerless in the political arena. The French Revolution was the decomposition of these two double disaffine strata and the creation of two new affine strata. Sorokin claimed that similar sets of circumstances prevailed in the case of the Russian Revolution of 1905, the Communist Revolution, and numerous other examples.

Toward a General Theory of Social Movements

The empirical relationship between status inconsistency and propensity toward revolutionary or protest activities is documented above. However, each of the temporal hypotheses included a rationale which accounted for the development of individual dissatisfaction sufficiently intense to produce protest. This is lacking in the preceding discussion of status consistency. This gap has been filled through an integration of the status consistency literature, Homan's Theory of Distributive Justice,[23] and Festinger's Theory of Cognitive Dissonance,[24] into an expanded theory.[25]

This integrated theory includes seven assumptions. The following are the relevant portions for an analysis of social movements and revolutions:

1. All individuals hold sets of cognitions which include some that are reality-based, some that are definitional, and some that are normative.
2. Any set of cognitions may stand in a relation of dissonance, consonance, or irrelevance, depending upon the internal relations which hold among reality-based and normative cognitions. If the conjunction of a reality-based and a normative cognition implies the negation of another reality-based cognition, then a state of dissonance exists.
3. Reality-based cognitions will include perceptions of one's status in the educational, occupational, income, and ethnic hierarchies. Definitional cognitions will include the definition of ethnicity as an ascribed investment, education as an achieved investment, occupation as a social reward, and income as a material reward. Normative cognitions will include the belief that rewards received should be proportional to investments.
4. Dissonance is an upsetting state and will produce tension for the individual. This tension will lead to an attempt to reduce dissonance by altering cognitions, adding new cognitions, or deleting old ones. Attempts to alter reality-based cognitions will involve attempting to change the real world.
5. Status inconsistents whose rewards received are less than believed to be proper for their investments will feel guilt. Anger is a sharper form of dissonance than guilt. The intensity of dissonance-reducing behavior will be directly proportional to the sharpness of dissonance.
6. Dissonance-reducing attempts will take the form of coping responses, attempts to change the real world, when possible.
7. Dissonance-reducing attempts will move from the simple to the complex. The most complex form of attempting to change reality is attempting to alter society.

These assumptions allow the derivation of predictions of specific behavioral responses to specific profiles of status inconsistency. Included are a number of predictions regarding the manner in which status inconsistency may contribute to the origin of social movements. More will be said on this below. The addition of the following assumptions will permit the derivation of predictions regarding the manner in which temporal changes in socioeconomic conditions may contribute to the origin of social movements:

8. Reality-based cognitions will include perceptions of present socioeconomic circumstances, past socioeconomic circumstances, and time lapse between the two. A higher level of socioeconomic circumstances will be defined as preferable to a lower level of socioeconomic circumstances.

9. Individuals whose present socioeconomic circumstances are at a higher level than past circumstances will be aware of the fact that they have experienced improvement and will define further improvement as possible and desirable. The discrepancy between anticipated future circumstances and present circumstances will produce dissonance. Anticipation of future rate of progress will be determined by rate of past progress (time lapse cognition).

10. Reality-based cognitions will include perceptions of present and past socioeconomic statuses of relevant reference groups. Comparisons will be made between rates of progress of self and relevant reference groups. Discrepancies between perceived rates of progress will produce dissonance.

11. Individuals whose present socioeconomic circumstances are at a lower level than past circumstances will be aware that they have experienced a worsening of conditions and will be fearful of further deterioration. A comparison of present circumstances and past circumstances will produce dissonance.

12. Attempts to reduce dissonance will take the form of attempting to change society when it is believed that sufficient power is, or can be, harnessed to bring this about. They will take a rightist direction when present circumstances are at a lower level than past circumstances and a leftist direction when present circumstances are at a higher level than past circumstances.

13. The intensity of dissonance experienced will be inversely proportional to the time span during which the discrepancies developed and will be directly proportional to the size of the discrepancies. The intensity of change attempts will be directly proportional to the intensity of dissonance.

14. Change-oriented, dissonance-reducing attempts on the part of status inconsistents will take a rightist orientation when high ethnic status is combined with lower levels of occupation or income: they will take a leftist orientation when high educational status is combined with a lower level of occupation or income.

Discussion

All of the patterns of temporal change which produce revolutionary activities may be explained within dissonance theory. Changes in objective conditions produce a state of mind in which individuals believe that they are unjustly deprived of a better way of life. First, they develop the image of a state of affairs which is possible of attainment. Second, they develop the belief that they are entitled to that state of affairs. Third, they know that they are not enjoying that state of affairs. The simultaneous possession of these three cognitions produces a state of dissonance. Dissonance is not comfortable and it produces pressures toward dissonance reduction. One means of reducing this dissonance is to alter the environment so as to produce the desired state of affairs. Therefore, dissonance-reducing activities often take the form of social protest or revolutionary behavior.

The fact that different individuals may experience different intensities of dissonance (or may have different levels of tolerance for dissonance) would lead to their engaging in protest activities at different points in time. It is conceivable that attempts to reduce dissonance (protest activities) on the part of the earliest and most severely affected will help to create dissonance in others similarly situated. Thus, the former group acts as agitators in helping to stir the latter to revolt.

It is also possible to predict the direction and intensity of the protest response with the aid of dissonance theory. It is reasonable to assume that the intensity of the response will be proportional to the intensity of dissonance experienced. Certain of the patterns would be likely to produce a more intense. state of dissonance than others. Davies' "rise and drop" hypothesis describes a set of circumstances which produces a large discrepancy between expected level of need satisfaction and actual level of need satisfaction. This discrepancy should be much smaller for those sets of circumstances described by the "rising expectations" hypothesis. The former might then be expected to produce a more intense form of dissonance, and, consequently, a more intense form of dissonance-reducing behavior (e.g., revolutionary rather than reform movements).

This can be illustrated by two types of Negro protest movements. The relationship between the "rising expectations" hypothesis and civil rights protest has been discussed above. The more extreme reaction to the "rise and drop" hypothesis can be illustrated with the Universal Negro Improvement Association of Marcus Garvey.[26]

Garvey had been actively, but unsuccessfully, attempting to recruit supporters prior to World War I. During the war opportunities for Negroes improved dramatically. As whites went into the armed services and defense needs expanded, many jobs were opened to Negroes for the first time. Other Negroes went into the service, and some went to Europe and saw that conditions prevailing in the United States were not necessarily inevitable. Their accounts were printed in Negro newspapers throughout the country. These circumstances produced an anticipation of, and a desire for, better conditions of life than those prevailing prior to the war. When the war ended whites returned from the armed services and defense spending was sharply curtailed. Negroes lost jobs gained during the war. Riots occurred all over the country to "put the Negro back in his place." The "rise and drop" circumstances had been experienced and Marcus Garvey found his recruits. The growth of the movement, until it was crushed, is history.

It is conceivable that the growth of the Nation of Islam after World War II and of Black Nationalism after the federal government's recent retreat on civil rights is the result of a similar "rise and drop" experience. This would illustrate the fact that different segments of the Negro community differentially experience the same societal changes. Middle-class Negroes have experienced a continual improvement in life circumstances and may be reacting in terms of the "rising expectations" hypothesis. Lower-class Negroes have had their aspirations raised simply to find the doors closed as tightly as ever. They may be reacting in terms of the "rise and drop" hypothesis.

Similarly, we would expect that those sets of circumstances described by the "relative deprivation" hypothesis and the "downward mobility" hypothesis would vary in the intensity of dissonance created, and in intensity of dissonance-reducing behavior, according to the degree of relative deprivation and the rate of downward mobility. The set of circumstances described by the "status inconsistency" hypothesis would produce varying intensities of dissonance and dissonance-reducing behavior according to the degree of discrepancy between relevant status dimensions.

The "rise and drop" hypothesis, the "rising expectations" hypothesis, and the "relative deprivation" hypothesis all describe sets of circumstances in which dissatisfaction results from a comparison of actual conditions with anticipated conditions. It involves a future orientation on the part of those affected. This future orientation is represented by a desire to bring about a better state of affairs—one which has never existed in reality. Thus, it may be predicted that protest movements and revolutions resulting from these sets of conditions are likely to be "progressive" or leftist in character.

The "downward mobility" hypothesis, whether absolute or relative mobility, described a set of circumstances in which dissatisfaction is created by comparing present conditions with conditions which existed in the past. Thus, it may be predicted that dissonance reduction would take the form of a "regressive" rightist protest movement.

The direction taken by movements resulting from circumstances described in the "status inconsistency" hypothesis would depend upon the nature of the inconsistency involved. Individuals who experience status inconsistency resulting from greater educational investments than income and/or occupational rewards will likely attempt to reduce dissonance in one of two ways. They may attempt to bring about consonance through individual mobility. If this is not possible and they shift to protest activities, it is likely to be in the direction of creating an equalitarian society in which rewards are based upon universalistic criteria—a "progressive" or leftist movement.

Those individuals who experienced dissonance resulting from their ethnic investment being greater than their income and/or occupational rewards are not likely to select either of these modes of dissonance reduction. Individual mobility is not possible without education, and rewards distributed upon the basis of universalistic criteria will not help. They are much more prone to support a movement emphasizing rewards based upon particularistic criteria—a "regressive" or rightist movement.

Just as not all revolutionary attempts succeed, Festinger acknowledged that not all attempts to reduce dissonance will be successful. If an attempted revolution or protest movement fails, the dissonant individuals will be forced to attempt to reduce dissonance by altering one of their cognitions (such as that of the desired state of affairs or the proper relation between investments and rewards), or by adding new cognitions (such as their lack of ability to bring about the desired state). This could produce the apathetic, disinterested, nonprotesting type of fatalistic behavior that we find among the severely downtrodden.

One of the assumptions presented above stated that social change would be perceived as a means of reducing dissonance if it is believed that sufficient power is, or could be, harnessed. It is also possible that the required intensity of dissonance may be present but the required perception of power absent. This combination cannot be expected to produce social movements or revolutions. However, the dissonance that has been generated will not simply dissipate and may not be reduced by cognitive reorganization. It is possible that this combination may produce hostile outbursts such as the ghetto riots currently occurring throughout the country.

Civil rights legislation, the "war on poverty," VISTA, and other governmental actions may lead ghetto-dwelling Negroes to drastically raise their levels of aspirations and expectations. The failure of these measures to bring about significant improvements may lead to disillusionment. The discrepancy between expectation and reality creates dissonance. No improvement is actually experienced; only hopes are raised. Thus, intense dissonance is combined with feelings of powerlessness that typify the ghetto dweller, and riots or explosions emerge.

Conclusions

It has been shown that the particular sequence of temporal changes described by Davies is only one of several sequences which produce in individuals the state of mind that tends to be expressed in revolutionary or other protest activities. The experiencing of status inconsistency is a nontemporal condition which also produces this same state of mind. Dissonance theory is capable of explaining the manner in which this state of mind is produced by these diverse sets of conditions and the manner in which it finds its expression in protest activities.

Hypotheses have been derived which predict the particular mode of dissonance reduction that will be attempted under certain sets of conditions, the direction of change attempts (rightist or leftist movements), the intensity of change attempts (revolutionary or reform), and the conditions under which change will not be attempted but hostile outbursts emerge or apathy and hopelessness set in. Research is needed to test these hypotheses and to detail the relationship between these and other possible sets of preconditions of revolutionary activity. Davies has taken a major step in the development of a theory of revolution and the present paper has helped to place this contribution into a more general context.

Acknowledgments

I am indebted to Frederick B. Waisanen for the hours of discussion which gave rise to many of the ideas included herein. I am also indebted to William A. Rushing, Lewis M. Killian, and Leland Axelson for the careful reading of an earlier version and the useful suggestions which they made.

NOTES

1. James C. Davies, "Toward a Theory of Revolution," *American Sociological Review,* 27 (February 1962), pp. 5–18.
2. *Ibid.,* p. 6 (italics added for emphasis).
3. Lyford P. Edwards, *The Natural History of Revolution* (Chicago: University of Chicago Press, 1927).
4. Crane Brinton, *The Anatomy of Revolution* (New York: W. W. Norton & Co., 1938).
5. Davies, *op. cit.,* p. 9.
6. Cited in *ibid,* pp. 5–6.
7. Edwards, *op. cit.,* pp. 34–35.
8. Brinton, *op. cit.,* p. 286 and pp. 78–79.
9. Cf. Dan Wakefield, *Revolt in the South* (New York: Grove Press, 1960).
10. Cited in Davies, *op. cit.,* p. 5.
11. James A. Geschwender, "The Negro Revolt: An Examination of Some Hypotheses," *Social Forces,* 43 (December 1964), pp. 248–256.
12. Emile Durkheim, *Suicide* (Glencoe, Illinois: The Free Press, 1951).
13. Lewis M. Killian, "The Adjustment of Southern White Migrants to Northern Urban Norms," *Social Forces,* 32 (October 1953), p. 61.
14. For a discussion of such countermovements see Ralph H. Turner and Lewis M. Killian, *Collective Behavior,* (Englewood Cliffs, New Jersey: Prentice-Hall, 1957), pp. 382–384; Lewis M. Killian, "The Purge of an Agitator," *Social Problems,* 7 (Fall 1959), pp. 152–156; and James W. Vander Zanden, "Resistance and Social Movements," *Social Forces,* 37 (May 1959), pp. 212–315.
15. Seymour M. Lipset, *Agrarian Socialism* (Berkeley: University of California Press, 1950).

16. *Ibid.,* p. 91, quoted from William Allen and E. C. Hope, *The Farm Outlook for Saskatchewan* (Saskatchewan: University of Saskatchewan, 1934), p. 2.

17. Theodore Draper, *The Roots of American Communism* (New York: Viking Press, 1957), p. 37.

18. William Kornhauser, *The Politics of Mass Society* (Glencoe, Illinois: The Free Press, 1959), p. 181. For a similar interpretation see also Emile Benoit-Smullyan, "Status, Status Types, and Status Interrelations," *American Sociological Review,* 9 (April 1944), pp. 353–359.

19. Gerhard Lenski, "Status Crystallization: A Non-Vertical Dimension of Social Status," *American Sociological Review,* 19 (August 1954), pp. 405–413. For a summary of some of the literature on the relationship between status inconsistency and participation in social movements see James A. Geschwender, "Continuities in Theories of Status Consistency and Cognitive Dissonance," *Social Forces,* 46 (December 1967), pp. 165–167.

20. Leonard Broom, "Social Differentiation and Stratification," in Robert K. Merton, Leonard Broom, and Leonard S. Cottrell (eds.), *Sociology Today* (New York: Basic Books, 1959), pp. 429–441.

21. Cf. E. Franklin Frazier, *Black Bourgeoisie* (Glencoe, Illinois: The Free Press, 1959), pp. 98–104; Robert Michels, *Political Parties* (New York: Dover Publications, 1959), pp. 260–261; and Lipset, *op. cit.,* p. 191.

22. Pitirim A. Sorokin, *Society, Culture and Personality* (New York: Harper & Brothers, 1947), pp. 289–294.

23. George C. Homans, *Social Behavior: Its Elementary Forms* (New York: Harcourt, Brace & World, 1961).

24. Leon Festinger, *A Theory of Cognitive Dissonance* (Evanston, Illinois: Row, Peterson & Co., 1957).

25. Geschwender, "Continuities . . .," pp. 160–171.

26. Gunnar Myrdal, *An American Dilemma* (New York: Harper & Row, 1962), pp. 745–749.

8

THE NORM-ORIENTED MOVEMENT

NEIL J. SMELSER

Introduction

Definition of a Norm-Oriented Movement

A norm-oriented movement is an attempt to restore, protect, modify, or create norms in the name of a generalized belief. Participants may be trying either to affect norms directly (e.g., efforts of a feminist group to establish a

private educational system for women) or induce some constituted authority to do so (e.g., pressures from the same group on a governmental agency to support or create a public co-educational system). Any kind of norm—economic, educational, political, religious—may become the subject of such movements. Furthermore, norm-oriented movements may occur on any scale—for instance, agitation by a group of nations to establish an international police force; agitation by groups of businessmen for tax legislation on the federal, state, or local level; agitation by the members of a local union to federate with other unions; agitation by a minority of members of a local chapter of the Society for the Prevention of Cruelty to Animals to amend the by-laws of the chapter. Finally, the definition includes movements of all political flavors—reactionary, conservative, progressive, and radical.

A normative innovation—a new law, custom, bureau, association, or segment of a political party—frequently appears as the result of a norm-oriented movement. Not all normative changes, however, are preceded by a movement with generalized beliefs. In fact, all normative changes could be located on a continuum from those routinely incorporated to those adopted as a result of an agitation based on a generalized belief.

The Value-Added Sequence of a Norm-Oriented Movement

We shall analyze norm-oriented movements under the set of categories—structural conduciveness, strain, generalized beliefs, precipitating factors, mobilization for action, and the response of agencies of social control. This treatment of the norm-oriented movement as a logical accumulation of determinants is similar to the study of the natural history of social movements. In this chapter, however, we are not interested primarily in the temporal accumulation of events; we are attempting to establish the conditions under which events become significant as determinants of a norm-oriented movement. The empirical succession of events may coincide with the analytic accumulation of determinants; for instance, conditions of structural conduciveness may arise first, conditions of strain next, and a generalized belief next. This coincidence need not be the case, however. A generalized belief may have lain dormant for a long time before any movement bearing its name arises; in order for this belief to become a determinant in such movement it must be activated by conditions of conduciveness and strain. While we shall refer occasionally to temporal sequences of events, *we are not attempting to formulate generalizations about natural histories, but to generate a systematic account of the activation of events and situations as determinants.*

Structural Conduciveness

The Structural Possibility of Demanding Normative Changes Alone

The most general condition of conduciveness concerns the possibility for demanding modifications of norms *without simultaneously appearing to demand a more fundamental modification of values.* If social arrangements permit these more limited kinds of demands, these arrangements are conducive to the development of norm-oriented movements; if social arrangements are such that all demands for normative change tend more or less immediately to generalize into conflicts over values, they are not conducive to the development of norm-oriented movements.

In specifying the kinds of social structures which meet these conditions of conduciveness we must distinguish between (1) the source demands for normative change in the population and (2) the kind of reception that these demands receive at the political level. Gabriel Almond has made essentially the same distinction in another context in his separation of the process of *interest-articulation* from the process of *interest-aggregation.* Interest articulation refers to the structures through which interests, grievances, and desires are made explicit. Such structures include lobbies, pressure groups, armies, bureaucracies, churches, kinship, and lineage groups, ethnic groups, and status and class groups. Interest-aggregation refers to the structures in which these articulated interests are combined, weighed, and forged into policy. Examples of structures for the aggregation of interests are legislatures, bureaucracies, political blocs, and coalitions. Although a single organization (e.g., a political party) may engage to a degree in both articulation and aggregation of interests, the analytic distinction between the two phases of the political process still holds.

If the expression of dissatisfaction is to be channeled into norm-oriented movements, both interest-articulation and interest-aggregation must be structurally differentiated to a high degree. First, with regard to articulation, if political, economic, and ethnic cleavages coincide, it is difficult to prevent specific grievances and interests from generalizing, thus giving protest a more diffuse character.

In short, if the social bases for conflict of interest (e.g., position in economic or political order) are not separate from kinship, ethnic, regional, or religious groups, *any* grievance is likely to become a conflict of values. If, however, the structures for articulating grievances are differentiated from one another demands tend to be formulated more in terms of specific programs for normative regulation which do not excite such a wide range of conflicts.

With regard to interest-aggregation as well, a high degree of differentiation between the machinery for interest-aggregation from other kinds of social control encourages the development of more specific demands for normative change. In a society with a fusion between religious and political authority— many medieval societies could serve as examples—protests against specific normative arrangements inevitably tend to generalize into heresies. Under such conditions the mechanisms for insulating specific demands from challenges to legitimacy itself are not highly developed. Similarly, in contemporary totalitarian societies, the legitimacy of the state and the political management of limited protests are relatively

undifferentiated. Totalitarian ideologies generally subordinate all institutions— labor, business, education, the military—to the political and ideological concerns of the state. Protest in these spheres tends to generalize into a political crisis. Deviance in many spheres tends to be treated as a political and ideological threat. This is because the claim to legitimate power is not differentiated from other kinds of social control.

By way of contrast, historical developments in parts of Western Europe and the United States have resulted in a high degree of differentiation of the claim to legitimacy from demands for institutional change. Even political leaders can be attacked severely without endangering the legitimacy of their office itself. When President Truman dismissed General MacArthur in 1951, the latter returned to the United States in great glory, rode through a ticker-tape parade in New York, mobilized all sorts of opposition to Truman, testified before Congress, and later delivered the keynote speech at the Republican National Convention. Yet through all this neither Truman's right to dismiss MacArthur, nor his right to hold the office of Presidency, nor the sanctity of the office itself was even questioned. The question of legitimacy was separated clearly from the question of political opposition. This series of events might be contrasted with the dismissal of General Zhukov in the Soviet Union a few years later. His removal was revealed amidst a shroud of secrecy. Once dismissed, furthermore, there was no possibility that he could defend his case publicly, or initiate a movement for reform. In fact, he later confessed publicly to *ideological* errors and acknowledged that he had deserved the dismissal. Political agitation on his behalf was unthinkable because it would have constituted a threat to the legitimacy of the regime.

More broadly, the democratic countries of Northwestern Europe and North America have institutionalized—with varying degrees of finality—this principle of differentiation under formulae such as "separation of church and state," "civil control of military power," "separation of church and school," "academic freedom," "freedom of expression," etc. These formulae imply maximum autonomy for each institutional sector, and great limitations on the ability of each sector to interfere with the central political "clearing-house" for grievances in society. This high level of differentiation accounts in part for the relative predominance of norm-oriented movements as the typical mode of expressing collective grievances in these countries, and the relative absence of revolutionary movements in the same countries in recent times.

The same principle applies to examples less extreme than the contrast between differentiated democratic systems and undifferentiated theocratic or totalitarian systems. When, for instance, a political party claims that it is the main instrument for guaranteeing the legitimacy of the state (as in the case of many nationalist parties in the developing nations) it is difficult for competing parties or interest groups to challenge this party on bases other than the claim to legitimacy.

In short, then, for norm-oriented movements to be possible in a society, the articulation of interests and aggregation of interests must be differentiated—both within themselves and from one another—to a high degree. This is not to say that grievances are not expressed and heard *at all* under less differentiated structural conditions; it is true, however, that under such conditions grievances will be less likely to take the form of a collective outburst based on generalized norm-oriented beliefs.

The Channels of Agitation for Norm-Oriented Movements

In the remaining discussion, we shall assume that the broadest conditions of conduciveness just discussed remain unchanged. Within such conditions, what kinds of channels for expressing dissatisfaction are most conducive for the development of norm-oriented movements rather than other kinds of outbursts?

In general, the discontented must have *some* degree of access to some method of affecting the normative order. Democratic systems possess various ways of passing information, sentiments, and desires to governmental and other agencies—petitions, elections, initiatives, referenda, letters to congressmen, letters to the press, demonstrations, public opinion polls, requests for court injunctions, etc. Through such channels citizens influence authorities, who in turn are responsible for influencing the character of laws, regulations, and other kinds of norms. Under decentralized democratic systems, aroused individuals or groups may be able to by-pass such authorities altogether and thus affect the normative order directly. Examples of this direct action are movements to establish private schools for the deaf or blind, to introduce playgrounds under private auspices, to establish consumer cooperatives, or to introduce a welfare scheme into a labor union's program. In such cases it is necessary to influence others privately to cooperate in building an enterprise; thus such movements have a political dimension. Still this kind of political action differs from agitating to influence governmental authorities.

For each channel available for influencing the normative order, it is possible to rely on one or more of many types of social organization—independent associations, political parties, pressure groups, clubs, political bosses, or informal gatherings.

The potential availability of many different channels for affecting normative arrangements, plus the potential availability of many different kinds of organizations, presents a vast array of alternative strategies and tactics for any given movement. The development of the prohibition movement in the United States illustrates this great variety of methods. At first, the movement was carried by the Protestant churches (1810–26). Shortly thereafter, however, local organizations devoted specifically to temperance began to arise and agitate for prohibition on the local level (1826–1840s). In the late 1860s Prohibition parties began to form, and between 1880 and 1893 these parties attempted to secure temperance legislation at the state level. The period between 1893 and 1906 marked a reversion to non-partisan political activity at the local level. Between 1906 and 1913 non-partisan activity continued, this time at the state level. Finally, beginning in 1913, the temperance forces shifted to the national level and ultimately secured the adoption of the Eighteenth Amendment to the Constitution. Later in the chapter we shall attempt to account for some of these shifts from one method to another.

Many norm-oriented movements crystallize when it appears to the discontented that *one* method of agitation has disappeared or is disappearing.

When *all* avenues of agitation for normative change are perceived to be closing or closed, moreover, dissatisfaction tends to find an outlet in a value-oriented movement or in expressions of hostility. All avenues of agitation cannot be closed, then, if a norm-oriented movement is to occur. Neither, however, can these avenues be completely free from obstacles. If they were, normative reorganization would occur quickly and smoothly, with no need to mobilize for action under a generalized belief.

What conditions, then, encourage the rise of generalized norm-oriented beliefs? Avenues for agitation must be open, but participants must perceive a precarious balance between their own power and the power of the opposition. Many norm-oriented movements, in fact, are driven into a flurry of excited activity when ambiguity is introduced into the battle between proponents and opponents. This ambiguity is created by an event or series of events which signifies a new chance for success in overcoming the opposition *or* a new danger of being defeated by the opposition. Note the operation of this principle in the following examples: (1) The rapid growth of the short-hours movement among American workers in many states in 1871 and 1872 "can be explained by its immediate successes in New York." Labor, previously unable to reduce hours by any known means, flocked to this method when it appeared to succeed in a single instance. (2) The Know Nothing Movement received a great impetus after its strong showing in the elections of 1854. (3) Henry George, who had been agitating for the single tax for a number of years, ran for the mayor of New York in 1866, and came in a surprising second. This success precipitated the most vigorous period of agitation in the single tax movement's history.

Among the conditions of structural conduciveness, then, is the presence of channels for affecting normative arrangements which are open, but within which the chances of success and the chances of failure are balanced precariously.

The Lack of Opportunities for Other Outbursts

So much for the existence of channels for attempting to effect positive normative changes by agitation. Any discussion of structural conduciveness must refer also to the lack of alternative channels for expressing dissatisfaction. If facilities conducive for (say) a craze are available for a distressed group, energy will be diverted away from norm-oriented attempts to modify existing structural arrangements.

Other channels of expression must be perceived as unavailable as well. The forces of social control must be able to prevent the use of mob violence, *coups d'état*, etc., as channels for gaining demands. Finally, if a society is gripped by an encompassing social movement which occupies the attention of large numbers of its citizens—as in the case of the slavery question in the United States at mid-nineteenth century—other norm-oriented movements are frequently muted by the overwhelming social crisis at hand. In sum, structural conduciveness for norm-oriented movements requires both the accessibility to avenues for affecting normative change and the inaccessibility to other avenues.

The Possibility of Communication

Like all collective outbursts, a norm-oriented movement requires a certain ability to communicate if beliefs are to be disseminated and action is to be mobilized. In this respect political control of the media of communication is important. So is the presence of common language and culture; diversity among natives and immigrants is no doubt partially responsible for the historical lag in the organization of American labor. Finally, past movements frequently establish patterns of communications among a class of people, thus giving future movements a head start in formulating, spreading, and acting on beliefs; the Grange, for instance, undoubtedly established a degree of organization among American farmers in the 1870s which facilitated the formation of future protest movements.

Strain

Strain and Facilities

Sometimes the appearance of new knowledge initiates a movement to apply this knowledge in order to eradicate a condition previously taken for granted. The increase in knowledge concerning the control of venereal diseases was one of the main factors which stimulated the movement to disseminate this knowledge through sex education in schools.

Strain and Organization: Deprivation

The history of social movements abounds with agitations on the part of groups who experience a real or apparent loss of wealth, power, or prestige. For example: (1) Farmers' movements have arisen in periods of depression and declined in periods of prosperity. (2) Dissatisfactions over land distribution have also been at the root of numerous agrarian movements. (3) As we have seen, the revival of old movements and the initiation of new ones among American laborers in the nineteenth century was closely related to their changing economic fortunes. (4) Movements to regulate speculation have been stimulated by the financial losses and market disorganization occasioned by financial crises. (5) The movement which culminated in the rise of the Progressive Party in the early twentieth century was based in large part on the apprehension that big business was acquiring too much economic and political power. (6) In the 1820s, many of the supporters of the anti-Masonry movement—among whose objectives was to prohibit Masons from holding public office—came from the ranks of ministers who felt their own religious influence waning and who resented the Masons' religious appeal.

Strain and Norms

Any disharmony between normative standards and actual social conditions can provide the basis for a movement whose objective it is to modify the norms. This is particularly true when either norms or social conditions undergo rapid change in a relatively short time.

Sometimes new legislation creates strains on existing normative arrangements. In the late eighteenth century, for instance, many states began to use imprisonment rather than death as punishment for criminals. The resulting conditions in the prisons—overcrowding, mixing of all ages and types of offenders, etc.—underlay various movements for prison reform. Finally, norm-oriented movements themselves, which threaten to alter the normative order, stimulate counter-movements (e.g., anti-socialized medicine) among those who feel endangered by the impending change.

Sometimes strain results not from changes in norms but from changing social conditions which render existing norms more offensive. Discriminatory norms concerning the employment of Negroes remained fairly stable through the late 1930s; with the onset of wartime conditions, however—which demanded patriotic sacrifices on the part of Negroes in the armed services and their labor in defense industries—many Negroes became more bitter about this discrimination and ultimately launched a movement which resulted in the establishment of the Fair Employment Practices Commission. To choose another example, the recruitment of both Negroes and whites into the tenancy system after Reconstruction threatened the existence of the two-caste system; whites' resentment over these conditions lay behind not only outbursts of scapegoating but also gave a white supremacist flavor to Southern Populism.

Strains and Values

The rise of new values frequently creates bases for defining certain social conditions as "evils"—social conditions which previously had passed less noticed. The twin strand of philosophical deism and evangelical piety, for instance, which consolidated in Britain in the second half of the eighteenth century, became the basis for condemning and agitating for the end of slavery, cruelty to animals, and the subordination of women. All these practices had existed for centuries without serious opposition.

In sum, norm-oriented movements are usually fostered by strains which create "demands for readjustment in the social situation." To this general formula we should add several qualifying and amplifying remarks:

First, strain need not involve "a change in objective external conditions or . . . material deprivation," but may stem from alterations in *expectations* concerning social life. To discuss strains in terms of discrepancies between social conditions and social expectations is preferable to the use of a concept such as "disorganization" as the basis for collective outbursts. This term is too strong for some of the very delicate shifts in determinants which trigger major outbursts.

Second, strains frequently appear in periods of rapid and uneven social change—when one subsystem of society changes more rapidly than others, or, to put it the other way around, when one subsystem, because of inflexibilities, resists change. Rapid industrial development in England during the Industrial Revolution, for instance, by demanding new and complex skills of the labor force, brought about a crisis in education, which lagged behind these economic changes. Similarly, the early institutionalization of universal suffrage in American history brought pressure to bear on popular education. In this case political change moved ahead of the ability of the society to prepare its citizens for responsible participation. This discrepancy between political and educational institutions preoccupied educational reformers in this country in the 1830s and 1840s.

Third, negative stereotypes associated with cleavages frequently mean that one group is convinced that another is conspiring to create conditions of strain. If these feelings are strong, a minor change in social conditions can fire a collective outburst. For instance, because a strong anti-Catholic prejudice already existed in the United States in the early nineteenth century, the economic and other kinds of competition from Catholic immigrants in the 1850s assumed magnified importance. Many of the dissatisfactions which give strength to a specific situation of strain, then, may have been in existence for a long time.

Fourth, any specific norm-oriented movement may be the product of many different kinds of strain. The Townsend movement, for instance, reflected simultaneously the strains resulting from long-term changes in the kinship structure which led to progressively greater isolation of the aged, and the strains arising from conditions of economic deprivation of the aged in the depression of the 1930s. Many social movements stem from the complex and multiple structural strains resulting from industrialization, urbanization, commercialization of agriculture, and colonial domination.

Finally, to become a determinant of a norm-oriented movement, a condition of strain must combine with appropriate conditions of structural conducivenss. For example, the conditions of strain which gave rise most directly to the British anti-slavery agitation was the discrepancy between the values of evangelism and the social conditions of slavery. These values had been fomenting for many decades during the eighteenth century. The actual rise of the anti-slavery movement, however, was delayed until appropriate conditions of conduciveness were established; in this case these conditions came into existence only after the American Revolutionary War had removed much slave-holding territory from the British Empire and thus diminished the opposition to abolition. (This example also shows that conditions of conduciveness need not precede conditions of strain temporally for the two to combine as determinants of a norm-oriented movement.)

The Growth of Generalized Beliefs and the Role of Precipitating Factors

Under the conditions of structural conduciveness and strain outlined above, generalized beliefs begin to come into play as determinants. This is not to say that beliefs are created temporally only *after* conditions of conduciveness and strain have developed. Frequently the belief—or at least some of its components—have existed for generations or centuries. In such a case the conditions of conduciveness and strain activate what has been latent, and thus draw it into the total value-added process as a determinant.

For a norm-oriented movement, the generalized belief includes a diagnosis of the forces and agents that are making for a failure of normative regulation. It also involves some sort of program—passing a law, creating a regulatory agency, scrapping an antiquated custom, etc. Those committed to the belief feel that adoption of this program will control, damage, or punish the responsible agent, and thus erase the source of strain. The combination of all these components results in a "cause" in the name of which the aggrieved mobilize and agitate for normative change.

What are the roles of precipitating factors in the development of beliefs? Most important, they mark the sudden establishment or symbolization of one of the conditions of conduciveness or strain. In this way precipitating factors focus the belief on a particular person, event, or situation. In addition, precipitating factors create a sense of urgency and hasten mobilization for action. Let us illustrate these general roles.

Many precipitating factors are interpreted as signs, either of the opponents' power or the proponents' chances of success. The following are instances of the power of limited setbacks to invigorate the movement: (1) The arrest of a leader. The birth control movement was given considerable impetus by the arrest of Margaret Sanger in New York in September, 1914, for distributing her pamphlet, *Family Limitation*. (2) An attack on one of the protagonists for a cause. Hiller argues that "a strike may be precipitated by a simple incident, such as an attack upon the group or one of its members. But ordinarily such an event is merely a point upon which attention is fixed. It is a symbol of cumulated grievances." (3) A rebuff to a movement by an authority who has the power to help in furthering its program. President Roosevelt's refusal in 1940 to push forward with racial integration in the armed forces was followed by a period of increasing bitterness in the Negro press and heightened agitation for a Negro march on Washington. (4) The appointment of James Campbell, a Catholic, as Postmaster-General, set off a tremendous hysteria and flurry of agitation within the Know Nothing movement. (5) The threat of success of a counter-movement. (6) An illegal act, such as a crime or riot. Especially if such an act "reveals" the insidious character of an enemy, it may quicken agitation for reform. Spectacular sex crimes, for instance, apparently invigorate the pressure for passage of more laws against sexual psychopaths.

As we have seen, limited successes of a movement, especially unanticipated successes, often "prove" the efficacy of a given method of agitation, and stimulate more agitation of this type.

Finally, a precipitating factor may create or underline a condition of strain. Most of the explosive movements among American farmers in the past century, for instance, have been boosted by financial crises and rapidly falling farm prices. In this case—as in all collective behavior—strain and precipitating factors shade into one another. Depending on the time perspective, a single event may be treated as a condition of strain or a precipitating factor, or both. This illustrates an important characteristic of collective behavior: a single empirical event or situation may be significant analytically in many ways.

Mobilization of the Movement for Action

The final determinant in the value-added process that results in a norm-oriented movement is the mobiliztion of its participants for action. In certain respects the pattern of mobilization may be standardized.

As a rule, mobilization to organize and push though a program takes a long time—a longer time than is generally required for the mobilization phases of panics, crazes, and hostile outbursts. For this reason the mobilization phase of a norm-oriented movement is likely to be very complicated; it has to adapt to the exigencies of maintaining an organization over long periods. Accordingly, we shall discuss the problem of mobilization under four distinct headings: (a) the role of leaders in organizing the movement for action; (b) the real and derived phases of mobilization; (c) the effect of the success or failure of the movement's specific strategies and tactics on the development of the movement; (d) the effect of the movement's overall success or failure on its development. Each heading poses a problem of potential instability and disunity for a movement; under each heading we shall discuss this problem.

Leadership

For all collective outbursts, including norm-oriented movements, we may distinguish between two kinds of leadership—leadership in formulating the beliefs and leadership in mobilizing participants for action. Sometimes the same person performs both functions; in other cases a division of leadership roles appears within a movement.

Because the organizations engaged in a movement frequently must endure over a long period, several new types of leadership appear as the movement progresses—leadership geared to the organizational exigencies of the movement rather than its ideals and goals.

As the collectivity becomes a going concern, even more types of leaders may appear—some engaged in the pursuit of power within the collectivity itself, others engaged in maintaining the prestige of the organization or movement in the public eye.

Many bases for internal conflict and fragmentation of the movement arise from this proliferation of leaders into formulators, promoters, bureaucrats, power-seekers, and prestige-seekers. Each type of leader develops vested interests which he seeks to safeguard. Furthermore, if a movement appears to be drifting in a direction which minimizes his own leadership role, power struggles over the course of the movement may develop.

The leader who is most important in the phase of active mobilization focuses on a set of strategies and tactics—to form a new political party; to influence existing parties; to stage a march or other kind of demonstration; to influence legislatures by conventional lobbying or letter-writing; to engage in "direct action" such as boycotts, lockouts, or sit-ins; to educate the public; and so on. Within a single movement, conflicts may arise among leaders who differ in their emphasis on particular strategies and tactics. Later we shall investigate the occasions upon which such conflicts are likely to become intensified.

As for the recruitment of leaders into movements, no single formula accounts for the source of leadership. Leaders may be marginal or respectable; they may come from "nowhere" or they may be permanently established in extremist groups which lie in wait for disturbances and then move in to assume leadership. The source of leadership for any given movement, then, depends on a number of factors—the availability of the qualities of leaders among the population suffering from strain, the prior existence of organizations with similar or related dissatisfactions, and the ability of these organizations to seize power in a movement.

The Real and Derived Phases of Mobilization

The development of a norm-oriented movement may be divided into three temporal phases—the incipient phase, the phase of enthusiastic mobilization, and the period of institutionalization and organization. The movement begins with slow, searching behavior; accelerates into a period of supercharged activity; then settles gradually into decline or routine, day-by-day activity. The enthusiastic phase displays a bulge of activity and membership which can be analyzed in terms of the real and derived aspects of a movement. Let us illustrate these aspects in several movements.

If the beliefs associated with a norm-oriented movement are sufficiently inclusive to encompass a wide variety of grievances, an initial success of the movement is likely to draw in a large, heterogeneous membership. "Americanism," for instance, is a vague and inclusive symbol; it can be a receptacle for anti-Negro-feelings, anti-foreign feelings, prohibitionist feelings, etc.—in short, any sentiment which can be labeled conveniently as "American." Adherents of entirely different stripes have rallied to this symbol during the past century.

Norm-oriented movements with vague, inclusive symbols, then, display three central characteristics: *(a)* diversity of motivation and grievances among the participants; *(b)* a period of very rapid growth and a period of equally rapid decline; *(c)* a fluid association among the strands of the same general movement, strands which continuously flow into one another, break off again, then join in some other guise.

The Success or Failure of Specific Tactics

Norm-oriented movements generally have access to a *variety* of channels for agitation and a *variety* of strategies and tactics for each channel. Because of this large number of alternative paths of action, several related movements frequently arise simultaneously, their major differences being in the realm of strategy and tactics. For instance, during and after World War I, the general movement by "native, Anglo-Saxon Protestant Americans" took a number of forms—the Ku Klux Klan revival, fundamentalism, agitation for prohibition, agitation for restricting immigration quotas, etc.

Furthermore, the history of any given movement—its ebbs and flows, its switches, its bursts of enthusiasm—can be written in large part as a pattern of abandoning one method which appears to be losing effectiveness and adopting some new, more promising method.

The problem of settling upon methods of agitation, then, is an important source of conflict, fragmentation, and turnover of leadership in norm-oriented movements. The same kinds of instability may appear when one branch of a movement exerts pressure to agitate for a policy to use a method considered by others in the movement to be beyond the legitimate scope of the movement. For instance, when some feminists in England took up a crusade to repeal the regulations for examining and prosecuting prostitutes, this shocked the sensibilities of other feminists. The result was a split in the movement which persisted through the 1860s and 1870s.

The Directions of Development after Success or Failure

Any movement which crusades under a fully developed set of generalized beliefs is bound to fail in one sense. Because its fears and hopes are likely to be exaggerated through the processes of generalization and short-circuiting, even the adoption of the concrete proposals it advocates does not approach its expectations. As a result of a century of feminist agitation and success, for instance, women have neither attained to the general level of leadership that the pioneers of the feminist movement insisted they would attain once the legal framework was provided, nor has the female invasion of strange pastures transformed those pastures into the Promised Land. In fact, the very fervor of the pioneers has become somewhat ludicrous in modern eyes, nowhere more in evidence than among groups of so-called emancipated women. The concerted demand of women's groups for more rights and privileges mounts apace, but the belief that a brave new world was a-borning, as a specific result, has waned.

Beyond this inherent tendency for even successful movements to leave a residue of disappointment, we can speak of the relative success of movements. Some movements, such as the short-ballot movement in the early twentieth century, have achieved their ends almost in their entirety. Other movements, such as the Townsend movement, fail to achieve their own ends, but see the adoption of related programs. Still other movements, such as the vegetarian movement, ultimately see neither their own program nor a substitute put into effect. Generally speaking, a successful movement usually begins to focus on other, related reforms, or becomes a guardian of the normative changes it has won; correspondingly, an unsuccessful movement usually declines. In many respects, however, successful and unsuccessful movements resemble each other in their later stages. Both continue to stay alive for long periods after the phase of active agitation. Furthermore, both tend to accumulate new functions—recreation, maintenance of the organization, civic contributions, etc.—in addition to, or even in place of, their original purposes.

At several points in this chapter we have observed the importance of social control. First, if a political authority that receives expressions of grievances is differentiated from other aspects of social control, this makes for greater toleration of specific, norm-oriented movements. Second, the success that a given agitation has in the political arena influences a movement's course of development. Now we shall ask what kinds of behavior on the part of agencies of social control encourage a norm-oriented movement to retain its norm-oriented character and what kinds of behavior tend to turn this kind of movement into another kind of collective behavior.

In the first place, a *general* encouragement of a norm-oriented movement by political authorities—whether or not the authorities approve its specific proposals—usually boosts and consolidates the movement. For example: (1) The continuous existence of the Society for the Prevention of Cruelty to Animals in England was guaranteed when in 1835 it received the patronage of the Duchess of Kent and Princess Victoria. (2) "Two factors which contributed to the rapid development of the playground movement were the support of the schools and [support] of agencies concerned with crime, especially juvenile delinquency."

Beyond general encouragement of a movement, what kinds of behavior on the part of authorities encourage a norm-oriented movement to retain its norm-oriented character? The agencies of social control must *(a)* permit expression of grievances but insist that this expression remain within the confines of legitimacy, and *(b)* give a hearing—as defined by institutionalized standards of "fairness"—to the complaints at hand. This does not mean that authorities must accede to the demands of the movement; rather they must leave open the possibility that these demands, along with others, will be heard, and that some responsible decision will be taken with regard to them.

In this way agencies of social control usually lift the issues from the hands of aggrieved groups and consider these issues in a setting apart from the heat of emotional commitment to generalized beliefs.

Other mechanisms for controlling a fiery movement can be found in the various kinds of political machinery. An aggrieved party seeking a court injunction must carry his demands through lawyers, and lawyers have to present them to judges, who have the right to ponder and delay before coming to a decision; legislatures utilize committees and commissions for investigating serious public issues before legislating on them; and so on.

Agencies of social control do not, however, always live up to these standards. They can, in effect, close off the avenues to normative change—thus encouraging alternative kinds of collective outbursts—in the following related ways:

(1) By consistently refusing to recognize one or more groups in a community.

(2) By appearing to vacillate in the face of pressure from the movement.

(3) By appearing to close off the avenues for norm-oriented agitation abruptly and directly.

(4) By appearing openly to "take sides" in a controversy.

(5) By openly encouraging some other kind of collective outburst, such as mob violence or revolutionary conspiracy.

Conclusions

In this chapter we have outlined a model value-added process in which several determinants combine to produce a norm-oriented movement. We have illustrated each determinant by referring to a variety of movements. Empirically, of course, any given movement does not follow such a neat sequence because the several determinants continuously combine and recombine as a movement progresses, thus giving it new directions. One tactic fails, and another is taken up; the movement is infused with new energy by the occurrence of some unexpected event; an authority rebuffs a movement crudely and drives it temporarily into a violent outburst. In this chapter, we have not tried to account for the evolution of any single movement, but rather to extricate from the histories of many movements the principles which shape the development of norm-oriented movements in general.

Two final observations on the empirical unfolding of norm-oriented movements are in order. First, the events that touch off a norm-oriented movement may simultaneously give birth to other collective outbursts. The movement of a Negro family into a white neighborhood, for instance, may trigger several distinct collective outbursts: (1) panic selling by neighbors who are convinced that property values will fall drastically; (2) a hostile outburst such as stoning the house or baiting the children of the new family; (3) a norm-oriented movement such as an agitation to modify the zoning laws to prevent Negro families from moving into the neighborhood in the future. For all these outbursts the conditions of structural strain and the precipitating factor are identical. The different character of each movement is imparted by the way in which the participants of each perceive—correctly or incorrectly—the conditions of structural conduciveness and the agencies of social control. The same concrete events, then, may be experienced by subgroups in different ways, and thus stimulate a rash of related but distinct outbursts.

Second, the same kinds of strain may produce different types of outbursts over time if the conditions of structural conduciveness and the behavior of authorities change.

9

TOWARD A THEORY OF SOCIAL MOVEMENTS

RALPH H. TURNER • LEWIS M. KILLIAN

In order to explain collective behavior we must explain its three distinctive features: (1) the occurrence of a disposition to transcend, bypass, or subvert established institutional patterns and structures; (2) the translation of perceptions, feelings, and ideas into action; (3) action that takes place collectively rather than singly. While doing so we must pay close attention to the interaction among these three features.

From *Collective Behavior*, 3/e, by Ralph H. Turner and Lewis M. Killian, pp. 241–261. Copyright © 1987. Reprinted by permission of Prentice Hall, Upper Saddle River, New Jersey.

1. Critical to extra-institutionalism is the justification and coordination derived from emergent norms. Emergent norms specify both behavior and conceptions of the situation that guide and justify extra-institutional action. Emergent norms range from the merely permissive to the obligatory. Social movements are complex and enduring phenomena in contrast to simple and transitory forms of collective behavior. Hence their emergent norms emphasize the obligatory nature of the movement's mission, and their normative conceptions of the situation are elaborated into ideologies and goal hierarchies. Essential to the understanding of social movements is therefore the understanding of processes leading to the development of movement ideology and goals, and the emergent sense of an obligatory mission.

2. Complementing the emergent normative sense of justification and obligation in fostering the translation of perceptions, feelings, and ideas into action is a sense of feasibility and timeliness. Feasibility includes a sense that it is possible to correct the unjust situation; impressions of the kind of support and opposition that will be encountered from all quarters, including the state and other "establishment" agencies; the facilities or resources needed for carrying out the action and dealing with opposition; and the ability of the potential actors to carry out the action successfully. Timeliness involves the urgency of the situation and the symbolic appropriateness of the occasion, as well as the sense that feasibility is greater now than it has been, or than it will be in the future.

   Because the objectives of social movements, in contrast to other forms of collective behavior, are to bring about lasting social change, the sense that it is possible to correct the situation necessarily involves at least some rudimentary image of a workable set of alternative arrangements. Anticipations of support and opposition incorporate confidence that significant latent support exists that can be mobilized as the campaign progresses. Similarly, much more concrete and reliable facilities and resources are required, and a constituency that can supply a continuous flow of dedicated movement adherents.

   People act partly on the basis of calculation but primarily on the basis of vague feelings that they can succeed in their objective and that the time is right. But because collective behavior in a social movement must be sustained for months or years, the sense of feasibility and timeliness is more extensively and continuously tested and revised as the enterprise progresses than is true for other forms of collective behavior, and there is more opportunity for calculation and planning. Images of workable alternative arrangements for correcting the unjust situation are subjected to searching public critique and the test of public credibility. Unrealistic assumptions about forthcoming support and opposition are exposed by the course of events. The objective adequacy of resources and the displayed capabilities of movement adherents intrude on the world of fantasy and wishful thinking as the movement achieves notable successes and disappointing setbacks. As experience accumulates and organizational centralization occurs, both the ideas and the strategies for action are refined and uniformized, leaving less room for spontaneous assessments.

3. People develop understandings and norms concerning the situations confronting them *collectively*, and translate feelings and perceptions into action *collectively*, because of the interaction of two circumstances. One is a condition or event suffi-

ciently outside the range of "ordinary" happenings that people turn to their fellow human beings for help and support in interpreting and responding to the situation. The other is the availability of pre-existing groupings through which communication can be initiated fairly easily.

Because of the nature of social movements in contrast to other forms of collective behavior, a social condition rather than merely a passing event is the necessary focus for collective concern. And the condition must be one that is seen as amenable to social manipulation. Because social movements are solidaristic rather than individualistic, complex communication and decision-making structures are necessary to facilitate cooperative action and to establish and maintain a division of labor. Because social movements are diffuse rather than compact, and require timely coordination of action in widely dispersed locations, both formal and informal communication networks are essential. In the modern world, access to mass communications is also indispensable. Because social movements are sustained rather than transitory, they require stable organization and leadership and stable constituencies from which adherents can be constantly recruited and replaced.

We can now look more closely at these three features of collective behavior as they develop and thus determine the growth and shape of social movements.

The Sense of Injustice as Emergent Norm

A movement is inconceivable apart from a vital sense that some established practice or mode of thought is wrong and ought to be replaced. To peace movement adherents it is intolerable to continue stockpiling potentially dangerous levels of nuclear weapons just because our potential enemies are still stockpiling theirs. To environmentalists we can no longer accept air and water pollution as the essential trade-off for industrial growth and full employment. To the cultist, prevalent doubts about the vitality of conventional churches and their impersonality take on an escalated meaning that makes it unacceptable to continue life as before.

Like the norms in other forms of collective behavior, the movement norm supplies a uniform packaging for diverse kinds of actions. Like the crowd, a social movement depends upon the contributions of many kinds of people, acting in varied ways, for diverse reasons. Also like the crowd, it must have some central norm that supplies a ready-made explanation and justification for these diverse elements. The emergent norm underlies the appearance of homogeneity that permits members and society to see the movement as a unit.

The common element in the norms of most, and probably all, movements is the conviction that existing conditions are unjust. The rule or norm that gains in importance, that is imposed upon members of the movement, and that the movement seeks to impose on the larger society is a specification that what has heretofore been accepted as an inescapable or even desirable condition must be viewed as *unjust.* The sense of what is just and unjust seems self-evident once it is established in a particular case.

The complex nature of the sense of justice can be illustrated in this way. Today, throughout the United States it is agreed that the denial of equal education or equal employment opportunity for equally qualified persons because of race is unjust. However, if two equally qualified men or women apply for a job, and the position is awarded to the physically more attractive one, there is seldom an organized sense of outrage. People of short stature occasionally complain that there is prejudice against them, that they must offer greater proofs to achieve equal recognition in competition with people who are moderately taller than average. The short man is likely to be introduced with the apologetic observation: "Though he is small, he packs a wallop" or "Don't be deceived by his size." If plain-looking people and short people experience widespread discrimination, there is yet no sign of any well-developed sense of injustice concerning their difficulties.

The problem posed for students of collective behavior is why there should be so clear a sense of injustice in the one case and not in the others, and why a set of circumstances that were not seen as unjust should come to be viewed in this fashion at a particular time in history. It is these questions that clarify the meaning of emergent norm in connection with social movements.

The emergent norm—the revised sense of justice—matures and crystallizes with the development of the movement. It is implemented through the strategy of the movement and diffused through the public that is concerned about the movement. The ultimate and most enduring product of a movement is either the repudiation of the revised conception of justice or its acceptance in the society. This end-result does not correlate perfectly with the success of the movement as an organization or with the success of the movement in securing specific programs of reform. Through the deliberations of publics, the revised conception of injustice may take hold in society, even though the specific plan of the movement is frustrated and the movement dies as an organization.

We propose that the revised sense of what is just and unjust comes principally from the positive effect of *new perspectives* in combination with the negative effect of *aroused indignation*.

Typically, a new perspective is the realization that an extant condition doesn't have to be, that it is not in the nature of things, and a reassessment of the costs and benefits of existing arrangements. The idea that women had not shown much public leadership because they had not been given the chance, and not because it was their biological nature to be passive and receptive, was an eye-opening perspective early in the twentieth century. The discovery that pollution of our rivers was reaching a level that had massive implications for public health was another recent perspective.

Aroused indignation fuels the fire that only smolders, so long as the realization of a new perspective stands alone. Indignation is typically aroused in the course of open conflict between those who question existing arrangements or assumptions and some oppressor. William Gamson speaks of "encounters with unjust authority."[1]

The development of new perspectives usually occurs gradually, often germinating for years before a substantial movement gets underway. Often a best-selling book or other media presentation serves dramatically to crystallize the evolving awareness. Betty Friedan's 1963 publication of *The Feminine Mystique*, issued in paperback the following year, crystallized the new perspectives on women's roles for the emerging women's movement.[2] The best-selling *Silent Spring*, by Rachel Carson, made the case dramatically for an environmental movement in 1962.[3] Both were best sellers because they were well-written, because they formulated what many were already thinking, and because their timing was right.

The arousal of indignation can take place in a much shorter time span than the development of new perspectives, and can thus be more predictive of just when a movement will develop. A rapid escalation of antagonism can occur when authorities meet public protest or disturbance with ineptness, obstinacy, deception, and oppression. When such an escalating antagonistic encounter takes place against the background of an appropriate and maturing new perspective, conditions are right for the emergent norm that is one essential aspect of any social movement.

Feasibility and Timeliness

New perspectives and unjust encounters alone cannot launch a movement without the conditions favorable for collective *action*. On the objective side a movement needs resources and outside support. On the subjective side there must be hope and self-confidence among potential adherents to the movement.

The indispensable movement resources in modern societies include such obvious things as financial backing, free use of facilities, and a great deal of free or inexpensive service, much of it unskilled but some of it quite skilled. Mailing lists, computer facilities and expert programmers, legal assistance in establishing tax-free status and eligibility for postal bulk mailing rates, and accountancy are mundane resource needs that cannot be overlooked. In addition, access to the mass media of communication and access to centers of power and decision making are essential.

Many resources are brought to the movement by adherents, who do so because they are persuaded of the importance of the movement's goals. Obviously, then, a potential movement whose constituency includes the wealthy and powerful has a great advantage over one that speaks only for the weak and the poor. And in either case, deeply committed adherents will bring more resources than weakly committed adherents. So long as these conditions prevail, the study of resources is simply a nat-

ural extension of the study of the potential adherents and the extent to which they find the movement's mission compelling.

But resources and support often come from outside of the obvious movement constituency. When the mass media find an emerging or established movement newsworthy, movement activities and personalities can receive free public exposure that would have cost millions of dollars to purchase. Coalitions and less formal mutual aid among movement organizations and among different movements are a common source of resources. The late 1960s saw a great deal of resource sharing among civil rights, peace, women's, and environmental movements. Public interest organizations and charitable foundations as well as government agencies have been generous supporters of movements in the United States in recent decades.

Why do these outside groups contribute or share their resources? Reasons include value-relatedness, gaining attention or a favorable public image, and more Machiavellian motives. Examples of value-relatedness include support for the battered-wives movement by women's organizations and mental health groups, cooperation between environmental and gun-control movements, and mutual help between creationists (a movement to require that the biblical version of creation be taught in public school biology courses) and the right to life movement (anti-abortion). A decision by the mass media to feature movement activities because the personalities involved or the bizarre nature of events guarantees a large and attentive audience illustrates the provision of resources to gain attention. Grants by government agencies hoping to enhance their image as humane, as was the case with much support for the battered-wives movement, illustrates the donation of resources for the sake of a favorable public image.

The availability of resources in the foregoing cases bears at least a modest relationship to public receptivity toward the movement's cause. But Machiavellian considerations bring resources with less relationship to belief in the movement's mission or public receptivity. Two examples will suffice. During the 1960s a great deal of money and other support came to Martin Luther King's Southern Christian Leadership Conference from government, foundations, and private industry. Some of this support was intended to bolster the SCLC as a bulwark against the more radical and potentially disruptive black movements, especially the Student Nonviolent Coordinating Committee (SNCC) and Congress of Racial Equality (CORE). More recently, federal government officials and allied conservative organizations have given surprising prominence to the movement to reinstate prayer in public school classrooms. Presumably this token support for an otherwise low-priority concern could help to retain the political support of a small but vocal segment of the electorate.

From the examples cited, two broadly sensitizing hypotheses can serve as a starting point for further investigation. First, the more intense the competition among established organizations and elites in a society, the more sponsorship of developing social movements will occur. Second, the more impressive the growth of movements that threaten radical change and serious disruption, the more resources will be made available to moderate alternative movements from establishment sources.

Hope

Hope and despair are intangible but nevertheless powerful states of mind. They are formed, diffused, and become normative for a population segment through rumor-like discussion in small family, neighborhood, workplace, and recreation-place groupings, and between these groupings through informal communication networks. Most evidence at our disposal indicates that despair and hopelessness block the formation of movements while hope opens the gates to movement formation.

Hope and despair can be more or less enduring attributes of population segments, reflecting their stable situation, or they can change with the course of events. In the former instance they help to explain which groups of people are likely to become constituencies for social movements; in the latter, they help to explain when a movement is likely to arise within a particular constituency.

Important elements in a stable condition of hope are a sense of group pride and group autonomy. Only when the group identity is one in which members can take pride are they able to assert themselves and feel confident that they can change an unacceptable situation by acting collectively. Pariah groups like the outcasts of India and the Eta of Japan have been slow to question their lot on a massive scale. Wulbert has observed that collective protest is less common in mental institutions than in prisons. He attributes the difference in part to the fact that there are aspects of being a criminal in which a person can take pride, whereas being a mental patient is almost without prideful aspects.[4] An important theme of the 1970s Black Power movement was the slogan "Black is beautiful!" The slogan, substitution of the term *black* for Negro, and other features of the movement were intended to combat the low racial esteem revealed by blacks' preference for light skins and deference to white leaders.

Individuals and groups who are totally dependent upon a dominant group are least likely to challenge the justice of their situation. In total dependence, the very basis for continuing existence is threatened when the terms of the relationship are challenged.

Even a state of slavery will be accepted by the majority of its victims without challenge when the slaves are taken out of reach of their homes, denied the skills necessary for independent existence, insulated from the practice of making significant decisions for themselves, and in other respects rendered totally dependent. Under American slavery, the memory of freedom in the recent past, the example of free blacks in the North, the opportunities for freedom nearby in Spanish Florida, and the identification with successful rebellion in Haiti kept the sense of impotence and dependency from being universal among the slaves. Consequently, there were many local and a few widespread movements of rebellion. The full extent and significance of these movements has been the subject of debate.[5] But most American slaves were unwilling to take the risks of rebellion. Even after slavery was abolished, most blacks did not seriously challenge their traditional position in the United States until they had been pushed off the plantations and out of paternalistic forms of service. So long as they lived on plantations, which constituted relatively total communities, serious questioning of the legitimacy of the system threatened blacks' only stable anchorage. Once they found themselves dealing in the open labor market, the dependency was broken, and they could afford to challenge their oppressors.

An indigenous nationality group constitutes an ideal medium for protest in this respect, especially when they have maintained their group integrity and remain in a traditional setting where the colonial power provides little towards their everyday needs. National pride and the memory of former autonomy are powerful forces conducive to challenging colonialism.

The arousal of hope and a sense of timeliness where hope was formerly lacking typically follows a period in which the condition and accomplishments of a population segment have been improving. We hypothesize that groups whose fortunes are rising are most likely to become movement constituencies, and groups whose fortunes are declining are least likely. Black power flourished at a time when prosperity and sympathetic federal government leadership encouraged hope, and declined when the combination of economic recession and a less sympathetic federal leadership dampened their hope.

In concluding this discussion, we must call attention to the interaction between feasibility and timeliness and the revised sense of injustice. Not only does the sense of feasibility and timeliness directly facilitate action; it also contributes to the sense of legitimacy, to the sense that the cause is just. A successful encounter with the opposition does not merely foster action by making the effort seem feasible. It also imparts a sense of legitimacy to the cause. There is a universal bias toward conceiving what succeeds as right and what fails as wrong, an expression of what psychologists have called the assumption of a *just world*.[6] Because of this bias, any dramatic success contributes to the essential normative underpinning of a budding movement.

Likewise, external support provides more than resources for an emerging movement. We offer the hypothesis that external legitimation is essential to convert the amoral pursuit of collective self-interest into a moral cause. A simple power struggle among self-interested groups evokes neither the sense of mission within the disadvantaged group, nor the sense of obligation to take their plight seriously among outsiders.

External legitimation takes place in at least two ways. First, support and sympathy from those who appear to have nothing directly at stake tells both the disadvantaged and members of larger publics that the issue is more than just one group trying to get a bigger share of the pie for themselves at the expense of other groups. Second, some of the public respect already accorded an established group rubs off on groups whose causes their spokespersons espouse. The surest technique for legitimating any moral claim is the "laying on of hands" through public support from an already respected group.

Forming and Sustaining the Collectivity

The processes of forming and sustaining collectivities can best be examined as they contribute to the crystallization of an emergent norm and as they facilitate action. Except in rare instances, social movements grow out of preexisting groupings of people because such groupings are necessary for both emergent norms and action and because they establish the basis for a continuing relationship between movement and constituency. In addition, each movement requires an emergent umbrella organization consisting of co-opted organizations such as the World Council of Churches in the peace movement or the Sierra Club in the environmental movement, organizations created as part of the movement such as NOW in the women's movement, and communication and decision-making structures to coordinate these component organizations and incorporate unattached adherents into movement activity.[7]

Membership in a Self-Conscious Group

The most obvious difference between categories of people whose problems are treated as injustices and people who are considered merely unfortunate is that the former constitute *groups* while the latter do not. We mentioned earlier that discrimination against less attractive people and short people is not treated as unjust in the same way as discrimination on the basis of race, religion, and sex, and increasingly on the basis of sexual orientation. There are no structural arrangements in society that sort people so that less attractive people regularly associate with other less attractive people, and so that short people regularly associate with each other. There is no internal communication network, no sense of group identity, and no embryonic subculture. A group is needed to provide the context in which intra-group communication can establish the sense that misfortune is shared. The embryonic subculture is needed as the foundation on which a norm can be erected, turning the misfortune into injustice.

It is a grass roots assumption that when a number of people experience shared misfortune, they form a bond because of their common plight and engage in collective action to remedy their grievance. This view treats the injustice as self-evident, as an objective fact in the situation. By contrast, we hypothesize that disadvantage or misfortune is transformed into injustice only when appropriate social definitions take place. The discovery by members of a preexisting self-conscious group that they share the disadvantage is one of the necessary conditions for defining the situation as unjust.

Consequently, revision in the sense of justice frequently follows a social change that separates a category of people from the heterogeneous groups in which they have been members and brings them together into a newly formed social unit. In modern times the loosening of extended family bonds has been an important precipitant for groups that have offered new perspectives on social justice. Separation of the aged from the family unit or segregation of their lives within the family has thrown the aged together. As membership in a multigenerational unit becomes less salient and fellowship with others of their own generation more central in their daily lives, the many limitations of their condition have come to seem less natural and more unjust. The idea that a division of labor under which male members cast ballots for the family unit was unjust developed after the women's sphere of activity outside the family had been greatly extended on a segregated basis. Women increasingly found themselves brought together in functioning units outside the family.

Modern labor movements did not appear until labor was moved out of the occupationally heterogeneous workshop into factories organized into occupationally homogeneous work groups. It is no accident that the first important organized outcries against the economic system in modern times came as peasant revolts rather than as worker uprisings. Peasants worked together in the fields and were integrated into the larger structure solely as a class and not as individuals long before the factory system made the same thing true of industrial laborers. Although urban and village workers were identifiable as a class, their work life occurred in groups that associated them closely with representatives of other classes, and their occupational identity was seldom translated into a vital and comprehensive group identity. The peasants, however, experienced the conjuncture of occupational class, work associates, and living associates that made it possible to view their collective lot as intolerable.

It is useful to search for clues to the emerging sense of injustice in the many investigations dealing with class consciousness. Class consciousness incorporates a burning conviction that members of a class suffer from a shared state of injustice. The theory of class consciousness should be viewed as a special case of a more general phenomenon including age-group consciousness, national consciousness, racial consciousness, and religious consciousness.

In Marxian analysis it is recognized that classes may exist without class consciousness. Members of an exploited economic class often fail to recognize their situation and consequently do not pursue their class interests. When they recognize their situation and begin to act collectively to right it, class consciousness has developed. David Lockwood observes:

> . . . . the development of class consciousness is rooted in two interrelated, yet possibly independent processes. The first is the consciousness of a division of interest between employer and employee, and the second a consciousness of a community of interest among employees. It is only when individual alienation becomes mobilized as collective solidarity that it is appropriate to speak of class consciousness as such.[8]

Recent analyses have suggested that class consciousness among laborers is on the decline and may have been the consequence of a unique and transitory set of circumstances in Western history. Contemporary research does not reveal a vital class consciousness among industrial workers. Labor units today limit their activities largely to bargaining that does not challenge the justice of the underlying relationship between employer and employee. Wilensky, among others, has proposed that class consciousness was a consequence of the correspondence between occupational class and religious, racial, or ethnic identity.[9] This observation illustrates a general proposition, namely, that a state of existence is most likely to be viewed as unjust when it is shared by people who are united into a group by the correspondence between two or more group identities. When people are already united by membership in a common ethnic group or participation in a common organized religion, their occupational class can readily become the point of reference for a vital sense of injustice over economic arrangements.

Prior Organization and Co-Optable Networks

If prior grouping is indispensable for the normative redefinition underlying a movement, it is equally essential for facilitating *action* on the redefinition. Prior organization supplies leadership, patterns for decision making, and an initial supply of indispensable resources. The emerging environmental movement relied heavily on such established organizations as the Sierra Club of California, which continues to play a crucial part in the now well established movement.

Jo Freeman asked why the women's movement flowered when it did, even though a twenty-year review indicated no apparent change in the role strains that might have provoked women to organize. She concluded that

> . . . . there appear to be four essential elements contributing to the emergence of the women's liberation movement in the mid-sixties: (1) the growth of a preexisting communications network which was (2) co-optable to the ideas of the new movement; (3) a series of crises that galvanized into action people involved in this network, and/or (4) subsequent organizing efforts to weld the spontaneous groups together into a movement.[10]

In 1961 President Kennedy established the President's Commission on the Status of Women, chaired by Eleanor Roosevelt. Following issuance of its report in 1963, commissions were established in the fifty states. By bringing together many politically sensitive and active women who would not otherwise have worked together on women's concerns, these commissions established a significant network that could be used in the formation of the National Organization for Women (NOW) in 1966. During the same period, many younger women were participating in the Civil Rights movement and the movement against the war in Vietnam. Networks and working relationships were established and converted increasingly to the service of a women's movement as the second-class status of women in these prior movements was increasingly impressed upon them.

The series of crises referred to by Freeman contributed to the sense of timeliness and the arousal of indignation already discussed. Freeman attributes the more extensive growth of the younger branch of the movement to the organizing skills acquired by women through their apprenticeship in the prior movements. She concludes that "the art of 'constructing' a social movement is something that requires considerable skill and experience. Even in the supposedly spontaneous social movement, the professional is more valuable than the amateur."[11]

Since movements often begin as small groups of concerned individuals in widely separated locations, the task of creating an organization that links these many units into a coordinated movement is critical in the translation of unrest into a significant force in society.

Fraternal Relative Deprivation

We have suggested that some frustrating conditions are more suitable for stimulating *collective* action than others. One important consideration is whether the individual's view of the situation is such as to make it seem a collective or an individual problem. A distinction is commonly made between the sense of *fraternal* deprivation and the sense of individual deprivation.

The theory of fraternal deprivation builds on *reference group* theory, especially as it was first developed by Robert Merton and Alice Kitt Rossi. Recognizing that the most objectively deprived groups are not necessarily those whose members feel the most deprived, Merton and Rossi proposed that feelings of deprivation depend upon what groups people compare themselves with. If they look at others who are better situated, they feel deprived; if they attend to less well situated others, they feel satisfied. Thus discontent is a consequence of *relative* deprivation rather than absolute deprivation. The important question, then, is why people choose the particular reference groups they do as the basis for assessing their own situations.[12]

W.G. Runciman expanded on the Merton and Rossi formulation in an effort to explain the presence and absence of class consciousness among British workers. Class consciousness combines the sense of injustice and the sense of class solidarity. We cite four principles suggested by Runciman as keys to the sense of collectivity and shared injustice.

1. People can normally compare themselves either with members of their own group or some other group. The former can lead to individual feelings of victimization, but stifles the development of any group solidarity or shared sense of injustice. So long as workers are chiefly jealous of benefits that come to some of their fellow workers as individuals, they are unlikely to join forces with their fellows or think of the worker's position in general as inherently unjust. Indeed the deliberate cultivation of internal jealousies is a control tactic sometimes used by persons in authority to forestall serious challenge to established patterns of organization. On the other hand, catastrophes that strike one class of people indiscriminately, exploitation that does not distinguish between friends and enemies within a particular group, and repressions that are applied to one category of people and not to others are the kinds of experience that divert attention away from internal dissension and redirect it toward other groups that are available for comparison.

2. Status inconsistency fosters unfavorable comparisons with other groups and consequently contributes to a sense of injustice and fellow feeling among the deprived. By status inconsistency we mean a lack of correspondence among the aspects of an individual's socioeconomic status, such as educational attainment and occupational level and income. College-educated blacks working as postal clerks compare themselves with college-educated whites who ply more rewarding occupations. The clear categorical basis for their deprivation forces them to rely on solidarity among similarly deprived blacks.

3. Sudden disappointment of a stable expectation when shared by members of a group is a third circumstance leading to unfavorable comparisons with another group. Economic depression hits the wage-earner and inflation hits the pensioner. In either case it forces a downward revision in living standards. Such revisions normally cause the victims to look about for other groups that are not similarly affected. There was a widespread conviction in the United States during the depression of the 1930s that the nation's wealth was concentrated in the hands of the well-to-do and that economic problems could be resolved by "soaking the rich." Discrepancies between the wealthy and the poor were probably no greater, and perhaps even less during the depression years than in

the preceding decade of prosperity. Yet there was a greater tendency for lower-income groups to use the wealthy as comparison groups and more questioning of the fundamental justice of the divisions between the wealthy and other income classes.

4. Finally, rising expectations may under some circumstances lead to comparison with a group that is better situated than one's own. Perhaps the significant instances are those in which the improved circumstances permit members of the rising group to assume many of the characteristics of a group above them. When they begin to dress like the higher group, drive similar automobiles, live in similar neighborhoods and speak with similar accents, they then adopt the higher category as a comparison group, which they would not otherwise have thought to do. If their progress is disappointing, they are thrown back onto bonds with fellow members of the rising group.[13]

Relative deprivation and especially fraternal deprivation have been difficult concepts to operationalize for research. Hence it is not yet clear how valuable these concepts will be in understanding social movements. But at present the fraternal-deprivation hypothesis is the best elaborated clue to what makes some situations more susceptible to collective rather than individual discontent and action.

Incorporating the Process Approach

Throughout our discussion of conditions that contribute to a revised sense of justice, to action, and to formation of a collectivity, questions of timing have arisen. Without attention to timing our discussion is like the list of ingredients included in every recipe for home cooking. With only the list of ingredients in hand, the inexperienced home chef could never produce a palatable lemon meringue pie or a gourmet omelet. Adding an essential ingredient too soon or too late, or applying maximum heat too long or too briefly spoils the product. In the same way, timing and order are critical in combining the ingredients for a social movement. Considerations of time and order bring us to the more general question of *process* in social movement theory. We shall look at *typical life cycle* and *interactive spiral* approaches to process in social movements.

Many investigators have attempted to describe a typical life cycle, applicable to all movements or to certain kinds of movements. It consists of an idealized series of stages from the origin to the success or other termination of the movement. Besides providing a process framework, the life cycle is a way of organizing our knowledge about movements so we can predict forthcoming events. The life cycle also offers a framework within which the many aspects of a movement can be seen working together—leadership, ideology, tactics, adherency, etc.—rather than each being studied separately. Finally, it provides a framework within which the causes for success can be approached.

A widely used formulation of a typical life cycle for social movements in general contains four stages of development. In the first or *preliminary stage of social unrest* there is unfocused and unorganized restlessness, evidence of increasing disorder, and susceptibility to appeals of agitators. In the second or *popular stage* unrest is brought into the open and given a positive focus that transforms it into collective excitement. A social myth characterizing the movement and its aims and supplying its justification is fabricated and disseminated. Prophets displace agitators as the principal leaders and are later (in the same stage) displaced by the reformers who attack more specific evils and offer more clearly developed programs of reform. In the *stage of formal organization* the movement is welded into a disciplined organization, capable of securing member commitment to stable goals and strategies and capable of working effectively on community centers of power to promote its aims. Now the reformers and prophets play second fiddle to the statesmen and stateswomen, who are masters of strategy. Finally, the *institutional stage* sees the movement established as an organic part of society, and leadership devolves on the administrator whose forte is keeping the system working.[14]

Each stage contains some but not all of the causal preconditions for the succeeding stage. No stage can occur before the prior stages have been achieved. But progression to the next stage is never inevitable, because there are unique contingencies for each stage.

As a product of development, each stage is a natural continuation of growth from the preceding stage. But internal and external contingencies either foster or impede the progression from each stage to the next, or alter the direction of development. Internal contingencies include decisions taken by movement leaders and actions taken by adherents. External contingencies include opposition and support from other organizations and the public images fostered largely through movement depiction in the mass media.

A different model of movement development, but one that is not necessarily incompatible with a flexible life cycle approach, pictures a series of episodes. The social actions and exchanges evoked in each episode escalate or deescalate movement development, and re-establish the direction of that development. The best elaborated application of this approach is the examination of free speech movement encounters at the University of California at Berkeley in 1964 and 1965. Although Max Heirich's analysis is focused on explaining the escala-

tion of conflict rather than the development of the movement, his model can be modified to serve the latter purpose.

Each of the 26 episodes culminated in some form of collective action. The action occurred because the acts by the university administration or other agents of established authority were perceived as creating a crisis with limited time for response, when the cause for the crisis appeared simple and a simple response promised to influence events in the desired direction. In the opening episode, political activity on a section of university property formerly thought to be city property was banned by the university. Students attributed the ban to politicians' having exerted pressure to remove political groups from access to students. Consequently, on September 21, the day the ban was to take effect, they established a picket line around Sproul Hall (the administration building) in order to mount public counterpressure to restore previous rights. Subsequent episodes culminated in sit-ins, trapping and holding a police car, "pack-ins," a strike, election of pro-free-speech-movement candidates to student body offices, physical action to block confiscation of a banned student publication, creation of a "Free Student Union," and other actions. The full analysis attempts to establish how each of the parties to the conflict saw the events leading up to each culminating action, and why they saw things as they did.[15]

A comparable analysis of movement development would likewise identify a succession of key episodes. Each episode would culminate in some enhancement or setback for the movement, or significant change in internal organization and orientation or in relations to outside forces. With each episode the investigator would examine the mutual interaction of emergent norm processes, action and dispositions to action, and changes in the strength and character of the collectivity. All of the circumstances affecting these key movement components would be re-examined for each episode. Thus instead of one grand analysis of the conditions affecting the rise and growth of a movement, there would be a series of mini-analyses. Rather than being predictable on the basis of a set of generalized stages, the course of a movement could only be predicted from episode to episode. Such an approach would realistically acknowledge that movement goals and ideology are constantly changing, as are their strategies for action and their organization. New perspectives, instead of simply maturing to a point of crystallization and fixity, would be seen as continuing to change and thus establishing constantly renewed ground for movement development. One encounter with authority would be succeeded by other encounters, each with a different effect as part of a distinctive episode in growth of the movement.

The Public Image of a Movement

In talking thus far of the parts of the movement and their interaction we have not acknowledged that the movement becomes an object in society. As people become aware of a movement they tend to reify it and assign it a transparent and unitary character. The 1960s women's movement quickly became known as "women's libbers," and a popular image crystallized. Once such a movement identity and image are established, they serve as reference for interpreting events and the actions of individuals. When a parishioner uses a period during Sunday morning church service that is set aside for announcements about church activities to make an impassioned speech for nuclear disarmament, members of the congregation explain to each other that the speaker is a *peacenik*.

Movement leaders and adherents frequently complain that their movements

are misunderstood and misrepresented. Women's movement spokespersons struggled to overcome an early image of unruly exhibitionists who burned their bras in public. Environmentalists protest that they have no wish to destroy industry and agriculture. Creationists who fight for mandatory teaching of the biblical account of creation in public schools insist that they do not oppose the parallel teaching of scientific views. Antinuclear activists denied that they wished to see America weakened so as to foster the expansion of international Soviet hegemony. The spokeswoman for MADD (Mothers Against Drunk Drivers) tries to reassure listeners that the movement has no interest in reinstating Prohibition. In all these instances, adherents object to a public image of extremism or irresponsibility that makes the movement unacceptable in the mainstream of American society. Movements with professional leadership hire public information experts to counter such damaging imagery and to cultivate more favorable images.

The Effects of Public Images

Two cases illustrate the dramatic effect that a changed image can have on a movement. In March 1966 U.S. Attorney General Katzenbach requested the Federal Subversive Activities Control Board to require the W.E.B. DuBois Clubs of America to register as a Communist-front organization. Many Americans who had never heard of this organization mistakenly thought he was referring to the Boys' Clubs of America. The result was a flood of hate mail and threatening telephone calls and a drop in public contributions to the Boys' Clubs. During the late 1960s Martin Luther King's Southern Christian Leadership Conference was widely supported by private and corporate donations from throughout the United States. King's dedication to nonviolence and moderation was seen as a crucial defense against more threatening black organizations such as SNCC and CORE. But in 1967 King announced that because of the war's unequal impact on blacks, the SCLC would henceforth include opposition to American military involvement in Vietnam among its leading objectives. Widely perceived as a shift in a more radical direction, this policy change was followed abruptly by a drop in receipts. Both illustrations underline resource mobilization theorists' emphasis on the importance of a steady flow of resources to a social movement. But they also reinforce traditional collective behavior emphasis on the public image of a movement.

The public issue in these two cases and in the several preceding examples is whether a movement (or an organization) seeks reform or revolution. The distinction between reform movements and revolutionary movements has always been important in the field of collective behavior because it corresponds to the way people think and talk about movements. The distinction usually refers to differences in both goals and methods. With respect to goals, a revolutionary movement challenges the fundamental values of a society. In America these values might be free enterprise, human rights, freedom of religious worship, or the sacredness of family life. A reform movement seeks improvements without challenging the existing value scheme. It advocates a change that will implement the existing value scheme more adequately than present conditions do, such as strengthening labor unions to improve the workers' lot within the free enterprise system. A revolutionary movement insists on replacing the underlying value scheme. For example, revolutionaries contend that the worker's lot will always be depressed until free enterprise is replaced by some form of communal ownership. At the same time, revolutionary movements are identified with the use of illegal and coercive strategies, with violence, secretiveness, and infiltration tactics. Reform movements are associated with the use of legal, socially approved, and nonthreatening strategies of persuasion, and operate openly.

Some movements fit clearly into one category or the other, like the short-lived revolutionary Symbionese Liberation Movement in California and guerilla movements in Latin America, or like the reform-oriented gun control movement. But many movements waver between goals of reform and revolution, and their activists employ a variety of tactics. Some adherents to the women's movement believe that women can achieve full equality while preserving the stable family ideal, but others see the family as inherently an agency for male domination. Some adherents to consumer movements find the production of high quality goods at reasonable prices irreconcilable with production for profit, while others are satisfied with policing private industry for the consumer. A peace movement pledged to nonviolence may nevertheless spawn a small cadre of impatient activists who bomb a munitions factory.

As shown by Todd Gitlin's analysis of the media and the New Left, publics debate a social movement's goals and define the character of the movement itself. *How the movement is publicly understood and defined will have more effect than the views and tactics of typical adherents* on the sources from which it can recruit adherents and accumulate resources, the type and tactics of opposition and official control with which it must cope, and the degree to which it can operate openly and through legitimate means.

If a movement is *respectable* (i.e., seen as a reform movement), its leaders can appeal for financial contributions and other resources from a wide spectrum of people and organizations, and recruit adherents and supporters broadly and openly. Opposition groups will have to tolerate the movement, and government agencies can be called upon to protect as well as regulate the movement's activities. Because the movement is legitimate and protected, it will have access to the mass media and other legitimate channels for advertising its goals, and can employ a wide range of tactics flexibly in attempting to bring about reform. If a movement is labeled *revolutionary*, appeals for support to any but a carefully selected and narrow population segment arouse public fears and consequent opposition. Recruitment of adherents must be attempted surreptitiously. The principal mass media will be closed to the movement and it will be forced to rely on "underground" newspapers and unlicensed radio stations. The movement will be met with public intolerance and often with violent government suppression. Movement advocates will be denied normal access to institutional and governmental decision-makers. It is hardly surprising, therefore, that a movement labeled revolutionary may resort to robbery and rackets to raise money, attempt to infiltrate influential, respectable organizations and the staffs of decision-making bodies, or resort to guerilla and terrorist tactics.

Thus the label of revolutionary attached to a movement can be a self-fulfilling prophecy. Denied legitimate means for building a movement and promoting their aims, leaders have no recourse but to abandon their effort or pursue it by illegitimate means. But when these methods are exposed to public view, the effect is to confirm the original label and strengthen the justification for intolerance and suppression.

Between respectable and revolutionary movements there is another category of movements viewed as odd, queer, or *peculiar*. Many religious cults and sects are seen in this way until they begin to recruit children from middle-class families, or until a sensational scandal such as the Jonestown mass suicide and execution provokes a redefinition as revolutionary. Similarly, "crackpot" schemes to change the world are more peculiar than threatening so long as they lack political clout and attract few adherents and sympathizers. Although they denounce major values in society, they are thought to be harmless and consequently are tolerated and granted considerable access to legitimate means for promoting their objectives. They are opposed largely through ridicule, isolation, and ostracism of their members, rather than repression or violence. Since the difference between a revolutionary and a peculiar definition is often simply a matter of apparent strength or weakness, change from one label to the other is frequent.

NOTES

1. William A. Gamson, Bruce Fireman, and Steven Rytina, *Encounters with Unjust Authority* (Homewood, IL: The Dorsey Press, 1982). Cf. also Barrington Morre, Jr., *Injustice: The Social Bases of Obedience and Revolt* (White Plains, N.Y.: M.E. Sharpe, 1978).

2. Betty Friedan, *The Feminine Mystique* (N.Y.: W. W. Norton, 1963).

3. Rachel L. Carson, *Silent Spring* (Boston: Houghton Mifflin, 1962).

4. Roland Wulbert, "Inmate Pride in Total Insitutions," *American Journal of Sociology*, 71 (July 1956), pp. 1–9.

5. Herbert Aptheker, *American Negro Slave Revolts* (New York: Columbia University Press, 1943).

6. Melvin J. Lerner, *The Belief in a Just World: A Fundamental Delusion* (New York: Plenum Publishing, 1980).

7. Russell R. Dynes and E. L. Quarantelli, "Group Behavior Under Stress: A Required Convergence of Organizational and Collective Behavior Perspectives," *Sociology and Social Research*, 52 (July 1968), pp. 416–29; Jack M. Weller and E. L. Quarantelli, "Neglected Characteristics of Collective Behavior," *American Journal of Sociology*, 79 (No. 1973), pp. 665–85.

8. David Lockwood, *The Blackcoated Worker: A Study in Class Consciousness* (London: George Allen and Unwin, 1958), p. 208.

9. Harold Wilensky, "Class, Class Consciousness, and American Workers," in William

Haber, ed., *Labor in a Changing America* (New York: Basic Books, 1966), pp. 12–44.

10. Jo Freeman, "The Origins of the Women's Liberation Movement," *American Journal of Sociology,* 78 (January 1973), p. 802.

11. *Ibid.,* p. 807.

12. Robert K. Merton and Alice S. Kitt, "Contributions to the Theory of Reference Group Behavior," pp. 40–105 in Merton and Paul F. Lazerfeld, eds., *Continuities in Social Research* (New York: Free Press, 1950).

13. W. G. Runciman, *Relative Deprivation and Social Justice* (Berkeley: University of California Press, 1966), pp. 9–35.

14. Herbert Blumer, "Collective Behavior," in Robert E. Park, ed., *An Outline of the Principles of Sociology* (New York: Barnes and Noble, 1939), pp. 259ff.; Carl A. Dawson and Warner E. Gettys, *An Introduction to Sociology* (New York: Ronald Press, 1948), pp. 689–709; Rex D. Hopper, "The Revolutionary Process: A Frame of Reference for the Study of Revolutionary Movements," *Social Forces,* 28 (March 1950), pp. 270–79; C. Wendell King, *Social Movements in the United States* (New York: Random House, 1956), pp. 11–24.

15. Max Heirich, *The Spiral of Conflict: Berkeley 1964* (Berkeley: University of California Press, 1971).

10

THE CLASSICAL MODEL OF SOCIAL MOVEMENTS EXAMINED

DOUG McADAM

During the past twenty years the accuracy of the pluralist model as a description of the American political system has been increasingly questioned. Yet pluralism represents more than just a description of institutionalized politics in America. In addition, the model is important for what it implies about organized political activity that takes place *outside* the political system.

The pluralist view of social movements follows logically from the way the model characterizes institutionalized politics. The central tenet of the pluralist model is that, in America, political power is widely distributed between a host of competing groups rather than concentrated in the hands of any particular segment of society. Thus Dahl tells us that, in the United States, "Political power is pluralistic in the sense that there exist many different sets of leaders; each set has somewhat different objectives from the others, each has access to its own political resources, each is relatively independent of the others. There does not exist a single set of all-powerful leaders who are wholly agreed on their major goals and who have enough power to achieve their major goals" (1967: 188–89).

This wide distribution of power has favorable consequences for the political system. The absence of concentrated power is held to ensure the openness and responsiveness of the system and to inhibit the use of force or violence in dealing with political

From *Political Process and the Development of Black Insurgency* by Doug McAdam, University of Chicago Press, pp. 5–19. Copyright © 1982 University of Chicago Press. Reprinted with permission.

opponents. With regard to the openness of the system, Dahl writes that "whenever a group of people believe that they are adversely affected by national policies or are about to be, they generally have extensive opportunities for presenting their case and for negotiations that may produce a more acceptable alternative. In some cases, they may have enough power to delay, to obstruct, and even to veto the attempt to impose policies on them" (1967: 23). The implication is clear: groups may vary in the amount of power they wield, but no group exercises sufficient power to bar others from entrance into the political arena.

Once inside the arena, groups find that other organized contenders are attentive to their political interests. This responsiveness is again a product of the wide distribution of power characteristic of the pluralist system. Groups simply lack the power to achieve their political goals without the help of other contenders. Instead, they must be constantly attuned to the goals and interests of other groups if they are to establish the coalitions that are held to be the key to success in a pluralist system.

Efficacious political interaction also requires that groups exercise tactical restraint in their dealings with other contenders. Any attempt to exercise coercive power over other groups is seen as a tactical mistake. Lacking disproportionate power, contenders are dependent on one another for the realization of their political goals. Thus, according to the pluralists, the exercise of force is tantamount to political suicide. A broad distribution of power, then, insures not only the openness and responsiveness of the system but its restrained character as well. "Because one center of power is set against another, power itself will be tamed, civilized, controlled and limited to decent human purposes, while coercion . . . will be reduced to a minimum" (Dahl, 1967: 24). In place of force and coer-

cion, the system will "generate politicians who learn how to deal gently with opponents, who struggle endlessly in building and holding coalitions together . . . who seek compromises" (Dahl, 1967: 329).

If the pluralist portrait is accurate, how are we to explain social movements? Why would any group engaged in rational, self-interested political action ignore the advantages of such an open, responsive, gentlemanly political system? One possible explanation would be that the group in question had simply made a tactical mistake. Yet the regularity with which social movements occur makes it difficult to believe that, as a historical phenomenon, they represent little more than a consistent strategic error made by countless groups.[1] However, pluralist theory implies another logical answer to the question. Movement participants are simply not engaged in "rational, self-interested political action." Accordingly their departure from the "proper channels" is not seen as evidence of tactical stupidity so much as proof that the motives behind their actions are somehow distinct from those leading others to engage in "ordinary" politics. This answer represents the underlying assumption of the "classical" model of social movements.

The Classical Model

As referred to here, the classical theory of social movements is synonymous with a general causal model of social movements rather than with any particular version of that model. For analytic purposes, the following variations of the model have been subsumed under the general designation of classical theory: mass society, collective behavior, status inconsistency, rising expectations, relative deprivation, and Davies' J-curve theory of revolution. No claim is made that these models are interchangeable.

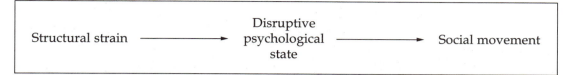

FIGURE 10.1   Classical Model

Each possesses features that are unique to the model. However, the idiosyncratic components of each are relatively insignificant when compared to the consistency with which a general causal sequence (see fig. 10.1) is relied on in all versions of the model to account for the emergence of social movements. This sequence moves from the specification of some underlying structural weakness in society to a discussion of the disruptive psychological effect that this structural "strain" has on society. The sequence is held to be complete when the attendant psychological disturbance reaches the aggregate threshold required to produce a social movement.

The various versions of the classical model agree on this basic sequence and differ only in their conceptualization of the parts of the model. That is, a variety of antecedent structural strains have been held to be casually related to social movements through an equally wide range of disturbed "states of mind." To appreciate the similarities underlying these various formulations, it will help to review briefly a number of them.

Mass Society Theory

According to proponents of this model, the structural condition known as mass society is especially conducive to the rise of social movements.[2] "Mass society" refers to the absence of an extensive structure of intermediate groups through which people can be integrated into the political and social life of society. Social isolation is thus the structural prerequisite for social protest. The *proximate*

causes of such activity, however, are the feelings of "alienation and anxiety" that are supposed to stem from social "atomization." Kornhauser tells us that "social atomization engenders strong feelings of alienation and anxiety, and therefore the disposition to engage in extreme behavior to escape from these tensions" (1959: 32). This sequence is diagrammed in figure 10.2.

Status Inconsistency

Another version of the classical model is status inconsistency (Broom, 1959; Laumann and Segal, 1971; Lenski, 1954).[3] Like "mass society," the term "status inconsistency" has both an objective and subjective referent. Objectively, status inconsistency refers to the discrepancy between a person's rankings on a variety of status dimensions (e.g., education, income, occupation). If severe, we are told, this discrepancy can produce subjective tensions similar to those presumed to "afflict" the "atomized" individual. For some proponents of the model, these tensions are explainable by reference to the theory of cognitive dissonance. Geschwender, for example, writes: "Dissonance is an upsetting state and will produce tension for the individual. This tension will lead to an attempt to reduce dissonance by altering cognitions . . . or deleting old ones. Attempts to alter reality-based cognitions will involve attempting to change the real world. . . . The set of circumstances described by the 'status inconsistency' hypothesis would produce varying intensities of dissonance and dissonance-reducing behavior according to the degree of discrepancy between relevant

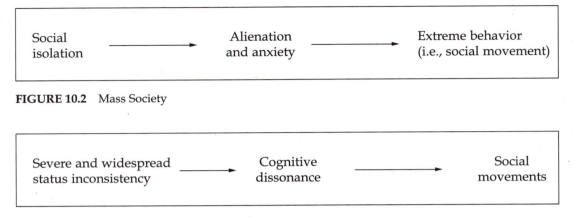

FIGURE 10.2   Mass Society

FIGURE 10.3   Status Inconsistency

status dimensions" (Geschwender, 1971b: 12, 15). As diagrammed in figure 10.3, status inconsistency is thus another variant of the basic causal sequence moving from structural strain, to discontent, to collective protest.

Collective Behavior

Collective behavior is the most general of all the classical models.[4] As a result, it approximates the causal sequence outlined in figure 10.1 quite closely. The model, as proposed by such theorists as Smelser, Lang and Lang, and Turner and Killian, does not specify a particular condition, such as status inconsistency or atomization, as the presumed structural cause of social movements. Instead, any severe social strain can provide the necessary structural antecedent for movement emergence. Thus, according to Smelser, "some form of strain must be present if an episode of collective behavior is to occur. The more severe the strain, moreover, the more likely is such an episode to appear" (1962: 48). Such strains are the result of a disruption in the normal functioning of society. The precise form this disruption takes is not specified, but frequent mention is made of such processes as industrialization, urban-

ization, or a rapid rise in unemployment. Indeed, any significant social change is disruptive in nature and therefore facilitative of social insurgency. Joseph Gusfield captures the essence of this argument: "We describe social movements and collective action as responses to social change. To see them in this light emphasizes the disruptive and disturbing quality which new ideas, technologies, procedures, group migration, and intrusions can have for people" (1970: 9).

In this model, then, social change is the source of structural strain. Social change is described as stressful because it disrupts the normative order to which people are accustomed. Subjectively this disruption is experienced as "normative ambiguity," which we are told "excites feelings of anxiety, fantasy, hostility, etc." (Smelser, 1962: 11). Once again, the familiar causal sequence characteristic of the classical model is evident in the theory of collective behavior (see fig. 10.4).

These brief descriptions of various classical theories demonstrate that, despite superficial differences, the models are alike in positing a consistent explanation of social movements. Specifically, all versions of the classical model seem to share three points. First, social movements are seen as a collec-

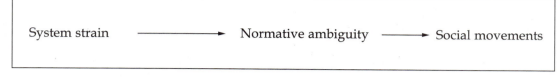

FIGURE 10.4   Collective Behavior

tive reaction to some form of disruptive system strain. Such strain creates tensions which, when severe enough—when some aggregate "boiling" point or threshold is reached—trigger social insurgency. Movement emergence is thus analogous to, and as inexorable as, the process by which water boils.

Second, despite the emphasis on system strain, the classical model is more directly concerned with the psychological effect that the strain has on *individuals*. In this view, individual discontent, variously defined as anxiety, alienation, dissonance, etc., represents the immediate cause of movement emergence. Some versions of the model account for discontent on the basis of the personal malintegration of movement participants. Such accounts depict movement participants as anomic social isolates. However, even if one discounts hints of personal pathology, the individual remains, in empirical analysis, the object of research attention. As seen in these formulations the social movement is an emergent group of discontented individuals.

Third, in all versions of the classical model, the motivation for movement participation is held to be based not so much on the desire to attain political goals as on the need to manage the psychological tensions of a stressful social situation. The functions ascribed to movement participation by various classical theorists support this contention. For the mass society theorist the movement offers the atomized individual the sense of community he lacks in his everyday life (Arendt, 1951: 316–17;

Kornhauser, 1959: 107–13; Selznick, 1970: 263–66). Selznick, for example, notes that for individuals in mass society:

> The need to belong is unfulfilled; insecurity follows and, with it, anxiety-laden efforts to find a way back to status and function and to a sense of relationship with society.
>
> But these efforts are compulsive: enforced by urgent psychological pressures, they result in distorted, pathological responses. There arises the phenomenon of the Ersatzgemeinschaft, the "substitute community," in which essentially unsatisfactory types of integration—most explicitly revealed in fascism—are leaned upon for sustenance (Selznick, 1970: 264).

Similarly, proponents of the status inconsistency model describe movement participation as one means by which the individual can reduce the dissonance produced by his inconsistent statuses (Geschwender, 1971b: 11–16). In a more general sense, the same argument is advanced by collective behavior theorists. The social movement is effective not as political action but as therapy. To be sure, movements are not unrelated to politics. Indeed, Smelser explicitly tells us that they frequently represent a precursor to effective political action (1962: 73). Nonetheless, in themselves, movements are little more than crude attempts to help the individual cope with the "normative ambiguity" of a social system under strain. The "therapeutic" basis of movement participation is implicitly acknowledged by Smelser in his discussion of the "generalized beliefs" that underlie collective behavior: "collective behavior is guided by various kinds of beliefs. . . . These beliefs differ, however, from those which guide many other types of behavior. They involve a belief in the existence of extraordinary forces—threats, conspiracies, etc.— which are at work in the universe. They also involve an assessment of the extraordinary consequences which will follow if the collective attempt to reconstitute social action is successful. The beliefs on which collective behavior is based (we shall call them *generalized beliefs*) are thus akin to magical beliefs" (Smelser, 1962: 8).

Movement participation is thus based on a set of unrealistic beliefs that together function as a reassuring myth of the movement's power to resolve the stressful situations confronting movement members. Movement participants, we are told, "endow themselves . . . with enormous power. . . . Because of this exaggerated potency, adherents often see unlimited bliss in the future if only the reforms are adopted. For if they are adopted, they argue, the basis for threat, frustration, and discomfort will disappear" (Smelser, 1962: 117). The message is clear: if the generalized beliefs on which the movement is based represent an inaccurate assessment of the political realities confronting the movement, it is only because they function on a *psychological* rather than a *political* level. The same can be said for the movement as a whole.

Weaknesses of the Classical Model

The classical model has not been without its critics (Aya, 1979; Currie and Skolnick, 1970; Gamson, 1975; Jenkins and Perrow, 1977; McCarthy and Zald, 1973; Oberschall, 1973; Rogin, 1967; Rule and Tilly, 1975; Schwartz, 1976; C. Tilly et al., 1975; Wilson and Orum, 1976). In general, I agree with the wide-ranging criticisms advanced in these works. The critique offered here, however, is limited to a discussion of the three general tenets discussed in the previous section.

Social Movements as a Response to Strain

The first proposition, that social movements are a reaction to system strain, is problematic because of the implicit assertion that there exists a simple one-to-one correspondence between strain and collective protest.[5] We are asked to believe that social movements occur as an inexorable response to a certain level of strain in society. But since widespread social insurgency is only an occasional phenomenon, we must conclude that system strain is also an aberrant social condition. The image is that of a normally stable social system disrupted only on occasion by the level of strain presumed to produce social insurgency. However, as others have argued, this view of society would appear to overstate the extent to which the social world is normally free of strain. The following passage by John Wilson represents an important corrective to the imagery of the classical model. "The lesson to be learned for the purposes of studying social movements is that since societies are rarely stable, in equilibrium, or without strain because change is constant, the forces which have the potential of producing social movements are always present in some degree. No great upheavals are needed to bring about the conditions conducive to the rise of social movements because certain tensions seem to be endemic to society" (Wilson, 1973: 55). If, as Wilson argues, the structural antecedents of social insurgency are "always present in some degree," then it becomes impossible to rely on them to explain the occurrence of what is a highly variable social phenomenon.[6] At best, system strain is a necessary, but insufficient, cause of social movements.

What is missing in the classical model is any discussion of the larger political context in which social insurgency occurs. Movements do not emerge in a vacuum. Rather, they are profoundly shaped by a wide range of environmental factors that condition both the objective possibilities for successful protest as well as the popular perception of insurgent prospects. Both factors, as we will see, are important in the emergence of organized protest activity. Together they comprise what Leites and Wolf have termed "cost push" factors in the generation of a social movement (1970: 28). By overlooking these factors, classical theorists are guilty of suggesting that the absence of social insurgency is a simple product of low levels of strain and discontent in society. This ignores the distinct possibility that movements may die aborning, or not arise at all, because of repression or rational calculations based on the imbalance of power between insurgents and their opponents. As Schattschneider reminds us, "People are not likely to start a fight if they are certain that they are going to be severely penalized for their effort. In this situation repression may assume the guise of a false unanimity" (1960: 8).

In short, the insistence that strain is the root cause of social movements has resulted in an overly mechanistic model that conceives of social movements as the result of a fixed and linear process rather than as the interplay of both "cost push" and "demand pull" factors. In John Wilson's view, the classical model "is based on the assumption that circumstances establish predispositions in people who are in turn drawn toward certain outcomes—more specifically, that structural conditions 'push' people into protest groups. But social movements are not a simple knee-jerk response to social conditions" (1973: 90). Wilson is right. Social movements are not simply a "knee-jerk response" to system strain.

Rather they emerge and develop as a product of the ongoing interaction of organized contenders within a shifting politico-economic environment. The important point is that social movements are not, as the classical theorists contend, only the product of factors endemic to the aggrieved population (alienation, dissonance, etc.). The characteristics and actions of opponents and allies, as well as those of movement groups, must be taken into consideration in accounting for any specific social movement. Insofar as classical theorists have failed to do so, they have diminished the utility of their model.

Individual Discontent as the Proximate Cause of Social Movements

While system strain, however defined, is seen by classical theorists as the structural cause of social movements, the motive force behind social insurgency remains some form of individual discontent. This atomistic focus is problematic on a number of counts.

Perhaps the most glaring weakness of this second proposition is the assertion that movement participants are distinguished from the average citizen by some abnormal psychological profile. In extreme versions of the model, nothing less than severe pathological traits are ascribed to movement participants (Hoffer, 1951; Lang and Lang, 1961: 275–89; Le Bon, 1960; McCormack, 1957). While perhaps effective as a means of discrediting one's political enemies, such formulations are less convincing as scientific accounts of social insurgency.[7] Maurice Pinard summarizes a number of objections to these models:

We do not see how such political movements could recruit a disproportionately large number of people characterized by pathological personality traits. For one thing, deep psychological traits are not necessarily translated into political beliefs, and the connections of these two with political action is not as simple as is often implied. Moreover, people affected by these traits are relatively few in the general population. . . . If such a movement were to draw only on such people, it would be small indeed and very marginal (Pinard, 1971: 225).[8]

By other accounts, movement participants are not so much distinguished by personal pathology as social marginality. This is the case with status inconsistents who, by virtue of their discrepant rankings on a number of status dimensions, are held to be poorly integrated into society. Similarly, mass society theorists attribute movement participation to the "uprooted and atomized sections of the population" (Kornhauser, 1959: 47). However, impressive empirical evidence exists that seriously challenges the assumption of individual malintegration. Especially significant are the many studies that have actually found movement participants to be better integrated into their communities than nonparticipants. Two examples will serve to illustrate the point. A study of the personal characteristics of participants in a right wing group in the early 1960s showed members to have higher rates of organizational participation, as well as higher incomes, levels of education, and occupational prestige, than a comparable national sample (Wolfinger et al., 1964: 267–75). In a finding more relevant to this study, Anthony Orum discovered participation in black student-protest activity to be highly correlated with integration into the college community (1972: 48–50).[9]

The lack of supportive evidence is not the only empirical weakness associated with the claim that movement participants are social isolates. Indeed, attempts to document the more general proposition that participa-tion in social insurgency is the product of particular psychological factors have traditionally foundered on a host of empirical/methodological deficiencies. For one thing, classical theorists have frequently inferred the presence of the presumed psychological state (alienation, dissonance, anxiety) from objective, rather than subjective, data. Thus, after comparing income, education, and occupational levels for whites and nonwhites, Geschwender concludes that, as an explanation for the emergence of the civil rights movement, " 'the Status Inconsistency Hypothesis' . . . is consistent with the data examined" (1971c: 40). His conclusion is empirically unwarranted, however. Wilson explains why:

> Status inconsistency is intended to describe the processes and product of social interactions in which perceptions, impressions, and responses to these play an important part in influencing attitudes. Underlying the whole model is a motivational scheme in which the perception of certain attitudes helps produce certain outcomes. And yet nowhere is data presented on these motivations. Despite the fact that the model contains crucial social-psychological variables, reliance is made exclusively on objective indexes of inconsistency (John Wilson, 1973: 80).

More damning is the consistent failure of classical theorists to document an aggregate increase in the psychological condition they are attempting to measure. The various versions of the classical model rely for their explanatory power on just such an increase. The claim is that social movements arise *only* when a certain level of psychological strain or discontent is present. This threshold can be conceived either as an increase in the proportion of the aggrieved population "suffering" the specified psychological state, or as an increase in the intensity of the psychological stress associated with the condition. Either way, a demonstrated increase in the presumed causal condition remains a basic requirement of any reasonable test of the model. Unfortunately, this "basic requirement" has been almost universally ignored.[10] In summarizing the findings of relative deprivation studies, a proponent of the model has remarked: "practically all of these studies fail to measure [RD] relative deprivation . . . over a period of time" (Abeles, 1976: 123). Instead, the usual approach has been to measure the degree of relative deprivation (or any of the subjective states deemed significant) in a specified population at a given point in time. On the basis of this analysis, the conclusion is drawn that relative deprivation is causally related to the protest activity of the population in question. But nowhere have we been shown data reporting comparable levels of relative deprivation *over time*.[11] That a certain proportion of the population is judged to be relatively deprived (or alienated, status inconsistent, etc.) at any point in time is hardly surprising. Indeed, it is likely that the incidence of these psychological conditions is relatively constant over time. If so, reliance on them to account for social insurgency is problematic indeed.

Finally, classical theorists have generally been remiss in failing to measure the incidence of these psychological conditions among comparable samples of movement participants *and* nonparticipants. Geschwender, for example, in the study discussed above, based his support for the status inconsistency hypothesis on aggregate data for the entire nonwhite population of the United States. Such data, however, are inadequate to test the theory. Insofar as movement involvement is held to stem from status inconsistency, a comparison of the

proportion of status inconsistents among movement participants *and nonparticipants* is required to assess the explanatory worth of the model. If we were provided with such a breakdown, we might very well find that the proportions were not significantly different. This was the case in one study that serves as a significant exception to the methodological weakness under discussion here. In his study of protest activity among black college students, Orum divided his sample into participants and nonparticipants and then compared the two groups on a variety of background variables. On the basis of this analysis, Orum concluded that: the "theory . . . of rising expectations, received no support in our data. Finally, the . . . interpretation, that the civil rights movement arose largely as a means of expressing the discontent of middle-class Negroes, who feel relatively deprived, was not confirmed" (1972: 45).

Orum's findings also illustrate what is perhaps the most serious, yet least acknowledged, weakness associated with the assertion that movements are a product of particular states of mind. While models based on personal pathology or social marginality have come under increasing fire, the same atomistic focus survives intact in less extreme formulations of the classical model. Geschwender illustrates this focus: "He [the Negro in America] is not experiencing as rapid a rate of occupational mobility as he feels he is entitled to. He is not receiving the economic rewards which he feels he has earned. As a result, he is becoming increasingly status inconsistent . . . He feels relatively deprived and unjustly so. Therefore, he revolts in order to correct the situation" (1971c: 42).

Social movements are thus viewed as emergent collections of discontented *individuals*. But to adopt this perspective requires that we ignore a fact that, on the surface, would appear to be obvious: social movements are *collective* phenomena. Obvious or not, classical theorists are guilty of failing to explain the collective basis of social insurgency. They offer no explanation of how individual psychological discontent is transformed into organized collective action. Rule and Tilly make the same point when they criticize Davies's variant of the classical model for treating "as automatic precisely what is most problematic about the development of revolutions: the transition from uncoordinated individual dissatisfactions to collective assaults on the holders of power" (1975: 50).

Quite simply, social movements would appear to be collective phenomena arising first among those segments of the aggrieved population that are sufficiently organized and possessed of the resources needed to sustain a protest campaign. Isolated individuals do not emerge, band together, and form movement groups. Rather, as numerous studies attest, it is within established interactional networks that social movements develop (Cameron, 1974; Freeman, 1973; Morris, 1979; Pinard, 1971; Shorter and Tilly 1974; C. Tilly et al., 1975). According to Shorter and Tilly, "individuals are not magically mobilized for participation in some group enterprise, regardless how angry, sullen, hostile or frustrated they may feel. Their aggression may be channeled to collective ends only through the coordinating, directing functions of an organization, be it formal or informal" (1974: 38).

Social Movements Represent a Psychological Rather than a Political Phenomenon

By claiming that the motive force behind movement participation is supplied by the disturbing effect of particular "states of mind," classical theorists are arguing that the proximate cause of social insurgency is psychological rather than political. Indeed, we are really being told that the movement as a whole is properly viewed as a psychological rather than a political phenomenon. Social movements are seen as collective attempts to manage or resolve the psychological tensions produced by system strain. In contrast, "ordinary," or institutionalized politics, is generally interpreted as rational group-action in pursuit of a substantive political goal. The contrast is clearly visible in the relationship that is presumed to exist, in each case, between the problem or strain to be resolved and the means taken to resolve it.

In the case of institutionalized politics, a straightforward relationship between the problem and the means of redress is assumed. If, for example, a government contract vital to the economic well-being of an area were terminated, we would expect the representatives of the affected constituency to initiate efforts to prevent the anticipated recession. Moreover, our interpretation of these efforts would, in most cases, be straightforward. In addition to ensuring their political survival, the elected officials of the region are simply trying to provide their constituents with jobs.

All of this may seem so obvious as to fail to merit such extensive attention. The important point is that classical theorists deny this straightforward link between problem and action when it comes to social movements. In fact, in some versions of the model, there is no logical connection whatsoever. Mass society theory provides us with such an example. According to proponents of the model, widespread isolation is the basic structural problem, or "strain," underlying social insurgency. The social movement is an attempt to resolve this problem, but it is, at best, an indirect attempt. To illustrate the point, let us return to our hypothetical example. Suppose, in addition to the institutionalized efforts of the area's elected officials, a protest movement emerged among workers who had lost their jobs as a result of the contract termination. How should we interpret their actions? Surely the workers are also engaged in instrumental political action designed to insure their means of livelihood. Not so, according to the mass society theorists. Quite apart from the movement's stated politico-economic goals, the primary motivation for participation remains psychological. Kornhauser is explicit on this point: "mass movements appeal to the unemployed on psychological . . . grounds, as ways of overcoming feelings of anxiety and futility, and of finding new solidarity and forms of activity" (1959: 167). Clearly, the functions ascribed to movements by Kornhauser are universal. That is, all movements offer their members a sense of community and an escape from the tensions engendered by social isolation. In this sense, movements are interchangeable. Following Kornhauser, the unemployed workers could as easily have solved their "problems" by joining a fundamentalist religious group as by engaging in political protest. The implication is clear: the political content of the movement is little more than a convenient justification for what is at root a psychological phenomenon.

We have thus come full circle. I began the chapter by raising the issue of the relationship between the pluralist view of the American political system and the classical model of social movements. At the heart of the issue was the puzzling question of how to account for social movements in the face of the open, responsive political system described by the pluralists. Why would any group engaged in rational political action ignore the benefits of this system in favor of noninstitutionalized forms of protest? The classical theorists have provided an answer

to this question: movement participants are not engaged in rational political action. Instead, the rewards they seek are primarily psychological in nature. The logic is straightforward. Social movements represent an entirely different behavioral dynamic than ordinary political activity. The pluralist model, with its emphasis on compromise and rational bargaining, provides a convenient explanation for the latter. Social movements, on the other hand, are better left, in Gamson's paraphrase of the classical position, to "the social psychologist whose intellectual tools prepare him to better understand the irrational" (1975: 133).

This distinction, however, raises serious questions about the accuracy of the classical model. It suggests, for example, that we need not take seriously the political goals of the movement. The substantive demands voiced by participants are more accurately viewed as epiphenomenal since the movement is, at root, a vehicle by which members resolve or manage their interpsychic conflicts. According to Kornhauser: "Mass movements are not looking for pragmatic solutions to economic or any other kind of problem. If they were so oriented, their emotional fervor and chiliastic zeal . . . would not characterize the psychological tone of these movements. In order to account for this tone, we must look beyond economic interests to more deep-seated psychological tendencies" (1959: 163).

And what of the participants in these movements? Are they aware of the "true" motivation behind their involvement? If not, how can we account for these periodic exercises in mass delusion? If, on the other hand, it is argued that they are aware, what explanation is there for their conscious rhetorical distortion of the "true" nature of the movement? Smelser offers the following explanation: "The striking feature of the protest movement is what Freud observed:

it permits the expression of impulses that are normally repressed. . . . The efforts—sometimes conscious and sometimes unconscious—of leaders and adherents of a movement to create issues, to provoke authorities . . . would seem to be in part efforts to 'arrange' reality so as to 'justify' the expression of normally forbidden impulses in a setting which makes them appear less reprehensible to the participants" (Smelser, 1973: 317).

The ideological implication of Smelser's account is none too flattering. At the same time, however, adherence to such a position makes it extremely difficult to explain the substantive impact social movements have had historically. If movement participants are motivated only by the desire to express "normally forbidden impulses," or to manage "feelings of anxiety and futility," then we would hardly expect social movements to be effective as social change vehicles. In fact, however, movements are, and always have been, an important impetus to sociopolitical change. The American colonists defeated the British on the strength of an organized insurgent movement. Mao, Lenin, Khomeini, and Castro all came to power as a result of similar movements. An incumbent president, Lyndon Johnson, was forced from office and this country's policy on Vietnam altered as a result of the antiwar movement. And through the collective protest efforts of blacks, the South's elaborate system of Jim Crow racism was dismantled in a matter of a decade. Are we to conclude that such significant historical processes were simply the unintended byproducts of a collective attempt at tension management? The argument is neither theoretically nor empirically convincing.

In summary, classical theorists posit a distinction between ordinary political behavior and social movements that is here regarded as false. At root, this distinction is based on an implicit acceptance of the plu-

ralist model of the American political system. Michael Rogin has cut to the heart of the matter: "Having denied the importance of a problem of power, pluralists do not treat mass movements as rational forms of organization by constituencies that lack power. . . . since the pluralists stress that power is shared in a pluralist democracy, movements that do not accept the normal political techniques of that society must be dangerous and irrational" (Rogin, 1967: 272–73). By assuming that all groups are capable of exercising influence through institutionalized means, the pluralists have made of social movements a behavioral phenomenon requiring "special" explanation. The classical theorists have, in turn, obliged with a host of such explanations based on any number of social psychological determinants. If, however, one rejects the pluralist model in favor of either an elite or Marxist view of power in America, the distinction between rational politics and social movements disappears.

NOTES

1. At the risk of lapsing into simplistic functionalism, I think that Durkheim was probably correct, when he wrote that "a human institution cannot rest upon an error and a lie" (Durkheim, 1965: 14).

2. My comments in this section are based largely on William Kornhauser's book *The Politics of Mass Society* (1959). For other writings in this tradition, see Arendt (1951) and Selznick (1970).

3. For a useful summary of the concept as applied to movement participation, see Louis Kriesberg, *The Sociology of Social Conflicts* (1973: 70–76).

4. In this section I draw heavily on Neil Smelser's *Theory of Collective Behavior* (1962). Other versions of the model can be found in Lang and Lang (1961) and Turner and Killian (1957).

5. At a more fundamental level, classical theorists can also be criticized for failing to adequately define strain. Indeed, in many

versions of the model the strains presumed to account for social movements are defined in such ambiguous fashion as to virtually guarantee their existence in the immediate premovement period. Thus, we appear to be engaged in little more than a form of post-hoc analysis. Rule and Tilly express this point nicely in reference to a particular version of the classical model, Davies's J-curve theory of revolution: "Davies appears to start with the accomplished fact of revolution, then cast about in the period immediately preceding it for evidence of the sharp reversal of some need within some part of the population, then look farther back for needs that have undergone increasing satisfaction for some length of time. Given that different groups in any population experience the satisfaction and frustration of various needs at various times, such a search has a high probability of success" (Rule and Tilly, 1975: 49).

6. Adoption of the classical perspective would force us to argue, for example, that the level of strain in American society was significantly lower in the 1980s than it was during the turbulent 60s. Quite apart from the methodological difficulties inherent in operationalizing the independent variable, I'm not sure there would be much intuitive support for this assertion.

7. Consistent with this point, it is entirely possible that the influence of the various models under discussion here are far more dependent on the ideological demands of the day than on the objective merits of the theories themselves. In this regard, the dominance of the classical model in the 1950s can be seen as stemming from the need of liberal academics to devise a "scientific" theory to discredit the antidemocratic movements (i.e., McCarthyism, Nazism) they were studying. The various classical models, with their heavy suggestions of irrationality, were ideally suited to the task. However, with the emergence of popular left-wing protest movements (i.e., civil rights, antiwar) in the 60s, liberal academia faced a new challenge: positing a revised perspective that cast these "progressive" movements in the favorable light of rationality and courageous resistance to oppression. In short, the development of both the resource mobilization and political process models must be seen in the context of the shift in political climate between the 1950s and 1960s and the consequent change in the ideological needs of the academic community.

8. In general, Pinard's summary and critique of psychological models of social movements is as good a one as can be found in the literature (Pinard, 1971: 223–42).

9. For other studies documenting the social integration of movement participants, see Caplan and Paige (1968); Flacks (1967); Fogelson and Hill (1968); Keniston (1968); Oberschall (1971); and Rogin (1967).

10. One exception is Geschwender's article "Social Structure and the Negro Revolt: An Examination of Some Hypotheses" (1964). Here the author attempts to document both a net increase in the proportion of status inconsistents in the black population and a rise in the aggregate level of relative deprivation for the same population. As I note though, Geschwender relies exclusively on objective data to infer the presence of the subjective states of mind he is concerned with.

11. A related weakness concerns the causal ordering of these various psychological states and movement participation. The classical model rests on the assumption that the former serves as the immediate cause of the latter. But empirical studies cited as supporting the classical model consistently lack the time-series data needed to document the causal ordering of the two variables. It may well be that movement participation actually triggers feelings of alienation, relative deprivation, etc., rather than the reverse. At least in the absence of unambiguous time-series data on both variables, this remains as likely a causal proposition as the classical interpretation.

REFERENCES:

Abeles, Ronald P. 1976. "Relative Deprivation, Rising Expectations, and Black Militancy." *Journal of Social Issues* 32 (no. 2): 119–37.

Arendt, Hannah. 1951. *The Origins of Totalitarianism.* New York: Harcourt, Brace.

Aya, Rod. 1979. "Theories of Revolution Reconsidered: Contrasting Models of Collective Violence." *Theory and Society* 8 (no. 1): 39–99.

Broom, Leonard. 1959. "Social Differentiation and Stratification." In Robert K. Merton, Leonard Broom, and Leonard S. Cottrell, eds., *Sociology Today.* New York: Basic Books, 429–41.

Cameron, David R. 1974. "Toward a Theory of Political Mobilization." *Journal of Politics* 36 (February): 133–71.

Currie, Elliott, and Jerome Skolnick. 1970. "A Critical Note on Conceptions of Collective Behavior." *Annals of the American Academy of Political and Social Science* 391 (September): 34–45.

Dahl, Robert A. 1967. *Pluralist Democracy in the United States.* Chicago: Rand McNally.

Freeman, Jo. 1973. "The Origins of the Women's Liberation Movement." *American Journal of Sociology* 78 (no. 4): 792–811.

Gamson, William A. 1975. *The Strategy of Social Protest.* Homewood, Ill.: The Dorsey Press.

Garfinkel, Herbert. 1959. *When Negroes March.* Glencoe, Ill.: The Free Press.

Geschwender, James A. 1971b. "Explorations in the Theory of Social Movements and Revolutions." In James A. Geschwender, ed., *The Black Revolt.* Englewood Cliffs, N.J.: Prentice-Hall, 6–17.

———. 1971c. "Social Structure and the Negro Revolt: An Examination of Some Hypotheses." In James A. Geschwender, ed., *The Black Revolt.* Englewood Cliffs, N.J.: Prentice-Hall, 33–43.

Gusfield, Joseph R. 1970. *Protest, Reform, and Revolt.* New York: John Wiley and Sons.

Hoffer, Eric. 1951. *The True Believer: Thoughts on the Nature of Mass Movements.* New York: Mentor Books, The New American Library.

Jenkins, Joseph Craig, and Charles Perrow. 1977. "Insurgency of the Powerless: Farm Worker Movements (1946–1972)." *American Sociological Review* 42 (no. 2): 249–68.

Kornhauser, William. 1959. *The Politics of Mass Society.* Glencoe, Ill.: The Free Press.

Lang, Kurt, and Gladys Lang. 1961. *Collective Dynamics.* New York: Crowell.

Le Bon, Gustave. 1960. *The Crowd: A Study of the Popular Mind.* New York: Compass Books, The Viking Press.

Leites, Nathan, and Charles Wolf, Jr. 1970. *Rebellion and Authority.* Chicago: Markham.

Lenski, Gerhard. 1954. "Status Crystallization: A Non-vertical Dimension of Social Status." *American Sociological Review* 19 (August): 405–13.

McCarthy, John D., and Mayer N. Zald. 1973. *The Trend of Social Movements in America: Profession-alization and Resource Mobilization.* Morristown, N.J.: General Learning Press.

McCormack, Thelma H. 1957. "The Motivation of Radicals." In R. H. Turner and L. M. Killian, eds., *Collective Behavior.* Englewood Cliffs, N.J.: Prentice-Hall, 433–40.

Morris, Aldon Douglas. 1979. "The Rise of the Civil Rights Movement and Its Movement Black Power Structure, 1953–1963." Ph.D. diss., State University of New York at Stony Brook.

Oberschall, Anthony. 1973. *Social Conflict and Social Movements.* Englewood Cliffs, N.J.: Prentice-Hall.

Orum, Anthony M. 1972. *Black Students in Protest.* Washington, D.C.: American Sociological Association.

Pinard, Maurice. 1971. *The Rise of a Third Party: A Study in Crisis Politics.* Englewood Cliffs, N.J.: Prentice-Hall.

Rogin, Michael Paul. 1967. *The Intellectuals and McCarthy.* Cambridge, Mass.: M.I.T. Press.

Rule, James, and Charles Tilly, eds. 1975. "Political Process in Revolutionary France: 1830–1832." In John M. Merriman, ed., *1830 in France.* New York: New Viewpoints, 41–85.

Schattschneider, E. E. 1960. *The Semisovereign People.* Hinsdale, Ill.: The Dryden Press.

Schwartz, Michael. 1976. *Radical Protest and Social Structure.* New York: Academic Press.

Selznick, Phillip. 1970. "Institutional Vulnerability in Mass Society." In Joseph R. Gusfield, ed., *Protest, Reform, and Revolt.* New York: John Wiley and Sons, 258–74.

Shorter, Edward, and Charles Tilly. 1974. *Strikes in France, 1830–1968.* London: Cambridge University Press.

Smelser, Neil J. 1962. *Theory of Collective Behavior.* New York: The Free Press.

———. 1973. "Social and Psychological Dimensions of Collective Behavior." In Ronald Ye-Lin Cheng, ed., *The Sociology of Revolution.* Chicago: Henry Regnery, 314–18.

Tilly, Charles, Louise Tilly, and Richard Tilly. 1975. *The Rebellious Century, 1830–1930.* Cambridge, Mass.: Harvard University Press.

Wilson, Kenneth L., and Anthony M. Orum. 1976. "Mobilizing People for Collective Political Action." *Journal of Political and Military Sociology* 4 (Fall): 187–202.

Wilson, John. 1973. *Introduction to Social Movements.* New York: Basic Books.

Wolfinger, Raymond, et al. 1964. "America's Radical Right." In David Apter, ed., *Ideology and Discontent.* Glencoe, Ill.: The Free Press, 267–75.

11

RESOURCE MOBILIZATION AND SOCIAL MOVEMENTS:
A Partial Theory

JOHN D. MCCARTHY AND MAYER N. ZALD

Past analysis of social movements and social movement organizations has normally assumed a close link between the frustrations or grievances of a collectivity of actors and the growth and decline of movement activity. Questioning the theoretical centrality of this assumption directs social movement analysis from its heavy emphasis upon the social psychology of social movement participants; it can then be more easily integrated with structural theories of social process. This chapter presents a set of concepts and related propositions drawn from a resource mobilization perspective. It emphasizes the variety and sources of resources, the relationship of social movements to the media, authorities, and other parties, and the interaction among movement organizations. Propositions are developed to explain social movement activity at several levels of inclusiveness—the social movement sector, the social movement industry, and the social movement organization.

For quite some time a hiatus existed in the study of social movements in the United States. In the course of activism leaders of movements here and abroad attempted to

enunciate general principles concerning movement tactics and strategy and the dilemmas that arise in overcoming hostile environments. Such leaders as Mao, Lenin, Saul Alinsky, and Martin Luther King attempted in turn to develop principles and guidelines for action. The theories of activists stress problems of mobilization, the manufacture of discontent, tactical choices, and the infrastructure of society and movements necessary for success. At the same time sociologists, with their emphasis upon structural strain, generalized belief, and deprivation, largely have ignored the ongoing problems and strategic dilemmas of social movements.

Recently a number of social scientists have begun to articulate an approach to social movements, here called the resource mobilization approach, that begins to take seriously many of the questions that have concerned social movement leaders and practical theorists. Without attempting to produce handbooks for social change (or its suppression), the new approach deals in general terms with the dynamics and tactics of social movement growth, decline, and change. As such, it provides a corrective to the practical theorists, who naturally are most concerned with justifying their own tactical choices, and it also adds realism, power, and depth to the truncated research on and analysis of social movements offered by many social scientists.

The resource mobilization approach emphasizes both societal support and constraint of social movement phenomena. It examines the variety of resources that must be mobilized, the linkages of social movements to other groups, the dependence of movements upon external support for success, and the tactics used by authorities to control or incorporate movements. The shift in emphasis is evident in much of the work published recently in this area (J. Wilson, 1973; Tilly, 1973, 1975; Tilly, Tilly, and Tilly, 1975; Gamson, 1975; Oberschall, 1973; Lipsky, 1968; Downs, 1972; McCarthy and Zald, 1973). The new approach depends more upon political sociology and economic theories than upon the social psychology of collective behavior.[1]

This chapter presents a set of concepts and propositions that articulate the resource mobilization approach. It is a partial theory because it takes as given, as constants, certain components of a complete theory. The propositions are heavily based upon the American case, so that the impact of societal differences in development and political structure on social movements is unexplored, as are differences in levels and types of mass communication of the left, ignoring, for the most part, organizations of the right.

The main body of the chapter defines our central concepts and presents illustrative hypotheses about the social movement sector (SMS), social movement industries (SMI), and social movement organizations (SMO). However, since we view this approach as a departure from the main tradition in social movement analysis, it will be useful first to clarify what we see as the limits of that tradition.

Perspectives Emphasizing Deprivation and Beliefs

Without question the three most influential approaches to an understanding of social movement phenomena for American sociol-ogists during the past decade are those of Gurr (1970) Turner and Killian (1972), and Smelser (1963).[2] They differ in a number of respects. But, most important, they have in common strong assumptions that shared grievances and generalized beliefs (loose ideologies) about the causes and possible means of reducing grievances are important preconditions for the emergence of a social movement in a collectivity. An increase in the extent or intensity of grievances or deprivation and the development of ideology occur prior to the emergence of social movement phenomena. Each of these perspectives holds that discontent produced by some combination of structural conditions is a necessary if not sufficient condition to an account of the rise of any specific social movement phenomenon. Each, as well, holds that before collective action is possible within a collectivity a generalized belief (or ideological justification) is necessary concerning at least the causes of the discontent and, under certain conditions, the modes of redress. Much of the empirical work that has followed and drawn upon these perspectives has emphasized even more heavily the importance of understanding the grievances and deprivation of participants. (Indeed, scholars following Gurr, Smelser, and Turner and Killian often ignore structural factors, even though the authors mentioned have been sensitive to broader structural and societal influences, as have some others.)[3]

Recent empirical work, however, has led us to doubt the assumption of a close link between preexisting discontent and generalized beliefs in the rise of social movement phenomena.[4] A number of studies have shown little or no support for expected relationships between objective or subjective deprivation and the outbreak of movement phenomena and willingness to participate in collective action (Snyder and Tilly, 1972; Mueller, 1972; Bowen et al., 1968; Crawford and Naditch, 1970). Other studies have failed to support the expectation of a generalized belief prior to outbreaks of collective behavior episodes or initial movement involvement (Quarantelli and Hundley, 1975; Marx, 1970; Stallings, 1973). Partially as a result of such evidence, in discussing revolution and collective violence Charles Tilly is led to argue that these phenomena flow directly out of a population's central political processes instead of expressing momentarily heightened diffuse strains and discontents within a population (Tilly, 1973).

Moreover, the heavy focus upon the psychological state of the mass of potential movement supporters within a collectivity has been accompanied by a lack of emphasis upon the processes by which persons and institutions from outside of the collectivity under consideration become involved; for instance, northern white liberals in the southern civil rights movement, or Soviets and Cubans in Angola. Although earlier perspectives do not exclude the possibilities of such involvement on the part of outsiders, they do not include such processes as central and enduring phenomena to be used in accounting for social movement behavior.

The ambiguous evidence of some of the research on deprivation, relative deprivation, and generalized belief has led us to search for a perspective and a set of assumptions that lessen the prevailing emphasis upon grievances. We want to move from a strong assumption about the centrality of deprivation and grievances to a weak one, which makes them a component—indeed, sometimes a secondary component—in the generation of social movements.

We are willing to assume (Turner and Killian [1972] call the assumption extreme) "that there is always enough discontent in any society to supply the grass-roots support for a movement if the movement is effectively organized and has at its disposal the power and resources of some established elite group" (p. 251). For some purposes we go even further: grievances and discontent may be defined, created, and manipulated by issue entrepreneurs and organizations.

We adopt a weak assumption not only because of the negative evidence (already mentioned) concerning the stronger one but also because in some cases recent experience supports the weaker one. For instance, the senior citizens who were mobilized into groups to lobby for Medicare were brought into groups only after legislation was before Congress and the American Medical Association had claimed that senior citizens were not complaining about the medical care available to them (Rose, 1967). Senior citizens were organized into groups through the efforts of a lobbying group created by the AFL-CIO. No doubt the elderly needed money for medical care. However, what is important is that the organization did not develop directly from that grievance but very indirectly through the moves of actors in the political system. Entertaining a weak assumption leads directly to an emphasis upon mobilization processes. Our concern is the search for analytic tools to account adequately for the processes.

Resource Mobilization

The resource mobilization perspective adopts as one of its underlying problems Olson's (1965) challenge: since social movements deliver collective goods, few individuals will "on their own" bear the costs of working to obtain them. Explaining collective behavior requires detailed attention to the selection of incentives, cost-reducing mechanisms or structures, and career benefits that lead to collective behavior (see, especially, Oberschall, 1973).

Several emphases are central to the perspective as it has developed.[5] First, study of the aggregation of resources (money and labor) is crucial to an understanding of social movement activity. Because resources are necessary for engagement in social conflict, they must be aggregated for collective purposes. Second, resource aggregation requires some minimal form of organization, and hence, implicitly or explicitly, we focus more directly upon social movement organizations than those working within the traditional perspective do. Third, in accounting for a movement's successes and failures one finds an explicit recognition of the crucial importance of involvement on the part of individuals and organizations from outside the collectivity a social movement represents. Fourth, an explicit, if crude, supply-and-demand model is sometimes applied to the flow of resources toward and away from specific social movements. Finally, there is a sensitivity to the importance of costs and rewards in explaining individual and organizational involvement in social movement activity. Costs and rewards are centrally affected by the structure of society and the activities of authorities.

We can summarize the emerging perspective by contrasting it with the traditional one as follows:

Support Base

Traditional Social movements are based upon aggrieved populations that provide the necessary resources and labor. Although case studies may mention external supports, they are not incorporated as central analytic components.

Resource Mobilization Social movements may or may not be based upon the grievances of the presumed beneficiaries. Conscience constituents, individual and organizational, may provide major sources of support. And in some cases supporters—

those who provide money, facilities, and even labor—may have no commitment to the values that underlie specific movements.

Strategy and Tactics

Traditional Social movement leaders use bargaining, persuasion, or violence to influence authorities to change. Choices of tactics depend upon prior history of relations with authorities, relative success of previous encounters, and ideology. Tactics are also influenced by the oligarchization and institutionalization of organizational life.

Resource Mobilization The concern with interaction between movements and authorities is accepted, but it is also noted that social movement organizations have a number of strategic tasks. These include mobilizing supporters, neutralizing and/or transforming mass and elite publics into sympathizers, and achieving change in targets. Dilemmas occur in the choice of tactics, since what may achieve one aim may conflict with behavior aimed at achieving another. Moreover, tactics are influenced by interorganizational competition and cooperation.

Relation to Larger Society

Traditional Case studies have emphasized the effects of the environment upon movement organizations, especially with respect to goal change, but have ignored, for the most part, ways in which such movement organizations can utilize the environment for their own purposes (see Perrow, 1972). This situation has probably been largely a result of the lack of comparative organizational focus inherent in case studies. In analytical studies emphasis is upon the extent of hostility or toleration in the larger society. Society and culture are treated as descriptive historical context.

Resource Mobilization   Society provides the infrastructure that social movement industries and other industries utilize. The aspects utilized include communication media and expense, levels of affluence, degree of access to institutional centers, preexisting networks, and occupational structure and growth.

Theoretical Elements

Having sketched the emerging perspective, our task now is to present a more precise statement of it. In this section we offer our most general concepts and definitions.

A *social movement* is a set of opinions and beliefs in a population representing preferences for changing some elements of the social structure or reward distribution, or both, of a society.[6] A *countermovement* is a set of opinions and beliefs in a population opposed to a social movement. As is clear, we view social movements as nothing more than preference structures directed toward social change, very similar to what political sociologists would term *issue cleavages*. (Indeed, the process we are exploring resembles what political scientists term *interest aggregation*, except that we are concerned with the margins of the political system rather than with existing party structures.)

The distribution of preference structures can be approached in several ways. Who holds the beliefs? How intensely are they held? In order to predict the likelihood of preferences being translated into collective action, the mobilization perspective focuses upon the preexisting organization and integration of those segments of a population that share preferences. Oberschall (1973) has presented an important synthesis of past work on the preexisting organization of preference structures, emphasizing the opportunities and costs for expression of preferences for movement leaders and followers. Social movements whose related populations are highly organized internally (either communally or associationally) are more likely than are others to spawn organized forms.

A *social movement organization* (SMO) is a complex, or formal, organization that identifies its goals with the preferences of a social movement or a countermovement and attempts to implement those goals.[7] If we think of the recent civil rights movement in these terms, the social movement contained a large portion of the population that held preferences for change aimed at "justice for black Americans" and a number of SMOs such as the Student Non-Violent Coordinating Committee (SNCC), the Congress of Racial Equality (CORE), the National Association for the Advancement of Colored People (NAACP), and Southern Christian Leadership Conference (SCLC). These SMOs represented and shaped the broadly held preferences and diverse subpreferences of the social movement.

All SMOs that have as their goal the attainment of the broadest preferences of a social movement constitute a *social movement industry* (SMI)—the organizational analogue of a social movement. A conception paralleling that of SMI, used by Von Eschen, Kirk, and Pinard (1971), the "organizational substructure of disorderly politics," has aided them in analyzing the civil rights movement in Baltimore. They demonstrate that many of the participants in a 1961 demonstration sponsored by the local chapter of CORE were also involved in the NAACP, the SCLC, Americans for Democratic Action (ADA) or the Young People's Socialist Alliance (YPSA). These organizations either were primarily concerned with goals similar to those of CORE or included such goals as subsets of broader ranges of social change goals. (The concept employed by Von Eschen et al. is somewhat broader than ours, however, as will be seen below.)

Definitions of the central term, *social movement* (SM), typically have included both elements of preference and organized action for change. Analytically separating these components by distinguishing between an SM and an SMI has several advantages. First, it emphasizes that SMs are never fully mobilized. Second, it focuses explicitly upon the organizational component of activity. Third, it recognizes explicitly that SMs are typically represented by more than one SMO. Finally, the distinction allows the possibility of an account of the rise and fall of SMIs that is not fully dependent upon the size of an SM or the intensity of the preferences within it.

Our definitions of SM, SMI, and SMO are intended to be inclusive of the phenomena analysts have included in the past. The SMs can encompass narrow or broad preferences, millenarian and evangelistic preferences, and withdrawal preferences. Organizations may represent any of these preferences.

The definition of SMI parallels the concept of industry in economics. Note that economists, too, are confronted with the difficulty of selecting broader or narrower criteria for including firms (SMOs) within an industry (SMI). For example, one may define a furniture industry, a sitting-furniture industry, or a chair industry. Close substitutability of product usage and, therefore, demand interdependence is the theoretical basis for defining industry boundaries. Economists use the *Census of Manufacturers* classifications, which are not strictly based on demand interdependence. For instance, on the one hand various types of steel are treated as one industry, though the types (rolled, flat, wire) are not substitutable. On the other hand, some products are classified separately (e.g., beet sugar, cane sugar) when they are almost completely substitutable (Bain, 1959, pp. 111–18).

Given our task, the question becomes how to group SMOs into SMIs. This is a difficult problem because particular SMOs may be broad or narrow in stated target goals. In any set of empirical circumstances the analyst must decide how narrowly to define industry boundaries. For instance, one may speak of the SMI that aims at liberalized alterations in laws, practices, and public opinion concerning abortion. This SMI would include a number of SMOs. But these SMOs may also be considered part of the broader SMI commonly referred to as the "women's liberation movement," or they could be part of the "population control movement." In the same way, the pre-1965 civil rights movement could be considered part of the broader civil liberties movement.

Economists have dealt with this difficulty by developing categories of broader inclusiveness, sometimes called *sectors*. Even this convention, however, does not confront the difficulties of allocating firms (SMOs) that are conglomerates, those that produce products across industries and even across sectors. In modern America there are a number of SMOs that may be thought of as conglomerates in that they span, in their goals, more narrowly defined SMIs. Common Cause, the American Friends Service Committee (AFSC) and the Fellowship of Reconciliation (FOR) are best treated in these terms as each pursues a wide variety of organizational goals that can only with difficulty be contained within even broadly defined SMIs.[8] The *social movement sector* (SMS) consists of all SMIs in a society no matter to which SM they are attached. (The importance of this distinction will become apparent below.)

Let us now turn to the resource mobilization task of an SMO. Each SMO has a set of *target goals*, a set of preferred changes toward which it claims to be working. Such goals may be broad or narrow, and they are the characteristics of SMOs that link them conceptually with particular SMs and SMIs. The SMOs must possess resources, however few and of whatever type, in order to work toward goal achievement. Individuals and other organizations control resources, which can include legitimacy, money, facilities, and labor.

Although similar organizations vary tremendously in the efficiency with which they translate resources into action (see Katz, 1974), the amount of activity directed toward goal accomplishment is crudely a function of the resources controlled by an organization. Some organizations may depend heavily upon volunteer labor, while others may depend upon purchased labor. In any case, resources must be controlled or mobilized before action is possible.

From the point of view of an SMO the individuals and organizations that exist in a society may be categorized along a number of dimensions. For the appropriate SM there are adherents and nonadherents. *Adherents* are those individuals and organizations that believe in the goals of the movement. The *constituents* of an SMO are those providing resources for it.

At one level the resource mobilization task is primarily that of converting adherents into constituents and maintaining constituent involvement. However, at another level the task may be seen as turning nonadherents into adherents. Ralph Turner (1970) uses the term *bystander public* to denote those nonadherents who are not opponents of the SM and its SMOs but who merely witness social movement activity. It is useful to distinguish constituents, adherents, bystander publics, and opponents along several other dimensions. One refers to the size of the resource pool controlled, and we shall use the terms *mass* and *elite* to describe crudely this dimension. Mass constituents, adherents, bystander publics, and

opponents are those individuals and groups controlling very limited resource pools. The most limited resource pool individuals can control is their own time and labor. Elites are those who control larger resource pools.[9]

Each of these groups may also be distinguished by whether it will benefit directly from the accomplishment of SMO goals. Some bystander publics, for instance, may benefit directly from the accomplishment of organizational goals, even though they are not adherents of the appropriate SM. To mention a specific example, women who oppose the preferences of the women's liberation movement or have no relevant preferences might benefit from expanded job opportunities for women pursued by women's groups. Those who would benefit directly from SMO goal accomplishment we shall call *potential beneficiaries.*[10]

In approaching the task of mobilizing resources an SMO may focus its attention upon adherents who are potential beneficiaries and/or attempt to convert bystander publics who are potential beneficiaries into adherents. It may also expand its target goals in order to enlarge its potential beneficiary group. Many SMOs attempt to present their goal accomplishments in terms of broader potential benefits for ever-wider groupings of citizens through notions of a better society, and so on (secondary benefits). Finally, an SMO may attempt to mobilize as adherents those who are not potential beneficiaries. *Conscience adherents* are individuals and groups who are part of the appropriate SM but do not stand to benefit directly from SMO goal accomplishment. *Conscience constituents* are direct supporters of an SMO who do not stand to benefit directly from its success in goal accomplishment.[11]

William Gamson (1975) makes essentially the same distinction, calling groups with goals aimed at helping nonconstituents *universalistic* and those whose beneficiaries and constituents are identical, *nonuniversalistic*. Gamson concludes, however, that this distinction is not theoretically important, since SMOs with either type of constituents have identical problems in binding them to the organization. It is not more "irrational," in Olson's sense, to seek change in someone else's behalf than in one's own, and in both cases commitment must be gained by other means than purposive incentives. The evidence presented by Gamson suggests that this dimension does not bear much relationship to SMO success in goal accomplishment or in the attainment of legitimacy. We argue below, however, that the distinction should be maintained: it summarizes important attachments and social characteristics of constituents. The problems of SMOs with regard to binding beneficiary and conscience constituents to the organization are different, not with regard to the stakes of individual involvement relative to goal accomplishment (the Olson problem) but with regard to the way constituents are linked to each other and to other SMOs, organizations, and social institutions (see also J. Q. Wilson, 1973).

An SMO's potential for resource mobilization is also affected by authorities and the delegated agents of *social control* (e.g., the police). While authorities and agents of control groups do not typically become constituents of SMOs, their ability to frustrate (normally termed *social control*) or to enable resource mobilization are of crucial importance. Their action affects the readiness of bystanders, adherents, and constituents to alter their own status and commitment. And they themselves may become adherents and constituents. Because they do not always act in concert, Marx (1974) makes a strong case that authorities and delegated agents of control need to be analyzed separately.

The partitioning of groups into mass or elite and conscience or beneficiary bystander publics, adherents, constituents, and opponents allows us to describe more systematically the resource mobilization styles and dilemmas of specific SMOs. It may be, of course, to the advantage of an SMO to turn bystander publics into adherents. But since SMO resources are normally quite limited, decisions must be made concerning the allocation of these resources, and converting bystander publics may not aid in the development of additional resources. Such choices have implications for the internal organization of an SMO and the potential size of the resource pool that can ultimately be mobilized. For instance, an SMO that has a mass beneficiary base and concentrates its resource mobilization efforts toward mass beneficiary adherents is likely to restrict severely the amount of resources it can raise. Elsewhere (McCarthy and Zald, 1973) we have termed an SMO focusing upon beneficiary adherents for resources a *classical SMO*. Organizations that direct resource appeals primarily toward conscience adherents tend to utilize few constituents for organizational labor, and we have termed such organizations *professional SMOs*.

Another pattern of resource mobilization and goal accomplishment can be identified from the writings of Lipsky (1968) and Bailis (1974). It depends upon the interactions among beneficiary constituency, conscience adherents, and authorities. Typical of this pattern is an SMO with a mass beneficiary constituency that would profit from goal accomplishment (for instance, the Massachusetts Welfare Rights Organization) but that has few resources. Protest strategies draw attention and resources from conscience adherents to the SMO fighting on behalf of such mass groups and may also lead conscience elites to legitimate the SMO to authorities. As a result of a similar pattern, migrant farmworkers benefited from the transformation of authorities into adherents (Jenkins and Perrow, 1977).

But an SMO does not have complete freedom of choice in making the sorts of decisions to which we have alluded. Such choices are constrained by a number of factors, including the preexisting organization of various segments of the SM, the size and diversity of the SMI of which it is a part, and the competitive position of the SMS (McCarthy and Zald, 1974; Zald and McCarthy, 1974). Also, of course, the ability of any SMO to garner resources is shaped by important events such as war, broad economic trends, and natural disasters.

The Elements Applied: Illustrative Hypotheses

Let us proceed to state hypotheses about the interrelations among the social structure, the SMS, SMIs, and SMOs. Occasionally, we introduce specifying concepts. Because the levels of analysis overlap, the subheadings below should be viewed as rough organizing devices rather than analytic categories.

Resources, the SMS, and the Growth of SMIs

Over time, the relative size of the SMS in any society may vary significantly. In general it will bear a relationship to the amount of wealth in a society. Hence:

> *Hypothesis 1:* As the amount of discretionary resources of mass and elite publics increases, the absolute and relative amount of resources available to the SMS increases.

This hypothesis is more of an orienting postulate than a directly testable hypothesis, but it is central to our perspective. And some related supporting evidence can be given.

By *discretionary resources* we mean time and money that can easily be reallocated, the opposite of fixed and enduring commitments of time and money. In any society the SMS must compete with other sectors and industries for the resources of the population. For most of the population the allocation of resources to SMOs is of lower priority than allocation to basic material needs such as food and shelter. It is well known that the proportion of income going to food and shelter is higher for low-income families, while the proportion of income going to savings and recreation increases among high-income families (Samuelson, 1964). The SMOs compete for resources with entertainment, voluntary associations, and organized religion and politics.

There is cross-sectional evidence that the higher the income, the larger the average gift to charitable activities and the greater the proportion of total income given (see Morgan, Dye, and Hybels, 1975; U.S. Treasury Department, 1965). Moreover, Morgan et al. (1975) show that (1) the higher the education, the more likely the giving of time, and (2) people who give more time to volunteer activities also give more money. As the total amount of resources increases, the total amount available to the SMS can be expected to increase, even if the sector does not increase its relative share of the resource pool. However, as discretionary resources increase relative to total societal resources, the SMS can be expected to gain a larger proportional share (see U.S. Treasury [1965], which shows a long-term secular increase in charitable giving). This argument is based upon our belief that, except in times of crisis, the SMS is a low priority competitor for available resources—it benefits from the satiation of other wants.[12]

Of course, the validity of this hypothesis depends upon a *ceteris paribus* proviso. What might the other factors be? First, the existing infrastructure, what Smelser (1963) terms *structural conduciveness,* should affect the total growth of the SMS. Means of communication, transportation, political freedoms, and the extent of repression by agents of social control, all of which may affect the costs for any individual or organization allocating resources to the SMS, serve as constraints on or facilitators of the use of resources for social movement purposes. Also, the technologies available for resource accumulation should affect the ability of SMOs within the sector to mobilize resources. For instance, the advent of mass-mailing techniques in the United States has dramatically affected the ability of the SMS to compete with local advertising in offering a product to consumers. The organization of the SMIs will support or hinder the growth of the sector as additional resources become available. The greater the range of SMOs, the more different "taste" preferences can be transformed into constituents.

Hypothesis 2: The greater the absolute amount of resources available to the SMS, the greater the likelihood that new SMIs and SMOs will develop to compete for these resources.

This and the previous proposition contain the essence of our earlier analysis (McCarthy and Zald, 1973). That study accounts in part for the proliferation in SMOs and SMIs in the 1960s in the United States by demonstrating both the relative and the absolute increases of resources available to the SMS. The major sources of increase in financial resources were charitable giving among mass and elite adherents, as well as government, church, foundation, and business giving among organizational adherents.

These two propositions attempt to account for the total growth of the SMS. They ignore variations in the taste for change over time. They imply nothing about which SMI will reap the benefits of sector expansion. Nor do they imply what types of SMOs will lead the growth of an expanding SMI. They explicitly ignore the relationship between the size of the SMS and the intensities of preferences within an SM.

Parallel hypotheses could be stated for the relationship of resources among different categories of SM adherents and SM growth. For instance:

Hypothesis 3: Regardless of the resources available to potential beneficiary adherents, the larger the amount of resources available to conscience adherents the more likely the development of SMOs and SMIs that respond to preferences for change.

The importance of this hypothesis in our scheme hinges upon the growing role of conscience constituents in American social movements. First, the greater the discretionary wealth controlled by individuals and organizations the more likely it is that some of that wealth will be made available to causes beyond the direct self-interest of the contributor. An individual (or an organization) with large amounts of discretionary resources may allocate resources to personal comfort and to the advancement of some group of which he or she is not a member. Second, those who control the largest share of discretionary resources in any society are also those least likely to feel discontent concerning their own circumstances.[13]

In a sense, Hypothesis 3 turns Olson (1965) on his head. Though it may be individually irrational for any individual to join an SMO that already fights on behalf of his preferences, the existence of an SM made up of well-heeled adherents calls out to the entrepreneur of the cause to attempt to form a viable organization (cf. Salisbury, 1969). To the extent to which SM beneficiary adherents lack resources, SMO support, if it can be mobilized, is likely to become heavily dependent upon conscience constituents.

This argument is also important in understanding the critique of interest-group pluralism as a valid description of modern America.[14] Many collectivities with serious objective deprivations, and even with preexisting preferences for change, have been highly underrepresented by social movement organizations. These SMOs tend to be very limited in their control of discretionary resources. It is only when resources can be garnered from conscience adherents that viable SMOs can be fielded to shape and represent the preferences of such collectivities.

Organization Structure and Resource Mobilization

How do the competitive position of the SMS, processes within an SMI, and the structure of an SMO influence the task of resource mobilization? Some aspects of these questions have been treated by Zald and Ash (1966). To discuss SMOs in detail we need to introduce assumptions about relevant SMO processes and structures.

Assume that SMOs operate like any other organization (J. Q. Wilson, 1973), and consequently, once formed, they operate as though organizational survival were the primary goal. Only if survival is ensured can other goals be pursued. Second, assume that the costs and rewards of involvement can account for individual participation in SMOs and that, especially, selective incentives are important, since they tend to raise the rewards for involvement.[15] Gamson (1975) and Bailis (1974) provide impressive evidence that selective material incentives operate to bind individuals to SMOs and, hence, serve to provide continuous involvement and thus resource mobilization.

For a number of reasons the term *member* has been avoided here. Most important, membership implies very different levels of organized involvement in different SMOs.

The distinction between inclusive and exclusive SMOs has been utilized in the past to indicate intensity of organizational involvement (Zald and Ash, 1966), but intensity of involvement actually includes several dimensions, usefully separated. Let us attempt to partition constituent involvement in any SMO. First there is the *cadre,* the individuals who are involved in the decision-making processes of the organization. Cadre members may devote most of their time to matters of the organization or only part of their time. Those who receive compensation, however meager, and devote full time to the organization, we term *professional cadre;* those who devote full time to the organization but are not involved in central decision-making processes, we term *professional staff;* those who intermittently give time to organizational tasks, not at the cadre level, we term *workers.* (Remember, constituents are those who give either time or money.)

A *transitory team* is composed of workers assembled for a specific task, short in duration. Transitory teams are typically led by cadre members. Members of transitory teams and cadre have more extensive involvement than other segments of an SMO constituency. What distinguishes these constituents from others is that they are directly linked to the organization through tasks—they are involved directly in the affairs of the SMO. Since involvement of this sort occurs in small, face-to-face groups, workers, whether through transitory teams or through continuous task involvement, can be expected to receive solidary incentives from such involvement—selective benefits of a nonmaterial sort.

Federated and Isolated Structure

An SMO that desires to pursue its goals in more than a local environment may attempt to mobilize resources directly from adherents or to develop federated chapters in different local areas. Federation serves to organize constituents into small local units. The SMOs that develop in this manner may deal with constituents directly, as well as through chapters or only through chapters. But many SMOs do not develop chapters but deal directly with constituents, usually through the mails or through traveling field staff. The important point is that constituents in nonfederated SMOs do not normally meet in face-to-face interaction with other constituents and hence cannot be bound to the SMOs through solidary selective incentives. We term these constituents *isolated constituents.*

Federation may occur in two ways. One strategy assigns professional staff the task of developing chapters out of isolated adherents or constituents. To some extent SDS and CORE (Sale, 1973; Meier and Rudwick, 1973) utilized this approach during the 1960s. Common Cause seems to have used it recently. Another strategy relies upon preexisting nonmovement local groups that have heavy concentrations of adherents or isolated constituents (Gerlach and Hines, 1970). This latter style, termed *group mobilization* by Oberschall (1973), was typical of several waves of recruitment by the Ku Klux Klan (Lipset and Rabb, 1970). Federation developing out of preexisting groups can occur quite rapidly, whereas organizing unattached individuals probably requires more time and resources. To the extent that it utilized mass involvement in the South, the SCLC operated through preexisting groups. We have argued elsewhere (McCarthy and Zald, 1973) that nonfederated SMOs dealing with isolated constituents accounted for much of the SMS growth during the burst of SMO activity during the decade of the 1960s.

Empirically, SMOs will combine elements of the two major organizational forms we have identified here. The manner in which the organization garners the bulk of

its resources should be used to characterize it during any time period. For instance, CORE would be deemed federated until the early 1960s, nonfederated at its peak during the early 1960s, and then federated again (Meier and Rudwick, 1973). It maintained a set of federated chapters during this entire period, but during the interim period its major resource flow was provided by isolated conscience constituents.

Hypothesis 4: The more an SMO is dependent upon isolated constituents, the less stable will be the flow of resources to the SMO.

Because isolated constituents are little involved in the affairs of the SMO, support from them depends far more upon industry and organizational (and counterindustry and counterorganizational) advertising than does support from constituents who are involved on a face-to-face basis with others. Advertising and media attention provide information about the dire consequences stemming from failure to attain target goals, the extent of goal accomplishment, and the importance of the particular SMO for such accomplishment.

Strickland and Johnston's (1970) analysis of issue elasticity is useful in understanding isolated constituent involvement in SM activities. At any time a number of target goals are offered to isolated adherents to any SM by one or more SMOs (and by other SMIs). Isolated adherents may choose to become constituents by allocating resources to one or another SMO according to the goals propounded. The SMOs within any SMI will tend to compete with one another for the resources of these isolated adherents. If they allocate resources, but remain isolated, their ties to the SMO remain tenuous. To the extent that any individual is an adherent to more than one SM, various SMIs will also be competing for these resources.

Treating SMO target goals as products, then, and adherence as demand, we can apply a simple economic model to this competitive process. Demand may be elastic, and its elasticity is likely to be heavily dependent upon SMO advertising. Products may be substitutable across SMIs. For example, while various SMOs may compete for resources from isolated adherents to the "justice for black Americans" SM, SMOs representing the "justice for American women" SM may be competing for the same resources (to the extent that these two SMs have overlapping adherent pools). Some adherents may have a high and inelastic demand curve for an SMO or SMI; others' demand curves may show great elasticity.

This state of affairs suggests that effective advertising campaigns may convince isolated adherents with high-issue elasticity to switch SMOs or SMIs, or both. Issue elasticity relates to what Downs (1972) terms *issue attention cycles*. These apparent cycles, he observes, include the stages of a problem discovered, dramatic increases in adherence as advertising alerts potential adherents, attempts at problem solution, lack of success of such attempts, and a rapid decline in adherence and advertising. Isolated adherents may purchase a target goal product when offered but can be expected to base decisions about future purchases upon their conception of product quality. Tullock (1966) has argued that the consumption of such products is vicarious, not direct; thus, perceived product quality is not necessarily related to actual goal accomplishment. Much publicity is dependent upon an SMO's ability to induce the media to give free attention, because most SMOs cannot actually afford the high cost of national advertising. They do, however, use direct-mail advertising. The point is that the media mediate in large measure between isolated constituents and SMOs.

Perceived lack of success in goal accomplishment by an SMO may lead an individual to switch to SMOs with alternative strategies or, to the extent that products are substitutable, to switch to those with other target goals. It must be noted, however, that there is also an element of product loyalty in this process. Some isolated constituents may continue to purchase the product (to support an SMO) unaware of how effective or ineffective it may be.

One could treat individual SMO loyalty in the same way as political party loyalty is treated by political sociologists, but most SMOs do not command such stable loyalties from large numbers of people. Certain long-lasting SMOs, the NAACP and the AFSC, for instance, may command stable loyalties, and the process of socializing youth into SMO loyalty could be expected to be similar to that of socialization into party loyalty (Converse, 1969). This process, however, most probably occurs not among isolated constituents, but among those who are linked in more direct fashion to SMOs.

Advertising by SMOs recognizes that isolated constituents have no direct way of evaluating the product purchased; therefore, it may stress the amount of goal accomplishment available to the isolated constituent for each dollar expended. The AFSC, for instance, informs isolated potential constituents in its mass mailings that its overhead costs are among the lowest of any comparable organization, and hence the proportion of each donation used for goal accomplishment is higher; the findings of an outside consulting firm that evaluated the organization support this claim (Jonas, 1971). Within an industry SMO products are normally differentiated by conceptions of the extremity of solutions required (Killian, 1972) and by strategies of goal accomplishment (passive resistance, strikes, etc.). When products are not differentiated in either of these ways, we can expect differentiation in terms of efficiency.

These considerations lead to a subsidiary proposition:

> *Hypothesis 4a:* The more dependent an SMO is upon isolated constituents, the greater the share of its resources that will be allocated to advertising.

As indicated, SMO advertising can take the form of mailed material that demonstrates the good works of the organization. Media bargaining (Hubbard, 1968; Lipsky, 1968; Turner, 1969) can also be conceptualized as SMO advertising. By staging events that will possibly be "newsworthy," by attending to the needs of news organizations, and by cultivating representatives of the media, SMOs may manipulate media coverage of their activities more or less successfully.[16] Some kind of information flow to isolated constituents including positive evaluation is absolutely essential for SMOs dependent upon them.

The foregoing reasoning, combined with Hypotheses 1 and 2, leads us to another related proposition:

> *Hypothesis 4b:* The more an SMO depends upon isolated constituents to maintain a resource flow, the more its shifts in resource flow resemble the patterns of consumer expenditures and marginal goods.

Stated differently, the hypothesis holds that if an SMO is linked to its major source of constituent financial support through the advertising of its products, isolated constituents will balance out their contributions with other marginal expenditures. Time of year, state of checkbook, mood, and product arousal value will influence such decision making.

The more attractive the target goal (product) upon which such a solicitation is based, the more likely that isolated adher-

ents will become isolated constituents. Consequently, SMOs depending heavily upon such resource mobilization techniques must resort to slick packaging and convoluted appeal to self-interest in order to make their products more attractive. This should be especially true within competitive SMIs. The behavior in the early 1970s of environmental groups, which depend heavily upon isolated constituents, appears to illustrate this point. Many of those SMOs took credit for stalling the Alaskan pipeline and attempted to link that issue to personal self-interest and preferences in their direct-mail advertising. Slick packaging is evident in the high quality of printing and the heavy use of photogravure.

Another technique advertisers utilize to appeal to isolated adherents is the linking of names of important people to the organization, thereby developing and maintaining an image of credibility (Perrow, 1970a). In the same way that famous actors, sports heroes, and retired politicians endorse consumer products, other well-known personalities are called upon to endorse SMO products: Jane Fonda and Dr. Spock were to the peace movement and Robert Redford is to the environmental movement what Joe Namath is to pantyhose and William Miller is to American Express Company credit cards.

The development of local chapters helps bind constituents to SMOs through networks of friendships and interpersonal control.[17] But note the following:

> *Hypothesis 5:* An SMO that attempts to link both conscience and beneficiary constituents to the organization through federated chapter structures, and hence solidarity incentives, is likely to have high levels of tension and conflict.

Social movement analysts who have focused upon what we have termed *conscience constituency participation* normally call it outsider involvement. Von Eschen et al. (1969), for instance, show that for a local direct action civil rights organization involvement on the part of geographical outsiders (both conscience and beneficiary) created pronounced internal conflict in the organization. Marx and Useem (1971) have examined the record of the recent civil rights movement, the abolitionist movement, and the movement to abolish untouchability in India. In these movements, "outsiders were much more prone to be active in other causes or to shift their allegiances from movement to movement" (p. 102). Ross (1975) has argued the importance of friendship ties based upon geographical and generational lines to the internal conflict of SDS. The more unlike one another workers are, the less likely there is to be organizational unity, and the more likely it is that separate clique structures will form. If conscience constituents are more likely to be active in other SMOs and to be adherents of more than one SM, we would expect their involvement to be less conscious.

Now the earlier discussion of conscience and beneficiary constituents can be combined with the analysis of SMI and SMO processes. First, conscience constituents are more likely to control larger resource pools. Individuals with more resources exhibit concerns less directly connected with their own material interests. Consequently, conscience constituents are more likely to be adherents to more than one SMO and more than one SMI.[18] Though they may provide the resources for an SMO at some point, they are likely to have conflicting loyalties.

This situation provides an account for why SMO leaders have been skeptical of the involvement of conscience constituents—intellectuals in labor unions, males in the women's liberation movement, whites in the civil rights movements. Conscience constituents are fickle because they have wide-ranging concerns. They may be even more

fickle if they are isolated constituents—they are less likely to violate personal loyalties by switching priority concerns. But organizations that attempt to involve them in face-to-face efforts may have to suffer the consequences of the differences in backgrounds and outside involvements from those of beneficiary constituents. On the one hand, involving only conscience constituents in federated chapters, which might be a method of avoiding such conflict, forces the SMO to pay the price of legitimacy—how can an SMO speak for a beneficiary group when it does not have any beneficiary constituents? On the other hand, depending exclusively upon mass beneficiary constituents reduces the potential size of the resource pool that can be used for goal accomplishment.

The involvement of conscience and beneficiary constituents may lead not only to interpersonal tensions, but also to tactical dilemmas. Meier and Rudwick (1976) document the extent to which the question whether the NAACP should use black or white lawyers to fight its legal battles has been a continuous one. Especially in the early days, the symbolic value of using black lawyers conflicted sharply with the better training and courtroom effectiveness of white lawyers. W. E. B. Dubois came out on the side of courtroom effectiveness.

Rates of Resource Fluctuation and SMO Adaptation

We have focused thus far upon the development of resource flows to SMOs, primarily in terms of how they link themselves to their constituents and the size of the resource pool controlled by constituents. What are the implications of larger or smaller resource flows for the fate of SMOs, for careers in social movements, and for the use of different types of constituencies?

An interesting question concerns the staying power of new and older entries into an SMI. Consider the following proposition:

Hypothesis 6: Older, established SMOs are more likely than newer SMOs to persist throughout the cycle of SMI growth and decline.

This state of affairs is similar to the advantage of early entry for a firm in an industry: A structure in place when demand increases improves the likelihood of capturing a share of the market. Stinchcombe (1965, p. 148) points out that "as a general rule, a higher proportion of new organizations fail than old. This is particularly true of new organizational *forms,* so that *if an alternative requires new organization,* it has to be much more beneficial than the old before the flow of benefits compensates for the relative weakness of the newer social structure." All the liabilities of new organizational forms that Stinchcombe elaborates—new roles to be learned, temporary inefficiency of structuring, heavy reliance upon social relations among strangers, and the lack of stable ties to those who might use the organization's services—beset new organizations of established forms as well, if to a lesser degree.[19] Moreover, a history of accomplishment is an important asset, and, as Gamson (1975) shows for his sample of SMOs, longevity provides an edge in the attainment of legitimacy. Older organizations have available higher degrees of professional sophistication, existing ties to constituents, and experience in fund-raising procedures. Thus, as factors conducive to action based upon SM preferences develop, older SMOs are more able to use advertising to reach isolated adherents, even though new SMOs may of course benefit from the experience of older ones. The NAACP, for instance, already had a fund-raising structure aimed at isolated adherents before the increase in demand for civil rights goals increased in the 1960s. And

CORE had the advantage of a professional staff member who was committed to the development of such techniques, but it took time for him to convince the decision makers of the organization to pursue such resource mobilization tactics (Meier and Rudwick, 1973). Newer SMOs may capture a share of the isolated constituent market, but they will be disadvantaged at least until they establish a clear image of themselves and a structure to capitalize upon it. J. Q. Wilson (1973) cogently argues that competition between SMOs for resources occurs between organizations offering the most similar products, not between those for which competition in goal accomplishment produces conflict. Since SMOs within the same SMI compete with one another for resources, they are led to differentiate themselves from one another. The prior existence of skilled personnel and preexisting images are advantages in this process. In the same way that name recognition is useful to political candidates it is useful to SMOs when issue campaigns occur.

Hypothesis 7: The more competitive an SMI (a function of the number and size of the existing SMOs), the more likely it is that new SMOs will offer narrow goals and strategies.

We have alluded to the process of product differentiation. As the competition within any SMI increases, the pressure to specialize intensifies. The decision of George Wiley (Martin, 1971, 1974) to present the National Welfare Rights Organization as an organization aimed at winning rights for black welfare recipients was apparently made partially as a result of the preexisting turf understanding of other civil rights organizations.

Hypothesis 8: The larger the income flow to an SMO, the more likely that cadre and staff are professional and the larger these groups are.

This proposition flows directly from an economic support model. It is obvious that the more money available to an organization, the more full- time personnel it will be able to hire. Though this is not a necessary outcome, we assume that SMOs will be confronted with the diverse problems of organizational maintenance, and as resource flows increase these will become more complex. As in any large organization, task complexity requires specialization. Specialization is especially necessary in modern America, where the legal requirements of functioning necessitate experienced technicians at a number of points in both resource mobilization and attempts to bring influence to bear. The need for skills in lobbying, accounting, and fund raising leads to professionalization.

It is not that SMOs with small resource flows do not recognize the importance of diverse organizational tasks. In them, a small professional cadre may be required to fulfill a diverse range of tasks such as liaison work with other organizations, advertising, accounting, and membership service. Large resource flows allow these functions to be treated as specialties, though organizations of moderate size may have problems of premature specialization. Economies of scale should be reached only at appropriate levels of growth. In CORE we have a good example of this process: early specialization required constant organizational reshuffling in order to combine functions and staff members in what seemed to be the most efficient manner (Meier and Rudwick, 1973).

Hypothesis 9: The larger the SMS and the larger the specific SMI, the more likely it is that SM careers will develop.

An SM career is a sequence of professional staff and cadre positions held by adherents in a number of SMOs or supportive institutions, or both. Such a career need not require continuous connection with an SMI, though the larger the SMI the more

likely such continuous involvement ought to be. Supportive institutions might be universities, church bodies, labor unions, governmental agencies, and the like (Zald and McCarthy, 1975). Moreover, target institutions sometimes develop positions for SM cadres, such as human-relations councils in local governments. Corporations have affirmative-action offices and antitrust lawyers.

When the SMI is large, the likelihood of SMI careers is greater simply because the opportunity for continuous employment is greater, regardless of the success or failure of any specific SMO. Though many of the skills developed by individuals in such careers (public relations, for instance) may be usefully applied in different SMIs, our impression is that individuals typically move between SMIs that have similar goals and hence have overlapping constituencies. Although we might find individuals moving between civil rights and labor SMOs, we would be unlikely to find movement from civil rights SMOs to fundamentalist, anticommunist ones. (But it should be remembered that communists have become anticommunists, and that an antiwar activist such as Rennie Davis later took an active role in the transcendental meditation movement.) The relevant base for SMO careers, then, is usually SMIs or interrelated SMIs.

Funding strategies affect not only careers but also the use of beneficiary constituents and workers.

Hypothesis 10: The more an SMO is funded by isolated constituents, the more likely that beneficiary constituent workers are recruited for strategic purposes rather than for organizational work.

This proposition is central to the strategy of the professional SMO. It leads to considering the mobilization of beneficiary constituent workers as a rational tool for attempts to wield influence, rather than as an important source of organizational resources. Earlier we mentioned the creation of senior citizen groups for purposes of bargaining by the AFL-CIO in the Medicare fight. The use of some poor people for strategic purposes by the Hunger Commission, a professional SMO, also illustrates the point (Brown, 1970). Also germane is the fact that of the groups in Gamson's study (1975), none that were heavily dependent upon outside sponsors provided selective material incentives for constituents. Binding beneficiary constituents to an SMO with incentives is not so important to an organization that does not need them in order to maintain a resource flow.

Much of this discussion has been framed in terms of discretionary money, but discretionary time is also of importance.

> *Hypothesis 11:* The more an SMO is made up of workers with discretionary time at their disposal, the more readily it can develop transitory teams.

The ability to concentrate large numbers of constituents and adherents is highly useful for SMOs in certain situations, such as demonstrations. But the occupational characteristics of constituents and adherents are crucial to an understanding of how an SMO or a coalition of SMOs is able to produce such concentrations. Producing large numbers can be used to impress bystanders, authorities, and opponents. In some nations (particularly authoritarian ones) authorities may, through control over employers or control of the work schedules of governmental employees, be able to produce large concentrations at will. But SMOs typically do not exercise such control; hence, it is the preexisting control adherents and constituents exercise over their own work schedules that shapes the possibility of concentration. The same mechanisms operate in peasant societies where the possibilities of concerted action are shaped by planting and harvesting schedules.

In modern society discretion over work schedules tends to be related to larger pools of discretionary income, allowing travel to distant sites as well. The discretion of constituents over work schedules, then, may be seen as a potential organizational resource useful in mounting short bursts of organizational activity. Students, college professors, and other professionals, for instance, probably find a three-day trip to Washington for a demonstration easier to bear than wage workers do. The March on Washington in support of the war in Vietnam, headed by the Rev. Carl McIntire, was poorly attended. For the reasons enumerated above, many of the adherents to which he appeals were probably unable to attend such a demonstration.[20]

Conclusion

The resource mobilization model we have described here emphasizes the interaction between resource availability, the preexisting organization of preference structures, and entrepreneurial attempts to meet preference demand. We have emphasized how these processes seem to operate in the modern American context. Different historical circumstances and patterns of preexisting infrastructures of adherency will affect the strategies of SMO entrepreneurial activity in other times and places. Our emphasis, however, seems to be useful in accounting for parallel activity in different historical contexts, including peasant societies, and in explaining the processes of growth and decline in withdrawal movements as well.

The history of the Bolshevik SMO (Wolfe, 1955) shows how important stable resource flows are to the competitive position of an SMO. The Bolsheviks captured the resource flow to the Russian Social Revolutionary movement and, at certain points in their history, depended heavily upon isolated conscience constituents. Free media are probably necessary to mass isolated constituent involvement in resource flows, so isolated adherents with control over large resource pools are probably more important to SMI growth in societies without mass media. Leites and Wolf (1970) make a similar analysis of the revolutionary SMI in its relationship to the constant rewards of participation by the peasants in Vietnam. Of course, the extent of discretionary resources varies considerably between that case and the modern American case, but so did the ability of authorities to intervene in the manipulation of costs and rewards of individual involvement in the revolutionary SMO. The flow of resources from outside South Vietnam was important in the SMO's ability to manipulate these costs and rewards. Extranational involvement in the American SMS seems almost nonexistent.

Moreover, Oberschall (1973) has shown how important communal associations may be for facilitating mobilization in tribal and peasant societies. Although the number of SMOs and hence the size of the SMI may be smaller in peasant societies, resource mobilization and SM facilitation by societal infrastructure issues are just as important.

Withdrawal movements are typically characterized primarily by the way in which constituents are bound to the SMO (Kanter, 1972). But SMOs in withdrawal SMs also encounter difficulties in developing stable resource flows, and they use a variety of strategies similar to those of other SMOs in response to their difficulties. The recent behavior of the Unification Church of America (led by the Reverend Sun Myung Moon) in the United States illustrates processes close to those we have focused upon for modern reform movements: heavy use of advertising and emphasis upon stable resource flows in order to augment the development of federated constituencies. The Father Divine Peace Mission (Cantril, 1941) utilized rather different strategies of resource mobilization, including a heavier dependence upon the constituents themselves, but the importance of maintaining flows for continued viability was recognized in both of these withdrawal movements.

Our attempt has been to develop a partial theory; we have only alluded to, or treated as constant, important variables: the interaction of authorities, SMOs, and bystander publics; the dynamics of media involvement; the relationship between SMO workers and authorities; the impact of industry structure; the dilemmas of tactics. Yet, in spite of the limitations of this brief statement of the resource mobilization perspective, it offers important new insights into the understanding of social movement phenomena and can be applied more generally.

ACKNOWLEDGMENTS

For critical, helpful, and insightful remarks upon earlier version of this chapter we are indebted to Gary Long, Anthony Oberschall, Anthony Orum, Kathy Pearce, Jack Seidman, and Benjamin Walter. This line of research and the preparation of the manuscript were supported by the Vanderbilt University Research Council.

NOTES

1. One reflection of this change has been discussion of the appropriateness of including the study of social movements within the social psychology section of the American Sociological Association (see the *Critical Mass Bulletin*, 1973–74). The issue is whether social movements research should consist largely of individual social psychological analysis (e.g., value, attitudes, and grievances of participants).

2. We are responding here to the dominant focus. Some analysts, most notably Rudolf Heberle (1951, 1968) among U.S.-based sociologists, have viewed social movements from a distinctly structural perspective. Of course, structural approaches have remained dominant in Europe.

3. For example, see Levy (1970). For an early attempt to move beyond a simple grievance model, see Morrison (1971): this article attempts to explain recruitment in social movement organizations rather than the attitudes of movement support of isolated individuals. Gurr's own empirical studies have led him to emphasize institutional-structural factors more heavily, because he has found that the structural characteristics of dissident groups are important factors in accounting for both violent and nonviolent civil strife (Gurr, 1972).

4. For a full and balanced review of research and theory about social movements during the past decade, see Marx and Wood (1975).

5. Other contributors to the research mobilization perspective, aside from those already noted, are James Q. Wilson (1973), Breton and Breton (1969), Leites and Wolf (1970), Etzioni (1968), Jenkins and Perrow (1977), Salisbury (1969), Strickland and Johnston (1970), and Tullock (1966).

6. There is by no means a clear consensus on the definition of the crucial term *social movement.* We employ an inclusive definition for two reasons. First, by doing so, we link our work to as much past work as possible. Second, there are important theoretical reasons that will be discussed below. Our definition of *social movement* allows the possibility that a social movement will not be represented by any organized groups but also allows for organizations that do not represent social movements at formation. Most earlier definitions have included both preferences and organizational factors. See Wilkinson (1971) for an extensive survey of definitions of *social movement.*

7. Making the distinction between a social movement (SM) and a social movement organization (SMO) raises the question of the relevance of the vast literature developed by political scientists on the subject of interest groups. Is an SMO an interest group? Interest group theorists often blur the distinction between the representative organization and the interest group (e.g., the AMA and doctors) (see Wootton [1970] for an extended discussion). Whereas political scientists usually focus upon interest groups' organizations and not the groups themselves, sociologists largely have focused upon social movements rather than upon social movement organizations. Though we are not fully satisfied with Lowi's (1971) distinction between the two terms, we will employ it for a lack of a better one. Lowi maintains that an SMO that becomes highly institutionalized and routinizes stable ties with a governmental agency is an interest group. This way of approaching the problem, of course, flows from Lowi's distinctive view of the functioning of pluralistic politics.

8. Although we can easily label the SMs these organizations relate to—political reform and peace, for instance—the diffuseness of their goals and the range of their concern seem to bring them closer to representing what Blumer (1946) calls *general movements.* Blumer's notion of general movements (as contrasted with specific ones) implies widespread appeal and attendant trends in culture and lifestyle, however, and the general peace-humanitarian organizations do not appear to generate such appeal today. In any case, Blumer's distinction is an early attempt to distinguish movements along dimensions of specificity of goals. (See Halloron's [1971] treatment of Common Cause, Jonas's [1971] treatment of the AFSC, and Hentoff's [1963] treatment of FOR for analyses of the wide range of goals pursued by these SMOs.)

9. Of course, the size of the resource pool controlled by an individual or an organization that might be allocated to an SMO is a dimension. We dichotomize the dimension only for purposes of discussion, and the appropriate cutting point will vary from situation to situation.

10. A potential beneficiary group has normally been termed an interest group. The distinction between beneficiaries and adherents recognizes that interests and preferences may not coincide.

11. We have borrowed this term from Harrington (1968, p. 291), who uses it to refer to middle-class liberals who have demonstrated strong sympathies for the interests of underdog groups. Our use broadens the meaning of the term.

12. The recent resource mobilization difficulties of the consumer movement as prosperity wanes provide support for these arguments. (See Morris [1975] for extensive evidence of the fund-raising difficulties of consumer groups—especially professional SMOs—and

the resulting organizational difficulties, and Pombeiro [1975] and the *New York Times* [1974] for similar material on a wide range of SMOs.)

13. Stouffer (1955) showed that among Americans the wealthier experienced fewest personal worries, though they were more concerned than the poorer with the problems beyond their immediate experience. In the United States wealth is positively related to happiness in general (Bradburn and Caplovitz, 1964). Cantril (1965) used a ladder technique to have respondents place themselves with respect to their closeness to "the best possible life." He shows that upper economic groups in a number of nations place their present circumstances closest to full satisfaction. Important for our analysis, when asked a similar question about their satisfaction with the nation, American respondents who were wealthy were no more satisfied than their counterparts.

14. For a review and statement of the critique, see Connolly (1969).

15. See Clark and Wilson (1961), J. Q. Wilson (1973), and Zald and Jacobs (1976), for a discussion of various types of incentives.

16. See *Organizer's Manual Collective* (1971) for a review of media manipulation techniques. The many "how to do it" books vary in their sophistication and comprehensiveness. Several others worthy of note are Kahn (1970), Walzer (1971), and Ross (1973).

17. Orum and Wilson (1975), and Freeman (1975) discuss the role of preexisting solidarity relations in SMO mobilization.

18. The empirical pattern of such ideological overlapping in choices of SMO and SMI provides a very different way of distinguishing SMIs from the one we have chosen. Ideological coherence is unusual, of course. See Campbell et al. (1960) for an empirical treatment of this problem, and Miller and Levitin (1976) for a more recent demonstration with regard to what has been termed the "new left" ideology. Even though conscience constituent involvement in an SMO or SMI may not imply involvement in another SMO or SMI through preexisting ideological coherence, any involvement increases the likelihood of adherence to another SM.

19. Stinchcombe's (1965) attempt to isolate the factors related to the rate of organizational formation in a society is quite similar to our own. He maintains that (1) new ways of doing things (technologies), (2) the belief on the part of organizational entrepreneurs that new organizations will have staying power, (3) a belief in direct benefits flowing from new technologies, (4) resource availability, and (5) the belief that opponents will not defeat organizing attempts are important factors in understanding the rate of organizational formation. Our analysis has stressed the first and fourth factors, but our formulation recognizes the importance of the other factors.

20. See Cicchetti et al. (1971) for an empirical demonstration of the costs of attendance and their effects upon recruitment patterns in an antiwar demonstration. For a study showing the minor importance of ideological commitment relative to structural and preorganizational factors for the McIntire-organized march, see Lin (1974–75).

REFERENCES

Bailis, L. 1974. *Bread and Justice.* Springfield, MA: Heath-Lexington.

Bain, J.S. 1959. *Industrial Organization.* New York: Wiley.

Blumer, H. "Collective Behavior." In *A New Outline of the Principles of Sociology,* ed. A.M. Lee. New York: Barnes & Noble, 1946, pp. 167–219.

Bowen, D., Bowen, E., Gawiser, S., & Masotti, S. "Deprivation, Mobility, and Orientation Toward Protest of the Urban Poor." In *Riots and Rebellion: Civil Violence in the Urban Community,* ed. L. Masotti and D. Bowen. Beverly Hills, CA: Sage, 1968, pp. 187–200.

Bradburn, N., & Caplowitz, D. 1964. *Reports on Happiness.* Chicago: Aldine.

Breton, A., & Breton, R. "An Economic Theory of Social Movements." *American Economic Review. Papers and Proceedings of the American Economic Association* 59 (2) (May 1969).

Brown, L. "Hunger U.S.A.: The Public Pushes Congress." *Journal of Health and Social Behavior* 11 (June 1970): 115–25.

Campbell, A., Converse, P.E., Miller, W.E., & Stokes, D.E. 1960. *The American Voter.* New York: Wiley.

Cantril, H. 1941. *The Psychology of Social Movements.* New York: Wiley.

_____. 1965. *The Pattern of Human Concern*. New Brunswick, NJ: Rutgers University Press.

Cicchetti, C.J., Freeman, A.M., III, Haveman, R.H., & Knetsch, J.L. "On the Economics of Mass Demonstrations: A Case Study of the November 1969 March on Washington." *American Economic Review* 61 (4) (September 1971): 719–24.

Clark, P.B. & Wilson, J.Q. "Incentive Systems: A Theory of Organizations." *Administrative Science Quarterly* 6 (September 1961): 129–66.

Connolly, W.E. 1969. *The Bias of Pluralism*. New York: Atherton.

Converse, P.E. "Of Time and Partisan Stability." *Comparative Political Studies* 2 (2) (July 1969): 139–71.

Crawford, T.J., & Naditch, M. "Relative Deprivation, Powerlessness, and Militancy: The Psychology of Social Protest." *Psychiatry* 33 (May 1970): 208–23.

Downs, A. "Up and Down with Ecology—the Issue Attention Cycle." *Public Interest* 28 (Summer 1972): 38–50.

Etzioni, A. 1968. *The Active Society*. New York: Free Press.

Freeman, J. 1975. *The Politics of Women's Liberation*. New York: McKay.

Gamson, W.A. 1975. *The Strategy of Social Protest*. Homewood, IL: Dorsey.

Gerlach, L., & Hine, V. 1970. *People, Power, and Change: Movements of Social Transformation*. Indianapolis, IN: Bobbs-Merrill.

Gurr, T.R. 1970. *Why Men Rebel*. Princeton, NJ: Princeton University Press.

_____. 1972. *Politimetrics: An Introduction to Quantitative Macropolitics*. Englewood Cliffs, NJ: Prentice-Hall.

Halloran, R. "The Idea That Politics Is Everybody's Business." *New York Times* (March 7, 1971): sec. 4, p. 3.

Harrington, M. 1968. *Toward a Democratic Left: A Radical Program for a New Majority*. New York: Macmillan.

Heberle, R. "Types and Functions of Social Movements." In *International Encyclopedia of the Social Sciences*, Vol. 14, ed. David Sills. New York: Macmillan, 1968, pp. 438–44.

_____. 1951. *Social Movements: An Introduction to Political Sociology*. New York: Appleton-Century Co.

Hentoff, N. 1963. *Peace Agitator: The Story of A.J. Muste*. New York: Macmillan.

Hubbard, H. "Five Long Hot Summers and How They Grew." *Public Interest* 12 (Summer 1968): 3–24.

Jenkins, C., & Perrow, C. "Insurgency of the Powerless: Farm Workers Movements (1946–72)." *American Sociological Review* 42 (2) (1977): 249–67.

Jonas, G. 1971. *On Doing Good: The Quaker Experiment*. New York: Charles Scribner's Sons.

Kahn, S. 1970. *How People Get Power: Organizing Oppressed Communities for Action*. New York: McGraw-Hill.

Kanter, R.M. 1972. *Commitment and Community: Communes and Utopias in Sociological Perspective*. Cambridge, MA: Harvard University Press.

Katz, H. 1974. *Give! Who Gets Your Charity Dollar?* Garden City, NJ: Doubleday.

Killian, L. "The Significance of Extremism in the Black Revolution." *Social Problems* 20 (Summer 1972): 41–48.

Leites, N., & Wolf, C., Jr. 1970. *Rebellion and Authority*. Chicago: Markham.

Levy, S. "The Psychology of Political Activity." *Annals* 391 (September 1970): 83–96.

Lin, N. "The McIntire March: A Study of Recruitment and Commitment." *Public Opinion Quarterly* 38 (Winter 1974–75): 562–73.

Lipset, S.M., & Raab, E. 1970. *The Politics of Unreason: Right-Wing Extremism in America, 1790–1970*. New York: Harper & Row.

Lipsky, M. "Protest as a Political Resource." *American Political Science Review* 62 (December 1968): 1144–58.

Lowi, T.J. 1971. *The Politics of Disorder*. New York: Basic Books.

Martin, G.T. "Organizing the Underclass: Findings on Welfare Rights," Working Paper No. 17. Human Side of Poverty Project, Department of Sociology, State University of New York at Stony Brook, 1971.

_____. "Welfare Recipient Activism: Some Findings on the National Welfare Rights Organization." Paper presented at the annual meeting of the Midwest Political Science Association, April 26, 1974, Chicago, IL.

Marx, G.T. "Thoughts on a Neglected Category of Social Movement Participant: The Agent Provocateur and the Informant." *American Journal of Sociology* 80 (September 1974): 402–42.

_____. "Issueless Riots." *Annals* 391 (September 1970): 21–33.

Marx, G.T., & Useem, M.M. "Majority Involvement in Minority Movements: Civil Rights, Abolition, Untouchability." *Journal of Social Issues* 27 (January 1971): 81–104.

Marx, G.T., & Wood, J. "Strands of Theory and Research in Collective Behavior." *Annual Review of Sociology* 1 (1975): 363–428.

McCarthy, J.D., & Zald, M.N. "Tactical Considerations in Social Movement Organizations." Paper delivered at the annual meeting of the American Sociological Association, August 1974, Montreal.

_____. 1973. *The Trend of Social Movements in America: Professionalization and Resource Mobilization.* Morristown, NJ: General Learning Press.

Meier, A., & Rudwick, E. 1973. *CORE: A Study in the Civil Rights Movement, 1948–1968.* New York: Oxford University Press.

_____. "Attorneys Black and White: A Case Study of Race Relations Within the NAACP." *Journal of American History* 62 (March 1976): 913–46.

Miller, W.E., & Levitin, T.E. 1976. *Leadership and Change: The New Politics of the American Electorate.* Cambridge, MA: Winthrop.

Morgan, J.N., Dye, R.F., & Hybels, J.H. 1975. *A Survey of Giving Behavior and Attitudes: A Report to Respondents.* Ann Arbor, MI: Institute for Social Research.

Morris, B. "Consumerism Is Now a Luxury Item." *Washington Star* (October 28, 1975): 1–7.

Morrison, D.E. "Some Notes Toward Theory on Relative Deprivation, Social Movements, and Social Change." *American Behavioral Scientist* 14 (May–June 1971): 675–90.

Mueller, E. "A Test of a Partial Theory of Potential for Political Violence." *American Political Review* 66 (September 1972): 928–59.

New York Times. "Social Action Hit by Financial Woes" (November 8, 1974): sec. 1, p. 20.

Oberschall, A. 1973. *Social Conflict and Social Movements.* Englewood Cliffs, NJ: Prentice-Hall.

Olson, M., Jr. 1965. *The Logic of Collective Action.* Cambridge, MA: Harvard University Press.

Orum, A.M., & Wilson, K.L. "Toward a Theoretical Model of Participation in Political Movements, I: Leftist Movements." Unpublished manuscript, Department of Sociology, University of Texas at Austin, 1975.

Perrow, C. 1972. *Complex Organizations: A Critical Essay.* Glenview, IL: Scott, Foresman.

_____. "Members as Resources in Voluntary Organizations." In *Organizations and Clients,* ed. W.R. Rosengren & M. Lefton. Columbus, OH: Merrill, 1970a, pp. 93–116.

Pombeiro, B.G. "Recession Cripples Social Aid Groups." *Philadelphia Inquirer* (October 12, 1975):1–2.

Quarantelli, E.L., & Hundley, J.R. "A Test of Some Propositions About Crowd Formation and Behavior." In *Readings in Collective Behavior,* 2nd ed., ed. R.R. Evans. Chicago: Rand McNally, 1975, pp. 317–86.

Rose, A. 1967. *The Power Structure.* New York: Oxford University Press.

Ross, D.K. 1973. *A Public Citizen's Action Manual.* New York: Grossman.

Ross, R.J. "Generational Change and Primary Groups in a Social Movement." Unpublished manuscript, Clark University, Worcester, MA, 1975.

Sale, K. 1973. *SDS.* New York: Random House.

Salisbury, R.H. "An Exchange Theory of Interest Groups." *Midwest Journal of Political Science* 13 (February 1969): 1–32.

Samuelson, P. 1964. *Economics: An Introductory Analysis.* New York: McGraw-Hill.

Smelser, N.J. 1963. *Theory of Collective Behavior.* New York: Free Press.

Snyder, D., & Tilly, C. "Hardship and Collective Violence in France." *American Sociological Review* 37 (October 1972): 520–32.

Stallings, R.A. "Patterns of Belief in Social Movements: Clarifications from Analysis of Environmental Groups." *Sociological Quarterly* 14 (Autumn 1973): 465–80.

Stinchcombe, A.L. "Social Structure and Organizations." In *Handbook of Organizations,* ed. James March. Chicago: Rand McNally, 1965, pp. 142–93.

Stouffer, S. 1955. *Communism, Conformity, and Civil Liberties.* Garden City, NY: Doubleday.

Strickland, D.A., & Johnston, A.E. "Issue Elasticity in Political Systems." *Journal of Political Economy* 78 (September–October 1970): 1069–92.

Thompson, J.D. "Revolution and Collective Violence." In *Macro Political Theory: Handbook of Political Science,* Vol. 3, ed. G. Greenstein & N. Polsby. Reading, MA: Addison-Wesley, 1975, pp. 483–555.

_____. "Does Modernization Breed Revolution?" *Comparative Politics* 5 (April 1973): 425–47.

Tilly, C., Tilly, L., & Tilly, R. 1975. *The Rebellious Century: 1830–1930.* Cambridge, MA: Harvard University Press.

Tullock, G. "Information Without Profit." In *Papers on Non-Market Decision Making,* ed. G. Tullock. Charlottesville: Thomas Jefferson

Center for Political Economy, University of Virginia, 1966, pp. 141–60.

Turner, R.H. "Determinants of Social Movement Strategies." In *Human Nature and Collective Behavior: Papers in Honor of Herbert Blumer,* ed. Tamotsu Shibutani. Englewood Cliffs, NJ: Prentice-Hall, 1970, pp. 145–64.

_____. "The Public Perception of Protest." *American Sociological Review* 34 (December 1969): 815–31.

Turner, R.H., & Killian, L. 1972. *Collective Behavior,* 2d ed. Englewood Cliffs, NJ: Prentice-Hall.

U.S. Treasury Department. *Report on Private Foundations.* Washington, DC: U.S. Government Printing Office, 1965.

Von Eschen, D,. Kirk, J., & Pinard, M. "The Organizational Substructure of Disorderly Politics." *Social Forces* 49 (June 1971): 529–44.

_____. "The Disintegration of the Negro Nonviolent Movement." *Journal of Peace Research* 3 (1969): 216–34.

Walzer, M. 1971. *Political Action: A Practical Guide to Movement Politics.* Chicago: Quadrangle.

Wilkinson, P. 1971. *Social Movements.* New York: Praeger.

Wilson, J. 1973. *Introduction to Social Movements.* New York: Basic Books.

Wilson, J.Q. 1973. *Political Organizations.* New York: Basic Books.

Wolfe, B. 1955. *Three Who Made a Revolution.* Boston: Beacon.

Wootton, G. 1970. *Interest Groups.* Englewood Cliffs, NJ: Prentice-Hall.

Zald, M.N., & Ash, R. "Social Movement Organizations: Growth, Decline, and Change." *Social Forces* 44 (March 1966): 327–40.

Zald, M.N., & Jacobs, D. "Symbols into Plowshares: Underlying Dimensions of Incentive Analysis." Unpublished manuscript, Vanderbilt University, 1976.

Zald, M.N., & McCarthy, J.D. "Organizational Intellectuals and the Criticism of Society." *Social Service Review* 49 (September 1975): 344–62.

_____. "Notes on Cooperation and Competition Amongst Social Movement Organizations." Unpublished manuscript, Vanderbilt University, 1974.

12

THE POLITICAL PROCESS MODEL

DOUG McADAM

The political process model represents an alternative to the classical and resource mobilization perspectives. The term "political process" has been taken from an article by Rule and Tilly entitled "Political Process in Revolutionary France,

From *Political Process and the Development of Black Insurgency* by Doug McAdam, University of Chicago Press, pp. 36–59. Copyright © 1982 University of Chicago Press. Reprinted with permission.

1830–1832" (1975: 41–85).[1] It should, however, be emphasized that the model advanced by Rule and Tilly is compatible but not synonymous with the perspective outlined here. The name has been adopted, not because the two models are identical, but because the term "political process" accurately conveys two ideas central to both perspectives. First, in contrast to the various classical formulations, a social movement is held to be above all else a *political* rather than a psychological phenomenon. That is, the factors shaping institutionalized political processes are argued to be of equal analytic utility in accounting for social insurgency. Second, a movement represents a continuous *process* from generation to decline, rather than a discrete series of developmental stages. Accordingly, any complete model of social insurgency should offer the researcher a framework for analyzing the entire process of movement development rather than a particular phase (e.g., the emergence of social protest) of that same process.

The Political Process Model and Institutionalized Politics

A point stressed repeatedly in this work is that theories of social movements always imply a more general model of institutionalized power. Thus, it was argued that the classical view of social movements is best understood as a theoretical extension of the pluralist model. By contrast, it was suggested that the resource mobilization perspective implies adherence to the elite model of the American political system. The political process model is also based on a particular conception of power in America. In many respects this conception is consistent with the elite model. Like the latter, the perspective advanced here rests on the fundamental assumption that wealth and power are concentrated in America in the hands of a few groups, thus depriving most people of any real influence over the major decisions that affect their lives. Accordingly, social movements are seen, in both perspectives, as rational attempts by excluded groups to mobilize sufficient political leverage to advance collective interests through noninstitutionalized means.

Where this perspective diverges from the elite model is in regard to the extent of elite control over the political system and the insurgent capabilities of excluded groups. While elite theorists display a marked diversity of opinion on these issues, there would seem to be a central tendency evident in their writings. That tendency embodies a perception of the power disparity between elite and excluded groups that would seem to grant the former virtually unlimited power in politico-economic matters. Excluded groups, on the other hand, are seen as functionally powerless in the face of the enormous power wielded by the elite. Under such conditions, the chances for successful insurgency would seem to be negligible.

By contrast, on both these counts, the political process model is more compatible with a Marxist interpretation of power. Marxists acknowledge that the power disparity between elite and excluded groups is substantial but hardly regard this state of affairs as inevitable. Indeed, for orthodox Marxists, that which is inevitable is not the retention of power by the elite but the accession to power by the masses. One need not accept the rigidity of this scenario, to conclude that it represents an improvement over elite theory insofar as it embodies a clear understanding of the latent political leverage available to most segments of the population. The insurgent potential of excluded groups comes from the "structural power" that their location in various politico-economic structures affords them. Schwartz explains the basis and significance of this power:

> Since a structure cannot function without the routinized exercise of structural power, any threat to structural power becomes a threat to that system itself. Thus, if employees suddenly began refusing to obey orders, the company in question could not function. Or if tenants simply disobeyed the merchant's order to grow cotton, the tenancy system would collapse. . . . Thus, we see a

subtle, but very important, relationship between structural power and those who are subject to it. On the one hand, these power relations define the functioning of any ongoing system; on the other hand, the ability to disrupt these relationships is exactly the sort of leverage which can be used to alter the functioning of the system. . . . *Any system contains within itself the possibility of a power strong enough to alter it* (Schwartz, 1976: 172–73; emphasis in original).

A second Marxist influence on the model outlined here concerns the importance attributed to subjective processes in the generation of insurgency. Marxists, to a much greater extent than elite theorists, recognize that mass political impotence may as frequently stem from shared perceptions of powerlessness as from any objective inability to mobilize significant political leverage. Thus, the subjective transformation of consciousness is appreciated by Marxists as a process crucial to the generation of insurgency. The importance of this transformation is likewise acknowledged in the political process model.

The perspective advanced here, then, combines aspects of both the elite and Marxist models of power in America. Central to the perspective is Gamson's distinction between "members" and "challengers": "the central difference among political actors is captured by the idea of being inside or outside of the polity. Those who are inside are *members* whose interest is vested—that is, recognized as valid by other members. Those who are outside are challengers. They lack the basic prerogative of members—routine access to decisions that affect them" (1975: 140). Gamson's distinction is not unique. Indeed, a similar notion is embodied in all versions of the elite model. What distinguishes this perspective from that advanced by most resource mobilization theorists, is

the latter's characterization of the relationship between "challengers" and "members." Proponents of the resource mobilization model depict segments of the elite as being willing, at times even aggressive, sponsors of social insurgency. By contrast, the political process model is based on the notion that political action by established polity members reflects an abiding conservatism. This conservatism, according to Tilly, encourages polity members to "resist changes which would threaten their current realization of their interests even more than they seek changes which would enhance their interests" (1978: 135). He goes on to state that these members also "fight tenaciously against loss of power, and especially against expulsion from the polity. They work against admission to the polity of groups whose interests conflict significantly with their own. Existing members tend to be more exacting in their demands of contenders whose very admission would challenge the system in some serious way" (Tilly, 1978: 135).

Tilly's remarks are reminiscent of Gamson's characterization of what he terms the "competitive establishment" in American politics (1968: 19). Gamson describes the competitive establishment as that "collection of represented groups and authorities" who control to a considerable degree the workings of America's institutionalized political system. According to Gamson, they are motivated by the same desires Tilly ascribes to established polity members. They seek to "keep unrepresented groups from developing solidarity and politically organizing, and . . . discourage their effective entry into the competitive establishment if and as they become organized" (Gamson, 1968: 20).

Tilly and Gamson's statements are instructive in view of the dominant resource mobilization characterization of member/challenger relations as facilitative of social protest activity. Their remarks serve to undermine this characterization by forcefully asserting the contradictory notion that established polity members are ordinarily not enamored of the idea of sponsoring any insurgent political activity that could conceivably threaten their interests. This conservative bias extends not only to those insurgents who advocate goals contrary to member interests but also to those protest groups—regardless of how moderate their goals—who simply pressure for membership in the competitive establishment. For any change in the makeup of the polity is inherently disruptive of the institutionalized status quo and thus something to be resisted. As Gamson asserts, "the competitive establishment is boundary-maintaining" (1968: 20).

Gamson and Tilly's discussion of the characteristic conservatism of established polity members implies an important point that is central to the political process model. If elite groups are unwilling to underwrite insurgency, the very occurrence of social movements indicates that indigenous groups are able to generate and sustain organized mass action. In positing the primacy of environmental factors, most resource mobilization theorists have seemingly rejected this point. This, of course, is not to suggest that such factors are unimportant. The strategic constraints confronting excluded groups should not be underestimated. The Tillys describe the rather unenviable position of the challenger:

> the range of collective actions open to a relatively powerless group is normally very small. Its program, its form of action, its very existence are likely to be illegal, hence subject to violent repression. As a consequence, such a group chooses between taking actions which have a high probability of bringing on a violent response (but which have some chance of reaching the group's goals) and taking no action at all (thereby assuring the defeat of the group's goals) (C. Tilly, L. Tilly, R. Tilly, 1975: 283).

Thus, while excluded groups do possess the latent capacity to exert significant political leverage at any time, the force of environmental constraints is usually sufficient to inhibit mass action. But this force is not constant over time. The calculations on which existing political arrangements are based may, for a variety of reasons, change over time, thus affording certain segments of the population greater leverage with which to advance their interests. The suggestion is that neither environmental factors nor factors internal to the movement are sufficient to account for the generation and development of social insurgency. I agree with Gary Marx that "social movements are not autonomous forces hurling toward their destiny only in response to the . . . intensity of commitment, and skill of activists. Nor are they epiphenomena completely at the mercy of groups in their external environment seeking to block or facilitate them" (Marx, 1976: 1). The political process model rests on the assumption that social movements are an ongoing product of the favorable interplay of *both* sets of factors. The specific mix of factors may change from one phase of the movement to another, but the basic dynamic remains the same. Movements develop in response to an ongoing process of interaction between movement groups and the larger sociopolitical environment they seek to change.

The Generation of Insurgency

The political process model identifies three sets of factors that are believed to be crucial in the generation of social insurgency. The first is the level of organization within the aggrieved population; the second, the collective assessment of the prospects for successful insurgency within that same population; and third, the political alignment of groups within the larger political environment. The first can be conceived of as the degree of organizational "readiness" within the minority community; the second, as the level of "insurgent consciousness" within the movement's mass base; and the third, following Eisinger, as the "structure of political opportunities" available to insurgent groups (Eisinger, 1973: 11). Before the relationships between these factors are outlined, each will be discussed in turn.

Structure of Political Opportunities

Under ordinary circumstances, excluded groups, or challengers, face enormous obstacles in their efforts to advance group interests. Challengers are excluded from routine decision-making processes precisely because their bargaining position, relative to established polity members, is so weak. But the particular set of power relationships that define the political environment at any point in time hardly constitutes an immutable structure of political life. As Lipsky points out:

> attention is directed away from system characterizations presumably true for all times and all places, which are basically of little value in understanding the social and political process. We are accustomed to describing communist political systems as "experiencing a thaw" or "going through a process of retrenchment." Should it not at least be an open question as to whether the American political system experiences such stages and fluctuations? Similarly, is it not sensible to assume that the system will be more or less open to specific groups at different times and at different places? (Lipsky, 1970: 14).

The answer offered here to both of Lipsky's questions is an emphatic yes. The

opportunities for a challenger to engage in successful collective action do vary greatly over time. And it is these variations that are held to be related to the ebb and flow of movement activity. As Eisinger has remarked, "protest is a sign that the opportunity structure is flexible and vulnerable to the political assaults of excluded groups" (1973: 28).

Still unanswered, however, is the question of what accounts for such shifts in the "structure of political opportunities." A finite list of specific causes would be impossible to compile. However, Eisinger suggests the crucial point about the origin of such shifts: "protest signifies changes not only among previously quiescent or conventionally oriented groups but also *in the political system itself*" (1973: 28; emphasis mine). The point is that *any* event or broad social process that serves to undermine the calculations and assumptions on which the political establishment is structured occasions a shift in political opportunities. Among the events and processes likely to prove disruptive of the political status quo are wars, industrialization, international political realignments, prolonged unemployment, and widespread demographic changes.

It is interesting to note that classical theorists have also described many of these same processes as productive of mass protest. In particular, industrialization and urbanization have been singled out as forces promoting the rise of social movements (Kornhauser, 1959: 143–58). The difference between the two models stems from the fact that classical theorists posit a radically different causal sequence linking these processes to insurgency than is proposed here. For classical theorists the relationship is direct, with industrialization/urbanization generating a level of strain sufficient to trigger social protest.[2]

In contrast, the political process model is based on the idea that social processes such as industrialization promote insurgency only indirectly through a restructuring of existing power relations. This difference also indexes a significant divergence between the two models in terms of the time span during which insurgency is held to develop. The classical sequence of disruption/strain depicts insurgency as a function of dramatic changes in the period immediately preceding movement emergence. By contrast, the perspective advanced here is based on the notion that social insurgency is shaped by broad social processes that usually operate over a longer period of time. As a consequence, the processes shaping insurgency are expected to be of a more cumulative, less dramatic nature than those identified by proponents of the classical model. The Tillys have nicely captured both these differences: "urbanization and industrialization . . . are by no means irrelevant to collective violence. It is just that their effects do not work as . . . [classical] theories say they should. Instead of a short-run generation of strain, followed by protest, we find a long-run transformation of the structures of power and of collective action" (C. Tilly , L. Tilly, R. Tilly, 1975: 254).

Regardless of the causes of expanded "political opportunities," such shifts can facilitate increased political activism on the part of excluded groups either by seriously undermining the stability of the entire political system or by increasing the political leverage of a single insurgent group. The significance of this distinction stems from the fact that the former pattern usually precipitates widespread political crisis while the latter does not.

Generalized political instability destroys any semblance of a political status quo, thus encouraging collective action by *all* groups sufficiently organized to contest the structuring of a new political order. The empirical literature offers numerous examples of this

process. Shorter and Tilly, for example, marshall data to show that peaks in French strike activity correspond to periods in which organized contention for national political power is unusually intense. They note that "factory and white-collar workers undertook in 1968 the longest, largest general strike in history as student unrest reopened the question of who were to be the constituent political groups of the Fifth Republic" (Shorter and Tilly, 1974: 344). Similarly, Schwartz argues that a period of political instability preceded the rise of the Southern Farmers Alliance in the post–Civil War South. With the southern planter aristocracy and emerging industrial interests deadlocked in a struggle for political control of the region, a unique opportunity for political advancement was created for any group able to break the stalemate (Schwartz, 1976).

Such situations of generalized political instability can be contrasted to instances in which broad social processes favorably affect the opportunities for insurgent action of particular challengers. In such cases, long-term socioeconomic changes serve simply to elevate the group in question to a position of increased political strength without necessarily undermining the structural basis of the entire political establishment. The Jenkins-Perrow study provides a good example of this latter process. In comparing the farmworker movements of the 1940s and the 1960s, the authors attribute the success of the latter to "the altered political environment within which the challenge operated" (Jenkins and Perrow, 1977: 263). Moreover, this all-important alteration of the political environment originated, they contend, "in economic trends and political realignments that took place quite independent of any 'push' from insurgents" (Jenkins and Perrow, 1977: 266). Successful insurgency, the authors suggest, was born, not of widespread political instability, but of broad social processes that strengthened the political position of the challenging group.

It remains only to identify the ways in which favorable shifts in the structure of political opportunities increase the likelihood of successful insurgent action. Two major facilitative effects can be distinguished. Most fundamentally, such shifts improve the chances for successful social protest by reducing the power discrepancy between insurgent groups and their opponents. Regardless of whether the broad social processes productive of such shifts serve to undermine the structural basis of the entire political system or simply to enhance the strategic position of a single challenger, the result is the same: a net increase in the political leverage exercised by insurgent groups. The practical effect of this development is to increase the likelihood that insurgent interests will prevail in a confrontation with a group whose goals conflict with those of the insurgents. This does not, of course, mean that insurgent interests will inevitably be realized in all conflict situations. Even in the context of an improved bargaining position, insurgent groups are likely to be at a distinct disadvantage in any confrontation with an established polity member. What it does mean, however, is that the increased political strength of the aggrieved population has improved the bargaining position of insurgent groups and thus created new opportunities for the collective pursuit of group goals.

Second, an improved bargaining position for the aggrieved population raises significantly the costs of repressing insurgent action. Unlike before, when the powerless status of the excluded group meant that it could be repressed with relative impunity, now the increased political leverage exercised by the insurgent group renders it a more formidable opponent. Repression of the group involves a greater risk of political reprisals than before and is thus less likely to be attempted even in the face of an increased threat to member interests. For, as Gamson notes in summarizing the evidence from his survey of challenging groups, insurgents "are attacked not merely because they are regarded as threatening—all challenging groups are threatening to some vested interest. They are threatening *and* vulnerable" (1975: 82). To the extent, then, that shifting political conditions increase the power of insurgent groups, they also render them less vulnerable to attack by raising the costs of repression. Or to state the matter in terms of the insurgent group, increased political power serves to encourage collective action by diminishing the risks associated with movement participation.

Indigenous Organizational Strength

A conducive political environment only affords the aggrieved population the opportunity for successful insurgent action. It is the resources of the minority community that enable insurgent groups to exploit these opportunities. In the absence of those resources the aggrieved population is likely to lack the capacity to act even when granted the opportunity to do so. Here I am asserting the importance of what Katz and Gurin have termed the "conversion potential" of the minority community (1969: 350). To generate a social movement, the aggrieved population must be able to "convert" a favorable "structure of political opportunities" into an organized campaign of social protest.

Conditioning this conversion is the extent of organization within the minority community. That indigenous structures frequently provide the organizational base out of which social movements emerge has been argued by a number of theorists. Oberschall, for instance, has proposed a theory of mobilization in which he assigns paramount importance to the degree of organization in the minority community. If no networks exist, he contends, the aggrieved population is capable of little more than "short-term, localized, ephemeral outbursts and movements of protest such as riots," (Oberschall, 1973: 119). Likewise Freeman (1973, 1977b) stresses the importance of an established associational network in the generation of social insurgency. Echoing Oberschall, she argues convincingly that the ability of insurgents to generate a social movement is ultimately dependent on the presence of an indigenous "infrastructure" that can be used to link members of the aggrieved population into an organized campaign of mass political action.

I agree with the importance attributed to existent networks or organizations in these networks. Specifically, the significance of such organizations would appear to be largely a function of four crucial resources they afford insurgents.

Members   If there is anything approximating a consistent finding in the empirical literature, it is that movement participants are recruited along established lines of interaction. This remains true in spite of the numerous attempts to explain participation on the basis of a variety of individual background or psychological variables.[3] The explanation for this consistent finding would appear to be straightforward: the more integrated the person is into the minority community, the more readily he/she can be mobilized for participation in protest activities. The work of Gerlach and Hine supports this interpretation. They conclude, "no matter how a typical participant describes his reasons for joining the movement, or what motives may be suggested by a social scientist on the basis of deprivation, disorganization, or deviancy models, it is clear that the original decision to join required some contact with the movement" (Gerlach and Hine, 1970: 79). The significance of indigenous

organizations—informal ones no less than formal—stems from the fact that they render this type of facilitative contact more likely, thus promoting member recruitment. This function can be illustrated by reference to two patterns of recruitment evident in empirical accounts of insurgency.

First, individuals can be recruited into the ranks of movement activists by virtue of their involvement in organizations that serve as the associational network out of which a new movement emerges. This was true, as Melder notes, in the case of the nineteenth-century women's rights movement, with a disproportionate number of the movement's recruits coming from existing abolitionist groups (1964). Curtis and Zurcher have observed a similar phenomenon in connection with the rise of two contemporary anti-pornography groups. In their study, the authors provide convincing data to support their contention that recruits were overwhelmingly drawn from the broad "multi-organizational fields" in which both groups were embedded (Curtis and Zurcher, 1973).

Second, indigenous organizations can serve as the primary source of movement participants through what Oberschall has termed "bloc recruitment" (1973: 125). In this pattern, movements do not so much emerge out of established organizations as they represent a merger of such groups. Hicks, for instance, has described how the Populist party was created through a coalition of established farmers' organizations (1961). The rapid rise of the free-speech movement at Berkeley has been attributed to a similar merger of existing campus organizations (Lipset and Wolin, 1965). Both of these patterns, then, highlight the indigenous organizational basis of much movement recruitment, and they support Oberschall's general conclusion: "mobilization does not occur through recruitment of large numbers of isolated and solitary individuals. It occurs as a result of recruiting blocs of people who are already highly organized and participants" (1973: 125).

Established Structure of Solidary Incentives

A second resource available to insurgents through the indigenous organizations of the minority community are the "established structures of solidary incentives" on which these organizations depend. By "structures of solidary incentives," I am simply referring to the myriad interpersonal rewards that provide the motive force for participation in these groups. It is the salience of these rewards that helps explain why recruitment through established organizations is generally so efficient. In effect, these established "incentive structures" solve the so-called "free-ride problem."

First discussed by Mancur Olson (1965), the "free-rider problem" refers to the difficulties insurgents encounter in trying to convince participants to pursue goals whose benefits they would derive even if they did not participate in the movement. The fact is, when viewed in the light of a narrow economic calculus, movement participation would indeed seem to be irrational. Even if we correct for Olson's overly rationalistic model of the individual, the "free rider" mentality would still seem to pose a formidable barrier to movement recruitment. The solution to this problem is held to stem from the provision of selective incentives to induce the participation that individual calculation would alone seem to preclude (Gamson, 1975: 66–71; Olson, 1965).

In the context of existent organizations, however, the provision of selective incentives would seem unnecessary. These organizations already rest on a solid structure of solidary incentives which insurgents have, in effect, appropriated by defining movement participation as synonymous with organizational membership. Accordingly, the myriad of incentives that have heretofore served as the motive force for participa-

tion in the group are now simply transferred to the movement. Thus, insurgents have been spared the difficult task of inducing participation through the provision of new incentives of either a solidary or material nature.

Communication Network
The established organizations of the aggrieved population also constitute a communication network or infrastructure, the strength and breadth of which largely determine the pattern, speed, and extent of movement expansion. Both the failure of a new movement to take hold and the rapid spread of insurgent action have been credited to the presence or absence of such an infrastructure. Freeman has argued that it was the recent development of such a network that enabled women in the 1960s to create a successful feminist movement where they had earlier been unable to do so:

> The development of the women's liberation movement highlights the salience of such a network precisely because the conditions for a movement existed *before* a network came into being, but the movement didn't exist until afterward. Socioeconomic strain did not change for women significantly during a 20-year period. It was as great in 1955 as in 1965. What changed was the organizational situation. It was not until a communications network developed among like-minded people beyond local boundaries that the movement could emerge and develop past the point of occasional, spontaneous uprising (Freeman, 1973: 804).

Conversely, Jackson et al. (1960) document a case in which the absence of a readily co-optable communication network contributed to "The Failure of an Incipient Social Movement." The movement, an attempted property tax revolt in California, failed, according to the authors, because "there was no . . . preestablished network of communication which could be quickly employed to link the suburban residential property owners who constituted the principal base for the movement" (Jackson et al., 1960: 38).[4]

These findings are consistent with the empirical thrust of studies of cultural diffusion, a body of literature that has unfortunately been largely overlooked by movement analysts despite its relevance to the topic.[5] To my knowledge, only Maurice Pinard (1971: 186–87) has explicitly applied the empirical insights of this literature to the study of social movements. He summarizes the central tenet of diffusion theory as follows: "the higher the degree of social integration of potential adopters, the more likely and the sooner they will become actual adopters . . . on the other hand, near-isolates tend to be the last to adopt an innovation" (1971: 187). The applicability of this idea to the study of social insurgency stems from recognition of the fact that a social movement is, after all, a new cultural item subject to the same pattern of diffusion or adoption as other innovations. Indeed, without acknowledging the theoretical basis of his insight, Oberschall has hypothesized for movements the identical pattern of diffusion noted earlier by Pinard: "the greater the number and variety of organizations in a collectivity, and the higher the participation of members in this network, the more rapidly and enduringly does mobilization into conflict groups occur" (Oberschall, 1973: 125).

Oberschall's statement has brought us full circle. Our brief foray into the diffusion literature only serves to amplify the basic argument by placing it in a theoretical context that helps explain the importance of associational networks in the generation of insurgency. The interorganizational linkages characteristic of established groups facilitate movement emergence by providing the means of communication by which the movement, as a new cultural items, can be disseminated throughout the aggrieved population.

Leaders All manner of movement analysts have asserted the importance of leaders or organizers in the generation of social insurgency. To do so requires not so much a particular theoretical orientation as common sense. For in the context of political opportunity and widespread discontent there still remains a need for the centralized direction and coordination of a recognized leadership.

The existence of established organizations within the movement's mass base ensures the presence of recognized leaders who can be called upon to lend their prestige and organizing skills to the incipient movement. Indeed, given the pattern of diffusion discussed in the previous section, it may well be that established leaders are among the first to join a new movement by virtue of their central position within the community. There is, in fact, some empirical evidence to support this. To cite only one example, Lipset, in his study of the Socialist C.C.F. party, reports that "in Saskatchewan it was the local leaders of the Wheat Pool, of the trade-unions, who were the first to join the C.C.F." His interpretation of the finding is that "those who are most thoroughly integrated in the class through formal organizations are the first to change" (1950: 197). Regardless of the timing of their recruitment, the existence of recognized leaders is yet another resource whose availability is conditioned by the degree of organization within the aggrieved population.

Existent organizations of the minority community, then, are the primary source of resources facilitating movement emergence. These groups constitute the organizational context in which insurgency is expected to develop. As such, their presence is as crucial to the process of movement emergence as a conducive political environment. Indeed, in the absence of this supportive organizational context, the aggrieved population is likely to be deprived of the capacity for collective action even when confronted with a favorable structure of political opportunities. If one lacks the capacity to act, it hardly matters that one is afforded the chance to do so.

Cognitive Liberation

While important, expanding political opportunities and indigenous organizations do not, in any simple sense, produce a social movement. In the absence of one other crucial process these two factors remain necessary, but insufficient, causes of insurgency. Together they only offer insurgents a certain objective "structural potential" for collective political action. Mediating between opportunity and action are people and the subjective meanings they attach to their situations. This crucial attribution process has been ignored by proponents of both the classical and resource mobilization perspectives. As Edelman has pointed out: "our explanations of mass political response have radically undervalued the ability of the human mind . . . to take a complex set of . . . cues into account [and] evolve a mutually acceptable form of response" (1971: 133). This process must occur if an organized protest campaign is to take place. One of the central problematics of insurgency, then, is whether favorable shifts in political opportunities will be defined as such by a large enough group of people to facilitate collective protest. This process, however, is not independent of the two factors discussed previously. Indeed, one effect of improved political conditions and existent organizations is to render this process of "cognitive liberation" more likely. I will explore the relation-

ship between this process and each of these factors separately.

As noted earlier, favorable shifts in political opportunities decrease the power disparity between insurgents and their opponents and, in doing so, increase the cost of repressing the movement. These are objective structural changes. However, such shifts have a subjective referent as well. That is, challengers experience shifting political conditions on a day-to-day basis as a set of "meaningful" events communicating much about their prospects for successful collective action.

Sometimes the political significance of events is apparent on their face as when mass migration significantly alters the electoral composition of a region. Thus, as early as the mid-1930s black leaders began to use the fact of rapidly swelling black populations in key northern industrial states as bargaining leverage in their dealings with presidential candidates (Sitkoff, 1978: 283). However, even when evolving political realities are of a less dramatic nature, they will invariably be made "available" to insurgents through subtle cues communicated by other groups. The expectation is that as conditions shift in favor of a particular challenger members will display a certain increased symbolic responsiveness to insurgents. Thus, in a tight labor market we might expect management to be more responsive to workers than they had previously been. Or, as regards the earlier example, should internal migration significantly increase the proportion of a certain population residing in a region, we could expect area politicians to be more symbolically attentive to that group than before.

As subtle and substantively meaningless as these altered responses may be, their significance for the generation of insurgency would be hard to overstate. As Edelman notes, "political actions chiefly arouse or satisfy people not by granting or withholding their stable substantive demands, but rather by changing the demands and the expectations" (1971: 7). In effect, the altered responses of members to a particular challenger serve to transform evolving political conditions into a set of "cognitive cues" signifying to insurgents that the political system is becoming increasingly vulnerable to challenge. Thus, by forcing a change in the symbolic content of member/challenger relations, shifting political conditions supply a crucial impetus to the process of cognitive liberation.

The existent organizations of the minority community also figure prominently in the development of this insurgent consciousness, lending added significance to their role in the generation of insurgency. Earlier the relevance of the diffusion literature for the study of social movements was noted. Based on the main finding derived from that literature, the argument was advanced that the importance of indigenous organizations stemmed, in part, from the fact that they afforded insurgents an established interaction network ensuring the rapid and thorough diffusion of social insurgency throughout the minority community. But that insight can now be extended even further. It is not simply the extent and speed with which insurgency is spread but the very cognitions on which it depends that are conditioned by the strength of integrative ties within the movement's mass base. As summarized by Piven and Cloward, these "necessary cognitions" are threefold:

> The emergence of a protest movement entails a transformation both of consciousness and of behavior. The change in consciousness has at least three distinct aspects. First, "the system"—or those aspects of the system that people experience and perceive—loses legitimacy. Large numbers of men and women who ordinarily accept the authority of their rulers and the legitimacy of institutional arrangements come to believe in some measure that these rulers and these arrangements are unjust and wrong. Second, people who are ordinarily fatalistic, who believe that existing arrangements are inevitable, begin to assert "rights" that imply demands for change. Third, there is a new sense of efficacy; people who ordinarily consider themselves helpless come to believe that they have some capacity to alter their lot (Piven and Cloward, 1979: 3–4).

It is important to recognize, however, that these cognitions "are overwhelmingly not based upon observation or empirical evidence available to participants, but rather upon cuings among groups of people who jointly create the meanings they will read into current and anticipated events" (Edelman, 1971: 32). The key phrase here is "groups of people." That is, the process of cognitive liberation is held to be both more likely and of far greater consequence under conditions of strong rather than weak social integration. The latter point should be intuitively apparent. Even in the unlikely event that these necessary cognitions were to develop under conditions of weak social integration, the absence of integrative links would almost surely prevent their spread to the minimum number of people required to afford a reasonable basis for successful collective action. More to the point, perhaps, is the suspicion that under such conditions these cognitions would never arise in the first place. The consistent finding linking feelings of political efficacy to social integration supports this judgment (Neal and Seeman, 1964; Pinard, 1971; Sayre, 1980). In the absence of strong interpersonal links to others, people are likely to feel powerless to change conditions even if they perceive present conditions as favorable to such efforts.

To this finding one might add the educated supposition that what Ross (1977) calls the "fundamental attribution error"—the tendency of people to explain their situation as a function of individual rather than situational factors—is more likely to occur under conditions of personal isolation than under those of integration. Lacking the information and perspective that others afford, isolated individuals would seem especially prone to explain their troubles on the basis of personal rather than "system attributions" (Ferree and Miller, 1977: 33).

The practical significance of this distinction comes from the fact that only system attributions afford the necessary rationale for movement activity. For movement analysts, then, the key question becomes, What social circumstances are productive of "system attributions"? If we follow Ferree and Miller, the likely answer is that the chances "of a system attribution would appear to be greatest among extremely homogeneous people who are in intense regular contact with each other" (1977: 34). This point serves to underscore the central thrust of the argument: the significance of existent organizations for the process of movement emergence stems from the expectation that cognitive liberation is most likely to take place within established interpersonal networks.

To summarize, movement emergence implies a transformation of consciousness within a significant segment of the aggrieved population. Before collective protest can get under way, people must collectively define their situations as unjust and subject to change through group action. The likelihood of this necessary transformation occurring is conditioned, in large measure, by the two facilitating conditions discussed previously. Shifting political conditions supply the necessary "cognitive cues" capable of triggering the process of cognitive liberation while existent organizations afford insurgents the stable group-settings within which that process is most likely to occur.

It is now possible to outline in broader fashion the alternative model of movement emergence proposed here. That model is shown in figure 12.1. As the figure shows, the generation of insurgency is expected to reflect the favorable confluence of three sets of factors. Expanding political opportunities combine with the indigenous organizations of the minority community to afford insurgents the "structural potential" for successful collective action. That potential is, in turn, transformed into actual insurgency by means of the crucial intervening process of cognitive liberation. All three factors, then, are regarded as necessary, but insufficient, causes of social insurgency.

The Development/Decline of Social Insurgency

The generation of social insurgency presupposes the existence of a political environment increasingly vulnerable to pressure from insurgents. Specific events and/or broad social processes enhance the bargaining position of the aggrieved population, even as insurgent groups mobilize to exploit the expanding opportunities for collective action. Over time the survival of a social movement requires that insurgents be able to maintain and successfully utilize their newly acquired political leverage to advance collective interests. If they are able to do so, the movement is likely to survive. If, on the other hand, insurgent groups fail to maintain a favorable bargaining position vis-à-vis other groups in the political arena, the movement faces extinction. In short, the ongoing exercise of significant political leverage remains the key to the successful development of the movement.

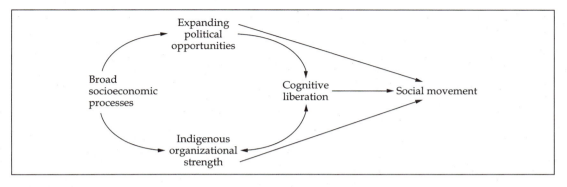

FIGURE 12.1   A Political Process Model of Movement Emergence

What is missing from the above discussion is any acknowledgment of the enormous obstacles insurgents must overcome if they are to succeed in this effort. This is not to say that social movements are doomed from the outset or that they are an ineffective form of political action. History contradicts both notions. Just the same, the fortuitous combination of factors productive of insurgency is expected to be short-lived. Even as insurgents exploit the opportunities this confluence of factors affords them, the movement sets in motion processes that are likely, over time, to create a set of contradictory demands destructive of insurgency. Of principal importance in this regard are two dilemmas on whose horns many movements seem to have been caught. (After a brief review of the factors shaping the ongoing development of insurgency, I will address these dilemmas.)

Conditioning the development of the movement over time is the same mix of internal and external factors that shaped the generation of insurgency. Indeed, with a few important modifications, the general causal model outlined in the previous section affords a useful framework for analyzing the ongoing development of insurgency. These modifications are reflected in figure 12.2.

Perhaps the most significant change evident in figure 12.2 is the emergence of the movement as an independent force shaping its own development. In analyzing the generation of insurgency, one considers the movement only as the end product of a specified causal sequence. Once under way, however, the pace and character of insurgency come to exercise a powerful influence on the development of the movement through the effect they have on the other factors depicted in figure 12.2. For example, the opportunities for insurgency are no longer independent of the actions of insurgent groups. Now the structure of political alignments shifts in response to movement activity, even as those shifts shape the prospects for future insurgency.

Much the same dynamic is evident in regard to the relationship between organizational strength and insurgency, with the pace, character, and outcome of collective protest shaping the availability of those organizational resources on which further movement activity depends. Reciprocal relationships also hold in the case of insurgency and the other two factors shown in figure 12.2. With the outbreak of insurgency, then, the movement itself introduces a new set of causal dynamics into the study of collective protest activity that are

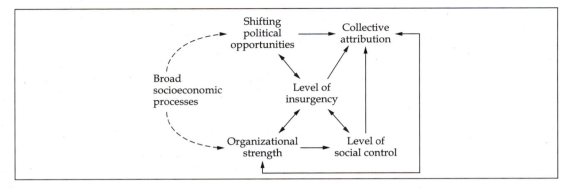

FIGURE 12.2   A Political Process Model of Movement Development/Decline

discontinuous with the process of movement emergence.

At the same time, however, there is a basic continuity between the generation and ongoing development of insurgency. The reader will note that all three factors discussed earlier in connection with the generation of insurgency are included in figure 12.2 as well. To these three factors I now add a fourth: the shifting control response of other groups to the insurgent challenge posed by the movement.

Little needs to be said about two of the original factors. It is enough simply to note that "the structure of political opportunities" and the process of "collective attribution" are expected to influence the development of the movement in much the same ways as they did in the generation of insurgency. The former conditions the ongoing vulnerability of the political system to pressure from the movement, while the latter determines the extent to which insurgents continue to share the particular mix of cognitions needed to sustain insurgency. As explained earlier, these cognitions involve the perception that conditions are unjust yet subject to change through group efforts.

The remaining two factors require more explanation. Though discussed earlier, the determinants of "organizational strength" are expected to shift, following the genera-

tion of insurgency, in accordance with an anticipated transformation of the movement's organizational structure. For that reason, the factor will be discussed anew. Finally, as the only factor set in motion by the emergence of the movement, "level of social control" merits attention if only because it has not been discussed previously. The importance of these remaining factors also results from their relationship to the two critical dilemmas alluded to above. That is, both factors index a set of cross-cutting pressures that must be carefully negotiated if the movement is to survive. In discussing these factors, then, I will not only be analyzing the ongoing process of movement development but also emphasizing the difficulties inherent in sustaining any insurgent challenge.

Sustaining Organizational Strength

Although social insurgency is expected to develop out of the established organizations of the aggrieved population, the movement cannot rely on such groups to sustain an ongoing protest campaign. It must be remembered that these organizations were not intended to serve as insurgent vehicles in the first place. Indeed, more often than not, the actual leadership of the burgeoning movement is supplied by ad hoc committees and loosely structured working coalitions with ill-defined and often indirect connections to these established organizations. The latter may function as sources of support and resources vital to the generation of insurgency but rarely as protest organizations per se.

For the movement to survive, insurgents must be able to create a more enduring organizational structure to sustain insurgency. Efforts to do so usually entail the creation of formally constituted organizations to assume the centralized direction of the movement previously exercised by informal groups. This transfer of power can only occur, however, if the resources needed to fuel the development of the movement's formal organizational structure can be mobilized. Accordingly, insurgent groups must be able to exploit the initial successes of the movement to mobilize those resources needed to facilitate the development of the more permanent organizational structure required to sustain insurgency. Failing this, movements are likely to die aborning as the loosely structured groups previously guiding the protest campaign disband or gradually lapse into inactivity.

This view is obviously at odds with Piven and Cloward's contention that organization is antithetical to movement success (1979: xxi–xxii). The authors base their pessimistic conclusion on a view that equates the development of movement organization with certain processes destructive of insurgency. The problem with their conclusion is in the inevitability they ascribe to these processes.

If Piven and Cloward overstate the negative effects of organization on insurgency, theirs is nonetheless an important thesis that indexes a major dilemma confronting movements. Without the minimal coordination and direction that organizations (informal no less than formal) afford, insurgency is

nearly impossible. This is true even in the case of the most disruptive forms of insurgency (riots, strikes, etc.) as the work of the Tillys and others makes clear (Feagin and Hahn, 1973: 48–49; C. Tilly, L. Tilly, R. Tilly, 1975). At the same time, the establishment of formal movement organizations does have the potential to set in motion any one (or some combination) of three processes ultimately destructive of the effectiveness of the movement as a social change vehicle.

The first process is that of oligarchization. One need not accede to the rigidity of the Weber-Michels view of this process to acknowledge the potential danger it poses.[6] Quite simply, the establishment of formal movement organizations *may* create a certain class of individuals who come to value the maintenance of that organization over the realization of movement goals. In such cases, the insurgent potential of the movement is sacrificed to ensure the survival of its organizational offshoot.

The creation of formal movement organizations also increases the likelihood of a second danger: co-optation. Having mobilized the resource support needed to create a formal organizational structure, insurgents still face the challenge of sustaining that structure over time. In this effort the resources of the movement's mass base are likely to be found wanting. The more impoverished the aggrieved population, the more likely this will be the case. In such instances, supplementary support must be drawn from outside sources. The establishment of external support linkages, however, grants considerable control over movement affairs to the source from which the resources are obtained. Of course, the control embodied in these support linkages need not be exercised in any particular case. If the movement organization uses the resource(s) in a manner consistent with the interests and goals of its sponsor(s), then support is likely to continue without interruption. Therein lies the dilemma. Owing to the impoverished state of the mass base, insurgents are likely to experience grave difficulties in trying to sustain insurgency solely on the basis of the limited resources of the movement's "beneficiary constituents." On the other hand, the establishment of external support linkages threatens to tame the movement by encouraging insurgents to pursue only those goals acceptable to external sponsors. The latter course of action may ensure the survival of the movement—or at least of its organizational offshoots—but only at the cost of reducing its effectiveness as a force for social change.

The final danger inherent in the creation of formal movement organizations is the dissolution of indigenous support. What amounts to a virtually inevitable by-product of the establishment of external support links, this process has been largely ignored by movement analysts. The dynamic is simple. As insurgents increasingly seek to cultivate ties to outside groups, their indigenous links are likely to grow weaker. The potential negative consequences of this process are threefold. First, it may encourage oligarchization as movement leaders are increasingly insulated from the indigenous pressures that would tend to ensure their responsiveness to the original goals of the movement. Second, the process increases the movement's dependence on external sources of support, thus rendering cooptation more likely. Third, and most important, the weakening of indigenous ties deprives the movement of the "established structures of solidary incentives" that earlier supplied the motive force for movement participation. Insurgents now face the difficult task of inducing participation through the provision of the sort of selective incentives that have been shown to correlate with movement success (Gamson, 1975: 66–71).

To summarize, sustained insurgency depends, in part, on the level of organizational resources that movement forces are able to maintain over time. Efforts to ensure a routinized flow of resources usually lead to the establishment of formal organizations to supplant the indigenous groups out of which the movement emerged. Although necessary, if the movement is to attain a degree of permanence, this transformation is nonetheless likely to set in motion several processes ultimately destructive of insurgency. Specifically, the creation of formal organizations renders the movement increasingly vulnerable to the destructive forces of oligarchization, cooptation, and the dissolution of indigenous support. Should insurgents manage somehow to avoid these dangers while maintaining an adequate flow of resources the movement is likely to endure. However, the long list of movements that have failed to negotiate these obstacles attests to the difficulties inherent in the effort.

The Social Control Response to Insurgency

The identification of this response as a crucial factor affecting movement development only serves to reemphasize the reciprocal relationship that exists between the movement and its external environment. If the likelihood of movement emergence is partly conditioned by shifting political conditions, the movement itself introduces new pressures for change into the political system. Other organized groups are expected to respond to these pressures in a fashion consistent with their own interests. Over time, the development of insurgency is expected to be profoundly affected by these responses.

Two factors are of principal importance in shaping these responses. The first is the strength of insurgent forces. In different ways, both Gamson and Tilly have argued as much in asserting that weakness encourages repression (Gamson, 1975: 81–82; Tilly, 1978: 111–15). When one reflects on it, the proposition, although not completely intuitive, makes sense. Quite simply, both the costs and risks involved in repressing a weak target are minimal when compared with those associated with the repression of a powerful opponent. Quite apart from the degree of threat each poses, the latter must be handled with greater caution because of the potentially graver repercussions associated with an unsuccessful attempt at repression. In part, then, the strength of insurgent forces conditions the responses of other groups to the movement by determining the costs associated with various alternative control strategies.

The second factor affecting the response of other parties to insurgency is the degree to which the movement poses a threat or an opportunity to other groups in terms of the realization of the latter's interests. In this regard, most movements confront an elite divided in its reaction to the insurgent challenge. Some components of the elite usually perceive the movement as a threat and seek through their actions to neutralize or destroy it. Others see in it an opportunity to advance their interests and thus extend cautious support to insurgents. Still others perceive their interests as little affected by the challenge and remain uninvolved. The mix of these three responses determines, for any particular movement, the relative balance of supporting and opposing forces it must confront at any given point in time. To oversimplify matters a bit, if the movement is to survive, it must retain (in consort with its allies) sufficient strength to withstand the control responses of the opposition.

What is absent in the above discussion is the element of time. The point to be made is that the level of threat or opportunity embodied in a movement is not constant over time. Not only are the interests of elite groups likely to change, but so are important characteristics of the insurgent challenge itself. Specifically, it is the goals and tactics of insurgents that are of crucial

importance, since together they largely define the degree of threat/opportunity posed by the movement.

Tactics The myriad tactics available to insurgents communicate varying degrees of threat to other organized groups in the political environment. The key distinction is between institutionalized and noninstitutionalized tactics. Even if used to pursue "radical" goals, the former implicitly convey an acceptance of the established, or "proper," channels of conflict resolution. Such tactics are, thus, viewed as nonthreatening by elite groups, both because they leave unchallenged the structural underpinnings of the political system and because it is within these "proper" channels that the power disparity between members and challengers is greatest.

Reliance on noninstitutionalized tactics represents the converse of the above situation and, as such, poses a distinct challenge to elite groups for at least two reasons. At a symbolic level, it communicates a fundamental rejection of the established institutional mechanisms for seeking redress of group grievances; substantively, it deprives elite groups of their recourse to institutional power. For both these reasons, elite groups are likely to view noninstitutionalized tactics as a threat to their interests. Thus, any significant shift in tactics on the part of insurgents will generally condition a commensurate shift in the response of elite groups to the movement. A greater reliance on noninstitutionalized forms of protest is likely to broaden opposition to the movement while decreased use of such tactics will usually diminish the intensity of movement opposition.

Goals Much the same dynamic applies to the goals of the movement. That is, substantive shifts in the goals embraced by insurgents profoundly affect the response of elite groups to the movement. The central distinction here is between those goals that embody a fundamental challenge to the existing political and economic structures of society (revolutionary goals) and those that merely call for piecemeal reform of those structures (reform goals). By virtue of their narrow focus, *reform* goals stand to engender the opposition of only those few elite groups whose interests are directly affected by the proposed changes. Moreover, such goals usually facilitate the mobilization of limited support from those components of the elite who stand to benefit either from the reforms themselves or from the defeat they would spell for their opponents. Thus, reform movements are frequently aided in their efforts by their ability to exploit existing divisions among the elite.

Truly *revolutionary* goals, on the other hand, are rarely the object of divided elite response. Rather, movements that emphasize such goals usually mobilize a united elite opposition whose minor conflicts of interest are temporarily tabled in deference to the central threat confronting the system as a whole. In terms of this discussion, then, shifts from reform to revolutionary goals will almost surely be accompanied by an intensification of movement opposition while a change in the reverse direction will usually diminish the strength of opposition forces.[7]

This indicates a second critical dilemma confronting insurgents. Although recourse to institutionalized tactics and moderate goals is likely to diminish opposition to the movement, it will just as surely reduce the overall impact of the movement. Indeed, with respect to tactics, it was their fundamental powerlessness *within* institutionalized channels that led insurgents to abandon "proper channels" in the first place. Accordingly, insurgents must chart a course that avoids crippling repression on the one hand and tactical impotence on the other. Staking out this optimal middle ground is exceedingly difficult. Yet failure to do so almost surely spells the demise of the movement.

Summary

The political process model represents an alternative to both the classical and resource mobilization perspectives. Rather than focusing exclusive attention on factors internal or external to the movement, the model describes insurgency as a product of both. Specifically, three sets of factors are identified as shaping the generation of insurgency. It is the confluence of expanding political opportunities, indigenous organizational strength, and the presence of certain shared cognitions within the minority community that is held to facilitate movement emergence. Over time these factors continue to shape the development of insurgency in combination with a fourth factor: the shifting control response of other groups to the movement.

NOTES

1. Besides the Rule-Tilly piece, other writings by political theorists have had considerable influence in shaping the perspective outlined here. Indeed, a rapidly growing body of literature on social movements has emerged in recent years and precipitated something of a conceptual revolution in the field. The political process model draws heavily on that literature, even as it reflects a critical stance toward much that has been written. Of those contributing to the literature, the following theorists have advanced specific insights that have been incorporated into the model proposed here: Aveni (1977); Edelman (1971); Ferree and Miller (1977); Freeman (1973); Gamson (1975); Gerlach and Hine (1970); Jenkins (1981); Jenkins and Perrow (1977); Marx (1976); McCarthy and Zald (1973); Oberschall (1973); Pinard (1971); Piven and

Cloward (1979); Schwartz (1976); and Wilson and Orum (1976).

2. Even such perceptive analysts as Piven and Cloward seem to echo this line of argument. They assert, for instance, "that it not only requires a major social dislocation before protest can emerge, but that a sequence or combination of dislocations probably must occur before the anger that underlies protest builds to a high pitch, and before that anger can find expression in collective defiance" (Piven and Cloward, 1979: 8). Consistent with the classical model, the image is that of disruptive social change, triggering a rise in aggregate discontent which eventually erupts into collective protest. This causal sequence remains problematic.

3. Indeed, the search for micro-level correlates of individual participation has frequently provided evidence of the central importance of existent associational networks. Orum, in his analysis of protest participation among black college students, compared nonparticipants and participants on a number of background variables such as family income, father's education, incidence of parental desertion, and size of place of residence. In general, the variables tested failed to produce any significant association with protest participation. There was, however, one exception. The variable that best distinguished participants from non-participants was simply the student's integration into the campus community, as measured by number of memberships in campus organizations (Orum, 1972: 27–50).

4. Judging from the passage of Proposition 13 in California we can be reasonably sure that the lack of a "pre-established communication network" was remedied in the twenty-odd years that intervened between the earlier tax revolt and the successful 1978 version.

5. For a general review or introduction to the literature on cultural diffusion, see Brown (1981), Lionberger (1960), or Rogers (1962).

6. Zald and Ash (1970) were but the first to challenge the inevitability ascribed to the process by Weber and Michels (Gerth and Mills, 1946: 297–301; Michels, 1959). Moreover, there now exists impressive empirical evidence supportive of the facilitating, rather than retardant, effect of organization on insurgency (Gamson, 1975: esp. chap. 7; C. Tilly, L. Tilly, and R. Tilly, 1975). Accordingly, current research in the field has shifted from describing the process of oligarchization to specifying the conditions under which movement organizations can be expected to develop in conservative or radical ways (Beach, 1977; Gillespie, 1980).

7. These observations are not made to suggest that insurgent groups should avoid goals and tactics that are likely to be seen by the political establishment as threatening. Indeed, my earlier assertion that the strength of insurgent forces is also a determinant of other groups' responses to the movement carries with it the implicit suggestion that insurgents can pursue any goal or tactic so long as they maintain the strength needed to withstand the social control response these choices produce. Instead, my aim has simply been to discuss the relationship between these various choices and the level of movement opposition they engender. The key point is that movement groups largely determine, by means of the goals and tactics they adopt, the level of opposition they must confront. As Schwartz notes, "in choosing movement activities, a protest group can attain a degree of control over who the opposition will be, and to what degree it will be mobilized" (1976: 162). It therefore behooves insurgents to base their choice of tactics and goals on some realistic assessment of their strength. If they are to survive, movement groups must avoid mobilizing an opposition that is capable of successfully repressing the movement.

REFERENCES

Abeles, Ronald P. 1976. "Relative Deprivation, Rising Expectations, and Black Militancy." *Journal of Social Issues* 32 (no. 2): 119–37.

Arendt, Hannah. 1951. *The Origins of Totalitarianism.* New York: Harcourt, Brace.

Aya, Rod. 1979. "Theories of Revolution Reconsidered: Contrasting Models of Collective Violence." *Theory and Society* 8 (no. 1): 39–99.

Broom, Leonard. 1959. "Social Differentiation and Stratification." In Robert K. Merton, Leonard Broom, and Leonard S. Cottrell, eds., *Sociology Today.* New York: Basic Books, 429–41.

Cameron, David R. 1974. "Toward a Theory of Political Mobilization." *Journal of Politics* 36 (February): 133–71.

Currie, Elliott, and Jerome Skolnick. 1970. "A Critical Note on Conceptions of Collective

Behavior." *Annals of the American Academy of Political and Social Science* 391 (September): 34–45.

Dahl, Robert A. 1967. *Pluralist Democracy in the United States.* Chicago: Rand McNally.

Freeman, Jo. 1973. "The Origins of the Women's Liberation Movement." *American Journal of Sociology* 78 (no. 4): 792–811.

Gamson, William A. 1975. *The Strategy of Social Protest.* Homewood, Ill.: The Dorsey Press.

Garfinkel, Herbert. 1959. *When Negroes March.* Glencoe, Ill.: The Free Press.

Geschwender, James A. 1971a. "Explorations in the Theory of Social Movements and Revolutions." In James A. Geschwender, ed., *The Black Revolt.* Englewood Cliffs, N.J.: Prentice-Hall, 6–17.

Geschwender, James A. 1971b. "Social Structure and the Negro Revolt: An Examination of Some Hypotheses." In James A. Geschwender, ed., *The Black Revolt.* Englewood Cliffs, N.J.: Prentice-Hall, 33–43.

Gusfield, Joseph R. 1970. *Protest, Reform, and Revolt.* New York: John Wiley and Sons.

Hoffer, Eric. 1951. *The True Believer: Thoughts on the Nature of Mass Movements.* New York: Mentor Books, The New American Library.

Jenkins, Joseph Craig, and Charles Perrow. 1977. "Insurgency of the Powerless: Farm Worker Movements (1946–1972)." *American Sociological Review* 42 (no. 2): 249–68.

Kornhauser, William. 1959. *The Politics of Mass Society.* Glencoe, Ill.: The Free Press.

Lang, Kurt, and Gladys Lang. 1961. *Collective Dynamics.* New York: Crowell.

Le Bon, Gustave. 1960. *The Crowd: A Study of the Popular Mind.* New York: Compass Books, The Viking Press.

Leites, Nathan, and Charles Wolf, Jr. 1970. *Rebellion and Authority.* Chicago: Markham.

Lenski, Gerhard. 1954. "Status Crystallization: A Non-vertical Dimension of Social Status." *American Sociological Review* 19 (August): 405–13.

McCarthy, John D., and Mayer N. Zald. 1973. *The Trend of Social Movements in America: Professionalization and Resource Mobilization.* Morristown, N.J.: General Learning Press.

McCormack, Thelma H. 1957. "The Motivation of Radicals." In R. H. Turner and L. M. Killian, eds., *Collective Behavior.* Englewood Cliffs, N.J.: Prentice-Hall, 433–40.

Morris, Aldon Douglas. 1979. "The Rise of the Civil Rights Movement and Its Movement Black Power Structure, 1953–1963." Ph.D. diss., State University of New York at Stony Brook.

Oberschall, Anthony. 1973. *Social Conflict and Social Movements.* Englewood Cliffs, N.J.: Prentice-Hall.

Orum, Anthony M. 1972. *Black Students in Protest.* Washington, D.C.: American Sociological Association.

Pinard, Maurice. 1971. *The Rise of a Third Party: A Study in Crisis Politics.* Englewood Cliffs, N.J.: Prentice-Hall.

Pinard, Maurice, Jerome Kirk, and Donald Von Eschen. 1971. "Process of Recruitment in the Sit-in Movement." In James A. Geschwender, ed., *The Black Revolt.* Englewood Cliffs, N.J.: Prentice-Hall, 184–97.

Rogin, Michael Paul. 1967. *The Intellectuals and McCarthy.* Cambridge, Mass.: M.I.T. Press.

Rule, James, and Charles Tilly, eds. 1975. "Political Process in Revolutionary France: 1830–1832." In John M. Merriman, ed., *1830 in France.* New York: New Viewpoints, 41–85.

Schattschneider, E. E. 1960. *The Semisovereign People.* Hinsdale, Ill.: The Dryden Press.

Schwartz, Michael. 1976. *Radical Protest and Social Structure.* New York: Academic Press.

Selznick, Phillip. 1970. "Institutional Vulnerability in Mass Society." In Joseph R. Gusfield, ed., *Protest, Reform, and Revolt.* New York: John Wiley and Sons, 258–74.

Shorter, Edward, and Charles Tilly. 1974. *Strikes in France, 1830–1968.* London: Cambridge University Press.

Smelser, Neil J. 1959. *Social Change in the Industrial Revolution.* Chicago: University of Chicago Press.

Smelser, Neil J. 1962. *Theory of Collective Behavior.* New York: The Free Press.

Tilly, Charles, Louise Tilly, and Richard Tilly. 1975. *The Rebellious Century, 1830–1930.* Cambridge, Mass.: Harvard University Press.

Turner, Ralph H., and Lewis Killian. 1957. *Collective Behavior.* Englewood Cliffs, N.J.: Prentice-Hall.

Wilson, Kenneth L., and Anthony M. Orum. 1976. "Mobilizing People for Collective Political Action." *Journal of Political and Military Sociology* 4 (Fall): 187–202.

Wilson, John. 1973. *Introduction to Social Movements.* New York: Basic Books.

Wolfinger, Raymond, et al. 1964. "America's Radical Right." In David Apter, ed., *Ideology and Discontent.* Glencoe, Ill.: The Free Press, 267–75.

13
<hr>

BEYOND RESOURCE MOBILIZATION?
Emerging Trends in Social Movement Theory

STEVEN M. BUECHLER

Resource mobilization (RM) theory is now the dominant theoretical framework for analyzing social movements and collective action within the discipline of sociology. This ascendancy may be traced from early programmatic statements (McCarthy and Zald 1973, 1977; Oberschall 1973) through subsequent critiques and reformulations (Ferree and Miller 1985; Fireman and Gamson 1979; Jenkins 1983; Klandermans 1984; Marx and Wood 1975; Perrow 1979; Piven and Cloward 1977; Snow et al. 1986) to a number of empirical studies which have sought to test and modify the theory (Cable et al. 1988; Gamson et al. 1982; McAdam 1982; Morris 1984; Rochford 1985; Walsh 1978, 1981; Walsh and Warland 1983; Zurcher and Snow 1981).

In this essay, I describe some problematic issues that have emerged from this fruitful period of work and that collectively pose a significant challenge to the theoretical dominance of the RM framework. Most of these issues can be exemplified by my own research into women's movements in the United States (Buechler 1986, 1990). My argument is that while there is no clearly defined contender for theoretical dominance, we are nonetheless entering a period of sustained debate and theoretical turmoil which may well lead to such an alternative.

<hr>

Reprinted from *The Sociological Quarterly*, Vol. 34, No. 1, pp. 217–235, by permission. Copyright © 1993 by Midwest Sociology Society.

I begin with brief overviews of the RM framework and my research on women's movements. I then identify a number of emerging trends in social movement theory which collectively imply the need for a new theoretical paradigm. I conclude with a brief evaluation of whether the RM framework will be able to respond effectively to these theoretical challenges.

The Resource Mobilization Framework

RM theory emerged in the 1970s as a distinctively new approach to the study of social movements. According to this perspective, social movements are an extension of politics by other means, and can be analyzed in terms of conflicts of interest just like other forms of political struggle. Movements are also seen as structured and patterned, so that they can be analyzed in terms of organizational dynamics just like other forms of institutionalized action (Oberschall 1973; McCarthy and Zald 1973, 1977; Tilly 1978). In sharp contrast to the earlier collective behavior tradition (Turner and Killian 1957; Smelser 1962), RM theory views social movements as normal, rational, institutionally rooted, political challenges by aggrieved groups. The border between conventional politics and social movements thus becomes blurred, but does not disappear altogether. Whereas established, special-interest groups have routine, low-cost access to powerful decision-makers, social movements must pay higher costs to gain a comparable degree of influence within the polity. RM theory thereby redefined the study of collective action from an example of deviance and social disorganization to a case study in political and organizational sociology (Buechler 1990).

RM theory also takes a distinct position on questions of recruitment, motivation, and participation. Based on a rational actor model, individuals are viewed as weighing the relative costs and benefits of movement participation and opting for participation when the potential benefits outweigh the anticipated costs (McCarthy and Zald 1977). When movement goals take the form of public goods which cannot be denied to nonparticipants, the free-rider dilemma is created because it is individually rational for each actor to let others win the goal and then share the benefits without the costs. In response to the free-rider dilemma, organizations may offer selective incentives for active participants which can be withheld from nonparticipants (Olson 1965). This logic has been criticized as economistic by those who argue that collective, moral, purposive, or solidary incentives often motivate people to join movements even if they could theoretically "ride free" on the efforts of others (Fireman and Gamson 1979). The role of different incentives remains a subject of debate, but the debate assumes rational actors on the individual level just as it assumes the normality of movements on the collective level (Buechler 1990).

Theoretical development never occurs in a sociopolitical vacuum. The emergence and increasing prominence of RM in the 1970s and 1980s was a response to the cycle of protest that was initiated in the United States by the civil rights movement and that spread to numerous other groups and issues during the 1960s and early 1970s. Many sociologists felt an affinity with the goals of these movements, and some were active participants in them. When they sought theoretical explanations of these movements, however, they found that existing theories were of limited utility and often contained both inaccurate and unflattering depictions of protest movements and their participants. Turner and Killian's (1957) formulation of the collective behavior tradition was oriented to short-term, spontaneous actions and was not well-suited to studying ongoing, organized, political forms of protest. Kornhauser's (1959) analysis of a mass society in which only the most marginal, socially isolated people would become involved in collective behavior seemed to fly in the face of mobilization patterns in 1960s movements. Smelser's (1962) assumptions that collective behavior involved a short-circuiting of institutional channels by irrational actors under the sway of generalized beliefs were an especially inappropriate way to analyze much (though not all) of the protest behavior of the 1960s. And Gurr's (1970) synthesis of relative deprivation approaches ultimately tested on psychological models of frustration-aggression which also distorted more than they revealed about many forms of activism. Against this theoretical backdrop, the RM framework offered an appealing alternative for many sociologists.

It is doubtful that RM theory would have emerged simply in response to the theoretical weaknesses of prior approaches. Such weaknesses were not fully apparent until a wave of protest movements appeared which dramatized the lack of fit between theoretical assumptions and forms of protest. The emergence of RM theory occurred at a particular, socio-historical moment when it became evident that the theoretical premises of prior approaches to collective behavior could no longer provide adequate analytical leverage or interpretive understanding of contemporary social movement activity. RM theory was well received almost from the beginning because it provided a set of assumptions and hypotheses which had a better fit with, and a readier application to emergent forms of social movement activity. Assumptions about the normality of protest challenged older theories and resonated with the sociopolitical climate. Assumptions about the rationality of activists rejected earlier premises about protesters and provided a more congenial view of their motives. RM theory therefore offered a satisfying resolution of the increasing tensions between prior theories and emerging movements.

Within the study of collective action, the appearance of the RM framework thereby constituted something of a paradigm shift which resolved a mounting crisis in this sociological subfield (Kuhn 1962). Since the rise and consolidation of this new paradigm in the mid-to-late 1970s, a great deal of sociological work on social movements has taken the form of "normal science" which operates within the assumptions of RM theory and examines the relative weight of various factors in the course of social activism. During this period, there has been considerable progress in clarifying questions about recruitment, mobilization, strategy, tactics, and the like. However, after a decade-and-a-half of more or less cumulative progress and theoretical development, the RM framework appears to be coming under increasing challenge in the form of new issues and questions which cannot readily be resolved within this framework. It is likely that these issues will precipitate another theoretical crisis in the study of social movements, and it is possible that a period of theoretical contestation will usher in a new paradigm for the study of social movement activism.[1] This essay does not attempt to predict these events. Rather, my goal is to identify some of the emerging issues which challenge and transgress the limits of RM theory, and

which will shape the contours of theoretical debate in the foreseeable future.

Women's Movements in the United States

These theoretical and metatheoretical issues are best illustrated by specific social movements. Women's movements provide an analytically interesting and empirically rich context for identifying and evaluating problematic issues for RM theory (Cott 1987; Rupp and Taylor; Staggenborg 1988, 1989; Taylor 1989a, 1989b). My own research has taken a comparative and historical approach to women's mobilization across two centuries. In the first phase of this work, I undertook extensive archival research into the woman suffrage movement in Illinois. This involved a detailed inspection of thousands of documents in the form of letters, diaries, novels, organizational records, movement publications, newspaper accounts, and the like. These efforts were complemented by selective primary research into the national suffrage movement and extensive reading of secondary sources (Buechler 1986). In the second phase of this work, I again undertook detailed archival research into the organizational records of the National Organization for Women and the Chicago Women's Liberation Union, complemented by extensive reading of the rapidly growing literature on the contemporary women's movement. These two phases of research culminated in a comparative anaysis of women's movements in the United States (Buechler 1990). This article builds on this research, as well as the work of others, to identify emerging new directions in the social movement theory.

Women's political mobilization began in the 1840s as a broadly oriented women's rights movement pursuing a radical agenda which went well beyond the right to vote and posed a major challenge to the sexual division of labor. Immediately after the Civil War, the movement experienced internal strife and interorganizational conflict which weakened its momentum and undermined its radical orientation. During the last three decades of the nineteenth century, the movement was in a period of relative dormancy and was eclipsed by the temperance movement. The latter's ideology of protecting the home and saving the family appealed to many women, and led to a more moderate ideological posture in the woman suffrage movement. After the turn of the century, a new generation of leaders brought strategic and tactical sophistication to the woman suffrage movement and aligned it with progressive politics. Efforts were made to expand the base of the movement, leading to significant growth in the membership of woman suffrage organizations after 1910. The movement also diversified ideologically, constructing a wide range of arguments for the vote. By 1915, the movement consisted of a sophisticated leadership, a diverse base, and a cross-class, multi-constituency alliance. As a result, the movement was able to take advantage of new political opportunities during and after World War I, and it thereby succeeded in winning the right to vote for women (Buechler 1986; DuBois 1978; Flexner 1975; O'Neill 1969).

The "second wave" of women's activism began in the 1960s. A women's rights sector emerged out of the Presidential Commission on the Status of Women and culminated in the formation of the National Organization for Women in 1966. A women's liberation sector appeared somewhat later, emerging out of the myriad dissatisfactions of women with sexist treatment in other social movements of the time. From the late 1960s to the mid-1970s, the contemporary women's movement was a genuinely mass movement, due in large part to the women's liberation sector and its emphasis on small,

decentralized groups and consciousness-raising activities. After passage of the Equal Rights Amendment in 1972 and the Roe v. Wade Supreme Court decision in 1973, factionalism began to undercut this mass mobilization and the first countermovements appeared. By the late 1970s, the balance was tipping and by the early 1980s, feminism was on the defensive in the face of a rising conservative tide and ongoing countermobilization. Despite these obstacles, the contemporary women's movement has survived, and it continues to wage strong battles for reproductive rights among other issues. Although the mass movement phase ended some time ago, the persistence of formal movement organizations and informal social movement communities testifies to the persistence of a women's movement into the last decade of the twentieth century (Buechler 1990; Freeman 1975; Ferree and Hess 1985).

The documentary record of women's activism across two centuries provides good examples of particular mobilizations in specific socio-historical contexts. As such, this record can help illustrate some of the emerging issues in social movement theory.

Emerging Trends

There are at least ten issues which pose some degree of challenge to the RM framework of studying social movements. While none of these issues are individually insurmountable, they collectively constitute a fundamental challenge to the RM framework. These issues may be loosely grouped into several categories. Some involve empirical generalizations on which there is conflicting evidence. Others involve aspects of collective action which appear increasingly important but are typically ignored by the RM framework. Still others involve core assumptions of the theory itself. By identifying and briefly describing these issues, we can understand the challenge confronting RM theory and identify emerging trends in social movement theory. The first three issues identified below are the subject of very extensive analysis elsewhere (Buechler 1990) and will be quickly summarized here; the latter seven issues reflect developments in the field generally, although most of these can also be illustrated by reference to women's movements.

Rethinking Grievances

From its origins, at least one strand of RM theory has consistently downplayed the role of grievances in the emergence of collective action (Buechler 1990; McCarthy and Zald 1973, 1977). This stance is typically defended by reference to many groups who have long-standing grievances but never are able to mount any collective challenge to the social arrangements which produce those grievances. RM proponents thus claim that grievances may be a necessary but are not a sufficient factor in explaining social movements; they proceed to argue that control over actual and potential resources is a more important determinant of the emergence as well as the likely success of collective action. In its most extreme form, the argument is that grievances can be assumed as a constant, background factor with no explanatory relevance, while changes in access to resources of many sorts will be the critical, variable factor which explains the periodic appearance of collective action. While other strands of the RM framework are somewhat more attentive to the issue of grievances (Tilly 1978), none would rank them on a par with resources in accounting for collective action and social protest.

Women's movements have typically emerged from "parent movements" like abolitionism, the civil rights movement, or the new left. As a result, women's movements have sometimes been presented as cases in which women derived both resources and grievances from their participation in parent movements and subsequently mobilized as women. However, a closer look suggests that the woman suffrage movement of the 19th century and the women's rights sector of the contemporary women's movement were both led by women with preexisting feminist grievances. When these longstanding grievances were combined with newfound resources from parent movements, women's movements emerged. These cases are thus consistent with the logic of the RM framework. However, the women's liberation sector of the contemporary women's movement did appear to formulate its grievances largely in the context of women's participation in parent movements which treated them unequally. Hence, the movement which has most radically challenged patriarchal power developed its grievances through interactive dynamics in parent movements which subsequently prompted the independent mobilization of women. This suggests that in some cases, grievances can be at least as important as access to resources in explaining the emergence of social movements (Buechler 1990).

These specific differences are best explained in generational terms. Members of the women's liberation movement tended to be younger women with relatively less exposure to systematic gender discrimination until their activist careers in other movements (Buechler 1990). The more general lesson is that grievances cannot be assumed to be a constant background factor in the study of social movements. Put differently, the social construction of grievances may be the critical step which allows members of socially dispersed groups to begin to mobilize for action. One of the core assumptions of the RM framework may thus lead its practitioners to gloss over what may be a fundamentally important part of the mobilization process.

Recognizing Ideology

Just as the RM framework has downplayed grievances, it has also marginalized ideology (Buechler 1990). This is a logical consequence of the emphasis placed on resources and opportunity in accounting for movement origins and persistence (Tilly 1978). This marginalization typically occurs by equating ideology with the expression of grievances, and then dismissing both as constant background factors with little explanatory relevance (McCarthy and Zald 1977). However, the expression of grievances does not exhaust the functions of ideology. In the broadest sense, ideology encompasses the ideas, beliefs, values, symbols, and meanings that motivate individual participation and give coherence to collective action. Ideological beliefs typically provide a critical diagnosis of the larger society, an idealized sketch of a positive alternative, and some suggestion as to how the problematic present may be replaced with a preferable future (Buechler 1990; see Wilson 1973 for a similar view). Ideology often performs multiple functions, including transforming vague dissatisfactions into a politicized agenda, providing a sense of collective identity, and defining certain goods as potential movement resources. It may be that for some constituencies, these processes may be taken for granted and do not require analysis. But it is also clear that for many others, the multiple roles of ideology are critical prerequisites for effective movement mobilization.

Women's movements provide a good test case of the importance of ideology. Indeed, the major accomplishment of feminist ideology is to create the very conditions which the RM framework takes for granted in the study of movement mobilization. It is through the development and diffusion of feminist ideology that grievances become politicized ("the personal is political"), that

women develop a collective identity rooted in gender, and that they reinterpret their social environment as consisting of potential movement resources. Over the history of women's movements in the United States, a variety of different ideological belief systems have contributed to these outcomes. The early suffrage movement was rooted in a radical ideology of women's rights which challenged many of the roots of patriarchal power. During its middle period, this radically egalitarian women's rights agenda was partially displaced by a social-feminist ideology which emphasized women's essential, underlying differences from men. In the final period, a plethora of ideological beliefs managed to successfully coexist in a manner which facilitated mass mobilization and the eventual success of the suffrage movement (Buechler 1986). The contemporary women's movement picked up with the same theme of ideological diversity with which the woman suffrage movement ended. Contemporary feminist ideologies range from liberal to radical to socialist to cultural to lesbian and beyond; the only fair generalization is that there has never been a significant movement sector which does not have a distinct and well-developed ideological position (Buechler 1990; Taylor and Whittier, unpublished).

Even in the supposedly pragmatic political culture of the United States, it is clear that women's movements have always operated with more-or-less explicit, ideological world views to foster mobilization, formulate goals, and debate strategy. The more general lesson is that for at least some constituencies, ideological work is a critical component of movement mobilization. It is often vital in politicizing discontent, fostering collective identity, and defining movement resources (Buechler 1990). Hence, the tendency of the RM framework to marginalize ideological issues may deflect critical attention from one of the most vital processes of movement formation.

Deconstructing Organization

RM theory has underscored the centrality of organization to the mobilization of movements in at least two major ways. First, all versions of the theory have identified preexisting forms of organization as critical in facilitating mobilization. This claim is richly confirmed by women's movements, all of which have built on preexisting networks. Second, some versions of RM theory have equated organization with formal, bureaucratic, centralized structures, as in McCarthy and Zald's distinctions between social movements (SMs), social movement organizations (SMOs), social movement industries (SMIs), and the social movement sector (SMS) (1977). Since they define SMs as "preference structures" in a population, the only actors in their conceptual scheme are SMOs, defined as complex or formal organizations whose goals match the preferences of a movement. There is an organizational bias in this implication that only formally organized bodies can act effectively. Once again, there are other strands of RM theory which are somewhat more receptive to the role of informal organizational structures, but the dominant tendency within the theory favors formal organization.

This organizational bias is particularly evident in the case of women's movements. To understand these movements, we need the concept of a social movement community (SMC) to designate informally organized networks of movement activists (Buechler 1990; see Gerlach and Hine [1970] for a related formulation). We need such a concept because in the history of women's movements, SMCs have probably played a larger role then SMOs in mobilizing women and pursuing movement goals. In the first

stage of the woman suffrage movement, there were no formal organizations which expressed women's emerging agenda, although there were many informal social networks and links among women's rights activists. In the middle stage, there were multiple SMOs which constituted a broader SMC of activist women which kept the suffrage issue alive. In the final stage. it was a combination of SMOs and SMCs which created the critical momentum needed to finally win the right to vote. At no stage can this history be understood without the notion of informal organization. In the contemporary women's movement, the women's liberation sector is perhaps the best example of an SMC because this sector consciously and explicitly repudiated formal organization on ideological grounds, and strove to discover and implement more egalitarian forms of organization. The women's rights sector offers more typical examples of SMOs (like the National Organization for Women) but even here, the periods of most successful activism by such organizations have been in conjunction with informally organized SMCs (Buechler 1990).

The history of women's movements in the United States suggests that SMCs have been critical in every major period of feminist mobilization, while SMOs have sometimes been nonexistent or marginal in these events (Buechler 1990). The more general lesson is that formal organization cannot be assumed to be the predominant or even the most common form for mobilizing collective action. Giving equal theoretical weight to SMCs can open up a series of important hypotheses about the conditions under which groups organize in one or another form and the relation between a group's ideological commitments and organizational form. Once again, one of the core assumptions of RM theory about formal organization can blind investigators to the theoretical value and strategic importance of different organizational forms.

Distinguishing Levels of Analysis

Sociological research within the RM framework has tended to operate on the meso-level of analysis to the relative exclusion of both macro-level and micro-level explorations of collective action.[2] This is a logical extension of RM's emphasis on the role of organization and the mobilization of resources as central to understanding such action. Given a historical context of sociological theories which traditionally approached collective behavior as a micro-level phenomenon to be explained in social-psychological terms or as the manifestation of macro-level social disorganization and breakdown, the establishment of the meso-level of analysis was an important step forward. By reorienting the study of collective action to this level, the connecting links between macro-structures and micro-processes were highlighted. However, there is a tendency within the RM framework to focus so exclusively on the meso-level of organizational analysis that "larger" questions of social structure and historical change and "smaller" issues of individual motivation and social interaction receive scant attention. The result is an image of movement organizations as reified social actors detached from larger structural constraints and historical contexts as they engage in collective action. Having developed such analytical strengths at the meso-level, it is now time for social movement theory to move both "up" and "down" by more thoroughly theorizing and studying the macro-level and micro-level determinants of collective action (for a related assessment, see McAdam, McCarthy, and Zald, 1988).

The study of women's movements illustrates the need for these theoretical moves.

The RM framework is quite helpful in understanding the inter-organizational dynamics of this (and other) movements, but it is less helpful in explaining their socio-historical determinants or the variable ability of such movements to recruit a committed membership. In analyzing the origins of women's movements in both the 19th and 20th centuries, I found it necessary to distinguish between "background conditions" and "proximate causes" (Buechler 1990). RM theory was applicable to the latter by orienting me to the role of parent movements, changing opportunity structures, newfound access to resources, and the like. But RM theory provides no particular guidance on the macro-structural determinants of such activism even though they were essential to understanding the origins and subsequent history of feminist activism. Such factors included capitalist industrialization, state consolidation, demographic changes, alterations in family structure, labor force participation, and educational attainment. Without these background conditions, the meso-level mobilization dynamics emphasized by RM theory would never have occurred. Although it was not a major focus of my research, RM theory was also unhelpful on questions of individual recruitment and commitment on the micro-level. Women's movements have had few of the resources required to overcome the free-rider problem by offering selective incentives, and yet they have experienced periods of intense recruitment and high commitment which the RM framework is ill-equipped to explain.

Understanding the relation between micro- and macro-levels of society is one of the most vexing problems in sociological theory today, but theorists of varying persuasions are nonetheless offering some intriguing ways to approach such questions. Social movement theory seems like a particularly fruitful area for pursuing such work because movements are fascinating microcosms of social constructions which require individual participation while also being embedded in larger, socio-historical contexts. Precisely because of RM's strengths in understanding the meso-level, social movement theory is well-positioned to begin attending to multiple levels of analysis by either elaborating or transcending the RM framework. Such development would not only help us understand social movements more clearly; it could also make significant contributions to more general sociological theory. In the next two sections, I identify some work that is already being done or that might be done to promote such theoretical development.

Interpreting the Micro-Level

Some of the most recent work within the RM framework has begun to move in the direction of closer scrutiny of micro-level processes in social movement activism. Indeed, RM appears more amenable to a synthesis of meso- and micro-levels than a comparable synthesis of meso- and macro-levels. In any case, the growing attention to the micro-level of analysis within the RM framework may contribute to the resolution of a paradox which has been at the center of RM theory from the beginning. The initial formulations of RM theory in the mid-1970s seemed to offer a succinct rebuttal to earlier theoretical approaches which tacitly assumed that participation in social movements indicated some degree of individual irrationality. The rebuttal was to posit the rational actor as a way of understanding movement participation based on a cost-benefit calculus. The new problem was the free-rider and the potential solution was selective incentives (Olson 1965). The lingering problem to the potential solution was that many movements have been able to recruit devoted followers without selective incentives while some others have not been able to

garner much support even with such incentives. The lingering problem casts doubt on the rational actor model at the heart of RM's understanding of individual participation.

These issues have been episodically identified and debated almost from the origin of the RM framework by those who have suggested that factors like solidarity, group interests, loyalty, responsibility, or urgency may be more fundamental in motivating individual participation than any utilitarian calculation of costs and benefits (Fireman and Gamson 1979). Other critics have argued that explaining movement participation on utilitarian grounds quickly becomes tautological if interpreted broadly or demonstrably false if interpreted narrowly. Such criticisms have led to calls for a recognition of the role of ideology as an intervening variable, for some attention to the effect of social organization on cognitive processes, and for a richer social psychological theory to complement RM's emphasis on resources and organization (Ferree and Miller 1985). Subsequent research within the RM framework has provided a clearer empirical understanding of micro-level processes in social movements. These efforts include work on framing activity and vocabularies of motive (Snow and Benford 1988; Benford 1993); work on the creation of a willingness to participate and on consensus mobilization (Klandermans 1984, 1988); work on the interactive role of spontaneity and direct democracy in movements (Rosenthal and Schwartz 1989); and work on understanding contexts of micro-mobilization as settings for collective attribution and frame alignment (McAdam, McCarthy, and Zald 1988).

Of all the issues identified in this paper, the interpretation of the micro-level has received the most attention and appears most amenable to a modified RM framework. This also reflects a cycle of attention in social movement theory. RM displaced a strong presumption about the irrationality of movement activists by positing the model of the rational actor and exorcising the premise of irrationality. This premise also helped reorient social movement theory to the meso-level of organizational analysis. Having established the general premise that social movement activism could be a reasonable thing for people to do, the specifically utilitarian image of the rational actor came under increasing scrutiny which in turn led to the identification of a number of important, micro-level, social-psychological processes of movement mobilization. Despite this work, the rational actor model has not been displaced by this new attention to the micro-level. As we will see in a moment, this model is also under attack on metatheoretical grounds.

Theorizing the Macro-Level

While there has been a sustained effort to move from the meso-level to the micro-level within the RM framework, there has been much less attention paid to the macro-level. Research in the organizational tradition of McCarthy and Zald may give fleeting attention to the macro-level to explain movement origins through changes in the availability of resources, but the subsequent analysis typically ignores this level. Research in the political tradition of Tilly may be somewhat more attentive to how macro-level change alters political opportunity structures for collective action, but once again the subsequent analysis tends to focus on the meso-level. Despite this difference in degree, both versions of RM theory take an eclectic and somewhat ad hoc approach to structural issues, and neither offers any systematic theory of how macro-level organization might affect movements (and vice versa) beyond resource availability or opportunity structures. Since these processes can really only be theoretically understood over significant periods of his-

torical time, this insensitivity to the macro-level also means a distinctly ahistorical approach to the study of social movements. While it may always be necessary to bracket some aspects of social reality so as to scrutinize others, the consistent tendency of the RM framework to ignore macro-structural and historical contexts has undermined its ability to understand the dynamics of collective action.

There has been no major effort to resolve this problem and theorize the macro-meso link in the way that some have begun to theorize the meso-micro link. In fact, it has become something of a cliche to accept this state of affairs by claiming that the RM framework can explain the "how" of movement mobilization while we must turn to other theoretical frameworks (typically new social movement theory) to understand the "why" of structural determination (Klandermans 1986). At this stage, it is less important which specific approach is taken to the macro-level than that the importance of taking some such approach be recognized. Three possibilities may be briefly mentioned here. First, Habermas's analysis of modern society as consisting of a technocratic system world of economic and political imperatives and a sociocultural lifeworld which is being colonized by systemic imperatives offers a highly general theory of the macro-structure which nonetheless has clear implications for social movement activism. For Habermas, such activism is most likely to occur along the "seams" between system and lifeworld and to congeal around the roles of employee, consumer, client, and citizen (1984/1987). Second, and at a less abstract level, recent work in political economy has attempted to delineate the contours of an emerging postindustrial society in the U.S. and Europe and to assess the prospects for social movement activism in these newly emerging social forms (Block 1987, 1990; Touraine 1981). Finally, recent work on multiculturalism and social diversity has suggested the utility of a conception of society as consisting of multiple structures of domination which are both the cause and the target of a good deal of contemporary social movement activism (Buechler 1990; Collins 1990).

The inattentiveness of scholars within the RM framework to the macro-level is particularly curious because contemporary social theory offers several promising approaches to the macro-level in general and to resolving the problems of the micro-macro gap in particular (Ritzer, 1992; Collins, 1988; Giddens 1984). The relative ease with which the RM framework has moved "down" to the micro-level needs to be complemented by moving "up" to the macro-level in some coherent theoretical fashion. Failure to do so will reinforce RM's implicit image of social movement activism as involving reified, free-floating organizations detached from larger socio-historical contexts as they pursue their collective goals.

Transcending the Rational Actor

When the model of the rational actor is problematized within the RM framework, it typically appears as a problem of motivation and recruitment exemplified by the free-rider dilemma. However, there is a more basic metatheoretical issue that is implicit in RM's entire approach to movement mobilization. The rational actor model of this theory reflects its heritage in exchange theory. Such models have always been criticized from a sociological perspective (Durkheim 1895; Parsons 1937; Zeitlin 1973), but new criticisms have recently been made by feminist standpoint theorists such as Nancy Hartsock (1985). According to these critics, rational choice theories presume a world "populated by fictive independent, isolated individuals" (Hartsock 1985, p. 67) who have conflicting interests and yet voluntarily enter into profit-seeking exchanges on a presumably equal footing with each other. From this perspective, the ontological assumptions of exchange theory may reflect masculine experience but they fail to capture the more nuanced, relational, communal, nurturant, and empathic world which is more typical of female experience. This perspective suggests that under the best of conditions, the ontological assumptions of RM theory fundamentally limit its utility for understanding the activism of any constituency whose orientation to the world departs from the "fictive" one implicity assumed by rational choice theory (Ferree 1992).

This ontological limit becomes readily evident when trying to understand some sectors of women's activism. The issue is most apparent in the contrast between the two sectors of the contemporary women's movement. The women's rights sector with its liberal feminist ideology and its focus on the public sphere presumes a world which resonates with many of the assumptions of rational choice theory. But the women's liberation sector with its radical feminist ideology presumes a fundamentally different world. Indeed, radical feminism has appealed to precisely those qualities (connection, empathy, intuition, concrete experience, interdependence) that most sharply divide male and female experience and that are most at odds with the assumptions of exchange theory. This ontological gulf between RM theory and radical feminism means that the theory cannot provide any definitive interpretation of this movement because the actors, goals, and actions which the theory presumes do not correspond to the actual actors, goals, and actions of this sector. Thus, what appears as either inexplicable or as a failure from the perspective of RM theory must rather be seen as the inability of this theory to grasp a movement which has explicitly repudiated rational choice principles as the foundation for social activism (Buechler 1990).

As we noted earlier, the rational actor model played an important historical function in reorienting social movement theory from a view of collective behavior as fundamentally irrational. However, by relying on an individualist and utilitarian conception of rational choice, RM theory created a set of analytical puzzles in the form of the free-rider problem which diverted attention from the larger, metatheoretical implications of this model. Upon closer scrutiny, these implications seem increasingly at odds with both sociological and feminist conceptions of the social actor. More recently, this conception has been challenged from another direction by interest in the problem of collective identity.

Analyzing Collective Identity

For RM theory, effective collective action requires gaining access to sufficient resources and motivating rational actors to become involved. Presuming that resources are sufficient and that the free-rider problem can be resolved, the RM framework implicitly assumes that the "preference structures" of individual actors will simply be aggregated until some critical mass is reached and a group constituency is created. With such premises, RM remains remarkably uninterested in who engages in collective action and how they view themselves and their allies in struggle. These questions are central in much work being done under the rubric of "new social movements" where such questions are approached through the concept of collective identity (Cohen 1985; Eder 1985; Melucci 1985, 1988, 1989). This work recognizes that people who participate in collective action do so only when such action resonates with both an individual and a collective identity that makes such action meaningful. For many mobilizations, the most central process is the social construction of a collective identity that is symbolically meaningful to participants and that logically precedes any meaningful calculation of the costs and benefits of joining in collective action. In contrast to the RM framework, such collective identities cannot be taken for granted nor viewed unproblematically; they are better seen as essential outcomes of the mobilization process and crucial prerequisites to movement success.

Women provide one example of a potential movement constituency whose members are not automatically predisposed to identify themselves as women with politicized grievances which can be redressed through collective action. This is one reason why even though gender dominance is virtually universal, collective resistance (at least in the form of mass movements) is relatively rare. One critical intervening process which must occur to get from oppression to resistance is the social construction of a collective identity which unites a significant segment of the movement's potential constituency. This process of socially constructing a collective identity based on gender is made all the more complicated because women are structurally dispersed throughout all other social groups, because they often live in close proximity with their "oppressors," and because their most salient collective identities may be based not on gender but on race, class, and the like. Given these realities, the collective identity of "women" is never firmly established. It rather must be continually constructed and reinforced as one vital aspect of mobilization in women's movements. It is also evident that such identities can never really be treated in isolation from other identities. Thus, those women who are most able to see themselves simply as "women" tend to be women from dominant racial and class groups (Cott 1987), while women from subordinate racial and class groups explicitly meld such identities with their gender identity (Buechler 1990). For all these reasons, a preexisting constituency of women cannot be taken for granted, but rather must be painstakingly constructed and maintained if women's movements are to be successful (for a somewhat parallel argument in the case of racial formation, see Omi and Winant 1986).

The theoretical importance of the social construction of collective identity is that it is logically prior to other social processes which the RM framework regards as central to collective action. Melucci argues that costs and benefits can only be calculated meaningfully after a sense of collective identity is established (1989). I have argued elsewhere that the identification of potential movement resources can only occur once members of a group consciously see themselves as a collectivity with politicized grievances (Buechler 1990). Hence, the RM framework may inadvertently take for granted some of the most central processes of collective action in order to focus on the role of resources and organization. Recent work on collective identity suggests that this focus needs readjustment.

Acknowledging Movement Diversity

If the social construction of collective identity is an ongoing, never-completed task in social movements, this is because movements are often composed of diverse and heterogeneous individuals and subgroups (Gerlach and Hine 1970). For all the reasons just discussed, this issue is also one that does not receive explicit attention within the RM framework although it may be one of the critical determinants of movement mobilization and outcomes. Intramovement diversity can be a potential asset or a liability, although it is perhaps most often viewed as a liability which will lead to factionalism and thereby reduce a movement's chances for success (Gamson 1975). However, diversity can also

be beneficial by expanding a movement's potential constituency and resource base as well as by broadening the arguments which can be made for movement objectives. Until such diversity is recognized as an important variable, however, these processes will likely go undetected (for a recent analysis of gender diversity in one movement, see McAdam 1992). In theoretical terms, the obstacle is a set of background assumptions that view social movements as unitary empirical objects with an underlying essence acting as a character or a personage on a historical stage (Melucci 1988). This movement-as-actor formulation can introduce an unwarranted teleological element if the movement is viewed as having an historical mission to perform, and it often introduces a reductionist element which obscures movement diversity. At the extreme, these problems may warrant replacing the concept of a social movement with alternative conceptions of collective action which carry less metatheoretical and metaphysical baggage (Melluci 1989).

The issue of movement diversity makes it difficult to utilize the RM framework to understand women's movements. Such diversity is evident on at least two levels, and in both cases it has been a central element in the course of women's movements across two centuries. One level of diversity concerns ideology, and the fact that women's movements typically are an ideologically contested terrain in which competing worldviews can always be found. A second level of diversity concerns identity, and the fact that women never mobilize strictly on the basis of gender but always on multiple and diverse bases of class, race, and other identities. The importance of recognizing and analyzing such diversity may be suggested by two counterintuitive examples in which it proved to be a movement asset. In the latter years of the woman suffrage campaign, leaders deliberately developed pro-suffrage arguments for women in almost every conceivable social situation. One could find pamphlets articulating why rural women, working women, wealthy women, homemaking women, and virtually every other subgroup of women required the ballot to protect some specific interest. This tactic helped to neutralize anti-suffrage sentiment and it contributed to the eventual suffrage victory (Buechler 1986). In the contemporary movement, much-publicized divisions around race and class have promoted an explosion of ideological and theoretical work on the nature of feminism which has helped to sustain the momentum of the contemporary movement in inhospitable times (Buechler 1990). In both these examples, diversity proved a movement asset rather than a liability.

While Melucci's suggestion about rejecting the very concept of a social movement may be too extreme, there is growing evidence that crosscurrents of diversity and unity are central to the origin, development, and transformation of collective mobilization. To the extent that the concept of social movement implies unity and homogeneity over diversity and heterogeneity, and to the extent that the RM framework relies on such a concept of social movements, the RM framework may once again be missing a vital element in the social construction of collective action.

Bringing Culture Back In

In the broadest theoretical terms, the RM framework might be characterized as emphasizing instrumental action oriented to political and economic subsystems utilizing generalized media of money and power while ignoring the cultural and symbolic lifeworld which necessarily underpins such strategic action and is increasingly a central focus of much movement activism (Habermas 1984/1987). Put more succinctly,

RM's concern with resources and organization leads it to ignore the role of culture in collective action. If we take culture to refer to symbolic systems of meaning construction, then it can serve as a master concept for many of the more specific issues already discussed in this essay. The formulation of grievances and the articulation of ideology are inseparable from cultural processes of framing, meaning, and signification which are prior to any utilization calculation of costs and benefits. The use of informal, egalitarian forms of organization is best understood not as the result of a strategic calculus but as the expression of some of the core values of a given movement constituency. The construction of collective identity and the inability of such an identity to completely overcome movement diversity cannot be understood without reference to cultural processes of identity formation and group solidarity. The rational actor is "fictive" precisely because this concept detaches social beings from their cultural contexts of values, norms, meanings, and significations. Hence, the call to bring culture back into the study of collective action is one way of summarizing much of what is missing in the conventional RM framework.

Once again, two examples from the history of women's movements will have to suffice to suggest the importance of culture in the study of collective action. In the woman suffrage movement, the period from 1870 to about 1900 has always appeared as a kind of "black hole" in the history of this movement because there were few strategic advances of any sort. However, a closer look suggests that this was an important period in which a movement culture was created that was critical in the eventual success of the movement. One form that this cultural work took involved writing a detailed history of the movement's efforts to date—a history that eventually filled six large volumes entitled *History of Woman Suffrage* (1969). By dedicating themselves to the creation of a cultural record of their activities in an otherwise inhospitable climate, movement leaders created a cultural resource which helped recruit subsequent generations of activists who were able to be more successful in achieving their goals (Buechler 1986; for a similar argument concerning the period from 1920 to 1960, see Rupp and Taylor 1987). In the contemporary women's movement, the creation of "women's culture" has become an explicit goal of some movement sectors. The rationale for this goal is to create a community of support and validation which can sustain alternative identities and visions for people seeking to resist dominant forms of sexism and heterosexism (Taylor and Rupp, unpublished). Such action makes little sense from the strategic calculus of the RM framework, but is eminently reasonable from a standpoint which recognizes the importance of cultural processes in collective action (Taylor and Whittier, unpublished).

The concept of culture conveniently summarizes numerous lacunas in the RM framework. While it is tempting to group these concerns under a generic heading like "expressive" to contrast with the "instrumental" approach of RM theory, such a formulation perpetuates an unfortunate dichotomy. The supposedly instrumental concerns of movement actors in the RM framework are always and inescapably embedded in a larger cultural framework of "expressive" elements concerning meaning, symbols, and signification. Until the cultural foundation of such strategic action is adequately theorized, the RM framework will offer us a very partial view of collective action at best.

Discussion

The issues identified above pose different challenges to the RM framework. Some are primarily empirical in nature, and could be resolved by further research to adjudicate between competing claims about observable processes in social movements. This may prove to be true for factors like grievances, ideology, and organization. Other challenges to the RM framework are more conceptual in nature because they involve its theoretical "silences." In these cases, the theory ignores important movement processes because they do not fit its conceptual schemata. Most of the issues identified in this essay fall into this category. Collective identity, movement diversity, and cultural construction are processes about which the RM framework is silent because its central concepts direct attention elsewhere. These conceptual silences cannot be resolved by collecting more data because conceptual presuppositions define what count as significant data in the first place. Such cases of theoretical contestation cannot be resolved in empirical arenas. Finally, some of the issues identified here pose a fundamental challenge to the core assumptions of the RM framework; the best example is the beleaguered career of the rational actor. This assumption makes not just a conceptual but an ontological claim about a social world of isolated, independent monads who freely enter in contractual arrangements based on self-interest. To the extent that collective action involves other foundations, RM may obscure more than it reveals about that action.

These challenges do not stand alone, but rather form an interconnected web of empirical, conceptual, and ontological issues which collectively imply that the RM framework is entering a period of crisis and that we may be in the early stages of a paradigm shift. There is not a clearly formulated contender for theoretical dominance at this moment, although some important work has been done by primarily European theorists studying "new social movements." If this is to become a competing paradigm, advocates will have to move beyond the preliminary work which is currently available toward a clearer specification of the core assumptions which could define a cohesive alternative to the RM framework. Of those working within this tradition, Alberto Melucci has probably moved further in this direction than anyone else (1989).

The emergence of any theoretical alternative to the RM framework will also be influenced by the current socio-historical context. Early approaches to the study of collective behavior with their distinctive premises about the irrationality of such episodes were, in part, elaborated against the backdrop of fascism. This historical moment was eclipsed by another in the 1960s, when a major paradigm shift toward the RM framework occurred which ushered in a different set of core assumptions about the nature, and in particular the rationality, of collective action. In the ensuing years we have seen the diffusion of social movement strategies, tactics, and ideologies across the entire political spectrum, eclipsing the historical moment of the 1960s cycle of protest. If collective behavior was the theoretical response to the sociopolitical climate of the 1930s, and if the RM framework was the theoretical response to the sociopolitical climate of the 1960s, it remains to interpret the sociopolitical climate of the 1990s and to reformulate social movement theory in ways which will enlighten us about this new historical moment.

NOTES

1. My use of the Kuhnian framework of paradigms, normal science, and scientific crisis is not entirely appropriate here because even proponents of RM have never claimed to be offering a fully articulated, scientific theory. Nonetheless, the RM framework does propose a sufficiently coherent set of core assumptions

and propositions that it can be at least loosely described as a scientific paradigm which may be entering a period of crisis.

2. This claim is more true for the economic-organizational version of RM represented by McCarthy and Zald than it is for the more political version of RM represented by Tilly. However, Tilly has never embraced the term "social movement," and those who study social movements within sociology rely more heavily on the McCarthy and Zald version of RM theory than on Tilly's version. For at least one partial exception and synthesis, see McAdam (1982).

REFERENCES

Benford, Robert D. 1993. "'You Could be the Hundredth Monkey': Collective Action Frames and Vocabularies of Motive within the Nuclear Disarmament Movement." *Sociological Quarterly* 34: 195–216.

Block, Fred. 1987. *Revising State Theory*. Philadelphia: Temple University Press.

———. 1990. *Post-Industrial Possibilities*. Berkeley: University of California Press.

Buechler, Steven M. 1986. *The Transformation of the Woman Suffrage Movement*. New Brunswick, NJ: Rutgers University Press.

———. 1987. "Elizabeth Boynton Harbert and the Ideological Transformation of the Woman Suffrage Movement, 1870–1896." *Signs* 13(1): 78–97.

———. 1990. *Women's Movements in the United States*. New Brunswick, NJ: Rutgers University Press.

Cable, Sherry, Edward J. Walsh, and Rex H. Warland. 1988. "Differential Paths to Political Activism: Comparisons of Four Mobilization Processes after the Three Mile Island Accident." *Social Forces* 66: 951–969.

Cohen, Jean. 1985. "Strategy or Identity: New Theoretical Paradigms and Contemporary Social Movements." *Social Research* 52: 663–716.

Collins, Patricia Hill. 1990. *Black Feminist Thought: Knowledge, Consciousness and the Politics of Empowerment*. Cambridge, MA: Unwin-Hyman.

Collins, Randall. 1988. *Theoretical Sociology*. New York: Harcourt Brace Jovanovich.

Cott, Nancy. 1987. *The Grounding of Modern Feminism*. New Haven: Yale University Press.

DuBois, Ellen. 1978. *Feminism and Suffrage*. Ithaca: Cornell University Press.

Durkheim, Emile. 1895. *The Division of Labor in Society.* New York: Free Press.

Eder, Klaus. 1985. "The 'New Social Movements': Moral Crusades, Political Pressure Groups, or Social Movements?" *Social Research* 52: 869–890.

Ferree, Myra Marx. 1992. "The Political Context of Rationality: Rational Choice Theory and Resource Mobilization." Pp. 29–52 in *Frontiers of Social Movement Theory,* edited by Aldon Morris and Carol Mueller. New Haven: Yale University Press.

Ferree, Myra Marx and Beth Hess. 1985. *Controversy and Coalition: The New Feminist Movement.* Boston: G. K. Hall/Twayne.

Ferree, Myra Marx and Frederick D. Miller. 1985. "Mobilization and Meaning: Toward an Integration of Social Psychological and Resource Perspectives on Social Movements." *Sociological Inquiry* 55: 38–61.

Fireman, Bruce and William Gamson. 1979. "Utilitarian Logic in the Resource Mobilization Perspective." Pp. 8–44 in *The Dynamics of Social Movements,* edited by Mayer N. Zald and John D. McCarthy. Cambridge: Winthrop.

Flexner, Eleanor. 1975. *Century of Struggle.* Cambridge: Harvard University Press.

Freeman, Jo. 1975. *The Politics of Women's Liberation.* New York: McKay.

Gamson, William. 1975. *The Strategy of Social Protest.* Homewood, IL: Dorsey Press.

Gamson, William A., Bruce Fireman, and Steven Rytina. 1982. *Encounters with Unjust Authority.* Homewood, IL: Dorsey Press.

Gerlach, Luther and Virginia Hine. 1970. *People, Power, Change.* New York: Bobbs-Merrill.

Giddens, Anthony. 1984. *The Constitution of Society.* Berkeley: University of California Press.

Gurr, Ted. 1970. *Why Men Rebel.* Princeton: Princeton University Press.

Habermas, Jürgen. 1984/1987. *The Theory of Communicative Action.* Translated by Thomas McCarthy. Boston: Beacon Press.

Hartsock, Nancy. 1985. "Exchange Theory: Critique from a Feminist Standpoint." Pp. 57–70 in *Current Perspectives in Social Theory,* edited by Scott McNall, Vol. 6. Greenwich, CT: JAI.

History of Woman Suffrage. 1969. Vols. One (1881), Two (1882) and Three (1886) edited by Elizabeth Cady Stanton, Susan B. Anthony, and Matilda Joslyn Gage; Vol. 4 (1902) edited by Susan B. Anthony and Ida Husted Harper; Vols. 5 (1922) and 6 (1922) edited by Ida Husted Harper. New York: Arno Press (Reprint).

Jenkins, J. Craig. 1983. "Resource Mobilization Theory and the Study of Social Movements." *Annual Review of Sociology* 9: 527–553.

Klandermans, Bert. 1984. "Mobilization and Participation: Social-Psychological Expansions of Resource Mobilization Theory." *American Sociological Review* 49: 583–600.

———. 1986. "New Social Movements and Resource Mobilization: The European and the American Approach." *International Journal of Mass Emergencies and Disasters* 4: 13–37.

———. 1988. "The Formation and Mobilization of Consensus." Pp. 173–196 in *International Social Movement Research,* Vol. 1: *From Structure to Action,* edited by Bert Klandermans, Hanspeter Kriesi, and Sidney Tarrow. Greenwich, CT: JAI.

Kornhauser, William. 1959. *The Politics of Mass Society.* Glencoe, IL: Free Press.

Kuhn, Thomas. 1962. *The Structure of Scientific Revolutions.* Chicago: University of Chicago Press.

Marx, Gary T. and James L. Wood. 1975. "Strands of Theory and Research in Collective Behavior." *Annual Review of Sociology* 1: 363–428.

McAdam, Doug. 1982. *Political Process and the Development of Black Insurgency.* Chicago: University of Chicago Press.

———. 1992. "Gender as a Mediator of the Activist Experience: The Case of Freedom Summer." *American Journal of Sociology* 97: 1211–1240.

McAdam, Doug, John D. McCarthy, and Mayer N. Zald. 1988. "Social Movements." Pp. 695–737 in *Handbook of Sociology,* edited by Neil Smelser. Newbury Park, CA: Sage Publications.

McCarthy, John D. and Mayer N. Zald, 1973. *The Trend of Social Movements.* Morristown, NJ: General Learning Press.

———. 1977. "Resource Mobilization and Social Movements." *American Journal of Sociology* 82: 1212–1241.

Melucci, Alberto. 1985. "The Symbolic Challenge of Contemporary Movements." *Social Research* 52: 789–816.

———. 1988. "Getting Involved: Identity and Mobilization in Social Movements." Pp. 329–348 in *International Social Movement Research,* Vol. 1: *From Structure to Action,* edited by Bert Klandermans, Hanspeter Kriesi, and Sidney Tarrow. Greenwich, CT: JAI.

————. 1989. *Nomads of the Present: Social Movements and Individual Needs in Contemporary Society*. Philadelphia: Temple University Press.

Morris, Aldon. 1984. *The Origins of the Civil Rights Movement*. New York: Free Press.

Oberschall, Anthony. 1973. *Social Conflict and Social Movements*. Englewood Cliffs, NJ: Prentice-Hall.

Olson, Mancur. 1965. *The Logic of Collective Action*. New York: Schocken.

Omi, Michael and Howard Winant. 1986. *Racial Formation in the United States from the 1960s to the 1980s*. New York: Routledge.

O'Neill, William. 1969. *Everyone Was Brave*. Chicago: Quadrangle.

Parsons, Talcott. 1937. *The Structure of Social Action*. New York: Free Press.

Perrow, Charles. 1979. "The Sixties Observed." Pp. 192–211 in *The Dynamics of Social Movements*, edited by Mayer N. Zald and John D. McCarthy. Cambridge: Winthrop.

Pichardo, Nelson A. 1988. "Resource Mobilization: An Analysis of Conflicting Theoretical Variations." *Sociological Quarterly* 29: 97–110.

Piven, Frances Fox and Richard Cloward. 1977. *Poor People's Movements*. New York: Vintage.

Ritzer, George. 1992. *Sociological Theory*, 3rd ed. New York: McGraw-Hill.

Rochford, E. Burke, Jr. 1985. *Hare Krishna in America*. New Brunswick, NJ: Rutgers University Press.

Rosenthal, Naomi and Michael Schwartz. 1989. "Spontaneity and Democracy in Social Protest." Pp. 33–59 in *International Social Movement Research*, Vol. 2: *Organizing for Change*, edited by Bert Klandermans. Greenwich, CT: JAI Press.

Rupp, Leila J. and Verta Taylor. 1987. *Survival in the Doldrums*. New York: Oxford.

Smelser, Neil. 1962. *Theory of Collective Behavior*. New York: Free Press.

Snow, David A., E. Burke Rochford, Steven K. Worden, and Robert D. Benford. 1986. "Frame Alignment Processes. Micromobilization, and Movement Participation." *American Sociological Review* 51: 464–481.

Snow, David A. and Robert Benford. 1988. "Ideology, Frame Resonance, and Participant Mobilization." Pp. 197–217 in *International Social Movement Research*, Vol. 1: *From Structure to Action*, edited by Bert Klandermans, Hanspeter Kriesi, and Sidney Tarrow. Greenwich, CT: JAI Press.

Staggenborg, Suzanne. 1988. "The Consequences of Professionalization and Formalization in the Pro-Choice Movement." *American Sociological Review* 1988: 585–606.

————. 1989. "Stability and Innovation in the Women's Movement: A Comparison of Two Movement Organizations." *Social Problems* 36: 75–92.

Taylor, Verta. 1989a. "Sisterhood, Solidarity and Modern Feminism. A Review Essay." *Gender and Society* 3: 277–286.

————. 1989b. "Social Movement Continuity: The Women's Movement In Abeyance." *American Sociological Review* 1989: 761–775.

Taylor, Verta and Leila J. Rupp. Unpublished paper. "Women's Culture and Lesbian Feminist Activism: A Reconsideration of Cultural Feminism."

Taylor, Verta and Nancy Whittier. Unpublished paper. "The Women's Movement in the 'Post-Feminist' Age: Rethinking Social Movement Theory from a Feminist Standpoint."

Tilly, Charles. 1978. *From Mobilization to Revolution*. Reading, MA: Addison-Wesley.

Touraine, Alain. 1981. *The Voice and the Eye*. New York: Cambridge University Press.

Turner, Ralph H. and Lewis M. Killian. 1957. *Collective Behavior*. Englewood Cliffs, NJ: Prentice-Hall.

Walsh, Edward J. 1978. "Mobilization Theory vis-á-vis a Mobilization Process: The Case of the United Farm Workers' Movement." Pp. 155–177 in *Research in Social Movements, Conflict and Change*, Vol. 1. Greenwich, CT: JAI Press.

————. 1981. "Resource Mobilization and Citizen Protest in Communities around Three Mile Island." *Social Problems* 29: 1–21.

Walsh, Edward J. and Rex H. Warland. 1983. "Social Movement Involvement in the Wake of a Nuclear Accident: Activists and Free Riders in the TMI Area." *American Sociological Review* 48: 764–780.

Wilson, John. 1973. *Introduction to Social Movements*. New York: Basic Books.

Zeitlin, Irving. 1973. *Re-thinking Sociology*. Englewood Cliffs, NJ: Prentice-Hall.

Zurcher, Louis, A. and David A. Snow. 1981. "Collective Behavior: Social Movements." Pp. 447–482 in *Social Psychology: Sociological Perspectives*, edited by Morris Rosenberg and Ralph H. Turner. New York: Basic Books.

14

FRAME ALIGNMENT PROCESSES, MICROMOBILIZATION, AND MOVEMENT PARTICIPATION

DAVID A. SNOW • E. BURKE ROCHFORD, JR.
STEVEN K. WORDEN • ROBERT D. BENFORD

A long standing and still central problem in the field of social movements concerns the issue of support for and participation in social movement organizations (SMOs) and their activities and campaigns. There is growing recognition that a thoroughgoing understanding of this issue requires consideration of both social-psychological and structural/organizational factors. This realization is reflected in recent literature reviews and critiques (Ferree and Miller, 1985; Gamson et al., 1982:7–12; Jenkins, 1983:527, 549; Zurcher and Snow, 1981) as well as in research on the correlates of support for or involvement in a variety of contemporary social movements (Isaac et al., 1980; Klandermans, 1984; McAdam, 1984; Useem, 1980; Walsh and Warland, 1983; Wood and Hughes, 1984). To date, however, little headway has been made in linking together social-psychological and structural/organizational factors and perspectives in a theoretically informed and empirically grounded fashion.

Our aim in this paper is to move forward along this line, both conceptually and empirically, by elaborating what we refer to as frame

From *American Sociological Review,* Vol. 51, August 1986, pp. 464–481. Reprinted by permission of American Sociological Association.

alignment processes and by enumerating correspondent micromobilization tasks and processes. By *frame alignment,* we refer to the linkage of individual and SMO interpretive orientations, such that some set of individual interests, values and beliefs and SMO activities, goals, and ideology are congruent and complementary. The term *"frame"* (and framework) is borrowed from Goffman (1974:21) to denote "schemata of interpretation" that enable individuals "to locate, perceive, identify, and label" occurrences within their life space and the world at large. By rendering events or occurrences meaningful, frames function to organize experience and guide action, whether individual or collective. So conceptualized, it follows that frame alignment is a necessary condition for movement participation, whatever its nature or intensity. Since we have identified more than one such alignment process, we use the phrase *frame alignment process* as the cover term for these linkages. By *micromobilization,* we refer simply to the various interactive and communicative processes that affect frame alignment.

We illustrate these processes with data derived primarily from our studies of the Nichiren Shoshu Buddhist movement (Snow, 1979, 1986), of Hare Krishna (Rochford, 1985), of the peace movement (Benford, 1984), and of urban neighborhood movements. Drawing upon these empirical materials, on Goffman's frame analytic perspective (1974), which we extend and refine for our purposes, and on a range of literature pertinent to the issue of movement participation, we discuss and illustrate the frame alignment processes we have identified, and elaborate related micromobilization tasks and processes. Before attending to this agenda, however, we consider several major problems that plague most extant analyses of participation in SMOs and movement-related activities and campaigns. This excursion will provide a more solid grounding for our utilization of Goffman's frame analytic scheme and our elaboration of the various frame alignment processes.

Neglect of Grievance Interpretation and Other Ideational Elements

The most striking shortcoming is the tendency to gloss questions concerning the interpretation of events and experiences relevant to participation in social movement activities and campaigns. This tendency is particularly evident in the treatment of grievances. Too much attention is focused on grievances per se, and on their social-psychological manifestations (e.g., relative deprivation, alienation), to the neglect of the fact that grievances or discontents are subject to differential interpretation, and the fact that variations in their interpretation across individuals, social movement organizations, and time can affect whether and how they are acted upon. Both the psychofunctional and resource mobilization perspectives ignore this interpretive or framing issue. The psychofunctional approaches do so by assuming an almost automatic, magnetic-like linkage between intensely felt grievances and susceptibility to movement participation. Lip

service is given to subjective/interpretive considerations, but they are rarely dealt with thoughtfully or systematically.

Resource mobilization perspectives also skirt this interpretive issue by assuming the ubiquity and constancy of mobilizing grievances. This assumption is stated most strongly by Jenkins and Perrow (1977:250–51, 266), McCarthy and Zald (1977:1214–15), and Oberschall (1973:133–34, 194–95). Tilly (1978:8) can be read as having reservations about the assumption, but deferring it to others for analysis. However, it is not so much this ubiquity/constancy assumption that we find troublesome, but rather the meta-assumption that this exhausts the important social-psychological issues and that analysis can therefore concentrate on organizational and macromobilization considerations. This leap skirts, among other things, "the enormous variability in the subjective meanings people attach to their objective situations" (McAdam, 1982:34). Questions concerning the interpretation of grievances and their alignment with social movement organizations' goals and ideologies are thus ignored or taken for granted.

Types of Frame Alignment Processes

Earlier we defined frame alignment as the linkage or conjunction of individual and SMO interpretive frameworks. We now propose and elaborate four types of frame alignment processes that are suggested by our research observations, and which attend to the blind spots and questions discussed above. The four processes include: (a) frame bridging, (b) frame amplification, (c) frame extension, and (d) frame transformation. For each variant of alignment we indicate correspondent micromobilization tasks and processes. The underlying premise is that frame alignment, of one variety or another, is a necessary condition for movement participation, whatever its nature or intensity, and that it is typically an interactional accomplishment.

Frame Bridging

By frame bridging we refer to the linkage of two or more ideologically congruent but structurally unconnected frames regarding a particular issue or problem. Such bridging can occur at the organizational level, as between two SMOs within the same movement industry, or at the individual level, which is the focal concern of this paper. At this level of analysis, frame bridging involves the linkage of an SMO with what McCarthy (1986) has referred to as unmobilized sentiment pools or public opinion preference clusters. These sentiment pools refer to aggregates of individuals who share common grievances and attributional orientations, but who lack the organizational base for expressing their discontents and for acting in pursuit of their interests. For these sentiment pools, collective action is not preceded by consciousness or frame transformation, but by being structurally connected with an ideologically isomorphic SMO.

This bridging is effected primarily by organizational outreach and information diffusion through interpersonal or intergroup networks, the mass media, the telephone, and direct mail. In recent years, opportunities and prospects for frame bridging have been facilitated by the advent of "new technologies," namely the computerization of lists of contributors or subscribers to various causes and literature (McCarthy, 1986). The micromobilization task is first, to cull lists of names in order to produce a probable adherent pool, and second, to bring these individuals within the SMO's infrastructure by working one or more of the previously mentioned information channels.

Evidence of frame bridging abounds in contemporary social movements. Indeed, for many SMOs today, frame bridging appears to be the primary form of alignment. Well-known examples include Common Cause, the National Rifle Association, the prolife and prochoice movements, and the Christian Right. In the case of the latter, for example, frame bridging was crucial to its rapid growth.

The use of such bridging techniques and avenues is not peculiar to the Christian Right. Research on the peace movement in Texas revealed, for example, that peace groups also utilize the direct mail and similarly develop their mailing lists from a variety of sources, including lists of individuals who attend events sponsored by other liberal organizations and who subscribe to left-oriented periodicals such as *Mother Jones*, *The Texas Observer*, and *The Progressive* (Benford, 1984).

The foregoing illustrations point to the widespread existence of frame bridging as an alignment process and suggest its salience for mobilizing participants and other resources. But frame bridging does not sufficiently explain all varieties of participation in all forms of movements or movement activities. Yet, most work within the resource mobilization tradition concerned with participation has approached it primarily in terms of frame bridging. The orienting assumption that grievances are sufficiently generalized and salient to provide support for SMOs turns subjective orientations into a constant, and thus focuses attention on the mechanistic process of outreach and bridging.

Networks frequently function to structure movement recruitment and growth, but they do not tell us what transpires when constituents and bystanders or adherents get together. Since a good portion of the time devoted to many SMO activities is spent in small encounters, an examination of the nature of those encounters and the interactional processes involved would tell us much about how SMOs and their constituents go about the business of persuading others, effecting switches in frame, and so on. McCarthy and Zald alluded to such concerns when they suggested that sometimes "grievances and discontent may be defined, created, and manipulated by issue entrepreneurs and organizations" (1977:1215), but this provocative proposition has neither been examined empirically nor integrated into a more general understanding of constituent mobilization. Our elaboration of the other variants of frame alignment addresses these considerations, thus moving us beyond the frame bridging process.

Frame Amplification

By frame amplification, we refer to the clarification and invigoration of an interpretive frame that bears on a particular issue, problem or set of events. Because the meaning of events and their connection to one's immediate life situation are often shrouded by indifference, deception or fabrication by others, and by ambiguity or uncertainty (Goffman, 1974), support for and participation in movement activities is frequently contingent on the clarification and reinvigoration of an interpretive frame. Our research experiences and inspection of the literature suggest two varieties of frame amplification: value amplification and belief amplification.

Value Amplification Value amplification refers to the identification, idealization, and elevation of one or more values presumed basic to prospective constituents but which have not inspired collective action for any number of reasons. They may have atrophied, fallen into disuse, or have been suppressed because of the lack of an opportunity for expression due to a repressive authority structure (Tilly, 1978) or the absence of an organizational outlet (McCarthy, 1986); they may have become taken for granted or clichéd (Zijderveld, 1979); they may not have been sufficiently challenged or threatened (Turner and Killian, 1972); or their relevance to a particular event or issue may be ambiguous (Goffman, 1974). If one or more of these impediments to value articulation and expression is operative, then the recruitment and mobilization of prospective constituents will require the focusing, elevation, and reinvigoration of values relevant to the issue or event being promoted or resisted.

The use of value amplification as a springboard for mobilizing support was evident in the peace movement. Fundamental values such as justice, cooperation, perseverance, and the sanctity of human life were repeatedly embellished. The movement's most frequently idealized values, however, were those associated with democracy, particularly the values of equality and liberty. Peace activists amplified such values by asserting their "constitutional right" to speak out on the nuclear arms race, national security, and foreign policy. A popular movement speaker, for example, often bracketed his speeches with the Preamble to the U.S. Constitution and excerpts from the Declaration of Independence. Similarly, the Texas Coordinator of the Nuclear Weapons Freeze Campaign, when asked in an interview what he thought needed to be done in order to achieve a nuclear freeze and move toward disarmament, responded succinctly, "just make the democratic system work."

By framing their mobilization appeals in the language of cherished democratic principles, peace activists not only attempt to build "idiosyncrasy credit" (Hollander, 1958; Snow, 1979), but they also seek to redefine their public image as a movement serving the best interests of their country, in part through revitalization of what they see as atrophied values such as the right to redress grievances and express dissent.

Belief Amplification   Broadly conceived, beliefs refer to presumed relationships "between two things or between some thing and a characteristic of it" (Bern, 1970:4), as exemplified by such presumptions as God is dead, the Second Coming is imminent, capitalists are exploiters, and black is beautiful. Whereas values refer to the goals or end-states that movements seek to attain or promote, beliefs can be construed as ideational elements that cognitively support or impede action in pursuit of desired values.

There are five kinds of such beliefs discernible in the movement literature that are especially relevant to mobilization and participation processes: (1) the previously discussed beliefs about the seriousness of the problem, issue, or grievance in question (Gamson et al., 1982; McAdam, 1982; Piven and Cloward, 1977; Turner, 1969); (2) beliefs about the locus of causality or blame (Ferree and Miller, 1985; Piven and Cloward, 1977; Zurcher and Snow, 1981); (3) stereotypic beliefs about antagonists or targets of influence (Shibutani, 1970; Turner and Killian, 1972); (4) beliefs about the probability of change or the efficacy of collective action (Klandermans, 1983, 1984; Oberschall, 1980; Olson, 1965; and Piven and Cloward, 1977); and (5) beliefs about the necessity and propriety of "standing up" (Fireman and Gamson, 1979; Oliver, 1984; Piven and Cloward, 1977).

Examples of the amplification of stereotypic beliefs about antagonists or targets of influence are not difficult to find in the social movement arena, especially since such beliefs frequently function as unambiguous coordinating symbols that galvanize and focus sentiment. The efforts of neighborhood organizers to mobilize citizens to oppose the relocation of the Salvation Army shelter provides a graphic illustration. Proximate relocation of the shelter was portrayed as a significant threat to the neighborhood ideal and to familistic values. The problem confronting organizers was to substantiate unambiguously the claim that the shelter would indeed "destroy our neighborhoods." Since the Salvation Army has long been identified with the values of Christian charity, it did not readily lend itself to rhetorical broadsides by neighborhood activists. Effective mobilization thus required a more negatively evaluated target of opposition. The growing number of homeless, transient males who had migrated to Austin and were served by the Salvation Army provided such a target.

Moving from beliefs about antagonists to beliefs about the efficacy of collective action, we turn to what has been the primary concern of recent efforts to integrate social-psychological considerations with the resource mobilization perspective. The basic proposition, rooted in value-expectancy theory, is that social action is contingent on anticipated outcomes (Klandermans, 1984). If people are to act collectively, it is argued, then they "must believe that such action would be efficacious, i.e., that change is possible but that it will not happen automatically, without collective action" (Oliver, 1985:21). Optimism about the outcome of a collective challenge will thus enhance the probability of participation; pessimism will diminish it. We do not quibble with this proposition, especially since it has received considerable empirical support from different quarters (Forward and Williams, 1970; Gamson, 1968; Klandermans; 1984; Paige, 1971; Seeman, 1975). But we do find troublesome the tendency to take for granted the process by which optimism or a sense of efficacy is developed and sustained. Our research observations suggest that such beliefs or expectancies are temporally variable and can be modified during the course of actual participation and by the micromobilization efforts of SMOs as well.

The problematic nature and processual development of efficacy were evident in our peace movement research. Nuclear disarmament activists were often heard to lament about finding themselves confronted by audiences who, on the one hand, agreed with the movement's assessment of the dangers of the nuclear arms race, but, on the other hand, did not seem to share the activists' beliefs that ordinary people can have any effect on the course of defense policy. Consequently, much of the micromobilization activity engaged in by peace activists involves the amplification of beliefs regarding the efficacy of their campaigns. Toward that end, disarmament leaders frequently cite and embellish the apparent successes of past movements. A favorite analogy is drawn between present attempts to rid the world of nuclear weapons and the nineteenth-century abolitionist movement. Parallels are drawn between those who believed that slavery would never be abolished and those who believe that nuclear weapons cannot be eliminated. Likewise, peace activists cite the presumed achievements of the anti–Vietnam War movement, as illustrated by the following excerpt from a campus rally speech:

> Some people think decisions are made in Washington and Moscow, but this is not necessarily the case. Decisions are made by the people. The decision that brought an end to the war in Vietnam was not made by politicians in Washington. The decision to stop it was made right here by people like you and me.

Such observations suffice to illustrate that beliefs about the efficacy of collective action are temporally and contextually variable and subject to micromobilization efforts to amplify them. Such is also the case with beliefs about the necessity and propriety of "standing up" and "being counted." Beliefs about necessity refer to beliefs about the instrumentality of one's own efforts in pur-

suit of some movement objective. Such beliefs are often of the "if-I-don't-do-it-no-one-will" genre, and are thus rooted in part in pessimism about the prospects of other potential participants "taking up the sword." As Oliver (1984:608–609) found in her research that compared active and token contributors to local collective action, activists were "more pessimistic about their neighbors' willingness to make active contributions" and therefore believed "that if they want(ed) something done they (would) have to do it themselves."

Our research on neighborhood movements and the peace movement similarly revealed pessimism on the part of activists about stimulating and sustaining constituent participation. But such pessimism was typically privatized. Moreover, it was frequently seen as something that might be neutralized in part through micromobilization activities to generate "a sense of necessity" on behalf of potential participants. Thus, organizers of a movement in opposition to expansion of the city airport exhorted proximate neighborhood residents to "speak up," emphasizing not only that their "voices count," but that it is a matter of necessity "because no one else will stand up for your home." In a similar vein, local peace activists emphasized repeatedly how critical it is to communicate to individuals that their contribution to the peace movement is of utmost necessity if nuclear war is to be prevented.

As Fireman and Gamson (1979:32) correctly note, "individuals exist in a climate of cultural beliefs about their obligations to those groups with which they identify." But since there is considerable variability in the salience of these beliefs both individually and culturally, it is often necessary to amplify them so as to increase the prospect that some potential participants will see their involvement as a moral obligation. The leadership of the Nichiren Shoshu movement seemed to understand this well. Members were constantly reminded of their obligation to carry out "a divine mission that was set in motion thousands of years ago." In the words of the movement's Master, "members were born into this world as Bodhisattvas of the Earth whose noble mission is to propagate true Buddhism throughout the world." Similarly, peace movement leaders often invoked notions of moral obligation and duty as mobilizing prods in their efforts to activate adherents, as illustrated by the comments of a media personality, before a crowd of demonstrators gathered at the gates of the Pantex nuclear weapons facility on the 40th anniversary of the Hiroshima bombing: "I've learned that we not only have a right, but a responsibility to tell our government . . . when they have gone against our wishes."

Frame Extension

We have noted how SMOs frequently promote programs or causes in terms of values and beliefs that may not be especially salient or readily apparent to potential constituents and supporters, thus necessitating the amplification of these ideational elements in order to clarify the linkage between personal or group interests and support for the SMO. On other occasions more may be involved in securing and activating participants than overcoming ambiguity and uncertainty or indifference and lethargy. The programs and values that some SMOs promote may not be rooted in existing sentiment or adherent pools, or may appear to have little if any bearing on the life situations and interests of potential adherents. When such is the case, an SMO may have to extend the boundaries of its primary framework so as to encompass interests or points of view that are incidental to its primary objectives but of considerable salience to potential adherents. In effect, the

movement is attempting to enlarge its adherent pool by portraying its objectives or activities as attending to or being congruent with the values or interests of potential adherents. The micromobilization task in such cases is the identification of individual or aggregate level values and interests and the alignment of them with participation in movement activities.

Evidence of this variety of frame alignment was readily discernible in the movements we studied. In the case of the peace movement, frame extension is commonplace. Movement leaders frequently elaborate goals and activities so as to encompass auxiliary interests not obviously associated with the movement in hopes of enlarging its adherent base. The employment of rock-and-roll and punk bands to attract otherwise uninterested individuals to disarmament rallies, and the dissemination of literature explicating the services sacrificed by a community as a result of an escalating defense budget are illustrative of this practice. A recent decision by the Austin Peace and Justice Coalition (APJC) illustrates this alignment process even more concretely. Since its inception four years ago, this citywide coalition of some 35 peace groups had organized most of its activities around the movement's goals of "nuclear disarmament, stopping military intervention, and redirecting military spending to the needy." During this period, the movement appealed primarily to "white middle-class baby-boomers." Efforts were made to mobilize racial and ethnic minorities under the banner of "peace and justice," but with little success. A recent APJC memo attributes the failure of this outreach campaign to two factors, and urges an expansion of the movement's framework:

> Two important reasons for this lack of interracial coalition are: (1) APJC's failure to actively work on issues important

to minority groups such as hunger, better public housing, and police brutality; and (2) APJC's stated goals and purposes do not clearly define its intention to oppose racism and unjust discrimination. . . . With the recent rapid growth of the anti-apartheid movement in Austin, it is time for APJC to definitively affirm its intentions and sympathies, which were previously only implied.

As a solution, APJC decided to add a fourth goal to its statement of purpose and promotional literature: "To promote social justice by nonviolently confronting racism, sexism, and all forms of discrimination and oppression." Whether this frame extension will broaden the movement's constituency remains to be seen, but it clearly illustrates the way in which the peace movement has attempted to enlarge its adherent pool.

Frame extension also surfaced on occasion during research on local neighborhood movements. The most vivid example occurred when the proprietors of bars and restaurants within a popular downtown nightlife strip were confronted with the prospect of the Salvation Army shelter being built in their area. In order to protect their interests, they quickly attempted to win the support of neighborhood residents throughout the city by invoking the already successful neighborhood frame and identifying their interests with those of Austinites in general. Thus, the rallying slogan became: "Let's Save 6th Street—Austin's Neighborhood." Once the frame was extended, organizers played upon and amplified the pieties of neighborhood in hopes of mobilizing support.

Frame extension was also operative in both the Nichiren Shoshu and Hare Krishna movements, but at a more interpersonal level. In the case of Nichiren Shoshu, the operation of this process was particularly evident at the point of initial contact between prospective recruits and movement members. The primary aim of these initial recruitment encounters was not to sell the movement or to get individuals to join, but simply to persuade the prospect to attend a movement meeting or activity. Toward that end, members attempted to align the prospect's interests with movement activities, practices, or goals. They did this by first trying to discover something of interest to the prospect, and then emphasized that this interest could be realized by attending an activity or chanting. In a similar manner, Hare Krishna devotees strategically attempted to assess the interests of persons contacted in various public places in an effort to relate the movement's religious philosophy to individual interests and concerns.

Since the purpose of such encounters is to encourage the prospect to attend or contribute to a movement function, members' appeals can vary widely, ranging from playing a musical instrument to meeting members of the opposite sex. Consequently, the reasons or interests prompting initial investigation of movement activity may not be relevant, if related at all, to the decision to join and become, at the very least, a nominal member.

And just as the interests that prompted investigation of movement activity were not always the same as those that motivated joining, so the latter were not always the same as the interests that sustained participation. This was clearly illustrated by comparison of the accounts of the same members over an extended period of time. What was found was that the interests associated with participation were frequently redefined or elaborated. The longer the member's tenure, the more likely he or she would articulate interest in world conditions and peace rather than in material or physiological matters, which was typically the case with novitiates.

These findings indicate that sustained participation in movements such as Nichiren Shoshu and Hare Krishna is frequently contingent on a change in interpretive frame, thus suggesting that for some individuals in some movements, frame extension is but a "hooking" (Lofland, 1977) process that functions as an initial step along the path to the more thoroughgoing type of alignment we refer to as frame transformation.

Frame Transformation

Thus far we have noted how the alignment of individuals and SMOs may be effected through the bridging, amplification, and grafting or incorporation of existing interpretive frames and their attendant values and beliefs. The programs, causes, and values that some SMOs promote, however, may not resonate with, and on occasion may even appear antithetical to, conventional lifestyles or rituals and extant interpretive frames. When such is the case, new values may have to be planted and nurtured, old meanings or understandings jettisoned, and erroneous beliefs or "misframings" reframed (Goffman, 1974:308) in order to garner support and secure participants. What may be required, in short, is a transformation of frame.

According to Goffman (1974: 43–44), such a transformation, which he refers to as a "keying," redefines activities, events, and biographies that are already meaningful from the standpoint of some primary framework, in terms of another framework, such that they are now "seen by the participants to be something quite else." What is involved is "a systematic alteration" that radically reconstitutes for participants what it is that is going on (Goffman, 1974:45).

We have identified two such transformation processes that are pertinent to movement recruitment and participation: transformations of domain-specific and global interpretive frames. We shall first consider the similarities between these two alignment processes, and then turn to their differences.

The obvious similarity is that both involve a reframing of some set of conditions, be they biographic or social, past, present, or future. The objective contours of the situation do not change so much as the way the situation is defined and thus experienced. Two analytically distinct aspects comprise this interpretive change. First, as noted earlier, there is a change in the perceived seriousness of the condition such that what was previously seen as an unfortunate but tolerable situation is now defined as inexcusable, unjust, or immoral, thus connoting the adoption of an injustice frame or variation thereof (Gamson et al., 1982).

But the development and adoption of an injustice frame is not sufficient to account for the direction of action. A life of impoverishment may be defined as an injustice, but its relationship to action is partly dependent, as attribution theorists would argue, on whether blame or responsibility is internalized or externalized. Thus, the emergence of an injustice frame must be accompanied by a corresponding shift in attributional orientation.

Evidence of such a shift manifested itself repeatedly in research on conversion to the Nichiren Shoshu Buddhist movement, as illustrated by the words of a 20-year-old convert:

> Before joining Nichiren Shoshu I blamed any problems I had on other people or on the environment. It was always my parents, or school, or society. But through chanting I discovered the real source of my difficulties: myself. Chanting has helped me to realize that rather than running around blaming others, I am the one who needs to change.

Since Nichiren Shoshu is a religious movement that emphasizes personal transformation as the key to social change, it might be argued that this feature of alignment is pertinent only to participation in religious, personal growth, and self-help movements. But this clearly is not the case; for a shift in attributional orientation is also frequently a constituent element of mobilization for and participation in movements that seek change by directly altering sociopolitical structures. In the case of participation in such movements, however, the shift involves a change from fatalism or self-blaming to structural-blaming, from victim-blaming to system-blaming, as documented by research on leftist radicalism in Chile (Portes, 1971a, 1971b), unemployed workers' movements in the U.S. (Piven and Cloward, 1977) and Cuba (Zeitlin, 1966), protest orientations among American blacks (Forward and Williams, 1970; Gurin et al., 1969; Isaac et al., 1980) and on the development of feminist consciousness (Bird, 1969; Deckard, 1979). Moreover, this literature suggests that this shift cannot be assumed.

Transformation of Domain-specific Interpretive Frames By transformation of domain-specific interpretive frames, we refer to fairly self-contained but substantial changes in the way a particular domain of life is framed, such that a domain previously taken for granted is reframed as problematic and in need of repair, or a domain seen as normative or acceptable is reframed as an injustice that warrants change. We construe "domain" broadly to include an almost infinite variety of aspects of life, such as dietary habits, consumption patterns, leisure activities, social relationships, social statuses, and self-perception. While each of these as well as other domains of life can be and frequently are interconnected, they can also be bracketed or perceptually bounded (Goffman, 1974:247–300), as often occurs in

the case of single-issue movements. The interpretive transformation that occurs with respect to one domain may affect behavior in other domains, but the change of frame is not automatically generalized to them.

Domain-specific transformations frequently appear to be a necessary condition for participation in movements that seek dramatic changes in the status, treatment, or activity of a category of people. Concrete examples include movements that seek to alter the status of a category of people such as women, children, the aged, handicapped, and prisoners, or that seek to change the relationship between two or more categories, as in the case of many ethnic and racial movements. In each case, a status, pattern of relationships, or a social practice is reframed as inexcusable, immoral, or unjust. In the case of Mothers Against Drunk Driving, for instance, the misfortune of the tragic loss of a loved one has been redefined as an injustice that demands an increase in the severity and certainty of penalties for drunk driving. However, as Turner (1983) has suggested, participation involves not only coming to see as an inexcusable tragedy what was formerly seen as an unfortunate accident, but also redefining the status of drunk driver in more negative terms than was previously the case.

While movements for the liberation or integration of negatively privileged status groups have considerably broader and more far-reaching goals, the success of their mobilization efforts also rests in part on effecting changes in the way their potential constituents view not only their life situation, but also themselves. As Carmichael and Hamilton argued in *Black Power* (1967:34–35):

. . .we must first redefine ourselves. Our basic need is to reclaim our history and our identity. . . . We shall have to struggle for the right to create our own terms through which to define ourselves and our relationship to society, and to have those terms recognized. This is the first right of a free people. . . .

Support for and participation in some SMOs is thus partly contingent on the refraining of some domain-specific status, relationship, practice, or environmental feature or condition. Yet there are still other movements for which a far more sweeping transformation is frequently required in order to secure more than nominal participation.

Transformations of Global Interpretive Frames In this final frame alignment process, the scope of change is broadened considerably as a new primary framework gains ascendance over others and comes to function as a kind of master frame that interprets events and experiences in a new key. What is involved, in essence, is a kind of thoroughgoing conversion that has been depicted as a change in one's "sense of ultimate grounding" (Heirich, 1977) that is rooted in the "displacement of one universe of discourse by another and its attendant rules and grammar for putting things together" (Snow and Machalek, 1983:265–66). Domain-specific experiences, both past and present, that were formerly bracketed and interpreted in one or more ways are now given new meaning and rearranged, frequently in ways that previously were inconceivable, in accordance with the new master frame. As a female convert to Nichiren Shoshu recounts:

> I am an entirely different person now. I never thought I would have much of a future or grow up to enjoy the world. I was against everything. I hated myself most of all, but I didn't know it until chanting and the Gohonzon (the sacred scroll) showed that there was a different kind of world. Now I see things totally different.

One of the major consequences of this more sweeping variety of frame transformation is that it reduces ambiguity and uncertainty and decreases the prospect of "misframings" or interpretive "errors" and "frame disputes" (Goffman, 1974:301–38). In short, everything is seen with greater clarity and certainty.

This pattern also manifested itself in discussions and interviews with some peace activists. One veteran activist noted, for example, that during the course of her involvement the perceptual boundaries between war and peace issues and other aspects of the world gradually dissolved until there were no longer any distinctive, mutually exclusive domains. Nearly every domain of life, from her interpersonal relations to global issues, came to be reframed in terms congruent with the peace movement.

> . . .The planet is all one system. And therefore it follows logically that we're all one people living on it. And, if people see that, how in the world could they get into a thing, you know, that's going to hurt each other? You've got to try to figure out how to make it all work. I mean, to me, it's a political, spiritual thing that's totally tied together. And I feel that it's the way it is whether or not people realize it. I'm sure of it. And the only real hope is for more people to realize it and to do whatever it takes to make them realize it.

What it takes, in those cases where there is little if any transparent overlap between the perspectives of potential adherents and SMOs, is frame transformation or conversion. In those cases, the micromobilization task is to effect conversion by "keying" the experiences of prospective participants, including events that they observe, so that what is going on for them is radically reconstituted

(Goffman, 1974:45), as reflected in the above activist's account of her transformation from a "right wing racist" into a peace movement activist:

> My senior year was the time when I changed from the extreme right to . . . left of liberal. . . . Everything I learned about it (the peace movement) convinced me how wrong and racist it was to be, you know, right wing. . . . I was in Oklahoma City then, and the peace movement was really late getting there.

While this radical transformative process may be a necessary condition for the participation of some individuals in an array of movements, it is undoubtedly more central to the participation process of some movements than others. Hare Krishna provides a case in point, as graphically illustrated by the following remarks routinely made to recruits at the New York ISKCON temple in 1980:

> As Krishna explains in the *Bhagavad-Gita*, our lives thus far have been in darkness, in the mode of ignorance. *All our learning up to now has been illusion, garbage.* This is because this past learning we have received does not allow us to know the Absolute, Krishna Consciousness (leader's emphasis).

Summary and Implications

We have attempted to clarify understanding of adherent and constituent mobilization by proposing and analyzing frame alignment as a conceptual bridge that links social-psychological and structural/organizational considerations on movement participation. We have pursued this task by identifying and elaborating six concrete points. First, participation in SMO activities is contingent in part on alignment of individual and SMO interpretive frames. Second, this process can be decomposed into four related but not

identical processes: frame bridging, frame amplification, frame extension, and frame transformation. Third, initial frame alignment cannot be assumed, given the existence of either grievances or SMOs. Fourth, frame alignment, once achieved, cannot be taken for granted because it is temporally variable and subject to reassessment and renegotiation. As we have noted, the reasons that prompt participation in one set of activities at one point in time may be irrelevant or insufficient to prompt subsequent participation. Fifth, frame alignment, in one form or another, is therefore a crucial aspect of adherent and constituent mobilization. And sixth, each frame alignment process requires somewhat different micromobilization tasks.

Taken together, these observations suggest several sets of questions and propositions that subsequent research ought to address. A first set of questions concerns the relationship between types of frame alignment and types of movements. While each of the frame alignment processes may be operative in varying degrees at some point in the life history of most movements, what we are hypothesizing is that there is a kind of elective affinity between forms of alignment and movement goals and perspectives, such that we can speak of modal types of alignment for particular types of movements. Investigation of this hypothesized relationship becomes especially important when we consider that the differential success of participant mobilization efforts may be due in part to variation in the capacity of SMOs to skillfully effect and then sustain a particular type of alignment.

A second issue concerns the relationship between types of frame alignment and what Tarrow (1983a, 1983b) has referred to as "cycles of protest." Cycles of protest are characterized by, among other things, "the appearance of new technologies of protest" that "spread from their point of origin to other areas and to other sectors of social protest" (Tarrow, 1983a:39), thus adding to what Tilly (1978) refers to as the "repertoire" of protest activity. *But* cycles of protest do not function only as crucibles out of which new technologies of social protest are fashioned; they also generate interpretive frames that not only inspire and justify collective action, but also give meaning to and legitimate the tactics that evolve. Just as some forms of innovative collective action become part of the evolving repertoire for subsequent SMOs and protesters within the cycle, so it seems reasonable to hypothesize that some movements function early in the cycle as progenitors of master frames that provide the ideational and interpretive anchoring for subsequent movements later on in the cycle. If so, then the corollary proposition follows that there ought to be cyclical variation in the predominance of particular types of frame alignment, such that transformation is more likely to be predominant in the early stages, followed by amplification and bridging.

Perhaps the occurrence, intensity, and duration of protest cycles are not just a function of opportunity structures, regime responses, and the like, but are also due to the presence or absence of a potent innovative master frame and/or the differential ability of SMOs to successfully exploit and elaborate the anchoring frame to its fullest. Hypothetically, the absence of innovative master frames may account in part for the failure of mass mobilization when the structural conditions seem otherwise ripe; or a decline in movement protest activity when the structural conditions remain fertile may be partly due to the failure of SMOs to exploit and amplify the anchoring frame in imaginative and inspiring ways. In either case, latent structural potential fails to manifest itself fully.

A third set of issues implied by the foregoing considerations concerns the factors that account for variation in the relative success or failure of framing processes in mobilizing potential constituents. In arguing that one or more varieties of frame alignment is a necessary condition for movement participation, we have proceeded as if all framing efforts are successful. But clearly that is not the case. Potential constituents are sometimes galvanized and mobilized; on other occasions framing efforts fall on deaf ears and may even be counter-productive. This obdurate fact thus begs the question of why framing processes succeed in some cases but not in others. There are least two sets of factors at work here.

One involves the content or substance of preferred framings and their degree of resonance with the current life situation and experience of the potential constituents. Does the framing suggest answers and solutions to troublesome situations and dilemmas that resonate with the way in which they are experienced? Does the framing build on and elaborate existing dilemmas and grievances in ways that are believable and compelling? Or is the framing too abstract and even contradictory? In short, is there some degree of what might be conceptualized as frame resonance? We propose that one of the key determinants of the differential success of framing efforts is variation in the degree of frame resonance, such that the higher degree of frame resonance, the greater the probability that the framing effort will be relatively successful, all else being equal. Many framings may be plausible, but we suspect that relatively few strike a responsive chord and are thus characterized by a high degree of frame resonance. Consideration of this issue calls for closer inspection than heretofore of not only the nature of the interpretive work and resources of SMOs, but also of the degree of fit between the resultant framings or products of that work and the life situation and ideology of potential constituents.

The second set of factors that we think bears directly on the relative success or failure of framing efforts concerns the configuration of framing hazards or "vulnerabilities" (Goffman, 1974:439–95) that confront SMOs as they go about the business of constructing and sustaining particular frame alignments. The excessive use of frame bridging techniques by SMOs, for example, may lead to an oversaturated market. Consequently, a movement may find itself vulnerable to discounting, particularly when potential adherents and conscience constituents are inundated by a barrage of similar impersonal appeals from a variety of competing SMOs.

Frame amplification, too, has its own vulnerabilities, as when a movement fails to consistently protect or uphold those core values or beliefs being highlighted. If, on the other hand, a value becomes discredited or loses its saliency, or a belief is popularly refuted, it may drag associated frames down along with it.

The foregoing observations suffice to illustrate that the frame alignment process is an uneasy one that is fraught with hazards or vulnerabilities throughout a movement's life history, and particularly at certain critical junctures, as when SMOs seek to establish coalitions or when they are attacked by countermovements. The ways in which SMOs manage and control these frame vulnerabilities, as well as interpretative resources in general, thus seem as crucial to the temporal viability and success of an SMO as the acquisition and deployment of more tangible resources, which to date have received the lion's share of attention by research informed by the resource mobilization frame.

By focusing on the role SMOs play in the frame alignment process, we have not intended to suggest that there are not other micromobilization agencies or contexts. Clearly, there is evidence that everyday social circles and local, non-movement communal organizations can function as important micromobilization agencies. The organizing role of the black churches in the early stages of the civil rights movement has been well documented (McAdam, 1982; Morris, 1984), as has the similar role performed by Islamic Mosques throughout the Middle East (Snow and Marshall, 1984). Mass protests that exist apart from SMOs have also been suggested as important mobilizing vehicles by European scholars (Melucci, 1980; Pizzorno, 1978; Touraine, 1981), and single protest events have been hypothesized to function in a similar manner as well (Tarrow, 1983a, 1983b). Precisely how these latent mobilizing structures and incidents of collective behavior affect frame alignment, and thereby facilitate consensus or action mobilization, is not clear, however. Thus, a fourth issue subsequent research ought to address concerns the relationship between extra-movement, micromobilization agencies, and the various types of frame alignment, focusing in particular on the processes and mechanisms through which frame alignment is effected in different contexts.

One might ask, of course, what difference it makes whether we can specify empirically how and in what contexts frame alignment of one variety or another is effected. Is it not enough to know that frame alignment is produced and constituents are mobilized? The answer is *no* for several reasons. As Tilly (1978) and his associates have shown, collective actors come and go. Some show up when not anticipated. Others fail to mobilize and press their claims, even when they appear to have a kind of natural constituency. And those that do show up vary considerably in terms of how successful they are. The argument here is that the reasons why some show up and others do not, why some stay in contention longer than others, and why some achieve greater and more enduring success, have to do not only with changes in opportunities and the expansion and appropriation of societal resources, but also with whether frame alignment has been successfully effected and sustained.

REFERENCES

Bateson, Gregory. 1972. *Steps to an Ecology of the Mind.* New York: Ballantine Books.

Bern, Daryl J. 1970. *Beliefs, Attitudes, and Human Affairs.* Belmont, CA: Brooks/Cole Publishing.

Benford, Robert D. 1984. *The Interorganizational Dynamics of the Austin Peace Movement.* Unpublished M.A. Thesis, Department of Sociology, University of Texas at Austin.

Berger, Bennet M. 1981. *The Survival of a Counterculture.* Berkeley: University of California Press.

Berger, Peter L., and Thomas Luckmann. 1966. *The Social Construction of Reality.* Garden City, NY: Doubleday.

Bird, Caroline. 1969. *Born Female.* New York: Pocket Books.

Borhek, James T., and Richard F. Curtis. 1975. *A Sociology of Belief.* New York: Wiley.

Bromley, David A., and Anson D. Shupe, Jr. 1979. *"Moonies" in America.* Beverly Hills: Sage.

Carmichael, Stokely, and Charles V. Hamilton. 1967. *Black Power: The Politics of Liberation in America.* New York: Vintage Books.

Coser, Lewis A. 1969. "The Visibility of Evil." *Journal of Social Issues* 25:101–109.

———. 1974. *Greedy Institutions.* New York: Free Press.

Crittenden, Kathleen S. 1983. "Sociological Aspects of Attribution." *Annual Review of Sociology* 9:425–46.

Deckard, Barbara Sinclair. 1979. *The Women's Movement.* New York: Harper and Row.

Fanon, Franz. 1967. *Black Skin, White Masks.* New York: Grove Press.

Ferree, Myra Marx, and Frederick D. Miller. 1985. "Mobilization and Meaning: Toward an Integration of Social Movements." *Sociological Inquiry* 55:38–51.

Fireman, Bruce, and William H. Gamson. 1979. "Utilitarian Logic in the Resource Mobilization Perspective." Pp. 8–45 in *The Dynamics of Social Movements*, edited by Mayer N. Zald and John D. McCarthy. Cambridge, MA: Winthrop Publishers.

Forward, John R., and Jay R. Williams. 1970. "Internal-external Control and Black Militancy." *Journal of Social Issues* 25:75–92.

Gamson, William A. 1968. *Power and Discontent.* Homewood, IL: Dorsey.

Gamson, William A., Bruce Fireman, and Steven Rytina. 1982. *Encounters with Unjust Authority.* Homewood, IL: Dorsey.

Goffman, Erving. 1974. *Frame Analysis*, Cambridge: Harvard University Press.

Granovetter, Mark. 1978. "Threshold Models of Collective Behavior." *American Journal of Sociology* 83:1420–43.

Gurin, Patricia, Gerald Gurin, Rosina Lao, and Muriel Beattie. 1969. "Internal-External Control in the Motivational Dynamics of Negro Youth." *Journal of Social Issues* 25:29–54.

Heirich, Max. 1977. "Change of Heart: A Test of Some Widely Held Theories about Religious Conversion." *American Journal of Sociology* 83:653–80.

Hollander, Edwin P. 1958. "Conformity, Status, and Idiosyncrasy Credit." *Psychological Review*, 65:117–27.

Institute for Social Research. 1979. "Americans Seek Self-Development, Suffer Anxiety from Changing Roles." *ISR Newsletter.* University of Michigan. Winter: 4–5.

Isaac, Larry, Elizabeth Mutran, and Sheldon Stryker. 1980. "Political Protest Orientations Among Black and White Adults." *American Sociological Review* 45:191–213.

James, William. 1950 (1890). "The Perception of Reality." Pp. 283–324 in *Principles of Psychology*, Vol. 2. New York: Dover Publications.

Jenkins, J. Craig. 1983. "Resource Mobilization Theory and the Study of Social Movements." *Annual Review of Sociology*, 9:527–53.

Jenkins, J. Craig, and Charles Perrow. 1977. "Insurgency of the Powerless: Farm Worker Movements (1964–1972)." *American Sociological Review* 42:249–68.

Jones, Edward E., and Richard E. Nisbet. 1971. *The Actor and the Observer: Divergent Perspectives on the Causes of Behavior.* Morristown, NJ: General Learning Press.

Katz, Alfred H. 1981. "Self-Help and Mutual Aid: An Emerging Social Movement." *Annual Review of Sociology* 7:129–55.

Kelley, Harold H. 1972. *Causal Schemata and the Attribution Process.* Morristown, NJ: General Learning Press.

Klandermans, Bert. 1983. "The Expected Number of Participants, the Effectiveness of Collective Action, and the Willingness to Participate: The Free-Riders Dilemma Reconsidered." Paper presented at the meetings of the American Sociological Association, Detroit.

―――. 1984. "Mobilization and Participation: Social-Psychological Expansions of Resource Mobilization Theory." *American Sociological Review* 49:583–600.

Leites, Nathan, and Charles Wolf, Jr. 1970. *Rebellion and Authority*. Chicago: Markham Publishing Company.

Liebman, Robert C. 1983. "Mobilizing the Moral Majority." Pp. 49–73 in *The New Christian Right: Mobilization and Legitimation*, edited by Robert C. Liebman and Robert Wuthnow. New York: Aldine Publishing Co.

Lofland, John. 1977. *Doomsday Cult*. 2nd edition. New York: Irvington.

Lofland, John, and Michael Jamison. 1984. "Social Movement Locals: Modal Member Structures." *Sociological Analysis* 45:115-29.

McAdam, Doug. 1982. *Political Process and the Development of Black Insurgency, 1930–1970*. Chicago: The University of Chicago Press.

―――. 1984. "Structural Versus Attitudinal Factors in Movement Recruitment." Paper presented at the meetings of the American Sociological Association, San Antonio.

McCarthy, John D. 1986. "Prolife and Prochoice Movement Mobilization: Infrastructure Deficits and New Technologies." In *Social Movements and Resource Mobilization in Organizational Society: Collected Essays*, edited by Mayer N. Zald and John D. McCarthy. New Brunswick, NJ: Transaction Books.

McCarthy, John D., and Mayer N. Zald. 1973. *The Trend of Social Movements in America: Professionalization and Resource Mobilization*. Morristown, NJ: General Learning Press.

―――. 1977. "Resource Mobilization and Social Movements: A Partial Theory." *American Journal of Sociology* 82:1212–41.

McHugh, Peter. 1968. *Defining the Situation: the Organization of Meaning in Social Interaction*. Indianapolis: Bobbs-Merrill.

Mead, George H. 1932. *The Philosophy of the Present*. Chicago: Open Court.

Melucci, Alberto. 1980. "The New Social Movements: A Theoretical Approach." *Social Science Information* 19:199–226.

Mills, C. Wright. 1940. "Situated Actions and Vocabularies of Motive." *American Sociological Review* 5:404–13.

Moore, Barrington. 1978. *Injustice: The Social Bases of Obedience and Revolt*. White Plains, NY: Sharpe.

Morris, Aldon. 1981. Black Southern Student Sit-In Movements: An Analysis of Internal Organization." *American Sociological Review* 45:744–67.

―――. 1984. *The Origins of the Civil Rights Movement: Black Communities Organizing for Change*. New York: Free Press.

Oberschall, Anthony. 1973. *Social Conflict and Social Movements*. Englewood Cliffs, NJ: Prentice-Hall.

―――. 1980. "Loosely Structured Collective Conflicts: A Theory and an Application." Pp. 45-88 in *Research in Social Movements, Conflict and Change*, Vol. 3. Edited by Louis Kreisberg. Greenwich, CT: JAI Press.

Oliver, Pamela. 1980. "Rewards and Punishments as Selective Incentives for Collective Action: Theoretical Investigations." *American Journal of Sociology* 84:1356–75.

―――. 1984. "If You Don't Do It, Nobody Will: Active and Token Contributors to Local Collective Action." *American Sociological Review* 49:601–10.

―――. 1985. "Bringing the Crowd Back In: The Non-organizational Elements of Social Movements." Paper presented at the meetings of the American Sociological Association at Washington, D.C.

Olson, Mancur. 1965. *The Logic of Collective Action: Public Goods and the Theory of Groups*, Cambridge: Harvard University Press.

Paige, Jeffrey M. 1971. "Political Orientation and Riot Participation." *American Sociological Review* 36:810–20.

Piven, Frances Fox, and Richard A. Cloward. 1977. *Poor Peoples' Movements*. New York: Vintage Books.

Pizzorno, Allesandro. 1978. "Political Exchange and Collective Identity in Industrial Conflict." Pp. 277–98 in *The Resurgence of Class Conflict in Western Europe since 1968*, Vol. II. Edited by Colin Crouch and Allesandro Pizzorno. London: Macmillan.

Portes, Alejandro. 1971a. "On the logic of Post-Factum Explanations: The Hypothesis of Lower-Class Frustration as the Cause of Leftist Radicalism." *Social Forces* 50:26–44.

―――. 1971b. "Political Primitivism, Differential Socialization, and Lower-Class Leftist Radicalism." *American Sociological Review* 36:820–35.

Rochford, E. Burke. 1982. "Recruitment Strategies, Ideology, and Organization in the Hare Krishna Movement." *Social Problems* 29:399–410.

———. 1985. *Hare Krishna in America.* New Brunswick, NJ: Rutgers University Press.

Rokeach, Milton. 1968. *Beliefs, Attitudes, and Values.* San Francisco: Jossey-Bass.

———. 1973. *The Nature of Human Values.* New York: Free Press.

Schutz, Alfred. 1962. "On Multiple Realities." Pp. 207–59 in *Collected Papers.* Vol. 1. The Hague: Martinus Nijhoff.

Seeman, Melvin. 1975. "Alienation Studies." *Annual Review of Sociology* 1:91–123.

Shibutani, Tamotsu. 1970. "On the Personification of Adversaries." Pp. 223–33 in *Human Nature and Collective Behavior: Papers in Honor of Herbert Blumer,* edited by Tamotsu Shibutani. Englewood Cliffs, NJ: Prentice-Hall.

Snow, David A. 1979. "A Dramaturgical Analysis of Movement Accommodation: Building Idiosyncrasy Credit as a Movement Mobilization Strategy." *Symbolic Interaction* 2:23–44.

———. 1986. "Organization, Ideology and Mobilization: The Case of Nichiren Shoshu of America." In *The Future of New Religious Movements,* edited by David G. Bromleyu and Phillip E. Hammond. Macon, GA: Mercer University Press.

Snow, David A., and Richard Machalek. 1983. "The Convert as a Social Type." Pp. 259–89 in *Sociological Theory,* edited by Randall Collins. San Francisco: Jossey-Bass.

———. 1984. "The Sociology of Conversion." *Annual Review of Sociology* 10:167–80.

Snow, David A., and Susan Marshall. 1984. "Cultural Imperialism, Social Movements, and the Islamic Revival." Pp. 131–52 in *Social Movements, Conflicts, and Change.* V.7. Edited by Louis Kriesberg. Greenwich, CT: JAI Press.

Snow, David A., Louis A. Zurcher, and Sheldon Ekland-Olson. 1980. "Social Networks and Social Movements: A Microstructural Approach to Differential Recruitment." *American Sociological Review* 45:787–801.

Stark, Rodney, and William S. Bainbridge. 1980. "Networks of Faith: Interpersonal Bonds and Recruitment to Cults and Sects." *American Journal of Sociology* 85:1376–85.

Stokes, Randall, and John P. Hewitt. 1976. "Aligning Actions." *American Sociological Review* 41:839–49.

Stryker, Sheldon, and Avi Gottlieb. 1981. "Attribution Theory and Symbolic Interactionism: A Comparison." Pp. 425–58 in *New Directions in Attribution Research,* Vol. 3. Edited by John H.

Harvey, William Ickes, and Robert F. Kidd. Hillsdale, NJ: Erlbaum.

Tarrow, Sidney. 1983a. *Struggling to Reform: Social Movements and Policy Change During Cycles of Protest.* Ithaca, NY: Cornell University.

———. 1983b. "Resource Mobilization and Cycles of Protest: Theoretical Reflections and Comparative Illustrations." Paper presented at the meetings of the American Sociological Association, Detroit.

Tilly, Charles. 1978. *From Mobilization to Revolution.* Reading, MA: Addison-Wesley Publishing Co.

Tilly, Charles, Louise Tilly, and Richard Tilly. 1975. *The Rebellious Century, 1830–1930.* Cambridge, MA: Harvard University Press.

Touraine, Alain. 1981. *The Voice and the Eye: An Analysis of Social Movements.* Cambridge, MA: Cambridge University Press.

Trotsky, Leon. 1959 (1932). *The History of the Russian Revolution,* edited by F. W. Dupre. New York: Doubleday.

Turner, Ralph H. 1969. "The Theme of Contemporary Social Movements." *British Journal of Sociology* 20:390–405.

———. 1983. "Figure and Ground in the Analysis of Social Movements." *Symbolic Interaction* 6:175–81.

Turner, Ralph H., and Lewis M. Killian. 1972. *Collective Behavior.* Englewood Cliffs, NJ: Prentice-Hall.

Useem, Bert. 1980. "Solidarity Model, Breakdown Model and the Boston Anti-Busing Movement." *American Sociological Review* 45:357–69.

Useem, Michael. 1975. *Protest Movements in America.* Indianapolis: Bobbs-Merrill.

Viguerie, Richard A. 1980. *The New Right: We Are Ready to Lead,* Falls Church, VA: The Viguerie Company.

Wallis, Roy, and Steve Bruce. 1982. "Networks and Clockwork." *Sociology* 16:102–107.

Walsh, Edward J. 1981. "Resource Mobilization and Citizen Protest in Communities around Three Mile Island." *Social Problems* 29:1–21.

Walsh, Edward J., and Rex H. Warland. 1983. "Social Movement Involvement in the Wake of a Nuclear Accident: Activists and Free-Riders in the Three Mile Island Area." *American Sociological Review* 48:764–81.

Williams, Robin M. 1970. *American Society: A Sociological Interpretation.* New York: Alfred A. Knopf.

Wood, Michael, and Michael Hughes. 1984. "The Moral Basis of Moral Reform: Status

Discontent vs. Culture and Socialization as Explanations of Anti-Pornography Social Movement Adherence." *American Sociological Review* 49:86–99.

Zeitlin, Maurice. 1966. "Economic Insecurity and the Political Attitudes of Cuban Workers." *American Sociological Review* 31:35–50.

Zijderveld, Anton C. 1979. *On Cliches: The Supersedure of Meaning by Function in Modernity.* London: Routledge and Kegan Paul.

Zurcher, Louis A., Jr., and David A. Snow. 1981. "Collective Behavior: Social Movements." Pp. 447–82 in *Social Psychology, Sociological Perspectives,* edited by Morris Rosenberg and Ralph H. Turner. New York: Basic Books.

Zygmunt, Joseph. 1972. "Movements and Motives: Some Unresolved Issues in the Psychology of Social Movements." *Human Relations* 25:449–67.

15

CONSTRUCTING SOCIAL PROTEST

WILLIAM A. GAMSON

Movement activists are media junkies. "Advocates of causes," Edelman reminds us, "are an avid audience for the political spectacle" (1988: 6). Along with other political actors, they eagerly monitor public discourse, using it along with other resources to construct meaning on issues they care about. Media discourse provides them with "weekly, daily, sometimes hourly triumphs and defeats, grounds for hope and for fear, a potpourri of happenings that mark trends and aberrations, some of them historic."

The more sophisticated among them recognize that many in their constituency— the potential challengers whom they would like to reach—are different from them. Hopes and defeats are defined by their

"Constructing Social Protest" by William A. Gamson, in *Social Movements and Culture,* Hank Johnston and Bert Klandermans, eds. Copyright © 1995 University of Minnesota Press. Reprinted by permission of the publisher.

everyday lives, not by public affairs, and their involvement with the political spectacle is more casual and haphazardly attentive. The trick for activists is to bridge public discourse and people's experiential knowledge, integrating them in a coherent frame that supports and sustains collective action.

General-audience media are only one forum for public discourse, but they are the central one for social movements. Activists may read a variety of movement publications and attend meetings and conferences where the issues that concern them are discussed. But they cannot assume that their constituency shares these other forums or is aware of this discourse. Only general-audience media provide a potentially shared public discourse.

Of course, one can assume more sharing than exists on many issues. Two people reading the same newspaper may end up with virtually no overlap in what they process from it. But on major events, the potential is often realized. Someone speaking on neglect of the cities and racial injustice in American society in the wake of the Rodney King verdict and the ensuing Los Angeles riot can reasonably assume media-based, shared images of these events. I do not mean to imply here that the *meanings* are shared, but one can draw on this public discourse to frame an issue with some assurance that potential challengers will understand the references and allusions.

This essay focuses on how the nature of media discourse influences the construction of collective action frames by social movements. Like Gitlin (1980), it asks how the media influence movements, but the focus is less on choice of mediagenic action strategies and the generation of media-based leadership and more on how this cultural tool affects the process of constructing meaning. It reverses the questions addressed by Gamson (1988) and Ryan (1991) on how movements attempt to influence media discourse as the central site of a symbolic struggle over which framing of an issue will prevail.

Media Discourse as a Framing Resource

Imagine a group of ordinary working people carrying on a conversation in which they are trying to figure out how they think about some complex public issue. The issue is a forest through which they must find their way—but not a virgin forest. The various frames in media discourse provide maps indicating useful points of entry, provide signposts at various crossroads, highlight the significant landmarks, and warn of the perils of other paths. Many people, however, do not stick to the pathways provided, frequently wandering off and making paths of their own.

From the standpoint of the wanderer, media discourse is a cultural resource to use

in understanding and talking about an issue, but it is only one of several available. Nor is it necessarily the most important one on some issues, compared, for example, with their own experience and that of significant others in their lives. Frequently, they find their way through the forest with a combination of resources, including those they carry with them.

Elsewhere I describe conversations among about forty groups of noncollege-educated people in the Boston area on four issues: troubled industry, affirmative action, nuclear power, and Arab-Israeli conflict. "Every group on every issue shows some awareness that there is a public discourse around them, even if they make minimal use of it and frequently apologize for not having better command of it" (Gamson 1992). On some issues, I found that media discourse was the main or even the exclusive resource used in constructing meaning, with experiential knowledge playing little role.

The public discourse on which people draw is much broader than the news. They quote advertising slogans and refer to movies. Nor do they confine the media discourse on which they draw to the issue under discussion but frequently bring in other related issues to make their point. They also make use of media discourse on the issue under discussion, employing catchphrases, making references to the players featured in news accounts, and bringing in a variety of informational elements to support the frames that spotlight these facts.

Any single resource has its limits. A frame has a more solid foundation when it is based on a combination of cultural and personal resources. Let me concede that no resource is purely personal or cultural. Even our personal experience is filtered through a cultural lens. "Big Brother is you, watching" is Miller's (1988) clever phrase. We walk around with hyperreal images from movies and television and use them to code our own experiences. Media discourse is not merely something out there but also something inside our heads.

Similarly, people bring their own experiences and personal associations to their readings of cultural texts. Media images have no fixed meaning but involve a negotiation with a heterogeneous audience that may provide them with meanings quite different from the preferred reading. Oppositional and aberrant readings are common and, hence, media images are not purely cultural but infused with personal meanings as well.

Nevertheless, the mix of cultural and personal varies dramatically among different types of resources. Our experiences may have cultural elements but they are overwhelmingly our own private resources, not fully shared by others. People distinguish between knowing something from having experienced it and knowing something secondhand or more abstractly, and they generally give a privileged place to their own experiential knowledge. Experiential knowledge is valued precisely because it is so direct and relatively unmediated. While there is plenty of selectivity in the memory of experiences, it is our own selectivity, not someone else's.

Media discourse, at the other extreme, is a useful resource precisely because it is public. In spite of personal elements, it is possible to talk about the beating of Rodney King, for example, on the basis of assumed common images and factual knowledge. If everyone may not know the particular element of media discourse referred to, it is nonetheless a matter of public record, available to anyone who wants to know: you can look it up—unlike personal experience. Media discourse, then, is predominantly a cultural resource.

Iyengar and Kinder (1987) offer experimental evidence of the special impact of integrating the personal and cultural. First, they review a large number of studies that show that Americans sharply distinguish the quality of their personal lives from their judgments about public issues. For example, crime victims do not regard crime as a more serious problem for society as a whole than do those who are personally untouched by crime; people's assessments of economic conditions are largely unrelated to the economic setbacks and gains in their own lives; and the war in Vietnam was not rated as a more important problem among those who had close relatives serving there than among Americans without personal connections to the war.

The researchers then designed a series of experiments to test more subtle connections between media coverage and personal effects. One experiment concentrated on three issues—civil rights, unemployment, and Social Security. They showed edited television news broadcasts to their subjects, varying the amount of coverage of these issues systematically. (Stories on a variety of other issues were included as well.) In different conditions, subjects saw either no coverage, intermediate coverage, or extensive coverage of each of the three issues.

The subjects varied on whether they were in a category that was personally affected. Blacks were contrasted with whites on civil rights, those out of work with those currently working on the unemployment issue, and the elderly with the young on Social Security. All subjects were asked at the end to name the most important problems that the country faced.

The researchers found that on two of the three issues—civil rights and Social Security—members of the personally affected group were especially influenced by the amount of television coverage they watched. On the unemployment issue, they found no differences between the employed and the unemployed. Only this last result is consistent with the earlier studies showing the lack of relationship between people's personal lives and their views on public issues.

Iyengar and Kinder interpret their results in ways that suggest the integration of personal and cultural resources. "We suspect," they write, "that the key feature distinguishing civil rights and social security is that they are experienced psychologically both as personal predicaments and as *group* predicaments." Although they do not use the term, collective identity processes that do not operate on unemployment come into play. Presumably, being an African-American or a senior citizen engages individuals in a collective identity, but being unemployed does not. On civil rights and Social Security, then, it is not merely that "I" am affected, but also that "we" are affected. And "we" are especially sensitive and responsive to media coverage that suggests that "our" problem is an important problem for the country.

In sum, by failing to use media discourse and experiential knowledge together in constructing a frame, people are unable to bridge the personal and cultural and to anchor their understanding in both. When they fail to link their media-based understanding of an issue with experiential knowledge, their issue understanding is ad hoc and separated from their daily lives. Hence, there is a special robustness to frames that are held together with a full combination of resources.

Collective Action Frames

We know, of course, that collective action is more than just a matter of political consciousness. One may be completely convinced of the desirability of changing a situation while gravely doubting the possibility of changing it. Furthermore, we know from many studies of social movements how important social networks are for recruiting people and drawing them into political action with their friends. People sometimes act first and only through participating develop the political consciousness that supports the action.

Personal costs also deter people from participating, their agreement with a movement's political analysis notwithstanding. Action may be risky or, at a minimum, require forgoing other more pleasurable or profitable uses of time. Private life has its own legitimate demands, and caring for a sick child or an aging parent may take precedence over demonstrating for a cause in which one fully believes.

Finally, there is the matter of opportunity. Changes in the broader political structure and climate may open and close the chance for collective action to have an impact. External events and crises, broad shifts in public sentiment, and electoral changes and rhythms all have a heavy influence on whether political consciousness ever gets translated into action. In sum, the absence of a political consciousness that supports collective action can, at best, explain only one part of people's quiescence.

Lest we be too impressed by the inactivity of most people, the history of social movements is a reminder of those occasions when people do become mobilized and engage in various forms of collective action. In spite of all the obstacles, it occurs regularly and frequently surprises observers who were overly impressed by an earlier quiescence. These movements always offer one or more *collective action* frames.

Collective action frames, to quote Snow and Benford (1992), are "action oriented sets of beliefs and meanings that inspire and legitimate social movement activities and campaigns."[1] They offer ways of understanding that imply the need and desirability of some form of action. Movements may have internal battles over which particular frame will prevail or may offer several frames for different constituencies, but they will all have in common the implication that those who share the frame can and should take action.

Gamson (1992) suggests three components of these collective action frames: injustice, agency, and identity. The injustice component refers to the moral indignation expressed in this form of political consciousness. This is not merely a cognitive or intellectual judgment about what is equitable, but is what cognitive psychologists call a "hot cognition"—one that is laden with emotion (see, for example, Zajonc 1980). An injustice frame requires a consciousness of motivated human actors who carry some of the onus for bringing about harm and suffering.

The agency component refers to the consciousness that it is possible to alter conditions or policies through collective action. Collective action frames imply some sense of collective efficacy and deny the immutability of some undesirable situation. They empower people by defining them as potential agents of their own history. They suggest not merely that something can be done but that "we" can do something.

The identity component refers to the process of defining this "we," typically in opposition to some "they" who have different interests or values. Without an adversarial component, the potential target of collective action is likely to remain an abstraction—hunger, disease, poverty, or war, for example. Collective action requires a consciousness of human agents whose policies or practices must be changed and a "we" who will help to bring about change.

To understand the role of media discourse in nurturing or stifling collective action frames, I will examine how it affects each of the individual components. Since different aspects of media discourse are relevant for each, we must distinguish between the framing and salience of the issue and the movement. While there is some mutual influence of issue- and movement-framing activities, they can vary independently. One can frame the anti-Vietnam War movement negatively while embracing an antiwar frame. One can repudiate the actions of rioters in Los Angeles and elsewhere while endorsing a racial injustice frame on the condition of U.S. cities. It is always possible to accept the message and reject the messenger.

Injustice

For injustice frames, it is the framing and salience of the issue, not the movement, that is relevant. The media role in fostering or retarding injustice frames is complex and double-edged. Hardships and inequities can be presented in ways that stimulate many different emotions: compassion, cynicism, bemused irony, and resignation, for example. Injustice focuses on the kind of righteous anger that puts fire in the belly and iron in the soul. Injustice, as I argued earlier, is a hot cognition, not merely an abstract intellectual judgment about what is equitable.

The heat of a moral judgment is intimately related to beliefs about what acts or conditions have caused people to suffer undeserved hardship or loss. The critical dimension is the abstractness of the target. Vague and abstract sources of unfairness diffuse indignation and make it seem foolish. We may think it dreadfully unfair when it rains on our parade, but bad luck and nature are poor targets for an injustice frame. When impersonal and abstract forces are responsible for our suffering, we are taught to accept what cannot be changed and make the best of it. Anger is dampened by the unanswerable rhetorical question, Who says life is fair?

At the other extreme, if one attributes undeserved suffering to malicious or selfish acts by clearly identifiable persons or groups, the emotional component of an injustice frame will almost certainly be there. Concreteness in the target, even when it is misplaced and directed away from the real causes of hardship, is a necessary condition for an injustice frame. Hence, competition over defining targets is a crucial battleground in the development or containment of injustice frames.

More specifically, an injustice frame requires that motivated human actors carry some of the onus for bringing about harm and suffering. These actors may be corporations, government agencies, or specifiable groups rather than individuals. They may be presented as malicious, but selfishness, greed, and indifference may be sufficient to produce indignation.

An injustice frame does not require that the actors who are responsible for the condition be autonomous. They may be depicted as constrained by past actions of others and by more abstract forces, as long as they have some role as agents in bringing about or continuing the wrongful injury. From the standpoint of those who wish to control or discourage the development of injustice frames, symbolic strategies should emphasize abstract targets that render human agency as invisible as possible. Reification helps to accomplish this by blaming actorless entities such as "the system," "society," "life," and "human nature."

If reification does not prevent the development of an injustice frame, a second line of defense involves accepting human agency while diverting the focus toward external targets or internal opponents. Righteous anger cannot always be prevented, but it may still be channeled safely and perhaps even used to further one's pur-

poses. Some sponsors of conservative frames claimed, for example, that the social welfare programs of the 1960s caused the 1992 Los Angeles riots.

For those who would encourage collective action, these strategies of social control provide a formidable dilemma. The conditions of people's daily lives are, in fact, determined by abstract sociocultural forces that are largely invisible to them. Critical views of "the system," however accurate, may still encourage reification just as much as benign ones as long as they lack a focus on human actors.

The antidote to excessive abstraction has its own problems. In concretizing the targets of an injustice frame, there is a danger that people will miss the underlying structural conditions that produce hardship and inequality. They may exaggerate the role of human actors, failing to understand broader structural constraints, and misdirect their anger at easy and inappropriate targets.

There is no easy path between the cold cognition of an overdetermined structural analysis and the hot cognition of misplaced concreteness. As long as human actors are not central in understanding the conditions that produce hardship and suffering, we can expect little righteous anger. Targets of collective action will remain unfocused. As long as moral indignation is narrowly focused on human actors without regard to the broader structure in which they operate, injustice frames will be a poor tool for collective action, leading to ineffectiveness and frustration, perhaps creating new victims of injustice.

To sustain collective action, the targets identified by the frame must successfully bridge the abstract and the concrete. By connecting broader sociocultural forces with human agents who are appropriate targets of collective action, one can get the heat into the cognition. By making sure that the concrete targets are linked to and can affect the broader forces, one can make sure that the heat is not misdirected in ways that will leave the underlying source of injustice untouched.

Media practices have a double-edged effect in both stimulating and discouraging injustice frames. The extent to which they do one or the other differs substantially from issue to issue. But some framing practices cut across issues and operate more generally.

Some encouragement of injustice frames is built into the narrative form that dominates news reporting. Most journalists understand that news writing is storytelling, but sometimes it is made explicit. Edward Epstein describes a memo that Reuven Frank sent to his staff at NBC News: "Every news story should, without any sacrifice of probity or responsibility, display the attributes of fiction, of drama" (1973, 241). Stories were to be organized around the triad of "conflict, problem, and denouement" with "rising action" building to a climax.

This dependence on the narrative form has implications for promoting an injustice frame. Narratives focus attention on motivated actors rather than structural causes of events. As new events unfold and changes appear in the conditions of people's daily lives, human agents are typically identified as causal agents in a morality play about good and evil or honesty and corruption. The more abstract analysis of sociocultural forces favored by social scientists is deemphasized if it enters the story at all.

Media emphasis on narrative form, then, tends to concretize targets in ways that would appear to abet injustice frames. Far from serving the social control needs of authorities in this instance, media coverage frequently gives people reasons to get angry at somebody. Of course, that "somebody" need not be the real source of grievance at all but merely a convenient surrogate. Nevertheless, however righteous indignation may get channeled, media discourse on many issues quite inadvertently helps to generate it by providing concrete targets. Hence it is an obstacle to social control strategies that diffuse a sense of injustice by moving the causes of undeserved hardship beyond human agency.

At the same time, the personalization of responsibility may have the effect of blurring broader power relations and the structural causes of a bad situation. Many writers have argued that the total media experience leads to the fragmentation of meaning. News comes in quotations with ever shorter sound bites. The preoccupation with immediacy results in a proliferation of fleeting, ephemeral images that have no ability to sustain any coherent organizing frame to provide meaning over time. The "action news" formula adopted by many local news programs packs thirty to forty short, fast items into a twenty-two-and-a-half-minute "newshole"—"one minute-thirty for World War III," as one critic described it (Diamond 1975).

Bennett analyzes the news product as a result of journalistic practices that combine to produce fragmentation and confusion. "The fragmentation of information begins," he argues, "by emphasizing individual actors over the political contexts in which they operate. Fragmentation is then heightened by the use of dramatic formats that turn events into self-contained, isolated happenings." The result is news that comes to us in "sketchy dramatic capsules that make it difficult to see the connections across issues or even to follow the development of a particular issue over time" (1988: 24). Hence the structure and operation of societal power relations remain obscure and invisible.

Iyengar (1991) provides experimental evidence on how the episodic nature of media reporting on most issues affects attributions of responsibility. He contrasts two forms of presentation—the "episodic" and the "thematic." The episodic form—by far the most common one—"takes the form of a case study or event-oriented report and depicts public issues in terms of concrete instances." In contrast, the much rarer thematic form emphasizes general outcomes, conditions, and statistical evidence.

By altering the format of television reports about several different political issues as presented to experimental and control groups, Iyengar shows how people's attributions of responsibility are affected. More specifically, he shows that exposure to the episodic format makes viewers less likely to hold public officials accountable for the existence of some problem and less likely to hold them responsible for alleviating it.

The implication of this line of argument is that if people simply relied on the media, it would be difficult to find any coherent frame at all, let alone an injustice frame. The metanarrative is frequently about the self-reforming nature of the system, operating to get rid of the rotten apples that the news media have exposed. If moral indignation is stimulated by fingering the bad guys, it is quickly and safely assuaged by their removal.

These complicated and offsetting characteristics force one to look closely at how media discourse treats the injustice theme on specific issues. Gamson (1992) found central and highly visible injustice frames in media discourse on affirmative action but very low visibility for injustice frames on nuclear power and Arab-Israeli conflict. Injustice frames were present in media discourse on the troubled steel industry, but the targets offered for indignation were selected ones, supporting some frames much more than others. Media-designated targets included the Japanese, for taking away the jobs of American workers, and the "Nader juggernaut," for forcing expensive health and safety regulations on American industry, but did not include the disinvestment decisions of U.S. steel companies.

Agency

What does it mean when demonstrators chant, "The whole world is watching"? It means that they matter—that they are making history. The media spotlight validates the fact that they are important players. Conversely, a demonstration with no media coverage at all is a nonevent, unlikely to have any positive influence on either mobilizing potential challengers or influencing any target. No news is bad news.

For this component of collective action frames, it is mainly attention that matters. How the issue is framed or even whether the movement is framed positively or negatively is irrelevant; the salience of the movement is the variable of interest. Potential challengers in the audience get the message that this group is taken seriously and must be dealt with in some way. Arrests and suppression only confirm the fact that they are important enough to be a threat to authorities. The content that matters with respect to agency is about the power of the movement and the ability of authorities to control it. The media role in this is, as usual, complicated.

The forces that discourage a sense of agency among ordinary citizens in most societies are overwhelming. Culture and social structure combine to induce collective helplessness. The vast majority seem condemned to remain subject to sociocultural forces that systematically remove from their consciousness any sense that they can collectively alter the conditions and terms of their daily lives.

Most of us, even those with political activist identities, spend most of our time and energy on sustaining our daily lives. Flacks points out that this includes not only meeting material needs but also "activity and experience designed to sustain one's self as a human being—to validate or fulfill the meaning of one's life, reinforce or enhance one's sense of self-worth, [and] achieve satisfaction and pleasure" (1988: 2). This daily activity typically takes for granted and reinforces the patterned daily life characteristic of a community or society; only very rarely do people have an opportunity to engage in activity that challenges or tries to charge some aspect of this pattern—what Flacks calls "making history."

As long as history making is centralized and hierarchical, with very little opportunity for people to participate in any of the institutions that set the conditions of their daily lives, they will inevitably feel "that they themselves are objects of historical forces alien to themselves, that they themselves are without power" (Flacks 1988: 5). Everyday life and history are experienced as separate realms because we have a national political economy that is dominated by centralized, hierarchical, national corporations and a national state.

This structural impediment to collective agency is reinforced by a political culture that operates to produce quiescence and passivity. Merelman tells us:

> [A] loosely bounded culture prevents Americans from controlling their political and social destinies, for the world which loose boundedness portrays is not the world of political and social structures that actually exists. It is, instead, a shadowland, which gives Americans little real purchase on the massive, hierarchical political and economic structures that dominate their lives. (1984: 1)

He analyzes the role of television in particular in promoting a loosely bounded culture that backs people away from politics and directs them toward a private vision of the self in the world.

Edelman (1988) points to the powerful social control that is exercised, largely unconsciously, through the manipulation of symbolism used in "constructing the political spectacle." Problems, enemies, crises, and leaders are constantly being constructed and reconstructed to create a series of threats and reassurances. To take it in is to be taken in by it. "For most of the human race," he writes in his conclusion, "political history has been a record of the triumph of mystification over strategies to maximize well-being." Rebellious collective action can even buttress the dominant worldview by helping political elites in their construction of a stable enemy or threat that justifies their policies and provides a legitimation for political repression.

Bennett observes how the structure and culture of news production combine to limit popular participation:

> As long as the distribution of power is narrow and decision processes are closed, journalists will never be free of their dependence on the small group of public relations experts, official spokespersons, and powerful leaders whose self-serving pronouncements have become firmly established as the bulk of the daily news. (1988: xii)

Furthermore, these "advertisements for authority" are surrounded by other reports "that convey fearful images of violent crime, economic insecurity, and nuclear war. Such images reinforce public support for political authorities who promise order, security, and responsive political solutions." Granting that people take it all with a grain of salt, he argues that even minimal acceptance of basic assumptions about political reality is enough to discourage most people from participating actively in the political process.

It is no wonder, Bennett concludes, that few Americans become involved politically and "most cannot imagine how they could make a political difference." One can break out by reading specialized publications with a broader range of discourse, but "those who take the time to do so may find themselves unable to communicate with the majority who remain trapped on the other side of the wall of mass media imagery" (1988: xv). Gans, reviewing the many reasons for people to avoid political activities, is led to conclude that "it is surprising to find any citizen activity taking place at all" (1988: 70).

And yet it does. There are clearly moments when people do take it upon themselves to do more than evade or transcend the terms and conditions of their daily lives and behave as collective agents who can change them. At some level, they harbor a sense of potential agency. Are social scientists, in emphasizing how this culture of quiescence is produced and maintained, themselves promulgating yet another set of reasons for inaction, another discouragement to agency? Where are the cracks in which some idea of collective agency stays alive, ready to grow and prosper under the proper conditions, as it did so dramatically and to everyone's surprise in Eastern Europe, for example?

I accept the claim that American media discourse systematically discourages the idea that ordinary citizens can alter the conditions and terms of their daily lives through their own actions. But this message comes through more equivocally on some issues than on others, and in some special contexts a sense of collective agency is even nurtured.

Among the four issues (troubled industry, affirmative action, nuclear power, Arab-Israeli conflict) discussed in Gamson (1992), the generalization seems strongest for media discourse on problems in the steel industry.

One media sample covered a moment of significant citizen action—a community effort by workers and other citizens in the Mahoning Valley area in Ohio to buy and run Youngstown Sheet and Tube Company. Sheet and Tube had been acquired in 1969 by a New Orleans-based conglomerate, the Lykes Corporation, which had used it as a "cash cow." Rather than modernizing the plant, Lykes used its cash flow to service the debt it had assumed in buying Sheet and Tube and to finance other new acquisitions.

By 1977, Lykes tried to sell the depleted company but found no buyers among other foreign and domestic steel companies; in September, it announced that it would permanently close its largest mill in the area and lay off 4,100 employees. An estimated 3,600 additional jobs would be lost through effects on local suppliers and retail businesses. Meanwhile, the United Steelworkers of America, with its primary weapon, the strike, rendered largely useless by changes in the worldwide steel industry, tried desperately to hold on to the gains it had won in the past but seemed incapable of any initiative.

In response, a broad group of religious leaders formed the Ecumenical Coalition of the Mahoning Valley to search for a solution to the crisis. At the suggestion of local steelworkers, they began to explore the possibility of a combined worker-community buyout. Alperovitz and Faux describe the action as embodying "concerns for jobs rather than welfare, for self-help and widespread participation rather than dependence on absentee decision-makers" (1982, 355).

The new company was to be known as Community Steel, directed by a fifteen-member board with six members elected by the company's workers, six by stockholders, and three by a broadly based community corporation. Thousands of residents pledged savings to a fund that would purchase the factory, and the coalition received a grant from the Department of Housing and Urban Development (HUD) to conduct a feasibility study. Eventually, the plan faltered when the Carter administration failed to support the needed loan guarantees, but the two-year Youngstown effort was clearly the largest and most significant attempt to convert a plant to worker-community ownership.

Was it visible in national media discourse? When they are covering a continuing issue such as the decline of the troubled steel industry, journalists look for a topical peg on which they can hang their stories. The Carter administration provided one when it offered a six-point plan to deal with the problems of the steel industry in the late fall of 1977. If there was a story in the Youngstown effort begun a couple of months earlier, this was an excellent opportunity to include it. It was receiving extensive coverage in local media. Grassroots efforts of this sort are novel enough, and it was too soon to know what the outcome would be. HUD secretary Patricia Harris was calling for "new models of community involvement to solve these problems" (Alperovitz and Faux 1982: 355). One might expect that the normal assumption in media discourse that citizen action is irrelevant might well be suspended in such an instance.

A two-week sample of media commentary in fifty daily newspapers, three major television networks, and three major newsmagazines found no references or allusions to citizen action in the Mahoning Valley in the heart of the steel industry. Workers who appear in this commentary are passive; they are never the subject of what is happening, always its unfortunate object. Even their status as victims is sometimes challenged. Columnist James Reston thought they partly brought it on themselves; he chided American workers who "increasingly con-

demn the integrity of work and reject the authority of their managers" and quoted approvingly from a former Nixon administration Labor Department official who claimed that workers "no longer think that hard work pays off" and "increasingly resist authority in their companies, communities, churches, or governments" (*New York Times*, December 2, 1977).

On affirmative action, citizen action was visible when an administration sympathetic to the civil rights movement was in power and became largely invisible when official discourse turned unsympathetic. Official sympathy for citizen action, then, may alter its normal disparagement or invisibility and encourage journalists to treat collective actors as if they were relevant players in the policy arena.

On nuclear power, citizen action became and remained visible in spite of an official discourse that belittled it and attempted to diminish its importance. Apparently, there are circumstances in which media discourse will portray a movement as a significant actor even without official encouragement. On nuclear power, in particular, a strong case could be made that media discourse has been more help than hindrance to the antinuclear movement. It serves no official agenda to have antinuke protesters taken so seriously that they provide potential models for the next community targeted for construction of a nuclear reactor. Indeed, officials in industry and government who might consider commissioning a new nuclear reactor must certainly be deterred by the likely prospect of prolonged local protest with extensive media coverage.

Media-amplified images of successful citizen action on one issue can generalize and transfer to other issues. The repertoire of collective action presented on a broad range of political issues in media discourse—of boycotts, strikes, and demonstrations, for example—can easily be divorced from the particular context in which it is presented and adapted to other issues. Gamson (1992) concludes that "the media role in portraying collective agency seems, to a substantial degree, issue specific and variable rather than constant."

But none of this evidence contradicts Gitlin's (1980) observations on the type of collective action that will draw the media spotlight. Between the sustained but unspectacular citizen action of the Mahoning Valley coalition and the flames of burning buildings in the Los Angeles riot, there is no contest. The media may offer occasional models of collective action that make a difference, but they are highly selective ones.

Identity

Being a collective agent implies being part of a "we" who can do something. The identity component of collective action frames is about the process of defining this "we," typically in opposition to some "they" who have different interests or values. As Melucci (1989) suggests, social movements elaborate and negotiate this meaning over time, and some even make the question of "who we are" an important part of their internal discourse.

Here it is the media framing of the movement, not the issue, that is relevant. Media images of a movement, as Gitlin (1980: 3) argues, "become implicated in a movement's self-image," and frequently the quality of the media images does not present the movement's intended identity. Since there are many aspects to a collective identity, it is quite possible for media coverage to reinforce one part that a movement wishes to encourage at the same time that it contradicts or undercuts other parts.

It is useful to think of collective identities as three embedded layers: *organizational,* *movement,* and *solidary group.* The organizational layer refers to identities built around movement carriers—the union maid or the party loyalist, for example. This layer may or may not be embedded in a movement layer that is broader than any particular organization. The identity of peace activists, for example, rarely rests on one organization; people support different efforts at different moments while subordinating all organizations to their broader movement identity.

Finally, the movement layer may or may not be embedded in a larger solidary group identity constructed around people's social location—for example, as workers or as black women. That constituents may come from a common social location does not itself mean that this will be relevant for movement or organizational identities. Environmental activists, for example, may be largely white and professional-managerial class, but they are likely to decry the narrowness of their base. Their internal discourse often focuses on how they can activate more workers and people of color.

Sometimes these different layers are so closely integrated that they become a single amalgam: a movement arises out of a particular solidary group with widespread support from it, and one particular organization comes to embody the movement. Often, however, the different layers are separate. Many working-class Americans, for example, personally identify with 49 working people, but have no identification with their union and think of the "labor movement" as something that happened fifty years ago.

Note that the locus of collective identity—for all three layers—is at the sociocultural, not the individual, level. It is manifested through the language and symbols by which it is publicly expressed—in styles of dress, language, demeanor, and discourse. One learns about its content by asking people about the meaning of labels and other cultural symbols, not about their own personal identity.

All social movements have the task of bridging individual and sociocultural levels. This is accomplished by enlarging the personal identities of constituents to include the relevant collective identities as part of their definition of self. The most powerful and enduring collective identities link solidary, movement, and organizational layers in the participants' sense of self. The movement layer is especially critical because it is a necessary catalyst in fusing solidary and organizational identification in an integrated movement identity.

Some movements attempt to mobilize their constituents with an all-inclusive "we." "We" are the world, humankind, or, in the case of domestic issues, all good citizens. Such an *aggregate* frame turns the "we" into a pool of individuals rather than a potential collective actor. The call for action in such frames is personal—for example, to make peace, hunger, or the environment your personal responsibility.

There is no clear "they" in aggregate frames. The targets are not actors but abstractions—hunger, pollution, war, poverty, disease. These abstractions do not point to an external target whose actions or policies must be changed. If pollution is the problem and we are all polluters, then "we" are the target of action. "We" are the "they" in such frames, and neither agent nor target is a collective actor.

Collective action frames, in contrast, are adversarial; "we" stand in opposition or conflict to some "they." "They" are responsible for some objectionable situation and have the power to change it by acting differently in some fashion. We and they are differentiated rather than conflated.

Aggregate frames are central to what Lofland (1989) and McCarthy and Wolfson

(1992) call "consensus movements." The latter define them as "organized movements for change that find *widespread support* for their goals and *little or no organized opposition* from the population of a geographic community." The movement against drunk driving provides an example. But widespread support for the broadest goals of a movement does not tell us much about whether there will be organized opposition. This depends on how a group translates its goals into action imperatives. Within the same movement, different social movement organizations will vary in how they frame the issue and in the form and targets of their action. The peace and environmental movements provide examples of a range of more consensual and more adversarial groups. It seems more useful to speak of consensus *frames* or consensus *strategies* rather than to treat this as a property of movements.

A blurry "they," by itself, does not imply an aggregate frame. It is quite possible to have a clear collective "we" while the "they" remains vague because it is so elusive. This is especially likely to be true when the main targets of change are cultural more than political and economic. If one is attacking, for example, the dominant cultural code of what is normal, the decisions of governments and powerful corporate actors may be secondary. In the pursuit of cultural change, the target is often diffused through the whole civil society and the "they" being pursued is structurally elusive.

In such a situation, the mass media are likely to become the ambivalent target of action. To the extent that they reflect the cultural code that the group is challenging, they are necessarily an adversary. But since they also are capable of amplifying the challenge and expanding its audience, helping it to reach the many settings in which cultural codes operate, they are necessarily a potential ally as well. Hence the characteristic ambivalence with which so many movement organizations approach the mass media as both a means for changing society and a target that epitomizes the objectionable cultural practices being challenged.

In sum, frames with a clear "we" and an elusive "they" are quite capable of being fully collective and adversarial; unlike aggregate frames, agent and target of action are not conflated. These frames, then, are simply a more complicated type of adversarial frame.

In one respect, media discourse works to encourage adversarial frames. Collective action by movement organizations helps to define an issue as controversial, triggering the balance norm of presenting quotes from two conflicting sides. The process, with its simultaneous advantages and disadvantages from the standpoint of movements, is well illustrated by media coverage of the 1977 site occupation of the Seabrook, New Hampshire, nuclear reactor by the Clamshell Alliance.

The television story is about a dyadic conflict between Governor Meldrim Thomson and his allies and the Clamshell Alliance over whether the Seabrook reactor will be completed. The central question addressed is who will win and, hence, there is very little direct commentary about nuclear power as such. But the coverage does present images of the anti-nuclear-power movement as it implicitly addresses the question, What kind of people are against nuclear power?

For a deaf television viewer, the answer would seem to be people who wear backpacks and play Frisbee. All three networks feature these images in more than one segment. One sees beards and long hair, bandanas, "no nuke" buttons, people playing guitars and doing needlepoint. Outside the courthouse, after the demonstrators have been released, we see happy family reunions, with many children.

These visual images do not have a fixed meaning. One who believes that the experts know best may see frivolous flower children and environmental extremists who look as if they will not be happy until they turn the White House into a bird sanctuary. A more sympathetic viewer may see loving, caring, earthy young people who are socially integrated and concerned about our shared environment.

There are network differences in the words accompanying these images. The CBS and NBC coverage leaves the interpretive work to the viewer, but ABC offers its own interpretation. We are told that these are the same kind of people who were involved in antiwar demonstrations, "demonstrators in search of a cause." The network allows two members of the Clam to speak for themselves, quoting their determination to win ("We have to stop it at any cost") while omitting any quotations dealing with their reasons for acting.

The demonstrators are presented relatively sympathetically in newsmagazine coverage. Both *Time* and *Newsweek* mention their commitment to nonviolence, and *Newsweek* adds their exclusion of drugs, weapons, and fighting. The accompanying photographs reinforce the television images of backpackers; *Newsweek* calls them scruffy and mentions Frisbees, guitars, and reading Thoreau. *Time* also quotes the publisher of the *Manchester Union Leader*, William Loeb, who likened the Clam to "Nazi storm troopers under Hitler," but characterizes him in a discrediting way as an "abrasive conservative."

Some media frames invite the viewer to see the anti-nuclear movement in adversarial class terms. Opponents of nuclear power are presented as indulged children of the affluent who have everything they need. They have secure professional jobs in hand or are awaiting them and can afford to ignore the imperatives of economic growth. These "coercive utopians" (McCracken 1977, 1979) are intent on imposing their anti-growth vision on others at the expense of the real interests of working people.

The adversarial frames offered by media discourse on nuclear power do not emphasize a collective movement identity that the movement would like to embrace. The movement's preferred identity cuts across racial and class lines. To the extent that it offers an adversarial frame at all, it is the people versus the nuclear industry and its allies in government. But when this adversarial frame appears in the media, it is in highly attenuated form, and it is often undercut by imagery that emphasizes the narrowness of the solidary group identities engaged by the movement.

On the issues discussed in Gamson (1992), media discourse is heavily adversarial only on affirmative action. Troubled industry and Arab-Israeli conflict are almost never framed as adversarial across solidary group cleavages in American society. And even on affirmative action, the adversarial framing is continually undercut by a discourse that assumes persons have rights as individuals. Although the term "equal rights," for example, could apply to the claims of a group as well, the discourse makes the articulation of collective claims problematic. The assertion of injustices based on social inequalities must contend with a culturally normative response that asserts that we are all individuals and implicitly denies the relevance of social location and group differences.

In spite of the tendency of media discourse to emphasize a fight, it narrows the basis of conflict, divorcing the movement level from the solidary group level. This works against the efforts of movements to integrate the different parts of a collective identity.

Conclusion

Qualifications and nuances notwithstanding, the overall role of media discourse is clear: it often obstructs and only rarely and unevenly contributes to the development of collective action frames. The good news for movement activists is that media discourse is only one resource. Selectively integrated with other resources—especially experiential knowledge—it remains a central component in the construction of collective action frames.

Using an integrated resource strategy is far from a sufficient condition for developing this political consciousness, but it helps. It is especially important in constructing the injustice component. Experiential knowledge helps to connect the abstract cognition of unfairness with the emotion of moral indignation. Media discourse is equally important in forging an injustice frame. Experiential knowledge of injustice in concrete form stimulates the emotions, but they may dissipate for lack of a clear target. Media discourse places the experienced injustice in context, making it a special case of a broader injustice. The experiential resource concretizes injustice; the media resource generalizes it and makes it shared and collective.

Relevant experiences, be they direct, vicarious, or the generalized sort embodied in popular wisdom, are not enough. They may be sufficient to guide people to some coherent frame on an issue but, if people are to become agents who influence the conditions that govern their daily lives, they must connect their understanding with a broader public discourse as well. Without an integrated understanding, relevant events and actors in the news will remain a sideshow—and a frequently bewildering one, having little to do with their daily lives.

The problem of linkage varies from issue to issue. Meaning on some issues is overly dependent on media discourse. The difficulty people face here is connecting their media-based understanding of the issue with their everyday lives. Understanding remains abstract and emotionally distant without the elements of collective identification and moral indignation that flow from experience. Integration does not happen spontaneously unless special conditions produce it—as they can, for example, when events in the news directly disrupt or threaten to disrupt their daily lives. More typically, the relevance is indirect and some cognitive leap is necessary to bridge the gap.

The organizer's task is more difficult on such issues. Abstract argument about complex indirect and future effects will not forge the emotional linkage even if people are convinced intellectually. Two alternative strategies seem more promising than presenting arguments about general causes and effects.

The first is to search for existing experiential knowledge that can be shown to be relevant for a broader collective action frame. It helps here if organizers share the life world of those who are being encouraged to make the linkage. Then they can draw on their own experience in pointing out connections with some confidence that others will have similar stories of their own. Some relevant experiences are universal enough to transcend a broad range of social backgrounds.

The second is to create situations where people can gain experiential knowledge of injustice. Public discourse facilitates knowledge through vicarious experience when it personalizes broader injustices by using exemplary cases to embody them. Hence, the concrete experience of Anne Frank conveys the meaning of the Holocaust in an experiential mode that no amount of factual information on the 6 million Jewish victims

of Nazi death camps can convey. Social movement organizations frequently try to make the link by bringing potential participants in contact with witnesses whose firsthand accounts provide listeners with vicarious experiential knowledge.

There is a well-laid cultural trap into which movement activists sometimes fall. They frame their primary task as marketing a product for consumers through the mass media. The product is a cause in which they sincerely believe but that, for a variety of reasons, they must "sell" to others. The constituency for this mobilization effort is thought of as a set of potential buyers whose response of vote, donation, signature, or other token marks a successful sales effort. The logic of this approach leads one to look for a more effective marketing strategy, expressed through catchy symbols that will tap an emotional hot button and trigger the desired response.

Emotion is an important component of collective action frames, as I have emphasized. Perhaps it is quite possible to trigger a burst of moral indignation by finding the right photograph or clever slogan. The problem with the hot-button approach is not that it does not work, but that it directly undermines the goal of increasing people's sense of agency.

Collective agency can hardly be encouraged by treating potential participants as passive objects to be manipulated. This simply decreases any tendency toward the development of a collective identity and sympathy with some sustained effort at social change. It provides good reason to extend the pervasive cynicism about those who run the society to include those who supposedly challenge their domination.

To increase a sense of agency, symbolic strategies should attempt to draw out the latent sense of agency that people already carry around with them. Organizers need to assume that a sense of agency is, at least, dormant and capable of being awakened. Their task is to listen for it and to nurture it where it occurs spontaneously. One does not transform people who feel individually powerless into a group with a sense of collective agency by pushing hot buttons. Direct, rather than mass-mediated, relationships are necessary.

ACKNOWLEDGMENT

I wish to thank Mary Katzenstein and the editors of this volume for their helpful comments on an earlier draft.

NOTES

1. They also define collective action frames as "emergent," but this seems an unwise inclusion. Changes in political consciousness can occur at various points, sometimes well in advance of mobilization. They may have already merged by the time mobilization occurs, awaiting only some change in political opportunity to precipitate action. In other cases, they may emerge gradually, developing most fully after some initial collective action. Emergence should not be made a matter of definition.

REFERENCES

Alperovitz, Gar, and Jeff Faux. 1982. "The Youngstown Project." In *Workplace Democracy and Social Change,* edited by Frank Lindenfeld and Joyce Rothschild-Whitt. Boston: Porter Sargent.

Bennett, W. Lance. 1988. *News: The Politics of Illusion.* New York: Longman.

Diamond, Edwin. 1975. *The Tin Kazoo: Television, Politics, and the News.* Cambridge, Mass.: MIT Press.

Edelman, Murray J. 1988. *Constructing the Political Spectacle.* Chicago: University of Chicago Press.

Epstein, Edward J. 1973. *News from Nowhere.* New York: Random House.

Flacks, Richard. 1988. *Making History.* New York: Columbia University Press.

Gamson, William A. 1992. *Talking Politics.* Cambridge: Cambridge University Press.

———. 1988. "Political Discourse and Collective Action." In *International Social Movement Research: From Structure to Action,* edited by Bert Klandermans, Hanspeter Kriesi, and Sidney Tarrow. Greenwich, Conn.: JAI Press.

Gitlin, Todd. 1980. *The Whole World Is Watching.* Berkeley and Los Angeles: University of California Press.

Iyengar, Shanto. 1991. *Is Anyone Responsible?: How Television News Frames Political Issues.* Chicago: University of Chicago Press.

Iyengar, Shanto, and Donald R. Kinder. 1987. *News That Matters.* Chicago: University of Chicago Press.

Lofland, John. 1989. "Consensus Movements: City Twinning and Derailed Dissent in the American Eighties." In *Research on Social Movements.* Vol. 11. Greenwich, Conn.: JAI Press.

McCarthy, John D., and Mark Wolfson. 1992. "Consensus Movements, Conflict Movements, and the Cooptation of Civic and State Infrastructures." In *Frontiers of Social Movement Theory,* edited by Aldon Morris and Carol McClurg Mueller. New Haven, Conn.: Yale University Press.

McCracken, Samuel. 1979. "The Harrisburg Syndrome." *Commentary* 67:27–39.

———. 1977. "The War against the Atom." *Commentary* 64:33–47.

Melucci, Alberto. 1989. *Nomads of the Present: Social Movements and Individual Needs in Contemporary Society.* Philadelphia: Temple University Press.

Merelman, Richard M. 1984. *Making Something of Ourselves: On Culture and Politics in the United States.* Berkeley: University of California Press.

Miller, Mark Crispin. 1988. *Boxed-In: The Culture of TV.* Evanston, Ill.: Northwestern University Press.

Ryan, Charlotte. 1991. *Prime Time Activism.* Boston: South End Press.

Snow, David. A., and Robert D. Benford. 1992. "Master Frames and Cycles of Protest." In *Frontiers in Social Movement Theory,* edited by Aldon Morris and Carol McClurg Mueller. New Haven, Conn.: Yale University Press.

Zajonc, Robert B. 1980. "Feeling and Thinking: Preferences Need No Inferences." *American Psychologist* 35 (February): 151–75.

16

SOCIAL MOVEMENTS AS COGNITIVE PRAXIS

RON EYERMAN • ANDREW JAMISON

Introduction

There is something fundamental missing from the sociology of social movements, something that falls between the categories of the various schools and is left out of their various conceptualizations. That something is what we mean by cognitive praxis. It is not that sociologists of social movements are not aware of a certain cognitive dimension in the activities of the movements they study, but it is something that they are unable to theorize in that it remains marginal to their main concerns. As it is for most social movement activists themselves, the cognitive interests and activities of the movements being studied by sociologists are largely taken for granted. They are the unreflected assumptions of analysis rather than the objects of investigation.

The problem begins in the very act of defining a social movement. For the particularists and for most resource mobilization sociologists, a social movement is defined empirically. Indeed it is seldom defined at all, but rather it is studied as an empirical phenomenon. For the particularists, a movement is seen from the vantage point of the actor and thus definition is made by those being studied: self-definition. For the resource

mobilization school of thought, a movement is defined in operational terms: organizations are distinguished from sectors, or industries, and the movement dissolves into the particular mechanisms of mobilization and recruitment that are being analyzed. In a recent survey article, Charles Tilly has written that "the proper analogy to a social movement is neither a party nor a union but a political campaign. What we call a social movement actually consists in a series of demands or challenges to power-holders in the name of a social category that lacks an established political position" (Tilly 1985: 735–6). Instead of focusing on cognitive activity, the meaning of a movement for Tilly is to be read out of its particular "framework of action repertoires." A movement is what it does and how it does it, not what its members think and why they think the ideas that they do.

In this empirical universe populated by most American sociologists, knowledge and for many even identity are seen as nonempirical objects and thus largely outside of the sociologist's area of competence. What we refer to as cognitive praxis is seen through the prism of "packages of ideas" or clusters of issues, or, perhaps most ambitiously, as organizational ideologies or profiles (Klandermans et al., 1988). But the problem, as we see it, is that knowledge becomes disembodied; it is relegated to a largely marginal, ephemeral, or superstructural level of reality, and not to the centrality of movement identity formation where we contend it belongs. The identity of the movement becomes disinterested, stripped of its driving ideas, its cognitive meaning. The particular historical interests that a movement aims to further are not analyzed in the process of being formed, as a central component of movement praxis. The knowledge interests of a social movement are frozen into static, ready-formed packages, providing the issues or ideologies around which movements mobilize resources or socialize individuals. Cognitive praxis is invisible for eyes that are directed elsewhere or focused through the wrong paradigmatic eyeglasses. For the currently dominant paradigms of social movement analysis, it is other components of movement praxis—the tactical, strategic, organizational, even emotional actions and interactions—which are subjected to the analytical gaze of the sociologist. They are thus not seen as important sources for new cognitive developments in the sciences and/or everyday life.

For many of the European students of social movements, the difficulties are of a different sort. Here it is the political meaning of a movement that is of most importance, its sociohistorical rather than its cognitive identity. What Jean Cohen calls identity theorists are those sociologists who define social movements as attempts to create new collective identities. The identities are, however, not derived from studying the cognitive praxis of movements themselves, but rather drawn from theories of social change and philosophies of history. Lurking behind the identity theorists are the classical social theorists of the nineteenth century, and behind them the positivist and idealist philosophies of Comte and Hegel. As such, identity in the sense used by many European sociologists is something superimposed on a social movement and used as a standard of evaluation to judge their potential and historical significance, even their status as a social movement. Thus Alain Touraine, after

investigating the French antinuclear energy movement, concluded that the movement was not a real social movement: it was not involved in the struggle for what he terms "historicity" (Touraine 1983).

In a similar vein, many political writers and social thinkers on both sides of the Atlantic have sought to characterize the ideological messages of the so-called new social movements. Carl Boggs (1985) has, for instance, attempted to place some of the new movements within what he calls a post-Marxist discourse. The terms of the discourse are, to a certain extent, derived from the activity of the movements, but they are interpreted as the ideological results of the movement, and are thus seen as products rather than processes. In any case, they are not studied in formation, as cognitive praxis. We do not challenge the legitimacy or even the value of such an exercise; our point is merely that Boggs and others are not so much analyzing the movements as incorporating them into their own ideals and ideologies. Such readings of social movements are by now rather common. The primarily ideological writings of, for instance, André Gorz (1982) in France and Rudolf Bahro (1984) in Germany can be considered significant political statements, pointing toward a postindustrial or even postmaterial future (Frankel 1987). But they unfortunately contribute little to our understanding of the actual cognitive significance of social movements. What gets lost from view is the dynamic role, the mediating role that movements play in what might be termed the social shaping of knowledge. Thus, while the empirical sociologists largely neglect the cognitive praxis of social movements because it cannot be easily reduced to empirical data, for the more theoretically minded the knowledge interests of the new social movements are transformed into ideological positions or organizational programs.

Jean Cohen has suggested, as part of her attempt to synthesize the different schools of social movement theory, that the "theory of communicative action" developed by Jürgen Habermas "allows one to see how the paradigms of collective action [i.e., resource mobilization and identity theory] . . . can be complementary." She distinguishes conceptually between normative and communicative interaction and contends that, at least on the abstract level, a concept of communicative interaction can inform all theories of social movements. "It refers to the linguistically mediated, intersubjective process through which actors *establish* their interpersonal relations and coordinate their action, through negotiating definitions of the situation (norms) and coming to an agreement" (Cohen 1985: 707). Such a concept, Cohen writes, obviously forgetting Blumer's symbolic interactionism, has not been applied directly to the analysis of social movements. In any case, the process of communicative interaction has not been explored empirically—indeed, this is one of the points in her criticism of Habermas's views on social movements. Our approach to reading social movements aims to examine historical and contemporary movements from the vantage point of such communicative interaction. It is what we mean by cognitive praxis.

Perhaps closest to our position among contemporary students of social movements is the Italian sociologist Alberto Melucci, who sees the challenge of the new social movements in primarily "symbolic" terms. Drawing on the terminology of semiotics and his own, practice as a psychotherapist, Melucci sees the identity formation of social movements as a kind of social dramaturgy; the "movements no longer operate as characters but as *signs*," Melucci writes. "They do this in the sense that they translate their action into symbolic challenges that upset the dominant cultural codes and reveal their irrationality and partiality by acting at the levels (of information and communication) at which the new forms of technocratic power also operate" (Melucci 1988: 249). Social movements make power visible, Melucci argues, and they challenge the dominant meaning systems or symbols of contemporary everyday life.

Our conceptualization of social movements as cognitive praxis seeks to grasp the symbolic, or expressive, significance of social movements. But we see that significance not merely as a challenge to established power, but also and more so as a socially constructive force, as a fundamental determinant of human knowledge. The cognitive praxis of social movements is not just social drama; it is, we might say, the social action from where new knowledge originates. It is from, among other places, the cognitive praxis of social movements that science and ideology—as well as everyday knowledge—develop new perspectives. In order to see that formative influence, however, it is necessary to read social movements in a particular cognitive way.

A Sociological Conception of Knowledge

Knowledge for us is a fundamental category, providing the basis or the working materials for what Berger and Luckmann (1967) termed the social construction of reality. Society is constructed by "re-cognition," by recurrent acts of knowing that go on all the time. Knowledge in this perspective is not only or even primarily the systematized, formalized knowledge of the academic world, nor (merely) the scientific knowledge produced by sanctioned professionals. It is rather the broader cognitive praxis that informs all social activity. It is thus both formal and informal, objective and subjective, moral and immoral, and, most importantly, professional and popular.

This broad conception of knowledge was characteristic of the period between the First World War and the Second World War when the social movements of fascism and communism were seen by many intellectuals to challenge the notions of enlightened reason that were central to Western civilization. Critical theory and sociology of knowledge were both born in a public space carved out by the social movements of the 1920s and 1930s. The Marxist intellectuals of the Frankfurt School sought to combat what Max Horkheimer was to call the "eclipse of reason" with a new conceptualization of consciousness in which intellectual activity was seen as dialectically related to social praxis (Horkheimer 1974).

The general ambition of the sociology of knowledge, as developed by Max Scheler and Karl Mannheim, was more academic; it was to find a synthesis between "objectivist" and "subjectivist" conceptions of knowledge in a kind of sociological intersubjectivity. The sociology of knowledge was an explicit attempt to rise above the passions of extremist belief and develop a rational understanding of all types of knowledge, both scientific and ideological. Indeed, as it came to be developed by Karl Mannheim (1948), a detached sociology of knowledge and a group of dispassionate free-floating intellectuals were seen as crucially necessary in an age in which knowledge had become all too emotional, all too partisan.

The sociology of knowledge that Mannheim developed was, in many ways, constrained by its context. From our perspective, it went too far in narrowing the original Schelerian ambition to a sociological subfield (Jamison 1982). Our conceptualization attempts to recombine the "precision" of Mannheim with the critical social theory of Lukács, Horkheimer, Marcuse, and Adorno, whose more critical conception of knowledge developed in the 1930s in a kind of opposition to the sociology of knowledge. As such, we want to reconnect sociology of knowledge to social theory. Based on Marxism as well as on German idealistic philosophy, Lukács and the later Frankfurt School sought to analyze the relations between social change and social consciousness. Rather than starting from the ideas themselves as did the sociologists of knowledge, the critical Marxists started from society and attempted to elucidate, as well as produce, the kind of knowledge that was necessary for revolutionary change. They attempted to articulate an alternative to the bourgeois rationality of capitalist society; by developing reflection and dialectical thinking as sociological tools, Horkheimer, Marcuse, Adorno, Fromm, and the other critical theorists sought to create an alternative to the sociology of knowledge, as well as to positivist thought more generally (Jay 1973). They also sought to reconnect to the critical, more anthropological conceptions of knowledge of the early Marx in opposition to the scientific Marxism that had so much come to dominate the communist movement.

For both the sociologists of knowledge and the critical theorists, knowledge was seen as the collective creation of social groups; it emerged on the basis of what might be termed sociohistorical interest. Common to both interwar projects was an ambition to contextualize the development of consciousness, to identify the social agents of new forms of knowledge. The challenge to universal reason embodied in the social movements inspired many intellectuals to reflect on the social basis of reason and to seek means to defend and eventually revitalize the social conditions necessary for the further development of rational thought.

Rediscovering Sociological Conceptions of Knowledge: the 1960s and Beyond

In the postwar era, knowledge has tended to be reduced by sociology to one or another of its component parts; there are thus sociologists of scientific knowledge, sociologists of religious belief systems, sociologists of everyday knowledge, and even sociologists of sociological knowledge. And, as with the study of social movements, sociologists of knowledge have tended to approach their subject at different levels of abstraction, with grand theorists at one extreme and students of particular knowers or knowledge contexts at the other.

The rediscovery of the sociology of knowledge in the 1960s was both externally and internally generated. On the one hand, it grew out of the student movement and the new left, perhaps especially among natural science and engineering students. The radical concerns of some scientists, participation in the antiwar movement, and the ensuing challenges to academic authority led to a rediscovery of the debates of the 1920s and 1930s, and to a new literature of "radical science" and "radical philosophy" published in new journals and eventually in books (for instance, Rose and Rose 1975). Influential also were the works of Herbert Marcuse, in particular his *One-Dimensional Man* (1964), which presented a modern version of the critique of technological rationality for a new generation. As one of the participants in the early development of critical theory in the 1930s, Marcuse represented, as well, a personal connection between the generations. The positivism debate in Germany between Karl Popper and Theodor Adorno also played a role in bringing the legacy of critical theory into the consciousness of social scientists. By the end of the 1960s, the criticism of science within the student move-

ment and new left had inspired a new movement of environmental activism and also led many scientists out of the laboratories to create courses in "social responsibility" and eventually programs and departments in science studies.

Internally, the rediscovery of sociological conceptions of knowledge was inspired by a number of influential works which challenged the limited and highly fragmented views of knowledge that dominated postwar philosophy, history, and sociology of science. Books such as Thomas Kuhn's *Structure of Scientific Revolutions* (1962) and Berger and Luckmann's *Social Construction of Reality* (1967) pointed to an area of sociological investigation that had been neglected but which seemed to call out for detailed investigation. In the 1970s, growing numbers of sociologists challenged the then dominant institutional approach of Robert Merton (1957) and Joseph Ben-David (1971) and called for sociological analysis of the contents of science, as well as its institutions.

If we are to consider social movements in terms of their cognitive praxis, it becomes necessary to recombine what are now disparate discourses in the sociology of knowledge. Even with the new perspectives that have emerged since the 1960s, the sociology of knowledge remains divided between those who study professional, scientific knowledge and those who study "everyday" knowledge. The division has led to separate theories, separate audiences, and separate social functions. It has also meant that social movements have difficulty finding a place in the conceptual and explanatory frameworks developed by sociologists of knowledge. Cognition is seen either as the work of professional cognizers or the work of everyone; and although the connections between the various types of knowledge production are recognized, they are seldom the topic of any sustained treatment. That is what we aim to do in the rest of this book. What we suggest is a mediating role for social movements both in the transformation of everyday knowledge into professional knowledge, and, perhaps even more importantly, in providing new contexts for the reinterpretation of professional knowledge. As such, we seek to link the new, micro-level approaches of sociologists of science to the broader macro-level approaches of (critical) social theorists.

The sociologists of science have sought to show how scientific knowledge is socially constructed (Knorr-Cetina and Mulkay 1983). They have gone into the laboratories, either as anthropologists visiting a foreign planet, or as ethnomethodologists analyzing ritualized behavior, or as discourse analysts decoding scientific texts. Sociologists have uncovered the processes of negotiation by which truth is established in scientific research, disclosing how scientific concepts and theories are manufactured according to complicated actor networks and institutional frameworks (Latour 1987).

In almost all cases, however, the sociologists of science have left the broader society outside their purview. The laboratory, or the scientific workplace, has become a surrogate society, a micro-level society that either represents a particular empirical universe of its own or is made to stand as a kind of microcosm for broader macro-level processes of social interaction. In both cases, however, the contextualizations of the sociologists of scientific knowledge have become ever more internal, the contexts of relevance being limited to the institutional and organizational frameworks within which scientists work.

On the epistemological level, social constructivism has led to a relativization of scientific truth. The attempt to demystify science or, as the title of one recent volume puts it, to take "science off the pedestal," has

led to a challenge to traditional, more positivist conceptions of knowledge (Chu and Chubin 1989). Where science was traditionally conceived as rational pursuit of valid knowledge, or reliable knowledge, or, perhaps most precisely, verifiable knowledge, the new sociology of science has shown that knowledge production is a social phenomenon. Among other things, this has raised the possibility of a social epistemology by which the "truth" of scientific knowledge is seen as dependent on its social context (Fuller 1988).

It has proved difficult, however, to move from the internal contexts of research laboratories and scientific institutions to the broader society; that is, the social construction of knowledge has not yet taken broader social forces into account in developing its social epistemologies. Where do new scientific ideas come from? From which social actors, through which social processes, at which historical moments do new approaches to scientific knowledge emerge? On these fundamental questions, the new sociology of science has as yet little to say. By focusing almost exclusively on scientific research at a micro level, the field has—perhaps unwittingly—made it all but impossible to answer the more fundamental question: where does scientific knowledge come from in the first place? In not problematizing this question, the sociologists of science appear to accept some of the assumptions that they criticize, that scientific knowledge is the product of individual genius and inspiration and that its validity is derived from internal, intrascientific criteria rather than from the wider social context.

What is needed, from our perspective, is a closing of the gap between the new sociology of science and the sociology of social movements. Certain preliminary steps have been taken, such as the recent work on the sociology of technology by Wiebe Bijker and others (Bijker et al., 1987). Here, the creation of technological artifacts is seen as the work of social networks of actors, and the values and interests of those actors are seen as having a fundamental determining role in the development of technological knowledge. Similarly, anthropologists and sociologists inspired by Foucault have looked at the relations between knowledge production and political power, exploring mechanisms of institutionalization as instruments of social control and discipline (Law 1986). The focus on intellectual strategies, so central to the work of Pierre Bourdieu, has also begun to influence sociologists, and has directed attention to the subtle forms of interaction between social stratification and knowledge production (Bourdieu 1988). In many respects, this approach echoes the Marxian attempts to attribute knowledge production to class interests.

Our cognitive approach to social movements is an attempt to integrate these diverse threads into a contextual theory of knowledge. Drawing on a synthetic or interactionist tradition of social theorizing, represented in recent years especially by the work of Habermas (1987b) and Giddens (1985), our perspective seeks to reconnect an individual or psychological level of analysis to a collective or sociological level of analysis. We aim, in other words, at providing a social theory which focuses on the interactions between individual, collective, and macro societal practices. In the case of social movements, this interaction, we suggest, can best be understood as cognitive praxis. Indeed, it is our claim that a social movement *is* its cognitive praxis, that is, what distinguishes one movement from another, but also, and more importantly, what gives a social movement its significance for broader social processes.

Our focus on cognitive praxis is directed both to sociologists of knowledge and to sociologists of social movements. On the one hand, we want to provide an important "missing link" in the social construction of science. Scientific knowledge, we contend, is directly dependent on social movements in a variety of ways. In the seventeenth century, the very idea of science, as experimental philosophy, emerged in the context of the religious movements of revolutionary Britain (Webster 1975). And in the eighteenth and nineteenth centuries, science after science, discipline after discipline emerged as a result of, or in answer to, questions about nature and society that were raised by social movements. In our own time, new fields, new conceptual frameworks, new intellectual roles, new scientific problems, new scientific ideas themselves are directly attributable to the "knowledge interests" of social movements. Through what we call movement intellectuals, who are formed as intellectuals in social spaces constituted by social movements, new ideas are able to be articulated.

On the other hand, our cognitive reading of social movements can help resolve the fragmentation that currently plagues the sociology of social movements. A social epistemology that directs attention to the role of social movements as cognitive actors can avoid the polarization between grand theories and particularist studies. It can also correct the instrumental bias that is so characteristic of resource mobilization and its many variants. We want to read social movements as producers of knowledge, not as rational operators in a world of competing movement industries.

Social Movements as Knowledge Producers

The collective articulation of movement identity can be likened to a process of social learning in which movement organizations act as structuring forces, opening a space in which creative interaction between individuals can take place. At a certain point in time, the interaction takes on a further dimension, as different organizations together carve out an actual societal space, transforming what began as interpersonal interests into interorganizational concerns, that is, from individual into wider social terms. This transition from a formative to an organizational phase, we contend, is what distinguishes social movements from action groups or single-issue protest organizations. A social movement is not one organization or one particular special interest group. It is more like a cognitive territory, a new conceptual space that is filled by a dynamic interaction between different groups and organizations. It is through tensions between different organizations over defining and acting in that conceptual space that the (temporary) identity of a social movement is formed.

This does not mean that social movements are only learning processes; but it rather means that the particular character of a movement, what distinguishes it from other movements and what sets it off in time, is its cognitive praxis. Having said this, it is apparent that cognitive praxis does not come readymade to a social movement. It is precisely in the creation, articulation, formulation of new thoughts and ideas—new knowledge—that a social movement defines itself in society. This means that other elements of social movement activity are not so much ignored as reinterpreted. As we will indicate in our case study on the American civil rights movement, campaigns or demonstrations are of interest to our cognitive approach not as particular historical events or moments but as illustrations of the formative tensions of cognitive praxis.

Cognitive praxis is, we contend, the core activity of a social movement. In analyzing it, it is useful to think in terms of the phases, or stages, of development that are so well established in the study of social movements. It is generally recognized (for instance, Smelser 1962, McAdam 1982) that social movements go through a kind of lifecycle, from gestation to formation and consolidation. Social movements seldom emerge spontaneously; instead they require long periods of preparation both at the individual, group, and societal level. No social movement emerges until there is a political opportunity available, a context of social problem as well as a context of communication, opening up the potential for problem articulation and knowledge dissemination. Not every social problem, however, generates a social movement; only those that strike a fundamental chord, that touch basic tensions in a society have the potential for generating a social movement. As such, our approach tends to limit the number of social movements to those especially "significant" movements which redefine history, which carry the historical "projects" that have normally been attributed to social classes. A movement conceptualizes fundamental contradictions or tensions in society—what Smelser called structural strains: in our day, for instance, the tensions between man and nature, between the sexes, as well as between "masters" and "slaves." Yet not even that is enough to determine the emergence of a social movement. Not until the theme has been articulated, not until the tensions have been formulated in a new conceptual space can a social movement come into being, and this is a very uncertain process involving many contingencies. Our point here is that among those contingencies the ability of "movement intellectuals" to formulate the knowledge interests of the emergent social movement is particularly crucial.

At the same time, no social movement can emerge until individuals are ready to take part in it, willing to transform what C. Wright Mills (1963) called private troubles into public problems, as well as to enter into a process of collective identity formation. No matter how objectively necessary a social movement might appear to be, real individuals must make it happen. All of these levels of motivation are significant in the later stages of social movement lifecycles, as well. The longevity of a social movement is largely the result of how long a society takes it seriously as a political force, and this, in turn, depends on the commitment of individual actors, their creative use of strategy and tactics, the response of the established political institutions, and the willingness and capacity of the entire social formation to absorb, incorporate, or reject the "message" of the movement.

Cognitive praxis does not appear all at once, but emerges over time; and in conceptualizing its cyclical development, it can be valuable to draw on theories of other cyclical processes, such as those studied by students of technological innovation (Dosi et al., 1988). Students of technology have come to see innovation as a process, often starting with the discovery of new ideas in the scientific research laboratory. From the "pool" of ideas only some, usually for economic reasons, are selected for a further stage of "applied research" and development, which takes place within a corporate space of commercially oriented establishments. Those ideas that actually lead to useful products are then transferred from the realm of research and development to a third stage of marketing, or diffusion of innovations.

Thinking of the cognitive praxis of social movements as a kind of product cycle, moving from discovery/articulation through application/specification to diffusion/institutionalization is not meant to imply any mechanical logic to social movement praxis. Rather, it is meant to suggest a congruence between different kinds of social learning processes. Social movement activists "learn by doing" as much as professional engineers; and their cognitive

praxis should be expected to reflect accumulated experience of the past as much as, if not more so, than the cognitive praxis of established knowledge producers. In the case of social movements, this experience is not only that of individual actors or even of the collective group composing the particular movement, but is as well the experience of previous movements and—not least—other movements acting concurrently.

Looking at social movements as cognitive praxis means seeing knowledge creation as a collective process. It means that knowledge is not the "discovery" of an individual genius, nor is it the determined outcome of systemic interactions within an established Research and Development system. Knowledge is instead the product of a series of social encounters, within movements, between movements, and even more importantly perhaps, between movements and their established opponents.

These creative learning processes of cognitive praxis occur on several levels. They take place in the unpredictable and often unintended interaction between movement activists in planning future and reflecting on past actions. Here the question is often how the project is to be operationalized, how a particular campaign or demonstration can best be used to put the message across. The heated debates over meeting agendas and demonstration slogans and specific organizational activities that are the stuff of all social movements are, for us, examples of cognitive praxis.

Other examples take place in the interaction between movement groups and their opponents, in the myriad of arenas of confrontation and dialogue that make up the public sphere. Here the cognitive praxis is often more strategic than communicative, more instrumental than expressive. In confronting the state or other agents of established power, social movements innovate tactics and organization forms. Indeed, a social movement can be thought of as one large social innovation, a new actor in society representing previously latent interests. In this, as in many other respects, there is nothing automatically progressive about social movements; as history itself is open and often regresses, social movements can re-act, as well as act, mobilizing interests that represent regressive as well as progressive values. Their ideological orientation need not affect their creativity; all social movements are producers of knowledge.

Cognitive praxis also takes place in interactions between contemporary social movements and "old" ones, in the direct sense of the interplay and competition between old and new social movements in the same time and place, as well as between contemporary social movements and the wide range of social movements of the past. Social movements are active in the continual reinvention of tradition, and in the recombination of the values or interests of past movements. This recombination involves both the reformulation of concepts and projects as well as the reinterpretation of intellectual roles and practices.

What focusing on the cognitive praxis of social movements means is to see them as creative forces in society, as sources of inspiration as well as new knowledge. This focus has not been entirely left out of social movement research. Structural-functional theorists of collective behavior with an interest in social change like Smelser have looked at the role social movements play in signaling areas of social "strain" for political elites. Identity theorists focus on the codes or symbols that are expressed by social movements in their various actions and activities. But nowhere is this interest in cognitive praxis systematized or connected to a contextual theory of knowledge.

In order to read social movements as cognitive praxis, we must look behind some of the fashionable reductionist perspectives among sociologists of knowledge and reconsider the totality of knowledge "types." It is certainly a positive achievement that Kuhn and others have opened up scientific knowledge to sociological analysis; it is valuable indeed to understand the social processes in scientific discovery and the social interests that condition scientific development. But a perhaps unintended effect has been a relative neglect of nonscientific knowledge. This is understandable enough in our highly scientific age, but it does represent a clear narrowing of sociological focus. And it makes it difficult to see the role that social movements play in the development of knowledge.

As we shall see, the cognitive praxis of many social movements lies between the disparate types of knowledge; social movements create new types of knowledge as well as recombine or connect previously separate types of knowledge with each other. Indeed, we want to argue that much if not all new knowledge emanates from the cognitive praxis of social movements, that new ideas both in and out of science are the often unconscious results of new knowledge interests of social movements. But this formative influence can only be uncovered if we have a broad notion of knowledge to begin with.

"Reading" Social Movements Cognitively: a Note on Method

Let us conclude this chapter by trying to draw some methodological conclusions. How can a conception of social movements as cognitive praxis be put to analytical use? What does it mean to "read" social movements in a cognitive way?

As mentioned earlier, a cognitive approach to social movements means having a processual focus, seeing social movements as processes in formation. One of the main barriers to recognizing social movements as producers of knowledge is the widespread tendency to reify them, to identify social movements with organizations, parties, sects, institutions, etc. Social movements are all too often reduced to specific empirical phenomena, and as such their "theory" as well as their inner dynamic fades from consideration. We contend, however, that the distinctiveness of social movements, indeed their very historical significance, lies in their impermanence, disorganization, transience, in short in their motion. A movement moves, it can be seen (for instance, Touraine 1981) as a kind of transition from one historical conjuncture to another; and, as such, its cognitive praxis can only be identified in formation. Once the ideas engendering movement become formalized either within the scientific community or in the established political culture, they have for all intents and purposes left the space of the movement behind.

This impermanent quality of social movements is central to our approach. A movement, by definition, lives and dies, or, more colorfully perhaps, it withers away as its cognitive project disintegrates into its various component parts and they become either adopted or discarded. Movements create for a time a space for social activity, a public space for interest articulation. Usually originating in protest of the established order, a social movement creates a public space that did not previously exist. And although movements usually involve the creation of organizations or the renovation of institutions, it is important not to mistake the one for the other. Organizations can be thought of as vehicles or instruments for carrying or transporting or even producing the movement's meaning. But the meaning, we hasten to add, should not be reduced to the medium. The meaning, or

core identity, is rather the cognitive space that the movement creates, a space for new kinds of ideas and relationships to develop.

It might be useful to say something more about our particular methods of reading. First of all, we read selectively, or, more precisely, we read epistemologically. Our approach does not claim to be comprehensive: we do not mean to be able to explain why social movements happen or, for that matter, why particular individuals choose to take part in them. What interests us is what a social movement represents for the development of human knowledge. And this knowledge, as discussed above, is both formal and informal, referring to organized scientific knowledge as well as broader aspects of political and social consciousness. Through our examples, we want to provide insights into the following questions: Which new ideas are produced in social movements and how do we go about characterizing those ideas? What do particular social movements contribute to social processes of knowledge production? And finally, and perhaps most centrally, what common processes or mechanisms of cognitive praxis can we identify in social movements from different historical periods and different countries? Our attempt to answer the final question is also our contribution to the broader discussion among sociologists about the character of social movements.

Secondly, we read critically. On the one hand, we distance ourselves from the movements we study, but the sociological distance that we seek to establish is not the objectivity that so many empirical sociologists strive to achieve. It is more like a qualified subjectivity, an evaluative or reflective distance that comes from our identification with a critical theory of society, or more broadly with an interpretative or qualitative tradition of sociology. Critical distance means placing movements in context, but it also means subjecting their praxis to reflection, to theorization. We try to locate the basic beliefs of a social movement, attempting, through critical reflection, to get to the core set of assumptions that gives a particular movement its identity. This means that our critical method of reading is a sort of deconstruction; we decompose the "text" of a movement into its component parts, its various dimensions, uncovering a hidden reality behind appearance. But unlike deconstructionists we also try to put the components back together again. More precisely, our critical method offers historical, contextual understanding for activist and scholar alike. We make no epistemological claims for the truth value of the reality that we understand, nor do we claim any privileged insight for our interpretation. Ours is a social epistemology, by which the truth of knowledge is contingent on the social context in which it is practiced. In relation to movements and movement activists, we aim to be interpreters rather than legislators (Bauman 1987). In relation to sociologists of social movements, we aim to be expansionist readers rather than reductionist analyzers. We attempt to reconstruct or remember the core identity of a social movement in the broad, historically informed context of a theory of social movements.

Cognitive praxis is an operational term, but it is also, we contend, an empirical term. It is however, a particular type of empirical phenomenon. Cognitive praxis takes place and can be studied empirically, but one should not necessarily look for it in the heads of the activists involved in social movements. As we discovered in our study of environmental movements, what we then called the "knowledge interests" of the movements under investigation did not present themselves to us readyformed. They had to be sifted out of movement documents and activist recollections, and their emergence and development had to be reconstructed. But they were not exclusively our creations, superimposed on the movement

from preconceived ideologies or beliefs. Nor were they planted by us in the heads of those we interviewed, and then later harvested in a fit of self-discovery. The cognitive praxis, or knowledge interests, of the new environmental movements were rather seen in the context of a social theory, a space of our own sociological creation, between actors and organizations. In short, cognitive praxis is there, but its dimensions must be found by someone looking for them. They guide actors but not necessarily consciously or explicitly. Even more importantly, they cannot exist without the actors being guided by them. They are a kind of glue that makes a social movement what it is.

We can conceive of social movements as cognitive praxis also because we read social movements historically; we read social movements in retrospect. We distance ourselves not merely through a technique of analysis, but also through time. In order to understand the historical projects of social movements, it is necessary to see them from within a dialectical theory of history; this means that social movements are at once conditioned by the historical contexts in which they emerge, their particular time and place, and, in turn, affect that context through their cognitive and political praxis. As the opponents of established patterns of thought and of politics, social movements are creators of history: out of their oppositional stance, their utopian critique, new historical opportunities arise and new syntheses or recombinations take place. But each movement or period of movement has its own historical meaning. There are continuities between old and new social movements, but there are also substantial differences.

History is not imposed on movements, but it conditions them, it provides their starting points as well as their range of operation. This means that the dimensions of cognitive praxis must be reconstructed in the context of their actualization. Our retrospective reading focuses on the interplay between movement identity formation and long-term social processes, that is, between internal knowledge push and external political pull. We read the tension between communicative and instrumental action, to speak with Habermas, or the interplay between cognitive development and structuration of society, to speak with Giddens.

It needs to be remembered that all social movements, according to our way of thinking, are transitory phenomena. The space they create is temporary, and continually invaded by other social actors. And yet, for a time, the cognitive praxis of a social movement or perhaps more accurately, of a period of social movement, open up new opportunities for thought. For us, it is less important to label particular social movements and distinguish them from each other, or to legislate when a period of social movement begins and ends, than it is to find common denominators within movements and among different movements in a particular time period. Our point is not that definition is unimportant but that it is less important than identifying the dimensions of cognitive praxis. Arbitrary or empirically based typologies and definitions often made it difficult to find what "different" movements have in common. We share with many American sociologists the assumption that social movements are empirical phenomena that exist independently of our theories about them; but we also share the ambition of many European sociologists to uncover a deeper meaning in social movement. That deeper meaning is what we mean by cognitive praxis.

There are thus historical periods characterized by social movement and there are periods of institutionalization and absorption, when movements more or less disappear as their ideas are incorporated to reform established patterns, or are discarded; the knowledge and the activists that were a social movement are then assimilated or rejected in processes of social reconstitution.

Empirically, social movements exist only through their particular historical manifestations. They emerge, take organizational form, and are more or less successful in their attempts to affect political and social processes.

The concept of cognitive praxis allows us to specify and distinguish among particular movements which occur contemporaneously within periods of social movement. Thus, one can distinguish, for example, the environmental movement from the student movements which more or less directly preceded it, showing the continuities and differences in their respective cognitive praxis as well as between activists and political strategies. In periods of social movement, particular movements tend to feed off and create each other, as well as producing, conceptually and practically, their opposition.

Gauging the relative success or failure of social movements, that is, measuring their ability to affect and transform established patterns of behavior has been an important issue in the empirical study of social movements. From our perspective, movement success is paradoxical. On the empirical level, the success or failure of a particular movement usually depends on its ability to mobilize resources and to exploit the "opportunity structures" of the surrounding political culture to achieve its strategic aims. In a broader historical sense, however, the success of a social movement depends on the effective diffusion of its knowledge production; but diffusion depends upon there being sufficient time and space for a movement identity to be articulated. Some movements are successful in one way while being failures in the other.

Thus, our reading of social movements focuses not so much on causation or political effect as on message: what is the kind of historical project that a social movement articulates? As our historical examples will indicate, we are not uninterested in understanding why social movements appear, but establishing cause or providing causal explanation is of less importance than deepening understanding. In this regard, our approach is more hermeneutic than positivistic: our aim is to understand rather than explain, although the two ambitions are often difficult to separate. In any case, our interest in explanation is of a more conditional character; social movements, we contend, are conditioned rather than caused by historical and contextual "factors." Movements create themselves and their own particular movement spaces, but their praxis is conditioned by the society around them.

Our historical examples will point to some of the ways in which this conditioning takes place. The social movements of the nineteenth century emerged at particular conjunctures; although they exist as local groups or even organizations throughout the century, it is in particular periods—in most countries, the 1830s and 1840s and then again in the 1880s and 1890s—that there is social movement. This is, of course, a matter of opinion; and there is by no means consensus among historians about the range or the appropriate connotations of the term social movement. Some apply it to any sign of popular mobilization, while others specify exacting criteria. From our perspective, the criteria of social movement are cognitive: that is, a social movement must articulate identifiable cognitive products or types of knowledge. But we also define social movements dynamically: they are, by our definition, impermanent, transient phenomena, which means that there are ebbs and flows, cycles if you will, of movement activity. Indeed, we could even talk of latent and active periods, or weak and strong periods, but the point would be the same; movements do not last forever, they come for a time, carve out their movement space, and get eventually "pulled" back into the society, as the space they create gets occupied by other social forces.

REFERENCES

Bahro, R. 1984: *From Red to Green.* London: Verso.

Bauman, Z. 1987: *Legislators and Interpreters.* Cambridge: Polity.

Ben-David, J. 1971: *The Scientist's Role in Society.* Englewood Cliffs: Prentice-Hall.

Berger, P. and Luckmann, T. 1967: *The Social Construction of Reality: A Treatise in the Sociology of Knowledge.* New York: Doubleday.

Bijker, W., Hughes, T. and Pinch, T. (eds) 1987: *The Social Construction of Technological Systems.* Cambridge, Ma.: MIT Press.

Boggs, C. 1985: *Social Movements and Political Power.* Philadelphia: Temple University Press.

Bourdieu, P. 1988: *Homo Academicus.* Cambridge: Polity.

Chu, E. and Chubin, D. (eds) 1989: *Science off the Pedestal: Social Perspectives on Science and Technology.* Belmont, Ca.: Wadsworth.

Cohen, J. 1985: "Strategy or identity: new theoretical paradigms and contemporary social movements. *Social Research,* 52.

Dosi, G. et al. (eds) 1988: *Technical Change and Economic Theory.* London: Frances Pinter.

Frankel, B. 1987: *The Post-Industrial Utopians.* Cambridge: Polity.

Fuller, S. 1988: *Social Epistemology.* Bloomington: Indiana University Press.

Giddens, A. 1985: *The Constitution of Society.* London: Macmillan.

Gorz, A. 1982: *Farewell to the Working Class.* London: Pluto.

Habermas, J. 1987: *The Theory of Communicative Action,* vol. 2. Cambridge: Polity.

Horkeimer, M. 1974: *Eclipse of Reason.* New York: Seabury.

Jamison, A. 1982: *National Components of Scientific Knowledge: A Contribution to the Social Theory of Science.* Lund: Research Policy Institute.

Jay, M. 1973: *The Dialectical Imagination.* London: Heinemann.

Klandermans, B., Kriesi, H. and Tarrow, S. (eds) 1988: *International Social Movement Research.* vol. 1: *From Structure to Action.* Greenwich, Conn.: JAI Press.

Knorr-Cetina, K. and Mulkay, M. (eds) 1983: *Science Observed: Perspectives on the Social Study of Science.* London: Sage.

Kuhn, T. 1962: *The Structure of Scientific Revolutions* (International Encyclopedia of United Science). Chicago: University of Chicago Press.

Latour, B. 1987: *Science in Action.* Milton Keynes: Open University Press.

Law, J. (ed.) 1986: *Power, Action and Belief: A New Sociology of Knowledge?* London: Routledge and Kegan Paul.

McAdam, D. 1982: *Political Process and the Development of Black Insurgency, 1930–1970.* Chicago: University of Chicago Press.

Mannheim, K. 1948: *Ideology and Utopia.* London: Routledge and Kegan Paul.

Marcuse, H. 1964: *One-Dimensional Man.* Boston: Beacon.

Melucci, A. 1988: Social movements and the democratization of everyday life. In J. Keane (ed.), *Civil Society and the State,* London: Verso.

Merton, R. 1957: *Social Theory and Social Structure.* New York Free Press.

Mills, C. Wright 1963: *Power, Politics and People.* New York: Ballantine Books.

Rose, H. and Rose, S. (eds) 1975: *The Radicalisation of Science.* London: Macmillan.

Smelser, N. 1962: *Theory of Collective Behavior.* New York: Free Press.

Tilly, C. 1985: Models and realities of popular collective action. *Social Research,* 52, winter.

Touraine, A. 1981: *The Voice and the Eye: An Analysis of Social Movements.* Cambridge: Cambridge University Press.

———1983: *Anti-Nuclear Protest.* Cambridge: Cambridge University Press.

Webster, C. 1975: *The Great Instauration: Science, Medicine and Reform 1626–1660.* London: Duckworth.

CONTEMPORARY APPROACHES: NEW SOCIAL MOVEMENTS

17

THE SYMBOLIC CHALLENGE OF CONTEMPORARY MOVEMENTS

ALBERTO MELUCCI

Action Systems

Sociological theory and research during the seventies have undoubtedly provided a deeper understanding of contemporary social movements. The forms of collective action which have emerged during the past twenty years in fields previously untouched by social conflicts (age, sex differences, health, relation to nature, human survival) are taking by now an increasing importance in sociological analysis and they become controversial and stimulating topics for both theory and research. The eighties seem to offer new material to this reflection, since collective action is shifting more and more from the "political" form, which was common to traditional opposition movements in Western societies, to a cultural ground.

Theoretical frameworks and empirical knowledge of contemporary complex societies suggest that:

(1) The emergent conflicts have a permanent and nonconjunctural nature; new forms of solidarity and action coexist with more traditional memberships (such as classes, interest groups, associations). Though their empirical features can vary widely, they become stable and irreversible components of contemporary social systems, because they are strictly connected to deep structural changes in these systems.

From *Social Research,* Vol. 52, No. 4 (Winter, 1985). Reprinted by permission of *Social Research* and the author.

(2) Widespread networks of conflictual solidarity fulfill a function of socialization and "submerged" participation. They open new channels for grouping and selecting elites, besides the more traditional ones. The ways of political socialization, the patterns of cultural innovation, the means of institutional modernization are therefore redefined outside the action of already established agencies.

(3) One of the main problems of "complexity" is the gap between institutional systems of representation and decision making and "civil society." Needs and forms of action arising from the society are not easily adaptable to the existing channels of political participation and to the organizational forms of political agencies; moreover, since the outcomes of collective action are difficult to predict, this increases the already high degree of uncertainty systems are confronted with.

A reflection on both theoretical and empirical dimensions of contemporary movements is thus a step which cannot be avoided in the debate on paradigms allowing a satisfactory understanding of complex systems.

In the field of social movements, sociology inherits a legacy of dualism from philosophies of history. Collective action has always been treated either as an effect of structural crises and contradictions or as an expression of shared beliefs and orientations. The dualism between structure and actors seems to be the common feature of traditional analysis of collective action, in both Marxist and functionalist approaches.

The duality can be formulated in terms of *breakdown/solidarity*.[1] The former approach is represented by theories of collective behavior and mass society[2] and holds collective action to be a result of economic crisis and social disintegration, particularly among the rootless. The latter considers social movements as expressions of shared interests within a common structural location (especially a class condition, as in any viewpoints derived from Marxism). Breakdown theories disregard the dimension of conflict within collective action and easily reduce it to pathological reaction and marginality. Solidarity models are unable to explain the passage from a given social condition to collective action. The classical Marxist problem (how to pass from class condition to class consciousness) still exists and can't be solved without taking into consideration how a collective actor is formed and how his identity is maintained.

Duality can be viewed also in terms of *structure/motivation*:[3] collective action is seen as a product of the logic of the system, or as a result of personal beliefs. The stress is in the first case on social-economic context, in the second on the role of ideology and values. Either actors are dispossessed of the meanings of their action, or they produce meanings and goals apparently without any constraints.

The seventies enabled sociological theory to move beyond the breakdown/solidarity or structure/motivation alternatives. In Europe the analyses of Touraine and Habermas, based on a systemic approach, tried to establish a link between the new forms of conflict and the emerging structure of postindustrial capitalism.[4] Some American authors focused their reflection on how a movement is made up, if and how it survives in time and in relation to its environment, in terms of *resource mobilization*.[5]

The seventies leave us what I would call a "skeptical paradigm" toward social movements: collective action is not a "thing," nor does it merely express what movements say of themselves; analysis has rather to discover the system of internal and external relationships which constitutes the action. but the seventies' theories also leave two problems unresolved. Structural theories, based on system analysis, explain *why* but not *how* a movement is set up and maintains its structure, that is, they only hypothesize about potential conflict without accounting for concrete collective action and actors. On the other hand, the resource mobilization approach regards such action as mere data and fails to examine its meaning and orientation. In this case, *how* but not *why.* Each question could be legitimate within its limits, but frequently authors tend to present their theories as global explanations of social movements.[6] In my view, the analysis should concentrate on the systemic relationships rather than on the simple logic of actors. But at the same time action cannot be considered only within structural contradictions. Action has to be viewed as an interplay of aims, resources, and obstacles, as *a purposive orientation which is set up within a system of opportunities and constraints.* Movements are *action systems* operating in a *systemic field* of possibilities and limits.[7] That is why the *organization* becomes a critical point of observation, an analytical level too often underestimated or reduced to formal structures. The way the movement actors set up their action is the *concrete link between orientations and systemic opportunities/constraints.*

Movements are social constructions. Rather than a consequence of crises or dysfunctions, rather than an expression of beliefs, collective action is "built" by an organizational investment. "Organization" is not here an empirical feature but an analytical level. Keeping together individuals and mobilizing resources for the action means allocating values, capabilities, decisions in a field which is delimited: possibilities and boundaries provided by social relationships shape the action, but neither resources nor constraints can be activated outside the action itself.

Social movements are thus action *systems* in that they have structures: the unity and continuity of the action would not be possible without integration and interdependence of individuals and groups, in spite of the apparent looseness of this kind of social phenomena. But movements are *action* systems in that their structures are built by aims, beliefs, decisions, and exchanges operating in a systemic field. A *collective identity* is nothing else than a shared definition of the field of opportunities and constraints offered to collective action: "shared" means constructed and negotiated through a repeated process of "activation" of social relationships connecting the actors.[8]

To consider a movement as an action system means to stop treating it just as an empirical phenomenon. The empirical forms of collective action are objects of analysis, and they are not meaningful in themselves. Currently one speaks of a "movement" as a unity, to which one attributes goals, choices, interests, decisions. But this unity, if any, is a result rather than a point of departure; otherwise one must assume that there is a sort of deep "mind" of the movement, instead of considering it as a system of social relationships. A collective action can't be explained without taking into account how internal and external resources are mobilized, how organizational structures are built and maintained, how leadership functions are assured. What empirically is called a "social movement" is a system of action, connecting plural orientations and meanings. A single collective action, moreover, contains different kinds of behavior, and the analysis has to break its apparent unity and to find out the various elements converging in it and possibly having different outcomes. Only by separating different analytical elements can one understand how they are kept together by an "organizational" structure; how a collective identity is built through a complex system of negotiations, exchanges, decisions; how action can occur as a result of systemic determinations *and* of individual and group orientations.

The field of social movements theory needs a shift away from empirical generalizations to analytical definitions. Just for a methodological purpose I will indicate the essential lines of my own theoretical path.[9] I assume that the meaning of collective action depends on its *system of reference* and on its *analytical dimensions*. The same empirical behavior can be viewed in different ways, whether or not it refers to an organizational system, to a political system, to a mode of production: claims against an ineffective authority are different from demands for broadening participation and are still different from action challenging the production and appropriation of resources in a system. Apart from the system of reference, action can be analyzed also according to its internal analytical dimensions. Using *conflict, solidarity*, and the *breaking of the system limits*, I have differentiated among various types of collective action.

I define conflict as a relationship between opposed actors fighting for the same resources, to which both give value. Solidarity is the capability of an actor to share a collective identity, that is, the capability of recognizing and being recognized as a part of the same system of social relationships. Limits of a system indicate the range of variations tolerated within its existing structure. A breaking of these limits pushes a system beyond the acceptable range of variations.

I define analytically a social movement as a form of collective action (a) based on solidarity, (b) carrying on a conflict, (c) breaking the limits of the system in which action occurs. These dimensions, which are entirely analytical, enable one to separate social movements from other collective phenomena which are very often empirically associated with "movements" and "protest": one can speak of deviance, regulated grievances, aggregated-mass behavior, according to which of these dimensions is present or absent. Moreover, different kinds of move-

ments and collective actions can be assessed according to the system of reference of action.

Beyond the actual content of a definition (which is always an operational tool and not a metaphysical truth), what is important to me is the methodological orientation. Since a movement is not a thing but a system of action, we have to improve our capability of going beyond the empirical unity through analytical instruments as sophisticated as possible. What I have outlined above is a way, still roughly designed, of making our tools more effective.

The Systemic Field and the Actors

Complex systems require a growing intervention in social relationships, in symbolic production, in individual identity and needs. Postindustrial societies no longer have an "economic" basis; they produce by an increasing integration of economic, political, and cultural structures. "Material" goods are produced and consumed with the mediation of huge informational and symbolic systems.

Social conflicts move from the traditional economic/industrial system to cultural grounds: they affect personal identity, the time and the space in everyday life, the motivation and the cultural patterns of individual action. Conflicts reveal a major shift in the structure of complex systems, and new contradictions appear affecting their fundamental logic. On the one hand, highly differentiated systems increasingly produce and distribute resources for individualization, for self-realization, for an autonomous building of personal and collective identities. And that is because complex systems are informational systems and they cannot survive without assuming a certain autonomous capacity in individual elements, which have to be able to produce and receive information. Consequently the system must improve the autonomy of individuals and groups and their capacity for becoming effective terminals of complex informational networks.

On the other hand, these systems need more and more integration. They have to extend their control over the same fundamental resources which allow their functioning, if they want to survive. Power must affect everyday life, the deep motivation of individual action must be manipulated, the process by which people give meaning to things and their action must be under control. One can speak of "power microphysics"[10] or of a shift in social action from external to "internal nature."[11] The conflicts of the eighties reveal these new contradictions, and they imply an intense redefinition of the location of social movements and of their forms of action. They involve social groups more directly affected by the processes outlined above. They arise in those areas of the system which are connected to the most intensive informational and symbolic investments and exposed to the greatest pressures for conformity. The actors in these conflicts are no longer social classes, that is, stable groups defined by a specific social condition and culture (as the working class was during capitalistic industrialization).

Actors in conflicts are increasingly *temporary,* and their function is to *reveal the stakes,* to announce to society that a fundamental problem exists in a given area. They have a growing symbolic function; one can probably speak of a *prophetic function.* They are a kind of *new media.*[12] They do not fight merely for material goals, or to increase their participation in the system. They fight for symbolic and cultural stakes, for a different meaning and orientation of social action. They try to change people's lives, they believe that you can change your life today while fighting for more general changes in society.[13]

Because it apprehends a movement only as a given empirical actor, resource mobi-

lization theory is unable to explain the meaning of these contemporary forms of action. The field of new social conflicts is created by the system and its contradictory requirements. The activation of specific issues depends rather on historical and conjunctural factors. Specific empirical conflicts are carried out by different groups which converge on the ground provided by the system. The field and the stakes of antagonistic conflicts must therefore be defined at the synchronic level of the system. Actors, on the contrary, can be identified only by taking into account diachronic, conjunctural factors, particularly the functioning of the political system. Resource mobilization theory can help in understanding how different elements converge in activating specific forms of collective action, but cannot explain why action arises and where it is going.

The resource mobilization approach avoids the macrolevel (which is the main interest of theories such as Touraine's or Habermas's), but in fact tends to reduce every collective action to the political level. But that way it misses the cultural orientation of the emerging social conflicts. Elsewhere I have spoken of "political overload" of many contemporary analyses on social movements.[14] Sometimes implicitly, very often explicitly, the relationship between movements and the political system becomes the focus of attention and debate. Of course this viewpoint is legitimate, unless it exhausts any possible consideration of other dimensions.[15] Contemporary social conflicts are not just political, since they affect the system's cultural production. Collective action is not carried out simply for exchanging goods in the political market or for improving the participation in the system. It challenges the logic governing production and appropriation of social resources.

The concept of movement itself seems increasingly inadequate, if referred to recent phenomena. I prefer to speak of *movement networks* or *movement areas* as the network of groups and individuals sharing a conflictual culture and a collective identity. This definition includes not only "formal" organizations but also the network of "informal" relationships connecting core individuals and groups to a broader area of participants and "users" of services and cultural goods produced by the movement.[16]

The inadequacy of the concept of social movement is a symptom of a more general epistemological problem. The concept of movement belongs to the same semantic and conceptual framework in which other notions, such as progress or revolution, were formed. In a world where change means crisis management and maintenance of systemic equilibrium, where "no future" is not only a slogan but the recognition that the system is both planetary and dramatically vulnerable, in such a world the historicist paradigm fades and reveals the need for new conceptual frames.

In the field of collective action the lack of more adequate concepts makes it difficult to get rid of a notion such as "social movement"; but I am aware that the concept of "movement network" is a temporary adjustment covering a lack of more satisfactory definitions and perhaps facilitating the transition to another paradigm.

But such a concept indicates also that collective action is changing its organizational forms, which are becoming fairly different from traditional political organizations. Moreover, they are increasingly autonomous from political systems; a proper space for collective action is created within complex societies as a specific subsystem. It becomes the point of convergence for different forms of behavior which the system cannot integrate (including not only conflicting orientations but also deviant behavior, cultural innovation, etc.).

The normal situation of today's "movement" is a network of small groups sub-merged in everyday life which require a personal involvement in experiencing and practicing cultural innovation. They emerge only on specific issues, as for instance the big mobilizations for peace, for abortion, against nuclear policy, etc. The submerged network, although composed of separate small groups, is a system of exchange (persons and information circulate along the network; some agencies, such as local free radios, bookshops, magazines provide a certain unity).[17]

Such networks (first outlined by Gerlach and Hine)[18] have the following characteristics: (a) they allow multiple membership; (b) militantism is only part-time and short-term; (c) personal involvement and effective solidarity is required as a condition for participation in many of the groups. This is not a temporary phenomenon but a morphological shift in the structure of collective action.

One can speak of a *two-pole model: latency* and *visibility,* each having two different functions. Latency allows people to experience directly new cultural models—changes in the system of meanings—which are very often opposed to the dominant social codes; the meaning of sexual differences, time and space, relationship to nature, to the body, and so on. Latency creates new cultural codes and makes individuals practice them. When small groups emerge to confront a political authority on a specific issue, visibility demonstrates the opposition to the logic underlying decision making with regard to public policy. At the same time, public mobilization indicates to the rest of society that the specific problem is connected to the general logic of the system, and also that alternative cultural models are possible.

These two poles, visibility and latency, are reciprocally correlated. Latency allows visibility in that it feeds the former with solidarity resources and with a cultural framework for mobilization. Visibility reinforces submerged networks. It provides energies to renew solidarity, facilitates creation of new groups and recruitment of new militants attracted by public mobilization who then flow into the submerged network.

The new organizational form of contemporary movements is not just "instrumental" for their goals. It is a goal in itself. Since the action is focused on cultural codes, the *form* of the movement is a message, a symbolic challenge to the dominant patterns. Short-term and reversible commitment, multiple leadership that can be challenged, temporary and ad hoc organizational structures are the bases for internal collective identity, but also for a symbolic confrontation with the system. People are offered the possibility of another experience of time, space, interpersonal relations, which opposes operational rationality of apparatuses. A different way of naming the world suddenly reverses the dominant codes.

The medium, the movement itself as a new medium, is the message. As prophets without enchantment, contemporary movements practice in the present the change they are struggling for: they redefine the meaning of social action for the whole society.

Peace Mobilizations: Political or Symbolic?

I will try now to apply the conceptual framework outlined above to the unexpected wave of mobilizations for peace which has been troubling all Western countries from the beginning of the eighties, with gigantic demonstrations crossing the main capitals of the Western world. Two general questions can be raised: What produces these forms of mobilization? What is the meaning of individual and collective action?

For both questions the answers might seem obvious: mobilization is a reaction to the changing political and military scene, after the decisions regarding nuclear weapons in Europe; peace is the goal, as a universal good threatened by the nuclear race and by the risk of total warfare.

These answers are as obvious as they are incomplete and partial: they contain the same simplification in the "peace movement" as that already applied to other recent collective mobilizations in complex societies.

So far I have spoken of peace *mobilizations* and not of peace movement because as I explained before I don't think that "peace movement" has any analytical unity. Empirical phenomena of recent years are multidimensional realities which converge, only in a specific conjuncture, on the ground offered by peace mobilization.

The changes in military policies offer the conjunctural opportunity for the emergence and coagulation of different elements:

(1) There is first of all a *reaction* to the changes in military policies which has two main aspects: (a) *mobilization of political actors* (in a broad sense of parties, unions, pressure groups, associations); (b) collective fear of an irreversible catastrophe. In the first case, the logic of action can be explained almost entirely within the national political systems. Inner dynamics, already operating in these systems, are activated by international conjuncture: the residual political "new left" of the seventies in West Germany, or the Communist party in Italy, find on the peace ground an opportunity for their political action. The second element of reaction is collective fear, which can be analyzed as a sum of atomized behaviors, following the classical analyses of crowd behavior or aggregative behavior.[19]

(2) A second component of peace mobilizations is what I would call a *moral utopianism* that is not just a contemporary phenomenon. Every social system contains a certain amount of moral and totalizing

expectations toward happiness, justice, truth, and so on. These claims do not have social attributions, do not involve specific social interests or practical-historical projects. They live on the borders of great religions or great cultural and political waves, in the form of small sects, heretical cults, theological circles. The great collective processes offer a channel to express this moral utopianism, which otherwise would survive in marginal enclaves.

The peace issue is a ground of expression for these totalizing aspirations, which become visible through a cyclical up and down wave. Contemporary international conjuncture offers a social and cultural opportunity for a phenomenon which has only an occasional link with the activating situation.

(3) But peace mobilizations are not only a reaction to the recent military policies. Political actors have only a minor role in mobilization. The fear of the bomb doesn't explain the patterns of solidarity, organization, identity of recent collective action, which is very different from an aggregative behavior such as a panic. Moral utopianism could not leave its marginality if it were not pushed by collective processes which have their roots elsewhere.

My hypothesis is that peace mobilizations also express conflicts of a complex society. There is a qualitative gap between recent mobilizations and pacifism of the fifties. There is, on the contrary, a continuity with other mobilizations of the seventies and early eighties (youth, women, ecological mobilizations).

An understanding of peace mobilizations of the eighties thus needs a consideration not only of the nuclear war threat but of the whole system in which this possibility occurs.

Information has today become a central resource, and contemporary systems depend on it for their survival and development. The capability of collecting, processing, transferring information has been developed in the last twenty years at a level which is not comparable to that of the whole history of mankind.

That increases the *artificial*, "built" characteristics of social life. A large amount of our everyday experiences occur in a socially produced environment. Media represent and reflect our actions; individuals incorporate and reproduce these messages in a sort of self-growing spiral. Where are "nature" and "reality" outside the cultural representations and images we receive from and produce for our social world?

Social system acquires a planetary dimension, and the events are not important in themselves or for the place and people where they occur but for their symbolic impact on the world system.

Informational societies develop a cultural production not directly connected to the needs for survival or for reproduction: in that they are "postmaterial" societies and they produce a "cultural surplus." Since information cannot be separated from human capability of perceiving it, social intervention affects more and more man himself. Large investments in biological research, motivational research, brain research, recent developments of neurosciences, particularly in the most developed countries, show that the deepest bases of human behavior become a field of exploration and intervention: biological and motivational structure of humans becomes a valuable resource.

A society based on information redefines *space* and *time*. Spaces loses its physical limits and can be extended or contracted at a degree that one could hardly imagine only a few years ago. A whole library can be stocked in a space smaller than a book, but the symbolic space everybody can be in touch with reaches the whole planet and even extraterrestrial space.

The time needed to produce and process information has been reduced so rapidly in recent years that we can already experience the dramatic gap regarding other human time experiences. The gap between the time a computer needs to process information and the time for human analysis of the output is still very high. However, research on artificial intelligence has been growing in the direction of the reduction of this lag. But the most dramatic is the gap concerning other times of our everyday experience: the inner times, times of feelings and emotions, times of questions without answers, times for unifying the fragments of personal identity.

Control over informational production, accumulation, and circulation depends on codes which organize and make information understandable. In complex societies, power consists more and more of operational codes, formal rules, knowledge organizers. In the operational logic, information is not a shared resource accessible to everybody, but an empty sign, the key of which is controlled by only a few people. The access to knowledge becomes a field of a new kind of power and conflicts. Moreover, the possibility of unifying individual experience beyond the operational rationality becomes more and more difficult: there is no place for questions concerning individual destiny and choices, life, birth, death, love.

The "nuclear situation" as the possibility of total destruction has to be considered within the framework I have just outlined.

(1) The nuclear situation is the extreme, paradoxical example of social capability of intervening on society itself. It is the ultimate expression of an "artificial," self-reflexive social life. Contemporary societies produce themselves to a degree that includes the possibility of final destruction.

(2) This situation, for the first time in human history, transforms peace and war into a *global social problem*. Society in itself is concerned with a question which affects the survival of mankind and which cannot therefore be restricted to the separate area of technical, military, or political decision. While the war, from the point of view of technology, becomes more and more a specialist's field, its meaning is paradoxically reversed and becomes a general social question concerning all of us and everybody.

(3) For the first time in history war and peace acquire a planetary dimension and break the limits of relations among the states which have maintained in modern history a monopoly over them. The complex system of relations we call society acquires the power of self-destruction but at the same time disposes of the chances of survival and development. "The social" becomes the field of power, risk, and responsibility.

(4) The "nuclear situation" brings the war threat to the informational field, particularly to a symbolic ground. The actual war would be the end of war, bringing with it the disappearance of mankind. So the confrontation within these limits is necessarily a symbolic fight and a struggle for controlling information. The concept of deterrence, a key concept in contemporary political and military international relations, operates mainly on symbolic ground. It intervenes in information and representations of opponents, by creating a mirror game in which every player tries to influence the other and to take advantage of the enemy's misperception.

The nuclear situation contains two paradoxes. First, if society produces the power of self-destruction, it shows both the highest level of self-reflection, of action on itself, *and* the potential and final end of this capability. Second, the nuclear situation is the product of an information society and, as such, it is no longer reversible. It is virtually impossible for information on the nuclear bomb and its production to disappear and therefore to come back to a prenuclear society. One has to imagine a catastrophe or situation in which there is total control over information and the erasing of facts and the rewriting of history, in Orwellian terms. Otherwise the bomb is an incumbent and irreversible possibility of human society, both a result of the largest widening of choices and opportunities ever produced by material and cultural evolution and an irreversible risk. We can only go beyond, confronting it.

The "nuclear situation" has substantial analogies with other contemporary forms of intervention of society on itself. Particularly genetic engineering, and all forms of voluntary action on biological bases of behavior, reproduction, thought, life itself are as radical interventions on human destiny as the nuclear threat. The difference is not the irreversibility (which could also be true for genetic manipulation or ecological disasters) but the specific characteristics of nuclear threat: *time* (destruction would be almost instantaneous) and *space* (destruction could be global), which make nuclear war incomparable with any other intervention on the future of mankind.

So what is at stake in contemporary movements, and particularly in peace mobilizations, is *the production of the human species,* at the individual and collective level: the possibility for men, as individuals and as species, to control not only their "products" but their "making," culturally and socially (and more and more biologically). What is at stake is the production of human existence and its quality.

In collective action for peace, one can find some dimensions of this emerging field of conflicts.

(1) Struggle against military policies reveals the *transnational* nature of contemporary problems and conflicts[20] and the *global interdependence* of the planetary system. Collective action challenges not only the actual shape of international relations but the logic governing them. The world system is formally a set of relations among sovereign states, but in fact it is dominated by the two-blocs logic and by the imbalances between North and South. Within the two empires, technocratic and military apparatuses control informational and decisional resources for change among different areas of the planet. The exhausting of the nation-state system is perhaps the fundamental message of contemporary pacifism, even if there are still a good deal of "national" questions unresolved.[21] Through the peace issue one can hear an appeal to give society the power of deciding and controlling its own existence, in a new set of relations among its elements (groups, interests, cultures, "nations"). A new *intersocietal* order is not a utopia but great aspiration of our planetary situation where the nation-states are extinguishing themselves not because of socialism (the myth of the end of the state) but because they lose their authority: from above, a planetary, multinational political and economic interdependence moves the center of actual decision making elsewhere; from below, multiplication of autonomous centers of decision gives "civil societies" a power they never had during the development of modern states.

The problem of political management of this new situation is not an easy one; but the planetary system has to start from the *social* transformation of its nature, if it wants to find new *political* means for its survival.

(2) Peace mobilizations point out the increasing *decisional* dimension of the contemporary situation. Society and its destiny are constructed, as a result of decisions and choices, products of social relationships and not of the apparently fatal logic of apparatuses, pretending they have a right to a monopoly of "rationality."

(3) Collective action for peace reveals, finally, the *contractual* nature of social life in complex systems: the survival of mankind depends on the capability of negotiating ends. Discussion on ends disappears from the scene of collective debates, nullified by

the operational criteria of efficacity or by the pure consumption of signs. Collective action says that the ends must be visible, negotiable, under control.

Acceptance of the contractual nature of contemporary societies means: (a) to recognize that the differences of interests and a certain amount of conflict can't be eliminated in complex systems; (b) to recognize the necessity of limits, that is, rules of the game, which can be established and changed by negotiation; (c) power is one of these limits and its negotiability depends on its *visibility*; (d) to recognize the *risk*, that is, the openness and temporariness of every decisional process reducing uncertainty. Risk, which in ethical terms means responsibility and freedom, is an irreversible component of the contemporary situation. It is not bigger for the nuclear situation than it is for other possibilities of destruction (biological, chemical, ecological) connected to the increasing intervention of society on itself. The risk points out definitely that the destiny of humans has been put into their hands.

Naming the World

The *form* of contemporary movements, and of peace mobilizations as well, is the most direct expression of the message collective action announces to the society. The meaning of the action has to be found in the action itself more than in the pursued goals: movements are not qualified by what they do but by what they are.

The legacy of industrial society is an image of social movements as tragic characters. They act on the historical scene, heroes or villains depending on the point of view, but always oriented toward great ideals or a dramatic destiny. The history of the nineteenth and twentieth centuries is full of these

images, not merely rhetorical. They have maintained their force until recent years. Movements of the sixties and also the first wave of feminism in the seventies still belong to this epic representation: in the struggle of progress against barbarism, everyone can choose his side and can be sure of the opponent's necessary breakdown!

At the beginning of the eighties almost nothing seems to survive of these epic representations. Movements are lost, and there is no character occupying the scene. But there are a lot of submerged networks, of groups and experiences that insist on considering themselves "against." But who cares about them? They seem more interested in themselves than in the outer world, they apparently ignore politics, they don't fight against power. They don't have big leaders, organization seems quite inefficient, disenchantment has superseded great ideals. Many observers consider these realities, which don't challenge the political system and are not interested in the institutional effects of their action, as residual, folkloristic phenomena in the big scenario of politics.

I am convinced, on the contrary, that these poor and disenchanted forms of action are the seeds of the qualitative change in contemporary collective action. Certainly contemporary movements produce some effects on political institutions, although they are not mainly oriented toward political change. They modernize institutions, they furnish them new elites who renew culture and organization. But conflict goes beyond institutional renewal and affects the meaning of individual action and the codes which shape behaviors. Thus contemporary movements have to be read on different levels.

There is in their action a component which influences institutions, governments, policies; there are pushes toward the renewal of cultures, languages, habits. All these effects facilitate the adaptation of complex systems to the transformations of the environment and to the accelerated pace of internal changes they are exposed to.

But beyond modernization, beyond cultural innovation, movements question society on something "else": who decides on codes, who establishes rules of normality, what is the space for difference, how can one be recognized not for being included but for being accepted as different, not for increasing the amount of exchanges but for affirming another kind of exchange?

This is the deepest and the most hidden message of the movements. Movements present to the rationalizing apparatuses questions which are not allowed. While the problem becomes to operationalize what an anonymous power has decided, they ask where we are going and why. Their voice is difficult to hear because they speak from a particularistic point of view, starting from a specific condition or location (as being young, being a woman, and so on). Nevertheless, they speak to the whole society. The problems they raise affect the global logic of contemporary systems.

Starting from a temporary biological and social condition, the youth movement has presented to society the problem of *time*. Youth is no more a simple biological condition but has become a symbolic definition. One is not young only because of one's age but because one assumes cultural characteristics of variability and temporariness proper to youth. The condition of the young is a mirror through which a more general appeal is raised: the right to reverse the life time, to make temporary existential and professional choices, to dispose of a time measured not only by the rhythm of operational efficacity.

Rooted in the particularism of a condition marked by biology and history, the women's movement has raised a fundamental question concerning everyone in complex systems: how communication is possible, how to communicate with "another" without denying the difference by power relations. Beyond the demand for equality, beyond the inclusion in the field of masculine rights, women are yet speaking of the right to difference and to "otherness." That is why they sometimes choose silence, because it is difficult to find words other than those of the dominant language.

The ecological nebula grown in the last decade collects different elements: modernization of the system, new elites in formation, but also conflictual orientations which challenge the logic of relationships between man and nature and between man and *his* nature. This ecological culture raises the question of how to deal with nature inside and outside ourselves. The body, the biological structure, the environment are the limits for the "destructive creation" of technological societies. Where can human intervention stop? What is the place for "nature" still constituting and surrounding human life?

Contemporary societies have eliminated from the field of human experience what was not measurable and controllable, what in the traditional world belonged to the dimension of the sacred. The final meaning of existence, questions on what escapes individual experience, feed a new "religious" research or simply a need for connecting the external change to an interior growth. A heterogeneous area emerges looking for a "new consciousness." It seems very far from traditional forms of conflictual movements. Nevertheless, when we are not confronted with multinational corporations selling security, we can observe a way of resistance to operational codes, an appeal to shadow, a search for an interior unity against the imperatives of efficacity.

All these forms of collective action challenge the dominant logic on a symbolic ground. They question definition of codes, *nomination* of reality. They don't ask, they offer. They offer by their own existence other ways of defining the meaning of individual and collective action. They don't separate individual change from collective action, they translate a general appeal in the here and now of individual experience. They act as new media: they enlighten what every system doesn't say of itself, the amount of silence, violence, irrationality which is always hidden in dominant codes.

At the same time, through what they do, or rather through how they do it, movements announce to society that something "else" is possible.

Peace mobilizations like other forms of mobilizations coagulate and make visible this submerged "nebula." They offer a field for external action to networks of solidarity which live in different areas of society and share the cultural reversal and the symbolic challenge to the system. Contractual and short-term involvements, coincidence between collective goals and individual experience of change, globalism of symbolic appeal and particularism of actors' social locations, all these are aspects of collective mobilizations. In the peace issue, as in other forms of contemporary mobilizations, we can see the end of a distinction between instrumental and expressive dimensions of action. Medium is the message, and action sends back to the system its own paradoxes.

Coming Back to Politics

Apparently the outcome of contemporary forms of collective action cannot be measured. Movements realize the paradox of being both winners and losers. Since they challenge the dominant cultural codes, their mere existence is a reversal of symbolic systems embodied in power relationships. Success and failure are thus meaningless concepts if referred to the symbolic challenge.

But movements don't exist only in their cultural message; they are also social organizations, and they confront political systems when they choose public mobilization. From this point of view they produce modernization, stimulate innovation, push to reform. They provide new elites, assure the change of the personnel in political institutions, create new patterns of behavior and new models of organization. Here their outcome can be measured, but one must not forget that this is only one part, and not always the most important, of contemporary collective action.

Those stressing the lack of efficacity of these forms of action not only don't catch the symbolic antagonism but also underestimate the political impact of mobilizations.

For instance, the peace mobilizations have fundamental *transnational effects:* for the first time action, also located in a specific national context, has effects at the planetary level and on the system of international relations. The lack of mobilizations in Eastern countries is paradoxically a part of the same scene: it reveals and makes clear the authoritarian structure of these societies and the amount of repression power has to use to control them.

Collective action acts also as a *symbolic multiplier:* since it is not aiming for efficacity, it challenges the operational logic of technocratic-military apparatuses and questions the bases of their power. It makes apparatuses to produce justifications, it pushes them to reveal their logic and the weakness of their "reasons." It makes the power *visible.* In systems where the power becomes increasingly anonymous and neutral, where it is incorporated in formal procedures, to make it visible is a fundamental *political* achievement: the only condition for negotiating the rules and for making social decisions more transparent.

What peace mobilizations propose to the collective consciousness is that survival of societies, like individual life, is not assured anymore by a metasocial order or by an historical law (progress or revolution). For the first time societies become radically aware of their contingency, they realize they "are thrown" in the world, they discover they are not necessary and thus they are irreversibly responsible for their destinies. Catastrophe, suffering, freedom, all belong to the possible future, and they are not fatal events. Moreover, no collective well-being can be assured as a final solution. It has to be renewed by decisions, negotiations, actions. That is, by *polis* activity.

But, if so, a critical problem of complex societies is the relationship between political institutions and actors and the emerging pattern of collective action. What kind of representation could offer political effectiveness to the movements without negating their autonomy? How can movements translate their messages into effective political changes? These questions can't find easy answers, of course. But if we assume that the structure and orientations of contemporary movements are likely to shift in the direction outlined above, two consequences can be pointed out.

First, the organizational forms of traditional political institutions, also those coming from the leftist inheritance, are in themselves inadequate to represent the new collective demands. Political organizations are shaped for representing relatively stable interests, for achieving long-term goals through the accumulation of short-term results, for mediating among different demands through the professional action of representatives. This structure, although submitted to increasing adjustments, still fulfills important functions in Western political systems. But it can't even hear the voice of movements, and when it does, it is unable to adapt itself to the variability of the actors and issues collective action involves.

Second, because of the fragmentation of collective action, social movements can't survive in complex societies without some forms of political representation. The existence of channels of representation and of institutional actors capable of translating in "policies" the message of collective action is the only condition preserving movements from atomization or from marginal violence. Openness and responsiveness of political representation keep clear an appropriate space for collective action and let it exist. But movements don't exhaust themselves in representation; collective action survives beyond institutional mediation; it reappears in different areas of the social system and feeds new conflicts.

Mobilizations of the eighties show that in the passage from latency to visibility a function is carried out by temporary organizations providing financial and technical resources for public campaigns on specific issues while recognizing the autonomy of submerged networks. It is a way of redefining and inventing forms of political representation, and also an opportunity for the more traditional political actors to meet new demands.

A new political space is designed beyond the traditional distinction between state and "civil society": an intermediate *public space,* whose function is not to institutionalize the movements nor to transform them into parties, but to make society hear their messages and translate these messages into political decision making, while the movements maintain their autonomy.[22]

Conflicts and power can't be held by the same actors. The myth of the movements transforming themselves into a transparent power has already produced tragic consequences. The distance between processes by which needs and conflicts are formed and structures performing systemic integration and goals is a condition for making power visible, that is, negotiable. The enlargement of the public space, between movements and institutions, is the task for a real "postindustrial" democracy, a task in which both movements and political actors are concerned.

NOTES

1. Following C. Tilly, L. Tilly, and R. Tilly, *The Rebellious Century, 1830–1930* (Cambridge: Harvard University Press, 1975), and B. Useem, "Solidarity Model, Breakdown Model, and the Boston Anti-Busing Movement," *American Sociological Review* 45 (1980).

2. See especially N. Smelser, *Theory of Collective Behavior* (New York: Macmillan, 1963), and A. Kornhauser, *The Politics of Mass Society* (Glencoe, Ill.: Free Press, 1959).

3. Following K. Webb, "Social Movements: Contingent or Inherent Phenomena?", paper presented at the Conference on Social Movements and Political Systems, Milan, June 1983.

4. A. Touraine, *Production de la société* (Paris: Seuil, 1973) and *La voix et le regard* (Paris: Seuil, 1978); J. Habermas, *Zur Rekonstruktion des historischen Materialismus* (Frankfurt: Suhrkamp, 1976).

5. J. D. McCarthy and M. N. Zald, *The Trend of Social Movements in America: Professionalization and Resource Mobilization* (Morristown, N.J.: General Learning Press, 1973) and "Resource Mobilization and Social Movements: A Partial Theory," *American Journal of Sociology* 86 (1977); M. N. Zald and J. D. McCarthy, eds., *The Dynamics of Social Movements* (Cambridge: Winthrop, 1979); W. A. Gamson, *The Strategy of Social Protest* (Homewood, Ill.: Dorsey, 1975); A. Oberschall, *Social Conflict and Social Movements* (Englewood Cliffs, N.J.: Prentice-Hall, 1973); C. Tilly, *From Mobilization to Revolution* (Reading, Mass.: Addison-Wesley, 1978). For a review and discussion of the resource mobilization approach, see J. C. Jenkins, "Resource Mobilization Theory and the Study of Social Movements," *Annual Review of Sociology* 9 (1983), and J. Freeman, ed., *Social Movements of the Sixties and Seventies* (New York: Longman, 1983).

6. For a wider discussion of the theoretical legacy of the seventies, see A. Melucci, ed., *Altri codici: Aree di movimento nella metropoli* (Bologna: Il Mulino, 1984) and "An End to Social Movements?", *Social Science Information* 24 (1984).

7. This concept is derived from different theoretical frameworks. Cf. Touraine, *Production de la société*; M. Crozier and E. Friedberg, *L'acteur et le système* (Paris: Seuil, 1977); J. S. Coleman, "Social Structure and a Theory of Action," *Polish Sociological Bulletin*, no. 1/2 (1975).

8. On the concept of collective identity, see A. Pizzorno, "Scambio politico e identità collet-tiva nel conflitto di classe," in C. Crouch and A. Pizzorno, eds., *Conflitti in Europa* (Milan: Etas Libri, 1977) and "Identità e interesse," in L. Sciolla, ed., *Identità* (Turin: Rosenberg, 1983); E. Reynaud, "Identités collectives et changement social: Les cultures collectives comme dynamique d'action," *Sociologie du Travail* 22 (1982). The construction of organizational settings as systems of action is pointed out by Crozier and Friedberg, *L'acteur et le système*.

9. I have developed my theoretical reflections in several works. See particularly A. Melucci, "The New Social Movements: A Theoretical Approach," *Social Science Information* 19 (1980), *L'invenzione del presente: Movimenti, identità, bisogni individuali:* (Bologna: Il Mulino, 1982), and "End to Social Movements?"

10. M. Foucault, *Microfisica del potere* (Turin: Einaudi, 1977).

11. Habermas, *Zur Rekonstruktion.*

12. J. H. Marx and B. Holzner, "The Social Construction of Strain and Ideological Models of Grievance in Contemporary Movements," *Pacific Sociological Review* 20 (1977); J. Sassoon, "Ideology, Symbolism and Rituality in Social Movements," *Social Science Information* 24 (1984).

13. A discussion of these topics connecting them to general changes in postindustrial societies is proposed in A. Melucci, "Ten Hypotheses for the Analysis of New Movements," in D. Pinto, ed., *Contemporary Italian Sociology* (Cambridge: Cambridge University Press, 1981) and "New Movements, Terrorism and the Political System," *Socialist Review* 56 (1981).

14. Melucci, "End to Social Movements?"

15. An analysis of social movements which takes account of systemic interaction and the political system responses is proposed by K. Webb et al., "Etiology and Outcomes of Protest: New European Perspectives," *American Behavioral Scientist* 26 (1983); S. Tarrow, "Movimenti e organizzazioni sociali: Che cosa sono, quando hanno successo," *Laboratorio politico* 2 (1982) and *Struggling to Reform: Social Movements and Policy Change During Cycles of Protest,* Western Societies Occasional Papers, no. 15 (Ithaca, N.Y.: Cornell University, 1983); D. Della Porta, "Leadership Strategies and Organizational Resources: The Crisis of the French Women's Movement," paper presented at the 6th EGOS Colloquium, Florence, November

1983; Y. Ergas, "Politica sociale e governo della protesta," in S. Belligni, ed., *Governare la democrazia* (Milan: Angeli, 1981); A. Marsh, *Protest and Political Consciousness* (London: Sage, 1977); J. Wilson, "Social Protest and Social Control," *Social Problems* 24 (1977); F. Fox Piven and R. Cloward, *Poor People's Movements* (New York: Pantheon, 1977). A "political" reduction of the women's movement can be found in J. Freeman, *The Politics of Women's Liberation* (New York: Longman, 1975), and J. Gelb, *Women and Public Policies* (Princeton: Princeton University Press, 1982). For a critique of this reduction, see Y. Ergas, "The Disintegrative Revolution: Welfare Politics and Emergent Collective Identities," paper presented at the Conference on Performance of Italian Institutions, Bellagio, June 1983.

Referring to contemporary movements, I have used the expression "postpolitical movements" (Melucci, *L'invenzione del presente*). Offe speaks of the "metapolitical paradigm" of these movements (C. Offe, "New Social Movements as a Metapolitical Challenge," unpublished paper, University of Bielefeld, 1983).

16. See also, although referred to more formal organizations, the concepts of "social movement industry" (McCarthy and Zald, "Resource Mobilization") and "social movement sector" (R. Garner and M. N. Zald, "Social Movement Sectors and Systematic Constraint," Working Paper no. 238, Center for Research on Social Organization, University of Michigan, 1981).

17. I am referring to the results of broad empirical research on new forms of collective action (youth, women, environmentalists, neoreligious) in the Milan metropolitan area. See Melucci, *Altri codici*; P. R. Donati, "Organization Between Movement and Institution," *Social Science Information* 24 (1984); Sassoon "Ideology, Symbolism, and Rituality."

18. L. P. Gerlach and V. H. Hine, *People, Power and Change* (Indianapolis: Bobbs-Merrill, 1970).

19. N. Smelser, *Theory of Collective Behavior*; F. Alberoni, *Movimento e istituzione* (Bologna: Il Mulino, 1981).

20. S. Hegedus, "Pacifisme, neutralisme ou un nouveau mouvement transnational pour la paix?", presented at Feltrinelli Foundation Conference, Milan, June 1983.

21. A. Melucci and M. Diani, *Nazione senza stato: I movimenti etnico-nazionali in Occidente* (Turin: Loescher, 1983).

22. See J. Cohen, "Crisis Management and Social Movements," Telos, no. 52 (1982): 24–41, and "Rethinking Social Movements," *Berkeley Journal of Sociology* 28 (1983): 97–113.

18

IDENTITIES, GRIEVANCES, AND NEW SOCIAL MOVEMENTS

HANK JOHNSTON   •   ENRIQUE LARAÑA   •   JOSEPH R. GUSFIELD

In the last two decades, the emergence of new forms of collective action in advanced industrial societies stimulated a provocative and innovative reconceptualization of the meaning of social movements. Its relevance has been highlighted by the process of delegitimization of major political parties in Europe at the end of the 1980s, as shown in recent electoral results that have demonstrated considerable support for new or nontraditional parties in Germany, Austria, Italy, and France. In both Europe

From *New Social Movements*, edited by E. Laraña, Hank Johnston, and Joseph R. Gusfield. Reprinted by permission of Temple University Press.

and North America, movements have arisen that stretch the explanatory capacities of older theoretical perspectives. Peace movements, student movements, the anti-nuclear energy protests, minority nationalism, gay rights, women's rights, animal rights, alternative medicine, fundamentalist religious movements, and New Age and ecology movements are but a sampling of the phenomena that have engaged the puzzled attention of sociologists, historians, and political scientists. What is significant for sociologists in such developments is the inability of these movements to be clearly understood within the European or American traditions of analysis. They constitute the anomalies of Kuhnian "normal science."

For much of this century sociological studies of social movements have been dominated first by theories of ideology and later by theories of organization and rationality. Especially in Western Europe, but also in the United States, sociologists have focused on the systems of ideas that movements have espoused. These have often been described in general terms, such as socialism, capitalism, conservatism, communism, fascism. The problem of the analyst has often been that of understanding the economic or class base of the movement or at least some set of discrete interests and sentiments, such as social status, that characterize a group in the social structure. The movement could then be seen as a response to a felt sense of injustice that the ideology specified and that provided the basis for mobilization. Partisanship and mobilization involved a commitment to the ideas and goals of the movement and its program.

The basic problem of many analysts was to understand the process of movement formation by analysis of the social structure that gave rise to the ideology and the problems to which it was addressed. The focus was directed toward groups that occupied spe-

cific places in the social structure from which derived objective interests and demands. The nineteenth-century emphasis on labor and capital fit well into this general paradigm, from which it was also derived. Labor movements and the rise of new political parties have long been the ideal-typical images of social movements and mobilization; through them, the revolutionary actions of communism and fascism were further examined.

Marxist-oriented scholars, as well as some others, have emphasized the class origins and interests of movements and the ideological programs accompanying them. This emphasis on elements of ideology, commitment, and partisanship led to the dominance of ideas as ideologies in understanding the emergence of social movements and collective action. It furthered a focus on the strains and conflicts in social structure as the sources of movement formation, dissent, and protest activity. What it ignored was the importance of organization and the consequences of organizing into group associations. It assumed that the existence of potential conflicts and strains would automatically generate associations of people to correct them.

An interest in the organizational aspects of movements tapped an existing vein of theoretical and empirical interests. Since Max Weber and Ernst Troeltsch there had been a keen interest in charisma and routinization through the functional and strategic considerations of organizational expansion. A series of studies of religious organizations focused on the pathos associated with loss of an original mission as sects became churches. Others, influenced by Weber's writings on bureaucratic organization, have emphasized the internal changes within the movement as an organization. In more recent years, guided in part by conceptions of rational choice, sociologists have gone well beyond Weberian insights into a focus on how collective action depended on the ability of associations to mobilize resources and to conduct the organization on the basis of planned and rational action.

As a corrective to the dominance of ideas and structural strain in the older theories, the resource mobilization perspective was a welcome addition and substitution. Sociologists, especially Charles Tilly and John McCarthy and Mayer Zald, pointed out that there was always strain in the society and that mobilization required both resources and a rational orientation to action. The actor in movements and in protest action was not under the sway of sentiments, emotions, and ideologies that guided his or her action, but rather should be understood in terms of the logic of costs and benefits as well as opportunities for action. When dealing with existent organized groups, as in labor unions or in the civil rights movement, the emphasis on organization could ignore the already existing ideologies. By treating the activities of collective actors as tactics and strategy, the analyst could examine movements and countermovements as engaged in a rational game to achieve specific interests, much like pluralist competition among interest groups in political analysis.

This broad canvas, theoretically spanning finer conceptual and empirical issues that have been debated for more than a century, nevertheless constitutes the painted backdrop for two fundamental questions about new social movements. Why did they create a theoretical problem for the sociologist? And what was lacking in either of the general perspectives outlined above? Such movements had certainly occurred in the past. Earlier this century, witness the Young Movements of Europe (Young Germany, Young Italy, etc.) and the temperance movements in the United States or suffrage movements and student movements on both sides of the Atlantic. In many ways, the student movements of the 1960s, by raising issues that were more than just "problems of interpretation," heralded the first challenges to these classic paradigms (Flacks 1967; Laraña 1982; Katsiaficas 1987).

The concept "new social movements" is a double-edged sword. On one side, it has contributed to the knowledge of contemporary movements by focusing attention to the meaning of morphological changes in their structure and action and by relating those changes with structural transformations in society as a whole. These changes are the source of these movements' "novelty" when compared with the model of collective action based in class conflict that prevailed in Europe since the industrial revolution (Melucci 1989). On the other side, there is a tendency to "ontologize" new social movements (Melucci 1989). This means using the term broadly, as if it captures the "essence" of all new forms of collective action. There is also a tendency to give the concept more explanatory power than is empirically warranted, which no doubt derives from its popularization. The concept, however, refers to an approach rather than a theory; it is not a set of general propositions that have been verified empirically but just an attempt to identify certain common characteristics in contemporary social movements and develop analytical tools to study them (Melucci 1989; Laraña 1993b). The bundle of new social movements mentioned earlier were difficult to conceptualize with either the imagery of the ideological movements of the past or the rationally organized interest group.

Conceived as such, the analysis of new social movements (NSMs) can be advanced by cross-cultural research and by contrasting them with movements of the past that originated in class conflict. To this end, a good starting place is the specification of the fundamental characteristics of NSMs. By no means do all current movements display the following characteristics of new social movements, nor can all current movements be designated new. In many cases, their appearance among current movements leads us to conceptualize them along dimensions of differences from earlier cases of collective action and social movements.

First, NSMs do not bear a clear relation to structural roles of the participants. There is a tendency for the social base of new social movements to transcend class structure. The backgrounds of participants find their most frequent structural roots in rather diffuse social statuses such as youth, gender, sexual orientation, or professions that do not correspond with structural explanations (Klandermans and Oegema 1987). This has been striking in two especially strong movements: the Greens in Europe and the ecological movement in America. It is evident also in such other movements as the anti-nuclear energy movement in Europe and America or the animal and children's rights movements in the United States.

Second, the ideological characteristics of NSMs stand in sharp contrast to the working-class movement and to the Marxist conception of ideology as a unifying and totalizing element for collective action. Especially in Europe but also in the United States, movements were characteristically perceived in accordance with overarching ideologies: conservative or liberal; right or left; capitalist or socialist. Marxist thought, always more dominant in Europe than in America, provided the paradigm for perceptions of action, either bourgeois or proletarian. The new social movements are more difficult to characterize in such terms. They exhibit a pluralism of ideas and values, and they tend to have pragmatic orientations and search for institutional reforms that enlarge the systems of members' participation in decision making (Offe 1985; Cohen 1985; Laraña 1992, 1993a). These movements have an important political meaning in Western societies: They imply a "democratization

dynamic" of everyday life and the expansion of civil versus political dimensions of society (Laraña 1993b).

Third, NSMs often involve the emergence of new or formerly weak dimensions of identity. The grievances and mobilizing factors tend to focus on cultural and symbolic issues that are linked with issues of identity rather than on economic grievances that characterized the working-class movement (Melucci 1985, 1989). They are associated with a set of beliefs, symbols, values, and meanings related to sentiments of belonging to a differentiated social group; with the members' image of themselves; and with new, socially constructed attributions about the meaning of everyday life. This is especially relevant to the ethnic, separatist, and nationalistic movements within existing states. The Catalan and Basque movements in Spain, the Asian and Hispanic movements in the United States, the ethnic movements in the former Soviet Union and even Palestinian nationalism are all examples of new identities emerging in the modern world. The women's movement and the gay rights movement also exemplify this trend. All of these new identities are formed as both private and public ones or old ones remade along new lines.

Fourth, the relation between the individual and the collective is blurred. Closely related to the above point, many contemporary movements are "acted out" in individual actions rather than through or among mobilized groups. The "hippie" movement is the most striking instance, but it is equally true of aspects of other movements where the collective and the individual are blurred, for example, in the gay rights and the women's movements. Another way of thinking about the same phenomena is that in and through movements that have no clear class or structural base, the movement becomes the focus for the individual's definition of himself or herself, and action within the movement is a complex mix of the collective and individual confirmations of identity. The student movements and various countercultural groups of the 1960s were among the earliest examples of this aspect of collective action.

Fifth, NSMs often involve personal and intimate aspects of human life. Movements focusing on gay rights or abortion, health movements such as alternative medicine or antismoking, New Age and self-transformation movements, and the women's movement all include efforts to change sexual and bodily behavior. They extend into arenas of daily life: what we eat, wear, and enjoy; how we make love, cope with personal problems, or plan or shun careers.

Sixth, another common feature of NSMs is the use of radical mobilization tactics of disruption and resistance that differ from those practiced by the working-class movement. New social movements employ new mobilization patterns characterized by nonviolence and civil disobedience that, while often challenging dominant norms of conduct through dramatic display, draw equally on strategies influenced by Gandhi, Thoreau, and Kropotkin that were successfully used in the past (Laraña 1979; McAdam 1988; Morris 1984; Klandermans and Tarrow 1988).

Seventh, the organization and proliferation of new social movement groups are related to the credibility crisis of the conventional channels for participation in Western democracies. This is especially true with regard to the traditional mass parties from which NSMs tend to have a considerable degree of autonomy—and even disdain. This crisis is a motivational factor for collective action in search of alternative forms of participation and decision making relating to issues of collective interest (Whalen and Flacks 1989; Melucci 1989).

Finally, in contrast to cadre-led and centralized bureaucracies of traditional mass parties, new social movement organizations tend to be segmented, diffuse, and decentralized. While there is considerable variation according to movement type, the tendency is toward considerable autonomy of local sections, where collective forms of debate and decision making often limit linkages with regional and national organizations. This has been called the "self-referential element" of the new movements, and it constitutes another sharp distinction with the hierarchical, centralized organization of the working-class movement and the role of the party organization in the Leninist model.

These characteristics of new social movements are not independent of links with the past. Nor is there an absence of continuity with the old, although that varies with each movement. The women's movement has its roots in the suffrage movement of the late nineteenth century in America. New Age movements can trace connections to earlier spiritualist teachings and Eastern philosophies; and contemporary health movements have roots in various quasi-medical orientations that proliferated earlier in this century. Even movements with old histories have emerged in new forms with more diffuse goals and different modes of mobilization and conversion. It is both the newness of expression and extension as well as the magnitude and saliency of such movements that constitutes the basis for needing revised frameworks of understanding.

The theoretical roots of social movement scholarship provide a backdrop to the contemporary discussion of new forms of social movements. Are the new movements as new as they seem? What social and cultural changes have led to the emergence of such movements? Are the ideologies of the past 150 years, with their general programs of reform and revolution, no longer operative in these movements? Has the fulcrum of social movement action shifted from a concern for large-scale societal change to narrower, more self-oriented goals of claiming and realizing new individual and group identities? As Alberto Melucci has written concerning the influence of a changed social structure on movements, "The freedom to have which characterized . . . industrial society has been replaced by the freedom to be" (Melucci 1989, 177–78).

This chapter joins the theoretical debate by focusing on three of the themes mentioned above: the role of identity in social movements, the place of ideology and its relation to collective identity, and issues arising from ideational and structural continuity in contemporary forms of mobilization. Our goals are to identify the key issues, to point out provocative junctures of theory and research, and to reassess where this new conceptual apparatus might take us.

Dimensions of Identity in Social Movement Theory

About twenty-five years ago several American sociologists noted the growing popularity of social movements concerned with the identity of their members. Ralph Turner (1969) observed that personal identity and personal transformation were increasingly themes of diffusely organized social movement organizations. Orrin Klapp (1969) also discussed the collective search for identity as a response to the impoverishment of interaction in modern society. He argued that modern, rationalized, social relations no longer provided reliable reference points from which to construct one's identity. The movements he observed—"identity seeking movements," such as religious and self-help groups, and less organized, trendy, collective behaviors—were attempts to reclaim a self robbed of its identity.

The new social movement perspective holds that the collective search for identity is a central aspect of movement formation. Mobilization factors tend to focus on cul-

tural and symbolic issues that are associated with sentiments of belonging to a differentiated social group where members can feel powerful; they are likely to have subcultural orientations that challenge the dominant system. New social movements are said to arise "in defense of identity." They grow around relationships that are voluntarily conceived to empower members to "name themselves." "What individuals are claiming collectively is the right to realize their own identity: the possibility of disposing of their personal creativity, their affective life, and their biological and interpersonal existence" (Melucci 1980, 218).

Both approaches seem to assume that the pursuit of collective identity flows from an intrinsic need for an integrated and continuous social self, a self that is thwarted and assaulted in modern society. The link between the "morphological social changes" described by Melucci and identity-seeking behaviors seems to result from four factors that are characteristic of postmodernism: material affluence, information overload, confusion over the wide horizon of available cultural alternatives, and system inadequacies in providing institutionally based and culturally normative alternatives for self-identification (see Inglehart 1990, 347). The issues that NSM groups advocate reflect the expanded horizons of personal choice and point out cracks in the system, often in the form of newly defined global concerns. Individuals seek out new collectivities and produce "new social spaces" where novel life-styles and social identities can be experienced and defined. Much as Klapp's explanation of the collective search for identity implicitly criticized modern society, NSM research points out the need for system adjustments via movement formation and the cultural challenges that new movements pose (Habermas 1981, 36–37).

NSM thinking and research so far has produced important insights about the nature of these groups, but to date these insights have not taken the form of an over-all theory. The four factors mentioned above are often left implicit; how they interrelate in the formation of new groups has not been developed. A cynosure of the new social movement perspective that needs further elaboration is the linkage between the broad structural changes that are said to character-ize postindustrial society and identity prob-lems for individuals. This task can begin with a systematic approach to the concept of identity itself. An understanding of who one is, in all its complexity, is fundamental to the formulation of goals, plans, assessments, accounts, and attributions that constitute making one's daily way. That it is so funda-mental may explain why, from the new social movements approach, there is a ten-dency to refer to the concept of identity in a taken-for-granted way. There has been much written in sociology about various aspects of identity, and in the last decade, psychological research has increasingly examined the relationship between individ-ual and group identity (Tajfel 1978; Tajfel and Turner 1985; Turner 1985; Turner et al. 1987). From this vast literature, three dis-tinct dimensions of identity stand out as central for participation in social move-ments: individual identity, collective iden-tity, and public identity. A more theoretical approach requires clear conceptualizations about how they are related.

Individual Identity

For most sociologists, the term individual identity is inherently contradictory. Apart from the "hard wiring" of gender and kin-ship—which we are only beginning to understand—who a person is and what he or she becomes are thoroughly social processes. Yet, in several ways individual identity is important in understanding social movement participation. It relates to the wholly personal traits that, although constructed through the interaction of bio-logical inheritance and social life, are inter-nalized and imported to social movement participation as idiosyncratic biographies. Psychologists studying group formation (Tajfel 1978, 1981; Turner et al. 1987) clearly separate individual identity from its social aspects derived from group membership, but a sociology of social movements must recognize that individual identities are brought to movement participation and changed in the process.

The degree to which they are changed can be used as a means to classify move-ments—from totalizing cults of personal transformation, where the individual iden-tity is taken over by the group, to checkbook quasi-movements like Greenpeace and Ross Perot's United We Stand America, where individual identification may not extend beyond a bumper sticker. Stephen Reicher has noted a parallel continuum regarding the degree to which group-based, socially constructed aspects of identity come to dominate the "imported" individual aspects (see Turner et al. 1987, 169–202).

The field of social movements has appro-priated symbolic interactionist approaches to social roles and social location (Stryker 1980) as the conceptual foundation for thinking about individual identity. The social self of a movement adherent is made up of several social identities that are, in part, shaped as they are acted out, but also that correspond to institutional and organizational roles that proscribe normative behaviors (Merton 1957). These insights have influenced subse-quent research in social psychology on role strain, role change, and role conflict. Another line of research has been directed at operationalizing and measuring individual identity in its various dimensions. A funda-mental problem is that most people can describe "who they are" in only limited terms. The verbal articulation of identity is often limited to counseling psychology or self-help psychologizing of a popular nature. Outside these contexts, and outside life-cycle influences that bring identity issues to the foreground, expression of individual identity in all its facets is not usually necessary. In the ebb and flow of everyday life, identity only becomes an issue when one's status quo is threatened.

In most sociological fields that touch on identity issues—social movements, deviance, family studies, health and medicine—discussions of individual identity are based on the basic framework described above. Erving Goffman's insights into the managed and situational nature of self-image (1959, 1967) have important implications for a sociological approach to individual identity, as does recent work on the relation between self-concept and spoken discourse (Perinbanayagam 1991), but these ideas have proven difficult to reconcile with positivistic research strategies. Recently, feminist research has broken new ground in specifying male-female differences in thinking about oneself and others that derive from biology and culturally defined gender influences.

One of the problems with this key concept is also a source of strength: its interdisciplinary nature in both sociology and psychology. One aspect of a psychological focus emphasizes pathological and unconscious forces and the developmental progress toward adulthood. The work of Erik Erikson (1958, 1968) has focused on the meaning of psychosocial identity as a subjective sense of "continuity and being oneself," and as a fundamental step in personal development. This subjective sense does not arise in isolation but requires the existence of a community. Sociologists and social psychologists have pointed out that personal identity emerges through the mirror of social interaction, that is, by playing different roles and by interpreting how others see us. Although the degree to which a core identity is estab-

lished and functions as an integrating concept will vary, the basic insight of Meadian social psychology also holds true: Individual identity is quintessentially social and its core—if it can be apprehended at all by a reflective self—is relativized according to interactive situations. If identity is difficult to grasp because so much of its content is locked away in the black box of mental life, then it is more difficult to specify because the contents are shifted and rearranged according to social context. The concept provides a tool to analyze a concrete set of facts and problems where the individual and the social realms intersect; this reinforces the need to integrate the biological and sociological models of human behavior.

The dichotomy of a core identity versus a malleable one—or individual versus social identity, to use Tajfel's terms (1981)—should be an important focus in future social movement research. A key question is the extent to which NSMs are disproportionately represented by a coming-of-age generation for whom questions of identity are paramount due to developmental psychological factors. In the three NSM groups studied by Melucci and his colleagues in *Altri Codici* (1984), in addition to the one that was characterized by Giovanni Lodi and Marco Grazioli (1984) as a "youth movement," all seem to be composed largely of people between the ages of eighteen and twenty-eight.

More than in other stages in one's life cycle, search for identity is a youthful activity. Erikson's (1968) fifth developmental stage occurs in late adolescence, when a process of solidification of a mature identity occurs through reconciliation of ascribed roles and new or emergent adult roles. He also pointed out that there is an intrinsic link between identity and ideology. An individual's identity becomes consistent when it is built in a common ideological orientation that renders it meaningful and gives it coherence. To take one example, in interviews with leftist and nationalist militants in Barcelona, Hank Johnston (1991) found that many spoke vividly of psychological dissonance that arose from reconciling a traditional, often religious, and middle-class upbringing with newfound Marxism. Identity reconciliation was the substance of interaction with dense interpersonal networks of young student and working-class militants. It forged a solidarity in these groups that imparted a resilience against state repression. It also provided for a unique flexibility and breadth that served to bridge different oppositional groups during mass mobilization. Sustained by intense discussions among friends, these networks were the functional equivalent of "new social spaces" discussed by Melucci.

It is our guess that among different social movements, the emphasis on identity quest results from the intersection of several factors, one of which is the coming of age of a cohort in an economic and social milieu that frees them from immediate material concerns and disposes them to intense introspection about who they are. Although research on new social movements recognizes that these factors are related to participation, identity search and temporariness of involvement are treated as something new, deriving from system changes in postindustrial society (Lodi and Grazioli 1984). To the extent that we are dealing primarily with youth movements, or at least movements that bear the imprint of a large youthful membership, then identity search cannot be explained exclusively by post-industrial changes.

Collective Identity

The concept of collective identity has recently been thrust into the foreground of social movement theory. Aldon Morris's and Carol Mueller's book, *Frontiers in Social Movement Theory* (1992), contains several chapters that either deal directly with this concept or have sections that discuss it. Taken together, these treatments point out the multifaceted and interrelated nature of the concept; the paradoxical result is that the theoretical spotlight simultaneously reveals many more angles, corners, niches, and shadows. Let us see if we can clarify the ways of talking about collective identity, and in particular point out the relationship between several closely related concepts like group boundaries, group membership, solidarity, and the organization of everyday life.

The concept of collective identity refers to the (often implicitly) agreed upon definition of membership, boundaries, and activities for the group. According to Melucci (1995), "Collective identity is an interactive and shared definition produced by several individuals (or groups at a more complex level) and concerned with the orientations of action and the field of opportunities and constraints in which the actions take place." It is built through shared definitions of the situation by its members, and it is a result of a process of negotiation and "laborious adjustment" of different elements relating to the ends and means of collective action and its relation to the environment. By this process of interaction, negotiation and conflict over the definition of the situation, and the movement's reference frame, members construct the collective "we."

This social constructionist definition has three dimensions that make collective identity an especially difficult concept to pin down empirically. First, it is predicated on a continual interpenetration of—and mutual influence between—the individual identity of the participant and the collective identity of the group. Second, by the very nature of the phenomena we study, the collective identity of social movements is a "moving target," with different definitions predominating at different points in a movement career. Third, distinct processes in identity creation and maintenance are operative in different phases of the movement.

In the midst of all this change and flux, this concept is often employed as if it was frozen in time and space, neglecting its process-based nature and shifting boundaries. A related problem refers to the "facticity" of collective identity and the way it serves as a predicate of behavior. A frequent usage, although one that seems to occur more as a rhetorical device than a conscious analytical position, is to speak of collective identity as something that stands above and beyond the individual social actors and takes on a life of its own. Suggestive of Herbert Blumer's early conceptualization of esprit de corps (1955) and other early collective behavior theorists that emphasized group consciousness, this is a definition that directs attention away from individual contributions and attaches it to a movement organization defined in the aggregate as a collective actor. In this usage, both "collective identity" and "social movement" can be spoken of without reference to the processes that constitute them. Rather, like Émile Durkheim's *conscience collective,* collective identity is the repository of movement values and norms that define movement behavior from some epistemological point beyond the individual participant. It is a "social fact" that dictates prohibitions and appropriate behaviors.

Yet there is a grain of insight that can be winnowed from the Durkheimian position. We have in mind the notion that an identity is both cognitively real—that is, based on lived experience and knowledge stored in memory—and idealized in Goffman's sense of ideal notions of how a role behavior should be. To share a collective identity means not only to have had a part in constituting it but also, in some instances, "obeying" its normative proscriptions. Clearly, this is an aspect of collective identity that meets Durkheim's external and constraining

criteria for social facts; and, from this perspective, to partake in a collective identity means also doing (and not doing) certain things. The key insight is that normative and valuational elements of external social relations are closely associated with how one thinks about oneself; these elements guide and channel behavior within—and without—the group. In this sense, doing (appropriate movement-related behaviors) and being (identity) are inextricably linked. This closely follows Stephen Reichter's treatment of identity and crowd behavior (see Turner et al. 1987, 169–202). He suggests that the more the individual identifies with the group, the more likely emergent group norms will constrain and shape behavior. The power of emergent norms works through the mechanism of collective identity and the intrinsic human tendency to affirm group identification (see Tajfel and Turner 1985).

Bearing this in mind, we can turn to the more common, constructionist usage that has been drawn on by NSM thinking. The constructionist view has been emphasized in current analyses of radical feminist, gay, and lesbian groups (Margolis 1985; Marshall 1991), as well as attempts to explain ethnic politics and nationalism (Johnston 1985; See 1986; Nagel and Olzak 1982; Anderson 1991). Characteristic of this approach, Melucci asserts that "collective identity is a product of conscious action and the outcome of self-reflection more than a set of given or 'structural' characteristics. [It] tends to coincide with conscious processes of 'organization' and it is experienced not so much as a situation as an action" (1992, 10–11). By stressing the "process-based, self-reflexive and constructed manner in which collective actors tend to define themselves today" (10), contemporary approaches to collective identity acknowledge a strong symbolic interactionist influence. This tradition points to interaction among social movement participants as the locus of research on identity processes. In Europe, one tendency has been to explore this avenue of investigation through "intervention research" (Touraine 1981; Melucci 1984). In North America, research has followed an identity-focused agenda via traditional interactionist issues: self-presentation, dramaturgical analysis, conversions, and gender and gender interaction. Regardless of research strategy, the global point is that collective actors define themselves in a social context, and any constructionist view of identity must make reference to both the interactive situations where identity is formed and shaped and to the other people who join in the task.

This raises inevitable questions about the relation between group membership and collective identity. Debra Friedman and Doug McAdam (1992, 169) have discussed how individual attachments to preexisting groups and interpersonal networks frequently function as sources of collective identity when these attachments are highly valued. The assumption of valued group attachments allows the authors to recast collective identity as a selective incentive, to use Mancur Olson's (1965) term, as a way of reconciling a microstructuralist focus with rational choice models. Collective identity becomes a valued commodity that is worth the commitment of time, resources, the "capital" of individual autonomy and the risk of presentation of self because the group from which it is derived is also valued.

The issue goes to the core of social movement formation, and there are several answers, which, taken together, can help the student of social movements think more systematically about the creation of collective identities. First, following the argument of Friedman and McAdam, one can consider organizational strategy. In their analysis, the organization "provides an identity" and "shapes it for consumption." This might be

called a "strategic constructionist perspective," to coin a term, that suggests, for some movements, there are leaders, committees, or cabals that plot the best collective identity for the movement, much like marketing executives strategizing the best way to present a product. It is a "top down" approach to collective identity that seems to be more useful in some movements than others. This approach would be especially useful in later stages of movement development when social movement organizations are established and likely to be thinking of these strategic terms. At earlier stages, however, when issues are being articulated and groups coalesce around issues, it makes sense that a more "bottom up" approach is, if not the entire answer, then at least deserving of a place in the theoretical equation. These issues are expanded in the next two sections.

Public Identity

While the two previous dimensions of identity involve self-assessments—either by an individual or by the group—the concept of public identity captures the influences that the external public have on the way social movement adherents think about themselves. Both individual identity and collective identity are affected by interaction with nonmembers and by definitions imposed on movements by state agencies, countermovements, and, especially in the contemporary movement environment, the media. There are different courses and different channels by which public definitions can influence movement identities, and it makes sense that, depending on the source, there can be different effects.

On the one hand, there is a long tradition of research on how impersonal influences affect movement identities. State repression can intensify we-them distinctions and fortify group identification and commitment (Trotsky 1957; Smelser 1962; Brinton 1965; Hierich 1971), especially in radical political movements (Knutson 1981; della Porta and Tarrow 1986; della Porta 1992; Pérez-Agote 1986). Particularly important in today's movement environment are the information media and the role of the media in shaping a movement's image (Gamson 1988; Gitlin 1980). Enrique Laraña observes how a split in the internal and external images of a movement can result from journalists' tendency to focus on professionalized movement representatives and visible aspects of movement activities. Another element of media identity is the process of influencing the assignment of meaning through framing activities by leaders. This occurred in the Basque and Catalan movements in Spain and in Spanish student mobilizations during the 1980s.

On the other hand, a neglected aspect of research on public identity is personal influence and social impact. By this we refer to concrete interaction between members of a movement and nonmembers. Research in social psychology has demonstrated that the more intimate, local, and personally relevant an informational input, the greater the influence it has on opinion (Latané 1981). If media images of a movement can influence personal or collective identity, their influence carries more weight if it comes via people who are close to and who are valued by the movement participant. With the exception of totalizing groups such as cults and radical cells, the collective aspect of identity formation tends to be at best a part-time endeavor; and what others (especially primary relations) think about the movement can carry great weight in a developing collective identity. An individual's social life will include others outside the movement group. This is even more relevant for movement participants who are deeply associated in community life, especially in the early phases of the movement when the demands on time and resources characteristic of the increasing pace of mobilization are just beginning. Then the relation between the public identity and the emergent collective identity is critical.

As a movement mobilizes, committed members will progressively exclude extraneous ties in favor of movement-based interaction. Boundary maintenance, a term used in ecological theory to understand the creation of resource niches, is another way of thinking about increasingly exclusionary behavior. Verta Taylor and Nancy Whittier (1992) discuss how radical feminists engage in a species of boundary maintenance by building alternative loci of affiliation called "feminist counterinstitutions" to affirm their collective identity. There is a time-budgeting dimension to these actions in that the larger proportion of daily activities that movement-related roles occupy in a social actor's overall identity—that is, the sum total of his or her roles—the sharper the boundaries, the clearer the we-they distinctions, and the stronger the collective identity. Boundaries can be thought of as activities and definitions that reinforce collective definitions through we-they distinctions, which are often marked by differences in physical appearance, dress, speech, demeanor, and other behaviors. There is variation in the panorama of movements regarding the sharpness of boundary distinctions. Taylor and Whittier review the efforts at exclusion among lesbian feminist groups, while other movements are less exclusionary and even may wax inclusive in later stages of their careers, with negative effects on collective identity and commitment (Zald and Ash 1966; Gerlach and Hine 1970). It makes sense that the strength of boundary maintenance (which is an activity) and we-they distinctions (which is a cognition) are related to collective identity in terms of the relationship between time and effort dedicated to movement activities.

We know a great deal about the social processes by which collective identity gathers strength, but our thinking about the topic has not been able to explain starting mechanisms, that is, the initial kick that moves potential participants to choose one set of social ties above others. This brings us to the third approach to the issue of emergent collective identities, and to what we see as a forgotten theoretical issue: the relation between what a social movement is about—its substance in the form of grievances, demands, and a program for change—and the way its collective identity can be codified in an ideology.

Ideology, Grievances, and Collective Identity

"Old movements" coalesced around shared grievances and perceptions of injustice. Programs for amelioration of these grievances and attribution of cause constituted the ideological base for mobilization. In the movement context, the link between ideology and grievances was strong, as it was conceptually in early theories of social movements. Ideology as a codification of wrongs and injustices was seen as a necessary process for mobilization to occur (Smelser 1962). In deprivation theories, the link between grievances and action was fundamental to explanatory logic, but typically it was left implicit. Research in the symbolic interactionist tradition emphasized the definition of a situation as unjust and warranting action; the specification of collective solutions was understood as key to mobilization processes. William Gamson, Bruce Fireman, and Steven Rytina's research into the emergence of injustice frames offers decisive insights into the earliest mechanisms by which grievances become articulated (1982; see also Gamson 1992).

In the 1960s, several observers—Daniel Bell, Ralph Turner, Joseph Gusfield, Orrin Klapp, among others—noted that an increasing number of movements and conflicts articulated grievances that were not based on economic and class interests. These movements were based on less "objective" elements such as identity, status, humanism, and spirituality. In a sense, the link between mobilization and grievances became less compelling. While not without their own ideological base and in varying degrees among different groups, these movements were less characterized by the extensive ideological articulation usually found in socialist and communist organizations. Shortly thereafter, the link between grievances and mobilization was further deemphasized as factors relating to resources, organization, and strategy gained theoretical predominance in the field.

The year 1990 brought the collapse of Marxist-Leninist states, and with it the debilitation of the most highly developed oppositional ideologies of the twentieth century. Richard Flacks points out that there is much more to the Left's vision than the way it was distorted by the communist parties of the socialist bloc. He argues that the grand tradition of the Left has both been an integral part of how generations of activists have thought about themselves and a transcendent view of what society could be. This tradition was internalized into one's social identity; it was lived in one's daily contacts and through the content of that interaction. Although ideology, grievances, and collective identity are analytically separate, there is a strong relationship between them, one that has been muted in the past but has been brought into the theoretical foreground by NSM research.

The traditional theories of social movements did not emphasize the link between grievances and identity as relevant to explaining movement formation, but it makes sense that the link was there. For laboring men and women, for peasants, and for anarchist militants, the substance of grievances, and their interpretation by ideologies, was embedded in everyday life. E. P. Thompson's (1963) study of the emergence of the English working class shows that identity as a tradesman permeated everyday life and that there were many instances when the collective identity deriving from a shared sense of injustice was particularly strong. In his study of protests of weavers in Rouen, France, William Reddy (1977) shows how structural changes outside village society threatened the way of life for seventeenth-century weavers. The forms of protest weavers instigated were closely linked with the defense of their traditional social statuses. Similarly, anarchist groups in nineteenth-century Spain first organized athenaeums where workers gathered at the end of the day to socialize, discuss issues, and take courses. Family activities such as picnics and choral groups were also organized (Esenwein 1989). In West Virginia, the identity of a united mine worker's organizer in the 1930s was closely linked to the injustices he and his compatriots faced in the mines, in the company towns, in company stores, and in seeing the ravages of poverty on their children. Although none of the militants would have characterized their involvement in terms of a quest for identity, through the newly ground lenses of NSM concepts, the degree to which close friends and everyday activities were linked with the movement becomes apparent. Collective identity and grievances are not the same, but their close association lies in the fact that the organization of how social movement adherents think about themselves is structured in important ways by how shared wrongs are experienced, interpreted, and reworked in the context of group interaction.

These observations are strikingly similar to recent work in feminist theory and the women's movement about the politicization of everyday life. Because gender stereotyping and discrimination permeates most modern social relations, there is a fundamental injustice embedded at the level of quotidian interaction. An important aspect of the feminist program has been to create new social spaces, ones that are equally quotidian, where women can respond to, and in the extreme, withdraw from, gender discrimination and interaction with men in order to nurture their own identities (Taylor and Whittier 1992). These kinds of groups, which are characteristic of the women's movement, are often considered prototypical of NSM organizations.

To understand how movements are distributed on the axis of grievances and identity, we suggest that the following reckoning is helpful. First, all movements, to some degree, are linked with issues of individual and collective identity via the way that focal grievances affect everyday life. In the United States, mobilizations in response to economic crisis and rising unemployment during the 1930s, often led by communist activists, followed the classic pattern of European workers' movements (Piven and Cloward 1971, 62). People participated massively in collective action because they were hungry and without jobs. These were matters that went to the core of their existence, and collective identity was not the focus of action. Yet, in the United States, status movements are closely linked with identity issues (Gusfield 1963; Zurcher and Kirkpatrick 1976; Luker 1984). Here the grievances are actuated by perceived threats to how one defines oneself, such as the way that the popularization of abortion threatens, for some women, traditional conceptions of motherhood. Status movements take action about "other people's business" because that business often poses a threat to how the mobilizing group defines itself. They might be seen as precursors of NSMs if we accept that identity issues become a basic mobilizing factor.

New social movements display a paradoxical relationship between identity and grievances. First, the very nature of grievances for NSMs merges them closely with the concept of identity. For movements about gender or sexual identity, for example, the collective grievances are inextricably linked with issues of identity quest in the group context. The support and identity-affirming functions of feminist and gay rights groups are well known. Second, where grievances have a more important place in group formation, such as in ecological groups, the NSM perspective tells us that identity quest co-occurs as a displaced (or unconscious) but nevertheless fundamental raison d'être of group formation. Third, for some NSM groups, such fundamental grievances as threats to the ozone level, nuclear proliferation, or saving whales are so distant from everyday life that they can only remain immediate through their ongoing social construction and reassertion in the group context. Indeed, one might speculate that in those instances when the goals of NSM groups are particularly global and distant from achievement, it is the intensely personal orientations and the close melding of the group with everyday life that provide the sustaining lifeblood of cohesion. In rational choice terms, identity defense and affirmation provide the necessary counterbalancing selective incentives where the more practical payoffs of the movement are small.

Continuity in New Social Movements

An important focus of recent research has been the informal organizational networks as the platform from which movement formation occurs. Joseph Gusfield (1981) emphasizes the role of "carry-ons and carry-overs" from one movement to another; Adrian Aveni (1977), Mark Granovetter (1983), and Doug McAdam (1982, 1988) all argue for the importance of preexisting networks of relations in collective action; and Aldon Morris (1984) looks at the role of established social organizations—"movement halfway houses"—in the growth of the civil rights movement. In a similar vein, Leila Rupp and Verta Taylor (1987) discuss "abeyance structures" during the recumbent periods of the women's movement in a hostile political climate. In the even more hostile setting of the authoritarian state, Hank Johnston examines the role of "oppositional subcultures" in several nationalist mobilizations (1991, 1992, 1993; see also Pérez-Agote 1990). These subcultures are comprised of well developed but, for the most part, private social networks that are built up in response to repression and the stilted discourse of public life in closed societies.

The theoretical import of this work on the "microstructural" factors prior to mobilization is that the temporal frame of analysis gets pushed back in order to focus on premobilization phases as partial explanations of the shape and course social movements take. This shift also tends to lay bare the role of cultural content since continuity arises not only through persistence of organizations but also through the shared meanings and beliefs of movement members. Its significance for current research on social movements might contribute to overcoming its structuralist bias and to framing research within the perspective of an "interpretative sociology" (Gamson 1988). This "epistemological reframing" would permit a deeper approach to the study of social movement formation that draws on the latent, nonvisible, cognitive dimensions instead of visible and political aspects (Melucci 1989). Consideration of the historical preconditions of mobilization is of course nothing new—seeking causes in itself implies temporal priority—but the search for a movement's origins has, in the past, focused either on intellectual currents or preexisting resources rather than on the nonvisible networks that function in everyday life as premobilization structures.

Prior to this research, the analysis of social movements had taken a more "volcanic" approach: It is attracted to an event when it erupts through the surface of social life, and it focuses on the flow of human, organizational, and resource-related magma. Taylor (1989, 761) points out that NSM research tends to succumb to this tendency as well. Her research with Rupp (1987) chronicles how organizational and cultural continuities can shape highly noninstitutionalized NSM forms of organization. Their study reviews how the intense commitment, rich and variegated culture, and strong activist networks facilitated the resurgent women's movement in the mid 1960s. Although their emphasis is on continuity in repertoires of contention, there are several points where one sees continuities in the shape of everyday organization within the retrenched movement, especially the solidarity, cohesiveness, and commitment within the abeyance networks they describe. These characteristics were important sources of personal support in the difficult postwar years of the women's movement and suggest that in periods of quiescence factors related to personal and collective identity may be at work to establish links of continuity (Taylor 1989). One is led to speculate the degree to which the prior organization stimulated smaller support groups that, in contrast to lobbying organizations, characterize the newness of contemporary feminism.

In a similar vein, the roots of the New Left in the United States have been traced by several researchers (Whalen and Flacks, 1984; Wood 1974; Isserman 1987) who have pointed out strong continuities with the Old Left. Taking the women's movement and

the New Left together, the point is that while events of greater or lesser magnitude punctuate history, there is an important thread of organizational and cultural continuity for many NSMs in the United States insofar as the focus of analysis shifts to everyday activities. On the other hand, research in the European tradition has stressed the special significance of great historical events and the path-breaking influence of ideas and persons. From this perspective, as analysts of new social movements in Europe sifted through the soil of postmodernism, they have located the first sprouts of new social movements among the relatively recent mobilizations of students and the New Left in the late 1960s (Habermas 1981; Kriesi 1992).

The fact that the NSM perspective has generated wider enthusiasm in Europe than in the United States provides evidence about the nature of theory construction and its patterns of diffusion in sociology. As we pointed out earlier, the European tradition of social movement research, reflecting the influence of Marxist thought, emphasized structural backgrounds of class to a greater extent than the American studies. In the United States, the situation has been historically different and there has never been a strong party representing the working class. Flacks attributes this fact to the peculiar characteristics of the American labor force, especially its multiethnic character, which is the result of waves of immigration. Instead of the unification of the people sharing the tradition of the Left, there has been a fragmentation of the working class in ethnic groups and trade unions based on ethnic solidarity. The growth of a unified working-class party was prevented by a system where the competition between ethnic groups created obstacles to class solidarity. The absence of strong leftist parties and socialist unions in the United States atomized working-class organization into local manifestations and decentralized civil society to a greater extent than in Europe.

If we search for cultural factors, there is a long tradition of individualism and self-help/self-improvement movements in the United States (Meyer 1975). These have roots in the broader cultural templates discussed over 150 years ago by Alexis de Tocqueville in *Democracy in America* and more recently by Bellah et al. (1985). In the words of de Tocqueville, the American propensity to "self-interest properly understood" fomented a wide array of interest groups and voluntary associations that exercised influence at local levels of government early in the nation's history. These local forms of participation continued to characterize American society throughout the nineteenth and twentieth centuries. In Europe, despite wide variations between countries, there were two social forces that shaped civil participation differently: the institutional church and the Left. While European society today is more secularized than the United States, the Catholic church and other religious groups played important roles in the development of social movement organizations, especially in some countries like Belgium, Italy, and Spain. The church in Europe enjoyed a quasi-monopoly on the kinds of transcendental questions that sects and cults in the United States have regularly taken up. These observations must be taken as generalizations that gloss many factors, but they stress that the utility of the NSM perspective is intimately related to the cultural and intellectual soil in which it germinates.

A final point regarding continuity in NSM groups is often overlooked, but it is central to cultural and organizational continuity over long periods. We have in mind the relations between generational cohorts alluded to earlier (see Braungart and Braungart 1984). Intergenerational relations are a key aspect of how continuity in culture, ideology, and organizational form is achieved (Mannheim 1952). This is not to imply a one-way relation from the wizened older generation to the young. Rather, in many movements there are opportunities for reciprocity where the older members mitigate the radicalism of youth, and youthful members open new horizons to the older generation (Johnston 1991). These are processes that are not examined in depth by new social movement research, despite methodological strategies, for example, participant observation and "intervention," that would seem to lend themselves to such questions (Touraine 1981; Melucci 1984). To the extent that the quest for identity is a youthful activity, theoretical concern with intergenerational relations will become more relevant for the study of contemporary movements. Whittier's (1993) treatment of generational relations in the women's movement may signal the beginning of a shift in interest in this area of research.

Conclusions

This chapter opens with a review of European and North American traditions in social movement scholarship and two questions about new social movements: Why have they posed such a challenge to traditional theories? And, What was it about the traditional theories that proved to be inadequate? From the NSM perspective, the answer to the first question centers on the link between structural change characteristic of postindustrial society and movements that emphasize identity in the context of a wide variety of grievances and forms of organization embedded in the everyday life of participants. The answer to the second question is that traditions of the past, perhaps colored by their particular ideological lenses, did not grasp the everyday and identity dimensions of the "old movements" they sought to explain.

The heart of this chapter focuses on the idea that a more systematic approach to NSMs requires stronger conceptual development regarding identity, especially if the linkages between the social actor and structural changes characteristic of postmodern society are to be specified. Identity has two central dimensions—individual and collective—both of which are shaped by a third—public identity. Both individual and collective identity are characterized by a dualistic epistemology in which continuity and change coexist as alternative approaches. Individual identity is composed of both its fixed aspects, which are "imported" by each participant to social movement groups, and by its fundamentally malleable quality, which is shaped in the course of interaction within the collectivity. Similarly, collective identity can be conceptualized at any point in time as a fixed content of meanings, frames of interpretation, and normative and valuational proscriptions that exercise influence over individual social actors. On the other hand, collective identity is also an emergent quality of group interaction, which is strengthened by group solidarity and boundary maintenance activities and shaped by public images of the group via interaction with nonmembers.

Part of the task we face is to refine both conceptual and methodological tools. Research strategies must permit the complexity of identity to unfold in the data-gathering process. This issue is echoed in Bert Klandermans's call for longitudinal research of movement activists (1992, 53–75). Batteries of questions focused wholly on identity issues will be required for meaningful comparisons over time. But the complexity of identity is such that fixed choice questions can access only some dimensions of the concept. More often than not, the raw data of identity is expressed in halting and fragmented accounts, platitudes, and monologues—sometimes spontaneous, sometimes

rehearsed—of "who we are" and "who I am." Moreover, aspects of identity can change in the course of data-gathering itself. In some instances, different aspects of identity are invoked for different behaviors being observed, or for different phases—and even responses—in the interview process. A woman may discuss issues of the environmental movement as an activist, as a mother, as a manager, as a spouse, or as a Latina. Sociological intervention, discourse analysis, informal interviewing, and qualitative research strategies, such as those suggested by Scott Hunt, Robert Benford, and David Snow would be very helpful.

Our examination of continuity and change in individual and collective identities suggests further research. First, in examining the "imported" qualities of individual identity, we note a potential correlation between identity quest and youthful composition of NSM groups. The degree to which there is a mix between young adults, for whom identity questions are important, and older members is an important dimension on which NSM groups might be distributed. The processes of intergenerational relations, reflected in the cohort composition of new social movements, while traced in several studies of the New Left and the women's movements, has not been pursued elsewhere.

Second, we note that the emphasis of "identity quest" will differ among NSMs and, given the centrality of the concept, it makes sense that this is a dimension on which NSM groups should be categorized. Comparisons require reliable measures of both individual and collective identity orientations that, by freezing concepts that are also inherently malleable and emergent, violate the dual nature of identity concepts. Nevertheless, there is much to be gained by inter-movement and cross-national comparisons. It may be necessary to shed prejudices about measures of individual identity deriving from susceptibility theories in order to establish a comparative data base about who joins NSMs.

Third, we also note that the link between grievances and everyday life of movement participants might vary between NSM groups. The extent to which grievances are tied to everyday concerns in contrast to more global issues that seem quite removed from mundane concerns is a provocative question, and it makes sense that there will be considerable variation in the panorama of NSM groups. A working hypothesis is that where global concerns are far removed from everyday life, movement cohesion requires the selective incentives of a strong identity component. Moreover, the relationship between identity and the immediacy/globalness of grievances may comprise another dimension on which NSMs can be analyzed.

A final observation arises from current events in Europe. The specter of violent skinheads and neofascist youth movements in Europe raises the question if these, too, somehow fit into the NSM equation of identity quest, everyday embeddedness, and broad structural change. When seen in the context of the crisis of credibility of the main traditional political actors, the emergence of xenophobic movements presents similarities with post-World War I Europe. In the past, NSMs have been discussed as a creative force of change, signifying directions for cultural and social innovation. Yet, there may be a darker side that parallels the dangers presented by collective identities in the mold of totalitarian movements of the past. Surely the rise of nationalist movements and ethnic hatred also go to the core of how social actors think about themselves. Unlike mass society theory, the NSMs represent alternative channels for participation in public life. If this is so, the revival of violent racist groups in the same European countries that gave birth to Nazism and fascism would confirm the Marxist dictum, "History repeats itself: the first time as a tragedy, the second as farce."

REFERENCES

Anderson, Benedict. 1991. *Imagined Communities.* 2d ed. London: Verso.

Aveni, Adrian F. 1977. "The Not-So-Lonely Crowd: Friendship Groups in Collective Behavior." *Sociometry* 40:96–110.

Bellah, Robert N., Richard Madsen, William M. Sullivan, Ann Swidler, and Steven M. Tipton. 1985. *Habits of the Heart.* Los Angeles: University of California Press.

Blumer, Herbert. 1955. "Collective Behavior." In *An Outline of the Principles of Sociology,* edited by Robert Park, pp. 68–121. New York: Barnes and Noble.

Braungart, Richard G. 1984. "Historical Generations and Generation Units: A Global Pattern of Youth Movements." *Journal of Political and Military Sociology* 12:113–35.

Braungart, Richard G., and M. M. Braungart, eds. 1984. Special issue, "Life Course and Generational Politics." *Journal of Political and Military Sociology* 12.

Brinton, Crane. 1965. *Anatomy of Revolution.* Rev. ed. New York: Knopf.

Cohen, Jean L. 1985. "Strategy or Identity: New Theoretical Paradigms and Contemporary Social Movements." *Social Research* 52, 4:663–716.

della Porta, Donatella. 1992. "Introduction: On Individual Motivations in Underground Political Organizations." In *Social Movements and Violence: Participation in Underground Organizations,* edited by Donatella della Porta, pp. 3–28. Vol. 4 of *International Social Movement Research.* Greenwich, Conn.: JAI Press.

della Porta, Donatella, and Sidney Tarrow. 1986. "Unwanted Children: Political Violence and the Cycle of Protest in Italy, 1966–1973." *European Journal of Political Research* 14:607–32.

Erikson, Erik. 1958. *Young Man Luther.* New York: Norton.

———. 1968. *Identity: Youth and Crisis.* New York: Norton.

Esenwein, George R. 1989. *Anarchist Ideology and the Working-Class Movement in Spain, 1869–1898.* Berkeley: University of California Press.

Flacks, Richard. 1967. "The Liberated Generation: An Exploration of the Roots of Student Protest." *Social Issues* 13, 3:52–75.

Friedman, Debra, and Doug McAdam. 1992. "Collective Identity and Activism: Networks,

Choices, and the Life of a Social Movement. In *Frontiers in Social Movement Theory*, edited by Aldon D. Morris and Carol McClurg Mueller, pp. 156–72. New Haven: Yale University Press.

Gamson, William A. 1988. "Political Discourse and Collective Action." In From *Structure to Action*, edited by Bert Klandermans, Hanspeter Kriesi, and Sidney Tarrow, pp. 219–44. Vol. 1 of *International Social Movement Research*. Greenwich, Conn.: JAI Press.

———. 1992. "The Social Psychology of Collective Action. " In *Frontiers in Social Movement Theory*, edited by Aldon D. Morris and Carol McClurg Mueller, pp. 53–76. New Haven: Yale University Press.

Gamson, William A., Bruce Fireman, and Steven Rytina. 1982. *Encounters with Unjust Authority*. Homewood, Ill.: Dorsey.

Gerlach, Luther P., and Virginia H. Hine. 1970. *People, Power, and Change: Movements of Social Transformation*. Indianapolis: Bobbs-Merrill.

Gitlin, Todd. 1980. *The Whole World Is Watching*. Berkeley: University of California Press.

Goffman, Erving. 1959. *The Presentation of Self in Everyday Life*. New York: Doubleday.

———. 1967. *Interaction Ritual*. New York: Doubleday.

Granovetter, Mark. 1983. "The Strength of Weak Ties: A Network Theory Revisited." In *Sociological Theory*, edited by Randall Collins, pp. 201–33. San Francisco: Jossey-Bass.

Gusfield, Joseph R. 1963. *Symbolic Crusade*. Urbana: University of Illinois Press.

———. 1981. "Social Movements and Social Change: Perspectives of Linearity and Fluidity." In *Research in Social Movements, Conflict, and Change*, edited by Louis Kreisberg, Vol. 3. Greenwich, Conn.: JAI Press.

Habermas, Jürgen. 1981. "New Social Movements." *Telos* 49:33–37.

Hierich, Max. 1971. *The Spiral of Conflict: Berkeley 1964*. New York: Columbia University Press.

Inglehart, Ronald. 1990. *Culture Shift in Advanced Industrial Society*. Princeton: Princeton University Press.

Isserman, Maurice. 1987. *If I Had a Hammer . . . : The Death of the Old Left and the Birth of the New Left*. New York: Basic Books.

Johnston, Hank. 1985. "Catalan Ethnic Mobilization: Some 'Primordial' Modifications of the Ethnic Competition Model." In *Cultural Perspectives in Social Theory*, edited by Scott McNall, 6:129–47. Greenwich, Conn.: JAI Press.

———. 1989. "Toward an Explanation of Church Opposition to Authoritarian Regimes: Religio-oppositional Subcultures in Poland and Catalonia." *Journal for the Scientific Study of Religion* 28:493–508.

———. 1991. *Tales of Nationalism: Catalonia, 1939–1979*. New Brunswick, NJ.: Rutgers University Press.

———. 1992. "Religion and Nationalist Subcultures in the Baltics." *Journal of Baltic Studies* 24, 2 (Summer): 133–48.

———. 1993. "Religio-Nationalist Subcultures under the Communists: Comparisons and Conceptual Refinements." *Sociology of Religion* 54, 4:237–55.

Katsiaficas, George. 1987. *The Imagination of the New Left*. Boston: South End Press.

Klandermans, Bert. 1992. "The Case for Longitudinal Research on Movement Participation." In *Studying Collective Action*, edited by Mario Diani and Ron Eyerman, pp. 55–75. London: Sage.

Klandermans, Bert, and Dirk Oegema. 1987. "Potentials, Networks, Motivations, and Barriers: Steps toward Participation in Social Movements." *American Sociological Review* 52:519–31.

Klandermans, Bert, and Sidney Tarrow. 1988. "Mobilization into Social Movements: Synthesizing European and American Approaches." In *From Structure to Action*, edited by Bert Klandermans, Hanspeter Kriesi, and Sidney Tarrow, pp. 1–38. Vol. 1 of *International Social Movement Research*. Greenwich, Conn.: JAI Press.

Klapp, Orrin. 1969. *Collective Search for Identity*. New York: Holt, Rinehart, and Winston.

Knutson, Jeanne N. 1981. "Social and Psychological Pressures toward a Negative Identity: The Case of an American Revolutionary Terrorist." In *Behavioral and Quantitative Perspectives on Terrorism*, edited by Yanov Alexander and J. M. Gleason. New York: Pergamon.

Kriesi, Hanspeter. 1992. "The Political Opportunity Structure of New Social Movements." Paper presented at the First European Conference on Social Movements, Wissenschaftszentrum Berlin für Socialforschung, Berlin, October 30.

Laraña, Enrique. 1979. "La Constitución y el derecho a la resistencia." In *Revista de la Facultad de Derecho de la Universidad Compultense de Madrid*. Monográfico sobre la Constitución Española, no. 2:183–203.

———. 1982. "La juventud contemporánea y el conflicto intergeneracional." *Revista de Juventud* 3:41–62.

———. 1992. "Student Movements in the U.S. and Spain: Ideology and the Crisis of Legitimacy in

Post-Industrial Society." Paper presented at the International Conference on Culture and Social Movements. University of California, San Diego, June 17–20.

———. 1993a. "Ideología, conflicto social y movimientos sociales contemporáneos." In *Escritos de teoría sociológica en homenaje a Luis Rodríguez Zúñiga*. Madrid: Centro de Investigaciones Sociológicas.

———. 1993b. "Los movimientos sociales en España (1960–1990). Análisis de tendencias." In *Tendencias sociales en la España de hoy*, edited by Salustiano del Campo. Madrid: Centro de Investigaciones Sociológicas.

Latané, B. 1981. "The Psychology of Social Impact." *American Psychologist* 36:343–56.

Lodi, Giovanni, and Marco Grazioli. 1984. "Giovani sul territorio urbano: l'integrazione minimale." In *Altri Codici: Aree di movimento nella metropoli*, edited by Alberto Melucci, pp. 63–125. Bologna: Il Mulino.

Luker, Kristin. 1984. *Abortion and the Politics of Motherhood*. Berkeley: University of California Press.

McAdam, Doug. 1982. *Political Process and the Development of Black Insurgency, 1930–1970*. Chicago: University of Chicago Press.

———. 1988. *Freedom Summer*. New York: Oxford University Press.

Mannheim, Karl. 1946. *Ideology and Utopia: An Introduction to the Sociology of Knowledge*. Translated by Louis Wirth and Edward Shils. New York: Harcourt, Brace.

———. 1952. "The Problem of Generations." In *Essays on the Sociology of Knowledge*, edited by Karl Mannheim. pp. 276–320. London: Routledge and Kegan Paul.

Margolis, Diane Rothbard. 1985. "Redefining the Situation: Negotiations on the Meaning of 'Woman'." *Social Problems* 32:332–34.

Marshall, Barbara L. 1991. "Reproducing the Gendered Subject." In *Current Perspectives in Social Theory*, Vol. 11. Greenwich, Conn.: JAI Press.

Melucci, Alberto. 1980. "The New Social Movements: A Theoretical Approach." *Social Science Information* 19:199–226.

———. 1985. "The Symbolic Challenge of Contemporary Movements." *Social Research* 52:789-816.

———. 1989. *Nomads of the Present: Social Movements and Individual Needs in Contemporary Society*. Philadelphia: Temple University Press.

———. 1995. "The Process of Collective Identity." In *Social Movements and Culture*, edited by Hank Johnston and Bert Klandermans, pp. 41–63. Minneapolis: University of Minnesota Press.

———, ed. 1984. *Altri Codici: Aree di movimento nella metropoli*. Bologna: Il Mulino.

Merton, Robert K. 1957. *Social Theory and Social Structure*. Rev. ed. New York: Free Press.

Meyer, Donald. 1975. *The Positive Thinkers*. Garden City, N.Y.: Doubleday.

Morris, Aldon D. 1984. *The Origins of the Civil Rights Movement*. New York: Free Press.

Morris, Aldon D., and Carol McClurg Mueller, eds. 1992. *Frontiers in Social Movement Theory*. New Haven: Yale University Press.

Nagel, Joane. 1986. "The Political Construction of Ethnicity." In *Competitive Ethnic Relations*, edited by Susan Olzak and Joane Nagel, pp. 93–112. Orlando, Fla.: Academic Press.

Nagel, Joane, and Susan Olzak. 1982. "Ethnic Mobilization in New and Old States: An Extension of the Competition Model." *Social Problems* 30:127–43.

Offe, Claus. 1985. "New Social Movements: Challenging Boundaries of Institutional Politics." *Social Research* 52:817–68.

Olson, Mancur, Jr. 1965. *The Logic of Collective Action*. Cambridge, Mass.: Harvard University Press.

Pérez-Agote, Alfonso. 1986. *La reproducción del nacionalismo vasco*. Madrid: Centro de Investigaciones Sociologicas/Siglo XXI Editores.

———. 1990. "El nacionalismo radical vasco. Mecanismos sociales de su aparición y desarrollo." Paper presented at "New Social Movements and the End of Ideologies," a seminar held at Universidad Internacional Menendez Pelayo, Santander, Spain, July.

Perinbanayagam, R. S. 1991. *Discursive Acts*. New York: Aldine de Gruyter.

Piven, Frances Fox, and Richard Cloward. 1971. *Regulating the Poor*. New York: Vintage Books.

Reddy, William M. 1977. "The Textile Trade and the Language of the Crowd at Rouen." *Past and Present* 74 (February): 62–89.

Rupp, Leila, and Verta Taylor. 1987. *Survival in the Doldrums: The American Women's Rights Movement, 1945 to the 1960s*. New York: Oxford University Press.

See, Katherine O'Sullivan. 1986. *First World Nationalism*. Chicago: University of Chicago Press.

Sewell, William H., Jr. 1980. *Work and Revolution in France*. Cambridge: Cambridge University Press.

Smelser, Neil. 1962. *Theory of Collective Behavior*. New York: Free Press.

Stryker, Sheldon. 1980. *Symbolic Interactionism: A Social Structural Version.* Palo Alto, Calif.: Benjamin/Cummings.

Tajfel, Henri. 1978. *Differentiation between Social Groups: Studies in the Social Psychology of Intergroup Relations.* London: Academic Press.

———. 1981. *Human Groups and Social Categories.* Cambridge: Cambridge University Press.

Tajfel, Henri, and John C. Turner. 1985. "The Social Identity Theory of Intergroup Behavior." In *The Social Identity Theory of Intergroup Behavior,* edited by W. G. Austin and S. Worchel, pp. 7–24, Chicago: Nelson-Hall.

Taylor, Verta. 1989. "Social Movement Continuity: The Women's Movement in Abeyance." *American Sociological Review* 54, 5:761–75.

Taylor, Verta, and Nancy Whittier. 1992. "Collective Identity in Social Movement Communities: Lesbian Feminist Mobilization." In *Frontiers in Social Movement Theory,* edited by Aldon D. Morris and Carol McClurg Mueller, pp. 104–29. New Haven: Yale University Press.

Thompson, E. P. 1963. *The Making of the English Working Class.* New York: Pantheon Books.

Touraine, Alain. 1981. *The Voice and the Eye: An Analysis of Social Movements.* New York: Cambridge University Press.

Trotsky, Leon. 1957. *The History of the Russian Revolution.* Translated by Max Eastman. Vols. 1–3. Ann Arbor: University of Michigan Press.

Turner, John C. 1985. "Social Categorization and the Self-Concept: A Social-Cognitive Theory of Group Behavior." In *Advances in Group Processes,* edited by E. J. Lawler, pp. 77–122. Greenwich, Conn.: JAI Press.

Turner, John C., with Michael A. Hogg, Penelope J. Oakes, Stephen D. Reicher, and Margaret S. Wetherell. 1987. *Rediscovering the Social Group: A Self-Categorization Theory.* New York: Basil Blackwell.

Turner, Ralph H. 1969. "The Theme of Contemporary Social Movements." *British Journal of Sociology* 20:390–405.

Whalen, Jack, and Richard Flacks. 1984. "Echoes of Rebellion: The Liberated Generation Grows Up." *Journal of Political and Military Sociology* 12:61–78.

———. 1989. *Beyond the Barricades: The Sixties Generation Grows Up.* Philadelphia: Temple University Press.

Whittier, Nancy. 1993. "Feminists in the 'Post-Feminist' Age: Collective Identity and the Persistence of the Women's Movement." Unpublished paper.

Wood, James L. 1974. *The Sources of American Student Activism.* Lexington, Mass.: Lexington Books, Heath.

Zald, Mayer N., and Roberta Ash. 1966. "Social Movement Organizations: Growth, Decay, and Change." *Social Forces* 44 (March): 327–41.

Zurcher, Louis A., Jr., and R. George Kirkpatrick. 1976. *Citizens for Decency: Antipornography Crusades as Status Defense.* Austin: University of Texas Press.

19

NEW SOCIAL MOVEMENT THEORIES

STEVEN M. BUECHLER

Over the last twenty years, resource mobilization theory has become the dominant paradigm for studying collective action in the United States. With

Reprinted from *The Sociological Quarterly*, Volume 36, Number 3, pages 441–464. Copyright © 1995 by The Midwest Sociological Society.

its characteristic premises of rational actors engaged in instrumental action through formal organization to secure resources and foster mobilization, this paradigm has demonstrated considerable theoretical and empirical merit for understanding social movements (McCarthy and Zald 1977; Tilly 1978). More recently, however, some have questioned the utility of this perspective for understanding at least some kinds of movements and constituencies, and others have lodged important criticisms against this approach (Buechler 1993). These developments have created an intellectual space for complementary or alternative perspectives for analyzing social movements. One such alternative is social constructionism, which brings a symbolic interactionist approach to the study of collective action by emphasizing the role of framing activities and cultural processes in social activism (Snow and Benford 1992; Gamson 1992; Hunt, Benford, and Snow 1994). This article examines another alternative to the resource mobilization perspective that has come to be known as new social movement theory. In what follows, I describe this perspective, summarize the work of some of its major theorists, discuss the central debates associated with it, offer a distinction between political and cultural versions of the theory, and provide an assessment of this paradigm for understanding collective action.

New social movement theory is rooted in continental European traditions of social theory and political philosophy (Cohen 1985; Klandermans 1991; Klandermans and Tarrow 1988; Laraña, Johnston, and Gusfield 1994). This approach emerged in large part as a response to the inadequacies of classical Marxism for analyzing collective action. For new social movement theorists, two types of reductionism prevented classical Marxism from adequately grasping contemporary forms of collective action. First, Marxism's economic reductionism presumed that all politically significant social action will derive from the fundamental economic logic of capitalist production and that all other social logics are secondary at best in shaping such action. Second, Marxism's class reductionism presumed that the most significant social actors will be defined by class relationships rooted in the process of produc-

tion and that all other social identities are secondary at best in constituting collective actors (Canel 1992). These premises led Marxists to privilege proletarian revolution rooted in the sphere of production and to marginalize any other form of social protest. New social movement theorists, by contrast, have looked to other logics of action based in politics, ideology, and culture as the root of much collective action, and they have looked to other sources of identity such as ethnicity, gender, and sexuality as the definers of collective identity. The term "new social movements" thus refers to a diverse array of collective actions that have presumably displaced the old social movement of proletarian revolution associated with classical Marxism. Even though new social movement theory is a critical reaction to classical Marxism, some new social movement theorists seek to update and revise conventional Marxist assumptions, while others seek to displace and transcend them.

Despite the now common usage of the term "new social movement theory," it is a misnomer if it implies widespread agreement among a range of theorists on a number of core premises. It would be more accurate to speak of "new social movement theor*ies*," with the implication that there are many variations on a very general approach to something called new social movements. As a first approximation to this general approach, however, the following themes may be identified. First, most strands of new social movement theory underscore symbolic action in civil society or the cultural sphere as a major arena for collective action alongside instrumental action in the state or political sphere (Cohen 1985; Melucci 1989). Second, new social movement theorists stress the importance of processes that promote autonomy and self-determination instead of strategies for maximizing influence and power (Habermas 1984–1987; Rucht 1988). Third, some new social movement theorists emphasize the role of postmaterialist values in much contemporary collective action, as opposed to conflicts over material resources (Inglehart 1990; Dalton, Kuechier, and Burklin 1990). Fourth, new social movement theorists tend to problematize the often fragile process of constructing collective identities and identifying group interests, instead of assuming that conflict groups and their interests are structurally determined (Hunt, Benford, and Snow 1994; Johnston, Laraña, and Gusfield 1994; Klandermans 1994; Melucci 1989; Stoecker 1995). Fifth, new social movement theory also stresses the socially constructed nature of grievances and ideology rather than assuming that they can be deduced from a group's structural location (Johnston, Laraña, and Gusfield 1994; Klandermans 1992). Finally, new social movement theory recognizes a variety of submerged, latent, and temporary networks that often undergird collective action rather than assuming that centralized organizational forms are prerequisites for successful mobilization (Melucci 1989; Gusfield 1994; Mueller 1994). Many of these themes signify a divergence from both classical Marxism and resource mobilization theory, as well as some points of convergence with social constructionism. But once again, various new social movement theorists give different emphases to these themes and have diverse relations with alternative traditions, thereby warranting a language that speaks of new social movement theories (in the plural).

Beyond these themes is another defining characteristic of new social movement theories that warrants special emphasis. In differing ways, all versions of new social movement theory operate with some model of a societal totality that provides the context for the emergence of collective action. Different theorists operate with different models (referring variously to postindustrial society, an information society, advanced capitalism, etc.), but the attempt to theorize a historically specific social formation as the structural backdrop for contemporary forms of collective action is perhaps the most distinctive feature of new social movement theories. Having offered a first approximation to this paradigm, it will be helpful to consider several scholars who exemplify the range of thinking among new social movement theorists.

Some Major Theorists

This overview of major new social movement theorists will serve several purposes. First, it will illustrate the range of orientations that may be found in this area, as well as the distortion that is introduced when these very different perspectives are referred to as a single paradigm. Second, it will provide a foundation for a more detailed examination of the major debates associated with new social movement theories in the next section. Third, it will suggest the need for some organizing typology that summarizes but does not oversimplify the diversity of social movement theories. Four theorists best exemplify the range of new social movement theories in the context of their own intellectual traditions: Manuel Castells (Spain), Alain Touraine (France), Alberto Melucci (Italy), and Jürgen Habermas (Germany).

Castells's focus is the impact of capitalist dynamics on the transformation of urban space and the role of urban social movements in this process. He argues that urban issues have become central because of the growing importance of collective consumption and the necessity of the state to intervene to promote the production of nonprofitable but vitally needed public goods. It is in this context that Castells sees the rise of urban social movements in a dialectical contest with the state and other political forces seeking to reorganize urban social life. He thus approaches the city as a social product that is a result of conflicting social interests and values. On the one hand, socially dominant interests seek to define urban space in keeping with the goals of capitalist commodification and bureaucratic domination; on the other hand, grassroots mobilizations and urban social movements seek to defend popular interests, establish political autonomy, and maintain cultural identity. While arguing that class relationships are fundamental, Castells recognizes that they exist alongside other identities and sources of change, including the state as well as group identities based on gender, ethnicity, nationality, and citizenship. For Castells, urban protest movements typically develop around three major themes. First, some demands focus on the forms of collective consumption provided by the state, thereby challenging the capitalist logic of exchange value with an emphasis on the provision of use values in community contexts. Second, other demands focus on the importance of cultural identity and its links to territoriality, thereby resisting the standardization and homogenization associated with bureaucratic forms of organization by establishing and defending genuine forms of community. Finally, still other demands express the political mobilization of citizens seeking more decentralized forms of government that emphasize self-management and autonomous decision making. For Castells, the goals of collective consumption, community culture, and political self-management may be found in a wide variety of cross-cultural settings that warrant the concept of urban social movements.

Castells's analysis of urban social movements exemplifies several new social movement themes while also bringing a distinctive framing to these themes. The emphasis on cultural identity, the recognition of nonclass-based constituencies, the theme of autonomous self-management, and the image of resistance to a systemic logic of commodification and bureaucratization all serve to illustrate dominant strains in new social movement theories. At the same time, Castells remains closer to some of the concerns of conventional Marxism than many other new social movement theorists, and he does so by offering a "both/and" rather than an "either/or" stance toward some familiar social movement dichotomies. Thus, rather than counterposing "old" class-based movements with "new" nonclass based movements, Castells recognizes the roles of both class-based and nonclass-based constituencies in urban social movements. Rather than contrasting "political" and "cultural" orientations, he recognizes that urban social movements contain a dialectical mixture of both orientations that finds expression in civil society and the state. Rather than dichotomizing between "instrumental" strategies and "expressive" identities, Castells acknowledges the mutual interplay between these themes in many urban social movements. Because of this more catholic and inclusive approach, Castells's version of new social movement theory is more attentive to the role of the state than some other versions of the theory that appear to eschew instrumental action altogether. As a result, he is more likely to recognize the role of political dynamics, such as changing political opportunity structures, than other scholars of new social movement theory. Finally, Castells's approach suggests the compatibility of a certain style of neo-Marxist analysis with at least some versions of new social movement theory.

Alain Touraine argues that with the passing of metasocial guarantees of social order, more and more of society comes to be seen as the product of reflective social action. The growing capacity of social actors to construct both a system of knowledge and the technical tools that allow them to intervene in their own functioning—a capacity Touraine calls historicity—makes possible the increasing self-production of society, which becomes the defining hallmark of postindustrial or programmed society. The control of historicity is the object of an ongoing struggle between classes defined by relations of domination. Such classes take the form of social movements as they enter into this struggle. In postindustrial society, the major social classes consist of consumers/clients in the role of the popular class and managers/technocrats in the role of the dominant class. The principal field of conflict for these classes is culture, and the central contest involves those who will control society's growing capacity for self-management. As the state becomes the repository of society's ever increasing capacity to control historicity, there is reason to believe that the central conflict in postindustrial society will come to center around this institution. In a recent formulation, Touraine (1992) locates new social movements between two logics: that of a system seeking to maximize production, money, power, and information, and that of subjects seeking to defend and expand their individuality.

Touraine's work anticipates several of the major debates associated with new social movement theory. One debate considers the likely constituency for such movements. In an empirical study of the workers' movement in France, Touraine and his associates (Touraine, Wieviorka, and Dubet 1987) reiterate his distinctive claim that there is one central conflict in every type of society. In industrial society, this conflict centered around material production and the workers' movement posed the obvious challenge. With the coming of postindustrial society, Touraine and his associates still expect one principal adversarial movement, although they remain uncertain about whether new social movements will fill this role. In a 1988 work, Touraine suggests both that there is no single class or group that represents a future social order and that dif-

ferent oppositional social movements are united simply by their oppositional attitude. Touraine's inability to define the constituency for collective action, despite his insistence that each societal type has a single central conflict, underscores the difficulties that new social movement theorists have in identifying the constituency for such movements. In Touraine's case, this uncertainty may be related to a second debate anticipated by his work concerning the seeming apolitical nature of these movements. He sees contemporary social movements as evidence of a displacement of protest from the economic to the cultural realm, accompanied by the privatization of social problems. The typical result is an anxious search for identity and an individualism that may exclude collective action (1985). In another context, Touraine (1985) suggests that movements based on difference, specificity, or identity may too easily dismiss the analysis of social relations and the denunciation of power, and in still another work (1988) he suggests that appeals to identity are purely defensive unless they are linked with a counteroffensive that is directly political and that appeals to self-determination. As we shall see, this uncertainty over the political status of new social movements is a defining theme within this paradigm.

Jürgen Habermas (1984–1987) proposes the most elaborate theory of modern social structure by distinguishing between a politico-economic system governed by generalized media of power and money and a lifeworld still governed by normative consensus. Whereas the system follows an instrumental logic that detaches media like money and power from any responsibility or accountability, the lifeworld follows a communicative rationality requiring that norms be justifiable through discussion and debate. The problem for Habermas is that in modern society, system imperatives and logic intrude on the lifeworld in the form of colonization, resulting in the media of money and power coming to regulate not only economic and political transactions, but also those concerning identity formation, normative regulation, and other forms of symbolic reproduction traditionally associated with the lifeworld. Habermas suggests that the relationship of clients to the welfare state is a model case for this colonization of the lifeworld, in that the welfare state monetarizes and bureaucratizes lifeworld relationships as it controls the extent and kind of spending on welfare policy to fit the imperatives of money and power. More generally, Habermas argues that the process of colonization alters each of the basic roles that arise from the intersection of the politico-economic system and public and private lifeworld: employee, consumer, client, and citizen. In each case, these dynamics locate more and more decision-making power in the hands of experts and administrative structures, which operate according to the system logic of money and power and whose decisions are correspondingly removed from contexts of justification and accountability within the lifeworld.

Given this conception of social structure, Habermas locates new social movements at the seams between system and lifeworld. This location leads him to identify two features of these movements that have shaped further debates within new social movement theory. First, Habermas seems to imply that new social movements will have a purely defensive character: at best, they can defend the lifeworld against the colonizing intrusion of the system and sustain the role of normative consensus rooted in communicative rationality that has been evolving within this sphere throughout the process of societal modernization. But Habermas offers little evidence that new social movements can contribute to any broader social transformation, particularly

concerning the dominance of system over lifeworld and the dominance of generalized media of exchange like money and power in the system world. As we shall see, while no one sees new social movements as bringing about complete societal transformation, many of its theorists envision a more extensive and progressive role for movements than simply defending the lifeworld. A second Habermasian theme, which is more broadly accepted among new social movement theorists, concerns the nature of the goals or demands associated with these movements. For Habermas, as for many others, the conflicts in which new social movements engage are less about material reproduction and more about cultural reproduction, social integration, and socialization. The new movements bring with them a new politics concerned with quality of life, projects of self-realization, and goals of participation and identity formation. Many of these movements are united around the critique of growth as a central ideological foundation, with ecology and peace movements playing central roles. Because these are not traditional distributional struggles, Habermas implies that they cannot be channeled by political parties or allayed by material compensation. The implication is that under some circumstances, the conflicts associated with new social movements may contribute to the larger legitimation crisis that Habermas (1975; 1984–1987) associates with advanced capitalism.

Alberto Melucci argues that the (post-) modern world brings new forms of social control, conformity pressures, and information processing to which new social movements respond. The movements are triggered by new sites of conflict that are interwoven with everyday life; the conflict itself involves symbolic codes, identity claims, and personal or expressive claims. Melucci would thus concur with Touraine that the political status of new social movements is unclear, but he is less troubled by this fact than Touraine. While these conflicts are far removed from the conventional political sphere, they are not without structural effects that are central in Melucci's argument. In a society increasingly shaped by information and signs, social movements play an important role as messages that express oppositional tendencies and modalities. The very focus on personal, spiritual, or expressive aspects of modern life typical of new social movements is an implicit repudiation of the instrumental rationality of the dominant society. Perhaps the most important systemic effect of new social movements is to render visible the peculiarly modern form of power that resides behind the rationality of administrative procedures; in this way, collective action emphasizes the socially constructed nature of the world and the possibility of alternative arrangements. Melucci's positive view of these movements and their messages underscores the importance of free spaces between the level of political power and everyday life in which actors can consolidate collective identities through both representation and participation.

Melucci's work also helps to define some of the central issues of new social movement theory. One such issue concerns the role of identity in modern collective action. Melucci's starting premise is that in modern society, the pace of change, the plurality of memberships, and the abundance of messages all combine to weaken traditional points of reference and sources of identity, thereby creating a homelessness of personal identity. This means that people's propensity to become involved in collective action is tied to their capacity to define an identity in the first place (Melucci 1988). It also means that the social construction of collective identity is both a major prerequisite and a major accomplishment of the new

social movements.[1] The fluidity of identity in the modern world and in its social movements is related to the fragility of organization in such movements. Melucci is insistent that new social movements be seen as ongoing social constructions rather than as unitary empirical objects, givens or essences, or historical personages acting on a stage. In contrast to these conceptions, whatever unity movements may achieve is a result of ongoing efforts rather than an initial starting point for collective action. On another level, Melucci steers attention away from formal organization by stressing that much collective action is nested in networks of submerged groups that occasionally coalesce into self-referential forms of organization for struggle—but often on a temporary basis. He thereby suggests that we speak less in terms of movements and more in terms of movement networks or movement areas to capture the transitory nature of much contemporary mobilization.

These sketches hint at some of the main contours of new social movement theory while also suggesting its diversity. This diversity derives in part from the different national settings in which theorists like Castells, Touraine, Habermas, and Melucci have operated, as well as the rather different histories of social protest within each nation. This diversity also derives from the different theoretical traditions that inform the work of these theorists: Castells extends Marxist analyses of collective consumption, Touraine builds on his pathbreaking work on postindustrial society, Habermas works out of the German tradition of critical theory, and Melucci introduces some semiotic and postmodern elements. As suggested earlier, this diversity warrants speaking of "new social movement theor*ies*" rather than a unitary "new social movement theor*y*." Yet there are important threads of continuity across these thinkers. Despite their differences, all concur that their societies have moved into a distinct social formation that might be designated as postindustrial, advanced capitalism and that the structural features of their societies have shaped the kinds of current collective action as decisively as the structural features of liberal capitalism shaped the dynamics of proletarian protest. While these sketches have hinted at some of the issues that define the paradigm of new social movement theory, a more systematic presentation of these debates is now in order.

The Major Debates

Many of the issues raised by new social movement theories may be framed in terms of four major debates that typify this general approach. The first concerns the meaning and validity of designating certain movements as "new" and others (by implication) as "old." The second debate involves whether new social movements are primarily or exclusively a defensive, reactive response to larger social forces or whether they can exhibit a proactive and progressive nature as well. The third debate concerns the distinction between political and cultural movements and whether the more culturally oriented new social movements are inherently apolitical. The fourth involves the social base of the new social movements and whether this base can be defined in terms of social class. These debates involve overlapping issues and are ultimately interconnected in various ways. The second and third debates are closely related because they hinge on the ability to provide meaningful definitions of increasingly problematic terms like "progressive" or "political." The first and the fourth are also related in that the definition of new movements implies the ability to designate a social base other than the old working class. While acknowledging these connections, each debate is sufficiently complex to warrant separate analytical treatment here.

What's New about New Social Movements?

A central dispute that has attracted considerable attention concerns the extent to which new social movements represent something demonstrably new, with critics suggesting that these movements are not as distinct as proponents of the paradigm suggest. Thus, David Plotke (1990) argues that new social movement discourse tends to overstate their novelty, to selectively depict their goals as cultural, and to exaggerate their separation from conventional political life. Sidney Tarrow (1991) points out that many new social movements aren't really all that new, because they often have grown out of preexisting organizations and have long histories that are obscured by new social movement discourse. In Tarrow's analysis, the supposed newness of these movements has less to do with the structural features of advanced capitalism and more to do with the fact that these movements were studied in their early stages of formation within a particular cycle of protest in the late 1960s and early 1970s. The implication is that with the ending of this cycle of protest and the political realignments it promoted, social movement activity has decreased and returned to more conventional forms; the proponents of "newness" thus mistook a temporary and cyclical phase for a new historical stage of collective action. The most sweeping critique of this sort is offered by Karl-Werner Brand (1990), who suggests that "new social movements" are the latest manifestation of a cyclical pattern that has been evident for well over a century. In this argument, new social movements and their predecessors appeared in cyclical phases in response to cultural crises and critiques of modernization. In the latest cycle, a mix of moral-idealistic and aesthetic-countercultural critiques of modernization, along with a pessimistic civilization critique, provided the stimuli for new social movements. However, Brand argues that similar periods of culture critique prompted similar movements around 1840 and 1900 in Britain, Germany, and the United States. In various ways, these critics suggest that new social movements are continuous with past movements and are simply the latest manifestation of a cycle or a long wave of social protest movements. These critics see all these movements as romantic, cultural, idealistic, and even antimodern responses to patterns of societal evolution and modernization, rather than being new.

These critical challenges have forced proponents of new social movement theories to specify convincingly wherein the newness may be found, and several responses have been forthcoming. For Russell J. Dalton and Manfred Kuechler (1990), new social movements may draw on a long-standing humanistic tradition but their genuinely new aspects include their postmaterialistic value base, their search for pragmatic solutions, their global awareness, and their resistance to spiritual solutions. For Claus Offe (1990), the newness of these movements involves their postideological, posthistorical nature as well as their lack of a positive alternative and specific target in the form of a privileged class; because of these features, they deny accommodation to existing power and resist standard forms of co-optation. For Klaus Eder (1993), new social movements are inherently modern because only in modernity can their distinctive challenge to the cultural orientation of society be formulated. In his view, new social movements provide an alternative cultural model and moral order that both defends normative standards against the strategic, utilitarian, and instrumental goal seeking and decision making of elites and points in the direction

of a more democratic formulation of collective needs and wants within society. For Russell J. Dalton, Manfred Kuechler, and Wilhelm Burklin (1990), these movements are new in their advocacy of a new social paradigm that challenges the dominant goal structure of Western societies by advocating postmaterialist, antigrowth, libertarian, and populist themes. In addition, the political style of these movements involves a conscious avoidance or rejection of institutionalized politics and a careful distance from established political parties. For these authors, it is the combination of ideological bonds and political style that distinguishes new social movements. Jean Cohen (1983) argues that new social movements can be distinguished from utopian and romantic movements of the past in terms of their visions or goals for social development. Whereas utopian and romantic movements typically sought the de-differentiation of society, economy, and state into a premodern utopian community, new social movements presuppose and defend the structural differentiation of modern society and attempt to build on it by expanding the social spaces in which nonstrategic action can occur.

As these responses indicate, while there is no consensus among new social movement theorists about what constitutes the newness of these movements, there are plenty of candidates for that category. Given the diversity of empirical, philosophical, and political frameworks that these authors bring to this debate, there is little prospect that it can be resolved in any definitive way. But such debates are instructive even if unresolvable. One of the lessons here is that the term new social movements inherently overstates the differences and obscures the commonalities between past and present movements (Johnston, Laraña, and Gusfield 1994; Melucci 1994). The term had a strategic value in trying to break from the Marxist tradition of looking to the "old" labor movement as the primary agent of history, but the unintended result of shifting the focus to other constituencies has been to imply that they somehow have no history prior to the cycle of protest in the 1960s. In point of fact, there are no social movements for which this claim can be plausibly defended. Whether the movements involve students, women, racial, ethnic, or sexual minorities and whether they involve peace, ecology, or justice themes, all have important historical predecessors that span at least the twentieth century and sometimes reach much further back into the nineteenth century. Hence, there is more continuity between supposedly old and new social movements than is typically implied (Johnston, Laraña, and Gusfield 1994; Johnston 1994; Laraña 1994; Shin 1994; Taylor 1989). The term also suggests a false dichotomy between new movements and old forms of labor organization that obscures compelling evidence for the new social movement character of many nineteenth-century labor movements (Calhoun 1993; Tucker 1991). The danger here is that the terminology we adopt can become a conceptual straitjacket that precludes certain lines of inquiry. Thus, while there are distinct combinations of genuinely new elements in the social movements emphasized by this perspective, these can only be carefully specified by locating these movements and their predecessors in their appropriate sociohistorical contexts and by looking for both similarities and differences woven throughout such histories.

Are New Social Movements Reactive or Progressive?

A second set of debates in new social movement discourse concerns both the extent to which these movements are characterized as either defensive or progressive and the extent to which they are seen as carrying a liberatory potential. The disagreement over the newness of these movements carries over into this second debate, with few unambiguously convincing arguments on either side. One strand in this debate begins with Habermas (1984–1987), who has characterized the new social movements as primarily defensive reactions to the colonizing intrusions of states and markets into the lifeworld of modern society. As vital as this role may be, Habermas has said relatively little about the prospect that new social movements can or will assume a larger and more progressive role in societal transformation. Other theorists working within this tradition have been somewhat more forthcoming. Thus, Dieter Rucht (1988) argues that, although movements are likely to emerge during qualitative breakthroughs in societal modernization (understood in Habermasian terms of increasing differentiation between and within the system and lifeworld), they may be proactive, reactive, or ambivalent with respect to these patterns. Rucht implies that modernization in the lifeworld produces conflicts around democratization, self-determination, and individualization and that the expressive, identity-oriented movements this provokes have a progressive character. At the same time, modernization in the system tends to provoke a more defensive kind of protest against the side effects of technological, economic, or political changes that can have an antimodernist cast. This vision of new social movements as progressive with respect to lifeworld rationalization and as defensive with respect to system intrusion is one logical way of addressing this debate from a Habermasian perspective.

Another response is offered by Jean Cohen (1982, 1983), who also expresses dissatisfaction with the somewhat marginal role envisioned by Habermas for social movements. In her view, this is because movements interest Habermas not in terms of their substantive claims but rather as carriers of universalistic cultural potentials. Thus, social movements are granted significance only if they become vehicles of societal modernization and cultural rationalization. Cohen argues that both past and present movements have played a vitally important role in helping to institutionalize civil society as a sphere that is both differentiated from and connected to the state and that gives social actors the space to translate lifeworld concerns into systemic priorities for change. This can be grasped through neither systems theory nor action theory but rather requires analysis of the process of institutionalization by which movements have contributed to civil society and the creation of new associational and democratic forms, thereby building up the space that allows them to operate more progressively as change agents. In her view, social movements can be more than defensive, antimodern reactions precisely because they have established a foothold in civil society in which they can pursue larger goals of progressive social change. These goals include both the self-defense and the further democratization of society, and Cohen implies that these goals are best seen as complementary rather than contradictory imperatives of new social movements.

Analysts of new social movements from a more traditionally Marxist perspective have not necessarily arrived at clearer answers or more internal agreement on these questions. For example, Joachim Hirsch (1988) argues that new social movements must be understood as part of the crisis of Fordism. Fordism was itself a response to an earlier capitalist crisis that introduced mass production and consumption, a Keynesian and corporatist welfare state, and a broader "stratification" of society that extended surveillance and control throughout the society. These developments promoted the commodification and bureaucratization of social life, and new social movements are a response to these developments. These movements thereby seek to overcome alienation and regulation by promoting individual emancipation and the recovery of civil society through a radically democratic form of politics. Despite this seemingly progressive agenda, Hirsch argues that the organizational forms and ideological premises of many new social movements still reflect the fundamental contradictions of the Fordist period to which they are a response. As a result, they transcend the conventional dichotomy between left and right, or progressive and conservative. Hirsch expects these movements to play complex and contradictory roles during the transition from the Fordist mode of accumulation to a new strategy of accumulation in advanced capitalism: they may simultaneously embody genuine opposition to the old order and become unconscious vehicles for establishing a new order (Steinmetz 1994). Colin Mooers and Alan Sears (1992) are more pessimistic about the prospects for new social movements. In their view, the focus on civil society is consistent with a political agenda of lowering the horizons and range of possibilities to what can be achieved within the limits of the existing market and state. To the extent that the new politics of social movements does indeed accept capitalist social relations and turns away from confronting the capitalist state, this politics is simply a new reformism in their view.

These debates are difficult to resolve. One difficulty is the diversity of stances adopted by new social movements, but a greater obstacle is that the conceptual yardsticks that frame the debate are breaking down. That is, notions of progressive or reactionary and the traditional dichotomy between left and right all presuppose (to one degree or another) a metaphysics of history and a directionality to social change that has become untenable in late modernity. Yet a third trouble is in the abstract frames in which these debates are conducted.

Movements exist in specific sociohistorical circumstances such that the same movement and the same agenda may well be characterized as progressive or reactionary (to the extent we can define these terms meaningfully) depending on the context in which it is embedded. Perhaps for these reasons, some theorists have come to rely less on the goals or ideologies of a given movement than on its potential for democratization as a yardstick for judging movements.

Two rather different examples may be cited. In a discussion of how and when resistance movements (which may arise out of conservative impulses and responses to external threats) become liberation movements (which make radical demands for change), Richard Flacks (1988) suggests that the critical step in making this transition is the cultivation of democratic consciousness. This consciousness seeks to narrow the gap between "everyday life" and "making history," thereby drawing the largest possible number of people into the process of history making. Reflecting a very different theoretical tradition, Ernesto Laclau and Chantal Mouffe (1985) offer their own version of an argument about the liberatory potential of new social movements that also emphasizes the centrality of democratic discourse to such liberation. If these disparate examples are at all typical, then the older debate over the progressive or defensive nature of the new social movements is being gradually displaced by new discussions focusing on the potential of these movements for expanding the range of democratic participation both within movements and within the larger society.

Are New Social Movements Political or Cultural?

A third set of debates (not unrelated to the first two) revolves around the question of whether new social movements are "politi-cal" in nature or are better classified in some other way (e.g., as "cultural"). One danger in these discussions is that such terminology can create and perpetuate unfortunate dichotomies that obscure more than they reveal about movements. That is, all movements rest on cultural foundations and play some representational or symbolic function—hence all movements are cultural in some basic way (McAdam 1994). Similarly, all movements take explicit or implicit political stances, and it can be argued that even those which opt out of any conventional contestation for power have taken a political stance of quietism—hence all movements are political in an equally basic way. These considerations should be taken as reminders that such distinctions can be no more than sensitizing devices that highlight features of movements that are inevitably more complex than any such binary classificatory system. Nevertheless, the discussions about the political dimension of new social movements tap profound questions about their transformative potential. The operative definition of political in most of these discussions seems to involve two fundamental dimensions: political movements are at least in part focused on influencing or altering state power, and such movements must thereby have some explicit strategy aimed at transforming power relations.

One way of challenging the political nature of new social movements is to argue that they are about something larger than conventional politics; Brand (1986) thereby casts new social movements as providing a metapolitical challenge to modernity through a new historical type of protest. He sees these movements as carriers of a classical critique of modern civilization as well as the very project of modernity. Even though he classifies them as metapolitical, he identifies them as having discrete, political effects in terms of consciousness-raising, political socialization, and the politicization of decision making. The more standard critique of new social movements is that they are an apolitical or at least a prepolitical form of social activism. These critiques typically use the protests of the 1960s as a positive benchmark, when movements combined political and cultural dimensions in a desirable balance that still attempted to transform power relations. In the 1970s and 1980s, however, some of these movements shifted to a predominantly cultural orientation in which questions of identity and "identity politics" became predominant. With this change, the notion of "the personal is political" became deformed in such a way that excessive attention to personal life came to substitute for any sustained form of political action aimed at institutionalized power, and lifestyle politics thereby replaced previous movement politics aimed at social transformation. As a result, such movements and their participants jettisoned any concern with influencing or altering state power, abandoned discussions of strategy, and withdrew into cultural cocoons of personal lifestyle issues as a replacement for a previously political orientation (Boggs 1986; Carroll 1992; Epstein 1991). In the sharpest version of this critique, L. A. Kauffman (1990) argues that such antipolitics of identity leads to apolitical introspection, an emphasis on politically correct lifestyles, and the substitution of personal transformation for political activity. Despite the radical veneer that may cover such stances, Kauffman argues that they actually mirror and promote the values of the marketplace.

The most interesting rejoinder to these arguments can be derived from the work of Alberto Melucci (1989), whose stance is not that the new social movements are political (in any conventional sense of the term) but rather that it is just as well that they are not. If the new movements were more political in the conventional sense of that term, they would be playing by sets of rules that ben-

efit existing power holders and they would in all likelihood be much easier to co-opt through the normal channels of political representation and negotiation. Hence, their apolitical or antipolitical stance should be regarded as a strength rather than a weakness. However, to be apolitical in this sense does not mean a retreat into excessively individualist orientations for Melucci. Although he operates with a culturalist reading of new social movements, he also believes that such culturalist movements can pose major challenges to existing social relations. In part, this is because these relations have come to be defined more and more in the cultural language of symbolic representation. Thus, if power has become congealed, particularly in media messages and administrative rationality, the most profound challenge to such power may come from cultural movements that challenge these messages and rationality. By rendering power visible and by repudiating the instrumental rationality of the dominant society, cultural movements may be more effective than conventionally political movements at, in Melucci's terms, breaking the limits of compatibility of the system.

Like other issues already discussed, this debate is about more than one issue, and sometimes it is not about the same thing. For example, the sharpest critics of the apolitical turn in some new social movements are writing in the context of the United States, but Melucci and new social movement theory generally has emerged from a European context. Hence, a peculiarly American factor—such as individualism as a dominant cultural theme—may be the target of these critics. The critics also tend to be affiliated with a New Left strain of democratic socialism that provides them with an implicit model of the political stances movements ought to take and forms the benchmark for their critiques of the movements that fall short of this standard. But the positions in this debate ultimately reflect the theoretical stances of its participants as well as the way their stances conceptualize the dominant society and its recent changes. Those who criticize the apolitical nature of (some) new social movements tend to see modern society as predominantly capitalist. Although they may have transcended traditional Marxist positions on the role of "old social movements," they remain wedded to a conception of capitalism as a systemic form of domination that must ultimately be challenged in political terms. Those who defend the apolitical or cultural dimensions of new social movements appear to subscribe to a different theory of modern society that leans more heavily on postmodern, semiotic, or generally culturalist themes. Thus, each theoretical school can claim to have identified the more fundamental kind of (political or cultural) challenge that new social movements might offer to the dominant society, but these claims reflect their prior theoretical stances as much as any consistent set of observations about the movements themselves.

What Is the Class Base of New Social Movements?

A fourth set of debates reflects yet another basic premise implicit in the notion of new social movements. If old social movements presupposed a solidly working-class base and ideology, then new social movements are presumed to draw from a different social class base. However, there is no consensus on how this social class base should be defined or even whether the concept of class should remain central to the definition of a movement's base. Thus, one line of argument suggests that any attempt to answer this question in class terms is itself a resid-

ual effect of an economistic reading of social movements in which a movement's social base is automatically defined by class structure. Part of what makes new social movements new is precisely the fact that class becomes much less important in determining the base, interests, or ideology of the movement than in the older economistic reading. It is only by jettisoning such economistic notions that we can appreciate the extent to which new social movements are defined by the dynamics of race, ethnicity, culture, gender, or age—social divisions that may well have transcended class in their relevance for shaping collective action. While this logic is compelling as a means of dispelling the lingering influence of economistic readings of sociopolitical activism, it is not a sufficient way of dealing with the question of class. While new social movements may not be economically determined in the straightforward manner that old social movements were presumed to be, they nevertheless have what a Weberian would call "economic relevance." For example, the goals and policies pursued by a movement may have a very different impact on diverse social classes, just as differing class positions are likely to shape people's definition of a grievable issue in the first instance. If movements can no longer be reduced to class, neither can they be understood apart from class, as one among several salient structures and identities in contemporary forms of collective action.

One strategy for side stepping the issue of class is thus to argue that the group identities undergirding collective action have shifted from class to status, race, gender, ethnicity, or nationality. Another theoretical strategy that marginalizes the role of class is to argue that new social movement constituencies derive more from an ideological identification with certain issues than membership in some homogeneous social base. An example of this strategy may be found in

Dalton, Kuechler, and Burklin (1990). They argue that the defining characteristic of new social movements is their advocation of a new social paradigm that challenges the dominant goal structure of Western societies. In their account, such movements draw on a socially diffuse base of popular support rather than any specific class or ethnic base. They see this as a shift from group-based politics rooted in instrumental interest to value-based politics rooted in ideological support for collective goods. The shift from interest to ideology may therefore be a reflection of the fact that in advanced capitalism, many deprivations and forms of domination have acquired a relatively classless character because their effects touch members of many different social groups and classes (Steinmetz 1994). Hence, movements responding to these effects will not have an exclusive class character but will recruit across a variety of social groups.

Despite these two theoretical strategies that shift attention away from class, the most common strategy within the new social movement literature is to argue that these movements do indeed have a social class base that can be conceptualized as a middle-class base in contrast to the working-class base of old social movements. Erik Wright's (1989, 1985) concept of "contradictory class locations" provides one promising analytical tool for addressing the complexity of contemporary class structure and its implications for movement mobilization. While Wright has not specifically addressed the issue of new social movements, Claus Offe (1985) has. He suggests that the social base of new social movements is threefold: the new middle class, elements of the old middle class, and "decommodified" groups outside the labor market. This unusual combination of groups derives from the structural features of advanced capitalist society, which include a broadening of the negative effects of the system beyond a single class, a deepening of the methods and effects of social control and domination, and the irreversibility of problems and crisis potentials in the society. These effects create a tripartite constituency for new social movements whose only common feature may be their distance from the old poles of capital and labor. The new middle class is a modern, class-aware group whose goals are more general than those of traditional class politics. The old middle-class elements and the decommodified elements more often draw upon premodern, particularistic ideologies that shape their role in new social movements. As a result, the complex politics of new social movements will depend on which of these three factions becomes dominant at any given moment, as well as the alliances that such groups might pursue with other political actors. The possibilities range from maintenance of the old, growth-oriented paradigm to a new form of corporatism to a genuinely new challenge to the prevailing social order. The latter, in Offe's view, would require new social movements rooted in new middle-class elements, which then ally with the traditional left and proceed to establish a positive relation with peripheral and decommodified groups. Only this alliance could effectively challenge the old paradigm of growth-oriented politics and replace it with a new paradigm rooted in distinctively new social movement values and goals.

A multifaceted response to the question of class and social movements may be found in the work of Klaus Eder (1993). His general approach to these questions is informed by the assumptions that class and collective action have been decoupled in advanced capitalism, that culture plays an increasingly important intervening role between class structure and collective action, that all collective actors are socially constructed rather than structurally determined, and that Pierre

Bourdieu's concept of a class habitus is a useful guide to the social construction of class actors and collective action. Based on these premises, Eder constructs his argument about the middle-class base of new social movements. Because this class has an intermediate position between upper and lower social classes, it blends bourgeois individualism and plebeian particularism in a class-specific defense of individualization and the middle-class lifeworld. Such a habitus can generate new social movements, but it can also generate moral crusades and political pressure groups. New social movements—as opposed to other forms of collective action—are most likely to derive from those niches of contemporary society that preserve old communitarian traditions and radically democratic projects while also seeking new social relations that transcend moralism and power (Eder 1985). In a more recent essay, Eder (1993) proposes a theory of middle-class radicalism that sees new social movements as a class-specific response to the middle-class realities of upward mobility, cultural capital, and the lack of a clear group identity. For Eder, new social movements are not class movements in the traditional sense, but they manifest a new type of class relationship in which the making of the middle class as a group with a distinct identity and consciousness is dialectically intertwined with the mobilization of new social movements.

A more finely textured version of this argument is proposed by Hanspeter Kriesi's (1989) study of new social movements in the Netherlands. Building on Wright's (1985) approach to classes, Kriesi identifies antagonisms within the new middle class between technocrats with organizational assets and specialists with professional identities. He proceeds to distinguish between occupational segments, offering a broad contrast between "social and cultural specialists," on the one hand, and "administrative and commercial personnel," "technical specialists,"

"craft specialists," and "protective services," on the other. It is the social and cultural specialists with professional identities but without organizational assets who constitute a genuinely new class, which is formed out of the underlying antagonism between technocrats who favor administrative rationality and specialists who seek noninstrumental uses for their knowledge. The struggles of new social movements, in turn, may be seen as both expressing and contributing to the formation of this new class. Kriesi thereby suggests that the notion of a generic oppositional new middle class is both too broad and too narrow. It is too broad because it is not the class as a whole but only the younger generation of social and cultural specialists that tend to support new social movements. It is too narrow because there are other groups beyond the middle class who often provide support to new social movements as well. Kriesi concludes that if new social movements indeed have such deep structural roots in a segment of the new class, then they cannot be dismissed as temporary, conjunctural phenomena but must be seen as fundamental manifestations of advanced societies.

Offe's, Eder's, and Kriesi's analyses also hint at a subterranean issue related to the broad question of the social base of new social movements. If it is generally accurate to see new social movements as rooted in some type of middle-class base, this raises the possibility that these movements may not be unrelated to the older class politics as much as they may operate in opposition to traditional working-class interests. This possibility is exemplified by the supposed trade-off between environmental protection and job creation that appears to pit the interests of ecologically oriented new social movements against those of traditional labor union movements. While the framing of such demands as mutually exclusive alternatives may tell us more about elite strategies of control than about the positions of movements themselves, beyond all the divide-and-conquer strategies there are likely to be significant and enduring conflicts between the class base of new and old social movements. If new social movements are really dedicated to a postmaterialist paradigm of limits to growth, and if older social movements remain tied to growth-oriented policies in which workers share in the benefits of such growth, then we would expect to see significant fissures between these movements. On the other hand, some have argued that rather than seeing an inevitable conflict between old worker movements and new social movements, it is possible to see the latter as expressing other needs of workers above and beyond their roles as laborers (Carroll and Ratner 1994).

The relatively small amount of research on this issue has typically taken the form of arguing that the success of new social movements will ultimately depend on their ability to form alliances and coalitions with traditional labor movements. Thus, Barbara Epstein (1990) concludes her overview of contemporary social activism by arguing that any successful movement will have to recruit from both the middle and the bottom third of modern society. In a more detailed analysis, Carl Boggs (1986) argues that any successful future social transformation will depend upon building a sustained connection between working-class struggles and new social movements. This connection is necessary to overcome the Achilles heel of new social movements—their lack of an effective strategy for confronting state power. While such points are well-taken, they side step the difficult questions of how extensive the class conflicts between different social movements really are and the related question of how such conflicts may be contained long enough to foster the kinds of alliances and coalitions envisioned by these theorists.

Thus, while there is no consensus on the question of class and new social movements, this debate provides several important lessons. First, these movements represent a major form of social activism whose social base is sometimes best defined in something other than class terms, whether that be gender, ethnicity, race, sexuality, or age. Moreover, new social movements require us to rethink how all collective identities (including class identities) are not structurally guaranteed but socially constructed (Hunt, Benford, and Snow 1994; Meyer and Whittier 1994). As such, they do not come in neat, mutually exclusive, one-dimensional packages but rather in dialectically interrelated combinations of positions and identities (Collins 1990; Morris 1992; Omi and Winant 1986; Taylor and Whittier 1992). We therefore need to think in terms of how all these identities may be experienced simultaneously and how that experience will shape movement participation. We also need to think in terms of how one status may influence the perception of another, as when a middle-class position prompts people to see the world in terms of gender rather than class (exemplified by the history of white, middle-class feminism [Buechler 1990]). A second lesson is that some movements may be best characterized not in terms of a social base rooted in conventional statuses but rather in terms of values and goals with which participants agree. Thus, alongside identity-based movements in which such statuses are central, there are issue-based movements in which identities are secondary to the question of congruence between individual and movement values and goals. A third lesson is that (despite the first two lessons) there does appear to be an elective affinity between a middle-class location and new social movements. Many have noted the problems of clearly defining the term middle class, which too often serves as a residual category for groups between the traditional poles of capital and labor. To some extent, this problem can be addressed by more careful and systematic research into the constituencies for various new social movements. But the more important point (following Eder's [1993] lead) is to recognize that the conceptual confusion over the term middle class is not just a theoretical shortcoming but rather a mirror image of the fluidity and fragility of contemporary class structures—at least as they affect those "in the middle." If social classes really are socially constructed and if this process is especially important in the making of the middle class, then our inability to clearly identify the middle-class base of new social movements may simply be an accurate reflection of the fact that the construction project is still underway in advanced capitalism.

A Typology of New Social Movement Theories

The preceding profiles of central theorists and major debates convey some of the complexities in new social movement theory. At one extreme we may speak in terms of a very general orientation called new social movement theory, based on the tenets identified in the introduction of this article. At the other extreme we may speak in terms of specific theorists or positions in debates, producing a multiplicity of new social movement theories with no more than family resemblances to one another. My goal here is to improve on these images of one very general approach and a plurality of particular positions by proposing a typology of new social movement theories. Like all such typologies, this one is offered as an ideal-typical sensitizing construct that cannot capture all the complexities of the field and will inevitably oversimplify some of its dimensions. Nevertheless, such sorting

devices would seem to be in order as heuristic tools for improving our understanding of new social movement theories.

The most promising typological distinction in this field is between what I call "political" and "cultural" versions of new social movement theory.[2] This is not a mutually exclusive distinction but rather a matter of the emphasis placed on these differing dimensions. Nevertheless, there appears to be a number of related characteristics that cluster around these different emphases, producing two rather distinct versions of new social movement theory (see Table 19.1).

The political version of new social movement theory is pro-Marxist in that it draws upon the most promising work in neo-Marxist scholarship and seeks to build upon the strengths of this tradition. Like all new social movement theory, this version has a model of the societal totality in which new social movements arise, but this version is likely to emphasize the (advanced) capitalist nature of that totality over any other designation. In so doing, it is likely to offer strong claims about the connections between macrolevel structural features of contemporary capitalism and the emergence of new social movements. The political version of new social movement theory is more macro-oriented in general and more state-oriented in particular. It retains a concern with strategic questions and instrumental action as the ultimate goals of social movements while recognizing the importance of identity formation, grievance definition, and interest articulation as intermediate steps in the process of movement activism. Of the major theorists reviewed above, Castells is closest to this ideal-typical political reading, although some of Touraine's work fits into this category as well.

In terms of the first debate over the newness of these movements, the political version of new social movement theory recognizes a role for new constituencies in social activism

TABLE 19.1 Political and Cultural Versions of New Social Movement Theory

Issue	Political Version	Cultural Version
General Orientation	Pro-Marxist	Post-Marxist
Representative Theorist	Manuel Castells	Alberto Melucci
Societal Totality	Advanced capitalism	Information society
Image of Power	Systemic, centralized	Diffuse, decentralized
Level of Analysis	Macro-, mesolevel, state-oriented	Meso-, microlevel, civil society, everyday life
Movement Activity	Retains role for instrumental action toward strategic goals	Eschews strategic concerns in favor of symbolic expressions
First Debate: View of New Movements	Recognizes their role without rejecting role of working-class movements	Regards new movements as having displaced working-class movements
Second Debate: Movement Orientations	Potential for progressive orientations if allied with working-class movements	Sees new movements as defensive or rejects category of "progressive"
Third Debate: Evaluation of Movements	Sees political movements as most radical, cultural movements as apolitical	Sees cultural movements as most radical, political movements as co-optable
Fourth Debate: Social Base of Movements	Analyzed in class terms via contradictory locations, new class, or middle class	Analyzed in terms of nonclass constituencies or issues and ideologies

based on race, gender, nationality, and other characteristics, but it does not jettison the potential for class-based or worker-based movements alongside these other groups. In terms of the second debate over movement orientations, the political version sees the potential for proactive and progressive change if appropriate alliances and coalitions between class-based and nonclass-based movements can be forged. In terms of the third debate over the challenges posed by new social movements, the political version is most likely to be critical of the apolitical nature of more culturally oriented new social movements, which this perspective would see as limiting their potential for producing meaningful social change. In terms of the fourth debate over the social base of these movements, this perspective is most likely to identify the social base of new social movements in class terms through attempts to theorize the complexity of con-

temporary class structure and its contradictory locations as the backdrop for social activism.

The cultural version of new social movement theory is post-Marxist in that it transcends this tradition by proposing a more radical break between past and present societal types and movement forms than may be found in the political version. Accordingly, while the cultural version still has a model of the societal totality, it does not identify this totality in terms of capitalism but rather in culturalist or semiotic terms as an information society whose administrative codes conceal forms of domination. Its claims about the links between social structure and movement form emphasize the decentralized nature of both power and resistance, so it is not particularly macro-oriented or state-centered but focuses on everyday life, civil society, and the creation of free spaces between state and civil society. The cultural version eschews strategic questions and instrumental action as pitfalls to be avoided, while emphasizing symbolic explorations and expressions of identity that precisely challenge the instrumental logic of systemic domination. Of the major theorists reviewed above, Melucci is closest to this ideal-typical cultural reading, although some of Habermas's work fits into this category as well.

In terms of the first debate reviewed above, the cultural version of new social movement theory not only recognizes new social constituencies but also argues that the old worker-based constituencies for social activism have been transcended along with industrial capitalism. In terms of the second debate, the cultural version tends to view activism as a defensive reaction to systemic domination that can potentially challenge systemic imperatives, but it eschews the language of "progressive" movements as invoking an unwarranted metaphysics of history. In terms of the third debate, this version rejects the apolitical label often attached to culturalist movements by arguing that political movements are the most easily co-opted and that cultural movements fighting on symbolic terrain can do more to expose contemporary forms of power than the more conventionally political movements. In terms of the fourth debate, this version is more likely to identify the social base of new social movements in nonclass terms, by referring either to other statuses and identities or to values and ideologies that define movement constituencies, rather than by class locations.

The advantage of this typological distinction between political and cultural versions of new social movement theory is that it appears to organize a variety of diverse dimensions and debates into two more or less coherent positions with a fair degree of internal consistency across various issues. The disadvantage is that some major theorists defy easy classification. Thus, differing aspects of the work of both Touraine and Habermas can be located in both schools of thought, emphasizing that such typological distinctions should not become conceptual straitjackets that deny the complexity of such theorists. On the other hand, if used properly, such typologies may also aid in identifying contradictions and inconsistencies in these and other theorists, as well as identifying shifts in their positions over time.

Conclusions

Having examined the diversity of new social movement theories by way of an overview of the major theorists and debates and offered one means of organizing this diversity through the distinction between political and cultural versions of new social movement theories, it remains to evaluate the overall status of this paradigm as a general approach. The core claim of all versions of this approach concerns the appearance of demonstrably new social movements, but this claim is problematic. The central conceptual question is whether the designated new movements are similar enough to one another and different enough from others to support the distinction. As we have seen, these movements differ from each other in terms of their issues and constituencies, so the claim for newness often comes down to something like postmaterialist values, informal organization, and a certain cultural orientation. At this point, the category can be challenged from the other direction by suggesting that many movements not designated as new social movements nonetheless share these features. Thus, it is not difficult to find earlier movements which were at least non- (if not "post-") materialistic, that shunned formal organization, or that articulated predominantly cultural themes. The claim for newness can also be challenged by pointing both to the historical predecessors of new movements and to how the category of new social movement obscures continuities and exaggerates differences between past and present movements. When all the criticisms have been lodged, a handful of movements remain that closely approximate the ideal type suggested by the category of new social movements, but they are a very small proportion of the forms of collective. action found in modern society.

While it is relatively easy to challenge the concept of new social movements in this way, it would be a mistake to dismiss the category prematurely. The very same sensitivity to the history of social movements that undermines any sharp distinction between past and present movements also supports the idea that something new *is* happening in collective mobilization in the late twentieth century. In part, this "something new" has to do with the public and at least quasi-political expression and exploration of supposedly private and subjective problematics, such as identity. But we need more subtle ways to capture this shift. It is not so much that one distinctive type of movement has replaced or been added to others as it is that many more movements have begun to explicitly thematize the kinds of issues identified by new social movement discourse. There has thus been a shift in emphasis and orientation in many (though not all) social movements, along with the appearance of a very few movements closely corresponding to the ideal-typical new social movement. These shifts in emphasis and orientation are not unrelated to changes in the macrolevel organization of contemporary society, such as the blurring of the distinction between public and private and the greater penetration of systemic imperatives into lifeworld contexts. While no single theoretical account has captured these shifts precisely, more work on these questions is warranted with an emphasis on greater specificity and a

richer contextualization of the character of new social movements in modern society.

A final means of assessing new social movement theory as a general approach involves identifying its characteristic strengths and weaknesses relative to other theories. At the most general level (as numerous commentators have noted), new social movement theory is better at explaining the "why" than the "how" of social movement activism (Melucci 1985; Klandermans and Tarrow 1988). Put differently, new social movement theory is a powerful tool for understanding the macrolevel social structures that shape contemporary activism. By offering historically specific formulations of societal totalities and the forms of domination they entail, new social movement theory has much to tell us about the roots of contemporary social activism and the dynamics of movement emergence. In the context of these general premises, the particular emphases on symbolic action, self-determination, postmaterialist values, collective identity, grievance articulation, and self-referential organization reflect fundamental features of contemporary social activism and the structures they challenge.

When seen from different angles these strengths also appear as limitations. Thus, the very historical specificity that gives new social movement theory much of its analytical power means that the theory (in all its variants) only applies to a limited number of movements in Western societies with mobilization biases toward white, middle-class participants pursuing politically or culturally progressive agendas. Alongside this empirical limitation is a theoretical one involving the type of questions new social movement theory has addressed (at least to date). By virtue of its focus on the "why" of movement emergence, new social movement theory has said relatively little about the "how" of ongoing movement processes. It also has not been particularly helpful in understanding the "when" or "where" of intermittent social movement formation across structurally similar societies (Tarrow 1994, p. 83). Like all theoretical frameworks, new social movement theory illuminates some issues while leaving others in the dark.

These double-edged strengths and limitations mean that new social movement theory can make its greatest contribution to understanding collective action when situated alongside other theoretical schools. In the most general terms, it may be that different theories speak most effectively to different levels of analysis. Thus, new social movement theory speaks to the macrolevel of structure and context; resource mobilization theory addresses the mesolevel of organization and strategy; and social constructionism accounts for the microlevel of identity and grievances. Theoretical progress within and between these paradigms is most likely to occur by identifying points of convergence and divergence between these levels and framing critical questions across these paradigms. This overview of new social movement theories suggests some linkages. The more political version of new social movement theory is more macro-oriented and has distinct affinities with some aspects of resource mobilization theory, while the more cultural version of new social movement theory is more micro-oriented and has equally strong affinities with social constructionism. By exploring the links across levels and paradigms, our theoretical understanding and empirical analysis of collective action are likely to be enhanced. New social movement theory promises to be a vital part of this process.

Acknowledgments

I gratefully acknowledge the helpful comments and suggestions of four anonymous *TSQ* reviewers. An earlier version of this article was presented at the annual meeting of the American Sociological Association, Los Angeles, 1994.

NOTES

1. In a somewhat similar argument, Anthony Giddens (1991) has proposed the concept of "life politics" to capture the inevitably political dimensions of self-actualization and identity formation in posttraditional contexts. In contrast to an emancipatory politics that challenges exploitation or oppression, life politics flows from the reflexive project of the self and emphasizes the interconnectedness of personal and global survival in late modernity.

2. In my earlier discussion of major debates, the contrast between political and cultural was used to refer to a specific debate about the political or apolitical nature of new social movements. In the present context of typological distinction, this contrast is used to refer to a broader pattern of interrelated differences that includes all the debates as well as other foundational assumptions that appear to cluster around political or cultural approaches to new social movements.

REFERENCES

Boggs, Carl. 1986. *Social Movements and Political Power*. Philadelphia, PA. Temple University Press.

Brand, Karl-Werner. 1986. "New Social Movements as a Metapolitical Challenge: The Social and Political Impact of a New Historical Type of Protest." *Thesis Eleven* 15:60–68.

——— 1990. "Cyclical Aspects of New Social Movements: Waves of Cultural Criticism and Mobilization Cycles of New Middle-Class Radicalism." Pp. 24–42 in *Challenging the Political Order*, edited by Dalton and Kuechler.

Buechler, Steven M. 1990. *Women's Movements in the United States: Woman Suffrage, Equal Rights and Beyond*. New Brunswick, NJ: Rutgers University Press.

———. 1993. "Beyond Resource Mobilization? Emerging Trends in Social Movement Theory." *The Sociological Quarterly* 34:217–235.

Calhoun, Craig. 1993. " 'New Social Movements' of the Early Nineteenth Century." *Social Science History* 17:385–427.

Canel, Eduardo. 1992. "New Social Movement Theory and Resource Mobilization: The Need for Integration." Pp. 22–51 in *Organizing Dissent*, edited by William K. Carroll. Toronto: Garamond Press.

Carroll, William K. 1992. "Introduction: Social Movements and Counter-Hegemony in a Canadian Context." Pp. 1–19 in *Organizing Dissent*, edited by William K. Carroll. Toronto: Garamond Press.

Carroll, William K., and R. S. Ratner. 1994. "Between Leninism and Radical Pluralism: Reflections on Counter-Hegemony and the New Social Movements." *Critical Sociology* 20:3–26.

Castells, Manuel. 1977. *The Urban Question*, Cambridge, MA: MIT Press.

———. 1978. *City, Class and Power*. New York: St. Martin's.

———. 1983. *The City and the Grassroots*. Berkeley: University of California Press.

Cohen, Jean. 1982. "Between Crisis Management and Social Movements: The Place of Institutional Reform." *Telos* 52:21–40.

———. 1983. "Rethinking Social Movements." *Berkeley Journal of Sociology* 28:97–113.

———. 1985. "'Strategy or Identity'? New Theoretical Paradigms and Contemporary Social Movements." *Social Research* 52:663–716.

Collins, Patricia Hill. 1990. *Black Feminist Thought*. Cambridge, MA: Unwin Hyman.

Dalton, Russell J., and Manfred Kuechler, eds. 1990. *Challenging the Political Order: New Social and Political Movements in Western Democracies*, New York: Oxford University Press.

Dalton, Russell J., Manfred Kuechler, and Wilhelm Burklin. 1990. "The Challenge of the New Movements." Pp. 3–20 in *Challenging the Political Order*, edited by Dalton and Kuechler.

Eder, Klaus. 1985. "The 'New Social Movements': Moral Crusades, Political Pressure Groups, or Social Movements?" *Social Research* 52:869–890.

———. 1993. *The New Politics of Class: Social Movements and Cultural Dynamics in Advanced Societies*. London: Sage.

Epstein, Barbara. 1990. "Rethinking Social Movement Theory." *Socialist Review* 20:35–65.

———. *Political Protest and Cultural Revolution: Nonviolent Direct Action in the 1970s and 1980s*. Berkeley: University of California Press.

Flacks, Richard. 1988. *Making History: The American Left and the American Mind*, New York: Columbia University Press.

Gamson, William A. 1992. "The Social Psychology of Collective Action." Pp. 53–76 In *Frontiers of Social Movement Theory*, edited by Morris and Mueller.

Giddens, Anthony. 1991. *Modernity and Self-Identity*. Stanford, CA: Stanford University Press.

Gusfield, Joseph A. 1994. "The Reflexivity of Social Movements: Collective Behavior and Mass Society Theory Revisited." Pp. 58–78 in *New Social Movements*, edited by Laraña, Johnston, and Gusfield.

Habermas, Jürgen. 1975. *Legitimation Crisis*. Boston: Beacon Press.

———. 1984–1987. *The Theory of Communicative Action*. (2 Volumes). Translated by Thomas McCarthy. Boston: Beacon Press.

Hirsch, Joachim. 1988. "The Crisis of Fordism, Transformations of the 'Keynesian' Security State, and New Social Movements." Pp. 43–55 in *Research in Social Movements, Conflicts and Change*, Vol. 10, edited by Louis Kriesberg. Greenwich, CT. JAI Press.

Hunt, Scott A., Robert D. Benford, and David A. Snow. 1994. "Identity Fields: Framing Processes and the Social Construction of Movement Identities." Pp. 185–208 in *New Social Movements*, edited by Laraña, Johnston, and Gusfield.

Inglehart, Ronald. 1990. "Values, Ideology and Cognitive Mobilization in New Social Movements." Pp. 43–66 in *Challenging the Political Order*, edited by Dalton and Kuechler.

Johnston, Hank. 1994. "New Social Movements and Old Regional Nationalisms." Pp. 267–286 in *New Social Movements*, edited by Laraña, Johnston, and Gusfield.

Johnston, Hank, Enrique Laraña, and Joseph Gusfield. 1994. "Identities, Grievances and New Social Movements." Pp. 3–35 in *New Social Movements*, edited by Laraña, Johnston, and Gusfield.

Kauffman, L. A. 1990. "The Anti-Politics of Identity." *Socialist Review* 20:67–80.

Klandermans, Bert. 1991. "New Social Movements and Resource Mobilization: The European and American Approaches Revisited." Pp. 17–44 in *Research on Social Movements* edited by Rucht.

———. 1992. "The Social Construction of Protest and Multiorganizational Fields." Pp. 77–103 in *Frontiers of Social Movement Theory*, edited by Morris and Mueller.

———. 1994. "Transient Identities? Membership Patterns in the Dutch Peace Movement." Pp. 168–184 in *New Social Movements*, edited by Laraña, Johnston, and Gusfield.

Klandermans, Bert, Hanspeter Kriesi, and Sidney Tarrow, eds. 1988. *International Social Movement*

Research, Vol. 1, *From Structure to Action.* New York: JAI Press.

Klandermans, Bert, and Sidney Tarrow. 1988. "Mobilization into Social Movements: Synthesizing European and American Approaches." Pp. 1–38 in *International Social Movement Research,* Vol. 1, *From Structure to Action,* edited by Klandermans, Kriesi, and Tarrow.

Kriesi, Hanspeter 1989. "New Social Movements and the New Class in the Netherlands." *American Journal of Sociology* 94:1078–1116.

Laclau, Ernesto, and Chantal Mouffe. 1985. *Hegemony and Socialist Strategy: Toward a Radical Democratic Politics.* London: Verso.

Laraña, Enrique. 1994. "Continuity and Unity in New Forms of Collective Action: A Comparative Analysis of Student Movements." Pp. 209–233 in *New Social Movements,* edited by Laraña, Johnston, and Gusfield.

Laraña, Enrique, Hank Johnston, and Joseph Gusfield, eds. 1994. *New Social Movements: From Ideology to Identity.* Philadelphia, PA: Temple University Press.

McAdam, Doug. 1994. "Culture and Social Movements." Pp. 36–57 in *New Social Movements,* edited by Laraña, Johnston and Gusfield.

McCarthy, John D., and Mayer N. Zald. 1977. "Resource Mobilization and Social Movements: A Partial Theory." *American Journal of Sociology* 82:1212–1241.

Melucci, Alberto. 1980. "The New Social Movements: A Theoretical Approach." *Social Science Information* 19:199–226.

———. 1981. "Ten Hypotheses for the Analysis of New Movements." Pp. 173–194 in *Contemporary Italian Sociology,* edited by Diana Pinto. Cambridge: Cambridge University Press.

———. 1984. "An End to Social Movements?" *Social Science Information* 23:819–835.

———. 1985. "The Symbolic Challenge of Contemporary Movements." *Social Research* 52:789–815.

———. 1988. "Getting Involved: Identity and Mobilization in Social Movements." Pp. 329–348 in *International Social Movement Research,* Vol. 1, *From Structure to Action,* edited by Klandermans, Kriesi, and Tarrow.

———. 1989. *Nomads of the Present: Social Movements and Individual Needs in Contemporary Society,* edited by John Keane and Paul Mier. Philadelphia, PA.: Temple University Press.

———. 1994. "A Strange Kind of Newness: What's 'New' in New Social Movements." Pp.

101–130 in *New Social Movements,* edited by Laraña, Johnston, and Gusfield.

Meyer, David, and Nancy Whittier. 1994. "Social Movement Spillover." *Social Problems* 41:277– 298.

Mooers, Colin, and Alan Sears. 1992. "The 'New Social Movements' and the Withering Away of State Theory." Pp. 52–68 in *Organizing Dissent,* edited by William K. Carroll. Toronto: Garamond Press.

Morris, Aldon D. 1992. "Political Consciousness and Collective Action." Pp. 351–373 in *Frontiers of Social Movement Theory,* edited by Morris and Mueller.

Morris, Aldon D., and Carol McClurg Mueller, eds. 1992. *Frontiers of Social Movement Theory.* New Haven, CT: Yale University Press.

Mueller, Carol McClurg. 1994. "Conflict Networks and the Origins of Women's Liberation." Pp. 234–263 in *New Social Movements,* edited by Laraña, Johnston, and Gusfield.

Offe, Claus. 1985. "New Social Movements: Challenging the Boundaries of Institutional Politics." *Social Research* 52:817–868.

———. 1990. "Reflections on the Institutional Self-transformation of Movement Politics: A Tentative Stage Model." Pp. 232–250 in *Challenging the Political Order,* edited by Dalton and Kuechler.

Omi, Michael, and Howard Winant. 1986. *Racial Formation in the United States from the 1960s to the 1980s.* New York: Routledge.

Plotke, David. 1990. "What's So New about New Social Movements?" *Socialist Review* 20:81–102.

Rucht, Dieter. 1988. "Themes, Logics and Arenas of Social Movements: A Structural Approach." Pp. 305–328 in *International Social Movement Research,* Vol. 1, *From Structure to Action,* edited by Klandermans, Kriesi, and Tarrow.

———, ed. 1991. *Research on Social Movements: The State of the Art in Western Europe and the USA.* Boulder, CO: Westview Press.

Shin, Gi-Wook. 1994. "The Historical Making of Collective Action: The Korean Peasant Uprisings of 1946." *American Journal of Sociology* 99:1596–1624.

Snow, David A. and Robert D. Benford. 1992. "Master Frames and Cycles of Protest." Pp. 133–155 in *Frontiers in Social Movement Theory,* edited by Morris and Mueller.

Steinmetz, George. 1994. "Regulation Theory, Post-Marxism, and the New Social Movements." *Comparative Studies in Society and History* 36(1):176–212.

Stoecker, Randy. 1995. "Community, Movement, Organization: The Problem of Identity Convergence in Collective Action." *The Sociological Quarterly* 36:111–130.

Tarrow, Sidney. 1991. *Struggle, Politics, Reform: Collective Action, Social Movements, and Cycles of Protest.* Western Societies Program, Occasional paper no. 21, Center for International Studies. Ithaca, NY: Cornell University Press.

———. 1994. *Power in Movement: Social Movements, Collective Action, and Politics,* Cambridge: Cambridge University Press.

Taylor, Verta. 1989. "Social Movement Continuity: The Women's Movement in Abeyance." *American Sociological Review* 54: 761–755.

Taylor, Verta, and Nancy Whittier. 1992. "Collective Identity in Social Movement Communities." Pp. 104–129 in *Frontiers of Social Movement Theory,* edited by Morris and Mueller.

Tilly, Charles. 1978. *From Mobilization to Revolution.* Reading, MA: Addison-Wesley.

Touraine, Alain. 1977. *The Self-Production of Society.* Chicago: University of Chicago Press.

———. 1981. *The Voice and the Eye: An Analysis of Social Movements,* New York: Cambridge University Press.

———. 1985. "An Introduction to the Study of Social Movements." *Social Research* 52:749–787.

———. 1988. *Return of the Actor: Social Theory in Post-Industrial Society.* Minneapolis: University of Minnesota Press.

———. 1992. "Beyond Social Movements." *Theory, Culture, and Society* 9:125–145.

Touraine, Alain, Michel Wieviorka, and Francois Dubet. 1987. *The Worker's Movement.* Cambridge: Cambridge University Press.

Tucker, Kenneth H. 1991. "How New Are the New Social Movements?" *Theory, Culture, and Society* 8:75–98.

Wright, Erik Olin. 1985. *Classes.* London: Verso.

———. 1989. *The Debate on Classes.* London: Verso.

PART III

Movement Issues

Power concedes nothing without demand.
—FREDERICK DOUGLASS

One purpose of the theories reviewed in Part Two is to provide conceptual tools for answering questions about social movements. However, there are many different questions that can be asked about such movements. In this part, we select a small sample of those questions for closer scrutiny. Whereas the readings in Part Two addressed theoretical issues in general, the readings in Part Three engage specific questions about mobilization obstacles, organizational dynamics, continuity and cycles, culture and collective identity, and future scenarios. Through these readings, we hope to illuminate these issues and to illustrate the role of theory in examining some central questions about social movements.

The first set of questions addressed concerns the various obstacles that movements must overcome if they are to mobilize in the first place. There are at least two sets of factors that can pose problems for movements—internal and external obstacles. Internal obstacles concern the group itself. Sometimes movements falter because of a lack of resources or a lack of commitment on the part of sympathizers. At other times, movements are unable to get started because the group cannot achieve sufficient organization, communication, or coordination to pursue its goals. This is why, as resource mobilization theory argues, successful movements often build on existing forms of social organization that already provide means of communication and coordination for people to use. This is also why disorganized groups face an especially diffi-

cult time in organizing collective action. Once a group is organized, there are additional internal obstacles that can derive from the organization itself, as we will see in the section on organizational dynamics.

Movements that overcome internal obstacles to mobilization may still face external obstacles. In some cases, these obstacles simply involve the nature of social organization and the fact that group needs cannot easily be expressed, heard, or responded to in the existing political and social system. In addition to this "unconscious" obstacle, there may be those who consciously oppose the movement and seek to block its progress. Because most movements have an oppositional quality to them, it is usually not hard to predict which groups will become active opponents of the movement if it appears likely to achieve some success. In addition to these opponents, the state may oppose the movement. Because the role of the state is often to preserve a social order that benefits some groups and not others, the state may become quite deliberate in devising strategies to repress a social movement. A final type of external factor concerns the timing of a movement's appearance and the issue of opportunity. Some historical moments are ripe for social change because elites are vulnerable or because other groups have become successful, but other moments offer virtually no prospect of success. Although movements can sometimes control internal factors that influence their likelihood of success, they can rarely exert much control over external factors, which often determine movement outcomes.

The readings in the section on mobilization obstacles provide some specific examples of the factors that movements must overcome if they are to achieve some success. Frances Fox Piven and Richard A. Cloward identify numerous ways in which social and political structures either preclude social movements altogether or channel their direction and limit their impact if they do appear. Although they address the prospects for poor people's movements, many of the issues they describe are important to the success or failure of other movements as well. Whereas Piven and Cloward address relatively disadvantaged groups, the reading by Bert Klandermans and Dirk Oegema suggests that even groups whose positions enjoy broad popular support have difficulty mounting effective protest. Their research reveals a "funnel effect" in which broad support of movement goals is funneled down to a relatively small percentage of people who are willing to become politically active on behalf of those beliefs. Finally, the selection by Gary Marx details the many tactics that governmental authorities can use to undermine the effectiveness of social movements. Taken together, these readings suggest some of the difficulties that movements must overcome if they are to have an impact on their societies.

The second set of questions addressed concerns organizational dynamics in social movements. Although some movements remain relatively unstructured, it is increasingly common for movements to assume some persisting organizational form. Such organization brings its own logic to the conduct of social movement activism. Whereas Piven and Cloward claim that organization inevitably means the end of effective protest (at least for poor people's movements), most theorists would argue that organization brings many potential benefits to social movement activism. Such benefits, however, involve certain trade-offs. There is considerable evidence to suggest that formally organized, bureaucratic, centralized organizations are effective at utilizing resources but do not elicit high levels of commitment from their members. Indeed, such organizations may create a major division between leaders and followers in a movement. Informal, decentralized organizations may lose something in their ability to marshal resources effectively, but they typically gain something in the commitment of their members and, hence, their willingness to engage in high-risk forms of activism. Although it is tempting to seek a formula for an effective movement organization, the evidence suggests that different forms of organization are suited to different purposes, and there is no simple recipe for an effective organization in all times and places.

It is also true that many movements consist of multiple organizations that support movement goals. The existence of multiple organizations within the same movement adds another level of organizational dynamics to the analysis of social movements. Once again, there is no simple formula for what kinds of organizations and interorganizational relations are most beneficial. Multiple organizations can be a drawback if they end up competing for the same scarce resources, but they can be an asset if they play somewhat different roles in the movement. A common example involves the coexistence of radical and moderate organizations within the same movement. Although this can be a source of friction, it is not uncommon for such pairings to work to the advantage of the movement. This happens when the radical organization makes the moderate one appear as a reasonable alternative to its own demands and hence as a sensible compromise. In many such situations, the moderate group would probably win nothing on its own, but it wins substantial concessions when it is perceived as occupying a middle ground between a radical alternative and the status quo. Another distinction is whether an organization derives from the indigenous group or from some group of outsiders. Once again, there are cross-pressures because organizations led by outside sympathizers can often provide resources and allies, but they can also redirect a movement away from its indigenous base and the needs of that base.

The broadest approach to organizational dynamics in social movements grows out of the recognition that social movements exist in multiorganizational fields. Such fields consist of an alliance system and a conflict system. The alliance system is composed of all movement organizations seeking the same goal, as well as those that may be devoted to different purposes but nevertheless support the movement. The conflict system is composed of all organizations that are likely to actively oppose the movement. The conflict system of a movement is likely to consist of both private organizations and agencies within the state that oppose the movement. Indeed, for some contemporary movements, different agencies within the state have been part of the alliance system and the conflict system of the movement, thereby translating movement demands into struggles between different groups within the state. The most intriguing element in a movement's conflict system may well be the countermovement. Although many groups may oppose a movement, a countermovement is created for the sole purpose of opposing an existing movement. Once organized, movements and countermovements engage in an elaborate dance as each seeks to deploy strategies to undermine the effectiveness of its opponent.

The readings in the section on organizational dynamics illustrate some of the different roles that organization can play in social movements. The lead article, by Seymour Martin Lipset, summarizes Robert Michels's "iron law of oligarchy," which claims that even democratic or representative organization will inevitably give rise to an elite leadership group that does not accurately represent the membership. The next reading, by Aldon

Morris, provides a dense analysis of interorganizational relationships within the civil rights movement, focusing on the Southern Christian Leadership Conference (SCLC), the National Association for the Advancement of Colored People (NAACP), and the Congress of Racial Equality (CORE). Although these distinct movement organizations were committed to similar overall goals, the relations between them exhibited conflict and rivalry as well as common purpose. The final reading, by Tahi L. Mottl, analyzes countermovements and offers a number of hypotheses about how they operate in opposition to an existing movement. Although hardly exhaustive, these readings suggest some of the organizational complexities to be found in many different social movements.

The third set of questions addressed concerns the longevity and the timing of social movements. For many years, students of social movements worked with a "natural history" model of collective action, in which movements were seen as following a predictable pattern of "rise and fall." Movements were presumed to begin with an identifiable "birth" and to conclude with a definitive "death," which allowed analysts to clearly distinguish a movement from its social environment and from other movements. However powerful they were at their peak, movements were typically seen as ending with their own collapse or absorption into the dominant society. Although the duration of a movement was recognized as variable, movements were presumed to be relatively short lived compared with periods of social calm.

Recent research on the continuity and cycling of social movements challenges many of the premises of the natural history model of collective action. The view of movements as short-lived phenomena with clear beginnings and endings has been partially replaced by a new image of movements as continuous, ongoing efforts for change that go through periods of overt activism and relative dormancy. This view reinterprets the "death" of movements as something closer to suspended animation in which old lessons are preserved and new strategies are devised. One indicator of such preservation is the persistence of movement organizations. It is remarkable how many movement organizations survive through long periods of relative inactivity. The metaphor of dormancy or suspended animation can be misleading because organizations often do a great deal to sustain the potential for future activism by consolidating their gains, preserving their history, socializing new generations, and nurturing activists' commitments, for example. Although some forms of collective action do culminate in a definitive ending, an increasing number of movements persist over long periods of time.

Recent attention to the temporal dimension of social activism also suggests that movements become highly active in cycles of protest and clusters of groups. Several patterns have become evident. The events that provide resources and create opportunities for one movement often do so for many other movements as well. Thus, a political crisis of leadership can make elite groups vulnerable to the demands of many different social movements at the same time, inviting a variety of groups to mobilize on behalf of their interests. On another level, the most general frames of meaning that express grievances can often be applied to many different groups with minor variations in the general frame. Thus, notions of "rights" or "justice" provide a way of expressing grievances that can be applied to many groups in many situations. Finally, one movement can create space and opportunity for other movements to follow its lead and agitate for change. A new appreciation of all these processes has led contemporary researchers to focus on how social movements often appear in cycles and clusters of activism.

The readings in the section on continuity and cycles explore some of these temporal dimensions of social movement activity. The lead article, by Verta Taylor, describes a positive role that organization can play by providing an "abeyance structure" that allows a movement to survive through bad times until the conditions for mobilization are better. The persistence of such abeyance structures requires that we rethink our notions of how and when movements begin and end. The next reading, by Sidney Tarrow, explores the concept of cycles of protest for understanding activism in many different times and places. Although the forms of activism he analyzes have a similar cyclical rhythm, their outcomes are highly diverse. The final reading, by David A. Snow and Robert D. Benford, explores the role of master frames in cycles of protest, offering a number of propositions about how these two aspects of social activism are linked. Taken together, these readings richly illustrate continuity and cycles in social movements.

The fourth set of questions addressed concerns the general role of culture and the particular issue of collective identity in social movements. In the last few years, cultural processes have received increasing attention in the social sciences. This "cultural turn" is apparent on at least three levels. First, at the level of general social theory, sociology has become much more attentive to cultural issues in the last two decades. Questions of meaning, subjectivity, identity, signs, and discourse have become central in contemporary social theory and many subfields of sociology. Second, at the level of social movement theory, there has been a gradual shift from the political and organizational concerns of the resource mobilization perspective to the more cultural emphases of both social constructionism and new social movement theory. This shift can be traced in the readings in the contemporary theory section of this book. Finally, at the level of activism, an increasing number of movements have oriented themselves around cultural issues. By conscious strategy or implicit focus, many contemporary movements engage in personal transformation, identity construction, or cultural activity in lieu of more traditional political struggle. For all these reasons, the role of culture now looms larger in the study of social movements than it has for a very long time.

Among the many cultural dimensions to social movements, none is more central than the construction of collective identities. For too long, the groups that constitute the social bases of movements were taken for granted by prevailing theories, as typified by the Marxist assumption that because workers occupied similar structural locations, they would eventually form a "class-for-themselves" and overthrow the exploitive system of capitalism. Although Marx recognized the complexity of this process, many of his followers assumed the existence of a mythical working class whose organization, identity, and ideology were ripe for revolution at any moment. In contrast to this view, both social constructionism and new social movement theory have reemphasized the complexity of the collective identities that undergird social activism. These perspectives make it clear that entire categories of people never act in unison, that it is always subgroups within broader categories that act collectively, that the solidarity of these groups is never automatic but is a movement accomplishment, and that all such solidarities have a fleeting character. Thus, like many forms of identity in modern society, the collective identity involved in social activism has a fragility that traditional theories of identity and solidarity never recognized. Although these insights are most evident in new social movements rooted in race, gender, sexuality, and generation, it is also evident that even the "old" social movements based on class underwent similar processes of social construction to arrive at an identity that would support working-class activism.

The construction of collective identities requires a meshing of individual and group through an identity that is personal enough to be deeply felt and collective enough to unite large numbers. On the individual level, this process requires tapping people's sense of themselves as well as the beliefs and forms of consciousness that provide them with a coherent understanding of their social world. On the group level, this process involves the creation of a solidarity that overrides individual differences and is reinforced by collective action frames that link individual fates and group fortunes. And on the intergroup level, this process often utilizes an outgroup as an "enemy" who is critical in creating a "we feeling" within a collectivity. Although these processes can have a rational or strategic quality, they also rely on the emotions and passions of people. Rather than treating reason and emotion as dualistic, cultural approaches to social movements are better equipped to recognize their intertwined nature, as both logic and passion contribute to the meanings that undergird collective identity in social movements.

The readings in the section on culture and collective identity illustrate these processes in contemporary social movements. The lead article, by Doug McAdam, identifies the various ways in which culture is salient to our understanding of social movements. He discusses the role of culture in the emergence of social movements, analyzes the kinds of "cultures" created by movements, and surveys some of the cultural consequences of social movements. This approach thus recognizes culture both as a "macro" element in the environment of movements and as a "micro" element that movements themselves create. The next selection, by William Gamson, discusses the social psychological dimensions of social movements. His reading describes the construction of collective identity and the role of solidarity and consciousness in this process and is thus applicable to many different kinds of movements. The closing selection, by Verta Taylor and Nancy E. Whittier, presents a more specific analysis of collective identity in lesbian feminist movements. Reflecting many of the notions advanced by Gamson, this article analyzes collective identity as a function of boundaries, consciousness, and negotiation. This rich case study provides a compelling example of the centrality of collective identity and the importance of culture in contemporary social activism.

The final set of questions addressed concerns the future of social movement activity. Social scientists have been notoriously unsuccessful at predicting the future, and few are willing to go out on a limb by making specific predictions about social activism. Even so, it is possible to speculate about plausible scenarios based on current knowledge. Perhaps what is most striking about present speculations is their broad differences from the speculations of earlier generations of social movement theorists. The natural history model of the "rise and fall" of movements implied that they were rare and isolated events. This model also presumed that social movements had few, if any, lasting effects on the larger society. The combination of these two presumptions shows why social movements were regarded as a marginal part of both society and sociology.

These presumptions about social movements have changed, and this in turn has changed sociologists' speculation about the future of social activism. Since the activism of the 1960s, it has been difficult to see social movements as isolated and rare. Social activism is now seen as a "normal," if not exactly predictable, feature of contemporary society. Current theory also recognizes a much broader range of effects that movements have on their societies. Sometimes these effects are evident during the peak mobilization of the movement. In other cases, the effects are less tangible but still represent significant traces left by movements after they subside. For all these reasons, social movement theorists now think differently about the future of social movements than earlier generations did.

Indeed, if there is a common thread in the very diverse readings in the section on future scenarios, it is the presumption that social movements will continue to be a major part of our societies. The lead article, by Mayer Zald, describes the trajectory of social movements in the United States. On the one hand, he expects a permanent social movement industry to remain a part of our society, but on the other hand, he expects most social activism to be reformist and limited in its orientation for the foreseeable future. The next reading, by Jackie Smith, describes the emergence of transnational social movements that operate on an international scale. Her analysis suggests that an increasing number of movements are both thinking and acting globally. The final reading, by Sidney Tarrow, assesses how much social activism has changed over the last two hundred years (including the trend toward transnational movements noted by Smith), with a striking contrast between 1789 and 1989. In posing the possibility that we are becoming a "movement society," Tarrow identifies potential risks and dangers in a permanently mobilized, international movement society. These provocative readings thus indicate several plausible scenarios for future activism.

There are many more questions that could be posed about social movements, but the ones addressed here speak to vital processes in social activism. At their best, these readings illuminate specific questions about social movements as well as the utility of theory in making sense of contemporary forms of social activism.

20

THE STRUCTURING OF PROTEST

FRANCES FOX PIVEN   •   RICHARD A. CLOWARD

Common sense and historical experience combine to suggest a simple but compelling view of the roots of power in any society. Crudely but clearly stated, those who control the means of physical coercion, and those who control the means of producing wealth, have power over those who do not. This much is true whether the means of coercion consists in the primitive force of a warrior caste or the technological force of a modern army. And it is true whether the control of production consists in control by priests of the mysteries of the calendar on which agriculture depends, or control by financiers of the large-scale capital on which industrial production depends. Since coercive force can be used to gain control of the means of producing wealth, and since control of wealth can be used to gain coercive force, these two sources of power tend over time to be drawn together within one ruling class.

Common sense and historical experience also combine to suggest that these sources of power are protected and enlarged by the use of that power not only

to control the actions of men and women, but also to control their beliefs. What some call superstructure, and what others call culture, includes an elaborate system of beliefs and ritual behaviors which defines for people what is right and what is wrong and why; what is possible and what is impossible; and the behavioral imperatives that follow from these beliefs. Because this superstructure of beliefs and rituals is evolved in the context of unequal power, it is inevitable that beliefs and rituals reinforce inequality, by rendering the powerful divine and the challengers evil. Thus the class struggles that might otherwise be inevitable in sharply unequal societies ordinarily do not seem either possible or right from the perspective of those who live within the structure of belief and ritual fashioned by those societies. People whose only possible recourse in struggle is to defy the beliefs and rituals laid down by their rulers ordinarily do not.

Briefly stated, the main argument of this chapter is that protest is not a matter of free choice; it is not freely available to all groups at all times, and much of the time it is not available to lower-class groups at all. *The occasions when protest is possible among the poor, the forms that it must take, and the impact it can have are all delimited by the social structure in ways which usually diminish its extent and diminish its force.* Before we go on to explain these points, we need to define what we mean by a protest movement, for customary definitions have led both analysts and activists to ignore or discredit much protest that does occur.

The emergence of a protest movement entails a transformation both of consciousness and of behavior. The change in consciousness has at least three distinct aspects. First, "the system"—or those aspects of the system that people experience and perceive—loses legitimacy. Large numbers of men and women who ordinarily accept the authority of their rulers and the legitimacy of institutional arrangements come to believe in some measure that these rulers and these arrangements are unjust and wrong. Second, people who are ordinarily fatalistic, who believe that existing arrangements are inevitable, begin to assert "rights" that imply demands for change. Third, there is a new sense of efficacy; people who ordinarily consider themselves helpless come to believe that they have some capacity to alter their lot.

The change in behavior is equally striking, and usually more easily recognized, at least when it takes the form of mass strikes or marches or riots. Such behavior seems to us to involve two distinguishing elements. First, masses of people become defiant; they violate the traditions and laws to which they ordinarily acquiesce, and they flaunt the authorities to whom they ordinarily defer. And second, their defiance is acted out collectively, as members of a group, and not as isolated individuals. Strikes and riots are clearly forms of collective action, but even some forms of defiance which appear to be individual acts, such as crime or school truancy or incendiarism, while more ambiguous, may have a collective dimension, for those who engage in these acts may consider themselves to be part of a larger movement. Such apparently atomized acts of defiance can be considered movement events when those involved perceive themselves to be acting as members of

a group, and when they share a common set of protest beliefs.

Institutional Limits on the Incidence of Mass Insurgency

Aristotle believed that the chief cause of internal warfare was inequality, that the lesser rebel in order to be equal. But human experience has proved him wrong, most of the time. Sharp inequality has been constant, but rebellion infrequent. Aristotle underestimated the controlling force of the social structure on political life. However hard their lot may be, people usually remain acquiescent, conforming to the accustomed patterns of daily life in their community, and believing those patterns to be both inevitable and just. Men and women till the fields each day, or stoke the furnaces, or tend the looms, obeying the rules and rhythms of earning a livelihood; they mate and bear children hopefully, and mutely watch them die; they abide by the laws of church and community and defer to their rulers, striving to earn a little grace and esteem. In other words most of the time people conform to the institutional arrangements which enmesh them, which regulate the rewards and penalties of daily life, and which appear to be the only possible reality.

Those for whom the rewards are most meager, who are the most oppressed by inequality, are also acquiescent. Sometimes they are the most acquiescent, for they have little defense against the penalties that can be imposed for defiance. Moreover, at most times and in most places, and especially in the United States, the poor are led to believe that their destitution is deserved, and that the riches and power that others command are also deserved. In more traditional societies sharp inequalities are thought to be divinely ordained, or to be a part of the natural order of things. In more modern societies, such as the United States, riches and power are ascribed to personal qualities of industry or talent; it follows that those who have little or nothing have only what they deserve. As Edelman observes in his study of American political beliefs:

> The American poor have required less coercion and less in social security guarantees to maintain their quiescence than has been true in other developed countries, even authoritarian ones like Germany and notably poor ones like Italy; for the guilt and self-concepts of the poor have kept them docile (1971, 56).

Ordinarily, in short, the lower classes accept their lot, and that acceptance can be taken for granted; it need not be bargained for by their rulers. This capacity of the institutions of a society to enforce political docility is the most obvious way in which protest is socially structured, in the sense that it is structurally precluded most of the time.

Sometimes, however, the poor do become defiant. They challenge traditional authorities, and the rules laid down by those authorities. They demand redress for their grievances. American history is punctuated by such events, from the first uprisings by freeholders, tenants, and slaves in colonial America, to the postrevolutionary debtor rebellions, through the periodic eruptions of strikes and riots by industrial workers, to the ghetto riots of the twentieth century. In each instance, masses of the poor were somehow able, if only briefly, to overcome the shame bred by a culture which blames them for their plight; somehow they were able to break the bonds of conformity enforced by work, by family, by community,

by every strand of institutional life; somehow they were able to overcome the fears induced by police, by militia, by company guards.

When protest does arise, when masses of those who are ordinarily docile become defiant, a major transformation has occurred. Most of the literature on popular insurgency has been devoted to identifying the preconditions of this transformation (often out of a concern for preventing or curbing the resulting political disturbances). Whatever the disagreements among different schools of thought, and they are substantial, there is general agreement that the emergence of popular uprisings reflects profound changes in the larger society. This area of agreement is itself important, for it is another way of stating our proposition that protest is usually structurally precluded. The agreement is that only under exceptional conditions will the lower classes become defiant—and thus, in our terms, *only under exceptional conditions are the lower classes afforded the socially determined opportunity to press for their own class interests.*

The validity of this point follows from any of the major theories of civil disorder considered alone. When the several theoretical perspectives are considered concurrently and examined in the light of the historical events analyzed in this book, the conclusion is suggested that while different theories emphasize different kinds of social dislocations, most of these dislocations occurred simultaneously in the 1930s and 1960s. One does not have to believe that the various major theoretical perspectives are equally valid to agree that they may all cast at least some light on the series of dislocations that preceded the eruption of protest, at least in the periods we study. This argues that it not only requires a major social dislocation before protest can emerge, but that a sequence or combination of dislocations probably must occur before the anger that underlies protest builds to a high pitch, and before that anger can find expression in collective defiance.

It seems useful to divide perspectives on insurgency according to whether the emphasis is on pressures that force eruptions, or whether the emphasis is on the breakdown of the regulatory capacity of the society, a breakdown that permits eruptions to occur and to take form in political protest. Thus among the "pressure" theorists one might include those who emphasize economic change as a precondition for civil disorder, whether economic improvement or immiseration. Sharp economic change obviously disturbs the relationship between what men and women have been led to expect, and the conditions they actually experience. If people have been led to expect more than they receive, they are likely to feel frustration and anger.

The major flaw, in our view, in the work of all pressure theorists is their reliance on an unstated and incorrect assumption that economic change or structural change is extraordinary, that stability and the willing consensus it fosters are the usual state of affairs. Economic change, and presumably also structural change, if one were clear as to what that meant, are more the usual than the occasional features of capitalist societies. Nevertheless, historical evidence suggests that extremely rapid economic change adds to the frustration and anger that many people may experience much of the time.

The other major set of theoretical perspectives on popular uprising emphasizes the breakdown of the regulatory capacity of social institutions as the principal factor leading to civil strife. These explanations also range broadly from social disorganization theorists such as Hobsbawm, who emphasizes the breakdown of the regulatory controls implicit in the structures and routines of daily life; to those such as Kornhauser, who argues that major societal changes—depression, industrialization, urbanization—break the ties that bind people to the multiple secondary associations that ordinarily control political behavior (1959); to those who focus on divisions among elites as the trigger that releases popular discontents. Taken together, these social disorganization perspectives provide a major insight, however general, into the links between societal change, the breakdown of social controls—what Ash calls the "deroutinization" of life (164–167)—and the eruption of protest. The disorganization theories suggest that periods of rapid change tend, at the same time as they build frustration, to weaken the regulatory controls inherent in the structures of institutional life.

Ordinary life for most people is regulated by the rules of work and the rewards of work which pattern each day and week and season. Once cast out of that routine, people are cast out of the regulatory framework that it imposes. Work and the rewards of work underpin the stability of other social institutions as well. When men cannot earn enough to support families, they may desert their wives and children, or fail to marry the women with whom they mate. And if unemployment is longlasting entire communities may disintegrate as the able-bodied migrate elsewhere in search of work. In effect daily life becomes progressively deregulated as what Edelman calls the "comforting banalities" of everyday existence are destroyed (95). The first signs of the resulting demoralization and uncertainty are usually rising indices of crime, family breakdown, vagrancy, and vandalism. Barred from conforming to the social roles they have been reared to live through, men and women continue to stumble and struggle somehow to live, within or without the rules.

Thus it is not only that catastrophic depression in the 1930s and modernization and migration in the 1960s led to unexpected hardships; massive unemployment and the forced uprooting of people and communities had other, perhaps equally traumatic effects on the lives of people. The loss of work and the disintegration of communities meant the loss of the regulating activities, resources, and relationships on which the structure of everyday life depends, and thus the erosion of the structures that bound people to existing social arrangements. Still, neither the frustrations generated by the economic change, nor the breakdown of daily life, may be sufficient to lead people to protest their travails. Ordinarily, when people suffer such hardships, they blame God, or they blame themselves.

For a protest movement to arise out of these traumas of daily life, people have to perceive the deprivation and disorganization they experience as both wrong, and subject to redress. The social arrangements that are ordinarily perceived as just and immutable must come to seem both unjust and mutable. One condition favoring this transvaluation is the scale of distress. This transvaluation is even more likely to take place, or to take place more rapidly, when the dislocations suffered by particular groups occur in a context of wider changes and instability, at times when the dominant institutional arrangements of the society, as people understand them, are self-evidently not functioning.

Finally, as these objective institutional upheavals lead people to reappraise their situation, elites may contribute to that reappraisal, thus helping to stimulate mass arousal—a process that has often been noted by social theorists. Clearly, the vested interest of the ruling class is usually in preserving the status quo, and in preserving the docility of the lower orders within the status quo. But rapid institutional change and upheaval may affect elite groups differently, undermining the power of some segments of the ruling class and enlarging the power of other segments, so that elites divide among themselves. This dissonance may erode their authority, and erode the authority of the institutional norms they uphold. If, in the ensuing competition for dominance, some among the elite seek to enlist the support of the impoverished by naming their grievances as just, then the hopes of the lower classes for change will be nourished and the legitimacy of the institutions which oppress them further weakened.

Our main point, however, is that whatever position one takes on the "causes" of mass unrest, there is general agreement that extraordinary disturbances in the larger society are required to transform the poor from apathy to hope, from quiescence to indignation. On this point, if no other, theorists of the most diverse persuasions agree. Moreover, there is reason to think that a series of concurrent dislocations underlay the mass protests of the 1930s and 1960s. And with that said, the implication for an understanding of the potential for political influence among the poor becomes virtually self-evident: *since periods of profound social dislocations are infrequent, so too are opportunities for protest among the lower classes.*

The Patterning of Insurgency

Just as quiescence is enforced by institutional life, and just as the eruption of discontent is determined by changes in institutional life, the forms of political protest are also determined by the institutional context in which people live and work. This point seems self-evident to us, but it is usually ignored, in part because the pluralist tradition defines political action as essentially a matter of choice. Political actors, whoever they may be, are treated as if they are not constricted by a social environment in deciding upon one political strategy or another; it is as if the strategies employed by different groups were freely elected, rather than the result of constraints imposed by their location in the social structure. In this section, we turn, in the most preliminary way, to a discussion of the ways in which the expression of defiance is patterned by features of institutional life.

The Electoral System as a Structuring Institution

In the United States the principal structuring institution, at least in the early phases of protest, is the electoral-representative system. The significance of this assertion is not that the electoral system provides an avenue of influence under normal circumstances. To the contrary, we shall demonstrate that it is usually when unrest among the lower classes breaks out of the confines of electoral procedures that the poor may have some influence, for the instability and polarization they then threaten to create by their actions in the factories or in the streets may force some response from electoral leaders. But whether action emerges in the factories or the streets may depend on the course of the early phase of protest at the polls.

Accordingly, one of the first signs of popular discontent in the contemporary United States is usually a sharp shift in traditional voting patterns. In a sense, the electoral system serves to measure and register the extent of the emerging disaffection. These early signs of political instability ordinarily prompt efforts by contending political leaders to placate the defecting groups, usually at this stage with conciliatory pronouncements. The more serious the electoral defections, or the keener the com-

petition among political elites, the more likely that such symbolic appeasements will be offered. But if the sources of disturbance and anger are severe—and only if they are severe and persistent—conciliations are likely merely to fuel mass arousal, for in effect they imply that some of the highest leaders of the land identify with the indignation of the lowly masses.

Moreover, just as political leaders play an influential role in stimulating mass arousal, so do they play an important role in shaping the demands of the aroused. What are intended to serve as merely symbolic appeasements may instead provide a focus for the still inchoate anxieties and diffuse anger that drive the masses. Thus early rhetorical pronouncements by liberal political leaders, including presidents of the United States, about the "rights" of workers and the "rights" of blacks not only helped to fuel the discontents of workers and blacks, but helped to concentrate those discontents on demands articulated by leading officials of the nation.

But when people are thus encouraged in spirit without being appeased in fact, their defiance may escape the boundaries of electoral rituals, and escape the boundaries established by the political norms of the electoral-representative system in general. They may indeed become rebellious, but while their rebellion often appears chaotic from the perspective of conventional American politics, or from the perspective of some organizers, it is not chaotic at all; it is structured political behavior. When people riot in the streets, their behavior is socially patterned, and within those patterns, their actions are to some extent deliberate and purposeful.

Social Location and Forms of Defiance

In contrast to the effort expended in accounting for the sources of insurgency, relatively little attention has been given to the question of why insurgency, when it does occur, takes one form and not another. Why, in other words, do people sometimes strike and at other times boycott, loot, or burn? Perhaps this question is seldom dealt with because the defiant behavior released often appears inchoate to analysts, and therefore not susceptible to explanation, as in the nineteenth-century view of mental illness. Thus Parsons characterizes reactions to strain as "irrational" (1965); Neil Smelser describes collective behavior as "primitive" and "magical"; and Kornhauser attributes unstable, extremist, and antidemocratic tendencies to mass movements. Many defiant forms of mass action that fall short of armed uprisings are thus often simply not recognized as intelligent political behavior at all.

Such perspectives have left us with images which serve to discredit lower-class movements by denying them meaning and legitimacy, instead of providing explanations. While the weakening of social controls that accompanies ruptures in social life may be an important precondition for popular uprisings, it does not follow either that the infrastructure of social life simply collapses, or that those who react to these disturbances by protesting are those who suffer the sharpest personal disorientation and alienation. To the contrary it may well be those whose lives are rooted in some institutional context, who are in regular relationships with others in similar straits, who are best able to redefine their travails as the fault of their rulers and not of themselves, and are best able to join together in collective protest. Thus while many of the southern blacks who participated in the civil rights movement were poor, recent migrants to the southern cities, or were unemployed, they were also linked together in the southern black church, which became the mobilizing node of movement actions.

Just as electoral political institutions channel protest into voter activity in the United States, and may even confine it within these spheres if the disturbance is not severe and the electoral system appears responsive, so do other features of institutional life determine the forms that protest takes when it breaks out of the boundaries of electoral politics. Thus, it is no accident that some people strike, others riot, or loot the granaries, or burn the machines, for just as the patterns of daily life ordinarily assure mass quiescence, so do these same patterns influence the form defiance will take when it erupts.

First, people experience deprivation and oppression within a concrete setting, not as the end product of large and abstract processes, and it is the concrete experience that molds their discontent into specific grievances against specific targets. Workers experience the factory, the speeding rhythm of the assembly line, the foreman, the spies and the guards, the owner and the paycheck. They do not experience monopoly capitalism. People on relief experience the shabby waiting rooms, the overseer or the caseworker, and the dole. They do not experience American social welfare policy. Tenants experience the leaking ceilings and cold radiators, and they recognize the landlord. They do not recognize the banking, real estate, and construction systems. No small wonder, therefore, that when the poor rebel they so often rebel against the overseer of the poor, or the slumlord, or the middling merchant, and not against the banks or the government elites to whom the overseer, the slumlord, and the merchant also defer. In other words, it is the daily experience of people that shapes their grievances, establishes the measure of their demands, and points out the targets of their anger.

Second, institutional patterns shape mass movements by shaping the collectivity out of which protest can arise. Institutional life aggregates people or disperses them, molds group identities, and draws people into the settings within which collective action can erupt. Thus factory work gathers men and women together, educates them in a common experience, and educates them to the possibilities of cooperation and collective action. Casual laborers or petty entrepreneurs, by contrast, are dispersed by their occupations, and are therefore less likely to perceive their commonalities of position, and less likely to join together in collective action.

Third, and most important, institutional roles determine the strategic opportunities for defiance, for it is typically by rebelling against the rules and authorities associated with their everyday activities that people protest. Thus workers protest by striking. They are able to do so because they are drawn together in the factory setting, and their protests consist mainly in defying the rules and authorities associated with the workplace. The unemployed do not and cannot strike, even when they perceive that those who own the factories and businesses are to blame for their troubles. Instead, they riot in the streets where they are forced to linger, or storm the relief centers, and it is difficult to imagine them doing otherwise. *It is our second general point, then, that the opportunities for defiance are structured by features of institutional life. Simply put, people cannot defy institutions to which they have no access, and to which they make no contribution.*

The Limited Impact of Mass Defiance

If mass defiance is neither freely available nor the forms it takes freely determined, it must also be said that it is generally of limited political impact. Still, some forms of protest appear to have more impact than others, thus posing an analytical question of considerable importance. It is a question, however, that analysts of movements, espe-

cially analysts of contemporary American movements, have not generally asked. The literature abounds with studies of the social origins of protestors, the determinants of leadership styles, the struggles to cope with problems of organizational maintenance. Thus protest seems to be wondered about mainly for the many and fascinating aspects of social life which it exposes, but least of all for its chief significance: namely, that it is the means by which the least-privileged seek to wrest concessions from their rulers.

It is our judgment that *the most useful way to think about the effectiveness of protest is to examine the disruptive effects on institutions of different forms of mass defiance, and then to examine the political reverberations of those disruptions.* The impact of mass defiance is, in other words, not so much directly as indirectly felt. Protest is more likely to have a seriously disruptive impact when the protestors play a central role in an institution, and it is more likely to evoke wider political reverberations when powerful groups have large stakes in the disrupted institution. These relationships are almost totally ignored in the literature on social movements; there are no studies that catalogue and examine forms of defiance, the settings in which defiance is acted out, the institutional disruptions that do or do not result, and the varying political reverberations of these institutional disruptions.

The Limits of Institutional Disruption

To refer to an institutional disruption is simply to note the obvious fact that institutional life depends upon conformity with established roles and compliance with established rules. Defiance may thus obstruct the normal operations of institutions. Factories are shut down when workers walk out or sit down; welfare bureaucracies are thrown into chaos when crowds demand relief; landlords may be bankrupted when tenants refuse to pay rent. In each of these cases, *people cease to conform to accustomed institutional roles; they withhold their accustomed cooperation, and by doing so, cause institutional disruptions.*

By our definition, disruption is simply the application of a negative sanction, the withdrawal of a crucial contribution on which others depend, and it is therefore a natural resource for exerting power over others. This form of power is, in fact, regularly employed by individuals and groups linked together in many kinds of cooperative interaction, and particularly by producer groups. Farmers, for example, keep their products off the market in order to force up the price offered by buyers; doctors refuse to provide treatment unless their price is met; oil companies withhold supplies until price concessions are made.

But the amount of leverage that a group gains by applying such negative sanctions is widely variable. Influence depends, first of all, on whether or not the contribution withheld is crucial to others; second, on whether or not those who have been affected by the disruption have resources to be conceded; and third, on whether the obstructionist group can protect itself adequately from reprisals. Once these criteria are stated, it becomes evident that the poor are usually in the least strategic position to benefit from defiance.

Thus, in comparison with most producer groups, the lower classes are often in weak institutional locations to use disruption as a tactic for influence. Many among the lower class are in locations that make their cooperation less than crucial to the operation of major institutions. Those who work in economically marginal enterprises, or who perform marginally necessary functions in major enterprises, or those who are unemployed, do not perform roles on which major institutions depend. Indeed, some of the poor are sometimes so isolated from

significant institutional participation that the only "contribution" they can withhold is that of quiescence in civil life: they can riot.

Moreover, those who manage the institutions in which many of the lower classes find themselves often have little to concede to disruptors. When lower-class groups do play an important role in an institution, as they do in sweatshops or in slum tenements, these institutions—operated as they often are by marginal entrepreneurs—may be incapable of yielding very much in response to disruptive pressure.

Finally, lower-class groups have little ability to protect themselves against reprisals that can be employed by institutional managers. The poor do not have to be historians of the occasions when protestors have been jailed or shot down to understand this point. The lesson of their vulnerability is engraved in everyday life; it is evident in every police beating, in every eviction, in every lost job, in every relief termination. The very labels used to describe defiance by the lower classes—the pejorative labels of illegality and violence—testify to this vulnerability and serve to justify severe reprisals when they are imposed. By taking such labels for granted, we fail to recognize what these events really represent: a structure of political coercion inherent in the everyday life of the lower classes.

Still, if the lower classes do not ordinarily have great disruptive power, and if the use of even that kind of power is not planned, it is the only power they do have. Their use of that power, the weighing of gains and risks, is not calculated in board rooms; it wells up out of the terrible travails that people experience at times of rupture and stress. And at such times, disruptions by the poor may have reverberations that go beyond the institutions in which the disruption is acted out.

The Limits of Political Disruption

It is not the impact of disruptions on particular institutions that finally tests the power of the poor; it is the political impact of these disruptions. At this level, however, a new set of structuring mechanisms intervenes, for the political impact of institutional disruptions is mediated by the electoral-representative system.

Responses to disruption vary depending on electoral conditions. Ordinarily, during periods of stability, governmental leaders have three rather obvious options when an institutional disruption occurs. They may ignore it; they may employ punitive measures against the disruptors; or they may attempt to conciliate them. If the disruptive group has little political leverage in its own right, as is true of lower-class groups, it will either be ignored or repressed. It is more likely to be ignored when the disrupted institution is not central to the society as a whole, or to other more important groups. Thus if men and women run amok, disrupting the fabric of their own communities, as in the immigrant slums of the nineteenth century, the spectacle may be frightening, but it can be contained within the slums; it will not necessarily have much impact on the society as a whole, or on the well-being of other important groups. Similarly, when impoverished mobs demand relief, they may cause havoc in the relief offices, but chaotic relief offices are not a large problem for the society as a whole, or for important groups. Repression is more likely to be employed when central institutions are affected, as when railroad workers struck and rioted in the late nineteenth century, or when the police struck in Boston after the First World War. Either way, to be ignored or punished is what the poor ordinarily expect from government, because these are the responses they ordinarily evoke.

But protest movements do not arise during ordinary periods; they arise when large-scale changes undermine political stability. It is this context, as we said earlier, that gives the poor hope and makes insurgency possible in the first place. It is this context that also makes political leaders somewhat vulnerable to protests by the poor.

At times of rapid economic and social change, political leaders are far less free either to ignore disturbances or to employ punitive measures. At such times, the relationship of political leaders to their constituents is likely to become uncertain. This unsettled state of political affairs makes the regime far more sensitive to disturbances, for it is not only more likely that previously uninvolved groups will be activated—the scope of conflict will be widened, in Schattschneider's terminology—but that the scope of conflict will be widened at a time when political alignments have already become unpredictable.

When a political leadership becomes unsure of its support, even disturbances that are isolated within peripheral institutions cannot be so safely ignored, for the mere appearance of trouble and disorder is more threatening when political alignments are unstable. And when the disrupted institutions are central to economic production or to the stability of social life, it becomes imperative that normal operations be restored if the regime is to maintain support among its constituents. Thus when industrial workers joined in massive strikes during the 1930s, they threatened the entire economy of the nation and, given the electoral instability of the times, threatened the future of the nation's political leadership. Under these circumstances, government could hardly ignore the disturbances. When government is unable to ignore the insurgents, and is unwilling to risk the uncertain repercussions of the use of force, it will make efforts to conciliate and disarm the protestors.

These placating efforts will usually take several forms. First and most obviously, political leaders will offer concessions, or press elites in the private sector to offer concessions, to remedy some of the immediate grievances, both symbolic and tangible, of the disruptive group. Thus mobs of unemployed workers were granted relief in the 1930s; striking industrial workers won higher pay and shorter hours; and angry civil rights demonstrators were granted the right to desegregated public accommodations in the 1960s.

Whether one takes such measures as evidence of the capacity of American political institutions for reform, or brushes them aside as mere tokenism, such concessions were not offered readily by government leaders. In each case, and in some cases more than in others, reform required a break with an established pattern of government accommodation to private elites. Thus the New Deal's liberal relief policy was maintained despite widespread opposition from the business community. Striking workers in the mid-1930s succeeded in obtaining wage concessions from private industry only because state and national political leaders abandoned the age-old policy of using the coercive power of the state to curb strikes. The granting of desegregated public accommodations required that national Democratic leaders turn against their traditional allies among southern plantation elites. In such instances concessions were won by the protestors only when political leaders were finally forced, out of a concern for their own survival, to act in ways which aroused the fierce opposition of economic elites. In short, under conditions of severe electoral instability, the alliance of public and private power is sometimes weakened, if only briefly, and at these moments a defiant poor may make gains.

Second, political leaders, or elites allied with them, will try to quiet disturbances not only by dealing with immediate grievances, but by making efforts to channel the energies and angers of the protestors into more legitimate and less disruptive forms of political behavior, in part by offering incentives to movement leaders or, in other words, by co-opting them. Thus relief demonstrators in both the 1930s and the 1960s were encouraged to learn to use administrative grievance procedures as an alternative to "merely" disrupting relief offices, while their leaders were offered positions as advisors to relief administrators. In the 1960s civil rights organizers left the streets to take jobs in the Great Society programs; and as rioting spread in the northern cities, street leaders in the ghettos were encouraged to join in "dialogues" with municipal officials, and some were offered positions in municipal agencies.

Third, the measures promulgated by government at times of disturbance may be designed not to conciliate the protestors, but to undermine whatever sympathy the protesting group has been able to command from a wider public. Usually this is achieved through new programs that appear to meet the moral demands of the movement, and thus rob it of support without actually yielding much by way of tangible gains.

Finally, these apparently conciliatory measures make it possible for government to safely employ repressive measures as well. Typically, leaders and groups who are more disruptive, or who spurn the concessions offered, are singled out for arbitrary police action or for more formal legal harassment through congressional investigations or through the courts. In the context of much-publicized efforts by government to ease the grievances of disaffected groups, coercive measures of this kind are not likely to arouse indignation among sympathetic publics. Indeed, this dual strategy is useful in another way, for it serves to cast an aura of balance and judiciousness over government action.

The main point, however, is simply that *the political impact of institutional disruptions depends upon electoral conditions.* Even serious disruptions, such as industrial strikes, will force concessions only when the calculus of electoral instability favors the protestors. And even then, when the protestors succeed in forcing government to respond, they do not dictate the content of those responses. As to the variety of specific circumstances which determine how much the protestors will gain and how much they will lose, we still have a great deal to learn.

The Demise of Protest

It is not surprising that, taken together, these efforts to conciliate and disarm usually lead to the demise of the protest movement, partly by transforming the movement itself, and partly by transforming the political climate which nourishes protest. With these changes, the array of institutional controls which ordinarily restrain protest is restored, and political influence is once more denied to the lower class.

We said that one form of government response was to make concessions to the protestors, yielding them something of what they demanded, either symbolic or material. But the mere granting of such concessions is probably not very important in accounting for the demise of a movement. For one thing, whatever is yielded is usually modest if not meager; for another, even modest concessions demonstrate that protest "works," a circumstance that might as easily be expected to fuel a movement as to pacify it.

But concessions are rarely unencumbered. If they are given at all, they are usually part and parcel of measures to reintegrate the movement into normal political channels and to absorb its leaders into stable institutional roles. This feature of government action deserves some explanation because the main reintegrative measures—the right to organize, the right to vote, black representation in city government—were also responses to specific demands made by the protestors themselves. To all appearances, government simply acted to redress felt grievances. But the process was by no means as straightforward as that. As we suggested earlier, the movements had arisen through interaction with elites, and had been led to make the demands they made in response to early encouragement by political leaders. Nor was it fortuitous that political leaders came to proclaim as just such causes as the right to organize or the right to vote or the right to "citizen participation." In each case, elites responded to discontent by proposing reforms with which they had experience, and which consisted mainly of extending established procedures to new groups or to new institutional arenas. Collective bargaining was not invented in the 1930s, nor the franchise in the 1960s. Driven by turmoil, political leaders proposed reforms that were in a sense prefigured by institutional arrangements that already existed, that were drawn from a repertoire provided by existing traditions. And an aroused people responded by demanding simply what political leaders had said they should have. If through some accident of history they had done otherwise, if industrial workers had demanded public ownership of factories, they would probably have still gotten unionism, if they got anything at all; and if impoverished southern blacks had demanded land reform, they would probably have still gotten the vote.

At the same time that government makes efforts to reintegrate disaffected groups, and to guide them into less politically disturbing forms of behavior, it also moves to isolate them from potential supporters and, by doing so, diminishes the morale of the movement. Finally, while the movement is eroding under these influences, its leaders attracted by new opportunities, its followers conciliated, confused, or discouraged, the show of repressive force against recalcitrant elements demolishes the few who are left.

However, the more far-reaching changes do not occur within the movement, but in the political context which nourished the movement in the first place. The agitated and defiant people who compose the movement are but a small proportion of the discontented population on which it draws. Presumably if some leaders were coopted, new leaders would arise; if some participants were appeased or discouraged, others would take their place. But this does not happen, because government's responses not only destroy the movement, they also transform the political climate which makes protest possible. The concessions to the protestors, the efforts to "bring them into the system," and in particular the measures aimed at potential supporters, all work to create a powerful image of a benevolent and responsive government that answers grievances and solves problems. As a result, whatever support might have existed among the larger population dwindles. Moreover, the display of government benevolence stimulates antagonist groups, and triggers the antagonistic sentiments of more neutral sectors. The "tide of public opinion" begins to turn—against labor in the late 1930s, against blacks in the late 1960s. And as it does, the definitions put forward by political leaders also change, particularly when prodded by contenders for political office who sense the shift in popular mood, and

the weaknesses it reveals in an incumbent's support. Thus in the late 1960s, Republican leaders took advantage of white resentment against blacks to attract Democratic voters, raising cries of "law and order" and "workfare not welfare"—the code words for racial antagonism. Such a change is ominous. Where once the powerful voices of the land enunciated a rhetoric that gave courage to the poor, now they enunciate a rhetoric that erases hope, and implants fear. The point should be evident that as these various circumstances combine, defiance is no longer possible.

The Residue of Reform

When protest subsides, concessions may be withdrawn. Thus when the unemployed become docile, the relief rolls are cut even though many are still unemployed; when the ghetto becomes quiescent, evictions are resumed. The reason is simple enough. Since the poor no longer pose the threat of disruption, they no longer exert leverage on political leaders; there is no need for conciliation. This is particularly the case in a climate of growing political hostility, for the concessions granted are likely to become the focus of resentment by other groups.

But some concessions are not withdrawn. As the tide of turbulence recedes, major institutional changes sometimes remain. Thus the right of workers to join unions was not rescinded when turmoil subsided (although some of the rights ceded to unions were withdrawn). And it is not likely that the franchise granted to blacks in the South will be taken back (although just that happened in the post-Reconstruction period). Why, then, are some concessions withdrawn while others become permanent institutional reforms?

The answer, perhaps, is that while some of the reforms granted during periods of turmoil are costly or repugnant to various groups in the society, and are therefore suffered only under duress, other innovations turn out to be compatible (or at least not incompatible) with the interests of more powerful groups, most importantly with the interests of dominant economic groups. Such an assertion has the aura of a conspiracy theory, but in fact the process is not conspiratorial at all. Major industrialists had resisted unionization, but once forced to concede it as the price of industrial peace, they gradually discovered that labor unions constituted a useful mechanism to regulate the labor force. The problem of disciplining industrial labor had been developing over the course of a century. The depression produced the political turmoil through which a solution was forged. Nor was the solution simply snatched from the air. As noted earlier, collective bargaining was a tried and tested method of dealing with labor disturbances. The tumult of the 1930s made the use of this method imperative; once implemented, the reforms were institutionalized because they continued to prove useful.

Similarly, southern economic elites had no interest in ceding southern blacks the franchise. But their stakes in disenfranchising blacks had diminished. The old plantation economy was losing ground to new industrial enterprises; plantation-based elites were losing ground to economic dominants based in industry. The feudal political arrangements on which a plantation economy had relied were no longer of central importance, and certainly they were not of central importance to the new economic elites. Black uprisings, by forcing the extension of the franchise and the modernization of southern politics, thus helped seal a fissure in the institutional fabric of American society, a fissure resulting from the growing inconsistency between the economic and political institutions of the South.

What these examples suggest is that *protestors win, if they win at all, what historical circumstances has already made ready to be conceded.* Still, as Alan Wolfe has said, governments do not change magically through some "historical radical transformation," but only through the actual struggles of the time (154). When people are finally roused to protest against great odds, they take the only options available to them within the limits imposed by their social circumstances. Those who refuse to recognize these limits not only blindly consign lower-class protests to the realm of the semirational, but also blindly continue to pretend that other, more regular options for political influence are widely available in the American political system.

A Note on the Role of Protest Leadership

The main point of this chapter is that both the limitations and opportunities for mass protest are shaped by social conditions. The implications for the role of leadership in protest movements can be briefly summarized.

Protest wells tip in response to momentous changes in the institutional order. It is not created by organizers and leaders.

Once protest erupts, the specific forms it takes are largely determined by features of social structure. Organizers and leaders who contrive strategies that ignore the social location of the people they seek to mobilize can only fail.

Elites respond to the institutional disruptions that protest causes, as well as to other powerful institutional imperatives. Elite responses are not significantly shaped by the demands of leaders and organizers. Nor are elite responses significantly shaped by formally structured organizations of the poor.

Whatever influence lower-class groups occasionally exert in American politics does not result from organization, but from mass protest and the disruptive consequences of protest.

Finally, protest in the United States has been episodic and transient, for as it gains momentum, so too do various forms of institutional accommodation and coercion that have the effect of restoring quiescence. Organizers and leaders cannot prevent the ebbing of protest, nor the erosion of whatever influence protest yielded the lower class. They can only try to win whatever can be won while it can be won.

In these major ways protest movements are shaped by institutional conditions, and not by the purposive efforts of leaders and organizers. The limitations are large and unyielding. Yet within the boundaries created by these limitations, some latitude for purposive effort remains. Organizers and leaders choose to do one thing, or they choose to do another, and what they choose to do affects to some degree the course of the protest movement. If the area of latitude is less than leaders and organizers would prefer, it is also not enlarged when they proceed as if institutional limitations did not in fact exist by undertaking strategies which fly in the face of these constraints. The wiser course is to understand these limitations, and to exploit whatever latitude remains to enlarge the potential influence of the lower class. And if our conclusions are correct, what this means is that strategies must be pursued that escalate the momentum and impact of disruptive protest at each stage in its emergence and evolution.

REFERENCES

Anderson, Gosta Esping, and Friedland, Roger. "Class Structure, Class Politics and the Capitalist State." Madison: University of Wisconsin, September 1974, mimeographed.

Ash, Roberta. *Social Movements in America.* Chicago: Markham Publishing Co., 1972.

Balbus, Isaac D. "The Concept of Interest in Pluralist and Marxian Analysis." *Politics and Society* 1 (1971).

Bloom, Howard S., and Price, Douglas H. "Voter Response to Short-Run Economic Conditions: The Asymmetric Effect of Prosperity and Recession." *American Political Science Review* 69 (December 1975).

Bridges, Amy. "Nicos Poulantzas and the Marxist Theory of the State." *Politics and Society* 4 (Winter 1974).

Burnham, Walter Dean. "The Changing Shape of the American Political Universe." *American Political Science Review* 59 (1965).

———. *Critical Elections and the Mainsprings of American Politics.* New York: W. W. Norton and Co., 1970.

Campbell, Angus; Converse, Philip E.; Miller, Warren E.; and Stokes, Donald E. *The American Voter.* New York: John Wiley & Sons, 1960.

Castells, Manuel. "L' Analyse Interdisciplinaire de la Croissance Urbaine." Paper presented at a colloquium of the Centre National de la Recherche Scientifique, June 1–4, 1971, in Toulouse.

Dahrendorf, Ralf. *Class and Class Conflict in Industrial Society.* Stanford: Stanford University Press, 1959.

Davies, James C. "Toward a Theory of Revolution." *American Sociological Review* 27 (1962).

Dollard, John, et al. *Frustration and Aggression.* New Haven: Yale University Press, 1939.

Edelman, Murray. *Politics as Symbolic Action.* New Haven: Yale University Press, 1971.

Engels, Frederick. "Socialism: Utopian and Scientific." In *Engels: Selected Writings,* edited by W. O. Henderson. Baltimore: Penguin Books, 1967.

———. "Introduction to Karl Marx's 'The Class Struggles in France, 1848–1850.'" In *Selected Works,* Vol. 1, by Karl Marx and Frederick Engels. New York: International Publishers, 1970.

Feierabend, Ivo; Feierabend, Rosalind L.; and Nesvold, Betty A. "Social Change and Political Violence: Cross National Patterns." In *Violence in America: A Staff Report,* edited by Hugh Davis Graham and Ted Robert Gurr. Washington, D.C.: U. S. Government Printing Office, 1969.

Flacks, Richard. "Making History vs. Making Life: Dilemmas of an American Left." *Working Papers for a New Society* 2 (Summer 1974).

Gamson, William A. *The Strategy of Social Protest.* Homewood, Illinois: Dorsey Press, 1975.

Geschwender, James. "Social Structure and the Negro Revolt: An Examination of Some Hypotheses." *Social Forces* 3 (December 1964).

Gordon, David M.; Edwards, Richard C.; and Reich, Michael. "Labor Market Segmentation in American Capitalism." Paper presented at the Conference on Labor Market Segmentation, March 16–17, 1973, at Harvard University.

Gurr, Ted Robert. "Psychological Factors in Civil Violence." *World Politics* 20 (January 1968).

——. *Why Men Rebel.* Princeton, N.J.: Princeton University Press, 1970.

Gusfield, Joseph R., ed. *Protest, Reform and Revolt: A Reader in Social Movements.* New York: John Wiley & Sons, 1970.

Hobsbawm, Eric. *Primitive Rebels.* New York: W. W. Norton and Co., 1963.

——, and Rudé, George. *Captain Swing.* New York: Pantheon Books, 1968.

Howard, Dick, ed. *Selected Writings of Rosa Luxemburg.* New York: Monthly Review Press, 1971.

Huntington, Samuel P. *Political Order in Changing Societies.* New Haven: Yale University Press, 1968.

James, C. L. R.; Lee, Grace C.; and Chaulieu, Pierre. *Facing Reality.* Detroit: Bewick Editions, 1974.

Katznelson, Ira. "The Crisis of the Capitalist City: Urban Politics and Social Control." In *Theoretical Perspectives in Urban Politics,* edited by W. D. Hawley and Michael Lipsky. New York: Prentice-Hall, 1976.

Kornhauser, William. *The Politics of Mass Society.* New York: The Free Press, 1959.

Kramer, Gerald H. "Short-Term Fluctuations in U. S. Voting Behavior, 1896–1964." *American Political Science Review* 65 (March 1971).

Lefebvre, Henry. *Everyday Life in the Modern World.* London: Allen Lane, The Penguin Press, 1971.

Lipsky, Michael. "Protest as a Political Resource." *American Political Science Review* 62 (December 1968).

——. *Protest in City Politics.* Chicago: Rand McNally, 1970.

Lodhi, Abdul Qaiyum, and Tilly, Charles. "Urbanization, Crime, and Collective Violence in 19th Century France." *American Journal of Sociology* 79 (September 1973).

Lupsha, Peter A. "Explanation of Political Violence: Some Psychological Theories Versus Indignation." *Politics and Society* 2 (Fall 1971).

Luxemburg, Rosa. "Mass Strike Party and Trade Unions." In *Selected Writings of Rosa Luxemburg,* edited by Dick Howard. New York: Monthly Review Press, 1971.

Marx, Karl. *The Eighteenth Brumaire of Louis Bonaparte.* New York: International Publishers, 1963.

——, and Engels, Frederick. *Manifesto of the Communist Party.* New York: International Publishers, 1948.

Michels, Robert. *Political Parties.* Glencoe: The Free Press, 1949.

Moore, Barrington. "Revolution in America?" *New York Review of Books,* January 30, 1969.

Ollman, Bertell. "Toward Class Consciousness Next Time: Marx and the Working Class." *Politics and Society* 3 (Fall 1972).

Parsons, Talcott. *The Social System.* New York: The Free Press, 1951.

——. "An Outline of the Social System." In *Theories of Society: Foundations of Modern Sociological Thought,* edited by Talcott Parsons, Edward Shils, Kaspar D. Naegele, and Jesse R. Pitts. New York: The Free Press, 1965.

Poulantzas, Nicos. *Political Power and Social Classes.* London: New Left Books and Sheed and Ward, Ltd., 1973.

Rudé, George. *The Crowd in History.* New York: John Wiley & Sons, 1964.

Rustin, Bayard. "From Protest to Politics." *Commentary* 39 (February 1965).

Schattschneider, E. E. *The Semi-Sovereign People.* New York: Holt, Rinehart, and Winston, 1960.

Schwartz, Michael. "The Southern Farmers' Alliance: The Organizational Forms of Radical Protest." Unpublished Ph.D. dissertation, Department of Sociology, Harvard University, 1971.

Smelser, Neil J. *Theory of Collective Behavior.* New York: The Free Press, 1962.

Snyder, David, and Tilly, Charles. "Hardship and Collective Violence in France, 1830–1960." *American Sociological Review* 37 (October 1972).

Spencer, Joseph; McLoughlin, John; and Lawson, Ronald. "New York City Tenant Organizations and the Formation of Urban Housing Policy, 1919 to 1933." Unpublished paper of The Tenant Movement Study, New York, Center for Policy Research, 1975.

Tilly, Charles. "Reflections on the Revolution of Paris: A Review of Recent Historical Writing." *Social Problems* 12 (Summer 1964).

Useem, Michael. *Conscription, Protest and Social Conflict: The Life and Death of a Draft Resistance Movement.* New York: John Wiley & Sons, 1973.

———. *Protest Movements In America.* Indianapolis: Bobbs-Merrill, 1975.

Weber, Max. *Essays in Sociology.* Translated, edited, and with an Introduction by H. H. Gerth and C. Wright Mills. New York: Oxford University Press, 1946.

Wilson, James Q. *Political Organizations.* New York: Basic Books, 1973.

Wilson, John. *Introduction to Social Movements.* New York: Basic Books, 1973.

Wolfe, Alan. "New Directions in the Marxist Theory of Politics." *Politics and Society* 4 (Winter 1974).

Zald, Mayer N., and Ash, Roberta "Social Movement Organizations: Growth, Decay, and Change." *Social Forces* 44 (March 1966).

21

POTENTIALS, NETWORKS, MOTIVATIONS, AND BARRIERS
Steps Towards Participation in Social Movements

BERT KLANDERMANS • DIRK OEGEMA

Social movements entail forming mobilization potentials, forming and motivating recruitment networks, arousing motivation to participate, and removing barriers to participation. It is important to distinguish these processes because they not only require very different activities of social movement organizations but they also require different theories of analysis. To create mobilization potentials, a social movement must win attitudinal support. The formation and activation of recruitment networks must increase the probability that people who are potentially mobilizable become targets of mobilization attempts. The arousal of motivation must favorably influence the propensity to participate of the targeted people. In removing barriers a movement organization increases the proba-

bility that motivated people eventually participate.

At the individual level, becoming a participant in a social movement can be conceived as a process with four different steps: becoming part of the mobilization potential, becoming the target of mobilization attempts, becoming motivated to participate, and overcoming barriers to participate. The first two steps are necessary conditions for the arousal of motivation. Motivation and barriers interact to bring about participation: the more motivated people are, the higher the barriers they can overcome.

Mobilization Potential

Mobilization potential refers to the people in a society who could be mobilized by a social movement. It consists of those who take a positive stand toward a particular social movement. Attitudes toward a move-

From *American Sociological Review*, 52 (August, 1987) pp. 519–531. Reprinted by permission of American Sociological Association.

ment involve the means and/or goals of the movement. With respect to attitudes toward the means, the concept of mobilization potential is related to that of protest potential, that is, the willingness to become engaged in unconventional forms of political behavior (Barnes and Kaase 1979). With respect to attitudes toward the goals, the concept of mobilization potential is related to Kriesi's (1985) concept of manifest political potential, that is, a group of people with a common identity and a set of common goals. The mobilization potential of a social movement is not identical to the social categories who will benefit by achievement of the goals of the movement (cf. McCarthy and Zald 1976; Jenkins and Perrow 1977), although such categories can easily become included. The mobilization potential of a social movement sets the limits within which a mobilization campaign can succeed. People who are not part of the mobilization potential will not consider participating in movement activities, even if they are reached by attempts at mobilization. The mobilization potential is the reservoir the movement can draw from. It is the result of often lengthy campaigns in which a movement propagates its view that certain states of affairs are unacceptable and can be changed and that collective action will be effective in enforcing changes. Campaigns like this, called consensus mobilization (Klandermans 1984) or frame alignment (Snow et al. 1986), are needed to convert relative deprivation or lack of trust in authorities into mobilization potential (Gurney and Tierney 1982).

Recruitment Networks and Mobilization Attempts

However successfully a movement mobilizes consensus, however large its mobilization potential, if it does not have access to recruitment networks, its mobilization potential cannot be realized. Networks condition whether people become targets of mobilization attempts. The more a movement's reach-out networks are woven into other organizations, the more people are reached by mobilization attempts.

A person can be targeted by mobilization attempts through one or more of the following routes: mass media, direct mail, ties with organizations, and friendship ties. The mass media are not very effective in convincing and activating people (McQuail 1983). McCarthy (1983) and Mitchell (1984) revealed how American environmental organizations managed to make effective use of direct mail to recruit participants. But recruitment through mass media and direct mail is less likely to work in cases of high-risk or high-cost participation (McAdam 1986a; Briet et al. 1987). Ties with organizations make "en bloc recruitment" possible (Oberschall 1973).

The importance of friendship networks for reaching potential participants has been repeatedly indicated in the literature. Gerlach and Hine (1970) found that people were much more inclined to join religious movements if they were approached by those whom they trusted on other grounds. Bolton (1972) showed how new members of peace groups were recruited in circles with a high proportion of people who were already members. Orum (1974) and Wilson and Orum (1976) pointed out the importance of friends or relatives who were already involved in a movement to explain participation. The introduction of network analysis in this field made more systematic analyses possible (Snow, Zurcher, and Ekland-Olson 1980; Knoke and Wood 1981; Granovetter 1983; Fernandez and McAdam 1989).

The formation of recruitment networks involves both extending the reaches of the organization, particularly at a local level, and forming coalitions with other organizations (Wilson and Orum 1976; Ferree and Miller 1985). During a mobilization campaign a movement organization has to mobilize and activate its recruitment networks by mobilizing persons who hold positions in it. When such persons back out, recruitment channels come to a dead end.

Motivation to Participate

The motivation to participate is a function of the perceived costs and benefits of participation (Oberschall 1973, 1980; Klandermans 1984; Muller and Opp 1986). The distinction between collective and selective incentives is fundamental (Olson 1965). With respect to collective incentives, a multiplicative relationship is assumed between the value of the collective good and the expectancy of success. Selective incentives are either soft (nonmaterial) or social, and hard (material) or nonsocial (Opp 1983; Klandermans 1984; McAdam 1986b). Soft or social incentives are important determinants of willingness to participate (Mitchell 1979; Opp 1983; Klandermans 1984; McAdam 1986b). Outcomes with respect to hard or nonsocial incentives are more ambiguous. Opp (1983) found that such incentives were important in activities in the antinuclear movement in the former West Germany. Klandermans (1984) found a moderate effect in union participation, and Mitchell (1979) found no effect in American environmental organizations. Differences in the nature of the participation seem relevant. Mitchell's case clearly involved low-cost participation, Opp's involved high costs, and Klanderman's moderate costs.

On the part of the movement the arousal of motivation requires control of costs and benefits of participation. In fact, since it is *perceived* costs and benefits, control is not sufficient. Movements must commu-nicate to potential participants the extent to which collective and selective incentives are controlled by the movement. Consequently, the mobilization of consensus is also an essential part of this stage of the mobilization process.

Barriers to Participation

Motivation can predict willingness to participate, but willingness is a necessary but insufficient condition of participation. It can predict participation when intentions can be carried out (Mitchell 1974). Motivation and barriers interact to activate participation. The more people are motivated, the higher the barriers they can overcome. This opens up two strategies for a movement: maintaining or increasing motivation and/or removing barriers. The former strategy is, of course, closely related to the arousal of motivation; the latter requires knowledge of barriers and resources to remove them. Although every organizer knows that many people do not participate despite their promises, there is little empirical data on actual participation. McAdam (1986a showed that among applicants to Freedom Summer Rides, those who eventually participated knew more participants than those who did not. He did not provide data on barriers, however. Klandermans (1984) and Klaassen (1986) asserted that nonparticipants who definitely intended to go to a union meeting mentioned more concrete obstacles than nonparticipants who were less motivated to go. Scarcity of empirical evidence reflects the lack of longitudinal studies on intended and actual participation. Post hoc comparison of participants and nonparticipants is inadequate in this regard.

In this paper we present data on all four steps of the mobilization process from a mobilization campaign for the peace demonstration in The Hague in 1983, the largest demonstration the Netherlands had ever experienced.

The 1983 Peace Demonstration in The Hague

On October 29, 1983, 1 out of every 25 inhabitants of the Netherlands joined the largest demonstration the country had ever seen. This was the climax of a campaign against nuclear armament started five years before. Nobody would have expected this event in the early seventies when the peace movement had all but died.

The structure and constituency of the contemporary peace movement differed from those that had appeared earlier: The movement was comprised of four national organizations (The Interdenominational Peace Council (IKV), Stop the Neutron Bomb, Women for Peace, Pax Christi) and a number of smaller groups. Hundreds of active local groups formed the base of the movement. Although most of these groups were connected with one of the national organizations, they were autonomous in defining their activities. Since over half of the communities in the Netherlands had at least one active peace group, the peace movement had at its disposal a network extending to the furthest reaches of the country. Local groups played a key role in the mobilization campaigns and were capable of mobilizing unprecedented support: 1.2 million signatures against the neutron bomb in 1978; 400,000 participants in an Amsterdam demonstration in 1981; 500,000 participants in a 1983 demonstration at The Hague; 800,000 participants in local peace week activities in 1984; and 3.75 million signatures against the deployment of cruise missiles in 1985. To evaluate these figures it is instructive to consider

that the Netherlands has a population of 14 million.

NATO's decision to deploy cruise missiles and Pershing IIs in Europe contributed to the rapid growth of the peace movement. The Achilles heel of the NATO decision was that each European government had to decide individually whether and where to locate the missiles. This gave the Dutch peace movement a concrete goal and a target to concentrate on: the prevention of the deployment of cruise missiles in the Netherlands and the Dutch government, which would ultimately have to decide whether and where to deploy.

From 1981 on, mobilization campaigns were organized by a coalition of political and social organizations. Apart from the four major peace organizations, the center-left and leftist political parties and the largest union federation formed a coalition that organized the campaign for the 1983 demonstration. Despite initial exploratory contacts, the Christian Democratic Party did not enter the coalition. At the local level, coalitions of local peace groups and organizations mobilized the population. The rest of this article is devoted to one such local campaign. We describe how it attempted to activate and expand the local recruitment network and to mobilize the population for the demonstration. This part of the article is based on a study carried out between January and November 1983.

The Campaign at the Local Level

Mobilization attempts often occur at different levels. National leaders of a movement mobilize local cadres, and local cadres mobilize others inside or outside the organization. Sometimes these persons represent other local organizations, which in turn attempt to mobilize members of their own organizations. Each step involves new interactions and new actors who have to decide whether they will participate. Here we briefly describe the campaign as it penetrated our research locale, a town in the environs of Amsterdam, which we call Smalltown. Here the first level of mobilization—mobilization of the local peace group, in this case a local chapter of the Interdenominational Peace Council—went without problems. Early in January, the national IKV announced its plan to hold a national demonstration on October 29 in The Hague. Part of the local mobilization campaigns was to assemble as many relevant local organizations as possible in a peace platform and to mobilize the local population. The local IKV group showed an unquestioning willingness to do this. The second stage, activating and expanding the recruitment network by mobilizing local political and social organizations, was much more difficult. Following the general IKV strategy, the IKV group set out to organize a peace platform. Every local organization was approached by letter announcing the formation of a peace platform, stating its goals, and inviting participation. At the first meeting on April 18, 1983, 30 people representing 13 organizations attended; ultimately 8 joined, including 3 out of the 5 parties (the Christian Democrats and the Conservatives did not participate), an organization of elderly people, a youth organization, and a women's organization. In not participating, the Christian Democrats and the Conservatives conformed to their national party organizations, who were opposed to the movement's goals. The women's organization and the youth organization decided to support the peace platform because they agreed with its goals and did not expect any problem with national leadership or local membership. The organization of elderly citizens and the union decided to withhold support until the first meeting. Later, the elderly citizens' organization joined, but the union local did not. Both organizations feared problems with their membership. Unlike the elderly organization, the union decided to withdraw for this reason. Altogether, the local IKV group assembled those organizations (with the exception of the union local) that already supported the peace platform but did not mobilize the others. This in turn was critical to the local mobilization campaign.

The proximate goal of the peace platform was to send two buses (100 people) to the demonstration. To keep financial thresholds low, the platform committee worked hard to get a cheap bus fare. Most of the effort, however, was put into publicity: distributing pamphlets; selling buttons, stickers, and posters; erecting a publicity stand downtown; sending a carrier tricycle with speakers around town; and securing local news coverage. This was reinforced by a national publicity campaign. By the end of June, the local campaign was in full swing. By late September, 75 bus tickets had been sold, and eventually three buses (150 people) went to the demonstration. An unknown number also went independently. The week before the demonstration, the authors conducted a telephone survey among a random sample of the local population to determine the support for the IKV campaign. Respondents were asked if they intended to participate in the demonstration. After the demonstration, they were asked in a follow-up survey if they had been to the demonstration. The remainder of this article analyzes both surveys.

Method

Telephone surveys have both advantages and disadvantages. The main reasons for us to use telephone surveys rather than

face-to-face interviews or mailed questionnaires were time and money. Telephone
surveys are relatively cheap and easy to
organize at short notice. Moreover, one has
a better control over time. In our case it was
important to conduct the survey in exactly
3 days before the demonstration. Mailed
questionnaires lack this precision, and face-
to-face interviewing is too time consuming.
The major disadvantage of telephone sur-
veying is of course bias due to the fact that
there are households without a telephone.
Fortunately, in the case of Smalltown this is
not too serious a problem. A suburban
community, Smalltown, has an extremely
low proportion of households without a
telephone. There may be some bias in our
sample, but not an alarming one.

Less important as a drawback are response rates. Although higher than those
with mailed questionnaires, response rates
of telephone surveys lag behind those of
face-to-face interviews. Adopting one of
Frey's (1983) devices, we sent an initial letter
informing respondents that they would be
contacted for an interview. In this way we
were able to attain reasonable response rates.
Since we needed the combination of telephone numbers *and* addresses for this strategy, we used telephone books to draw our
sample. This has the disadvantage of missing unlisted telephone numbers (fortunately
not yet widespread in the Netherlands) but
the advantage that private numbers can be
distinguished from business numbers.

We mailed letters to 175 randomly selected addresses a few days before the interviews asking the addressees to cooperate. In 9 cases there was no answer after
repeated attempts to reach the addressees.
No interview could be made in 52 cases for
various reasons (refusals, illness, impossible to make an appointment). Ultimately
114 (69 percent) interviews were held.
After the demonstration we reached three-

TABLE 21.1 Party Votes

	Sample Votes (%)	Population of Smalltown (%)
VVD	28	34
CDA	22	29
D66	5	5
PvdA	30	22
Small Left	10	6
Others	5	4
	100	100
Total	(94)	

Note: VVD: Volksparty voor Vrijheid en Democratie
(conservatives); CDA: Christelijk Democratisch Appèl
(Christian Democrats); D66: Democraten 66 (Progressive Democrats); PvdA: Party van de Arbeid (Social
Democrats).

quarters of our original respondents for a
second interview. Respondents who had
said they would go to the demonstration
were asked if they had actually done so.
Unfortunately, for some unexplained reason, those reached included only half of
the respondents who had said they would
go to the demonstration. Both interviews
lasted about 15 minutes. We used structured questionnaires, asking about collective and selective costs and benefits of participation, attitudes on nuclear armament,
peace movement goals, government policies, and demographics. Forty-four percent
of the respondents were women, 55 percent
men. The average age was 44.4 (s.d. = 16.9).
Respondents were normally distributed
over educational levels. Compared to the
local statistics in recent elections respondents sympathetic to left or center-left parties were slightly overrepresented (Table
21.1). Obviously, such a small sample cannot be used to draw firm conclusions about
the Dutch population as a whole. Our object
here is to examine processes affecting selective recruitment to collective action.

Measurement

1. *Mobilization potential.* The following question was used to determine whether individuals belonged to the mobilization potential of the peace movement: "The coming demonstration is directed against deployment of cruise missiles in Europe, and especially against deployment in the Netherlands. How do you feel about this goal of the demonstration?" Respondents could disagree absolutely, disagree, agree, and agree absolutely. Only two respondents had no opinion. Respondents who agreed with the goal of the demonstration were assigned to the mobilization potential of the movement.

2. *Mobilization target.* Whether persons were targets of mobilization attempts was deduced from their answers to several questions. We assumed that people who had never heard of the local IKV group, nor of the peace platform in their community, and who did not know any individual who was planning to take part in the demonstration, were not targets of mobilization attempts. Although they might have been contacted in national appeals, our concern was the effectiveness of the local campaign.

3. *Motivations.* The motivation to participate was ascertained by asking the following question: "Do you plan to go to the demonstration?" (Yes, I intend to go; no, I will not go.)

4. *Participation.* Actual participation was measured from the second interview.

5. *Attitudes.* Attitudes toward peace and war were measured by questions regarding NATO, governmental policy, the negotiations in Geneva, and the influence of the Dutch government on the arms race.

6. *Incentives.* Collective benefits were measured by questions about the effectiveness of the demonstration both in terms of changing the policy of the government and in terms of the number of participants. Together with the attitude toward the goal of the demonstration, they indicate the collective benefits of the demonstration. Social incentives were measured by asking about the expected reactions of significant others and by asking if many friends and acquaintances would go to the demonstration. The nonsocial selective incentives were captured by the perceived value of sacrifice of leisure and the risk of violence.

7. *Participation barriers.* Respondents who intended to go to the demonstration, but eventually did not go, were asked why they did not go. This was an open-ended question.

8. *Leftism of party vote.* Party votes in recent elections were ascertained. Table 21.1 presents the parties that were present in Smalltown, ordered on a right-left continuum, together with the distribution of votes in the last election of the population in Smalltown and our respondents. The figures indicate that people voting for parties to the left are overrepresented at the expense of voters for parties to the right. Our voting behavior variable indicates a person's rightism vs. leftism of party vote, ranging from –1 (VVD/CDA), 0 (D66/PvdA) to –1 (Small Left).

9. *Demographics.* Sex, age, and education of respondents were recorded.

Results

The major research findings are summarized in Figure 21.1. Twenty-six percent of those interviewed did not belong to the mobilization potential of the peace movement; 74 percent did. About one-fifth of those were not targets of a mobilization

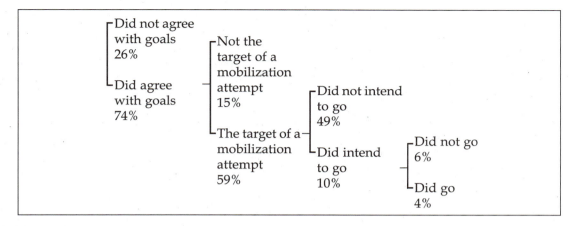

FIGURE 21.1   Mobilization Potential, Recruitment Networks, Motivations to Participate, and Actual Participation (*N* = 114)

attempt, whereas four-fifths were. One-sixth of those who supported the campaign *and* who were targets of mobilization attempts actually intended to go to the demonstration. Two-fifths of those who intended to go to the demonstration eventually did go, whereas three-fifths did not.

These results suggest some preliminary conclusions. With each step of the mobilization process, considerable numbers drop out. This underscores the importance of the four conditions that we distinguished. Those who had not been targets of a mobilization attempt were without exception unwilling to participate, regardless of their opinion of the goals of the demonstration. The fact that three-fifths of those who, only a few days before the demonstration, had said that they intended to go, eventually did not go, underscores the importance of overcoming participation barriers. The biggest drop-off occurs, however, in the motivation stage. Here almost half of the sample got lost. Clearly, the local movement organization has been unable to arouse motivation to participate on a large scale. In the following paragraphs we exam-

ine each of the four steps and their determinants.

The Mobilization Potential

Almost three-quarters of the respondents were involved in the mobilization potential of the movement against cruise missiles, and one quarter was not. Respondents who did not belong to the mobilization potential were somewhat older, and voted almost without exception for parties to the right. No differences in education and gender were found (Table 21.2).

The attitudinal comparisons validate the distinction between the two groups. Individuals from the mobilization potential were more concerned about deployment, more inclined to fight against deployment even if a decision were made to deploy, and, contrary to individuals outside the potential, announced almost without exception that they would sign a petition to pass a freeze motion in their town. The two groups did not differ with regard to their views on the possibility to control the arms race either through efforts by the Dutch government

TABLE 21.2   Demographic and Attitudinal Comparison of People within and outside the Mobilization Potential of the Peace Movement (Means and Standard Deviations)

	Belongs to Mobilization Potential			
	Yes		No	
Demographics				
Age	43.1	(18.2)	49.6*	(13.6)
Gender (male = 2)	1.5	(.50)	1.6	(.49)
Education	5.3	(2.65)	5.9	(2.77)
Vote in last election (rightist/center right = –1; center left = 0; leftist = 1)	–.25	(.69)	–.96**	(.20)
Attitudinal				
Is deployment a matter of deep concern to you? (no = 1, yes = 3)	2.50	(.57)	2.24*	(.74)
If deployment is pushed through, will you continue to fight against it (3), accept it regretfully (2), or approve it (1)?	2.66	(.50)	1.68**	(.48)
Does the Dutch government have any opportunity to influence the arms race? (no = 1, many = 3)	1.74	(.52)	1.76	(.51)
Do you believe that the negotiations in Geneva will lead eventually to arms reduction? (definitely not = 1, definitely = 4)	1.81	(.90)	2.04	(1.00)
Would you sign a petition to pass a freeze motion in your city council? (no = 0, yes = 1)	.86	(.35)	.08**	(.27)

Note: $N = 109$.   *$p < .10$.   **$p < .001$.

or through negotiations in Geneva. These figures demonstrate that it is concern for nuclear armament rather than strong beliefs in possibilities to control the arms race that makes the difference between individuals who do and who do not belong to the mobilization potential of the movement against cruise missiles. These concerns are conflated with political party preferences (Table 21.3). Because our dependent variable was dichotomous, we used logistic regression analyses. Equation (1) clearly shows the significance of voting behavior as a distinguishing feature of the two groups, as compared to age and education. In equation (2) the effect of voting behavior is no longer present. The attitudinal factors take its place.

Individuals who stayed outside the mobilization potential of the movement against cruise missiles were primarily from the right wing of Dutch society, although voters for parties to the right were not guaranteed opponents. A fair number of the supporters of right-wing parties (11 percent of the Conservatives and 30 percent of the Christian Democrats) could be counted among the sympathizers with the movement against cruise missiles. Virtually the entire left wing of Dutch society was part of the mobilization potential (100 percent of the Progressive Democrats, 86 percent of the Social Democrats, and 100 percent of Small Left).

Apart from political party alignment there are small independent effects of age and education. The effect of age is not dif-

TABLE 21.3 Logistic Regression Analysis Predicting Who Belongs to the Mobilization Potential of the Peace Movement (Standard Errors in Parentheses)

	Equation (1)		Equation (2)	
Demographics				
Age	−.03*	(.02)	−.04	(.02)
Gender	−.45	(.53)	−.43	(.63)
Education	−.23*	(.11)	−.24*	(.13)
Vote in last election	3.08**	(.74)	1.38	(.93)
Attitudinal				
Is deployment a matter of deep concern to you?			.43	(.53)
If deployment is pushed through will you continue to fight against it, accept it regretfully, or approve it?			3.09**	(.93)
Constant	3.42	(1.37)	10.72	(2.96)
Log likelihood	−45.86		−33.41	

Note: $N = 109$. *$p < .05$. **$p < .001$.

ferent from what we found with the zero order relationships; the effect of education is. If we control for age, gender, and voting behavior, education is related to sympathy with the peace movement. The sign is negative, however, indicating that people who do not belong to the mobilization potential are more highly educated than people who do.

In summary, the mobilization potential of the movement against cruise missiles covered a broad spectrum of social categories. It clearly did not restrict itself to categories thought to be typical of the mobilization potential of new social movements, like the new middle class, highly educated professionals, and youth (Brand 1982; Klandermans 1986; Kitschelt 1985; Melucci 1980). In the case of education we even found the opposite relationship. We will come back to this in the next section.

Target of Mobilization Attempts

In order to establish whether persons have been targets of mobilization attempts, we asked our respondents what formal and informal links they had with the local peace movement. Given the intensity of the mobilization campaign, we assumed that everybody who was linked in one way or another to the movement had been a target of mobilization attempts. However, the two sets (individuals being linked and individuals being targeted) need not necessarily be identical, and there might be situations where they are rather different indeed.

Almost 60 percent of the mobilization potential was reached by mobilization attempts through formal networks: they visited the peace stand downtown (31 percent), read appeals in local newspapers (23 percent), were reached through organizations linked with the movement (16 percent), or saw posters, billboards, banners (4 percent). A brochure that was delivered at every address was mentioned by only 13 percent of the respondents. We assumed that individuals with several or even many acquaintances or friends who planned to go to the demonstration were tied with informal recruitment networks of the movement.

TABLE 21.4   Links between the Local Peace Movement Networks and Intention to Participate, Education, Voting Behavior, and Gender

	Intention to Participate[a]	Education	Voting Behavior[b]	Gender[b]
No links (N = 17)	—	3.82	−.73	1.29
Formal links only (N = 15)	1	4.27	−.45	1.40
Informal links only (N = 17)	4	5.88	−.14	1.59
Formal and informal links (N = 32)	6	6.38	−.03	1.72

Note: ANOVA for education: $p < .01$; voting behavior, gender: $p < .05$. N = 81.
[a]In absolute numbers.
[b]Means (see Table 21.2).

Some 40 percent of our respondents had no such ties, and about 30 percent had several.

If we merge the two tracks, 20 percent of the mobilization potential had virtually no links at all with peace movement networks; 19 percent were reached through formal links only; 21 percent had only informal links; and 40 percent reported both formal and informal links to the movement. People who belonged to the mobilization potential had been as frequently targets of mobilization attempts as people outside the mobilization potential. There is, however, an interesting difference between the two groups: people outside the potential have, compared to those within, more formal links (chisquare = 4.811, $p < .05$). Obviously, outside the mobilization potential individuals are less likely to have friends or acquaintances who intend to go to the demonstration. This does not prevent local movement organizations from approaching these people, and apparently with some success. However, these are "wasted" mobilization attempts, since nobody from this category will participate. Women had less links with the local peace movement networks (Table 21.4). People reached were more highly educated and voted for parties to the left. We found no relation to age. The results in Table 21.5 show that three independent variables account for

27 percent of the variance in linkages to local peace movement networks. The beta coefficient for gender reveals that there is no independent gender effect. Controlling for education and voting behavior, we find no significant relation between gender and links to local movement networks.

The strong positive relationship with education confirms the findings in the literature that participants in movements like the peace movement are highly educated, young professionals (Brand 1982; Klandermans 1986; Kitschelt 1985; Melucci 1980). The findings on mobilization potential and recruitment networks suggest, however, that the explanation for this is not to be found in the stage of the formation of mobilization potentials but in the forming and activating of recruitment networks. It is not that more highly educated individuals who are sensitive to political or economic developments create new mobilization potentials but that these individuals are more connected with the social networks engaged in recruitment.

The data on voting behavior demonstrate the importance of political alignment in recruitment. The negative sign and the size of the mean of the group without any link show that people who have not been reached are located at the right side of the

TABLE 21.5 Stepwise Regression of Education, Gender, and Voting Behavior Linked to Local Peace Movement Networks

	Beta	*p*
Education	.30	.005
Voting behavior	.23	.025
Gender	.20	.06
$R^2 = .27$		

Note: N = 81.

political spectrum. Apparently, recruitment networks did not reach this part of the mobilization potential. The means in Table 21.4 of the two categories having informal links indicate that the categories are densely populated with voters of the small leftist parties. This points out that the informal networks were to a large extent networks among adherents of the small parties to the left.

In our theoretical introduction we assumed that participation in movement activity would only be considered by individuals who belong to the mobilization potential *and* have been targets of mobilization attempts. This leads to the straightforward hypothesis that people who have not been targets of mobilization attempts will not intend to participate in the demonstration, even if they belong to the mobilization potential of the movement.

The data fit the theory perfectly; without exception every person who intended to participate had in one way or another been the target of a mobilization attempt (Table 21.3). More interestingly, the figures in Table 21.4 demonstrate that the informal recruitment networks are far more important than the formal. The data suggest that informal networks are necessary conditions for the arousal of motivation to participate. In this respect our data confirm earlier findings on differential recruitment (Orum 1974; Gerlach

and Hine 1970; Snow, Zurcher, and Ekland-Olson 1982; McAdam 1986b).

In conclusion, network factors entailed important biases in the mobilization potential reached by mobilization attempts. On the one hand, they excluded to a large extent the rightist sectors of the mobilization potential, which were not reached by mobilization attempts; on the other hand, informal networks restricted themselves to a large extent to the small leftist parties. The composition of the peace platform reproduced itself in the composition of the group reached by mobilization attempts. As a consequence, the subset of the mobilization potential reached by mobilization attempts was biased to the more highly educated, radical left, a makeup much more characteristic for new social movements than the mobilization potential, demonstrating that network factors were responsible for this typical makeup of the constituency rather than factors generating mobilization potentials.

Motivation to Participate

Although links with informal networks seem to be a necessary condition for the arousal of motivation to participate in the demonstration, it is definitely not a sufficient condition, as the outcomes in Figure 21.1 show. Structural factors like positions in networks increase the likelihood that a person will be a target of mobilization attempts but do not guarantee that these attempts will be successful. Mobilization attempts make individuals consider costs and benefits of participation. The outcome of this weighing process depends on the specific blend of costs and benefits perceived.

Collective Incentives None of the respondents was very optimistic about the effectiveness of the demonstration; those who intended to demonstrate were no exception. None of them believed that deployment of the cruise missiles could be stopped. Potential participants and nonparticipants did not show many differences in their expectations about the number of participants either. But it is interesting to note that the former estimated the number of participants higher than the latter. This runs counter to Olson's (1965) assumptions but confirms ours (Klandermans 1984) that people show more of a tendency to participate in collective action if they expect that others will do so as well. Oliver (1984) reports a condition in which people are less likely to participate the more they believe others will. These are in her terms forms of participation with a decelerating production function. Participation in demonstrations has an accelerating production function; that is, more participation does help in achieving the collective goal. Only one-tenth of the potential demonstrators said they expected their own contribution to have no effect. In this respect they differed from nonparticipants among the supporters, one-fourth of whom said they expected their own participation to have no effect. Since values and expectations are multiplicatively related, under such circumstances the extent to which a person agrees with the goal of the demonstration should play a large role. This turned out to be the case. Three-quarters of the potential participants belonged to the group that absolutely agreed with the goal of the demonstration, while only one-third of the nonparticipants among the supporters belonged to this group. But something must be added to this. In sharp contrast to the nonparticipants, the potential participants were of the opinion that there were ways open to the Dutch government of influencing the arms race (m = 1.72 and 2.53, p < .001, $\eta2$ = .17). This is what gave substance to the demonstration and their participation in it. If the cruise missiles cannot be stopped, then at the very least it ought to be made clear to the government that it should exert its influence to oppose the arms race.

Selective Cost and Benefits—Social People who intended to go to the demonstration knew more people who were also going than nonparticipants among the supporters (p < .001, $\eta2$ = .13). The implication of this is obvious: those who knew many others who were also going to the demonstration stood a much higher chance of being asked if they participated and of getting negative reactions if it turned out that they did not participate than those who knew only a few others or none at all.

Nonsocial The costs of participation were low. The demonstrator had to give up a free Saturday, and like any other demonstration, there was some risk of disturbances. The potential participants had no objections to the first, and they did not expect any disturbances. One-fifth of the supporters who did not intend to demonstrate did object to these costs and/or they expected disturbances.

Table 21.6 presents the outcomes of logistic regression analyses with willingness to participate as the dependent variable. Because of the small N, we restricted the number of variables in the equation by alternately including different subsets of independent variables.

The expectancy variables are not included in the equations because of low zero-order correlations (ranging from .02 to .06). It is clear from equations (5), (6), and (7) that collective incentives were more important than selective incentives in determining the motivation to participate (the log likelihood for social and nonsocial incentives = –24.3— not presented in Table 21.6—as compared to –18.8 for collective incentives). Among the selective incentives the social incentives were more important than the nonsocial. The same conclusions can be drawn from equations (2), (3), and (4) after controlling for the

TABLE 21.6 Logistic Regression Analysis Predicting Willingness to Participate in the Demonstration (Standard Errors in Parentheses)

	Equation (1)	Equation (2)	Equation (3)	Equation (4)	Equation (5)	Equation (6)	Equation (7)
Demographics							
Age	.04 (.03)	.05 (.06)	.03 (.03)	.04 (.03)			
Gender	−.32 (.88)	.92 (1.40)	−.17 (.88)	−.54 (.92)			
Education	.37 (.21)*	.84 (.48)*	.33 (.22)*	.39 (.21)*			
Voting behavior	2.33 (.90)**	3.07 (1.67)*	2.06 (.91)**	2.22 (.90)**			
Collective Incentives							
Attitude toward goal of demonstration		1.23 (1.15)			1.58 (.83)*		
Does the Dutch government have the potential to influence the arms race?		15.47 (3.97)***			8.46 (1.67)***		
Selective Incentives							
Social							
How many acquaintances/friends will go to the demonstration?			.89 (.71)			1.37 (.64)**	
Nonsocial							
Sacrificing free time				−.78 (.72)			−.79 (.63)
Fear of disturbances				−.77 (1.61)			−.42 (1.16)
Constant	−7.53 (2.92)	12.33	−5.60 (3.27)	10.41 (4.49)	10.04 (2.96)	.62 (.97)	−4.43 (2.79)
Log likelihood	−22.63	−11.55	−21.78	−21.79	−18.77	−26.13	−27.82

Note: $N = 64$.　　*$p < .05$.　　**$p < .001$.　　***$p < .001$.

demographic variables. Both social and nonsocial incentives add significantly to the variance explained by the collective incentives; (log likelihood: −16.2 for collective and social incentives, −15.6 for collective and nonsocial incentives; improvement of goodness of fit $p < .05$ in both cases). Finally, motivational factors are much more important than demographics in explaining willingness to participate in the demonstration.

In summary, the motivation to participate was produced primarily by collective and social incentives. Participants wanted to protest against the deployment of cruise missiles and to put pressure on the government to use its influence to reduce nuclear armaments. Together with the awareness that nonparticipation had to be justified to friends and acquaintances, these motives pushed individuals toward participation. Since nobody firmly believed in the effects of the demonstration, the collective incentives were basically ideological: acting according to one's principles. The awareness that nonparticipation had to be justified to one's friends urged even more to participate.

Barriers to Participation

The intention to participate is by no means a sufficient condition, as demonstrated by the proportion of motivated individuals that eventually did not participate (60 percent). At this stage numbers are too small to allow us to draw any firm conclusion. Although it is worthwhile to remark that those who did not go mentioned concrete barriers to participation (they had to work, they were sick, or their wife was sick), obviously the reliability of those answers is questionable.

Conclusions

Each step in the mobilization process produced another group of individuals dropping out, and as a result not even 1 out of 20

sympathizers eventually participated in collective action. This proportion is not spectacular and in line with the percentages presented by Walsh and Warland (1983) and Oliver (1984). Both focused on the free-rider problem (that is, nonparticipation by people who sympathize with the movement goals), the former describing noncontributors as free riders, and the latter by explaining participation on the part of activists resulting from the awareness of the free-rider problems. As Oliver (1984) showed in her study, the awareness that others will not participate is capable of motivating participation in activities with decelerating production functions. Free riding is pertinent as an explanation of nonparticipation in these activities. Nonparticipation in activities with accelerating production functions, however, requires more complex explanations. Walsh and Warland (1983) conclude from their analysis that "both the structural variables advocated by resource mobilization theorists *and* more social psychological ones such as ideology and discontent should be considered by analysts seeking a better understanding of the factors inclining people toward activism" (p. 778, emphasis in original). Our paper is an attempt to systematically expand and elaborate this argument.

In Walsh and Warland's papers nonparticipation is made identical to free riding. Our research presents a much more differentiated picture. Nonparticipation in collective action can result from four different grounds: lack of sympathy for the movement, not having been the target of mobilization attempts, not being motivated to participate, and the presence of barriers. Free riding is a pertinent explanation only in the motivational stage where costs and benefits of participation are weighed. Elsewhere Klandermans (1987) argued that only in situations where collective action is expected to be effective can free riding be a valid explanation of nonparticipation. Otherwise nonparticipation results from perceived inefficacy of collective action, distrust of the behavior of others, or costs of participation that are not outweighed by benefits.

Students of social movement participation must be aware of what aspect of mobilization they are studying; otherwise results can easily be misinterpreted. To illustrate, we refer to our finding that participants in the peace movement are young, highly educated, and professionals. From similar observations, new social movement literature concluded that movements like the peace movement draw from new mobilization potentials created by modernization and industrialization (cf. Klandermans 1986). Our results made clear, however, the dangers of inferences about mobilization potentials from characteristics of participants. In our case, aspects other than the formation of mobilization potentials were responsible for the typical participant.

The four facets of mobilization imply different processes, both theoretically and practically. Mobilization potential presupposes grievance interpretation; the formation and activation of recruitment networks imply coalition formation and the linking of movement organizations to existing formal and informal networks; the arousal of motivation to participate rests on calculations of cost and benefits of participation; and securing actual participation entails the maintenance of motivation and the elimination of barriers. With regard to each step, important questions need to be answered. Recent literature on social movements in Europe and the United States has concentrated on different aspects of mobilization (cf. Klandermans 1986). European literature focused on the formation of new mobilization potentials, whereas American literature paid much attention to motivation to participate and attempts of movement organizations and authorities to control the

costs and benefits of participation. By assuming that grievances are ubiquitous, it neglects to a large extent the creation and interpretation of grievances and the formation of mobilization potentials. As a consequence several steps in the process of mobilization remain insufficiently examined in the literature, like grievance interpretation, or more general consensus mobilization, targeting potential participants, and participation vs. nonparticipation among motivated individuals.

Unlike previous research on union participation (Klandermans 1984), the present study reveals that attitudes toward the goal were important determinants of willingness to participate. This points to the significance of the multiplicative relation of values and expectations. In the case of the peace movement, people had almost unanimously modest expectations about the efficacy of the demonstration. Because of the multiplicative relations of values and expectations with willingness to participate, differences in attitude toward the goal become more important in this situation. In the case of the union actions it was just the other way around. On the whole, attitudes toward the goal were favorable and opinions on the effect of action were divided. Under such circumstances, expectations become of greater importance for the willingness to participate.

Ideological and social incentives appeared to be the primary motivations to participate in the peace demonstration. Our results make us speculate about the interaction of ideological incentives and informal networks: the more important ideological incentives are in a movement, the more informal networks linked to the movement act as guardians of the principles by forcing people to act according to their principles. Knowing other participants turned out to be an important variable in the mobilization process, not only in the case of high-risk activities like McAdam (1986a) demonstrated but in the case of low-risk activities as well. Ideological incentives presuppose the presence of ideological and attitudinal support for a movement in a society. This brings us back to the very beginning of the mobilization process: the formation of mobilization potentials. Recent work on micromobilization points to the relevance of informal social networks in this regard (McAdam 1986b; Snow et al. 1986; see Klandermans, Tarrow, and Kriesi (1988) for a compilation of contributions from both Europe and the United States), but many questions remain to be answered.

Our model combines structural and cognitive factors, and there is clear evidence that both interact in determining whether people participate or not in collective action. We spelled out the four different grounds nonparticipation can have. Influenced by events, circumstances, and movement strategies, the number of people prevented from participation by one or more conditions fluctuates. It would be of interest to study which factors influence those fluctuations and to what extent mobilizing organizations can control them.

REFERENCES

Barnes, Samuel H. and Max Kaase. 1979. *Political Action: Mass Participation in Five Western Democracies.* London: Sage.

Bolton, Charles D. 1972. "Alienation and Action: A Study of Peace Group Members." *American Journal of Sociology* 77:537–61.

Brand, K.W. 1982. *Neue soziale Bewequngen, Entstehung, Funktion und Perspektive neuer Protestpotentiale, Eine Zwischenbilanz.* Opladen: West Deutscher Verlag.

Briet, Martien, Bert Klandermans, and Frederike Kroon. 1987. "How Women Become Involved in the Women's Movement." In *The Women's Movement in the U.S. and Western Europe: Feminist Consciousness, Political Opportunity and Public Opinion,* edited by Mary Katzenstein and Carol Mueller. Philadelphia: Temple University Press.

Fernandez, R. and D. McAdam. 1989. "Multi-organizational Fields and Recruitment to Social Movements." In *Organizing for Change: Social Movement Organizations in Europe and the United States,* edited by Bert Klandermans. Greenwich, CT: JAI Press.

Ferree, Myra M. and Frederick D. Miller. 1985. "Mobilization and Meaning: Toward an Integration of Social Psychological and Resource Perspectives on Social Movements." *Sociological Inquiry* 55:38–61.

Fireman, Bruce and William A. Gamson. 1979. "Utilitarian Logic in the Resource Mobilization Perspective." Pp. 8–45 in *The Dynamics of Social Movements,* edited by M.N. Zaid and J.D. McCarthy. Cambridge, MA: Winthrop Publishers.

Frey, J.H. 1983. *Survey Research by Telephone.* London: Sage.

Gerlach, L.P. and V.H. Hine. 1970. *People, Power, Change: Movements of Social Transformation.* Indianapolis, IN: Bobbs-Merrill.

Granovetter, M. 1983. "The Strength of Weak Ties: A Network Theory Revisited." Pp. 201–33 in *Sociological Theory 1983,* edited by R. Collins. San Francisco: Jossey-Bass.

Gurney, J.N. and K.J. Tierney. 1982. "Relative Deprivation and Social Movements: A Critical Look at Twenty Years of Theory and Research." *Sociology Quarterly* 23:33–47.

Jenkins, J.C. and C. Perrow. 1977. "Insurgency of the Powerless Farm Worker Movements." *American Sociological Review* 42:249–68.

Kitschelt, Herbert. 1985. "New Social Movements in West Germany and the United States." Pp. 273–324 in *Political Power and Social Theory,* vol. 5, edited by Maurice M. Zeitlin.

Klaassen, Rob. 1986. "Participatie van kaderleden in besluitvormingsprocessen van de vakbond." Unpublished thesis, Social Psychology, Vrije University.

Klandermans, Bert. 1984. "Mobilization and Participation: Social Psychological Expansions of Resource Mobilization Theory." *American Sociological Review* 49:583–600.

———. 1986. "New Social Movements and Resource Mobilization: The European and the American Approach." *Journal of Mass Emergencies and Disasters,* Special Issue on Collective Behavior and Social Movements, Gary Marx (ed).

———. 1987. "Union Action and the Free Rider Dilemma." In *Social Movements as a Factor of Change in the Contemporary World,* edited by Janusz Mucha, Louis Kriesberg, and Bronislaw Misztal. Greenwich, CT: JAI Press.

Klandermans, Bert, Sidney Tarrow, and Hanspeter Kriesi. 1988. *From Structure to Action: Comparing Social Movement Research Across Cultures.* Greenwich, CT: JAI Press.

Knoke, David and James R. Wood. 1981. *Organized for Action: Commitment in Voluntary Associations.* New Brunswick, NJ: Rutgers University Press.

Kriesi, Hanspeter. 1985. *Bewegungen in der schweizer Politik, Fallstudien zu politischen Mobiliseringsprozessen in der Schweiz.* Frankfurt: Campusverlag.

McAdam, Doug. 1986a. "Recruitment to High-Risk Activism: The Case of Freedom Summer." *American Journal of Sociology* 92:64–90.

———. 1986b. "Micro Mobilization Contexts and Recruitment to Activism." Paper presented at the International Workshop on Participation in Social Movements: Transformation of Structure into Action. Amsterdam: 12–14 June.

McCarthy, John D. 1983. "Social Infrastructure Deficits and New Technologies: Mobilizing Unstructured Sentiment Pools." Working paper, Department of Sociology and Center for the Study of Youth Development. Washington, D.C.

McCarthy, John D. and Mayer N. Zald. 1976. "Resource Mobilization and Social Movements: A Partial Theory." *American Journal of Sociology* 82:1212–93.

McQuail, Denis. 1983. *Mass Communication Theory: An Introduction.* London: Sage.

Melucci, Alberto. 1980. "The New Social Movements: A Theoretical Approach." *Social Science Information* 19:199–226.

Mitchell, Robert C. 1979. "National Environmental Lobbies and the Apparent Illogic of Collective Action." Pp. 87–121 in *Collective Decision Making Applications from Public Choice Theory,* edited by Clifford S. Russell. Baltimore: Johns Hopkins University Press.

———. 1984. "Moving Forward vs. Moving Backwards: Motivation for Collective Action." San Antonio, TX: Paper presented at the 79th Annual Meeting of the American Sociological Association.

Mitchell, T.R. 1974. "Expectancy Models of Job Satisfaction, Occupational Preference and Effort: A Theoretical, Methodological and Empirical Appraisal." *Psychological Bulletin* 81:1053–77.

Muller, Edward N. and Karl Dieter Opp. 1986. "Rational Choice and Rebellious Collective Action." *American Political Science Review* 80:471–88.

Oberschall, Anthony. 1973. *Social Conflict and Social Movements.* Englewood Cliffs, NJ: Prentice-Hall.

———. 1980. "Loosely Structured Collective Conflicts: A Theory and an Application." Pp. 45–68 in *Research in Social Movements, Conflict and Change,* edited by Louis Kreisberg. Greenwich, CT: JAI Press.

Oliver, Pamela. 1984. "If You Don't Do it, Nobody Else Will: Active and Token Contributors to Local Collective Action." *American Sociological Review* 49:601–10.

Olson, Mancur. 1965. *The Logic of Collective Action, Public Goods and the Theory of Groups.* Cambridge, MA: Harvard University Press.

Opp, Karl Dieter. 1983. *Soft Incentives and Collective Action: Some Results of a Survey on the Conditions of Participating in the Anti-Nuclear Movement.* Hamburg: Institut für Soziologie.

Orum, Anthony M. 1974. "On Participation in Political Protest Movements." *Journal of Applied Behavioral Science.* 10:181–207.

Snow, David A., E. Burke Rochford, Steven K. Worden, and Robert D. Benford. 1986. "Frame Alignment and Mobilization." *American Sociological Review* 51:464–82.

Snow, David A., Louis A. Zurcher, and Sheldon Ekland-Olson. 1980. "Social Networks and Social Movements: A Micro-Structural Approach to Differential Recruitment." *American Sociological Review* 45:787–801.

Walsh, Edward J. and Rex H. Warland. 1983. "Social Movement Involvement in the Wake of Nuclear Accident: Activists and Free Riders in the Three Mile Island Area. *American Sociological Review* 48:764–81.

Wilson, Kenneth and Anthony M. Orum. 1976. "Mobilizing People for Collective Political Action." *Journal of Political and Military Sociology* 4:187–202.

22

EXTERNAL EFFORTS TO DAMAGE OR FACILITATE SOCIAL MOVEMENTS
Some Patterns, Explanations, Outcomes, and Complications

GARY T. MARX

In spite of the impression left by much of the literature through the 1960s, social movements are not autonomous forces hurling toward their destiny only in response to the oppression, intensity of commitment, and skill of activists. Nor are they epiphenomena at the mercy of groups in their external environment that seek to block or facilitate them. Instead movements represent a complex interplay of external and internal factors. Until recently researchers have tended to focus much more on the latter than the former, but both must be considered.

McCarthy and Zald (1973), in focusing on external factors, have helped to redress the balance. They note how broad social trends in the United States are conducive to the emergence and growth of social movements, regardless of the nature and type of deprivation felt by the beneficiaries of the movement. However, we can also note that many of the same factors are equally conducive to the emergence of countermovements and to efforts on the part of the government or private groups to block, damage,

inhibit, or destroy social movements. The resources are clearly there in greater abundance than ever before; how they will be used is another question. Our perspective on the external environment must be broad enough to include repressive as well as facilitative actions.

I will consider how selected elements of the external environment may seek to affect social movements by examining some strategies and tactics intended to facilitate or damage social movements, looking at some questions raised by these activities and some efforts at explanation, and showing some of their intended and unintended outcomes. My attention will focus on the actions of government because more is known about this area and a consideration of it can suggest concepts more generally applicable to the actions taken by nongovernmental groups. Beyond this, one of the insights to emerge from recent hearings and court cases is that some elements of the media, some interest groups, and some social movements can be extensions of government.

My concern is primarily with social control or facilitation efforts that have appeared with respect to specific movements in the United States. Of less concern are aspects of culture and social structure or general actions taken prior to the appearance of a movement that affects grievances and possibilities for collective action.[1] For example,

"External Efforts to Damage or Facilitate Movements: Some Patterns, Explanations, Outcomes, and Complications" by Gary T. Marx from *The Dynamics of Social Movements: Resource Mobilization, Social Control, and Tactics,* Mayer Zald and John D. McCarthy, eds. Reprinted by permission of the editors.

our legal system, with the protected freedoms of the Bill of Rights and local ordinances regarding parade permits, is a more distant form of facilitation and control. It is part of the societal framework within which a movement operates. In principle such forms of control and facilitation apply universally. They can be separated from the specific actions at the micro-level taken by government in response to a given movement.

Strategies and Tactics Intended to Facilitate or Damage Social Movements

To highlight the issues involved, let us take the least ambiguous, extreme case where an outside group such as the government either wants to damage or facilitate a movement. A review of the last two decades suggests a number of broad strategies and specific tactics that have been undertaken to achieve the desired goal. Many of the actions taken with the aim of damaging a movement are the reverse of those taken to enhance a movement. These can be characterized in terms of opposing organizational, tactical, and resource mobilization tasks. The actions of those seeking to further the cause of the social movement lie on the left side of Table 22.1, and those seeking to damage the movement lie on the right side.

Although analytically distinct, these factors are obviously related. Some—such as inhibiting the capacity for corporate action, directing energies to maintenance needs, and damaging morale—are general and include most of the others. Obtaining one end, such as the application of legal sanctions, can be a means to other ends, such as creating an unfavorable public image or destroying leadership. One end can be pursued by multiple means, and the same means, such as the use of agents provoca-teurs, can serve a number of ends. These represent the point of view of the outside analyst, although they are likely to overlap considerably with the point of view of the actor.[2] Let us first consider the far more prevalent efforts to damage movements.

Creation of an Unfavorable Public Image

Public labeling of a social movement, its leaders, and its activities is affected by what leaders say about it (Nixon's references to antiwar protesters as bums and Johnson's "we shall overcome" speech are examples), as well as by more covert actions designed to affect how its image is projected by the media. What and how the media report are crucial topics for understanding social movements, independent of government pressures. For example, advertisers and the beliefs of those working in the media can be crucial to what is said—and not said—about a social movement.[3] Our concern here, however, is government actions.

We do not know with certainty what effect recent Federal Communication Commission pressure or Vice-President Agnew's attack on the "liberal media" had. Yet real or anticipated pressures from government on the media may make it more difficult for a movement to communicate accurately with the public. Easier to identify than self-censorship in the presentation of news are more direct tactics that may be undertaken by social control agents in efforts to affect actual media content.

Image-damaging information may be given to friendly journalists or supplied anonymously. This may involve passing on information about arrest records, associations, lifestyles, and statements of the targeted person or group that are thought likely to hurt the movement. For example, information obtained from electronic surveillance supposedly dealing with Martin

TABLE 22.1 Some General Strategies for Facilitating or Inhibiting a Social Movement

To Facilitate the Movement	To Inhibit the Movement
Facilitate capacity for corporate action	Inhibit capacity for corporate action
Make it possible for energies of movement to go toward pursuit of broader social change goals, as well as maintenance needs	Direct energies of movement to defensive maintenance needs and away from pursuit of broader social goals
Create favorable public image; develop and support ideology	Create unfavorable public image and counterideology
Give information to movement	Gather information on movement
Facilitate supply of money and facilities	Inhibit supply of money and facilities
Facilitate freedom of movement, expression, and action; offer legal immunity	Inhibit freedom of movement, expression, and action; create myth and fact of surveillance and repression; apply legal sanctions
Build and sustain morale	Damage morale
Recruit supporters	Derecruitment
Build leaders	Destroy or displace leaders
Encourage internal solidarity	Encourage internal conflict
Encourage external coalitions with potential allies and neutral relations (or conflict only insofar as it is functional) with potential opponents	Encourage external conflict with potenital allies and opponents
Facilitate particular actions	Inhibit or sabotage particular actions

Luther King's sexual behavior was offered by the FBI to various journalists. Or control agents may write their own stories and editorials, which they pass on to the media. For example, the FBI planted a series of derogatory articles about the Poor People's Campaign (Select Committee, book II, 1976, p. 16). The media are not necessarily aware of the source of such material.

The information given to the media may be fabricated; it may be accurate yet privileged information known to authorities only as a result of wiretaps, informers, and other forms of surveillance; or it may be accurate but only in a contrived sense (as when authorities have taken covert action to create events whose reporting will reflect negatively upon the movement). Examples of this would be provoking the movement to illegal actions, carrying out illegal actions themselves that will then be attributed to the movement, or tempting leaders with vice opportunities.

Efforts may be undertaken to block or counter the publication of materials favorable to the movement. "Disinformation" and counterpropaganda arguing that the movement's ideology and claims are empirically wrong, illogical, in conflict with basic American values, or linked to foreign or disreputable sources may be published.

For the FBI, such activities go back at least thirty years. In 1946 the head of the FBI Intelligence Division suggested that "educational material" be released through "available channels [to] influence public opinion" about American communists. Propaganda efforts were carried out that aimed to bring the U.S. Communist party and its leaders "into disrepute before the American public" (ibid., p. 66).[4] In the case of the New Left, FBI agents were told that "every avenue of possible embarrassment must be vigorously and enthusiastically explored." In efforts "to discredit the New Left and its adherents," agents were requested to send information for "prompt dissemination to the news media" (ibid., p. 16). Among specific instructions given agents were:

> a. Prepare leaflets designed to discredit student demonstrators, using photographs of New Left leadership. . . . Naturally, the most obnoxious picture should be used.

> b. Send . . . articles from student newspapers or the "underground press" which show the depravity of the New Left to university officials, donors, legislators, and parents. Articles showing advocation of the use of narcotics and free sex are ideal.

Many examples indicate that this advice was followed for the New Left, as well as for other groups. For example, the FBI circulated a flyer headlined "Pick the Fag Contest," which contained a list of mock prizes and pictures of four New Left leaders (Wise, 1976, p. 317). It also sent an anonymous letter to a Hollywood gossip columnist claiming that activist Jane Fonda led a Black Panther rally in obscene and violent chants involving Richard Nixon. Fonda has denied this charge and filed a $2.8 million lawsuit. The agent in charge of the Los Angeles FBI office wrote to J. Edgar Hoover, "It is felt that knowledge of Fonda's involvement would cause her embarrassment and detract from her status with the general public" (ibid., p. 316).

The CIA in its foreign activities appears to have gone even farther in media manipulation by becoming, rather than merely trying to influence, the media. The CIA supported two European news services used by U.S. newspapers, and as of February 1976, about fifty U.S. journalists and other news organization workers were employed by or had a covert relationship with the CIA. In a few cases regular CIA agents also posed as journalists (Select Committee, book I, 1976). When asked whether the CIA ever planted stories with foreign news organizations, former director William Colby replied, "Oh, sure all the time" (*New York Times,* February 4, 1976). When foreign sources such as Reuters are used, this material can help shape American public opinion, as can books paid for or affected by the CIA.[5]

Information Gathering

The largest single activity of control agents with respect to social movements has probably been in information gathering. Indeed it is a prerequisite for most other activities. Information-gathering techniques developed for criminal investigations have been applied to social movements. In roughly decreasing frequency, they include:

- Collection of news items, movement documents, and membership lists.
- Informers developed through infiltration, *"turning around"* those already in the movement, or drawing upon individuals in the movement's milieu.
- Attendance at public meetings and demonstrations.
- Still photography and videotape.
- Background investigations using public and private records and interviews.
- Wiretaps and other forms of auditory electronic surveillance, often requiring breaking and entering and monitoring international telephone calls.
- Physical surveillance of persons or places.
- Police posing as journalists and photographers or the latter giving information to police.
- Grand jury investigations.
- Mail openings.

The reasons for which such information is collected vary: search for subversion, conspiracy, and espionage; information needed in a criminal investigation; harassment; names to put on a dangerous persons or organizations list and in computer banks; information to aid in the preparation of counterintelligence actions; or ritualized bureaucratic work to meet information quotas, which are taken as evidence that agents are working. The vast majority of the information gathered is not used, is often of questionable validity, and is rapidly dated. To be useful beyond its harassment function, it must be organized, evaluated, and interpreted. Knowing that agents are gathering information on it may make the social movement less open and democratic, require that limited resources be devoted to security, and may deter participation.

Inhibiting the Supply of Resources and Facilities

Social movement organizations need money, means of communication services and supplies, and physical space. Government actions may be taken to deny or restrict a movement's access to these, particularly insofar as they come from sources external to the movement. Where the government was the sponsor and an organization comes to be seen as too threatening, funds may simply be withdrawn, as was the case with Office of Economic Opportunity programs (Donovan, 1970). The social movement organization may experience direct pressure and threats from private funding agencies, which themselves may anticipate government sanctioning. As Goulden (1971) has noted for the Ford Foundation, even the accusation that a foundation is funding a radical group can lead to pressure on the group to become more moderate.

The government may seek to discover the source of an organization's funding. Efforts of varying degrees of legality may then be carried out to dry up larger sources of contribution. For example, the FBI considered its attempts to put a stop to a South-

ern Christian Leadership Conference funding source as "quite successful" (Select Committee, book II, 1976, p. 15).

The tax-exempt status of social movement organizations or those contributing to them may be chosen for auditing on strictly political grounds and then revoked. Contributors and activists may be subjected to special audits (ibid.). Recent general congressional inquiries into laws regarding the tax-exempt status of foundations appear to have resulted in greater caution in their funding activities.

Those renting offices or providing office or meeting space to a movement may be encouraged by the government not to do so. For example, the FBI tried to prevent the holding of a forum by an alleged Communist front on a Midwest campus. It then investigated the judge who ordered that the meeting be permitted (ibid., p. 17). The FBI claimed in a 1965 report that "as a result of counterintelligence action, many meeting places formerly used on a regular basis by the communists have been barred from their use" (Berman and Halperin, 1975, p. 28).

As McCarthy and Zald (1973) note, the more-than-subsistence income, fringe resources, leisure, and flexibility offered by many jobs can indirectly be important in facilitating social movement participation. Conversely the denial of such employment to activists can be a means of indirectly damaging a movement. Authorities have attempted to get activists fired from their jobs and to affect their credit standing negatively. Those whose names are in security files may have difficulty finding new employment.

During the McCarthy era, more than 490 persons lost government jobs on loyalty grounds though no cases of espionage were found. More recently, the Select Committee to Study Governmental Operations with Respect to Intelligence report cites examples such as FBI records being given to employers and their receiving anonymous letters about activist employees.

Such activities can damage morale, shrink resources, and make sustained actions difficult or impossible. For some activists, the cost of continued participation may become too great, and they may quit. But more direct efforts toward this end may also be undertaken in the form of explicit derecruitment activities.

Derecruitment

One way to create an unfavorable public image is to keep potential recruits away. The public sanctioning of activists may also be a means of deterring new recruits. But beyond trying to stop a movement from expanding, the government may try to reduce the movement's size and weaken the morale and degree of commitment among those currently active. Obtaining membership and mailing lists have been given high priority by authorities, even where this practice necessitated breaking and entering.

Once the identity of activists is known, employers, parents, neighbors, friends, or spouses may be contacted, sometimes anonymously, in hopes of encouraging them to dissuade or threaten activists. A policy directive advising FBI agents to make such contacts expressed the hope that "this could have the effect of forcing the parents to take action" (Select Committee, book III, 1976, p. 26). For example, in 1968, the FBI sent anonymous letters to the parents of two Oberlin College students involved in a campus hunger strike against the Vietnam War urging them to intervene to prevent their children from becoming dupes of the Young Socialist Alliance (Berman and Halperin, 1975, p. 30). It has also sent anonymous letters to the spouses of activists in the Ku Klux Klan, the Black Panthers, and other groups accusing their marital partners of infidelity (ibid., p. 51). A Klan informant testified that he was instructed "to sleep with as many wives as I could" in attempts to break up

marriages and gain information (Select Committee, Hearings, 1976, 6:118).

Activists may encounter direct appeals from government agents who point out the risks they face, argue matters of ideology, give them damaging information about others in the movement, and threaten them. There may be efforts to maneuver activists into situations (such as of a sexual nature) from which they can then be controlled under threat of exposure or arrest. They may seek to persuade them to become informants. An FBI directive tells agents, "There is a pretty general consensus that more interviews with these [New Left] subjects and hangers-on are in order for plenty of reasons, chief of which are it will enhance the paranoia endemic in these circles and will further serve to get the point across that there is an FBI agent behind every mailbox" (Wise, 1972).

In at least one case, FBI agents appear to have kidnapped an antiwar activist in hopes of scaring him into ceasing his protest actions (*New York Times,* July 11, 1976). During preparation for a large Washington, D.C., antiwar demonstration, another activist recalls: "We were followed more and more. The Feds came to a lot of different people's apartments in the middle of the night with keys. They grabbed people as they were getting into their cars in parking lots and threw them into the car and drove around for a few hours, bribing them, telling them they'd give them thousands of dollars and a new passport if they'd only sing a song. And it didn't make any difference whether they did or not, cause their goose was cooked, they had information on us—it just went on and on" (Wise, 1976, p. 377).

An example of derecruitment efforts in a private context is provided by attempts to deprogram youthful converts to religious movements, such as Reverend Sun Myung Moon's Unification church. A new class of countersocial movement specialist has emerged here, the functional equivalent of those playing recruitment roles from within the movement. In the rural South there were many privately initiated efforts to apply, and threats of applying, economic sanctions against civil rights activists. Private police in their campaign against labor radicals and union organizing had a marked degree of success here, at least until the reforms of the New Deal. For example, according to one estimate, labor spying was a major factor in a one-third decline in labor union membership between 1920 and 1929 (Bernstein, 1960).

Destroying Leaders

Because social movement leaders are symbolically and instrumentally important, movement-damaging activities often focus on weakening them as the most visible and presumed central part of a movement.[6] Visibility as a social movement leader may offer the person some protection from some of the more nefarious and illegal tactics, yet leaders have been targets for most of the movement-damaging strategies we are considering. They may be subject to image-damaging efforts, surveillance, harassment, assaults, and threats. They may face a variety of legal sanctions, such as injunctions against demonstrating, grand jury inquiries of a fishing expedition nature, arrest on false or vague conspiracy charges, and excessive bail and sentences. Tax difficulties may be created for them. They may be the principal figures in efforts to create internal and external conflict. There may be efforts to maneuver them into compromising positions where they can be made informers or at least be forced into cooperation with the government. Co-optive efforts may be undertaken. There may be efforts to displace them, as the government infiltrates its own people into the movement who become leaders or builds up a rival group. The campaign against Martin Luther King included

most of these tactics—plus some others—and Communist, Klan, black militant, and New Left leaders have faced similar efforts.

Internal Conflict

A major aim of domestic counterintelligence activities has been to create internal conflict by encouraging factionalism, jealousy, and suspicion among activists. Schisms based on disagreements over tactics, goals, or personalities may be created and encouraged. Agents were encouraged to create "personal conflicts or animosities" between leaders (Select Committee, book III, 1976, p. 26). In some cases government agents within opposing factions exacerbated tensions between them. This was apparently the case with the major split in the Black Panthers between the Newton and Cleaver factions and splits within the New Left between Students for a Democratic Society and groups such as the Progressive Labor party.

Key activists or those known to be violent may be anonymously and falsely accused of being informants or set up to make it appear that they are, in the hope that they will be attacked, isolated, or expelled. Beyond generating internal conflict, this tactic can be a means of derecruitment and efforts to destroy leadership.

William Albertson, a Communist party leader and member for almost thirty years, was drummed out of the party as a "stool pigeon" and one who had led a life of "duplicity and treachery." The FBI had planted "snitch jackets" (forged documents) on him to make it appear that he was an informer. One letter offered an FBI agent information in exchange for a "raise in expenses." After this episode, Albertson was unable to find work or to remain active in the movement he had given his life to, he was ostracized by his friends, and his home was burned after arson threats. He was ironically later approached by the FBI about becoming an informer and refused. Its assumption perhaps was that he would cooperate out of anger in response to the group's falsely accusing him (Donner, 1976). In describing this action and assessing its consequences, an FBI memo noted:

> The most active and efficient functionary of the New York District of the Communist Party USA and leading national officer of the party, through our counterintelligence efforts has been expelled from the party. Factors relating to this expulsion crippled the activities of the New York State communist organization and the turmoil within the party continues to this date. Albertson's exposure as an FBI informant has discouraged many dedicated communists from activities and has discredited the party in the eyes of the Soviets (p. 12).[7]

Encouraging External Conflict

Conflict between the movement and groups in its environment may be encouraged in the hope of damaging it and diverting it from the direct pursuit of broader social change goals. In extreme cases, this strategy involved the encouragement of armed conflict. In San Diego, four people were wounded and two killed during a summer of clandestinely encouraged FBI fighting between rival black groups (U.S. and the Black Panthers). A 1969 memo to J. Edgar Hoover on this episode stated, "Shootings, beatings, and a high degree of unrest continues to prevail in the ghetto area of southeast San Diego. Although no specific counterintelligence action can be credited with contributing to this overall situation, it is felt that a substantial amount of unrest is directly attributable to this program" (Wise, 1976, p. 319).

Actions aimed at preventing coalitions and cooperative actions may be undertaken. For example, after Malcolm X's assassina-tion, the Socialist Workers party attempted to gain new recruits from the Black Muslims. FBI informers within the New York Black Muslims were encouraged to speak out against the "anti-religious" Socialist Workers party and to thwart their recruitment efforts (Berman and Halperin, 1975, p. 26).

Rather than encouraging conflict between organizations under the umbrella of the same social movement, conflict may also be encouraged among social movements with very different ideologies. Thus an FBI informant organized the right-wing Secret Army Organization in San Diego, a group that attacked leftists (Viorst, 1976). In Operation Hoodwink, the FBI sought to encourage conflict between the Communist party and elements of organized crime. According to an FBI memo, it was hoped that this action "would cause disruption of both groups by having each expend their energies, time, and money attacking each other" (Donner, 1976, p. 19).

A related tactic involves creating alternative social movement organizations. For example, during the 1960s and early 1970s, U.S. authorities created Communist, student, Klan, and anti-Communist type groups. These may compete with the target group for a limited resource base, fight with it over matters of doctrine and policy, and offer authorities unprecedented control over the movement since it is a government front. There are some parallels to the trade unions sponsored by the Russian police.

Sabotaging Particular Actions

When social movements take public action, they often seek to expand their base to include sympathetic but nonactivist members of their presumed mass constituency, as well as enter into coalitions with other social movement organizations whose members are not well known to them. Movements often have a loose and shifting nature, are geographically dispersed, and frequently lack specialized internal resources. When national or regional meetings or demonstrations are held, out-of-town members must be housed and fed. Goods and services must be obtained from secondary sources. Strangers are brought together ostensibly in cooperative action but without the usual means of verifying identity. These factors make public social movement events vulnerable to disruption. Those seeking to disrupt a movement are offered a rich field for intervention.

Tactics of misinformation have been used to notify members falsely that events were cancelled, that they were being held elsewhere, or that times had been changed (Select Committee, book II, 1976, p. 10). Fake orders have been broadcast over the same citizen's band frequency used by marshals trying to control demonstrations, and CB communications have been jammed.

For large demonstrations planned in Chicago and Washington, FBI agents obtained and duplicated housing supply forms, which they filled in with fictitious names and addresses of people supposedly willing to offer housing to demonstrators. After "long and useless journeys to locate these addresses," demonstrators found themselves with no housing (ibid., p. 10).

Particular protest events are often affected by social control activities such as restrictive parade routes, permit denials, police provocation, and police failure to restrain those bent on attacking demonstrators. The government may pay and encourage counterdemonstrators, though only in a few recent cases have such actions been used. As one example, Bernard Barker and six other Cubans later to be involved in Watergate were flown in from Miami on White House orders to disrupt an antiwar demonstration on the Capitol steps. According to one of those involved, they were to punch Daniel Ellsberg, call him a traitor, and run. They did not succeed, but they did

fight with some other demonstrators. Two of them were taken by police but were soon released (Wise, 1976, p. 174). The Secret Service roughed up and prevented demonstrators with antiwar and anti-Nixon signs from attending a Billy Graham rally in North Carolina. Demonstrators were told their admission tickets were counterfeit (*New York Times,* April 22, 1975).

In labor struggles, there have been many alliances between management and local and state authorities. In labor struggles up to the 1930s, goon squads and private police hired to break strikes and attack organizers sometimes avoided prosecution and were even deputized. Police and National Guard were also called out to break strikes.

Some of the actions taken or contemplated would be worthy of humorous appreciation for the imagination involved were they not on behalf of legally and morally questionable ends. The FBI in Newark suggested an action that would result in "confusion and suspicion" during a Black Panther party convention. The idea was to send a telegram warning that food donated to the convention contained poison and that one of its symptoms was stomach cramps. The FBI laboratory then planned to "treat fruit such as oranges with a mild laxative-type drug by hypodermic needle or other appropriate method." The oranges were apparently not injected because of the FBI's lack of control over the fruit during shipment, though Hoover felt that the idea "has merit" (Wise, 1976, pp. 318–19).

Efforts to Facilitate Social Movements

It appears that government actions aimed at damaging rather than facilitating movements have been much more formalized and prevalent. At least many more examples of the former have become public. It is hard to identify equivalent government agencies such as the police or FBI, or programs such as COINTELL, concerned with facilitating domestic social movements. The actions of nonpolice government agencies, courts, or legislators with implications for social movements are much more likely to be of a general and overt nature, rather than being at the specific micro-level in response to a given movement. When micro-level facilitative actions do occur, they are often indirect, and reactive; examples are courts' overturning or inhibiting police efforts to damage a movement.

Many of the facilitative actions that police use are of a rather special nature. They may be part of an indirect strategy to strengthen or create (in order to control) a group that is the opponent, or rival, of the real target group. The government's aim is not to help the aided group obtain its goals as such. Or in the classic tradition of the provocateur, authorities may covertly encourage a group in order to sanction it later. A separate issue is that some actions by authorities inadvertently end up being facilitative.

It is easier to illustrate the right than the left side of Table 22.1. Nevertheless there are some domestic examples of intended facilitation involving anti-Communists, the Klan, and the labor, civil rights, and women's movements. There are also many examples of facilitation in the activities of the CIA outside the United States.

Until the 1960s when the federal government legitimated the civil rights movement and put resources into voter registration and initiated the War on Poverty and community action, and the 1970s when women's rights gained considerable support, the major beneficiaries of facilitative efforts were right-wing, anti-civil rights, and management groups. Such groups have tended to involve countermovements and often vigilante-like action. The predominant forms of support were immunity and information. Periods of intense anticommunism—the red scare,

the Palmer raids, and McCarthyism—have seen increased alliances and cooperative actions of government-investigating committees, police, and private groups, such as the American Protective League, the American Legion, and the American Security Council. Some retired FBI members or local police who have worked in intelligence units go to work for Americanism committees. Sometimes it appears that the social movement is primarily helping the government to a much greater extent than the reverse.

The granting of de facto legal immunity can be seen in some Latin American countries in attacks of the right on the left, which the government tends to ignore. Another example is the relation between the police and the Klan, where, in some parts of the South, the Klan was given what amounted to a license to break the law. Police in a sense delegated authority to Klansmen to carry out racial status quo–preserving activities that police could not legally carry out. Police behavior in many instances of earlier American racial violence has involved offering a de facto legal immunity to whites attacking blacks and some examples of the direct facilitation of particular actions by actually joining in the attacks (Marx, 1970).

The CIA gave large sums of money to domestic student, business, labor, church, and cultural groups. By strengthening moderate groups, such actions may have indirectly hurt more radical groups. Although these moderate groups are not social movements as usually defined, they often give money and support to them. Ironically money given to the National Student Association may have helped build up an infrastructure and national student networks that were important to the later student movement.

A major way that government has aided recent movements such as those concerned with consumer and environmental issues has been through information leaks of various kinds. Groups such as Common Cause and Ralph Nader's consumer groups that seek to mobilize public opinion often appear to have allies within the government who pass on important technical and political information. Sometimes these efforts are part of a strategy by top administrators to build public support for goals shared with the movement. At other times, they stem from movement sympathizers within the government. As the cohort that reached adulthood during the late 1960s and early 1970s enters the government, this practice may become even more common. The Freedom of Information Act is likely to have important facilitative implications.

In a special category of pseudofacilitative activities, the government helps a movement (or segments of it) but not out of a desire to have it obtain its goals. Rather it can be a means of exercising partial control over it. Assumptions may be made about the extensiveness of mass anger and the predisposition to join a movement. A government-controlled movement able to obtain some concessions may be considered the best alternative.

The police-initiated Russian trade unions and some company unions are examples, as are the moderate Klan-type organizations created by the FBI. However hostile the FBI was to the Communist party, it took actions to keep it in its traditional form rather than to see it reorganized under a new label. Some observers would also place community action organizations created under the War on Poverty in this category.

Efforts by Other Groups and Countries

Recent congressional hearings offer much information on the extent to which the CIA has attempted to be a resource or a constraint for social movements in other countries (Commission on CIA, 1975; Select Committee, book I, 1976). Concomitantly many foreign countries have a strong interest in U.S. internal affairs.

A number of government investigations have been unable to find strong links between broad American movements such as the New Left, antiwar, and civil rights movements and the U.S.S.R., China, or Cuba. Yet it is unlikely that a lack of foreign intervention (in supportive or adversarial form) could be found for more narrowly based movements concerned with U.S. policy toward, and the nature of the government in, countries such as Cuba, Chile, Korea, Iran, Israel, and Yugoslavia and other countries of Eastern Europe. Such movements are often formed around a nucleus of immigrants. Depending on their orientation, they are likely to receive resources or face constraints from the country in question. We must ask questions about the Cuban government, as well as the CIA, in seeking to understand the Fair Play for Cuba Committee, or current struggles in Miami between groups with opposing views of Cuba. This also holds even for what appear to be strictly domestic issues—for example, the pro-Nixon demonstrations organized by Reverend Moon, who is apparently linked in complex ways to the Korean government.[8]

Another fascinating and almost completely unstudied source of external mobilization and constraint is the corporation. For example Samuel Zemurray, the man primarily responsible for building the United Fruit empire, created a 1910 revolution in Honduras. His hired bands swept through the country and established a puppet president sympathetic to the needs of United Fruit. Many years later, several United Fruit ships carried men and weapons to the Bay of Pigs (McCann, 1976). In the age of the multinational corporation, increased overt and covert intervention efforts may be expected.

Questions, Patterns, and Explanations of Government Behavior

In trying to account for the behavior of the government (rather than looking at what it tried to do or what the consequences were) a number of questions arise:

- What are the historical roots of such behavior?
- What conditions the decision to intervene?
- What conditions the direction and form of the intervention—for example, whether it moves from information gathering to trying to affect outcomes; whether it aims to facilitate, redirect, or damage a movement; whether it is done overtly or covertly, legally or illegally, and directly on the group itself or indirectly on its environment?
- How do officials justify and protect themselves with respect to actions they take?
- Once government action has appeared, what factors affect its course and the frequent tendency for it to expand?

These are the kinds of questions that must be answered if we are to understand how external groups attempt to facilitate or damage a movement. Some of the answers may emerge after considering three empirical patterns of particular interest: (1) movements on the Left have received the most attention, followed by those on the Right, with relatively little attention being paid to movements or organizations in the center (except insofar as they were thought to be infiltrated by those from the Left or the Right); (2) efforts to damage social movements seem far more common than efforts to facilitate them; (3) the tendency for the government to intervene in social movement affairs has expanded over the last forty years.

The much greater emphasis on the Left than the Right may be explained by the fact that there are possibly more social movements on the Left than the Right; yet the imbalance of governmental attention appears to go far beyond this. For example, of the political cases in the Media, Pennsylvania, FBI files, more than two hundred involved Left and liberal groups, and only two involved right-wing groups. It could also be argued that the Left is more prone to illegal actions; yet the relative absence of successful prosecution of those on the Left would not support this theory. A General Services Administration audit of domestic intelligence investigations notes that only about 1 percent resulted in convictions. More likely, the pattern represents a carryover from a cold war ideology where the Left is defined as the enemy and the Right as the enemy of the enemy; it thus appears in a more benign light. In addition, the Left attacked J. Edgar Hoover while the Right praised him. With his highly personalized style of directing the FBI, Hoover often used its resources against those he defined as enemies, whether or not they had broken laws or were clearly security threats. Authorities in general are closer in terms of social characteristics, ideology, and lifestyle to those on the Right. Cases where the government has intervened with right-wing groups have, in general, been more likely to involve manifest illegality that cannot be ignored, and often, as with Klan-type groups in the South, disagreements between local and national social-control agents. Cases where the Right turns on the government, as with Joseph McCarthy's attacks on the army or the John Birch

Society's attacks on President Eisenhower, have also elicited responses.

The much greater emphasis on damage than facilitation (regardless of whether the Left or Right is involved) may be because social movements with their goals of change and their less institutionalized form are more likely to be seen as threats, rather than assets, by authorities tied to the status quo. Even where this is not the case, authorities may find it easier to justify illegal actions against those seen as subversive than to justify illegal actions on behalf of those seen as patriots. In addition, domestic social control agencies concerned with enforcing the criminal law have a conflict-apprehension ethos that is probably more conducive to combative than facilitative forms of interaction.

In other countries, covert U.S. actions have involved facilitation to a much greater extent than has been the case domestically. For example, U.S. interests in Communist, left-leaning, or anti-American countries are likely to be defined in opposition to the status quo. As such, the logic is to help elements wanting change, while in the United States (or in cases where its allies are weak or threatened) it has generally been the reverse: to damage social movements, some of which in a foreign context may themselves be facilitated by the Soviet Union or other countries.

The Expansion of Social Control

The government's ability and willingness to monitor and intervene in domestic social movement affairs has increased significantly in the last forty years.[9] According to the Select Committee, there has been "a relentless expansion of domestic intelligence activity beyond investigation of criminal conduct toward the collection of political intelligence and the launching of secret offensive actions against Americans" (Select Committee, book II, 1976, p. 21). There has

been an expansion with respect to criteria for defining who is to become a target, the number of agencies involved, and the tactics used.

Those considered appropriate targets for FBI intelligence activities have expanded from Communist party members and groups, to those allegedly under Communist influence, to those taking positions supported by Communists, to those who might become subject to Communist influence. A wide range of domestic groups who broke no laws and had nothing to do with Communists, fascists, or foreign threats became subjects for intelligence activities and covert action. From a concern with Communists, government attention was broadened in the 1960s to include "racial matters," the "New Left" "student agitation," and alleged "foreign influence" on the antiwar movement. Counterintelligence activities and investigations were undertaken against "rabble-rousers," "agitators," "key activists," and "key black extremists." The women's liberation, gay, and ecology movements have also received attention, as have PTAs and religious groups.

Government intervention in social movements affairs spread from the FBI to the Internal Revenue Service, the National Security Administration, and military intelligence agencies. Local police have also become much more involved. Their activities are particularly relevant to understanding the struggles of blacks, students, and the peace movement during the 1960s and early 1970s. A significant expansion of political policing at the local level occurred, partly in response to encouragement and resources from the Justice Department. The IRS in response to White House pressure created a program to audit certain politically active persons and organizations. Army intelligence collected massive amounts of data and carried out surveillance on citizens. The CIA used its vague mandate to protect its intelligence sources and methods to set up Operation Chaos and to engage in electronic surveillance, break-ins, and the use of informers among domestic protest groups.

By 1975 this expansion had halted and, according to public accounts, was being reversed.[10] In the post-Watergate period and following the decline of mass demonstrations (and new austerity programs in many municipalities), authorities at both the local and national level have lessened, sometimes significantly, their efforts to monitor and intervene in social movement affairs in destructive ways. Formal policies were established and updated, dossiers destroyed, intelligence units reduced in size or disbanded, and new accountability measures created.

What best explains the general expansion of government intervention, particularly at the federal level, in social movement affairs since its revival in the late 1930s? Many different government agencies, different types of intervention, and thousands of different groups across the country expanded over almost four decades. The topic is highly complex and multifaceted. No single theory is sufficient. Yet the broad pattern indicates at least five types of explanations that may be relevant: (1) a reactive crisis-response model, (2) a proactive anticipation-prevention model, (3) a bureaucratic and individual aggrandizement model, (4) a resource expansion-temptation model, and (5) a society-needs-devils model.

Crisis Response

This model assumes that systems operate to protect themselves and respond to threats to their equilibrium. Authorities are compelled to take the actions they do because of what the social movement does or claims it wants to do. As laws are broken, symbols attacked, and revolutionary rhetoric expressed, authorities respond in kind. They are seen (and publicly often see themselves) as reactive to subversive system-damaging social movements. Conditions for the emergence of such social control efforts and their expansion or contraction are found in the extent of the threat posed by a change-seeking social movement. If social control efforts have generally expanded over the last forty years, it is because the threats, or at least the perception of them, have also. As the threats decrease, so do social control activities.

To test this model, some objective means of threat assessment is needed, though it is likely to be difficult to get agreement on just who and what a threat is, particularly when laws have not been broken. A better measure might be authorities' perceptions of the extent of threat, though here one must be careful to separate actual from self-serving beliefs. National security and subversion offer easy rationalizations, as Watergate demonstrated. The threat-crisis argument seems consistent with the expansion of intelligence activities just prior to and during World War II; the creation of COINTELL programs against white hate groups, black nationalists, and the New Left, and the Huston plan, following the killing and intimidation of civil rights workers, civil disorders, and widespread antiwar and campus demonstrations; and the significant reduction in government efforts to damage social movements as relative calm returned in the mid-1970s.

Anticipation-Prevention and Inherent Pressures in the Role

Tendencies to expand may be inherent in intelligence gathering and crime or subversion prevention roles. The role may be defined in such a way as to create an appetite that can never be satiated. Unlike the crisis-response model, the response here comes because a crisis is anticipated, or at least can be conceived of. This ability to imagine future threats calls forth action. The emphasis is put on offensive action. Factors conducive to this response are the vagueness of concepts like subversion and conspiracy, the absence of obvious states of goal achievement, and the fact that one can never be certain that an investigation has turned up all the relevant information. Those charged with such open-ended tasks may find it in their interest to cast the widest possible net and to operate as indiscriminate intelligence gatherers.

Officials can always imagine future scenarios that require new data-gathering tasks and preventive efforts (some of the actions directed against Martin Luther King, Jr., seem to have been of this sort). Proving hypotheses in intelligence work presents all the problems of data collection, interpretation, and validity found in proving them in a scientific inquiry. In addition, the subject may be consciously engaging in deceptive action. According to this rationale, an investigation that suggests minimal threat and no outside conspiracy may be part of a carefully designed trap to confuse the investigator, or the conclusion may stem from insufficient and careless investigation. Can you trust your own agents? Can one ever be too prepared in a context thought likely to become a war or when dealing with enemies that one's ideology may describe as utterly ruthless, cunning, and driven to subvert you?[11]

Recent government hearings offer abundant examples consistent with this model. In 1940 Hoover wrote that those advocating foreign "isms" "had succeeded in boring into every phase of American life, masquerading behind 'front' organizations" (Select Committee, book II, 1976, p. 31). The FBI's "theory of subversive infiltration" meant that Communists and other domestic enemies might be found anywhere. A belief that individuals are guilty until proven innocent calls for eternal vigilance. The FBI, with little statutory justification, came to define itself in a 1966 memo to all its field offices as an "intelligence agency . . . *expected to know what is going on or is likely to happen* [italics added]" (ibid., p. 70).

Vague, all-inclusive definitions became the rule. For example, the FBI manual stated that it was "not possible to formulate any hard-and-fast standards [for measuring] the dangerousness of individual members or affiliates of revolutionary organizations." The manual further stated, "Where there is doubt an individual may be a current threat to the internal security of the nation, the question should be resolved in the interest of security and investigation conducted" (ibid., p. 47). In the case of groups such as the New Left, efforts to define it were vague and were "expanded continually." The agent in charge of intelligence on the New Left stated, "It has never been strictly defined . . . it's more or less of an attitude" (ibid., p. 72). A memo to all FBI field offices noted that the term does not refer to "a definite organization" but a "loosely-bound, free-wheeling, college-oriented movement" and to the "more extreme and militant anti-Vietnam war and antidraft protest organizations" (ibid., p. 73).

There is always abundant room for ideological predispositions and/or contrary expectations on the part of supervisors to generate pressure for more information. In a large investigation of the civil rights movement, J. Edgar Hoover pressured one of his top assistants to keep investigating until he found the link between the civil rights movement and the Communist party that Hoover was convinced existed. His insistence came after an initial investigation found no such connection. President Johnson, unhappy over investigations concluding that there was almost no link between the antiwar movement and foreign countries, pressured for more vigorous and extensive investigations.

The source of this proactive model may go beyond conspiratorial ideologies to a managerial model involving planning and the anticipation of demand (Graber, 1976). Galbraith's argument that the modern corporation has moved from passively being at the mercy of market forces of supply and demand to trying actively to affect those forces by intervention may apply here. Social control activities may also spiral because authorities increasingly feel a need to cover, protect, and justify their actions.[12]

Bureaucratic and Individual Aggrandizement

Factors that explain the origin of a phenomenon may not necessarily explain its continuance. Thus the origin of government programs for social movement intervention may generally lie in events that most members of a society would define as a crisis or a serious threat. However, the programs can take on a life of their own as vested interests develop around them, and new latent goals may emerge. Rather than social control as repression, deterrence, or punishment, it can become a vehicle for career advancement and organizational perpetuation and growth. The management and even creation of deviance, rather than its elimination, can become central. Intelligence and crime or subversion prevention roles offer rich possibilities to an entrepreneurial administrator or employee seeking to expand his or her domain. J. Edgar Hoover offers a clear example of this, but there are also many examples at the local level. The FBI increased from 500 to 4,000 employees by the end of World War II. Hoover, faced with the prospect of a greatly reduced agency with the end of the war effort, may have felt pressure to justify its size. The problem of Communist subversion offered a means of doing this. The bureau now has 25,000 employees.

Hoover skillfully manipulated the threat of domestic communism to gain continued support and increased resources from Congress, as his predecessors Attorney Generals Palmer and Dougherty had done with the red scare around World War I. Hoover was a moral entrepreneur with respect to both targets and tactics. He was a genius at using subtle language; he stressed "endeavors," "attempts," and "goals" of the target groups such as Communists, rather than their successes, because there were so few of the latter (Select Committee, book II, 1976, p. 49). Documents now available suggest that Hoover did not believe much of his own rhetoric and that he had accurate assessments of how weak and ineffective the Communist party was. When the size of the party began declining sharply, the FBI stopped reporting its strength and told inquirers that such information was classified (*Boston Globe*, November 19, 1975). Hoover also knew that whatever their rhetoric (which stopped short of incitement to violence), the Socialist Workers party did not engage in criminal acts over the thirty years that the FBI investigated it (Halperin et al., 1976, pp. 102–05).

Yet although this model fits some of the data, particularly J. Edgar Hoover's activities with respect to the Communist party, other data do not fit it. Thus Hoover appeared hesitant to move against the New Left, preferring to focus on the Old Left. When he finally did approve COINTELL operations, it was in response to a memo that rather than showing how the New Left was a threat to national security, argued that "the New Left has on many occasions viciously and scurrilously attacked the Director and the Bureau" (Select Committee, book II, 1976, p. 73). Vindictiveness rather than resource expansion seems the motive. However, an aggrandizement model would seem to fit the middle-management officials on the New Left desk who sought to extend COINTELL activities.

This model must also be tempered by noting that social control agencies operate within a broader political and social environment. Actions taken are partly in response to pressures perceived (both correctly and incorrectly) from this environment. Hoover, for example, was formally subordinate to the president and the attorney general, and he was very concerned with the public image of the bureau. His hand was not completely free. Some of the actions he took were in direct response to orders from superiors. In many of his actions, he may have anticipated what they wanted and not gone beyond that.

The bureau's reentry into political intelligence actions in the later 1930s was undertaken at the direction of President Roosevelt. The Johnson and Nixon administrations wanted information on and action against student, antiwar, and militant black protesters. Other actions that Hoover refrained from taking appear related to his concern with the public image of the FBI. His formal abolition of FBI break-ins, his reducing wiretaps by half in 1966, and his rejection of the Huston plan in 1970 are examples. With increased citizen and congressional concern, Hoover apparently believed such activities were too risky.

Yet to explain intervention in social movement affairs in light of the wishes of higher authorities has a question-begging potential.[13] The explanation is simply pushed up a level. We must then ask what conditions the behavior of higher authorities. Response to a perceived crisis and a desire to prevent a crisis are, of course, relevant. But as was the case with Richard Nixon and to a much lesser extent Lyndon Johnson and Franklin Roosevelt, a desire for the information gained from political intelligence and counterespionage, independent of any threats to national security, may also be involved. As the technology for these evolves, so too may the temptation to use it. Among the most interesting of questions are the links between having secret information and the desire to take covert action on the basis of it. Leaders, like the rest of us, may find that they can resist anything but temptation. An opportunity structure approach to deviance may apply to them as well as to more traditional deviants.

Governmental Expansion and New Resources

This century has seen a major expansion of government at all levels, and increased authority and centralization at the federal level. In this sense, increased government involvement—whether in health care, communications, or social movements—is part of a broader trend. But beyond this trend, the expansion of social control activities no doubt is also related to increased resources for doing this.

New opportunities and temptations have been created by ever more sophisticated technology for data gathering (bugging, electronic surveillance, and photography are examples), data storing, retrieving, and analyzing (computers as well as forms of analysis such as game theory or in-depth psychological profiles that call for data); and scientific developments permitting ever more subtle covert action.

An increasing pool of veterans of the cold war skilled in covert operations would also seem to be a factor. With respect to personnel, for example, all of those involved in the Watergate break-in were former CIA or FBI employees. John Caulfield and Anthony Ulasewitz, who did secret political investigations for the White House, were formerly of the New York City Police Department's Bureau of Special Services and Investigations. The absolute number of retired CIA, military intelligence agents, and local police increases each year. Thus in 1973, CIA director Schlesinger asked Congress to increase from 830 to 1,200 the number of

CIA agents who could retire after twenty years of service at the age of fifty (*New York Times,* May 2, 1973). Lucrative pension plans at the municipal level also mean that an increasing number of local police are retiring at an early age after twenty or twenty-five years of service.

What line of work such retired agents choose, if any, is conditioned by many factors, but their availability offers new resources for covert social movement intervention and intelligence gathering on the part of government (which may choose to delegate out some of this work to its own private police, as Nixon did), private interest groups, or other social movements. Such former agents are in some ways the counterpart of the new group of social movement professionals noted by McCarthy and Zald (1973). Both have specialized career skills independent of any specific social movement.

Society "Needs" Devils

This approach draws on a functionalist perspective on deviance from Durkheim (1960) and Erikson (1966). The creation of disvalued symbols is seen to help integrate a loosely organized society with considerable strain. Sanctioning of activists ("dangerous radicals," "subversives," "aliens," "reds," "hippies," "communists," "Klansmen," "militants," "fascists") who go too far from basic norms, even if they break no laws, can serve as a reminder to others to stay in line and can help bring a heterogeneous society together in shared condemnation of the outsiders.

Devil creation can also be seen as part of a scapegoating phenomenon wherein authorities' conscious manipulation of the threat of a social movement takes mass attention away from more basic sources of grievance, although with the increased education and sophistication of the American

public and increased resources for mobilization, this becomes more difficult to do.

This model is the most difficult to test. It can involve teleological assumptions and the reification of the concept society. It is likely most useful for considering some of the consequences of government sanctioning of social movements rather than the expansion or contraction of such activities.

Outcomes: Intended and Unintended

I have noted ways in which authorities may seek to help or damage a movement and have offered examples to illustrate the relevant concepts. I have assumed authorities know what they wanted to do and were able to do it. Sometimes this is the case; often it is not. In considering efforts to damage or facilitate a movement, it is important to ask what the actual (rather than intended) consequences of such efforts are; whether the government achieves the result it seeks; if it does not, what factors prevent it; and what other results are possible.

Let us turn to some of the complicating factors that may result in consequences other than those intended by authorities. That there is frequently a gap between formal and informal factors and intended and actual consequences is not surprising. Indeed much sociological research is directed toward understanding this general issue. In this regard, it is necessary to inquire what is unique about the situation of authorities' responding to the social movements. At least six somewhat exceptional factors that increase the likelihood of the government's intervention having unintended consequences can be identified: the secrecy involved; the frequent illegality of the actions; the lack of effective intervention techniques in the face of the diffuse, noninstitutionalized collective-behavior character of much social movement activity; the need to establish credibility through seemingly loyal actions; and the reactive neutralization processes inherent in many social control efforts.

Secrecy has meant a lack of accountability and usual standards of performance evaluation. There are problems in controlling agents, and occasional scenarios take place in which secret agents (unbeknown to each other) engage in mutual intelligence gathering and provocation.

It is more difficult to damage social movements in a context with a tradition of civil liberties and with levels and branches of government that are not monolithic. Many of the actions taken by authorities have been illegal. When authorities take illegal or morally questionable actions in a nonconsensual context, they run the risk of helping the movement should they be exposed. The government's legitimacy and credibility may be damaged, and court cases may be filed because of illegal procedures.

But even if government actions are not exposed or there is widespread public support, the nature of the phenomenon and our lack of social engineering knowledge may result in effects on group processes, or individual motivation, that are quite different from those authorities sought. Attention directed toward a movement may convince activists that they are a genuine threat and that what they are doing is of vital importance. By clearly focusing external conflict for the movement, authorities may heighten the sense of group boundaries and increase internal solidarity. Surveillance may make participation more exciting. It may increase the will, resolve, and anger of some activists. It may call forth martyrs who become important rallying symbols. It may make activists more radical and push them away from the reformist belief that change within the system is possible.

Infiltrators may be an important resource for the movement. To establish and maintain credibility, they must take actions that help it. For example, FBI informant Robert Hardy provided leadership, training, and resources to those involved in the Camden draft board raid (*New York Times*, March 16, 1972). He stated, "I taught them everything they knew . . . how to cut glass and open windows without making any noise. . . . How to open file cabinets without a key. . . . How to climb ladders easily and walk on the edge of the roof without falling. . . . I began to feel like the Pied Piper" (*Washington Post*, November 19, 1975). A Klan informant has reported how while performing duties paid for by the government, he had "beaten people severely, had boarded buses and kicked people, had [gone] into restaurants and beaten them [blacks] with blackjacks, chairs, and pistols." FBI informants were formally told that they could not be involved in violence; nevertheless he understood that in the Klan "he couldn't be an angel and be a good informant" (Select Committee, book III, 1976, p. 13).

As a movement comes under increased attack, it may be able to obtain increased resources for defense or a counteroffensive from its mass constituency and other sympathetic audiences.[14] Rival groups may make covert attempts to neutralize and disrupt the activities of government agents. The conflict may escalate.

Recent social movement repression in the United States clearly has some unique elements. Judged in a historical and international context, much of it was relatively benign, particularly at the federal level. It is hard to imagine national police forces in most of the rest of the world today, let alone in the past, responding to opposition social movements by injecting oranges with a laxative, tattling about sexual affairs, or printing and circulating false offers of housing for demonstrators. If a group is judged worthy of attention, violence against activists, threats, and arrests are far more common and effective. For American police at the federal level (in the absence of legal violations), such actions were too risky and morally unacceptable to many agents in a domestic context. The lesser availability of these overtly repressive tactics helps explain the tactics that emerged and the receptivity to agents capable of provoking illegal actions to justify government intervention. Many of the FBI COINTELL actions are best seen as expressive and symbolic; they were a way of doing something when there was often little that could be done legally. The local, relatively spontaneous, mass-based, collective-behavior-like quality of much activism also made traditional social-movement monitoring and breaking tactics less applicable.

In broad outline, several conclusions can be made about the effect of government efforts to damage the social movements of the 1960s and early 1970s. Let us take goal attainment and organizational viability as our criteria and consider the movements that received the most attention from the FBI's COINTELL program. There is a varied pattern. In the case of the Klan, Communist party, Socialist Workers party, and more radical black groups like the Panthers, the evidence is consistent with the argument that social control efforts were effective. These groups did not obtain their goals and did not increase with respect to organizational viability; indeed most seemed to decrease. These groups tended to be ideologically extreme and to recruit from marginal sources. As a result, they may have been more vulnerable to government efforts to damage them because they could not draw on mass audiences for support and sympathy to the extent that the more moderate groups could. The Klan and more radical black groups also

appear more likely to have been involved in felonious actions and to have used violent rhetoric, offering authorities greater possibilities for legal interventions. Relative to many of the other movements, they also seem to have in lesser abundance the organizational skills and sophistication needed to run a national movement.

Authorities appear to have been least successful against the antiwar, student, and moderate civil rights movements, groups that maintained, and even increased, strength until their major goals were obtained. In the case of the student and antiwar movements, this was in spite of massive efforts to damage them on a scale unprecedented in American history. With the exception of black groups, these movements have now declined, yet this is partly as a result of their very success.

In the case of the early civil rights movement, especially in the South, efforts by local authorities to damage the movement were more than matched by the facilitative efforts of the federal government (though efforts of nonsupport and even to damage can also be seen). The civil rights movement sought basic rights that had long been part of the American tradition for other groups, and it did so with nonviolent action in the name of Christianity. Its successes were the continuation of civil rights trends evident since before World War II. Only later, following the ghetto riots, did the federal government attempt covert action to damage the more radical black groups.

With the ending of the Vietnam War and the draft, greater flexibility and democratization on college campuses, and more sensitive college administrators who learned how not to be provoked and overreact to the small cadre of fully committed student radicals, the mass-based antiwar and more moderate student movements practically disappeared. They were at best heterogeneous and loosely held together by opposition to particular policies that were changed. They did not draw on shared interests growing out of historic or enduring cleavages and a culture of opposition within the society. As such, with victory came organizational defeat. Their large-scale, decentralized, participatory, fluid, shifting, and spontaneous collective behavior character did not lend itself well to the kinds of movement-damaging tactics the FBI had used against the bureaucratically organized Communist party. Yet even with better tactics, the level of mass support for stopping the war became so great and included so many powerful and respected business and political leaders that it is doubtful the movement could have been stopped within the traditional American framework. The same applies to the demands of the civil rights groups through 1964.

In response to the question of what happened to the student and antiwar movements, one is tempted to say they never really existed beyond the evening news and the immorality of the war or the incompetence of college administrators. They did not resolve the problems of structure noted by Jo Freeman (1977). At least they did not exist in the sense that the NAACP, Communist party, Socialist Workers party, Klan, and Black Panthers did. These groups had more ideological coherence and unity and a steadier organizational structure, and they were capable of mobilizing members and sympathizers in other than a reactive sense. They knew what they were for, as well as what they were against. Yet even in the case of those groups such as the Klan, radical blacks, and the Communist party, where the results desired by authorities appeared, can we conclude that authorities were responsible? Many factors beyond the efforts of external groups to facilitate or inhibit social movement processes affect them so there is a major difficulty in separating correlation from causation in natural field settings. Determining the effect of efforts at social control or facilitation on a given outcome is difficult. Where a major social change goal sought by a movement is obtained (and this is infrequent, particularly in the short run), it is difficult to tell how important the movement was to this end, what the causal link was, whether it occurred in spite of the movement's efforts, and whether the appearance of both the social change and the social movement were accounted for by some third set of factors.

Is the splintering of a sectarian group into two rival groups more a function of the efforts of authorities to create internal conflict, or of the seemingly endemic tendency of such groups to factionalism, even where no social control efforts are present? Is a high degree of turnover, sporadic participation, and ebbs and flows in mass participation more a function of authorities' ability to damage morale and create an unfavorable public image and the myth of surveillance and repression, or of the general problems involved in sustaining a mass movement, where many of the rewards for participation may be minimal and some may be available (if the movement succeeds) to nonparticipants as well?

With respect to the movements in question, it could be argued that government actions contributed to their failings but were not really decisive. The black power and black pride groups that grew out of the moderate civil rights groups failed when they opted for more radical goals and means. They moved from demands for inclusion and basic rights of a political and symbolic nature that could be granted without direct economic loss to whites (the right to vote, equal justice, nondiscrimination in hiring and public services, and racial dignity) to more controversial and zero-sum issues of an economic nature involving redistribution, retribution, quotas, nonachievement criteria, and, in many cases, racialism if not always racial separation. Matching the shift in goals were (primarily at the level of media rhetoric) calls for revolution, violence, and ties to the Third World. This shift in the nature of the black movement does not seem to be something directly initiated by agents of social control. It developed out of previous victories and defeats and the structure of American society. It had also occurred several times earlier in the history of the black movement. However, authorities were soon in the thick of it and no doubt encouraged (whether they intended to do so is less clear) through self-fulfilling effects the radicalism and violence of some groups such as the Black Panthers and the Student Nonviolent Coordinating Committee.

Like the more radical black groups, the Klan seemed on the wrong side of historical trends (something that was not always true). It failed to obtain its goals of halting civil rights gains for blacks, and its membership declined significantly. Once it became the subject of concentrated government attention, its well-documented pattern of criminal conspiracy and violence markedly declined. Government intervention efforts seem most successful here.[15] However, the same broad consequences might have been forthcoming, although they may have taken longer and at a greater toll of life, if the government had not been involved in preventive and disruptive efforts. The escalation of the conflict that characterized authorities' response to radical blacks did not seem to occur here, perhaps because the Klan started out violent and often correctly saw local authorities as their allies, or at least as being neutral.

In the case of groups such as the Communists and Socialist Workers party that sought radical economic change or black groups that sought separatism, one can argue that they would have failed anyway

as their counterparts have throughout the twentieth century before efforts at social movement repression became so developed and commonplace.

The structure of American society and natural social movement processes seem to work toward the weakening of ideologically extreme movements and those not organized around fundamental societal cleavages. It is difficult to sustain less institutionalized collective behavior phenomena under the best of circumstances. This would seem to be even truer for movements resisting broad historical trends. External efforts seeking to facilitate such movements (and beyond local support for movements seeking to counter the civil rights movement, there was not much of this) would seem to have much more difficulty and would in general appear to be less effective than those seeking to destroy them. Many of the outcomes sought by authorities seeking to damage social movements were likely to happen anyway, though perhaps not as rapidly or to the same degree.

Some inferences might also be made from what happened between 1924 and 1936 when the FBI ceased domestic intelligence. There was not a sudden upsurge in movement effectiveness, although given the conditions of the depression, social movements proliferated. Movements such as those of Townsend, Long, Smith, and Coughlin gained in popularity and then almost disappeared for reasons that appear to have little to do with federal-level social control intervention (or its absence). Nor in the period since 1975, when both the FBI and local police seem to have significantly reduced their policing of social movements, have movements suddenly flourished.

To be sure with respect to the local level and for particular people, groups, and events they were often decisive, though not always in ways that they hoped. Social control efforts certainly had some effect on the style and direction of many movements. The humanitarian community of love, trust, and openness sought by early student, pacifist, and civil rights groups becomes difficult to sustain in the milieu of paranoia, suspicion, and violence that authorities contributed to. Activists became more cautious in their dealings with strangers. The need to be suspicious of strangers is an obvious liability for a movement that seeks to build a mass base. But considering the broad national pattern, agents are only one among a variety of historical, cultural, social structural, and resource and grievance factors to be considered.

Not by Resources Alone

Just as there were clear limits to what social control agents could accomplish, there were limits to what the social movements could do. Both are bounded by historical, cultural, structural, and psychological factors that have not been well conceptualized.

Thus, the course of the Moon movement with millions of dollars, Madison Avenue techniques, and superb organization was roughly parallel to that of other youth-oriented religious movements lacking their resources (Lofland, 1977). Such movements recruited poorly during the 1960s, significantly expanded during the early and mid-1970s as disillusionment with politics spread, and now are contracting. The availability of resources or social control does not help much in explaining this pattern, though it may be useful for intramovement comparisons.

A major future challenge for analysts of social movements lies in bringing together the resource mobilization perspective with its emphasis on organizational variables and rational self-interest, with the collective behavior perspective with its emphasis on emotion, expression, symbols, and the fluid nature of mass involvement.

I think the prime significance of government efforts to damage recent movements lies not in the all-too-easily available conspiracy theories of social movement failure or success. Rather it lies in calling attention to an important and neglected variable, the increased ability of government to engage in practices that are abhorrent to a free society. Our liberties are fragile, and we must be prepared to ask with Yeats, "What if the Church and the State are the mob that howls at the door?"

Acknowledgments

I am grateful to Jo Freeman, John Howard, Bob Ross, and Dick Wilsnack for their suggestions. A longer version is available from the author.

NOTES

1. I am thus taking prior structural conduciveness and strain (Smelser, 1963) or the kinds of social controls that may be operating through the culture, education, and "false" need creation noted by Gramsci (Genovese, 1967) and Marcuse (1964) as givens, even though these may be affected by those seeking to create or forestall the appearance of a social movement; they may have such effects.

2. This, of course, depends on how terms are defined and events assessed. What, for example, are we to make of the government's War on Poverty and community action programs? Were they an effort to facilitate poor people's movements by building alternative sources of local power that could fight city hall, or were they efforts to damage and defuse the civil rights movement through co-optation? I will start here with cases whose meaning is more manifest.

3. See, for example, work by Turner (1969), Morris (1973), Molotch and Lester (1974), and Estep and Lauderdale (1977).

4. In the investigation of the entertainment industry in the early 1950s, such activities went beyond merely releasing educational material to direct and indirect media censorship. Blacklisting, self-censorship, and anti-Communist crusades carried out through the media helped create an image of American society that was not conducive to left activism.

5. More than a million dollars had been spent by the CIA on its book development program by the mid-1960s. By 1967 the Senate Select Committee estimated that the CIA was responsible for "well over 1,000 books."

6. In part this may stem from undue reliance on an agitator theory of social movements: leaders and organizers, not social conditions, are seen as the key to movement unrest. In part it may stem from the inability of agents to do much else: leaders offer tangible specific targets for intervention in a way that mass sympathizers (many of whom are unknown to authorities) or broad social conditions do not.

7. For authorities, the power of such techniques lies in their self-perpetuating quality. Once the myth of the informer gains currency and seeds of doubt are planted, cooperation and trust are made more difficult, for anyone potentially could be one. The accusation of informer becomes available as a tool in intra-group struggle, and informers become an explanation for failures that may lie elsewhere.

8. With secret budgets, determining causal links is always difficult. According to some sources, money from Nixon in 1974 may have been channeled to Moon, who then provided pro-Nixon crowds, as at the White House Christmas tree lighting in 1974.

9. My concern is primarily with domestic affairs. However, a similar process of expansion occurred for the CIA. The CIA was created as an intelligence agency and not given clear authority or capability for covert action. Yet it quickly went beyond gathering intelligence to covert action. It moved from reporting on events to trying to influence them, at first abroad and later at home.

10. Not only may authorities on occasion be less than truthful, but given the context of secrecy and the morass of huge bureaucracies, they may find it difficult to know all that is going on in their own agencies, or whether policies are being followed. Note FBI Director Kelley's claim that FBI breaking and entering had stopped when it had not, or a CIA scientist's failure to destroy shellfish toxin after orders to do so from the president and the head of the CIA.

11. This voracious skepticism also applies to one's own efforts to maintain security. For example, the CIA was so concerned that someone might plant electronic surveillance devices in the walls of its new buildings in Langley, Virginia, that it developed a network of paid informers among construction workers on the job (Wise, 1976, p. 145).

12. Wilsnack (1977), in considering four information control processes (espionage, secrecy-security, persuasion, and evaluation), suggests the following hypothesis: "The more that a group or organization develops specialized, full-time roles for carrying out one process of information control, the more resources that group or organization will invest in each of the other control processes" (p. 14).

13. Empirically documenting this is also difficult. For example, the efforts of the Select Committee to find out who authorized CIA assassination attempts were, in the words of Senator Walter Mondale, "like trying to nail Jello to the wall." CIA agents spoke to each other in "riddles and circumlocutions." He continued, "I believe the system was intended to work that way: namely, things would be ordered to be done that should it be made public, no one could be held accountable" (Wise, 1976, pp. 214, 209).

14. In a nongovernmental context, Anita Bryant's campaign against homosexuals seems to have given the gay movement a significant boost. We can also wonder what such actions did to the self-image and work satisfaction of those in the FBI (many trained as accountants and lawyers) who carried them out.

15. Former Attorney General Nicholas deB. Katzenbach observed that following the killing of the three civil rights workers, "a

full scale investigation of the Klan was mandated. Agents of the FBI interrogated and reinterrogated every known member of the Klan in Mississippi. Many were openly followed, using surveillance techniques that the bureau had developed in connection with organized crime cases. We learned more about the Klan activities in those months than we had known in years. I have no doubt that as an integral part of that investigation, members of the Klan on whom we were focusing our efforts became disoriented, distrustful of other members, and ultimately persuaded that cooperation with the ubiquitous FBI agents was the only safe recourse" (Select Committee, Hearings, 1976, 6:215). In 1976 an estimated 2,000 of 10,000 Klan members were paid FBI informants. Seventy percent of new Klan members that year were informants (ibid., p. 144).

REFERENCES

BERMAN, J., AND M. HALPERIN (eds.) (1975) The Abuses of Intelligence Agencies. Washington: Center for National Security Studies.

BERNSTEIN, I. (1960) The Lean Years: A History of the American Worker, 1920–1933. Boston: Houghton Mifflin.

BOSTON GLOBE (1975) 19 November.

COMMISSION ON CIA ACTIVITIES WITHIN THE UNITED STATES (1975) Report to the President. Washington, D.C.: U.S. Government Printing Office.

DONNER, F. (1976) "Let him wear a wolf's head: what the FBI did to William Albertson." Civil Liberties Review (April/May).

DONOVAN, J. C. (1970) The Politics of Poverty. New York: Pegasus.

DURKHEIM, E. (1958) Rules of the Sociological Method. Glencoe, Ill.: Free Press.

ERIKSON, K. (1966) The Wayward Puritans. New York: Wiley.

ESTEP, R., and P. LAUDERDALE (1977) "News blackout: the bicentennial protest." Unpublished paper, University of Minnesota.

FREEMAN, J. (1977) "Networks and strategy in the women's liberation movement." Paper presented at this conference.

GOULDEN, J. (1971) The Money Givers. New York: Random House.

GRABER, E. (1976) "Politics' undercover agents." In Police Roles in the Seventies (Forthcoming).

HALPERIN, M., and R. BOROSAGE (1976) The Lawless State. Baltimore: Penguin.

LOFLAND, J. (1977) "The boom and bust of a millenarian movement." Preface, Doomsday Cult. New York: Irvington.

MCCANN, T. (1976) An American Company: The Tragedy of United Fruit. New York: Crown.

MCCARTHY, J. D., and M. N. ZALD (1973) The Trend of Social Movements in America: Professionalization and Resource Mobilization. Morristown, N.J.: General Learning Corporation.

MARCUSE, H. (1964) One-Dimensional Man. Boston: Beacon Press.

MARX, G. T. (1970) "Civil disorder and the agents of social control." Journal of Social Issues 26 (Winter): 19–57.

MOLOTCH, H., and M. LESTER (1975) "Accidental news: the great oil spill as local occurrence and national event." American Journal of Sociology 81, 2:235–60.

MORRIS, M. (1973) "The public definition of a social movement: women's liberation." Sociology and Social Research 57: 526–43.

NEW YORK TIMES (1976) 4 February; 11 July.
———(1975) 22 April.
———(1973) 2 May.
———(1972) 16 March.

SELECT COMMITTEE TO STUDY GOVERNMENTAL OPERATIONS WITH RESPECT TO INTELLIGENCE FINAL REPORT (1976) Bks. 1–6; Hearings. Vols. 1–7. Washington, D.C.: U.S. Government Printing Office.

SMELSER, N. J. (1963) Theory of Collective Behavior. New York: Free Press.

TURNER, R. H. (1969) "The public perception of protest." American Sociological Review 34:815–31.

VIORST, M. (1976) "FBI mayhem." New York Review of Books 22 (18 March).

WASHINGTON POST (1975) 19 November.

WILSON, J. (1977) "Social protest and social control." Social Problems 24 (April): 469–481.

WISE, D. (1976) The American Police State. New York: Random House.

ORGANIZATIONAL DYNAMICS

23

THE IRON LAW OF OLIGARCHY

SEYMOUR MARTIN LIPSET

Introduction

It is organization which gives birth to the domination of the elected over the electors, of the mandataries over the mandators, of the delegates over the delegators. Who says organization says oligarchy.

These words, first published in 1911, sum up Michels' famous "iron law of oligarchy." In *Political Parties,* Robert Michels, then a young German sociologist, laid down what has come to be the major political argument against Rousseau's concept of direct popular democracy which underlay much of the traditional democratic and socialist theory. For Michels argued that the malfunctioning of existing democracy, in particular the domination by the leadership over the society and popular organizations, was not primarily a phenomenon which resulted from a low level of social and economic development, inadequate education, or capitalist control of the opinion-forming media and other power resources, but rather was characteristic of any complex social system. Oligarchy, the control of a society or an organization by those at the top, is an intrinsic part of bureaucracy or large-scale organization. Modern man, according to him, is faced with an unresolvable dilemma: he cannot have large institutions such as nation states, trade unions, political parties, or churches, without turning over effective power to the few who are at the summit of these institutions.

To demonstrate his thesis that democracy and large-scale social organization are incompatible, Michels examined the behavior of the Socialist parties in Germany and elsewhere which appeared to be, at that time, the most committed to the extension of democracy. Long active personally in the German socialist movement, he presented an intensive analysis of the oligarchic structure of the German Social Democratic Party, then the largest socialist party in the world. An argument that centered on showing the more conservative parties to be internally undemocratic would not have proven his point, since most German and other European conservatives did not believe in democracy, in the right or the ability of the majority to determine social policy. The socialists, however, fought for adult suffrage, free speech, and for popular participation in the operation of government and economic institutions at every level. If such parties were themselves undemocratic in their internal structure, presumably the effort to completely democratize society must fail.

What are the causes of this trend to oligarchy? To this question, Michels provided an answer.[1]

Michels' Theory of Organization

Large-scale organizations give their officers a near monopoly of power.

Political parties, trade unions, and all other large organizations tend to develop a bureaucratic structure, that is, a system of rational (predictable) organization, hierarchically organized. The sheer problem of administration necessitates bureaucracy. As Michels stated: "It is the inevitable product of the very principle of organization. . . . Every party organization which has attained to a considerable degree of complication demands that there should be a certain number of persons who devote all their activities to the work of the party." But the price of increased bureaucracy is the concentration of power at the top and the lessening of influence by rank and file members. The leaders possess many resources which give them an almost unsurmountable advantage over members who try to change policies. Among their assets can be counted: a) superior knowledge, e.g., they are privy to much information which can be used to secure assent for their program; b) control over the formal means of communication with the membership, e.g., they dominate the organization press; as full-time salaried officials, they may travel from place to place presenting their case at the organization's expense, and their position enables them to command an audience; and c) skill in the art of politics, e.g., they are far more adept than nonprofessionals in making speeches, writing articles, and organizing group activities.

The masses are incapable of taking part in the decision-making process and desire strong leadership.

These occupational skills which inhere in the leader's role are power assets which are further strengthened by what Michels called the "incompetence of the masses." Any effort to sustain membership influence requires, among other things, that the members be involved in the activities of the organization, participating in meetings and being aware of and concerned with the major problems affecting the life of the movement. In actuality, however, relatively few members attend party or union meetings. The pulls of work, family, personal leisure activities, and the like severely limit the amount of actual time and psychic energy which the average person may invest in membership groups or politics. The lower interest and participation are also due to the fact that the membership of any mass organization necessarily has less education and general sophistication than the leadership.

> In the mass, and even in the organized mass of the labor parties, there is an immense need for direction and guidance. . . . This . . . is explicable owing to the more extensive division of labor in modern civilized society, which renders it more and more impossible to embrace in a single glance the totality of the political organization of the state and its ever more complicated mechanism. To this misoneism are superadded, and more particularly in the popular parties, profound differences of culture and education among the members. Those differences give to the need for leadership felt by the masses a continually increasing dynamic tendency.[2]

If the facts of organizational life help account for the power of the leaders, they do not explain why there should be conflict between the interests of the officials and the members. Michels specifically rejected the assumption of a representative leadership. He argued that those who become full-time officials of unions, political parties, or who serve as parliamentary representatives, "whilst belonging by social position to the class of the ruled, have in fact come to form part of the ruling oligarchy." That is to say, the leaders of the masses are themselves part of the "power elite," and develop perspectives and interests derived from their position among the more privileged elements. Hence, many of the policies of mass organizations reflect not the will or interests of the masses, but the will and interests of the leaders. Furthermore Michels stated, in a political party, "it is far from obvious that the interests of the masses which have combined to form the party will coincide with the interests of the bureaucracy in which the party becomes personified The interests of the body of employees [that is, the party officials] are always conservative, and in a given political situation these interests may dictate a defensive and even a reactionary policy when the interests of the working class demand a bold and aggressive policy; in other cases, although these are very rare, the roles may be reversed. By a universally applicable social law, every organ of the collectivity, brought into existence through the need for the division of labor, creates for itself, as soon as it becomes consolidated, interests peculiar to itself. The existence of these special interests involves a necessary conflict with the interests of the collectivity."

Because the leaders of mass organizations are part of the dominant "political class" this does not necessarily mean that they will not continue to oppose other sections of the political elite. In order to maintain and extend their influence, they must command support from a mass following. Hence they will continue to oppose other elements of the ruling strata such as business and the aristocracy. The objective, however, of the mass-based elite is to replace the power of one minority with that of another, themselves.

When faced with a threat to their authority or office from within the organization, the leaders will become extremely aggressive and will not hesitate to under-mine many democratic rights. To lose command of their organization is to lose that which makes them important individuals, and hence they are strongly motivated to preserve their position even if it requires using repressive methods. They legitimize such behavior by pointing out that a mass organization is inevitably an organization maintaining itself by its struggle with powerful and evil opponents. Therefore all efforts to introduce factionalism into the organization, to challenge the appropriateness of party or organization policy, result in aid and comfort to its enemies. Serious criticism of the leadership is thus defined as treachery to the organization itself.

Fifty years ago, Michels sent out a warning to the socialist movement: "The problem of socialism is not merely a problem in economics. . . . Socialism is also an administrative problem, a problem of democracy." He made the prognosis that if socialists adhered to the existing simple relationship between political revolution and social change, a socialist revolution would result in a "dictatorship in the hands of those leaders who have been sufficiently astute and sufficiently powerful to grasp the sceptre of dominion in the name of—socialism. . . . Thus the social revolution would not effect any real modification of the internal structure of the mass. The socialists might conquer, but not socialism, which would perish in the moment of its adherents' triumph."

Michels' predictions that the behavior of the party leaders would reflect bureaucratic conservatism rather than adherence to ideology or defense of their members' interests, were seemingly validated just three years after the book was published. The great German Social Democratic Party, the pride of the Socialist International, the defender of international peace, which opposed the policies of the Kaiser's government and promised to call a general strike in the event of war, supported the war as soon as it was declared in 1914. Even Lenin, critic though he was of the leadership of the German party, could not believe that it was possible for the party to turn so quickly from a violent opponent of German militarism to a jingoistic supporter. He was convinced that the issue of the party newspaper *Vorwarts* calling for support of the war effort was a forgery.

To Michels, this abrupt about face by the Marxist leaders of German socialism was a natural consequence of their social position, for as he put it in the second edition of the book published in 1915, "the life of the party . . . must not be endangered. . . . The party gives way, hastily sells its internationalist soul, and impelled by the instinct of self-preservation, undergoes transformation into a patriotic party. The world war of 1914 has afforded the most effective confirmation of what the author wrote in the first edition of this book concerning the future of socialist parties."

The reaction of most socialist parties to World War I demonstrated that socialist party leaders placed the needs of organizational survival over adherence to doctrine. The Russian Revolution offered an even more dramatic confirmation of his other prediction that a successful socialist revolution would mean not the triumph of democracy for the working class but the replacement of one set of rulers by another.[3] The Revolution led by Nicolai Lenin, a strong advocate of a completely free and democratic society, quickly resulted in one party rule. The Bolsheviks seized power and suppressed all others, even those groups that had supported the Revolution and fought with the Bolsheviks against their military opponents. In 1920, just three years after taking power, the Bolshevik Party began to purge its own ranks. It denied its own members the right to form groups to advocate policies within the party, and within a decade had expelled some of its most important leaders for "the crime" of opposing the will of the party secretary, Joseph Stalin.[4]

Over-Deterministic Aspects of the Theory

Michels has been criticized for being over-deterministic, for seeing only the restrictive side of bureaucracy and failing to see it also as a means through which groups may achieve desired objectives. Thus, many of the recent analyses by social scientists have been concerned not only with bureaucratization as a determinant of organizational behavior which is self-interested, but also with specifying the factors which make certain types of organizations more successful than others. They have been interested to consider factors which make organizations *vary* in their behavior.[5] And among the variables noted are the nature of goals, the ways in which goals and methods are absorbed into the *modus operandi*, the way in which the multifunctions of organizations affect behavior, and the extent to which different kinds of members or clients modify the actions of bureaucrats.[6] Maurice Duverger, Sigmund Neumann, and Robert McKenzie, among others, have shown that Michels has been over-deterministic in his analysis of party behavior. There are clearly significant variations in the organizational structure of different political parties. For example, the two major political parties in the United States differ greatly from the German Social Democratic Party which served Michels as a model, in that they lack central control at the national level and exhibit comparatively little centralization even at the state level. Moreover factionalism is replete in American parties, and turnover in party control is relatively common as compared with most European parties. This variation is partly the result of the two-party pattern in America which, in turn, is largely a consequence of constitutional forms that virtually require the various politically relevant interests throughout the country to unite into two large electoral coalitions. (The primary executive power is determined by the election of a single man, the president or governor, rather than members of parliament.) Diverse groups, which in multiparty nations have independent parties with relatively little internal changes in leadership, form the basis for factions in two-party political systems.[7]

Leaving the problem of oligarchy aside, there still remains the question of representativeness. Some analysts of trade union activities who acknowledge that almost all unions are controlled by an entrenched administration argue that these unions still fulfill their primary function from the point of view of their members' interests. Thus the English student of unions, V. L. Allen, states in answer to Michels that "the end of trade union activity is to protect and improve the general standards of its members and not to provide workers with an exercise in self-government."[8] He goes on to suggest, however, that this end will be fostered only when "the penalty [to union leaders] for inefficiency, the misuse of resources, or the abuse of power is severe. . . . The voluntary nature of trade unions provides such a penalty. A trade union leader who is in continual fear of losing his members will inevitably take steps to satisfy their wants. . . . A failing membership is a much greater stimulant than a strongly worded resolution."[9]

Some evidence for this thesis may be adduced from the United Mine Workers of America, which for some time in the late 1920s and early 1930s followed conservative trade union policies which jibed with the social doctrines of its dictatorial president, John L. Lewis. Faced with a rapidly declining union membership and the

growth of left-wing rivals, Lewis adopted tactics whose militancy has been more marked than those of miners' unions in some other countries under Communist or left-wing socialist leadership. This argument has been made on the most general level of institutional analysis. According to Alvin Gouldner, in all organizations there is *"a need that consent of the governed be given—at least in some measure—to their governors. . . .* And if all organizations must adjust to such a need for consent, is there not built into the very marrow of organization a large element of what we mean by democracy? This would appear to be an organizational constraint that makes oligarchies, and all separation of leaders from those led, no less inherently unstable than democratic organizations."[10]

Furthermore, the problem of representativeness is confused by the absence of genuine alternatives from which members may choose. The absence of any organized opposition group in most unions and other private associations prevents the members from choosing a leader who shares their views. It is difficult to believe, for example, that the differences in the behavior of the two Jewish dominated garment unions in the 1930s and 1940s represented variations in the predominant sentiment of their members. The Amalgamated Clothing Workers' Union under Sidney Hillman was a pillar of the CIO and cooperated with the Communists in New York's American Labor Party. The International Ladies' Garment Workers' Union under David Dubinsky joined the A.F. of L., and formed the vigorously anti-Communist Liberal Party. John L. Lewis endorsed the Republican candidate for U. S. President in 1940, while the large majority of his members were obviously for Franklin Roosevelt.[11] A survey conducted of the membership of the British Medical Association at a time in which the leaders of the association were strongly fighting all proposals for state medicine showed that a majority of the members of the B.M.A. agreed with the government on most issues rather than with their officials.[12] The largest single British union, the Transport and General Workers' Union, shifted from being a stronghold of right-wing Labor politics, under the leadership of Ernest Bevin and Arthur Deakin, to the most important source of strength for the left-wing of the Labor Party, under the General Secretaryship of Frank Cousins. Cousins' succession to this post was not a result of a change in the attitudes of the members, but rather occurred following the death of the two preceding secretaries in one year.[13]

It is difficult to objectively adduce when there is actually a serious cleavage between the interests and conscious objectives of members and those of their leaders. Michels argued that the shift to the "right" prior to World War I of the German trade unions and the Social Democratic Party, demonstrated the way in which the inherent bureaucratic conservatism of leaders deflects organizations from their goals and the beliefs of their members. However, Rose Laub Coser has accumulated evidence which suggests instead that the goals and beliefs of the members changed first.[14] She points out that the rapid improvement in the social and economic position of the German working class in the two decades prior to World War I produced a relatively conservative, contented lower stratum, to whom the traditional revolutionary and internationalist ideology advanced by the party leadership up to 1914 had little appeal. Recent public opinion surveys in Britain show that the large majority of the British trade unions and Labor Party membership have supported the policies of the right wing parliamentary leadership of the party, though the left wing was able in 1960 to gain a majority vote on some issues at the Labor Party conference, and continues to retain strength far out of proportion to its

actual policy support among the members.[15] In the United States, the International Longshoremen's Association, described by all observers as corrupt, racket-ridden, and dictatorial, expelled from the AFL-CIO and attacked by various public agencies, has been able to win three secret-ballot elections conducted by the government against a well-financed rival backed by the resources and prestige of the AFL-CIO.[16] Similarly, the Teamsters' Union led by Jimmy Hoffa, although also expelled from the AFL-CIO as corrupt, and denounced by government agencies as dictatorial, has been the most rapidly growing union in the United States. This paradox of trade-union membership support for oligarchy, corruption, Communism, Republican politics, or other policies which are clearly at variance with their sentiments and/or interests, may be explained by the way in which unions are perceived by the members. If they are seen primarily as single-purpose organizations, and if the organization fulfills its primary purpose—in the case of unions this is clearly collective bargaining—its leaders are permitted considerable leeway in other areas, viewed as less salient policy areas.

Though organizations must in some general sense "represent" their members in the struggle for better wages, higher farm prices, greater profits, and dividends, the basic assumption of Michels regarding the effect of the division of labor within organizations remains valid. This division, as he said, results in the delegation of effective power to a small group of leaders who are able under most conditions to remain in power. It also appears to be true that such leadership groups develop aims which are often at variance with the original objectives of the organizations and the interests and attitudes of their members.

These generalizations obviously raise important problems concerning the viability of political democracy. Michels, himself, felt that he had proven democracy and socialism to be structurally impossible. When he wrote *Political Parties,* he still strongly favored the struggle for more democracy as a means of reducing oligarchic tendencies. Once having demonstrated that democracy was impossible, that democratic leaders were, in effect, hypocrites, Michels found it difficult to retain any sustained belief in democratic ideologies and movements, even as lesser evils. Theoretically, his analysis posed a problem. *If* in fact all leaders of mass organizations were inherently self-interested conservative oligarchs, from where does the polity secure the leadership to deal with major problems and with the need for social change?

The answer, Michels found years later, was in strong charismatic leaders, "persons endowed with extraordinary congenital qualities, sometimes held to be justly supernatural and in every way always far superior to the general level. By virtue of these qualities such persons are deemed capable (and often they are) of accomplishing great things, and even miraculous things."[17] Only a charismatic leader has the ability to break through the inherent conservatism of organization and to excite the masses to support great things. It is from charisma, rather than democracy or bureaucracy, that greatness can be expected. And it must be related that Michels found his charismatic leader in Benito Mussolini. For him, Il Duce translated "in a naked and brilliant form the aims of the multitude." Not for the charismatic Il Duce and fascism were the vulgar compromises and conservatism dictated by the constraints of bureaucratic and oligarchic democracy. "Rather, its perfect faith in itself, essential basis of this form of charismatic government, furnishes an inherent dynamic tendency. And that for two reasons. The charismatic leader has a past of struggles—victorious struggles. Therefore he is conscious of his qualities which he has demonstrated capable of valuable use. . . . On the other side his future is bound to the proofs that he may furnish of the faithfulness of his star."[18] And Michels, who had been barred from academic appointment in Germany for many years because of his socialism, left his position at the University of Basle to accept a chair at the University of Perugia offered to him personally by Benito Mussolini in 1928.

NOTES

1. Detailed efforts to summarize and respecify Michels' theory in terms of latter developments may be found in the following: Philip Selznick, "An Approach to a Theory of Bureaucracy," *American Sociological Review* (1943), pp. 47–54; James Burnham, *The Machiavellians* (New York: The John Day Co., 1943), pp. 135–70; C. W. Cassinelli, "The Law of Oligarchy," *American Political Science Review,* 47 (1953), pp. 773–84; and S. M. Lipset, "The Political Process in Trade Unions: A Theoretical Statement," in M. Berger, C. Page, and T. Abel, eds., *Freedom and Control in Modern Society* (New York: D. Van Nostrand Co., 1954), pp. 82–124.

2. Michels' assumptions concerning the "incompetence of the masses" corresponded greatly with those of Lenin, who justified his belief in the need for an elitist party of professional revolutionists who would lead the masses into socialism by the description of them as "slumbering, apathetic, hidebound, inert, and dormant." V. I. Lenin, *Left Wing Communism: An Infantile Disorder* (New York: International Publishers, 1940), pp. 74–75. For a summation of more recent evidence concerning the propensity of the underprivileged to rely on strong leadership and to participate less in political activities see S. M. Lipset, *Political Man* (New York: Doubleday and Co., 1960), pp. 97–130, 179–219.

3. Thus the editors of *Dissent,* Irving Howe and Lewis Coser find that they can quote *Political Parties* to describe changes in the Communist movement. "'As the party bureaucracy increases,' wrote Robert Michels in his classic study of early twentieth-century socialism, 'two elements which constitute the essential pillars of every socialist conception undergo

an inevitable weakening: an understanding of the wider and more cultural aims of socialism, and an understanding of the international multiplicity of its manifestations. *Mechanism becomes an end in itself.'* In these brilliant sentences Michels anticipated the basic curve of the historical development from the Leninist to the Stalinist movement." *The American Communist Party. A Critical History* (Boston: Beacon Press, 1957), p. 501.

4. As the Yugoslav formerly second-in-command to Tito, Milovan Djilas, has put it, "the Communist revolution, conducted in the name of doing away with classes, has resulted in the most complete authority of any single new class. Everything else is sham and an illusion." *The New Class. An Analysis of the Communist System* (New York: Frederick A. Praeger, 1957), p. 36.

5. See Reinhard Bendix, "Bureaucracy: The Problem and its Setting," *American Sociological Review,* 12 (1947), esp. pp. 493–95. In his most recent work, Selznick also has elaborated in detail the effect which variations in leadership behavior have on the ways in which organizations respond to their environment and vary in propensity to attain their goals. See *Leadership in Administration* (Evanston: Row, Peterson and Co., 1957).

6. For a good sample of the type of work which has been done in this field of inquiry see the articles reprinted in Amitai Etzioni, ed., *Complex Organizations* (New York: Holt, Rinehart and Winston, 1961) and in R. K. Merton, A. P. Gray, B. Hockey, and H. C. Selvin, eds., *Reader in Bureaucracy* (Glencoe: The Free Press, 1952).

7. Some of the factors which determine the number and type of parties in different countries are discussed in S. M. Lipset, "Party Systems and the Representation of Social Groups," *European Journal of Sociology,* 1 (1960), pp. 50–85.

8. *Power in Trade Unions* (London: Longmans, Green and Co., 1954), p. 15.

9. *Ibid.,* p. 63.

10. Gouldner, "Metaphysical Pathos and the Theory of Bureaucracy," in S. M. Lipset and N. W. Smelser, eds., *Sociology: The Progress of a Decade* (Englewood-Cliffs: Prentice-Hall, 1961), p. 88.

11. Irving Bernstein, "John L. Lewis and the Voting Behavior of the C.I.O." *Public Opinion Quarterly* 5 (1941), pp. 233–49.

12. Harry Eckstein, "The Politics of the British Medical Association," *The Political Quarterly,* 26 (1955), pp. 345–59; see also Oliver Garceau, *The Political Life of the American Medical Association* (Cambridge: Harvard University Press, 1941) and Anonymous, "American Medical Association: Power, Purpose and Politics in Organized Medicine," *Yale Law Journal* 63 (1954), pp. 938–1022.

13. For a detailed study of the sources and nature of oligarchy and membership apathy in this union see Joseph Goldstein, *The Government of British Trade Unions* (London: George Allen and Unwin, 1952).

14. *An Analysis of the Early German Socialist Movement* (M.A. Thesis: Department of Sociology, Columbia University, 1951).

15. A public opinion survey conducted in September 1960 about the time that a majority of the delegates to the Trades Union Congress and to the Labor Party Conference endorsed the left program favoring unilateral disarmament by Great Britain found that only 16 per cent of the trade union members supported the proposal that Britain unilaterally give up its nuclear weapons, while 83 per cent favored the policy that Britain should retain such arms until other powers agreed to disarm. See Research Department, Odhem's Press, *Report on a Survey of Opinions Concerning Nuclear Disarmament* (London: 1960). A survey conducted about the same time by the British Gallup Poll on the same issues, also reported relatively little support (24 per cent) among Labor voters for unilateral disarmament. (Gallup did not separate out trade union members in his report.) See *The Gallup Political Index,* Report No. 9, September, 1960. Given these results, it is perhaps not surprising that when the anti-unilateralists within the unions and the Labor Party formed an organization, the Campaign for Democratic Socialism, to reverse party policy, they were able within a year to change the policies which seemingly had had majority support at conventions.

16. See Daniel Bell, *The End of Ideology* (Glencoe: The Free Press, 1960), pp. 159–60. The election results are presented on pages 186–87.

17. Robert Michels, *First Lectures in Political Sociology* (Minneapolis: University of Minnesota Press, 1949), pp. 122–23. This book contains many of his writings in the 1920s and thirties.

24
_____

ORGANIZATIONAL RELATIONSHIPS
The SCLC, the NAACP, and CORE

ALDON D. MORRIS

SCLC-NAACP

The SCLC and the NAACP were closely linked. Indeed, most of SCLC founders were members of the NAACP, and many were current or former NAACP leaders at the time of the SCLC's formation. So closely linked were the two organizations that it was common for a community leader to function as president of both the local NAACP branch and the local SCLC affiliate. Moreover, the mass movements led by the SCLC founders did not arise outside of the NAACP's influence. The NAACP often provided substantial sums of money for the expensive legal cost of these movements, and in many cases it was NAACP lawyers who defended movement participants in court. Many NAACP branches sent money directly to the headquarters of these movements to help finance their overall efforts. Thus the NAACP, as a preexisting national organization with branches throughout the South, served as a vital resource for the mass movements. But even though NAACP officials assisted the direct action movements, many of them thought it unwise to form a new protest organization for the explicit purpose of organizing direct action.

_____

NAACP officials and many members generally believed that the NAACP was the organization through which to free blacks. Indeed, James Weldon Johnson, the NAACP's first black Executive Secretary, wrote in 1934 that in order for blacks to be liberated they should pool their resources and protest into a single unit, which he referred to as a central machine. "I believe we have that machine at hand," he wrote, "in the National Association for the Advancement of Colored People. I believe we could get the desired results by making that organization the nucleus, the synthesis, the clearinghouse, of our forces."[1] The idea that the NAACP was the only proper vehicle to achieve racial equality was widespread throughout the organization in the late 1950s. James Farmer, a founder of CORE, who served as the National Program Director of the NAACP from 1959 through 1961, recalled the thinking of that period:

> The NAACP staff, bureaucracy . . . and it was a heavy bureaucracy there . . . most of the persons had been there for many, many years and they had been conditioned to perceive the NAACP as being the civil rights organization. And all others were viewed as interlopers. So they viewed the SCLC as a potential rival . . . as an interloper. And felt it was not needed because they [NAACP] were doing what needed to be done.[2]

So top NAACP officials did not welcome the formation of the SCLC. Reverend Lowery recalls one occasion as SCLC was being organized:

We met with strong opposition from the NAACP. Well, the thing got so bad, that Martin, Ralph and I went to New York and had a meeting with Roy Wilkins [then NAACP Executive Secretary], John Morsell [then Assistant to the Executive Secretary], and Gloster Current [then Director of Branches]. [We] met half the day and night. Roy was very sophisticated, you know. He wouldn't dare show any antipathy. John Morsell was a little bit more matter-of-fact, but Gloster was the hatchet man. Gloster said, "To tell you the truth, gentlemen, at the end of the bus boycott, you all should have disbanded everything, and been back in NAACP."[3]

Lowery concluded that Gloster Current's view reflected the official NAACP position when Wilkins "didn't say 'Amen,' neither did he say 'Nay.' " This resentment toward the SCLC was reflected in an editorial in the *Pittsburgh Courier*, a prominent black newspaper:

Another Civil Rights organization would seem to be one thing that colored America does not need, and yet representatives from 12 states and the District of Columbia meeting in Montgomery, Alabama, answering the call of Dr. Martin Luther King, have set up the Southern Christian Leadership Conference. . . . Are the organizers of the Southern Christian Leadership Conference implying by their action that the NAACP is no longer capable of doing what it has been doing for decades because it is now under attack in several Southern states? . . . What sound reason is there for having two organizations

with the same goal when one has been doing such an effective job?[4]

The reluctance of NAACP officials to endorse the SCLC became evident when King asked a number of prominent Americans to join the SCLC's National Advisory Committee. Those who accepted were not expected to do extensive work, but their names were needed to add prestige and legitimacy to the young SCLC. Ralph Bunche and Herbert Lehman, both highly visible board members of the NAACP, refused to join the SCLC's Advisory Committee on the grounds of their affiliation with the NAACP. Lehman sent a $250 check with his letter of refusal to show his personal interest in the work of the SCLC.[5] Clearly, the NAACP was attempting to protect its organizational monopoly over black protest. The NAACP leadership's fears about the rise of the SCLC were not unfounded. The emergence of the SCLC represented a threat to the NAACP's local leadership, its financial base, and its patiently cultivated strategy of working within the law. To add to the NAACP's fears, the SCLC was being organized at precisely the time when the NAACP was losing strength in the South as the result of attacks by the Southern white power structure.

The formation of the SCLC threatened to drain away some of the NAACP's local leadership because, as Reverend Lawson has noted, "most of the people who began to surround King and saw him as the symbol of what we hoped for and wanted to happen, would have been people who, for lack of any other tool, would have been in the NAACP just as common procedure."[6] With the rise of the SCLC it was unclear whether the leaders on whom the NAACP had relied in the past would shift their allegiance to the new organization. It would be difficult to find people in the South willing to take on the harassment and sacrifices that association with the NAACP would automatically entail at a time when the NAACP was being treated as a radical organization by the white power structure. James Farmer indicated that a problem would remain even if leaders stayed with the NAACP, "because if church members, ministers, and others became active in SCLC they might become less active in the NAACP branches."[7]

The SCLC was a threat to the NAACP's financial base because much of that base was anchored in the church. Any NAACP leader who gravitated to the SCLC represented not only a loss of leadership but, in most cases, the loss of a minister in control of a congregation, hence the loss in turn of the substantial financial support forthcoming to the NAACP from that congregation. In 1947 the NAACP created a Church Department for the express purposes of coordinating activities between churches and the NAACP and acquiring NAACP memberships and financial support from the church. Ten years later, when the SCLC was being organized, the NAACP's Church Department began an aggressive campaign to win and consolidate Southern church support. To this end local NAACP branches established church committees and conducted ministers' workshops. The NAACP annual report for 1957 contains this comment:

> The branch church committees, it was learned, have been invaluable sources for securing memberships, mobilizing the support of local church leadership and giving concrete expression to the social concern of church groups by involving them in the struggle for equality on the community level.[8]

James Farmer, who worked in the NAACP during the late 1950s, was in a good position to observe how the NAACP and the SCLC drew from the same financial base in the South. He says the NAACP felt financially threatened because the SCLC's "base was the Baptist church in the South . . . and that black Baptist church was . . . one source of funds which the NAACP branches traditionally tapped. So SCLC was viewed as a threat in that sense. Because the money which went to SCLC might have gone to the NAACP had SCLC not been around."[9] The SCLC was in a better position to capitalize on the NAACP's church base by virtue of being a church organization with clergy leadership and being indigenous to the South.

Finally, the SCLC's strategy of nonviolent direct action by the masses was threatening to the NAACP's legal approach because of its mass appeal and wider effectiveness, as demonstrated by the Montgomery bus boycott and similar confrontations. The lack of a mass base has always been a problem for the NAACP. During the 1950s NAACP membership comprised less than 1 percent of the total black population, and the legal method itself served as one barrier to mass involvement. Dr. King was well aware that the NAACP's legal approach discouraged mass participation when he wrote, "when legal contests were the sole form of activity . . . the ordinary Negro was involved as a passive spectator. His interests were stirred, but his energies were unemployed."[10] James Farmer, hired in 1959 by the NAACP precisely for the purpose of reviving local activity, found that the NAACP chapters "didn't seem to be doing much except raising funds, raising the freedom budget each year. And many of the chapter branches had become essentially collection agencies."[11]

On the other hand, the SCLC's approach depended directly on mass involvement. Reverend Lawson accurately characterized this important difference between the two organizations' approaches:

> The point of the whole problem is that when people are suffering they don't

want rhetoric and processes which seem to go slowly. . . . Many people, when they are suffering and they see their people suffering, they want direct participation. They want to be able to say, what I'm doing here gives me power and is going to help us change this business. . . . That's one of the great successes when you do something like a school boycott . . . or an economic boycott. Because here I am, mad already, with the racism I see, and now you tell me, okay . . . here's a chance for us to do something. So you stay out of that store until they do XYZ. . . . Just stay out of that store. So you put into the hands of all kinds of ordinary people a positive alternative to powerlessness and frustration. That's one of the great things about direct action.[12]

The SCLC's strategy advocated a new method of mass protest. The mass movements that gave rise to the SCLC stood as proof that masses could be organized for collective protest through the churches. Thus the SCLC was capable of mobilizing a mass base, which the NAACP had never been able to do.

Shortly after the Montgomery bus boycott the effects of the direct action strategy began to be felt within the NAACP. The new approach was especially appealing to the young adults and teenagers associated with the NAACP Youth Councils. The NAACP was not a monolithic organization; it housed a range of protest leaders, some of them cautious, others aggressive, and a few militant. The diverse leadership clustered in the NAACP generated differences between NAACP chapters on the local level. Some NAACP members were dissatisfied with the pace of change resulting from the legal approach and felt that their branches functioned primarily as collection agencies for the national office rather than as effective

social change organizations. Members of the young, aggressive wing of the NAACP often served as adult advisers to NAACP Youth Councils. A disproportionate number of these advisers were women: Rosa Parks, Daisy Bates, Clara Luper, and Vera Pigee. Men like Floyd McKissick, Hosea Williams, and Ronald Walters also served as leaders of NAACP Youth Councils. These were the NAACP leaders who were impressed by the direct action strategies used in the Montgomery bus boycott, and they were not hesitant in adopting and implementing these strategies. The aggressive wing of the NAACP had always existed, but it was given new life after the mass movements began to be organized. Indeed, in the late 1950s numerous NAACP Youth Councils were reorganized after disappearing early in the decade for lack of support, and many of them began functioning as direct action organizations.

Some of the Youth Councils became involved in highly organized direct action projects, such as sit-ins, in the late 1950s. In 1957 the Oklahoma City NAACP Youth Council, headed by Mrs. Clara Luper, began formulating plans to sit-in at local stores with segregated dining facilities. Mrs. Luper wrote that "for eighteen months, the members of the NAACP Youth council had been studying non-violence as a way of overcoming injustices."[13] She pointed out that the group followed what it called Martin Luther King's nonviolent plan, which specified seven steps of action:

[R]esist the evil of segregation in a passive, non-violent way . . . . mobilize for an all out fight for first class citizenship. [T]he church must be awakened to its responsibility. Religion is the chief avenue to the minds and the souls of the masses. [C]ontinue our struggles in the courts, and above all things, we must remember to support the National

Association for the Advancement of Colored People. [A]t the same time we must support other organizations that are molding public opinion.[14]

Dr. Benjamin Mays, who worked on NAACP membership drives, clearly captured the impact of the aggressive wing of the NAACP: "You must remember that the local chapter was bringing pressure upon the NAACP to get out and do the kind of thing that Martin Luther and his group were doing because they're [SCLC] getting the prestige and they are being called the movement that is struggling for the masses."[15] The wing of the NAACP that Luper's group represented had obviously begun to emphasize the direct action method symbolized by King, E. D. Nixon, and thousands of nonviolent protesters rather than the legal method symbolized by such personalities as Thurgood Marshall and Roy Wilkins.

The discussion so far has shown how the emergence of the SCLC threatened the NAACP's leadership structure, financial base, legal strategy, and monopolistic status as *the* black civil rights organization. These were the underlying organizational reasons why the NAACP did not welcome the presence of the SCLC. In many instances members of the NAACP responded by spreading negative information about the SCLC in the community, as they did in the vote drive. In some situations the national NAACP attempted to prevent local chapters from engaging in direct action. Lawson, who assisted in training Luper's group to conduct sit-ins in 1957, recalls the NAACP's response: "The NAACP opposed [sit-ins]. The parent body, the branch body, chastised the school teacher [Luper] who was responsible for it, chastised them, told them to desist."[16] Specific strategies were pursued by the SCLC to overcome the attacks by the NAACP and promote cooperation between the two organizations. Because most SCLC

leaders were either former or current leaders of the NAACP, they were able to understand its attitude toward the SCLC. That understanding was an important aid to SCLC leaders in formulating effective strategies of cooperation.

First, the SCLC's leadership seized every opportunity to praise the NAACP as an organization both privately and publicly and to plead for continuing support of it. On May 17, 1957, a number of organizations, including the SCLC and the NAACP, conducted a Prayer Pilgrimage on Washington, D.C., that attracted 25,000 people. King told the gathering:

> We have won marvelous victories through the work of the NAACP. We have been able to do some of the most amazing things of this generation, and I come this afternoon with nothing but praise for this great organization. Although they outlawed the NAACP in Alabama and other states, the fact still remains that this organization has done more to achieve Civil Rights for Negroes than any other organization we can point to.[17]

King expressed the same sentiment to Thurgood Marshall privately: "NO sane, objective, intelligent individual can deprecate the work of the NAACP."[18] It was common for SCLC leaders to back their words of respect by taking out life memberships in the NAACP. King and the MIA each took out a life membership at a cost of $500 each. King then persuaded his church to take out a life membership and promised NAACP officials that he would urge other Montgomery churches to do likewise. The intention was plainly to promote harmonious relations with the NAACP.

Second, the SCLC pursued strategies aimed at convincing the NAACP that the SCLC's presence would not erode NAACP membership or weaken its financial base.

SCLC leaders constantly reminded the NAACP that the SCLC was not seeking individual members or chapters but affiliates that were preexisting organizations, hence was no threat to draw away NAACP members. For the NAACP's benefit many of the SCLC's printed materials proclaimed in bold print, "SCLC DOES NOT establish local units nor solicit individual membership."[19]

To avoid conflicts over funding, the SCLC and the NAACP developed a strategy of raising money jointly and dividing it. Evidence of this strategy is clear in Ella Baker's report to the SCLC in 1959:

> In order to generate real interest throughout the state in the fund raising aspects of the Columbia meeting, it seems highly desirable to follow something of the pattern that was used in the promotion of the Norfolk meeting. As you know, the NAACP and S.C.L.C. shared in proceeds from the Norfolk Mass Meeting.[20]

This was an ideal strategy from which the SCLC gained use of the NAACP's networks for organizing fundraising rallies and the NAACP gained the presence of the charismatic figure. During the late 1950s and early 1960s King played an important role in NAACP fundraising activities. It is safe to say that during this period King spoke for the NAACP more than for any other organization. He spoke for local NAACP branches across the country during their membership drives, often delivered the main address at NAACP annual conventions, and, in 1957, became a member of the National Advisory Committee for the NAACP Freedom Fund Campaign.[21] The importance of King's presence at NAACP fundraising events is evident in a letter from the Executive Secretary of the Detroit NAACP branch, written when he learned that King could not attend the branch's 1958 Freedom Fund Campaign:

> In view of your public acclaim and the unusually valuable position you now hold, I hope that you will be ever mindful that a helping hand from you is ten, twenty-five, one hundred times more productive than that of countless other friends whose resources and influence can never quite measure up to their interest in this work.[22]

In short, the financial strategy devised by the SCLC and the NAACP benefited them both and minimized the potential for a destructive conflict between two organizations whose personnel and funding bases were so intertwined.

Finally, the SCLC mitigated the NAACP's fears that direct action would replace the legal strategy. The SCLC emphasized that a division of labor was sorely needed in the movement, and the NAACP was superbly qualified for the legal role, leaving the SCLC to specialize in direct action at the community level. This effort took some force out of the NAACP's complaint that SCLC leaders were opportunists seeking to establish an organization while NAACP was under heavy attack in the South. SCLC officials reached to the heart of the matter by arguing: "A strong mass organization indigenous to the South is the greatest assurance for restoring the legal and emotional atmosphere in which the NAACP can again fully operate in the South."[23] The SCLC further pointed out that its approach complemented the legal strategies of the NAACP: Because "it is on the community level that court decision must be implemented," the SCLC's direct action approach was designed to make sure that the NAACP's legal victories were actually enforced. King often assured top NAACP legal experts, "you continue winning the legal victories for us and we will work passionately and unrelentingly to implement these victories on the local level through nonviolent means."[24]

Although the SCLC emphasized the necessity of an organizational division of labor, it still had to assert itself strongly as a new force capable of transforming the racial caste system of the South. But its assertiveness had to be established while maintaining a harmonious relationship with the NAACP. It did so by challenging NAACP to accept direct action as a useful approach. At the Prayer Pilgrimage of 1957, where the NAACP's highest officials gathered, King, after praising the accomplishments of the NAACP, warned: "We must also avoid the temptation of being victimized with a psychology of victors. We have won marvelous victories through the work of NAACP. . . . Certainly this is marvelous. We must not, however, remain satisfied with a court victory over our white brothers."[25]

In conclusion, the SCLC deployed a complex array of arguments to decrease NAACP animosity toward the new civil rights organization. Such defenses were necessitated by the fact that the two organizations overlapped in fundamental ways. Although tensions and conflicts remained between the NAACP and the SCLC, those specific strategies promoted cooperation and prevented the two organizations from engaging in destructive interorganizational rivalry.

SCLC-CORE-NAACP

The Congress of Racial Equality (CORE) also had an important role in the modern civil rights movement, and the interorganizational relationship that developed among CORE, the NAACP, and the SCLC calls for analysis.

In the 1950s CORE had no mass base in the South or the North. Before the late 1950s CORE had a national office consisting of one paid official and a number of small local Northern chapters. The chapters usually included five or six dedicated activists who periodically demonstrated against racial discrimination. Masses were not involved in the demonstrations. Rather, in attorney Stanley Levison's apt words, CORE activities were carried out in a "witness fashion by small groups."[26]

In the South during the early and mid-1950s CORE was unknown to the black masses; in fact, it was no better known to middle-income Southern blacks than to the poor and unemployed. CORE's first full-time field secretary, who was educated and had been a superintendent of public schools in South Carolina, acknowledged that before being hired by CORE in 1957, he "had never heard about it." This Southern black man, James McCain, who for years had been fighting for racial equality, went on to say: "At that time [1957] no. I didn't know anything about any other organizations. The only thing we knew about was the National Association, NAACP."[27] The reasons blacks had not heard of CORE are obvious. First, CORE was a Northern organization founded in Chicago in 1942. Most of its members were pacifist graduate students at the University of Chicago. One of its principal founders was James Farmer, a black man trained as a minister who had never pastored a church. The organization from the start was interracial, with whites far outnumbering blacks. That by itself is a strong indication that CORE was organized to function in the North, for something bordering on a revolution would have to occur in the South before interracial protest groups could function.[28] After its emergence, CORE's small groups sporadically attacked racism in a few Northern cities, at times with success. Yet CORE, the organization, was unknown to Southern blacks.

CORE was an intellectually oriented organization, concerned as much with broad philosophical issues as with racial equality. CORE members usually came from pacifist backgrounds or had adopted pacifist ideals and principles. The overriding goal of CORE members was to demonstrate that large social problems could be solved through nonviolent means. Gordon Carey, the second full-time field secretary hired by CORE, makes this point clearly:

> Most of the people involved in CORE in the early days were there because they saw a means of working out their own political and social ideologies. It was not a struggle for freedom. They looked upon what they were doing as working on huge social problems. Now, that's a very impersonal theoretical kind of thing. . . . The idea was that you came into CORE or you were in CORE and you believed in nonviolent direct action. That's really what you believed in.[29]

James Farmer, who became CORE's National Director in 1961, emphasized:

> CORE, you must remember, from its early days was a means-oriented organization. It was oriented toward the techniques of nonviolent direct action. That was perhaps more important in the minds of many of the persons there than the ends which were being sought . . . it was means, finding some way to use nonviolence to show the world that nonviolence can solve racial problems.[30]

Farmer also maintained that CORE usually attracted middle-class white intellectuals, because they were interested in finding alternatives to violence in resolving social conflict. He added that very few blacks had the interest, desire, or background required in CORE. James Robinson, national Executive Director of CORE until 1961, agreed that CORE members were "Looking for a method, developing a method, popularizing a method. . . . CORE

used nonviolence as a tactic, but I think a lot of the people including myself, thought of nonviolence as a value in and of itself."[31] In the middle and late 1950s the primary goals of Southern blacks were to desegregate buses, public schools, and voting booths; to prevent lynchings and beatings; and to overthrow racial domination. For CORE, on the other hand, the most important endeavor was to locate a set of social problems appropriate to its goal of demonstrating that a particular method could work. Although not necessarily incompatible, the two sets of goals were not the same.

Prior to the Southern mass movements of the 1950s CORE had concluded that the South was an impossible place to prove the efficacy of the nonviolent method. According to Farmer, the South was considered a "never-never land" by CORE's staff.[32] When masses of blacks began protesting nonviolently in the south, CORE became interested. As James Robinson recalls, the Montgomery movement demonstrated that something could be done in the South and "that there were people who would follow and take action in the South."[33]

CORE's staff explored ways to enter the South. Before 1957 CORE had no chapters in the South and had not succeeded in proving the efficacy of nonviolent protest on a large scale. In fact, CORE had a difficult time finding a favorable testing ground for the method of nonviolence. Carey shows the essence of the problem:

> Now, where can you apply that? Well, you can't apply it in the international scene, you can't apply it in the labor relations very much. Hell, they've been doing that in unions long before CORE was ever heard of, you know, with sit-down strikes and all this sort of thing. So a good place in which to practice your ideologies, so to speak, would be in race relations. And that's what really happened, I think.[34]

If one wanted to apply the method of nonviolence to problems of race relations during the late 1950s, the South was indeed the place that presented the challenge.

However, the CORE of the mid-1950s had greater problems than finding a testing ground for its method. With few resources and no national image, it was an organization more in spirit and commitment than in reality. CORE's Executive Secretary decided that the organization should enter the South in quest of organizational stability, national stature, and the development of a method.

CORE and the South

In 1957 CORE made its first attempt to establish a base in the South. Because CORE was largely led by middle-class white intellectuals during the late 1950s, it entered the South with a paternalistic attitude about how poor blacks should fight for liberation. James Farmer recalls:

> My friends in CORE at that time did view CORE as being their property. . . . It was paternalistic, very paternalistic. . . . They viewed the black brother as the junior partner in the alliance, not quite of age. So, thus they viewed themselves as senior partners, obviously. . . . CORE was a small organization that was standing outside of the ghetto, the minority community, working in its behalf.[35]

Farmer maintained that CORE leaders resisted having meetings in the black community because they favored taking blacks outside the ghetto into integrated situations. To illustrate CORE's paternalism, Farmer told of a time he proposed that CORE hold a rally in Representative Adam Clayton Powell's church in Harlem. Marvin Rich, a long-time activist with CORE who became

Community Relations Director in 1959, opposed the rally, whereupon Farmer exploded. He argued: "'This will tie in the black community.' [Marvin Rich's] argument was, 'We're not interested in the whole black community.' [Is that right?] Yes. 'We're only interested in the activists in the black community.'"[36]

Floyd McKissick, a black attorney from North Carolina who had participated in CORE's 1947 "Journey of Reconciliation" project, an attempt to integrate buses in the border states, and who became its National Chairman in 1964 and its National Director in 1966, agreed that most whites in CORE were not directly concerned with "the causes of freedom of black people." He added: "Now certainly, they did not appreciate blacks who asserted themselves. And some particular people who asserted themselves as I did."[37] Gordon Carey, the white field secretary, also agreed that CORE in the early days of the movement was paternalistic. The whites in CORE were not affected by problems that confronted blacks, he observed, so they were unable to view the situation from the vantage point of blacks.[38] This is not to say that CORE did not work tenaciously to bring about black liberation. It does mean, however, that the effective implementation of nonviolent strategies was as important a goal to CORE as black liberation.

Finally, Jim McCain, CORE's first full-time field secretary, immediately encountered problems with CORE's Executive Secretary over how blacks should struggle for freedom. McCain says he thought the quickest route to black liberation was acquiring the vote: "I felt that voter registration was one of the main thrusts with the blacks in the South, because we . . . had been disenfranchised."[39] From CORE's viewpoint, a protest centered on voting was not direct action. CORE officials explained to McCain that CORE was a direct action organization, and in voting protests "you don't picket." McCain replied, "Don't tell me you don't picket for the vote." He pointed out to the Executive Secretary that before CORE entered the South blacks were picketing for the vote in "Williamsburgh County and several counties." McCain explained to Robinson, who was issuing directives from CORE's headquarters in New York: "Plenty of black people down here don't feel like doing what you have in mind."[40] They knew that "some white people might come in and knock you off the stool" while you sat in. "James Robinson and I differed on that," McCain relates. "And so I told him, 'okay you're the boss. I'm working for you. I'll try to do it your way.'"[41]

Evidence about CORE's paternalism has been presented because it had a fundamental bearing on the organizational activity and the interorganizational relationships CORE established in the movement. It also has a direct bearing on one major thesis of this book: Because the SCLC functioned as the decentralized arm of the black church and its leadership was all black, it did not have to devote important resources, time, and energy to in-house racial bickering. By 1964 so much racial fighting had occurred in CORE that Farmer concluded: "There are many Negroes who will not work with an interracial organization because of their suspicion of whites. . . . White liberals must be willing to work in roles of secondary leadership and as technicians."[42]

Social movements and their organizations are rooted in the social structures they seek to change. Racism, sexism, and classism will therefore be found in American movements, because they are deeply rooted in American society. Social movements display existing social contradictions when they are pushed to the foreground by activists constrained by them. Often those who gain power in social change groups do not realize that the dynamics of a movement may eventually call their own privileges and leadership positions into question. Thus, even though the SCLC did not suffer from racial bickering, it did have to deal with problems and conflicts generated by sexism.

We are now in a position to analyze CORE's relations with the NAACP and the SCLC. CORE's entrance into the South in 1957 was facilitated by the organizational attack that white Southerners leveled against the NAACP, which again suggests that that attack is central to understanding the origins of the modern civil rights movement. CORE's initial entrance into the South was effected through one man, James McCain. Mr. McCain obtained his bachelor's degree from Morris College, a black institution in his hometown of Sumter, South Carolina, and did graduate work at Temple University in Philadelphia. After completing his education he returned to Sumter and taught at Morris College for more than a decade. In the meantime, when NAACP came to South Carolina, he became one of the youngest members on the State Board and the first president of its Sumter branch. He remained the president of the local NAACP for ten years and was re-elected after two years off the job.

After a successful stay at Morris College, where he was promoted to dean and served in that capacity about seven years, McCain accepted a job as supervising principal of a school district in Marion, South Carolina. After five productive years there he received a shock. "Because of my connection with NAACP, I was fired."[43] He was accused of having written an NAACP petition back in 1954, when the school desegregation case was being decided.

"Black parents in Mullens wrote a letter to the School Board, asking them if the Supreme Court decision was favorable on the school desegregation decision, would they start making plans now to admit black children to all white schools," McCain recalls.[44] Although he did not write the petition, he continues, "I was told if I would recant and apologize that most likely I could keep my job. But I refused to do it because I didn't have anything to do with it. So my contract was terminated."[45]

Following his dismissal, McCain was hired as a high school principal in Clarendon County, South Carolina. After one year, a reporter from Charleston asked McCain if he would teach white students if the school was forced to integrate. "I told him I was certified to teach, and it wasn't on my certificate, black or white. Any child that would come to school had a right to be taught by all of us."[46] McCain then uttered words that are quite revealing:

> So then he asked me the $64 question. He asked me whether I was a member of NAACP. And I told him, "yes." And in less than ten days I got a letter from the School Board that my contract was expired. [So in those days the question as to whether you were a NAACP member was a $64 question?] That's it exactly—most likely your job in the public school system depended upon your denying it or not getting a job.[47]

This is an individual account, but it portrays an environment created to destroy the NAACP and its protest activities. It also shows how the attack freed NAACP activists, making it possible for them to join direct action organizations.

After being fired, McCain became Assistant Director for South Carolina Council of Human Relations. He held that job for two years, long enough for him to meet a visiting woman CORE member, who sent his name to the Executive Secretary of CORE. In the meantime she told McCain he probably could get a job in CORE, because the "movement was heating up" and "CORE wanted to have a national image." From then on McCain was linked with the organization that he "had never heard about."[48]

After the Montgomery bus boycott CORE's Executive Secretary decided that the organization could become important in the movement if it could find a competent black organizer capable of building CORE chapters in the South. McCain was ideal for CORE, because he had stature in the black community and he knew that community. His education enabled him to speak CORE's language and write solid field reports, and he had acquired organizing experience while holding offices in the NAACP and a black college. McCain was popular with young people in South Carolina, having worked with them at both the college and the high school levels. CORE was particularly interested in a link with Southern young people, because it believed that the young were better suited to do CORE-type work. Finally, the organizational experience and contacts McCain had amassed as local president and State Board member of the NAACP were invaluable for his new post. Indeed, the early CORE activity of South Carolina would be closely tied to NAACP groups.

By October 1958, a year after McCain was hired by CORE, he had established seven CORE groups spanning the State of South Carolina. Unwittingly, he was developing a base through which the Carolina sit-ins of 1960 would spread. In many respects CORE chapters in the late 1950s resembled NAACP chapters, and most of their early work centered on voter registration. This reflects the reality that protest organizations entering new situations must adapt to the social context they seek to change. But it also meant that tensions would persist between blacks on the local level and whites who represented CORE at the national level because of differences over approaches and goals.

Funding Base

Up to 1960 the relationship CORE established with the SCLC and the NAACP was largely one of cooperation. The fact that CORE had no mass black base and had funding sources distinct from those of the SCLC and the NAACP made cooperation possible. According to James Robinson, CORE's Executive Secretary during the late 1950s, "SCLC was more important in the South than CORE ever was, because it had a predominantly black base. Through the churches it had a mass base, which CORE never really had."[49] The fact that CORE was a secular organization removed it even farther from the black church base. Farmer has noted: "CORE was a secular organization. It was nonreligious. In fact, when we set it up, I insisted that CORE not be a religious organization."[50] Farmer had reasoned that a secular social change organization could best serve his goal of creating a mass movement in the North.

Having no mass base, CORE depended largely on funds from middle-class whites living in Northern and Western states. Small proportions of the funds came from the top level of the white working class and from a few wealthy individuals, who also resided predominantly in Northern and Western states. A small amount of CORE's funds did come as a result of mail appeals from what are known as the border states.[51]

To understand important aspects of modern social movements, an organizational perspective is valuable. Leaders in pacifist organizations, such as George Houser of the Fellowship of Reconciliation, who already possessed valuable information (e.g., ad-dresses, phone numbers, size of contributions), including mailing lists, made it possible for CORE to locate some of its original financial contributors. Once these supporters were located, CORE began to build its own lists, which it then had to share with other related organizations.[52] In the early years of the movement CORE had no basic conflict with either the SCLC or the NAACP, because its money did not come from the South or from black churches. In fundamental ways, however, the financial development necessary for CORE to become a national organization depended on the activities of the Southern church-based mass movements.

Before the Montgomery bus boycott CORE barely raised the funds to pay its one full-time employee, its Executive Secretary. Following the Montgomery movement CORE changed this situation by "exploiting the headline-making development in the Southern black protest movements."[53] For example, in 1956–57 CORE sent forty thousand copies of King's pamphlet on the Montgomery movement with its mail appeals. Meier and Rudwick found this strategy to have been so successful that "the number of individual contributors nearly doubled between 1954 and 1957."[54]

The SCLC, and Dr. King in particular, played a key financial role in CORE's expansion between 1957 and 1959. For example, CORE was involved with a school integration project in Nashville. Anna Holden, Chairman of the Nashville CORE, wrote a lengthy pamphlet entitled *A First Step Toward School Integration*, in which she described the integration project and the central role that CORE played in it. Dr. King wrote the foreword to the pamphlet and signed a CORE appeal letter for funds. Both of these items received large circulation thanks to King's assistance, enabling CORE to double its list of contributors.[55]

King joined CORE's Advisory Committee in 1957. This meant his name could be added to the letterhead on CORE's correspondence and financial appeals. James Robinson explained that it was extremely important to have respected individuals on CORE's letterhead so that, "when appeals went out across the country, recipients could look down through the list, and see that there were prominent people who supported the organization."[56] CORE needed prominent people on its letterhead who were clearly not communists to defuse accusations that the organization was communistic, while soliciting financial support from contributors who were usually, according to Robinson, slightly left of center politically.[57]

Marvin Rich, whose duties included fundraising and public relations, said that as soon as he became Community Relations Director of CORE in 1959, he "helped to increase the size of the Advisory Committee. Not simply increase the size but add key people to it to be helpful in our relations with other organizations and with the public generally. . . . These are people who gave us entry into various segments of society."[58] An organizational perspective here is again important. In order for CORE to expand and acquire national status, it needed respectable names on its letterhead to facilitate fruitful connections with other organizations. Marvin Rich explained that his job in CORE was "to enhance the prestige and influence of CORE both within the civil rights movement and in the larger community." He was equipped to accomplish this because "I also knew how other organizations worked and therefore I was able to interpret CORE to a wider audience."[59] King's name, along with such others as the famous writer Lillian Smith, the protest leader and union organizer A. Philip Randolph, and the peace organizer A. J. Muste, made CORE's organizational task easier.

Finally, King was important to CORE's finances in another respect. On a number of occasions potential donors approached CORE to say that they wanted to make substantial contributions to the organization, but with the stipulation that CORE

demonstrate that King had an interest in the organization and approved of its work. CORE officials wrote King asking him to convince such individuals that CORE was deserving. In reference to a potential donor, Robinson asked King to write a brief note explaining that "you serve on the CORE Advisory Committee, have confidence in the organization, and that a substantial contribution would be much appreciated."[60] King wrote the potential donor strongly praising the organization and its work. Thus, mass movements of the South and King's influence were critical to CORE's finances and expansion between the years 1955 and 1960. Indeed, King's view of the movement usually enabled him to rise above narrow organizational interests and support all civil rights organizations fighting for black liberation. James Robinson provided insight into this aspect of King by recalling a television interview that included both King and a representative of CORE:

> I shall never forget watching that program, and over and over and again our field secretary mentioned CORE. King, who talked quite a bit, never once mentioned the SCLC. He was not an empire builder, as Wilkins to some extent was, and as I to some extent was with CORE. He was interested in the movement and the organization was just a means of pushing the movement. He always struck me as having extraordinarily little ego. He didn't need to have, because he was so superior.[61]

CORE and the Black Church

Turning from money to action, we find that the black church played an important role in CORE's protest activities in the South. Black ministers were essential to McCain's early organizing. He recalls: "I knew quite a few of the ministers because every place I went as a field secretary, the first person I most likely talked with was a minister who was a member of SCLC."[62] McCain did more than talk with ministers in his initial organizing in South Carolina in 1958. Indeed, in Clarendon County, Sumter, Spartanburg, and Greenville the chairmen of the local CORE groups were ministers.[63] On August 1, 1958, Gordon Carey, who was white, joined McCain as a full-time field secretary for CORE and helped organize local CORE groups in the South. In 1958, while organizing in Virginia, they persuaded the Reverend Wyatt Walker to become the State Director of Virginia CORE while at the same time heading the local SCLC and NAACP groups. In 1959 the two field secretaries traveled to Tallahassee, and with the assistance of Reverend Steele they established an affiliate there. Contrary to claims that outside elites (e.g., organizations, resource groups, and individuals) create movements by themselves, the data here clearly demonstrate that blacks possessed the key resources CORE, an "outside" organization, needed to become a solid organization with a national constituency. In a 1960 CORE document referred to as CORE's "Contact List," intended to "include all local CORE officers and *other key people* in local groups," we find that black ministers in Tallahassee, Florida; Charleston, Florence, Clarendon County, Greenville, Rock Hill, Spartan-burg, and Sumter, South Carolina; Norfolk, Virginia; and Charleston, West Virginia, held important leadership positions in CORE chapters.[64] The bulk of CORE Southern chapters were situated in those cities, and activist ministers were central to their activities.

Thus, CORE's activities in the South during the late 1950s were linked with and facilitated by black indigenous institutions, especially the churches and local NAACP chapters. It was the expertise and contacts of black leaders like McCain and the ministers that enabled CORE to be linked with the movement. CORE's expansion and building of a national image was so dependent on these groups that often CORE watched helplessly while the NAACP received the credit for activities CORE had initiated, because the local CORE leader was also an NAACP president and a black minister.

Besides, much of CORE's early Southern work resembled that being performed by the NAACP and the SCLC (e.g., voter registration activities carried out by black groups as opposed to "direct action" performed by interracial teams), because it had to be adapted to the Southern black base and the patterns of Southern race relations before it could acquire distinctiveness. The Southern brand of racism prevented close interactions between blacks and whites, and this included protest groups. Hence CORE, with important assistance from black organizations and activists, emerged as an organizational actor in the Southern movement and carved out a central niche for itself in the social conflict, which was to become more intense and pervasive. In the process CORE contributed to the building of movement centers during the late 1950s. It was another force, along with the SCLC and the direct action wing of the NAACP, that had begun to prepare the Southern black community for nonviolent confrontation with white racists.

NOTES

1. James Weldon Johnson, *Negro Americans, What Now?* (New York: Viking Press, 1934), pp. 36–37.
2. James Farmer interview, November 9, 1978, Washington, D.C.
3. Joseph Lowery interview, September 21, 1978, Atlanta.

4. *Pittsburgh Courier,* August 24, 1957.

5. Herbert H. Lehman, letter to Martin Luther King, Jr., December 20, 1957, and Ralph Bunche, letter to Martin Luther King, Jr., December 31, 1957, *MLK:BU.*

6. James Lawson interview, October 2 and 6, 1978, Los Angeles.

7. Farmer interview.

8. NAACP, *Annual Report,* 1957, p. 68.

9. Farmer interview.

10. Martin Luther King, quoted in Adam Fairclough, "A Study of the Southern Christian Leadership Conference and the Rise and Fall of the Non-Violent Civil Rights Movement," Ph.D. dissertation, University of Keele, 1977, p. 14.

11. Farmer interview.

12. Lawson interview.

13. Clara Luper, *Behold the Walls* (Jim Wire, 1979), p. 7.

14. *Ibid.,* pp. 10–11.

15. Benjamin Mays interview, September 20, 1978, Atlanta.

16. Lawson interview.

17. Martin Luther King, Jr., speech, May 17, 1957, Washington, D.C. *MLK:BU.*

18. Martin Luther King, Jr., letter to Thurgood Marshall, February 6, 1958, *MLK:BU.*

19. SCLC, Constitution and By-Laws, *MLK:BU.*

20. Ella Baker, memorandum to the Reverend Martin Luther King, Jr.; the Reverend Ralph D. Abernathy; the Reverend Samuel W. Williams; the Reverend J. E. Lowery; and Dr. L. D. Reddick, July 2, 1959, p. 3, *MLK:BU.*

21. Martin Luther King was so successful at fundraising that top NAACP officials attempted to persuade him to become an officer or board member of the NAACP. On the NAACP's attempt to persuade King to accept an official position with the NAACP, see the extensive correspondence between Kivie Kaplan and Martin Luther King in *MLK:BU.*

22. Arthur L. Johnson, letter to Martin Luther King, Jr., March 6, 1958, *MLK:BU.*

23. SCLC, "Crusade for Citizenship," 1957, *MLK:BU.*

24. King, letter to Thurgood Marshall, 1958, *MLK:BU.*

25. King, speech, 1957, *MLK:BU.*

26. Stanley Levinson, letter to Aldon Morris, March 21, 1979.

27. James McCain interview, November 18, 1978, Sumter, S.C.

28. For a discussion of the problems that Southern interracial CORE groups encountered, see Inge P. Bell, *CORE and the Strategy of Nonviolence* (New York: Random House, 1968), pp. 150–60.

29. Gordon Carey interview, November 18, 1978, Soul City, N. C.

30. Farmer interview.

31. James Robinson interview, October 26, 1978, New York.

32. Farmer interview.

33. Robinson interview.

34. Carey interview.

35. Farmer interview.

36. *Ibid.*

37. Floyd McKissick interview, November 18, 1978, Soul City, N. C.

38. Carey interview.

39. McCain interview.

40. *Ibid.*

41. *Ibid.*

42. August Meier and Elliott Rudwick, *CORE: A Study in the Civil Rights Movement 1942–1968* (New York: Oxford University Press, 1973), p. 295.

43. McCain interview.

44. *Ibid.*

45. *Ibid.*

46. *Ibid.*

47. *Ibid.*

48. *Ibid.*

49. Robinson interview.

50. Farmer interview.

51. Robinson interview.

52. *Ibid.*

53. Meier and Rudwick, *CORE,* p. 78.

54. *Ibid.*

55. See *ibid.,* p. 81.

56. Robinson interview.

57. *Ibid.*

58. Marvin Rich interview, October 24, 1978, New York.

59. *Ibid.*

60. James Robinson, letter to Martin Luther King, Jr., July 12, 1959, *MLK:BU.*

61. Robinson interview.

62. McCain interview.

63. For information on the black clergy functioning as CORE leaders in these cities, see Meier and Rudwick, *CORE,* pp. 88–90.

64. CORE, Contact List, September 15, 1960, pp. 1–9, *MLK:BU.*

25

THE ANALYSIS OF COUNTERMOVEMENTS

TAHI L. MOTTL

During the 1970s the United States experienced a series of "anti" movements, reactions to reforms following the 1960s protests. Although observers have discussed these movements, few sociologists have analyzed them as *countermovements*, a particular kind of protest movement which is a response to the social change advocated by an initial movement.[1] In fact, the analysis of reaction as an inevitable part of social conflict and change has not received sufficient analytical treatment in the social movements literature.

Building on a case study of the anti-busing counterreform movement in Boston, this paper conceptualizes the sources, forms and outcomes of countermovements. Examples are also drawn from other movements, the analysis of which might benefit from their reconceptualization as countermovements, thus placing these "anti" movements in the context of broader sociohistorical developments. That changes in the socioeconomic positions of groups generate protest, followed by counterprotest, can be seen as a dialectical process to be examined in its entirety as part of the continuity of development, conflict and social change.

Conceptual Orientation

A *social movement* is "a conscious, collective, organized attempt" to bring about social change (Wilson, 1973:8). It is useful to define a *countermovement* as a conscious, collective, organized attempt to resist or to reverse social change. The burden of this paper is to demonstrate that the unity of this conceptualization is greater than the sum of its parts. (My central propositions will appear in italics.)

Turner and Killian (1972) used the image of definitions and mirrored interest-group counterdefinitions of situations as a springboard for a preliminary analysis of countermovements. Tilly (1978) and Zald (1979) consider the resource mobilization of reactive protests and countermovements.[2] I extend the view that movements and countermovements ought to be seen as elements of common social processes of collective action centering on reform.

The literature on revolution and counterrevolution is rich with ideas for understanding the sources of countermovements. Tilly's

Reprinted from *Social Problems,* Vol. 27, No. 5, pp. 620–34 by permission. Copyright © 1980 by the Society for the Study of Social Problems.

(1964) analysis of late eighteenth-century counterrevolution in France pointed to rapid growth—in the form of industrialization and urbanization (see also Kornhauser, 1959: 142–158)—and to its uneven outcomes as sources of counterrevolution in the Vendée region. More recent studies (Garner, 1977; Germani, 1978; Skocpol, 1979) underline the importance of macrosocioeconomic transformations, state structures and international crises as sources of national political upheaval.

> *Movements and countermovements may become more international as states continue to be incorporated within a worldwide socioeconomy (see Zald, 1979). (1)*

The relevance of these studies is evident when the analyst inquires as to whether all "anti" movements are countermovements.

> *Movements challenge groups higher up in the stratification hierarchy, while countermovements are oriented against challenges from below.* (2)

This proposition leads me to differ with Zald (1979) in that I do not consider the recent anti-nuclear protests to constitute a countermovement, but rather to consist of a middle-class reform movement (see Barkan, 1979). Proposition 2 mandates the consideration of the nuclear industry as the potential source of a countermovement to protect vested interests (compare the reactions of challenged grape growers studied by Jenkins and Perrow, 1977). The 1960s antiwar protests were also part of a middle-class reform movement. Smelser (1960) and Scott (1974) described the reaction of crafts workers to their dislocation by the introduction of machines; I consider this "reaction" of workers to reflect labor movements, not countermovements (see also Huizer, 1970, with regard to some peasant "reaction"). On the other hand, vigilantism, nativist movements, and the Ku Klux Klan, usually analyzed as social movements, involved mobilization of rural and small town men from a variety of class positions to protect vested interests. Following Proposition 2, it is evident that vigilante activity results from countermovements.

The demand for new advantages versus resistance to the loss of advantages leads to Proposition 3.

> *While movements and revolutions are related to social divisions emergent from urban industrial growth, countermovements are related to social divisions resulting from socioeconomic decline, threatening the position of those who mobilize.* (3)

Studies of "right wing authoritarianism" in the nineteen-forties and fifties explained Nazism, fascism, McCarthyism, Poujadism and other forms of "extremism on the right" (e.g., Loomis and Beegle, 1946). Following Hofstadter (1955), Lipset (1960) argued that working- and middle-class "authoritarianism" expressed itself as a "status politics" of frustrated, "status inconsistent" individuals laboring under the "strains of prosperity" in changing (and often declining) socioeconomic situations. Kornhauser (1959) claimed that "marginal" individuals in mass society were those most accessible to mass movements. A literature on "status politics" emerged to examine ways in which such threatened groups defend their "lifestyles" (Gusfield, 1963; Zurcher *et al.*, 1971; Page and Clelland, 1978). A conflict over threatened cultural styles among groups in different socioeconomic positions is viewed here as a movement-countermovement conflict.

I consider the "state" as an important category for the analysis of movement-countermovement dynamics.[3] Skolnick (1969:xxiii) observed that collective reaction in the United States, "often aided by community support and encouragement from political leaders, is embedded in our history." Brown (1969:176) showed how "frontier entrepreneurs" traditionally assumed the leadership of law and order movements throughout the Midwest, South and West during the 19th century (also see Waskow, 1966). I would add that an important part of traditional movement-countermovement conflict is the intragovernmental power struggle among officials of various levels.

The next proposition concerns the conflict among institutional leaders.

A dual "structure" within government is found in successful movement-countermovement dynamics (as observed by such scholars of revolution as Trotsky, 1959; Garner, 1977; and Stinchcombe, 1978). (4)

When initial movements achieve success, some leaders are recruited into institutional slots, which creates "dual authorities" (see Mottl, 1979). These leaders and their allies organize against countermovement leaders and their allies within government.

Each locus of mobilization recruits politicians from other levels, while the national administration is often neutralized by the more successful forces. (5)

Jenkins and Perrow (1977:265) argue that neutral political elites are a requisite for "insurgent" mobilization (see also Freeman, 1973). This holds as well for countermovement mobilization. For example, the President, the Governor and the "Chicago machine," all public supporters of Equal Rights Amendment ratification in Illinois, were "not prepared to go all-out for passage," signalling anti-ERA forces that the amendment could be defeated (*New York Times,* 1978). Earlier, local officials around the country sought to "get off the hook" by removing themselves from participation in anti-fluoridation conflicts (e.g. Davis, 1959–60; Plaut, 1959; Brand, 1971).

The actions of the institutional leadership of movements and countermovements then suggest Proposition 6.

Institutional conflict draws in rank-and-file participants through pre-existent organizational institutional affiliations[4] (e.g., neighborhood political party organizations, local parent-teacher associations, church organizations; see also, Coleman, 1957; Freeman, 1975). (6)

To mobilize supporters, successful countermovement leaders usually find an ideological key to activate their angry constituents (political party members, voters, church members) who disagree with a particular social change.

A definitive feature of countermovements is the use of a single idea as an ideological lever for the mobilization of disparate constituents to preserve the status quo (see also Ferree and Miller, 1979).[5] (7)

An examination of the life cycles and outcomes of movements and countermovements in interaction (e.g., the pro- and anti-textbook conflict or the pro- and anti-women's liberation movements) yields further propositions.

When movements and countermovements are blocked they transform, attempting to mobilize at the next higher level of government or organizational support, and employing direct action protest (see also Jenkins and Perrow, 1977). (8)

If a countermovement fails it may continue sub rosa within institutions. (9)

This was the case with California's (Jarvis-Gann Proposition 13) anti-property-tax mobilization (see *Facts on File,* 1978).

If a countermovement succeeds, then protest personnel reconsolidate within the institution. (10)

However, few movements or countermovements achieve full success.

> *There remain elements of the original order, elements of reform, and elements of countermovement within government and as institutionalized movement and countermovement organizations.* (11)

Analyses of movement-countermovement genesis and interaction must therefore combine analytical rigor with detailed, historically grounded studies of what I will call a "conflux" of movements: that is, movements and countermovements in interaction (see also Blumer, 1951; Rothschild-Whitt, 1976). The conflux of reform movements and countermovements—during the antislavery period, the Progressive era, the New Deal, the civil rights era—and the closer examination of their interaction within periods of socioeconomic development (e.g., Hobsbawm, 1952; Garner, 1977) is a matter for amplification through continued research.

Busing in Boston: A Case Study The general analytical framework developed in this paper will be illustrated by a case study of the school desegregation movement and the anti-busing countermovement in Boston (Mottl, 1978). Pertinent studies based on large-scale survey data include those of Ross (1974), Taylor and Stinchombe (1978) and Useem (1979b). Here I outline an alternative conceptual approach: the application of a unified movement-countermovement perspective to the conflict. Events transpiring in this major American city over several decades have received wide attention from sociologists and other observers of urban social change (e.g., Cottle, 1976; Lupo, 1977; Hillson, 1977; Useem, 1979a; and the studies cited above). A brief chronology of relevant events introduces the more general discussion in this paper.

Direct action protest in Boston's initial movement emerged in 1963 as part of the nationwide civil rights movement. A major lobbying effort in 1964–1965 brought the passage of a landmark state school desegregation law which was not strenuously enforced by local officials. By 1965, blacks in Boston began to voice an ideology of local institutional control—developing community-run voluntary busing programs within the city and to the suburbs, community protest "free schools," and neighborhood projects funded through the federal and state governments. Ultimately the Boston NAACP and its allies went to court seeking mandatory institutional change. In 1974, after several years of litigation, the federal court ordered large-scale school desegregation.

For almost a decade, the school desegregation movement was effectively resisted by local elected officials on behalf of their constituents. Imminent desegregation, however, brought the mobilization of overt anti-busing protest within the context of national administration approval of the countermovement, the rise of general anti-busing support around the country, and the deepening urban fiscal crisis. Local resistance to school desegregation was encouraged by federal administrative policy. Conversely, the anti-busing movement in Boston was seen nationally as the vanguard for similar countermovements in other cities. From 1972 on, President Nixon—not a leader of the anti-busing movement but a politician drawn into the conflict—actively opposed busing, and President Ford specifically singled out Boston to exemplify the deleterious consequences of this means of achieving desegregation.[6] Congress was drawn into the conflict with annual consideration of anti-busing legislation from 1972 to date. Such was the national situation that interacted with the mobilization of mass anti-busing protest in several cities across the country during the mid-1970s.

Countermovement Forms

A countermovement mobilizes human, symbolic and material resources to block institutional social change or to revert to a previous *status quo*. The categories of countermovement analysis are the same as those for movements, but the patterns within categories are unique. I will consider six aspects of the forms taken by countermovements: strategies and tactics, organizations, rank and file, leadership, ideology, and countermovement life cycles.

Strategy and Tactics[7] William A. Gamson (1975:191) found that fewer than half of the initial movement groups he studied ("the challengers") "attempted to utilize the electoral system during their period of challenge," and that the success of these movements was not substantial. On the other hand, resistance at the polls is a major resource of countermovements. As was observed earlier, Boston's anti-busing movement began its public life as the institutional resistance of elected officials. It later shifted to direct action, and ultimately turned to violence.

> *Countermovement participants develop strategies (institutional resistance, non-violent direct action, violence) for the overall conduct of the movement in reaction to the successes of the initial movement and to the amount of social control exerted against them* (see Snyder and Tilly, 1972; Turner and Killian, 1972; Wilson, 1977).   (12)

Thus, the legislative strategy of the feminist movement at the national level has been opposed in state after state by an anti-ratification countermovement (Brady and Tedin, 1976; Tedin *et al.*, 1977; Arrington and Kyle, 1978).

In Boston, when institutional resistance did not succeed, the militance of countermovement strategies escalated.

> *Countermovements can move from institutionally sanctioned strategies to non-violent direct action to violence if the particular movement goal is not attained.*   (13)

In another example, Kanawha County anti-textbook protesters began with institutional opposition to reform, then adopted a direct action strategy; ultimately, some protesters (not restrained by police) turned to violence (Faigley, 1975:8).

> *Specific tactics (lobbying, letter-writing, boycotts, sit-ins) respond to the range of tactics employed by the initial movement, and the countermovement may even adopt elements of the movement's program* (Turner and Killian, 1972:409).   (14)

One example is the anti-United Farm Worker grape growers who used tactics of non-negotiation, "gradual workforce replacement by ethnic rivals," and recruitment of illegal aliens in response to worker strikes and boycotts (Jenkins and Perrow, 1977:264–266); another example is that countermovements defeated the Townsend social security movement during the 1930s, but ultimately accepted state support for the aged (Turner and Killian, 1972:419).

In Boston, activists lobbied and demonstrated for repeal of the statewide school desegregation law, for anti-busing legislation, and a referendum; deluged officials and editors with letters; jammed call-in talk shows with angry protest phone calls; attempted to draw in suburbs by advocating the expansion of one-way voluntary busing (a program of the initial movement); and established a nationwide anti-busing network. Tactics thus included a national dimension—visits to and from the surrounding metropolitan area and other cities undergoing desegregation, demonstrations and lobbying in Washington. Citywide events included weekly demonstrations, Sunday motorcades and candlelight prayer vigils. At neighborhood protests school buses were often stoned. Boycotts and school disruptions early in the week were followed by walkouts at the week's end. Militants in the countermovement inflamed student disruptions within high schools (Bing, 1978); bathroom and cafeteria brawls became commonplace.

Later, when violence had been repressed by local, state and federal police, covert forms of resistance were employed. Within schools, "black pushout"—seen previously in southern school desegregation—became evident as a disproportionate number of the minority students were suspended and arrested or designated "problem children." School budget cutbacks by city officials threatened to impede desegregation. City property tax rates were raised to support schools and police protection, generating an additional outcry from the public and a new backlash. A Boston white parent (reflecting the opinions of others) lamented, "For three years I've been worried about busing. But it's over now and now I'm worried about taxes" (*Boston Globe*, 1976).

Countermovement Organizations Boston's decentralized parent-teacher association was easily converted for anti-busing protest. Organized systematically, like political party wards, the South Boston Home and School Association acknowledged referendum supporters:

> On this issue—you're either with us or against us; . . . our sincere appreciation to our block captains and area captains for a job well done (*South Boston Tribune*, 1974).

The most powerful and militant anti-busing organization, Restore Our Alienated Rights (ROAR), had been organized in 1973 as a loosely structured umbrella group in which elected officials held important and highly visible leadership positions. When desegregation was implemented, the city and pro-desegregation groups opened information hotlines to answer questions and to calm fears about the process. In mirrored re-sponse, anti-busers (often from Home and School groups) opened "Information Centers" in many neighborhoods to disseminate resistance information. As the local pro-desegregation movement had done five years earlier, neighborhood protest schools were created for parents who refused to participate in busing (see also, Rothschild-Whitt, 1976).

> *Like social movements, countermovements put into effect extant organizational affiliations and draw from these to create new protest organizations. But "anti" movements are more likely to form from coalitions of pre-existent organizations with ties to major institutions (e.g., Oberschall, 1973; Freeman, 1977).* (15)

An incipient 1957 anti-tax movement in Los Angeles failed in part because it did not activate widespread networks, did not have the support of existent taxpayers' organizations representing business and industrial property owners, and generated no new umbrella organization (Jackson *et al.*, 1960: 37–38). The 1978 taxpayers revolt, on the other hand, had its most significant impact on large businesses and owners of farm property, and was sponsored (among others) by the Apartment [Owners] Association of Los Angeles County, the United Organization of Taxpayers (headed by State Representative Jarvis) and the People's Advocate (headed by retired real-estate salesman State Representative Gann), a taxpayer's organization with 30,000 members (*Facts on File*, 1978).

Rank and File Observers of local pro- and anti-Equal Rights Amendment conflict have found that the "pros" were of slightly higher middle-class status than the "antis" (Huber *et al.*, 1976; Tedin *et al.*, 1977; Arrington and Kyle, 1978). Similarly, Page and Clelland analyzed letters to the editor of the *Charleston-Gazette* and found that textbook proponents and opponents seemed to be of approximately the same educational strata. "The difference in median family income between the two sections is not remarkably great" although the "protest region" was more rural, had fewer wealthy residents, more variation in educational attainment, and more older people (1978: 272–273). This corresponds with Proposition 16.

> *While movement participants are interested in workers benefits or in the "bourgeoisifica-tion" of movement beneficiaries, counter-movement participants attempt to prevent "proletarianization" (see also Tilly, 1979; Sennett, 1972).* (16)

Likewise, Giles *et al.* (1976) found that anti-school desegregation protesters tended to be of two sorts: upper-middle-class, class-biased protesters (i.e., prejudiced against persons of other social classes) and racially prejudiced protesters who were high on either income or education and low on the other. Protesters were fending off challenges to their socioeconomic positions.

In Boston, the most active countermove-ment participants were Home and School Association parents, rank-and-file partici-pants were neighborhood parents mobilized by countermovement activists to join large tactical events (see Cottle, 1976), and periph-eral supporters were parents, neighbors and other voters who were opposed to busing (Taylor and Stinchcombe, 1978; Useem, 1979a,b).

Like movements, rank-and-file partici-pants of countermovements can be visual-ized as being relatively more or less actively mobilized.

> *Organized in circles of participation around the most committed core activists, rank-and-file members of organizations are activated to carry out countermovement tactics, but are not involved full-time; peripheral supporters agree with the countermovement ideology and may vote in its support (see Turner and Killian, 1972; Oberschall, 1973).* (17)

Anti-busing forces, organizing nation-wide rank-and-file support, deluged the Internal Revenue Service with 100,000 let-ters protesting its new rules against alterna-tive segregated "white flight" schools, a "groundswell" created by computerized mailing-list solicitation of the American Conservative Union and the National Chris-tian Action Coalition (Witte, 1978). Similarly, the Conservative Caucus, working from Washington, D.C., sent 90,000 letters to North Carolina voters and 150,000 to Florida voters with charges against the Equal Rights Amendment (*New York Times,* 1978). Calls and letters flooded into legislators' offices, and the group claimed responsibility for de-feat of the E.R.A. in those states.

Conflict centering on institutions related to health, education and social welfare may involve an overrepresentation of women, compared to their actual institutional leader-ship. Fainstein and Fainstein (1974) discuss this feature of the 1960s urban protest move-ments. Family-related countermovements (Gordon and Hunter, 1978) such as the anti-E.R.A., anti-abortion, and anti-gay protest also have mobilized women. This is true for educa-tion backlash movements: anti-busing (Mottl, 1977) and anti-textbook countermovements. Countermovement women can be seen to express concern about their possible "proletar-ianization" through the reduction of their hus-bands' status (see Huber *et al.,* 1976) or by being cast into the labor market themselves.

Leadership Oberschall (1973) discussed the elite origins of many protest and revolu-tionary leaders (see also Skocpol, 1979). Countermovement leaders, too, are often drawn from elite backgrounds.

> *Countermovement leaders are elites within existing institutions who strongly oppose change; they perceive their power as threat-ened by change or as augmented by their resistance to change.* (18)

The head of the national "Stop E.R.A." organization, Phyllis Schlafly, an upper-middle-class "housewife," was also a regular candidate for political office in Illinois (Wohl, 1974; *New York Times*, 1978). More to the point, the West Virginia anti-textbook countermovement was initiated in 1974 by newly elected school board member, Mrs. Alice Moore, the wife of a fundamentalist minister (Faigley, 1975; Burger, 1978). Other early leaders of the textbook countermovement were fundamentalist ministers with roots in the "old entrepreneurial middle class, subsistence farming, and the 'secondary market' working class" (Page and Clelland, 1978:275). Within a few months, the leadership began to change (Faigley, 1975): several small town mayors proposed to secede from their part of the county (Page and Clelland, 1978); and "spokesmen from outside the community representing extremist right-wing organizations" came to the fore (Faigley, 1975:8). Both movement and countermovement leaders were drawn from the middle class, although pro-textbook leaders were slightly better educated (Page and Clelland, 1978).

Gusfield (1957) specifically described the generations of protest leaders in the Temperance Movement and the shift from upper-middle-class to lower-middle-class origins over the generations. Boston's anti-busing countermovement recruited at least two generations of protest leaders. First there were office holders (self-employed professionals) like charismatic Louise Day Hicks who was a lawyer and the daughter of a judge (see also, Taylor and Stinchcombe, 1978). Second generation leaders included neighborhood civic and political party officers and heads of neighborhood Home and School Associations. For example, Elvira Palladino, a middle-class leader (with working-class origins) of the East Boston Home and School Association, emerged at the forefront of the militant stage of Boston's anti-busing countermovement. Palladino eventually was elected to the Boston School Committee. Secondary leaders included radio personalities such as talk-show host Avi Nelson who was an unsuccessful anti-busing candidate for governor in 1979. In the same vein, California's anti-taxation countermovement, led by state level politicians, was also mobilized in part by radio personalities. Garner (1977:186) points out that radio particularly lends itself to mass mobilization—for example, during the McCarthy era.

Ideology Like movements, the symbolic resources of the countermovement are organized for the coercion of target groups, to activate third parties to join the side of protesters, or to generate material resources for the countermovement (Lipsky, 1968).

> *Countermovement ideology* (like the ideology of movements) *includes ideas about the movement's goals, how they are to be attained, symbols, and underlying assumptions concerning social order and social change* (Heberle, 1951: 25–29). (19)
>
> *Countermovement goals are particularistic. They focus on a single grievance. Politicians attempt to increase their power by taking dramatic, clear, one-issue stands.* (20)

A number of one-issue movements emerged during the 1970s. It is important to view them as particularistic countermovements, and to understand that their general intent was to uphold the *status quo* (e.g., Hillocks, 1978). Countermovement ideologies adopt specific aspects of the institutions they seek to uphold—for example, the woman's role as homemaker and childbearer in the traditional family (Gordon and Hunter, 1978).

Chafe asserts that "the consistency of anti-feminist arguments constitute one of the most striking facts of the entire debate in America over women's place": since the mid-19th century, the ideology has centered on "woman's place in the home," admonishing that "equality will lead to the destruction of home and family" (Chafe, 1972: 231–232). Postwar anti-feminism, communicated through channels as varied as women's magazines and the social sciences (e.g., Freudian psychology), demanded that women return to the home and to traditional family structures as men returned to the workforce (Chafe, Chapter 9). Current anti-E.R.A. activists, with attitudes consistent with the Radical Right, have focused on legalized abortions and lesbianism as threats to the traditional family to generate opposition to the Equal Rights Amendment (*New York Times*, 1978).

Turner and Killian (1972:318-319) argue that countermovement ideology:

—is "preoccupied with opposing rather than promoting a particular program";

—tends to focus on the means proposed by the initial movement, rather than the ends;

—will change if the initial movement succeeds or fails (if the initial movement succeeds, then the counter movement often adopts "popular elements of the initial movement's ideology as its own");

—will be militant if the initial movement is seen as weak; or if the initial movement is perceived as strong, will respect initial movement participants and depict them as "well-meaning but misguided";

—depends on "evoking the established myths of the society to oppose change," and often absorbs elements from the initial movement's ideology and blends the new additions into societal myths, thus changing those myths.

The anti-busing movement evoked a number of "societal myths" in its ideational scheme (see also, Myers, 1948; Green, 1961; Hillocks, 1978). Protection of the neighbor-

hood and the family was a central theme of the anti-busing counterprotest. Particularly salient was the belief that the rights of parents were being abused (*South Boston Tribune*, 1974); "mother" was adopted as a symbolic figure (*East Boston Community News*, 1973). The widespread belief that schools in black neighborhoods are "dangerous" was compounded by resistance to the intrusion of "outsiders" into white neighborhoods and the protection of ethnic identity (*East Boston Community News*, 1973). "Suburbanites" represented the opposed and dominant class, while "white flight" to the suburbs was depicted as an indicator of unsuccessful desegregation.

Emblems like the orange, white and green flag with a shamrock in the center suggested a symbolic Irish-American constituency of the countermovement (just as the ritual display of the American flag had earlier symbolized anti-"peacenik" sentiment; Turner and Killian, 1972: 141; see also, Wilsnack, 1979). The "Here We Go Southie" football cheer, often heard at rallies, aligned the countermovement with a symbolically working-class neighborhood.[8] The ideology of the countermovement defined anti-busing advocates as an embattled, cohesive group, unified in the defense of a threatened traditional way of life (see Rubin, 1972). (In California the "embattled taxpayer" was depicted as a homogeneous group in the rapid mobilization behind Proposition 13.) Underlying these ideas were assumptions of the existence of stable, traditional institutions—families, neighborhoods, neighborhood schools—that were considered to have been violated.[9]

Countermovement Life Cycles There are regular stages in the development of countermovements.

A countermovement life cycle typically has four stages:

I. *Electoral and intrainstitutional resistance to change;*

II. *Mobilization of overt protest against change (when change seems inevitable);*

III. *Transformation to militant protest (if goals are blocked);*

IV. *Reinstitutionalization (if the countermovement succeeds) or covert resistance to change (if the countermovement is repressed).*   (21)

In the first phase of Boston's anti-busing countermovement, the resistance of School Committee Chairperson Louise Day Hicks to demands for school desegregation stimulated a new multiethnic coalition of middle- and lower-middle-class white voters (Ross, n.d.). This coalition survived more than a decade of biannual school committee elections. Similarly, in Charleston, West Virginia in 1974, a vote of the school board over the objections of an anti-textbook board member was the "precipitating factor" for overt protest (Page and Clelland, 1978).

The second phase of Boston's countermovement—mobilization for overt protest—began in 1972 when it became evident that school desegregation was probable. Federal government officials (from the Departments of Justice and Health, Education and Welfare) acted with state officials and civil rights organizations (particularly the Boston branch of the NAACP) to converge on the School Committee. School Committee officials responded by organizing to repeal the state Racial Imbalance Law, to lobby state and federal legislative bodies against busing, and to appeal lower court judgments. Likewise, in the second phase of the Kanawha County countermovement, anti-textbook protest forces "organized groups, attended rallies, and distributed leaflets condemning the books" and called a boycott for the opening of school in September, 1974 (Burger, 1978:155).

Countermovements such as the Ku Klux Klan and McCarthy anti-communism were crippled when "traditional power groups"

became antagonistic (Lipset, 1955:368). However, faced with the probable federal court school desegregation mandate in 1974, Boston's anti-busing countermovement accelerated. This militant phase lasted until the fall of 1977, when Hicks and other anti-busing candidates were defeated at the polls and the first black was elected to the School Committee. It was during this time that Boston's "fiscal crisis" became apparent; its credit rating dropped and the state reorganized its financial underpinnings in association with the region's major banks (*Wall Street Journal,* 1975). Since that time, militant protest has diminished.

In Kanawha County, the "incomplete success" of a school boycott led some anti-textbook protesters to attempt "violence to halt work at construction projects, factories, and chemical plants and to stop trains and buses" (Faigley, 1975:8). For two months there were bus drivers' and coal miners' strikes, and "general widespread violence" (Burger, 1978:145). As a result, the school board formally recognized the protest groups, closed the schools for three days, and removed the controversial books from classrooms pending their review by a special citizens committee (Burger, 1978:157). Violence accelerated and a month later a divided citizens committee produced two reports. Soon afterward, the school board building was dynamited.

Messinger (1955) discussed the organizational transformation of a declining movement (the Townsend social security movement) "outside" of a public institution. In a different manner, the fourth phase of Boston's anti-busing movement was characterized by a return to phase I strategies. While such organizations as the neighborhood information centers continue to exist in some areas (the South Boston Information Center was principal organizer in the July 1979 congressional vote on a constitutional amendment to halt "forced busing"), tactics now involve the reinstitutionalization of segregation through bureaucratic means: budget cutbacks, incomplete programming, imbalanced within-school tracking, particularistic school transfer decisions, and white departures from the school system.

Countermovement Outcomes

Outcomes are the effects that follow as the result or consequences of movement-countermovement conflict. (22)

Gamson considers "two basic clusters" of protest outcomes: "one concerned with the fate of the challenging group . . . and one with the distribution of new advantages to the group's beneficiary" (1975:28). Countermovements have outcomes for themselves as well as important effects upon initial social movements and on the social changes they attempt to create. I consider three kinds of consequences of countermovements: 1) their effect on institutional inequality, 2) the stabilization of the situation through the coexistence of movement and countermovement forces, and 3) the reconsolidation of "state" authority.

Inequality Countermovements aim to preserve the *status quo*, so they generally do not yield outcomes that reduce societal and institutional inequality. If such movements have broad effects, it is to reverse changes that ostensibly aimed to redistribute resources. Hence, their successes do not terminate the process of social change. In all probability, countermovement gains create pathways for future protest.

Stabilization of the Situation Countermovements, even when they do not attain their goals, often succeed in bringing about a relative stabilization of the change process generated by the initial movement. This neutralization is expressed as the coexistence of parts of both movements and countermovements within ongoing bureaucratic institutions (see Jenkins and Perrow, 1977, for neutralization of federal officials by the farm workers' movement). Any effects of institutional change may be reversed through mass nonparticipation (e.g., the "white flight" phenomenon). Hence one observes the legacies of the reforms (gains of the proactive movement—often in the form of new bureaucratic elements) existing simultaneously with reversals brought about by the countermovement. Thus, the outcome of countermovements for some politicians, officials, and administrators is that the situation is "stabilized." But the effects of countermovements for the great majority of citizens are at best negligible, at worst regressive.[10]

Reconsolidation of Bureaucratic Authority Not only do countermovements leave societal inequalities intact or sometimes enlarged, but they often generate a reconsolidation of bureaucratic authority. Target officials respond to attack and counterattack by shoring up defenses and cutting away unnecessary programs and agencies. Thus, the dual authority created by coexistence of old elites, new movement, and countermovement bureaucrats creates a higher level of consolidation.[11] For example, 19th century vigilantes created dual mechanisms to challenge political opponents who were in control, to save time and the costs of democratic social change, with the support of national "conservative" elites (Brown, 1969:188–195).

Today, lesser employees of the bureaucracy are "let go." Many parts of the bureaucracy are reorganized along more "rationalized" lines, often at the level of authority above the one under contention. For example, California's Proposition 13 bankrupted a number of local agencies and programs, forcing a consolidation of those services at the state level.

In this way, a counterprotest whose ideology often argues for local control (neighborhood schools, property owner rights) sometimes facilitates centralization of decision making at higher levels of government. In Boston, trenchant bureaucratic resistance at one level of government paradoxically made restructuring from higher levels easier. The authority of the local school committee was superceded by the federal court that began to administer the schools. The countermovement succeeded in mobilizing large-scale nonparticipation in change, continued bureaucratic resistance *(sub rosa)* and the election of militant anti-busing officials. Meanwhile, the crisis facilitated the restructuring of finances by lending institutions (*Wall Street Journal,* 1975). While widespread nonparticipation and protracted bureaucratic resistance continues to the present day, several local countermovement politicians have been defeated at the polls. Other anti-busing politicians have changed issues—to tax reform—in order to be reelected.

Summary and Implications

Social scientists have often turned their attention to "right wing movements" (Heberle, 1951; Bell, 1955; Skolnick, 1969; Lipset and Raab, 1970) and to the analysis of counterrevolution (Tilly, 1964; Garner, 1977). Past studies have not analyzed reactive movements as part of a movement-countermovement dialectic. The study of reform movements may well be enriched by reconceptualizing them in this way.

The contribution of the present paper has been to identify the movement-countermovement dynamic; to show that the analysis of both movements and countermovements can be greatly enriched by recognizing the historical relationship between them as they arise out of changing socioeconomic situations; to suggest some specific dimensions which might serve to differentiate movements and countermovements; to illustrate the applica-

tion of this developing schema with reference to a study of social change and resistance to change (the civil rights desegregation and anti-busing movements in Boston); and to suggest some relation to other anti-reform movements of the past and present.

A local countermovement may arise not only in response to the probable success of an initial movement focused on persistent inequality, but also in response to a shift in national policy which signals openings (or active support) for counterprotest and the rise of backlash.

The ideology of countermovements is particularistic—focused on the means for change advocated by the first movement. Furthermore, if the countermovement does not meet its objective, its ideology and tactics may escalate and become more militant (as is the case of many blocked political movements; Smelser, 1962).

Countermovements are frequently mobilized by elected officials and other elites in the name of their constituents whose prerogatives are superceded by the success of the initial movement. Leaders tend to rally grass roots support through pre-existent political, institutional, civic and religious organizations—an already highly aligned constituency. In this mobilization, committed core activists, part-time activists (who are less committed), and a large number of protest participants are activated through existing groups and new counterprotest organizations. New generations of leaders emerge if counterprotest is blocked and secondary leaders mobilize militant tactics.

If a countermovement does not dissipate for internal reasons but is frustrated in its aims, four phases of protest are likely to emerge: 1) bureaucratic resistance by elected officials; 2) the mobilization of overt protest; 3) transformation of protest to militant forms (attempts to reclaim power against heightened social control efforts); and 4) a return to protracted bureaucratic resistance.

This discussion suggests that additional systematic research should be undertaken on movement "confluxes"—the interaction of movements and countermovements—and on the generation of such confluxes out of socioeconomic changes in which some groups in society gain and other groups feel that they may lose, especially now when the American middle class is threatened with proletarianization. Such research should further clarify the features that differentiate movements and countermovements as well as those they share, and further elaborate the outcomes of movement-countermovement conflict.

The analytical framework presented and illustrated in this paper is based on the view that the study of movements and countermovements may usefully be conceptualized as a continuous dialectic of social change.

Acknowledgments

This is the revised version of a paper presented at the Institute for the Study of Social Change, University of California, Berkeley, August 1978. My thanks to the many colleagues who have commented on the paper. Specific new criticisms and encouragement were provided by Ronald Breiger, Roberta Garner, Clarence Lo, John McCarthy, Bert Useem, William J. Wilson and the editor.

NOTES

1. The most important exception to this statement is Zald (1979).
2. Tilly (1978:42) argues for the more generic term "collective action" to describe protest because it implies a logical connected outgrowth of class relations. Tilly is a persuasive critic of the view that the social movements literature depicts protest as "autonomous and separate" from ongoing politics.
3. My consideration of the role of the state has greatly benefitted from Theda Skocpol's study

(1979) of states and revolutions in France, Russia and China. Identification of the role of governmental infrastructure in the genesis, mobilization and outcomes of American movements and countermovements is central to the analysis developed in this paper.
4. This analysis is compatible with Traugott's (1978) article which focuses on the anti-institutional aspect of movements.
5. Villmoare (1977:597), for example, argues that the "law and order" ideological response to movements of the 1960s amounted to a "preventative counterrevolution."
6. Observe that the Nixon administration was "neutral" with respect to the United Farm Workers movement (Jenkins and Perrow, 1978) and the congressional passage of the Equal Rights Amendment, which was a tactic of the women's movement (Freeman, 1977), while it supported the anti-busing countermovement. The reasons for this occurrence are a subject for further research.
7. Here I distinguish between broad strategies and specific protest event tactics; see Heberle (1959:259).
8. South Boston High School (known as "Southie"), a segregated high school attended by whites, became a major target of counterprotest following the court-mandated desegregation of Boston's schools.
9. "Neighborhood schools" were found by the Boston federal district court in 1974 to be virtually nonexistent because numerous white children had voluntarily transferred to schools in other neighborhoods to avoid racial desegregation (*Morgan vs. Hennigan,* CA No. 72-911-G).
10. In Kanawha County, for instance, a "compromise" was reached: "the books were returned to the schools" but "much stricter guidelines were established for the selection of textbooks in the future" (Burger, 1978: 144). The school board president resigned, the countermovement leader was returned to office, and students were not required to use the controversial textbooks (Faigley, 1975:9; Page and Clelland, 1977:270).
11. Garner (1977) argues that only twice in American history—the Revolution and the Civil War—have dual structures of authority successfully been created in this society. She argues that cities offer "little time or space for experimentation with dual structures" because the "urban population is integrated into

the central institutions of the society" (1977: 103). I contend that a modified form of dual authority exists when reform and counter-reform movements meet within institutions.

REFERENCES

Arrington, Theodore S. and Patricia A. Kyle. 1978. "Equal Rights Amendment activists in North Carolina." Signs (Spring):666–680.

Barkan, Steven E. 1979. "Strategic, tactical and organizational dilemmas of the protest movement against nuclear power." Social Problems 27:19–37.

Bell, Daniel (ed.). 1955. The New American Right. New York: Criterion.

Bing, Steven R. 1978. "Going to school in Boston." Pp. 15–19 in R.C. Edwards (ed.), The Capitalist System: A Radical Analysis of American Society. Englewood Cliffs, N.J.: Prentice-Hall.

Blumer, Herbert. 1951. "Collective behavior." Pp. 166–222 in A. M. Lee (ed.), New Outline of the Principles of Sociology. New York: Barnes and Noble.

Boston Globe. 1976. "Political circuit: Hub politics beyond busing." Sept. 15:19.

Brandy, David W. and Kent L. Tedin. 1976. "Ladies in pink: Religion and political ideology in the anti-E.R.A. movement." Social Science Quarterly 56:564–575.

Brand, J. A. 1971. "Politics of fluoridation: A community conflict." Political Studies 19:430–439.

Brown, Richard Maxwell. 1969. "The American vigilante tradition." Pp. 154–226 in H. D. Graham and T. R. Gurr (ed.), Violence in America: Historical and Comparative Perspectives. New York: Bantam.

Burger, Robert H. 1978. "The Kanawha County textbook controversy: A study of communication and power." Library Quarterly 48:143–162.

Chafe, William Henry. 1972. The American Woman: Her Changing Social, Economic, and Political Roles, 1920–1970. New York: Oxford University Press.

Coleman, James S. 1957. Community Conflict. New York: The Free Press.

Cottle, Thomas J. 1976. Busing. Boston: Beacon.

Davis, Morris. 1959-1960. "Community attitudes toward fluoridation." Public Opinion Quarterly 23:474–482.

East Boston Community News. 1973. "Elvira Paladino fights busing full-time." July 17:5.

Facts on File: World News Digest with Index. 1978. "U. S. affairs: California voters pass initiative cutting property taxes by 57%." June 9:425–428.

Faigley, Lester I. 1975. "What happened in Kanawha County." The English Journal 64:7–9.

Fainstein, Norman I. and Susan S. Fainstein. 1974. Urban Political Movements: The Search for Power by Minority Groups in American Cities. Englewood Cliffs, N.J.: Prentice-Hall.

Ferree, Myra Marx and Frederick D. Miller. 1979. "Mobilization and meaning: Toward an integration of social psychological and resource perspectives on social movements." Unpublished paper, University of Connecticut, Storrs.

Freeman, Jo. 1975. The Politics of Women's Liberation. New York: David McKay.

Gamson, William A. 1975. The Strategy of Social Protest. Homewood, Ill.: Dorsey.

Garner, Roberta Ash. 1977. Social Movements in America. Chicago: Rand McNally.

Germani, Gino. 1978. Authoritarianism, Fascism, and National Populism. New Brunswick, N.J.: Transaction Books.

Giles, Michael, Douglas S. Gatlin and Everett F. Cataldo. 1976. "Racial and class prejudice: Their relative effects on protest against school desegregation." American Sociological Review 41:280–288.

Gordon, Linda and Allen Hunter. 1977-1978. "Sex, family and the new right: Anti-feminism as a political force." Radical America 12(1):9–25.

Green, Arnold L. 1961. "The ideology of anti-fluoridation leaders." Journal of Social Issues 17:13–15.

Gusfield, Joseph. 1975. "The problem of generations in an organizational structure." Social Forces 35:323–330.

———. 1963. Symbolic Crusade: Status Politics and the American Temperance Union. Urbana, Ill.: University of Illinois Press.

Heberle, Rudolf. 1951. Social Movements; An Introduction to Political Sociology. New York: Appleton-Century-Crofts.

Hillocks, George, Jr. 1978. "Books and bombs: Ideological conflict and the schools: A case study of the Kanawha County book protest." The School Review 86:632-654.

Hillson, Jon. 1977. The Battle of Boston: Busing and the Struggle for School Desegregation. New York: Pathfinder.

Hobsbawm, E. J. 1952. "Economic fluctuations and some social movements since 1800." Economic History Review (second series) 5:1-25.

Hofstader, Richard. 1955. "The pseudo-conservative revolt." In Daniel Bell (ed.), The New American Right. New York: Criterion.

Huber, Joan, Cynthia Rexroat and Glenna Spitze. 1976. "E.R.A. in Illinois: A crucible of opinion on women's status." Unpublished paper, University of Illinois, Urbana-Champaign.

Huizer, Gerritt. 1970. "Resistance to change and radical peasant mobilization: Foster and Erasmus reconsidered." Human Organization 20:303-313.

Jackson, Maurice, Eleanora Peterson, James Bull, Sverre Monsen and Patricia Richmond. 1960. "The failure of an incipient social movement." Pacific Sociological Review 3:35-40.

Jenkins, J. Craig and Charles Perrow. 1977. "Insurgency of the powerless: Farm worker movements (1946-1972). " American Sociological Review 42:249-268.

Kornhauser, William. 1959. The Politics of Mass Society. New York: The Free Press.

Lipset, Seymour Martin. 1955. "The sources of the radical right." pp. 397-372 in Daniel Bell (ed), The New American Right. New York: Criterion.

———. 1960. Political Man; the Social Bases of Politics. New York: Doubleday.

Lipset, S. M. and Earl Raab. 1970. The Politics of Unreason: Right Wing Extremism in America, 1790-1970. New York: Harper and Row.

Lipsky, Michael. 1968. "Protest as a political resource." American Political Science Review 62:1144-1158.

Loomis, C. P. and J. A. Beegle. 1946. "The spread of German Nazism in rural areas." American Sociological Review 11724-734.

Lupo, Alan. 1977. Liberty's Chosen Home: the Politics of Violence in Boston. Boston: Little, Brown.

Messinger, Sheldon L. 1955. "Organizational transformation: A case study of a declining social movement." American Sociological Review 20:3-10.

Mottl, Tahi L. 1977. "School movements as recruiters of women leaders." Urban Education 12:3:14.

———. 1978. "Conditions for black protest: The civil rights movement as school protest in a northern city." Working Paper Series #105. Berkeley, Calif: Institute for the Study of Social Change.

———. 1979. "When protest succeeds: Protest leaders after the institutionalization for a movement." Paper presented to the annual meeting of the American Sociological Association, August, Boston.

Myers, Robert C. 1948. "Anti-communist mob action: A case study." Public Opinion Quarterly 12:57-67.

New York Times. 1978. "Battle over Equal Rights Amendment: Emotional tactics, confused issues and broken promises." May 28:44.

———. 1978. "What rights amendment could— and couldn't do." May 29:D5.

Oberschall, Anthony. 1973. Social Conflict and Social Movements. Englewood Cliffs, N.J.: Prentice-Hall.

Page, Ann L. and Donald A. Celland. 1978. "The Kanawha County textbook controversy: A study of the politics of life style concern." Social Forces 57:265-281.

Plaut, Thomas F. A. 1959. "Analysis of voting behavior on a flouridation referendum." Public Opinion Quarterly 23:213-222.

Ross, Michael. n.d. "Political controversy and resistance to racial change: The Boston school committee elections, 1963–1965." Unpublished paper, Boston University, Boston, Mass.

Rothschild-Whitt, Joyce. 1976. "Conditions facilitating participatory-democratic organizations." Sociological Inquiry 46:75–86.

Rubin, Lillian B. 1972. Busing and Backlash; White Against White in a California School District. Berkeley: University of California.

Scott, Joan Wallach. 1974. The Glassworkers of Camaux: French Craftsmen and Political Action in a Nineteenth-Century City. Cambridge: Harvard University Press.

Sennett, Richard and Jonathan Cobb. 1972. The Hidden Injuries of Class. New York: Knopf.

Skocpol, Theda. 1979. State and Social Revolutions: A Comparative Analysis of France, Russia, and China. New York: Cambridge University.

Skolnick, Jerome H. 1969. The Politics of Protest. New York: Ballantine.

Smelser, Neil J. 1960. Social Change in the Industrial Revolution; An Application of Theory to the British Cotton Industry. Chicago: University of Chicago Press.

———. 1962. Theory of Collective Behavior. New York: The Free Press.

Snyder, David and Charles Tilly. 1972. "Hardship and collective violence in France, 1830 to 1960." American Sociological Review 42:105–123.

South Boston Tribune. 1974. "South Boston Home and School Association wishes to acknowledge those who supported us in our anti-busing fight and expose those who did not." (Advertisement.) March 28:7.

———. 1974. "City hall scene." May 23:1.

Stinchcombe, Arthur L. 1978. Theoretical Methods in Social History. New York: Academic Press.

Taylor, Garth and Arthur L. Stinchcombe. 1978. "A paradigm for studying the role of public opinion in community reactions to school desegregation." Unpublished paper, University of Chicago, Chicago, Ill.

Tedin, K. L., David W. Brady, Mary E. Buxton, Barbara W. Gorman and Judy L. Thompson. 1977. "Social background and political differences between pro-E.R.A. and anti-E.R.A. activists." American Politics Quarterly 5(3):395–408.

Tilly, Charles. 1964. The Vendée. Cambridge, Mass.: Harvard University Press.

———.1978. From Mobilization to Revolution. Reading, Mass.: Addison-Wesley.

———.1979. "Proletarianization: Theory and research." Paper presented at the annual meeting of the American Sociological Association, August, Boston.

Traugott, Mark. 1978. "Reconceiving social movements." Social Problems 26:38–49.

Trotsky, Leon. 1959 (1932). The Russian Revolution; the Overthrow of Tsarism and the Triumph of the Soviets. (Translated by Max Eastman.) Garden City, N.Y.: Doubleday.

Turner, Ralph H. and Lewis M. Killian. 1972. Collective Behavior. Englewood Cliffs, N.J.: Prentice-Hall.

Useem, Bert. 1979a. "The Boston anti-busing movement and social movements theory." Unpublished doctoral dissertation, Brandeis University, Waltham, Mass.

———.1979b. "Solidarity model, breakdown model, and the Boston anti-busing movement." Unpublished paper, Center for Research on Social Organization, University of Michigan, Ann Arbor.

Villmoare, Adelaide H. 1977. "Preventative counterrevolution: The ideological response to the 1960s." American Behavioral Scientist 20:597–616.

Wall Street Journal. 1975. "States try harder to persuade buyers that bonds are safe." Sept. 24:1.

Waskow, Arthur J. 1966. From Race Riot to Sit-In. Garden City, N.Y.: Doubleday.

Wilsnack, Richard W. 1979. "Counterfads: Episodes of collective disbelief." Paper presented at the annual meeting of the American Sociological Association, August, Boston.

Wilson, John. 1973. Introduction to Social Movements. New York: Basic Books.

———.1977. "Social protest and social control." Social Problems 24:469–481.

Witte, Ann G. 1978. "Subsidizing segregation; the IRS tries to close loopholes for racists." The New Republic, December 23 and 30:11–13.

Wohl, Lisa Cronin. 1974. "Phyllis Schlafly, 'The sweetheart of the silent majority'." Ms. Magazine (March):55–57, 85–89.

Zald, Mayer N. 1979. "Macro issues in the theory of social movements; SMO interaction, the role of counter-movements and cross-national determinants of the social movement sector." Working Paper No. 204. Ann Arbor, Mich.: Center for Research on Social Organization.

Zurcher, L. A., Jr., R. G. Kirkpatrick, R. G. Cushing and C. K. Bowman. 1971. "The anti-pornography campaign: A symbolic crusade." Social Problems 19:217–238.

CONTINUITY AND CYCLES

26

SOCIAL MOVEMENT CONTINUITY
The Women's Movement in Abeyance

VERTA TAYLOR

Introduction

Scholars of the social movements of the 1960s have by and large held an "immaculate conception" view of their origins. These "new so-

From *American Sociological Review*, 54 (October 1989) pp. 761–775. Reprinted by permission of American Sociological Association.

cial movements" (Klandermans 1986) seemingly emerged out of nowhere and represented a sudden shift from the quiescent 1940s and 1950s (Flacks 1971; Touraine 1971; McCarthy and Zald 1973; Jenkins 1987). Recent empirical work, however, challenges this view, suggesting that the break between the sixties movements and earlier waves of political activism was not as sharp as previously assumed (e.g., Isserman 1987; McAdam 1988). The overemphasis on movement origins and on new elements in the sixties movements has blinded students of social movements to the "carry-overs and carry-ons" between movements (Gusfield 1981, p. 324). What scholars have taken for "births" were in fact breakthroughs or turning points in movement mobilization.

This paper develops a framework that specifies the processes of movement continuity. The framework is grounded in research on the American women's rights movement from 1945 to the mid-1960s. Most accounts trace its origins to the civil rights movement (Freeman 1975; Evans 1979). Yet the women's movement, like the other movements that blossomed in the 1960s, can also be viewed as a resurgent challenge with roots in an earlier cycle of feminist activism that presumably ended when suffrage was won. My approach relies heavily on the central premises of resource mobilization theory: political opportunities and an indigenous organizational base are major factors in the rise and decline of movements (e.g., Oberschall 1973; McCarthy and Zald 1977; McAdam 1982; Jenkins 1983). The paper makes a new contribution by elaborating certain abeyance processes in social movements and by specifying features of social movement abeyance organizations. The term "abeyance" depicts a holding process by which movements sustain themselves in nonreceptive political environments and provide continuity from one stage of mobilization to another.

After discussing data sources, the analysis briefly describes the history of the American women's movement and the persistence of a small band of feminists who, in the 1940s and 1950s, continued to remain faithful to the political vision that had originally drawn them into the suffrage movement nearly a half century earlier. Because the cultural and political climate had changed, these women found that their ideals and commitment to feminism marginalized and isolated them from the mainstream of American women. I argue that their form of activism is best understood as a social movement abeyance structure. Finally, I delineate the features of abeyance structures that were a source of movement continuity by tracing the consequences of postwar activism for the contemporary women's movement. I conclude by exploring the implications of the abeyance hypothesis for understanding the organizational and ideological bridges between earlier activism and the development of other movements of the 1960s.

Abeyance Processes in Social Movements

The term "abeyance" is borrowed from Mizruchi (1983) and is central to a theory of social control. Abeyance structures emerge when society lacks sufficient status vacancies to integrate surpluses of marginal and dissident people. The structures that absorb marginal groups are abeyance organizations. They temporarily retain potential challengers to the status quo, thereby reducing threats to the larger social systems. Abeyance organizations have certain properties that allow them to absorb, control, and expel personnel according to the number of status positions available in the larger society (Mizruchi 1983, p. 17).

Although Mizruchi recognizes the social change potential of abeyance organizations, he does not address this aspect systematically (Kimmel 1984). I both challenge and extend Mizruchi's thesis to hypothesize that social movement abeyance organizations, by providing a measure of continuity for challenging groups, also contribute to social change. I hold that the abeyance process characterizes mass movements that succeed in building a support base and achieving a measure of influence, but are confronted with a nonreceptive political and social environment. A central tenet of resource mobilization theory concerns the role that changing opportunity structures play in the emergence and the attenuation of collective action (McCarthy and Zald 1973; Barkan 1984; Jenkins 1983). As a movement loses support, activists who had been most intensely committed to its aims become increasingly marginal and socially isolated. If insufficient opportunities exist to channel their commitment into routine statuses, then alternative structures emerge to absorb the surplus of people. These structures both restrain them from potentially more disruptive activities and channel them into certain forms of activism. In short, a movement in abeyance becomes a cadre of activists who create or find a niche for themselves. Such groups may have little impact in their own time and may contribute, however unwillingly, to maintenance of the status quo. But, by providing a legitimating base to challenge the status quo, such groups can be sources of protest and change.

The following factors are relevant to the abeyance process. First, certain factors external to a movement create a pool of marginal potential activists. These include *changes in opportunity structures* that support and constrain the movement and an *absence of status vacancies* to absorb dissident and excluded groups. Second, there are internal factors or organizational *dimensions of social movement abeyance structures: temporality commitment, exclusiveness, centralization,* and *culture.* Since these dimensions were inductively derived, I elaborate them with the case at hand. The significance of abeyance lies in its linkages between one upsurge in activism and another. I delineate three ways that social movement abeyance structures perform this linkage function: through promoting the survival of *activist networks,* sustaining a repertoire of *goals and tactics,* and promoting a *collective identity* that offers participants a sense of mission and moral purpose.

Data

Most accounts describe the American women's movement as peaking in two periods (Chafe 1972; Freeman 1975; Klein 1984). The first wave, generally referred to as the suffrage movement, grew out of the abolitionist struggle of the 1830s, reached a stage of mass mobilization between 1900 and 1920, and declined after the passage of the suffrage amendment. The second wave emerged in the mid-1960s, reached a stage of mass mobilization around 1970, and continued into the 1980s (Carden 1974; Evans 1979; Ferree and Hess 1985).

Curiosity about what happened to the organizations and networks of women who participated in the suffrage campaign led to the research described here. There are two reasons for focusing on the period from 1945 to the mid-1960s. First, other researchers have explored the period from 1920 to 1940 (Lemons 1973; Becker 1981; Cott 1987). Second, most researchers see the civil rights movement as the major predecessor to the contemporary women's movement (e.g., Freeman 1975; Evans 1979; McAdam 1988). By examining feminist activity in the decades just prior to the resurgence of feminism as a mass movement, I hoped to shed light on the accuracy of this view.

The data for this study come from documentary material in public and private archival collections and interviews with women who were activists from 1945 to the 1960s. Fuller description of the movement in this period and complete documentation are available in Rupp and Taylor (1987).

1. Archival data included the papers of the National Woman's Party and the League of Women Voters, the two major factions of the suffrage movement, and the papers of the President's Commission on the Status of Women (1961–63), whose activities facilitated the resurgence of the contemporary

women's movement. Other material examined were unofficial and official organizational documents, publications, personal letters, and memos in public and private collections, most of which are housed at the Schlesinger Library at Radcliffe College or the Library of Congress. The papers of individual women provided an important source of information, not only about their organizational careers, but also about the activities of diverse women's organizations.

2. The second source of data was 57 open-ended, semistructured, tape-recorded interviews, conducted between 1979 and 1983, with leaders and core members of the most central groups involved in women's rights activities. Twelve of the women were active at the national level and thirty-three at the local level. Twelve other transcribed interviews conducted by other researchers and available in archival collections were used.

The Women's Movement in the Postsuffrage Decades: The Transformation of Feminist Activism

Feminism activism continued in the years after the suffrage victory but was transformed as a result of organizational success, internal conflict, and social changes that altered women's common interests (Lemons 1973; Becker 1981; Buechler 1986; Cott 1987). Deradicalization and decline of the women's movement left militant feminists limited avenues through which to pursue their political philosophy.

In 1920, with the vote won, the women's movement was left with no unifying goal. Moreover, tactical and ideological differences divided militant from moderate suffragists and those who saw winning the vote as a means from those who viewed it as an end. As a result, the major social movement organizations of the suffrage movement evolved in two opposing directions.

The militant branch of the movement, the National Woman's Party (NWP), launched a relentless campaign to pass an Equal Rights Amendment (ERA) to the constitution. The NWP was never a mass organization but saw itself as a feminist vanguard or elite (Lunardini 1986). Hoping to enlist the support of former suffragists, NWP leader Alice Paul instead alienated both socialists and moderate feminists by her dictatorial style and the decision to focus on the ERA. The vast majority of suffragists feared that the ERA would eliminate the protective labor legislation that women reformers had earlier struggled to achieve (Balser 1987).

The mainstream branch of the movement, the National American Woman Suffrage Association, formed the nonpartisan League of Women Voters. It spearheaded the opposition to the ERA, educated women for their new citizenship responsibilities, and advocated a broad range of reforms. Other activists in the suffrage campaign channeled their efforts into new or growing organizations that did not have an explicitly feminist agenda but promoted a vast range of specific causes that, in part, grew out of the expanded role options available to women (Cott 1987). Thus, even though the women's movement was rapidly fragmenting, feminist activism continued throughout the 1920s and 1930s. But in the face of increasing hostility between the two camps of the suffrage movement, cooperation developed on only a few issues.

In addition to goal attainment and internal conflict, a third factor contributed to the dissipation of the mass base of the women's movement. Ironically, the role expansion for which the movement had fought fractured the bonds on which the solidarity of the movement had been built. As women's lives grew increasingly diverse, the definition of what would benefit women grew less clear.

As a result, the NWP—which alone continued to claim the title "feminist"—had become increasingly isolated from the mainstream of American women and even from women's organizations. With the demise of the large mass-based organizations that propelled the suffrage movement, the more radical feminists sought out the NWP. When the NWP captured the feminist agenda, however, the broad program of emancipation narrowed to limited goals and tactics pursued by an elite group of women (Cott 1987). This spelled the final demise of feminism as a mass movement.

Feminist Activism from 1945 to the 1960s: The Women's Movement in Abeyance

From 1945 to the 1960s, women's rights activists confronted an inhospitable political and social environment. Women who advocated equality found few outlets for their activism and became increasingly marginal and isolated from the mainstream of American women. Two social processes had this effect: first, advocates of women's rights lacked access to and support from the established political system; and, second, the cultural ideal of "the feminine mystique" that emerged after World War II affirmed the restoration of "normal family life" and discredited women who protested gender inequality.

Changing Opportunity Structure: Nonreceptive Political Elites

Despite an increase in the female labor force and the female student body in institutions of higher education, support for women's rights and opportunities declined sharply following the Second World War. By 1945, the women's movement had further fragmented into three overlapping interest groups, each with a different political

agenda (Harrison 1988, p. 7). Because women's issues were not generally salient, the three groups lacked political access and influence. Just as important, when they did gain access to political elites, they often canceled out each other's influence.

One interest group consisted of a coalition of women's organizations associated with the Women's Bureau of the Department of Labor. Throughout the 1940s and 1950s, this coalition sought to improve women's working conditions and defeat the ERA. Despite its governmental status, the Women's Bureau had little political clout, and the coalition used much of its influence to fight supporters of the ERA.

A second group consisted of a network of women in politics, including women active in the women's divisions of both the Democratic and Republican parties. They advocated the election and appointment of women to policy-making positions despite a dramatic decline in women's political opportunities after the Second World War. For the most part, the selection of women for policy-making positions was done by party women without regard for their position on women's issues (Harrison 1988, p. 64). Since women officials generally had no policy role and little influence on women's issues, advocating token appointments of women diverted attention from major policy questions such as the ERA.

A third group, the National Woman's Party, remained furthest outside the established political order. By 1944, the NWP had begun a major campaign to get Congress to pass the ERA and had managed to garner support from a few women's organizations. Confronted with the establishment of the National Committee to Defeat the Unequal Rights Amendment, spearheaded by the Women's Bureau, the NWP sought the support of both political parties. Presidents Truman and Eisenhower endorsed the ERA, both party platforms advocated it, and

Congress considered it in 1946, 1950, and 1953. Yet such support was more a nod to women than a serious political consideration (Freeman 1987).

None of these three groups made much progress in attaining their goals in the 1940s and 1950s. Although women's organizations succeeded in having 236 bills pertaining to women's rights introduced into Congress in the 1950s, only 14 passed (Klein 1984, p. 18). This reflected not only organized women's lack of political access and their conflicts, but also the exaggerated emphasis on sex roles that emerged on the heels of the Second World War.

Status Vacancy and Marginality

Following the war, a variety of social forces helped to reinstitutionalize traditional family life supported by rigid sex role distinctions (Friedan 1963; Breines 1985; May 1988). Women whose roles did not center on the home and family were considered deviant. In 1957, 80 percent of the respondents to a national poll believed that people who chose not to marry were sick, immoral, and neurotic (Klein 1984, p. 71). As a result of the pressure, fewer married women remained childless in the 1950s than in the 1900s—only 6.8 percent compared to 14 percent (Rupp and Taylor 1987, p. 15). Indicative of the tide, in 1945 only 18 percent of a Gallup Poll sample approved of a married woman's working if she had a husband capable of supporting her (Erskine 1971).

In addition to criticizing women who did not conform to the cultural ideal, the media denounced feminism, discredited women who continued to advocate equality, and thus thwarted the mobilization of discontented women (Rupp 1982). The most influential attack came from Ferdinand Lundberg and Marynia Farnham's popular and widely quoted book, *Modern Woman: The Lost Sex* (1947), which denounced feminists as severe neurotics responsible for the problems of American society. In the face of such criticism, only the NWP continued to claim the term "feminist." In fact, the core group of women in the NWP differed in major respects from the cultural ideal. An analysis of the 55 leaders and most active members of the NWP indicates that, by 1950, the majority were white, middle- or upper-class, well educated, employed in professional or semiprofessional occupations (especially law, government, and higher education), unmarried or widowed, and older, (in their fifties, sixties, or seventies).[1] Specifically, 71 percent of the women were employed; 97 percent were over the age of 50; and 60 percent were unmarried or widowed. In short, the lifestyles of the women, while relatively advantaged, were not normative. Feminists were largely unattached women with time, money, and other resources that facilitated their activism. Yet the retreat of a broad-based women's movement left few outlets to express their views either inside or outside the established political arena.

In summary, as the political and cultural wave that had once carried feminism forward receded, members of the NWP paid for their lifelong commitment with a degree of alienation, marginality, and isolation. Nevertheless, the NWP provided a structure and status capable of absorbing these intensely committed feminists and thus functioned as an abeyance organization.

Dimensions of Social Movement Abeyance Structures

The abeyance process functions through organizations capable of sustaining collective challenges under circumstances unfavorable to mass mobilization. Properties of abeyance organizations help an organizational pattern to retain potentially dissident populations. My analysis of the women's rights movement in the postwar period suggests that the most relevant variables with respect to the abeyance process are: temporality, purposive commitment, exclusiveness, centralization, and culture. Since these variables are derived from a single case, each dimension is treated as a hypothetical continuum with respect to other cases.

Temporality   By definition, of course, an abeyance structure persists throughout time, but temporality refers to the length of time that a movement organization is able to hold personnel. Activism provides a community that is an alternative source of integration and, thus, can have an enduring effect beyond a particular period in an individual's life (Coser 1974; White 1988).

During the 70-odd years of the first wave of the women's movement, a number of women's rights groups emerged and provided alternative status vacancies for large numbers of mainly white and middle-class women (Flexner 1959; Buechler 1986; Chafetz and Dworkin 1986). Among the 55 leaders and core activists of the NWP, 53 percent had been recruited at least four decades earlier during the suffrage campaign.

For NWP members, early participation in high-risk activism (McAdam 1986), including picketing the White House, engaging in hunger strikes while imprisoned, and burning President Wilson's speeches, kept them involved long after the suffrage victory. Lamenting the passage of that period, Florence Kitchelt asked a fellow suffragist in 1959 whether she ever felt "as I do that the modern woman is missing something very thrilling, uplifting as well as unifying in not being able to take part in a suffrage campaign? Those were the days!"[2] Katharine Hepburn, mother of the actress, in a speech to women's rights activists, described her experiences in the suffrage struggle. "That whole period in my life I remember with the greatest delight," she said. "We had no doubts. Life was a great thrill from morning until night."[3] Involvement in the suffrage movement had a powerful and enduring effect on participants, so much so that they continued even into the 1950s to promote

women's rights in a society antagonistic to the idea. The strong and lasting effects of participation in high-risk activism is supported by McAdam's (1988) study of participants in the 1964 Freedom Summer project.

By the 1940s and 1950s, a core of women in the NWP had devoted a major portion of their lives to feminist activity. Typical participation patterns are reflected in the comments of two members . In 1952, one woman wrote, "Since 1917 I have devoted all my spare time to feminism."[4] Another woman asked in 1950 for a "cure for giving too much of one's time to one thing," although she still continued to devote herself to passage of the ERA.[5] Not surprisingly, the most striking characteristic of the NWP membership was advanced age. Isserman (1987, p. 24) found a similar age structure in another organization that provided continuity between two stages of mass mobilization, the American Communist Party in the 1940s and 1950s. Constant numbers—even if small—are better for morale than steady turnover, so temporality enhances the likelihood that an organization will continue to endure.

Purposive Commitment   Commitment refers to the willingness of people to do what must be done, regardless of personal rewards and sacrifices, to maintain a collective challenge and is essential for holding an organizational pattern alive between stages of mass mobilization. Research on social movement involvement has focused primarily on the types of incentives that induce activists to make an initial commitment to a movement (e.g., Pinard 1971; Fireman and Gamson 1979; Oliver 1983; McAdam 1986). In exploring movement continuity, we must pose a different question: why do individuals maintain radical or unpopular convictions over time?

The few studies that have explored this question suggest that the nature of and incentives for commitment depend on a movement's stage in the mobilization process. Kanter's (1972) research on American communes concludes that groups characterized by high commitment are more likely to retain participants and to endure. Other research suggests that, although individuals may become activists through solidary or material incentives, continued participation depends upon high levels of commitment to group beliefs, goals, and tactics (Hirsch 1986; White 1988).

From its inception, the NWP appealed to women with strong feminist sympathies. By the 1950s, continued participation depended largely on the singleness of members' devotion to the principle of sexual equality embodied in the Equal Rights Amendment. Rejecting all other proposals for a feminist program, NWP leaders insisted that ideological integrity and the dogged pursuit of legal equality, not membership gain, would guarantee triumph.

A dedicated core of NWP members worked for the ERA by lobbying Congress and the President, seeking endorsements from candidates for political office and from other organizations, establishing coalitions to support the amendment, and educating the public through newspaper and magazine articles, letters to the editor, and radio and television appearances. Commenting on the persistence of feminists' lobbying efforts, one Representative from Connecticut wondered in 1945 "whether or not the Congress meets for any other purpose but to consider the Equal Rights Amendment."[6] Since the NWP depended entirely on the volunteer work of members, commitment was built on sacrifices of time, energy, and financial resources. Recognizing the impact of such high levels of commitment, one new recruit commented that "the secret of the ability of the group to do so much in the face of such odds is that it can attract just such devotion and loyalty."[7]

Commitment, then, contributes to the abeyance process by ensuring that individuals continue to do what is necessary to maintain the group and its purpose even when the odds are against immediate success. Moreover, such intense commitment functions as an obstacle to participation in alternative roles and organizations.

Exclusiveness Organizations vary according to their openness to members, some having more stringent criteria than others. Mizruchi (1983, p. 44) hypothesizes that the expansion-contraction of an abeyance organization's personnel occurs in response to changes in the larger social system's requirements for absorption, mobility, or expulsion of marginal populations. To absorb large numbers of people who are unattached to other structures requires organizations to be inclusive, as happens during the peak mobilization of social movement organizations. In cycles of decline, however, when challenging groups lack widespread attitudinal support, organizations become exclusive and attempt to expel or hold constant their membership. Zald and Ash (1966) contend that exclusive movement organizations are more likely to endure than inclusive ones.

At the peak of the suffrage struggle, the NWP was inclusive across the class and political spectrum (Cott 1987, pp. 53–55). It attracted wage-earning women from a variety of occupations as well as elite women social activists. Its members had ties to political parties, government, and industry, as well as to the socialist, peace, labor, and antilynching movements. But when the NWP launched its ERA campaign, many bodies organized on occupational, religious, and racial grounds and devoted to other policy issues began to absorb women from mainstream suffrage groups and siphon off NWP members. This left the NWP with a small and relatively homogeneous permanent core of feminists.

By the end of World War II, the NWP had lost most of its members and was not attracting new ones. Compared to its 60,000 members in the last years of the suffrage campaign, the NWP had about 4000 "general" members by 1945 and only 1400 by 1952. More revealing, it listed 627 "active" members in 1947 and 200 by 1952. Although the NWP also lost members as a result of an internal conflict over whether to expand membership in 1947 and again in 1953, the leadership preferred to keep the organization a small elite vanguard. As one member put it, "no mass appeal will ever bring into the Party that type of woman who can best carry forward our particular aims. We are an 'elect body' with a single point of agreement."[8]

Just as important, the membership of the NWP also grew increasingly homogeneous and socially advantaged over the decades. Of 55 core activists, 90 percent of the employed held professional, managerial, or technical positions. Several researchers have noted that intellectuals and other privileged groups are likely to be overrepresented among the leadership and supporters of neo-liberal and communal movements. Some have attributed this to the risks and resources that participation entails (Lenin 1970; McCarthy and Zald 1973; Oberschall 1973, p. 161), while others look to the unique political culture of intellectuals and professionals (Pinard and Hamilton 1988).

Despite the fact that the NWP leaders preferred a small homogeneous membership, they recognized the significance of size and diversity for public impact. In order to give the appearance of a mass constituency, the NWP devised certain strategies. Members maintained multiple memberships in women's organizations in order to win endorsements for the ERA; they established coalitions to give the impression of a large membership; they financed a "front" organization to give the appearance of cooperation between feminists and labor women; and they recruited leaders of the National

Association of Colored Women in order to obtain its endorsement of the ERA. Yet, despite attempts to appear inclusive, the NWP did not seriously try to build an indigenous base of support.

Organizational exclusivity is closely related to the commitment variable. Organizations that insist upon high levels of purposive commitment and make stringent demands of time and financial resources cannot absorb large numbers of people. They are, however, good at holding constant those members that they have. Thus, exclusiveness is an important characteristic of abeyance organizations because it ensures a relatively homogeneous cadre of activists suited to the limited activism undertaken.

Centralization Organizations vary in their centralization of power. Some operate through a "single center of power," whereas decentralized groups distribute power among subunits (Gamson 1975, p. 93). Although centralization contributes to a decline in direct-action tactics (Piven and Cloward 1977; Jenkins and Eckert 1986), it has the advantage of producing the organizational stability, coordination, and technical expertise necessary for movement survival (Gamson 1975; Wehr 1986; Staggenborg 1989).

By the end of World War II, the NWP functioned almost entirely on the national level with a federated structure in which local and state chapters had little control. State branches, which had been active in the 1920s, consisted in most cases of little more than a chairman and served the organization primarily as letterheads to use in lobbying senators and representatives.[9]

A national chairman headed the NWP. The Party's founder and leading light, Alice Paul, however, directed and kept a tight reign on its activities, even though she formally occupied the chair for only a brief period from 1942 to 1945. As one member described it, Paul "gave the chairman all deference. But if you were a wise chairman, you did what Alice Paul wanted, because she knew what was needed."[10] The chairman headed a national council that met periodically at the Washington headquarters. There was also a national advisory council composed of prominent women who lent their names to the group's work.

Paul, reputedly a charismatic leader committed to the point of fanaticism, maintained tight control over the ERA campaign. She decided when it was time to press Congress and when to maintain a low profile and, according to members' reports, worked from six in the morning until midnight. On at least two occasions serious conflict erupted over the lack of democratic procedures in the Party. It focused specifically on Alice Paul's autocratic leadership style and on the refusal of the national leadership to allow state branches to expand membership. A letter, circulated in 1947, contained charges typical of those directed against Paul: "You have made it clear that you consider yourself and the small group around you an elite with superabundant intellect and talents, and consider us, in contrast, the commonfolk."[11] Thus centralization of leadership, like exclusiveness, had the potential to provoke conflict among members. But it also had advantages in a nonreceptive political environment.

Paul used her influence to direct a small group of activists with highly specialized skills—lobbying and researching, testifying, and writing about policy issues—who viewed themselves as an embattled feminist minority. The NWP was able to finance its activities with some invested funds, dues, contributions from members, and revenue from the rental of rooms in its Washington property. As a result, activists did not have to expend energy generating resources to maintain the organization.

This kind of central direction allowed the NWP to sustain the feminist challenge through the years by concentrating on a single strategy that could be carried out by a dedicated band of activists with highly specialized skills. Thus, centralization contributes to the abeyance process by ensuring the maintenance of organization and at least minimal activity during periods when conditions do not favor mass mobilization.

Culture The culture of a social movement organization is embodied in its collective emotions, beliefs, and actions. Although all social movements create and bear culture, movement organizations vary in the character and complexity of their cultures (Lofland 1985).

The effectiveness of an organization with respect to its abeyance function depends, in part, on its capacity to motivate persons to assume certain positions. As the larger political and cultural atmosphere becomes less hospitable to the social movement, recruitment of personnel becomes difficult. In order to make participation more attractive, organizations must elaborate alternative cultural frameworks to provide security and meaning for those who reject the established order and remain in the group. Previous research suggests that the more highly developed an organization's culture, the more it offers members the satisfaction and other resources necessary for its survival (Kanter 1972; Lofland 1985).

The NWP developed an elaborate and expressive culture through activities at the Alva Belmont House, its national headquarters in Washington, D.C. Belmont House served not only as an office for national council meetings, but also as a center where lobbying efforts were coordinated and where the monthly newsletter was published. It also created the kind of female world essential to the maintenance of feminism (Freedman 1979; Rupp 1985). A few women lived at Belmont House and in two other Party-owned houses, while lobbyists stayed there from a few days to several months. In addition, Belmont House was the site of feminist events and celebrations: teas to honor women politicians or sponsors of the ERA, victory celebrations, and parties on Susan B. Anthony's birthday or on the anniversary of the suffrage victory. The activities and relationships women formed at Belmont House provided both ideological and affective support for participation in women's rights work.

Although NWP members believed in the pervasiveness of discrimination against women, the Party did not develop and advance a well-articulated ideological and theoretical position. Rather, feminism was defined principally through a culture that promoted a feminist worldview. One member expressed her worldview, complaining of "Masculinity running rampant *all over the earth!*" and rebelling at the "utter man-mindedness" she saw all around her.[12] Alice Paul characterized women's rights advocates as sharing a "feeling of loyalty to our own sex and an enthusiasm to have every degradation that was put upon our sex removed."[13] Despite occasional conflict over whether men should be brought into the movement, the NWP retained a separatist strategy. To ensure that the Party remain committed to its original vision—collective action by women for women—wealthy benefactor Alva Belmont included a clause in her bequest revoking her legacy if men ever joined or participated in the organization.

In addition to reinforcing feminist beliefs, the culture harbored at Belmont House fulfilled expressive and symbolic functions that contributed to the survival of feminism. Women who lived and worked at the house became, for some, the "Woman's Party family." Many who could not live at the house, because of family, work, and financial constraints, made regular pilgrimages in order to remain a part of the women's community. One member wrote that she was "looking forward with joy to my return home, and *Home* to me now, means the dear Alva Belmont House."[14] In fact, bringing friends to Belmont House was the primary way that women recruited new members.

Personal ties of love and friendship among members were an important cultural ideal. A willingness to shape personal relationships around the cause was, in large measure, what made possible the intense commitment of members. NWP members described their ties as mother-daughter or sororal relationships, and members' letters to one another were filled with expressions of intimacy and friendship. Ties among members took the form of close friendships, intense devotion to Alice Paul, and couple relationships. Having another woman as life partner seemed to facilitate feminist work because these women's personal lives meshed well with their political commitments.

Movement organizations that cultivate and sustain rich symbolic lives, then, enhance the abeyance function by helping to hold members. This finding is consistent with other research that demonstrates that commitment to peers and to a shared political community promotes sustained involvement in social movements (Rosenthal and Schwartz 1989; McAdam 1988; White 1988).

In summary, I have described the NWP in the post-1945 period as an organizational pattern characterized by high longevity of attachment; intense levels of individual commitment to movement goals and tactics; high exclusiveness in terms of membership; high centralization that ensures a relatively advanced level of specialized skills among core activists; and a rich political culture that promotes continued involvement in the movement. This appears to be the ideal combination of factors necessary to hold a movement in abeyance until the external forces make it possible to resume a more mass-based challenge.

Consequences For The Resurgent Women's Movement

However movement success is measured, the women's rights movement from 1945 to the mid-1960s was not successful in its own time. But a more important question is: what consequences, if any, did the actions of feminists in this period have for the revitalized movement for gender equality in the late 1960s? The founding of the National Organization for Women (NOW) in 1966 serves as a useful signpost marking the rise of the contemporary women's movement. NOW brought together labor union activists, government employees, and longtime feminist activists and took leadership of the liberal branch of the movement (Freeman 1975). At about the same time, younger women involved in the civil rights and New Left movement formed the more locally organized radical branch.

Studies have not generally recognized connections between the existing women's rights movement and the resurgent one. My analysis suggests three ways in which the activism of the NWP shaped the feminist challenge that followed. It provided preexisting *activist networks,* an existing repertoire of *goals and tactics,* and a *collective identity* that justified feminist opposition. These elements constitute the most important consequences of abeyance structures for future mobilization around persistent discontents.

Activist Networks

A substantial body of research documents the significance of preexisting links and organizational ties among individuals for the rise of collective action (e.g., Snow, Zurcher, and Ekland-Olson 1980; Freeman 1979, 1983; Rosenthal et al. 1985). The feminist network of the 1940s and 1950s affected the resurgent movement of the 1960s in two ways. First, activism by NWP members played a crucial role in two key events: the establishment of the President's Commission on the Status of Women, convened by President Kennedy in 1961, and the inclusion of sex in Title VII of the Civil Rights Act of 1964, which forbade discrimination in employment. Second, many women who participated in the struggle for women's rights in the 1940s and 1950s became active in the resurgent women's movement, especially the liberal branch. NWP members were among the founders and charter members of NOW. Of the 10 individuals who signed NOW's original Statement of Purpose, 4 were members of the NWP (Friedan 1976). In her account of the early years of NOW, founder Betty Friedan (1976, pp. 110–17) describes an "underground network" of longtime committed feminists who provided crucial resources necessary for the formation of NOW. Even Alice Paul joined NOW, although she criticized NOW members for acting "as if they've discovered the whole idea."[15]

Although less common, a few NWP members established ties to the radical branch. One member met with the women's caucus of the National Conference on New Politics in Chicago in 1967, a conference that helped spark the formation of the radical branch. Another member attended a speech by Kate Millett at Purdue University in the early 1970s and handed out ERA literature to the crowd. Contrasting vividly the feminists of her generation with those of the 1970s, she noted that she was the only one there in a hat and that everyone else, including Millett, had long hair.[16] Thus a committed core of activists helped to provide resources for a resurgent more mass-based movement.

Goals and Tactical Choices

Tilly's (1979) concept of repertoires of collective action provides the greatest insight into the ways that actions of a challenging group at a given point in time can affect actions of a subsequent group. Thus, the forms of action available to a group are not unlimited but are restricted by time, place, and group characteristics. Movement goals and strategies are learned, and they change slowly. Extending Tilly's hypothesis, the array of collective actions that a movement develops to sustain itself should influence the goals and tactics adopted by the same movement in subsequent mass mobilizations.

This is indeed the case with respect to the American women's rights movement. Although the NWP abandoned disruptive and militant strategies after the suffrage victory, it retained the same goal—a constitutional amendment. Largely as a result of NWP pressure, NOW voted at its second conference in 1967 to endorse the ERA, which became the most unifying goal of the movement by the 1970s (Ferree and Hess 1985; Taylor 1989). Further, NOW adopted many of the NWP's institutionalized tactics, such as lobbying, letter writing, and pressuring the political parties. NOW even made use of the NWP's political connections and its list of ERA sponsors.

The ERA example illustrates the ways that existing repertoires of action can both facilitate and constrain a movement. The final campaign for the ERA in the late 1970s and early 1980s mobilized massive numbers of participants, swelling the ranks of NOW to almost 200,000 and its budget to nearly 3 million dollars (Gelb and Palley 1982; Mueller unpublished). During its early years, with its equal rights emphasis which appealed mainly to white and middle-class women, NOW alienated black and union women (Giddings 1984). Thus, the liberal branch of the contemporary women's movement, by adopting the goals and strategies of earlier feminists, found it difficult to shake the class and race limitations of its predecessors.

For a movement to survive periods of relative hiatus, it must develop a battery of specialized tactics that can be carried out by an activist cadre without the support of a mass base (Oliver and Marwell 1988). These become a part of a group's repertoire of collective action and influence the subsequent range of actions available to future challenges.

Collective Identity

Collective identity is the shared definition of a group that derives from its members common interest and solidarity. Although resource mobilization theorists minimize the importance of group identity and consciousness in the rise of social movements (McCarthy and Zald 1973, 1977; Jenkins and Perrow 1977), these factors are central to theorists of the "new social movements" (e.g., Pizzorno 1978; Cohen 1985; Melucci 1985; Klandermans 1986). They suggest that, by definition, social movements create a collective oppositional consciousness. Mueller's (1987, p. 90) research on the women's movement suggests that changes in consciousness can have long-term significance because they can serve as a resource for future mobilization.

The creation of a shared collective identity requires the group to revise its history and develop symbols to reinforce movement goals and strategies (Gusfield 1970, p. 309–13). For the 1960s women's movement, the NWP, because of its ties to suffrage, became an important symbol of the long history of women's oppression and resistance. As a result of its historical significance and prime location, Belmont House was used throughout the 1970s for celebrations of women's movement history, as a temporary residence for scholars and students engaged in feminist research, and as a place for ERA lobbyists to meet. Moreover, Alice Paul, who earlier had sparked so many conflicts, became the quintessential symbol of feminist commitment. In 1977, NOW sponsored a birthday benefit for her at Belmont House that was attended by members of a wide range of feminist organizations. Even after Paul's death in 1977, the NWP continued to list her as founder on its letterhead and to advertise "Alice Paul Jail Jewelry," a replica of the famous jailhouse door pin proudly worn by imprisoned suffragists.

The significance of the NWP grew as younger and more radical women discovered the legacy of militant feminism. Even in 1981, the NWP's symbolic importance remained great enough to inspire an attempted takeover by a group of younger feminists, led by Sonia Johnson, who claimed the militants who first formed the NWP as their foremothers and even adopted the original name of the Party. Ironically, as the contemporary women's movement grew stronger and more militant, the actual heirs of the early militants grew increasingly isolated and less central in the struggle for women's rights.

In an abeyance phase, a social movement organization uses internally oriented activities to build a structure through which it can maintain its identity, ideals, and political vision. The collective identity that it constructs and maintains within a shared political community can become an impor-

tant symbolic resource for subsequent mobilizations.

Conclusion

This reading presents new data that challenge the traditional view that no organized feminist challenge survived in the 1940s and 1950s. I have used the NWP case to highlight the processes by which social movements maintain continuity between different cycles of peak activity. I analyze the factors associated with adaptations of Mizruchi's (1983) abeyance process. Abeyance is essentially a holding pattern of a group which continues to mount some type of challenge even in a nonreceptive political environment. Factors that contribute to abeyance are both external and internal to the movement. Externally, a discrepancy between a surplus of activists and a lack of status opportunities for integrating them into the mainstream creates conditions for abeyance. Internally, structures arise that permit organizations to absorb and hold a committed cadre of activists. These abeyance structures, in turn, promote movement continuity and are employed in later rounds of mass mobilization.

Although any theory based on a single case is open to challenge, recent research points to the utility of the abeyance model for understanding other movements of the 1960s, particularly the civil rights (McAdam 1988), New Left (Gitlin 1987; Isserman 1987; Hayden 1988), and gay rights (D'Emilio 1983) movements. But this work has not yet had major impact on revising theory about the sixties movements or on social movement theory in general.

Why have scholars of social movements neglected sources of continuity between cycles of movement activity and, instead, preferred an "immaculate conception" interpretation of social movements? First, scholars generally are more interested in movements undergoing cycles of mass mobilization and have done little research on movements in decline and equilibrium. Second, the limited conceptualization of movement organization in the literature has perpetuated classical conceptions of social movements as numerically large and mass-based. Research on a variety of organizational forms, including becalmed movements (Zald and Ash 1966), professional movements (McCarthy and Zald 1973), movement halfway houses (Morris 1984), elite-sustained movements (Rupp and Taylor 1987), and consensus movements (McCarthy and Wolfson unpublished), is now challenging the classical view by suggesting that these types of movements are capable of sustained activism in nonreceptive political climates (Staggenborg 1988). Third, existing approaches overlook social movement continuity by neglecting to think about outcomes (Gamson 1975). Focusing on short-term gains ignores the possibility that social reform proceeds in a ratchetlike fashion, where the gains of one struggle become the resources for later challenges by the same aggrieved group (Tarrow 1983).

The research presented above specifies the ways that organizational and ideological bridges span different stages of mobilization. Most movements have thresholds or turning points in mobilization which scholars have taken for "births" and "deaths." This research suggests that movements do not die, but scale down and retrench to adapt to changes in the political climate. Perhaps movements are never really born anew. Rather, they contract and hibernate, sustaining the totally dedicated and devising strategies appropriate to the external environment. If this is the case, our task as sociologists shifts from refining theories of movement emergence to accounting for fluctuations in the nature and scope of omnipresent challenges.

Acknowledgments

This reading is part of a larger collaborative study of the American women's rights movement conducted by Leila J. Rupp. The research was supported by a Basic Research Grant (RO-*0703-81) from the National Endowment for the Humanities and by grants from The Ohio State University. A Radcliffe Research Scholars fellowship awarded to Rupp supported a great deal of the documentary research. I thank Joan Huber, Craig Jenkins, Carol Mueller, Laurel Richardson, Leila Rupp, Mayer Zald, and the *ASR* reviewers for helpful comments on earlier drafts.

NOTES

1. This analysis of the leadership and core membership is based on a careful reading of archival material, particularly correspondence, as well as research in biographical sources. For 55 women identified as leaders and core members, information was recorded about race, class, education, occupation, age, place of residence, political affiliation, political views, marital status, presence and number of children, living situation, and time of first involvement in the women's movement. In addition, any comments made by participants about the social characteristics of the membership were noted.

2. Florence Kitchelt to Katharine Ludington, August 14, 1950, Florence Kitchelt papers, box 6 (175), Schlesinger Library (SL), Radcliffe College, Cambridge, Massachusetts.

3. Katharine Hepburn, speech to the Connecticut Committee, n.d. [1946], Kitchelt papers, box 6 (153), SL.

4. Betty Gram Swing to Ethel Ernest Murrell, October 3, 1952, National Woman's Party (NWP) papers, reel 99.

5. Mary Kennedy to Agnes Wells, July 12, 1950, NWP papers, reel 97.

6. Joseph E. Talbot to Florence Kitchelt, February 12, 1945, Kitchelt papers, box 8 (234), SL.

7. Mamie Sydney Mizen to Florence Armstrong, October 25, 1948, NWP papers, reel 94.

8. Open letter from Ernestine Bellamy to Ethel Ernest Murrell, May 24, 1953, NWP papers, reel 99.

9. I use the term "chairman" because that was the term used at the time. It seems historically inaccurate to change this usage.

10. Interview no. 2.

11. Laura Berrien and Doris Stevens, "An Open Letter to Miss Alice Paul," Committee on Information, Bulletin No. 4, July 30, 1947, Katharine A. Norris papers, box 2 (7), SL.

12. Rose Arnold Powell, diary entry, Nov. 2, 1960, Powell papers, box 1, v. 8, SL; Rose Arnold Powell to Mary Beard, June 23, 1948, Powell papers, box 2 (27), SL.

13. Alice Paul, "Conversations With Alice Paul: Woman Suffrage and the Equal Rights Amendment," an oral history conducted in 1972 and 1973 by Amelia R. Fry, Regional Oral History Office, University of California, 1976, p. 197.

14. Mary Alice Matthews to Alice Paul, March 24, 1945, NWP papers, reel 85.

15. Interview no. 12.

16. Mary Kennedy to Alice Paul, February 11, 1971, NWP papers, reel 112.

REFERENCES

Barkan, Steven E. 1979. "Strategic, Tactical and Organizational Dilemmas of the Protest Movement against Nuclear Power." *Social Problems* 27:19–37.

Basler, Diane. 1987. *Sisterhood and Solidarity: Feminism and Labor in Modern Times*. Boston: South End.

———. 1984. "Legal Control of the Southern Civil Rights Movement." *American Sociological Review* 49:552–69.

Becker, Susan. 1981. *The Origins of the Equal Rights Amendment: American Feminism between the Wars*. Westport, CT: Greenwood.

Breines, Wini. 1985. "Domineering others in the 1950s: Image and Reality." *Women's Studies International Forum* 8:601–8.

Buechler, Steven M. 1986. *The Transformation of the Woman Suffrage Movement: The Case of Illinois, 1850–1920*. New Brunswick, NJ: Rutgers University Press.

Carden, Maren Lockwood. 1974. *The New Feminist Movement*. New York: Russell Sage.

Chafe, William H. 1972. *The American Woman: Her Changing Social, Economic, and Political Roles, 1920–1970*. New York: Oxford University Press.

Chafetz, Janet Saltzman and Anthony Gary Dworkin. 1986. *Female Revolt: Women's Movements in World and Historical Perspective*. Totowa, NJ: Rowan and Allanheld.

Cohen, Jean L. 1985. "Strategy or Identity: New Theoretical Paradigms and Contemporary Social Movements." *Social Research* 52:663–716.

Coser, Lewis. 1974. *Greedy Institutions*. New York: Free Press.

Cott, Nancy F. 1987. *The Grounding of Modern Feminism*. New Haven: Yale University Press.

D'Emilio, John. 1983. *Sexual Politics, Sexual Communities*. Chicago: University of Chicago Press.

Erskine, Hazel. 1971. "The Polls: Women's Role." *Public Opinion Quarterly* 35:282–87.

Evans, Sara. 1979. *Personal Politics: The Roots of Women's Liberation in the Civil Rights Movement and the New Left*. New York: Knopf.

Ferree, Myra Marx and Beth B. Hess. 1985. *Controversy and Coalition: The New Feminist Movement*. Boston: Twayne.

Fireman, Bruce and William A. Gamson. 1979. "Utilitarian Logic in the Resource Mobilization Perspective." Pp. 8–44 in *The Dynamics of Social Movements*, edited by M. Zald and J. McCarthy. Cambridge, MA: Winthrop.

Flacks, Richard. 1971. *Youth and Social Change*. Chicago: Markham.

Flexner, Eleanor. 1959. *Century of Struggle*. Cambridge: Harvard University Press.

Freedman, Estelle. 1979. "Separatism as Strategy: Female Institution Building and American Feminism, 1870–1930." *Feminist Studies* 5:512–29.

Freeman, Jo. 1975. *The Politics of Women's Liberation*. New York: David McKay.

———. 1979. "Resource Mobilization and Strategy: A Model for Analyzing Social Movement Organization Actions." Pp. 167–89 in *The Dynamics of Social Movements*, edited by M. Zald and J. McCarthy. Cambridge, MA: Winthrop.

———. 1983. *Social Movements of the Sixties and Seventies.* New York: Longman.

———. 1987. "Whom You Know versus Whom You Represent: Feminist Influence in the Democratic and Republican Parties." Pp. 215–44 in *The Women's Movements of the United States and Western Europe,* edited by M. Katzenstein and C. Mueller. Philadelphia: Temple University Press.

Freidan, Betty. 1963. *The Feminine Mystique.* New York: Dell.

———. 1976. *It Changed My Life.* New York: Dell.

Gamson, William A. 1975. *The Strategy of Social Protest.* Homewood, IL: Dorsey.

Gelb, Joyce and Marian Lief Palley. 1982. *Women and Public Policy.* Princeton: Princeton University Press.

Giddings, Paula. 1984. *When and Where I Enter: The Impact of Black Women on Race and Sex in America.* New York: Bantam.

Gitlin, Todd. 1987. *The Sixties.* New York: Bantam.

Gusfield, Joseph R. 1970. *Protest, Reform, and Revolt.* New York: Wiley.

———. 1981. "Social Movements and Social Change: Perspectives of Linearity and Fluidity." Pp. 317–39 in *Research in Social Movements, Conflict and Change.* Vol. 4, edited by Louis Kriesberg, Greenwich, CT: JAI Press.

Harrison, Cynthia. 1988. *On Account of Sex.* Berkeley: University of California Press.

Hayden, Tom. 1988. *Reunion.* New York: Random House.

Hirsch, Eric L. 1986. "The Creation of Political Solidarity in Social Movement Organizations." *Sociological Quarterly* 27:373–87.

Isserman, Maurice. 1987. *If I Had a Hammer: The Death of the Old Left and the Birth of the New Left.* New York: Basic.

Jenkins, J. Craig. 1983. "Resource Mobilization Theory and the Study of Social Movements." *Annual Review of Sociology* 9:527–53.

———. 1987. "Interpreting the Stormy 1960s: Three Theories in Search of a Political Age." *Research in Political Sociology* 3:269–303.

Jenkins, J. Craig and Craig M. Eckert. 1986. "Channeling Black Insurgency: Elite Patronage and Professional Social Movement Organizations in the Development of the Black Movement. *American Sociological Review* 51:812–29.

Jenkins, J. Craig and Charles Perrow. 1977. "Insurgency of the Powerless: Farmworkers Movement (1946–1972)." *American Sociological Review* 42:249–68.

Kanter, Rosabeth Moss. 1972. *Commitment and Community.* Cambridge, MA: Harvard University Press.

Kimmel, Michael. 1984. Review of *Regulating Society* by Ephraim H. Mizruchi. *Society,* July/August:90–92.

Klandermans, Bert. 1986. "New Social Movements and Resource Mobilization: The European and the American Approach." *Mass Emergencies and Disasters* 4:13–38.

Klein, Ethel. 1984. *Gender Politics: From Consciousness to Mass Politics.* Cambridge, MA: Harvard University Press.

Lemons, J. Stanley. 1973. *The Woman Citizen: Social Feminism in the 1920s.* Urbana: University of Illinois Press.

Lenin, V. I. 1970. "What is to be Done?" Pp. 458–72 in *Protest, Reform, and Revolt,* edited by Joseph R. Gusfield. New York: Wiley.

Lofland, John. 1985. "Social Movement Culture." Pp. 219–39 in *Protest: Studies of Collective Behavior and Social Movements,* edited by John Lofland. New Brunswick, NJ: Transaction.

Lunardini, Christine A. 1986. *From Equal Suffrage to Equal Rights.* New York: New York University Press.

Lundberg, Ferdinand and Marynia F. Farnham. 1947. *Modern Woman: The Lost Sex.* New York: Harper.

May, Elaine Tyler. 1988. *Homeward Bound: American Families in the Cold War Era.* New York: Basic.

McAdam, Douglas. 1982. *Political Process and the Development of Black Insurgency, 1930–1970.* Chicago: University of Chicago Press.

———. 1986. "Recruitment to High-Risk Activism: The Case of Freedom Summer." *American Journal of Sociology* 92:64–90.

———. 1988. *Freedom Summer.* New York: Oxford University Press.

McCarthy, John D. and Mayer N. Zald. 1973. *The Trend of Social Movements in America: Professionalization and Resource Mobilization.* Morristown, NJ: General Learning.

———. 1977. "Resource Mobilization and Social Movements: A Partial Theory." *American Journal of Sociology* 82:1212–41.

McCarthy, John D. and Mark Wolfson. Unpublished. "Exploring Sources of Rapid Social Movement Growth: The Role of Organizational Form, Consensus Support, and Elements of the American State." Paper presented at the Workshop on Frontiers in Social Movement Theory, June 1988, Ann Arbor, MI.

Melucci, Alberto. 1985. "The Symbolic Challenge of Contemporary Movements." *Social Research* 52:789–816.

Mizruchi, Ephraim H. 1983. *Regulating Society.* New York: Free Press.

Morris, Aldon. 1984. *The Origins of the Civil Rights Movement: Black Communities Organizing for Change.* New York: Free Press.

Mueller, Carol McClurg. 1987. "Collective Consciousness, Identity Transformation, and the Rise of Women in Public Office in the United States." Pp. 89–108 in *The Women's Movements of the United States and Western Europe,* edited by M.F. Katzenstein and C.M. Mueller. Philadelphia: Temple University Press.

———. Unpublished. "The Life Cycle of Equal Rights Feminism: Resource Mobilization, Political Process, and Dramaturgical Explanations." Paper presented at the 1987 Annual Meetings of the American Sociological Association, Chicago.

Oberschall, Anthony. 1973. *Social Conflict and Social Movements.* Englewood Cliffs, NJ: Prentice-Hall.

Oliver, Pamela. 1983. "The Mobilization of Paid and Volunteer Activists in the Neighborhood Movement." Pp. 133–70 in *Research in Social Movements, Conflict and Change.* Vol. 5. Greenwich, CT: JAI Press.

Oliver, Pamela E. and Gerald Marwell. 1988. "The Paradox of Group Size in Collective Action: A Theory of the Critical Mass. II." *American Sociological Review* 53:1–8.

Pinard, Maurice. 1971. *The Rise of a Third Party: A Study in Crisis Politics.* Englewood Cliffs, NJ: Prentice-Hall.

Pinard, Maurice and Richard Hamilton. 1988. "Intellectuals and the Leadership of Social Movements: Some Comparative Perspectives." *McGill Working Papers on Social Behavior.*

Piven, Frances Fox and R. A. Cloward. 1977. *Poor People's Movements.* New York: Pantheon.

Pizzorno, Allessandro. 1978. "Political Science and Collective Identity in Industrial Conflict." Pp. 277–98 in *The Resurgence of Class Conflict in Western Europe since 1968,* edited by C. Crouch and A. Pizzorno. New York: Holmes and Meier.

Rosenthal, Naomi, M. Fingrutd, M. Ethier, R. Karant, and D. McDonald. 1985. "Social Movements and Network Analysis: A Case of Nineteenth Century Women's Reform in New York State." *American Journal of Sociology* 90:1022–54.

Rosenthal, Naomi and Michael Schwartz. 1989. "Spontaneity and Democracy in Social Movements." Pp. 33–59 in *International Social Movement Research.* Volume 2. Greenwich, CT: JAI Press.

Rupp, Leila J. 1982. "The Survival of American Feminism." Pp. 33–65 in *Reshaping America,* edited by R.H. Bremner and G.W. Reichard. Columbus: Ohio State University Press.

———. 1985. "The Women's Community in the National Woman's Party, 1945 to the 1960's." *Signs* 10:715–40.

Rupp, Leila J. and Verta Taylor. 1987. *Survival in the Doldrums: The American Women's Rights Movement, 1945 to the 1960s.* New York: Oxford University Press.

Snow, David A., Lewis A. Zurcher, and Sheldon Eckland-Olson. 1980. "Social Networks and Social Movements: A Microstructural Approach to Differential Recruitment." *American Sociological Review* 45:787–801.

Staggenborg, Suzanne. 1988. "Consequences of Professionalization and Formalization in the Pro-Choice Movement." *American Sociological Review* 53:585–606.

———. 1989. "Stability and Innovation in the Women's Movement: A Comparison of Two Movement Organizations." *Social Problems* 36:75–92.

Tarrow, Sidney. 1983. *Struggling to Reform: Social Movements and Policy Change during Cycles of Protest.* Center for International Studies, Western Societies Occasional Paper no. 15. Ithaca, NY: Cornell University.

Taylor, Verta. 1989. "The Future of Feminism: A Social Movement Analysis." Pp. 473–90 in *Feminist Frontiers II,* edited by Laurel Richardson and Verta Taylor. New York: Random House.

Tilly, Charles. 1979. "Repertoires of Contention in America and Britain, 1750–1830." Pp. 126–55 in *The Dynamics of Social Movements,* edited by M. Zald and J. McCarthy. Cambridge, MA: Winthrop.

Touraine, Alain. 1971. *The Post-Industrial Society.* New York: Random House.

Wehr, Paul. 1986. "Nuclear Pacifism as Collective Action." *Journal of Peace Research* 22:103–13.

White, Robert. 1988. "Commitment, Efficacy, and Personal Sacrifice Among Irish Republicans. *Journal of Political and Military Sociology* 16:77–90.

Zald, Mayer and Roberta Ash. 1966. "Social Movement Organizations: Growth, Decay, and Change." *Social Forces* 44:327–41.

27

CYCLES OF PROTEST

SIDNEY TARROW

The powers of social movements are a mix of internal and external resources. If movement organizers succeed in mobilizing the base of their movements, this depends not on formal organization, but on the social networks in which supporters are found, and on the mobilizing structures that link them to one another. If leaders frame collective action with their demands and ideologies, their proposals are woven into a cultural matrix and, in modern societies, depend on the mass media to be communicated to allies and enemies. If movements innovate in the forms of collective action that they use, most innovations are marginal changes in the conventional repertoire that they use to reach a broader audience. And finally, it is the political opportunities created by modern states and the changing opportunities in their environments that give movements the incentives to mobilize and diffuse collective action to broader movements. It is to an understanding of these broader movements and the cycles of protest in which they arise that this chapter is devoted.

When I use the phrase, cycle of protest, I am referring to a phase of heightened conflict and contention across the social system that includes: a rapid diffusion of collective action from more mobilized to less mobilized sectors; a quickened pace of innovation in the forms of contention; new or

transformed collective action frames; a combination of organized and unorganized participation; and sequences of intensified interaction between challengers and authorities which can end in reform, repression, and sometimes revolution.

When we turn to social scientists' research on waves of collective action, we find an odd paradox. Although recognizing their importance for social movements, they are more apt to pay attention to individuals, movements, and especially to social movement organizations. Even students of revolution have often ignored the relationship between cycles and revolutionary situations, as Charles Tilly has noted in his recent *European Revolutions* (1933b: 13–14). If protest cycles are such major watersheds of social and political change as I have claimed, why do we have so few studies of such periods?

One reason is that movement organizations are easier to fix in place and time than broader protest cycles and are more accessible to investigators—many of whom come from within their ranks. Protest cycles, in contrast, often begin within institutions, spread into confrontations among ordinary people, and bring the scholar face-to-face with some of the less edifying aspects of collective action—the crowd, the mob, the armed insurrection. When they end in repression and disillusionment, as the revolutions of 1848 did, they make depressing reading for movement sympathizers.

A second reason for the neglect of cycles is that they occupy no clearly demarcated space with respect to institutional politics. Students of "collective behavior," for example, distinguish it from behavior in institutions. But a brief reflection on 1848 and other cycles will show that insurgencies often begin within institutions, and that even organized movements become rapidly involved in the political process where they interact with interest groups, unions, parties, and the forces of order. To encompass cycles, our account must link social movements to struggles for power both in institutions and outside of institutions, and this requires us to adopt a degree of methodological syncretism that runs across the grain of the division of labor of contemporary social science.

The idea that entire systems go through cyclical change has been found among three main groups of scholars: Cultural theorists who see changes in culture as the source of political and social change (Brand 1990; Swidler 1986); political historians and historical economists who look for cycles of political or economic change (Schlesinger 1986; Hirschman 1982); and social theorists who see changes in collective action resulting from changes in states and capitalism (Tilly 1984: ch. 1).

The first school emphasizes the global nature of cycles, the second, their regularity, and the third, their derivation from configurations of structural change. All three can prove useful, but they all focus on macropolitical and macrosociological relations *between* cycles; none examines the structure of the cycle itself. What is most important about this structure is the broadening of political opportunities by early risers in the cycle, the externalities that lower the social transaction costs of contention for even weak actors, the high degree of interdependence among the actors in the cycle, and the closure of political opportunities at its end.

Organizations and authorities, movements and interest groups, members of the polity and challengers interact, experience conflict, and cooperate in such periods, and

the dynamic of the cycle is the outcome of their interaction. "Actions," as sociologist Pam Oliver writes, "can affect the likelihood of other actions by creating occasions for action, by altering material conditions, by changing a group's social organization, by altering beliefs, or by adding knowledge" (1989: 2). These actions create uncertainty and undermine the calculations on which existing commitments and alliances are based, leading supporters of the regime to trim their sails and opponents to make new calculations of interest and alliance. The outcome of such many-sided interactions depends less on the balance of power and the resources of any pair of actors, than on the generalized nature of contention and its multipolar nature. This is why, as we will see, although the beginnings of protest cycles are similar, their endings are far more disparate.

In what follows, I will sketch the main elements within a protest cycle to help us to understand how cycles unfold and how they end. The key concept is the opening, diffusion and the closure of political opportunities. I will then trace the main lineament of the first major international cycle of protest—the 1848 Revolution—before comparing three cycles in recent history, the 1930s, the 1960s and the liberation movements in Eastern Europe in the last decade.

Opportunities and Cycles

The generalization of conflict into a cycle of protest occurs when political opportunities are opened up for well-placed "early risers," when they make claims that resonate with those of others, and when these give rise to objective or explicit coalitions among disparate actors and create or reinforce instability in the elite. The early demands that appear in a cycle do two things: First, they demonstrate the vulnerability of authorities to such demands, which signals to other contenders that the time may be ripe for their own demands. And, second, "they inevitably challenge the interests of other contenders, either because the distribution of benefits to one group will diminish the rewards available for another, or because the demands directly attack the interests of an established group" (Tilly 1993b: 13).

Although cycles do not have a uniform frequency or extend equally to entire populations, a number of features characterize such periods in recent history.[1] These include heightened conflict, broad sectoral and geographic diffusion, the expansion of the repertoire of contention, the appearance of new movement organizations and the empowerment of old ones, the creation of new "master frames" linking the actions of disparate groups to one another, and intensified interaction between challengers and the state.

Conflict and Diffusion

Protest cycles are characterized by heightened conflict: not only in industrial relations, but in the streets; not only there, but in villages and schools. In such periods, the magnitude of conflictual collective action of many kinds rises appreciably above what is typical both before and after. Particular groups recur with regularity in the vanguard of waves of social protest (for example, miners, students); but they are frequently joined during the peak of the cycle by groups that are not generally known for their insurgent tendencies (for example, peasants, workers in small industry, white-collar workers).

Cycles of protest also have some traceable paths of diffusion from large cities to the rural periphery, or—as is often the case—from periphery to center. They often spread from heavy industrial areas to adjacent areas of light industry and farming, along river valleys or through other major routes of communication. They appear among members of the same ethnic or national group whose identities are activated by new opportunities and threats. The uncertainty created by widespread contention increases the importance of ethnicity or other communal characteristics in people's mutual recognition, trust, and cooperation (Bunce 1991).

What is most distinctive about such periods is not that entire societies "rise" in the same direction at the same time (they seldom do); or that particular population groups act in the same way over and over, but that the demonstration effect of collective action on the part of a small group of "early risers" triggers a variety of processes of diffusion, extension, imitation, and reaction among groups that are normally quiescent.

Diffusion is misspecified if it is seen only as a contagion of collective action to similar groups that are making the same claims against equivalent opponents. A key characteristic of protest cycles is the diffusion of a propensity for collective action from its initiators to both unrelated groups and to antagonists. The former respond to the demonstration effect of a collective action that succeeds or at least is not suppressed, while the latter produce the countermovements that are a frequent reaction to the onset of collective action.

Repertoires and Frames

Protest cycles are the crucibles out of which new weapons of social protest are fashioned. The barricades in the French revolutions of the nineteenth century; the factory councils of 1919–20; the sitdown strikes of the French Popular Front and the American New Deal; the "direct actions" of the

1968–72 period in Italy: In the uncertainty and experimentation of a cycle of protest, innovation accelerates and new forms of collective action have space to develop and be refined.

Of course, not all of the collective action innovations that appear in these periods of generalized contention survive past the end of the cycle. Some are directly linked to the peak of contention, when it seems to some that anything is possible and the world will be transformed (Zolberg 1972); others are the result of the very high levels of participation characteristic of cycles and cannot be sustained when mobilization declines. As participation declines and utopia recedes, more conventional forms come to dominate, and those who thought a brave new world was coming either retreat into private life or engage in increasingly desperate acts of violence. The most successful new forms become part of the future repertoire of collective action.

With a similar logic, protest cycles produce new or transformed symbols, frames of meaning, and ideologies to justify and dignify collective action and help movements to mobilize a following. These typically arise among insurgent groups—which is how the traditional concept of "rights" expanded in the United States in the 1960s—and then spread elsewhere in the system—for example, as the American "rights" frame spread to women, gay men and lesbians, Native Americans, and to campaigns for the rights of the unborn and even animals in the 1970s and 1980s. Waves of mobilization are the crucibles within which new cultural constructs are born, tested, and refined. These may then enter the political culture in more diffuse and less militant form and can serve as a source for the symbols around which future movement entrepreneurs mobilize a following.

Movement Organizations

The increase in collective action towards the peak of a cycle creates incentives for new organizations to form and for old ones to radicalize their tactics. Protest cycles almost never fall under the control of a single movement organization. The high point of the wave is marked by the appearance of "spontaneous" collective action; but in fact, both previous traditions of organization and new organized movements structure their strategies and outcomes. Nor is it the case that "old" organizations necessarily give way to new ones in the course of the cycle—many of them adopt the radical tactics of their competitors and adjust their discourse to reflect a broader, more aggressive public stance.

To the extent that organizations become the major carriers of a protest wave, contention will not cease just because a particular group has been satisfied, repressed, or becomes tired of life in the streets. Organizations born in collective action continue to use it. Once formed, movement organizations compete for support through collective action. The common spiral of radicalization observed in many protest cycles is the outcome of such competition for support. A key element in the decline of movements is the dispute over tactics, as some militants insist on radicalizing their strategy while others try to consolidate their organizations and deliver concrete benefits to supporters.

Increased Interaction

Finally, during periods of increased contention, interactions between groups of challengers and authorities increase in frequency and intensity and become multipolar rather than bipolar. Conflicts between elites widen into deep cleavages between social groups; new centers of power develop—however temporary and ephemeral—convincing insurgents that the old system is collapsing and producing new and sometimes bizarre alliances between challengers and supporters of the regime. These coalitions sometimes form the bases of new governing coalitions. More often, they split apart as some branches of the movement seek more radical change and others try to institutionalize their gains.

These characteristics can be found in many modern protest cycles, beginning with the revolutions of 1848 which we will examine. That conflict produced major watersheds of turbulence, collective action, and political conflict almost everywhere in Europe. In each country grassroots insurgency was encouraged by opportunities at the summit, expanded by conflicts within the elite, and mobilized by organized groups that took advantage of these opportunities to threaten order, challenge opponents, and in some cases attack the regime. But like twentieth-century cycles, the revolutions also contained elements of political mediation, reform, and adaptation. Out of them, later movements were formed, new collective action frames were fashioned, and future political cleavages were etched.

The First Modern Cycle

In the winter and spring of 1848, rebellions were breaking out all over Europe.[2] On parts of the continent, the bad crop yields of the past few years appeared to be the main cause of the uprisings, but in other areas, harvests had been improving since the disastrous one of 1846.[3] In some countries, disputes over the suffrage were the trigger for the agitations of issue; but in others, the suffrage had already been expanded and in still others it only became an issue after the revolution. Finally, religious and ethnic cleavages were the source of important struggles in some countries, but in others there was no visible communal conflict.[4]

Although they sprang from a variety of sources, the uprisings of 1848 struck observers as a single event of continental importance. Engels devoted considerable resources to raising insurrections in Germany just as Bismarck's career as an opponent of democracy was being launched. Mazzini made his way to Rome where he helped to hasten the end of the Roman Republic, while Garibaldi returned from Latin America to raise insurrections in the Italian states. Tocqueville saw the revolution as the last chance for France to combine popular representation with limited government (1987: 61 ff.). In his 1847 program for the moderate opposition, he had foreseen the vast nature of the imminent conflagration. "The time is coming when the country will again be divided between two great parties," he prophesied; "Soon the political struggle will be between the haves and the have-nots; property will be the great battlefield." (pp. 12–13).

By the middle of 1848 in every major European country, regimes were threatened or overturned. People marched, met, organized assemblies and committees, and erected barricades. Rulers either scurried to places of safety or rushed through reforms to forestall further rebellion. Figure 27.1 demonstrates the dramatic rise and fall in conflict and response by combining the number of public events from Jacques Godechot's chronology for all the major European states for which he provides information on collective action in the 1848 revolutions.[5]

Godechot's series begins in March 1847, when the first major events occurred, and continues for thirty months through the end of August 1849. He includes a detailed outline of events of national importance for Austria–Hungary, Belgium, Britain, France, the German and Italian states, the Netherlands, Poland, Spain, and Switzerland. Some of these events were

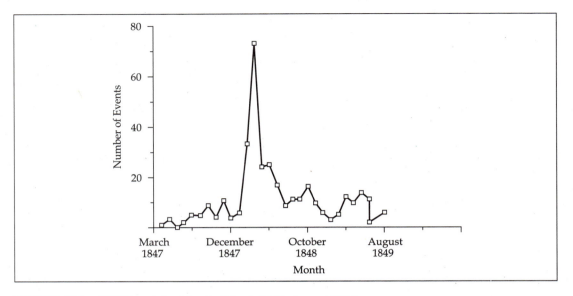

FIGURE 27.1   1848 Events by Month, March 1847–August 1849

Source: Sarah Soule and Sidney Tarrow, "Acting Collectively, 1847–1849: How the Repertoire of Collective Action Changed and Where it Happened," paper presented to the annual conference of Social Science History Association, New Orleans, Louisiana. 1991.

contentious and violent; others were routine electoral and legislative acts; others were the actions of public authorities; still others, the interventions of foreign powers. His chronology allows us to record only the *number* of events and not their duration or the number of participants, but it provides us with a graphic picture of the rapid spread of contention and the political and military responses to it across Europe in the revolutions of 1848, and will help us to introduce the dynamics of protest cycles.

A Transnational Movement

By aggregating these events across Europe, Figure 27.1 disguises the transnational nature of the 1848 revolutions. I will focus, here, only on the four major continental units—Italy, France, Germany, and the regions of the Hapsburg Empire. The time–series of events in each country from Godechot's chronology are represented for

France and Italy in Figure 27.2 and for Germany and Austria in Figure 27.3.

The national data reported in Figures 27.2 and 27.3 show a fitful rise in contention prior to February 1848 in most of the countries—with the exception of Italy—a near-simultaneous explosion of conflict in the spring of 1848, and a variety of national patterns for the remaining period. The pattern of similar beginnings and different endings of the cycle depended, in part, on the incidence of foreign intervention late in the period; but it will remain a salient characteristic of the twentieth century cycles we will turn to later in this chapter.

Although France has received the lion's share of attention, the events of February 1848 in Paris were presaged in three less central areas—Switzerland, Belgium, and Italy. Not for the first time in history, a revolution that attacked the core of the European power system began in its periphery. In Switzerland, divisions among Catholics, lib-

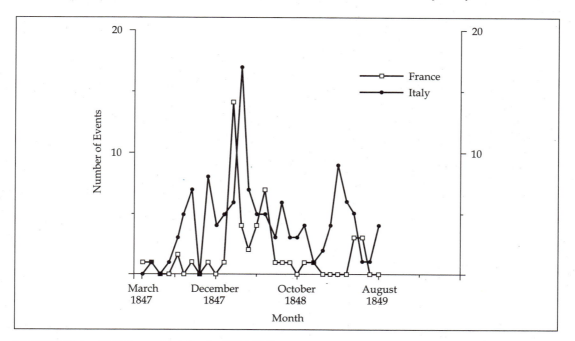

FIGURE 27.2   1848 Events by Month, 1847–1849

Source: Sarah Soule and Sidney Tarrow, "Acting Collectively, 1847–1849: How the Repertoire of Collective Action Changed and Where it Happened," paper presented to the annual conference of Social Science History Association, New Orleans, Louisiana. 1991.

erals, and radicals gave the more liberal Protestant cantons unusual margins for maneuver over their Catholic opponents. Their military successes in November of 1847, the support they enjoyed from the British, and the inability of the Austrians to intervene encouraged the party of change throughout Europe. No less French a historian than Halèvy would later assert that "the revolution of 1848 did not arise from the Parisian barricades but from the Swiss civil war" (Sigmann: 193).

Events in Brussels—so recently linked to Paris by rail—were another source of encouragement to the French opposition. If the king of the Belgians could appoint a liberal government, liberal parliamentarians in France were challenged to press the French government for expansion of France's limited suffrage. Though a "Belgian legion"

made a futile attempt to cross into Belgium from France in March, this time it was Belgium that influenced France, rather than vice versa.[6]

The Italian events of 1847 were even more remarkable, given that they began in benighted Rome, where an apparently liberal pope had just been chosen, and reached their peak in Sicily which was ruled from Naples by an anything-but-liberal Bourbon dynasty. From April to July 1847, Pope Pius conceded reforms to the papal states, triggering agitations both in Rome and in the Po valley towns, leading the rattled Austrians to occupy Ferrara. This was followed in the southern kingdom by an insurrection in Messina, riots in Naples, and the concession of a liberal ministry in the South by a frightened King Ferdinand.[7] Even in the peasant backwaters of Puglia and Calabria, "clubs"

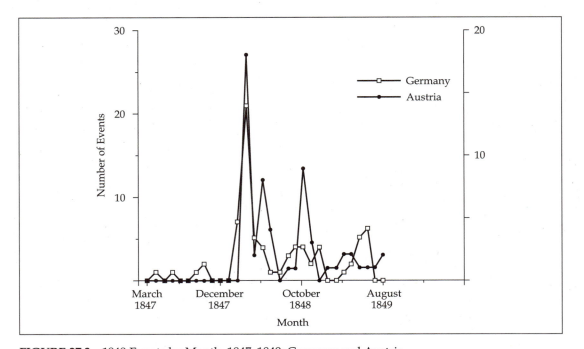

FIGURE 27.3   1848 Events by Month, 1847–1849; Germany and Austria

Source: Sarah Soule and Sidney Tarrow, "Acting Collectively, 1847–1849: How the Repertoire of Collective Action Changed and Where it Happened," paper presented to the annual conference of Social Science History Association, New Orleans, Louisiana. 1991.

and "circles" were formed along French lines (Soldani 1973).

Communications moved in both directions. As word of the agitations in Rome and Messina spread northward, they were studied in Milan and Venice, and were covered in detail in the French and German press. Agitations broke out in the Austrian-occupied parts of Northern Italy; and in the Kingdom of Sardinia, King Carlo Alberto was pressured to accord his people a constitution. The peace of Europe established at the Congress of Vienna was breaking down at the periphery where its vulnerability was demonstrated to reformers and radicals at its core.

Politically that core had always been Paris, and in February 1848, Paris did not disappoint the radicals. Although France was outpaced by Italy in the early sequence of events, Figures 27.2 and 27.3 suggest its importance in touching off rebellions in the other major areas of Europe. The most dramatic sign that an international protest wave was afoot was the rise in contentious events outside of France following the collapse of the July Monarchy. Paris was not the trigger for all the European revolts of these years, but it was a catalyst for its most intensive phase.

Creating Opportunities

Narrative histories of revolutions often concentrate on either their structural preconditions or their enthusiastic heights. But the immediate conditions of such explosions are found in the opening of opportunities within the polity—not only in the sense that the system is shown to be "ripe" for change, but in the more dynamic sense that alignments within it shift, access opens, elites divide and allies appear for challengers outside the system.

In the revolutions of 1848, conflicts at the summit provided opportunities first to moderates, then to organizations outside the elite and eventually to ordinary people. These changes were not begun by the downtrodden masses but by institutional and social elites whose conflicts provided opportunities for others to organize and mobilize. Incentives spread from elites to masses through the press, through legal and illegal political organizations, and increasingly, through collective actions that demonstrated the boldness of the opposition and the vulnerability of the regimes.

On the eve of the "springtime of peoples," such struggles were opening up in many of the countries of Europe. Of the major capitals, only Vienna doesn't appear in Godechot's chronology until 1848—except for the defeats it suffered in Switzerland and Italy.[8] In Paris, Berlin, and Rome, popular insurrection was presaged by realignments in the political class that opened opportunities for others. The French developments of 1847–8 can be used to illustrate this process.

By the early 1840s, most Central and Western European regimes, including France's, had semiconstitutional governments which provided a good deal of scope for elite debate, focusing increasingly on the issue of the suffrage (Anderson and Anderson: 307–17). French reformers were not so foolhardy as to wish to extend the vote universally, but the agitation around the suffrage revealed cracks in the elite and uncertainty in the government that were key factors in triggering contention among the poor.

The first stage in the unraveling of the Regime was its response to the parliamentary opposition's demand for reform. Rejection of its modest proposals threw the moderates into the arms of the Republicans, launching the campaign of "banquets" that were thinly disguised demonstrations for reform that took the debate from the Chamber to the streets, and from Paris to the provinces. Because these banquets were sponsored by the legitimate opposition and were entirely peaceable, the government hesitated to repress them. But because they bridged the tactical interests of parliamentary and extra-parliamentary groups, the campaign passed rapidly from the parliamentary opposition into the hands of a coalition of extra-parliamentary agitators and journalists who suddenly published a program calling for the National Guard to attend the final banquet as a body (Tocqueville 1987: 26–7). The liberals tried to pull back, but by the day scheduled for the biggest banquet of all—in Paris on February 22—it was too late, and the initiative passed into the hands of the Guard and the urban poor (p. 20).

The first stage of the revolution was centered on the Chamber, but before it had gone very far, barricades were raised on the streets of Paris, diligence drivers were taking advantage of the tumult to destroy the railway lines, Jews were attacked in the eastern provinces, and forest preserves were invaded. But the walls of the July Monarchy had been sapped from within before they were attacked from without. As Ronald Aminzade writes, "as soon as we look even a little deeply into the historical context of the 1848 events, the continuities between institutionalized and movement politics become more evident" (1994: 4).

The Peak of the Cycle

As in many of the protest cycles that followed, the peak of contention in the spring of 1848 was marked by an expansion of the forms of collective action. In 1848, these were the public meeting, the demonstration, the barricade, and violence against others. Although the 1848 Revolution has been remembered for its most confrontational movements, the co-occurrence of these collective action forms tells us just how broad participation was. As liberal and conservative gentlemen were holding sober meetings and learned conferences, radicals were organizing demonstrations, workers and artisans were building barricades, and peasants were attacking landlords and taking over forest reserves.

The barricades were the disruptive centerpieces of the various Parisian *journées* (Traugott 1990; 1993). They were mounted in the February days when the Monarchy was overthrown; in April in Rouen, when workers took to them after the defeat of the Republican candidates they had supported in the elections; during the June days, after the Assembly dissolved the national workshops; and again in June 1849, when a French army landed at Civitavecchia to reinstate the pope. Barricades spread rapidly across Europe wherever the Revolution took on a radical character.

But the peaks of protest cycles are also marked by an increase in violence. The attacks on Jews in the spring of 1848 were a presentiment of the ethnic conflicts that marked the passage of the revolution eastward. In Germany the first months of the revolution were marked by scores of such attacks. When Hungarian landowners shook off the rule of Vienna, they quickly put their boot on the necks of subject Serbs. As in Yugoslavia after the 1989 revolution, in Eastern Europe, the breakdown of order in 1848 opened a Pandora's box of opportunities for interethnic violence.

But the revolutions also produced endless public meetings and learned conferences and parliamentary gatherings. What did the Sicilian rebels do when they took over Palermo in January 1848? They formed committees for restoring order, ensuring provisions, securing finance, and controlling information (Tilly, Tilly, and Tilly: 130). How did German liberals respond when the king of Prussia dissolved the *landtag* in June 1847? They met in Offenberg in September and in Oppenheim in October to discuss future actions (Godechot: 199–200). Even in Austrian-ruled Serbia, Croatia, and Transylvania, the revolutionary events of February and March 1848 produced meetings and committees. The most long-lasting, and the least productive, was the "professors' parliament" in Frankfurt that was at first tolerated and then broken up.

Mass demonstrations were a third important part of the repertoire of 1848—in fact, the demonstration came into its own in France in that year. If we can assume a resemblance between Godechot's "*manifestation*" and our term "demonstration,"[9] we will find in his chronology thirty-one major demonstrations in the twelve months from July 1847 to June 1848. But it was from February through April 1848 that we find the greatest density of demonstrations. In France and Italy, Germany and Austria there were mass demonstrations by liberals and democrats, students and workers. The peaceful occupation of public space, the public meeting and the barricade, as well as traditional attacks on others were a hallmark of the intensive peak of the cycle.

Cyclical Decline

As the revolutions progressed beyond the effervescence of the spring of 1848, the peaceful demonstration and the public meeting begin to disappear from Godechot's chronology, to be replaced by terms like "attack," "clash," "dissolve," "intervene," and "defeat." The last public demonstration he lists was a demand for work in Berlin on October 31, followed soon after by the retraction of the reforms that the Kaiser conceded in the previous spring. People stopped demonstrating when armed force began to be employed against them.

Increasingly, armed clashes took on an international dimension. Austrian marines attacked the liberals in Northern Italy, the French intervened in Rome, and Russian troops moved against the Hungarians in aid of the Hapsburgs. By the end of 1849, Godechot's chronology provides a picture of almost unrelieved armed strife, foreign intervention and a collapse of popular collective action. In France, the cycle dragged on through the Second Republic and ended only with Louis Napoleon's coup in 1851.

Like many other protest cycles, the 1848 Revolution left the most bitter memories where the hopes it had generated were highest. At first welcomed by radicals and democrats across Europe, the revolutionaries of 1848 were soon denounced for their "hollow rhetoric, their mystical idealism . . . and their generous illusions" (Sigmann: 10). In Germany, the year was soon labeled "*das tolle Jahr*," while the British ambassador to Paris, Lord Normanby, wrote that 1848 left "almost every individual less happy, every country less prosperous, every people not only less free but less hopeful of freedom hereafter" (Postgate: 266). The memory it left in Italy was of confusion and chaos; even today, the expression to "*fare un quarantotto*" means to create confusion. "What we remember most" after the intoxication of a "moment of madness," writes Aristide Zolberg, "is that moments of political enthusiasm are followed by bourgeois repression or by charismatic authoritarianism, sometimes by horror but always by the restoration of boredom" (1972: 205).

Three Modern Cycles

The same characteristics found in the revolution of 1848 can be found in three cycles in recent history for which we have significant information: the period of the Popular Front in France and the American New Deal; the movements of the 1960s in Western Europe and the United States; and the Eastern European democratization wave that began in Poland in 1980 and ended in the collapse of the USSR in 1991. The first was centered in organized labor, although other occupational groups, like farmers and the unemployed, also appeared in it; the second was centered among students, although workers and urban movements were also present in Western Europe; and the third, though it began among workers and intellectuals, rapidly spread to entire populations.

Popular Front and New Deal

From 1934 to 1936, a wave of protests swept across France, leading democrats to fear an assault on the Republic from the right, and propertied interests to fear anarchy from the Left. While peasant leagues threatened order in the provinces, right wing formations reminiscent of the German brownshirts filled the squares of Paris. Faced by these pressures, the government fell, new elections were called, and a Popular Front headed by socialist Léon Blum came to power. As if by prearranged signal, workers all over France occupied their factories and brought the economy to a halt.[10]

Spain had a Popular Front in the mid-1930s too. As the result of a strike wave in Asturias and Catalonia, the center-right wing government fell and a left wing coalition came to power. Strikes were legalized, participation was extended to the workplace, and the separatist claims of Basques and Catalans received support from the government. As in France, the Popular Front gave the Spanish Communist Party the first government it could support since its creation in the early 1920s.

About the same time, factory workers in Flint, Michigan, and Akron, Ohio, were employing sit-down tactics like those of French workers, paralyzing production and occupying the premises of Fisher Body and Goodyear Rubber (Piven and Cloward 1979: ch. 3). Their grievances were different and their ideologies less articulate than those of their European counterparts, but they too acted in the midst of a political reform movement of national scope—the New Deal of Franklin Roosevelt.

The European and American Student Movements[11]

From 1968 to 1972, a wave of student and labor unrest arose in Europe that would eventually envelop almost every area of society. Two movements in particular reached historic proportions: in France, the short but explosive "movement of May" nearly toppled the self-assured Gaullist regime, while in Czechoslovakia, a short spring of reform was followed by a brutal military crackdown. At about the same time, an Italian *maggio strisciante* (sliding May) shut down schools, universities, and factories, while in Germany, a wave of protest jarred that country's complacent political class. Even in Poland, the dramatization of Adam Mickiewicz's play, *Forefathers,* touched off a series of events that led to a movement of university students (Weinert 1994).

In the United States, the years of hope began earlier, in the Civil Rights movement of the early 1960s and in the anti-Vietnam War agitations that culminated in the "Days of Rage" at the Chicago Democratic Party convention. As in Europe, university students were in the vanguard of the American movements, but the workers who played a central role in France and Italy were largely absent.

What is most striking in thinking back to the movements of the sixties is the common frames of collective action in what Doug McAdam and Dieter Rucht call "the cross-national diffusion of movement ideas" (1993). Not only ideas, but movement tactics crossed the Atlantic in the 1960s. Although—also in retrospect—movements of the 1960s were far from revolutionary, they aptly illustrate what Tilly writes about the cross-national diffusion of revolutionary situations; "The demonstration that one important state is vulnerable . . . signals the possibility of making similar demands elsewhere" and makes available transferable expertise and doctrine (1993b: 14). This was spectacularly the case in Eastern Europe in 1989 and after.

The Collapse of State Socialism

In Poland in the summer of 1980, a workers' protest exploded in the shipyards along the Baltic coast. It began in workplace disputes and—as in earlier Polish strikes—was triggered by the government's announcement of price increases. But this time, an interfactory committee born of working class solidarity made it no longer possible for the authorities to divide and conquer. Before it was over, the wave of protest had spread through the country, to farmers and students, creating an institution unique to the Communist world—an independent union called *Solidarność.*[12]

Nine years divided the early strikes on the Baltic coast from the collapse of state socialism in Eastern Europe, so we cannot really talk about an integrated cycle. But Poland's "self-limiting revolution" was not so much different from, as it was a prefiguration of, the patterns that emerged elsewhere in the region. That workers in the heart of the Lenin shipyard could organize resistance with other workers and intellectuals, maintaining an underground life under martial law, told dissidents throughout Eastern Europe that their turn would eventually come. When it did, it was triggered from the source of authority in Moscow with the promise of Gorbachev's reforms and his warning that his East European allies were on their own.

Variations in Movement Dynamics

Though each of these protest waves took a different form, they appear, in retrospect, to be international waves of mobilization and reform. France's 1934–6 agitations were a response to the 1933 victory of fascism in Germany; the student protests of the 1960s were an expression of a movement that began at Berkeley and spread through the common opposition to the Vietnam War; the Polish strikes, though unprecedented in scope, capped five years of labor unrest and, in retrospect, were the first signs of the impending collapse of the Soviet Union's Eastern European empire.

At the peak of each wave, citizens developed particular forms of collective action. The factory occupations that marked the French 1936 strikes were similar to the sitdown strikes of Flint and Akron; while the university occupations of Berlin, Turin, and Paris in 1968 linked European students to their American homologues. As for Solidarity, its most striking feature would prove to be the roundtable discussions between Solidarity leaders and the government that foreshadowed the form of negotiation that swept Eastern Europe in 1989.

In each of the cases, a spiral of demands spun outward from conflicts that began within the elite and produced political opportunities for outsiders. Early claims grew out of concrete conflicts of interest. But

as the protests spread, coalitions of challengers formed organizations and broadened their claims, often radicalizing them into general challenges to authority. The breadth of these movements and their rapid diffusion seemed to threaten the established order, giving rise to countermovements, demands for law and order, and sometimes to reform. In the end, what began as conflicts over claims became interlaced with struggles for power.

Diverse Endings

Viewed from a distance, each wave of collective action described a parabola; from institutional conflict to enthusiastic peak to ultimate collapse. After gaining national attention and state response, they reached peaks of conflict that were marked by the presence of movement organizers who tried to diffuse the insurgencies to broader publics. As participation was channeled into organizations, the movements, or parts of them, took on a more political logic—engaging in implicit bargaining with authorities. In each case, as the cycle wound down, the initiative shifted to elites and parties.

But the multipolarity of the interactions in these cycles made their endings far less similar than their beginnings. The diffusion of collective action from early risers to latecomers, and the shift of political opportunities from challengers to their allies and then to elites, increased the number of interactions and sent the cycles off in divergent directions. Especially the involvement of foreign powers turned the ends of these cycles into different directions.

The French Popular Front responded to the 1936 strikes by increasing minimum wages, limiting working hours, and ending the tradition of settling strikes with police truncheons, while in Spain it ended in civil war. The reforms that accompanied the 1968 student protests in Europe were carried out by different governmental coalitions and each ended differently. In France, this was a conservative coalition; in Germany, a Social Democratic one; and in Italy a shifting sequence of center-left and center-right wing governments. Some of the same differences were reflected in the "new" social movements of the 1970s and 1980s (Koopmans 1993). In Poland, the Jaruzelski government declared martial law in 1981, clapping Solidarity leaders into jail and attempting to put the stopper on dissent. Its greatest success was negative—it avoided the threat of Soviet military intervention.

Nor did the differential paths of these mobilization waves end with their collapse. In France, the Popular Front was soon defeated. But after the war, the Fourth Republic turned to its reforms for the model of its welfare state. In Italy, France, and Germany, the movements of 1968 split into a number of strands with some elements entering the political parties and unions, others flowing into cultural and religious movements, and the most extreme turning to armed violence. The outcomes of protest cycles are found in political struggle. It is the nature of that struggle and the strategies of the actors in each country that determine the outcome of the cycle.

NOTES

1. The outline below reflects experience in Western Europe and the United States since the 1960s and was developed in the context of research on Italy, perhaps not a typical case. It will be for empirical investigation to determine whether and in what ways the picture resembles waves of collective action in other systems and other periods of history. For a comparison of the West German experience, see Koopmans' "The Dynamics of Protest Waves."

2. The following section summarizes parts of the analysis in Soule and Tarrow, "Acting Collectively, 1847–1849: How the Repertoire of Collective Action Changed and Where it Happened," presented in 1991 to the Annual Conference of the Social Science History Association, New Orleans. I am grateful to Sarah Soule for her collaboration in analyzing the data on which this section is based, and for her helpful comments on a draft of this chapter.

3. For a survey of the main "background causes" of the revolutions in the various European countries, see Roger Price, *The Revolutions of 1848,* and the excellent basic bibliography he provides.

4. Generally speaking, religious cleavages were dominant in Switzerland, ethnic and nationalist ones in the Hapsburg Empire outside of Austria, and issues of political representation in France and Germany. Although the national question came to dominate the Italian *quarantotto,* it began with agitations for liberal reform in Rome and the Kingdom of the Two Sicilies, and only as it moved northward to areas controlled by the Hapsburgs, did it take on a nationalist coloration. In France and Germany, although food riots occurred in the early stages of the conflagration, the major axes of conflict were over representative institutions and workers' rights.

5. From Jacques Godechot's rich compendium, *Les Révolutions de 1848.* No information is provided by Godechot for Scandinavia (except for the brief war between Denmark and Prussia over Schleswig-Holstein); none for Greece and Portugal; and none for the European parts of the Ottoman Empire. For a more detailed analysis of this data and of some of the problems that they present see Soule and Tarrow, "Acting Collectively."

6. Based on an unpublished manuscript kindly provided to the author by Aristide Zolberg, and eventually published in shorter form in his "Belgium," in Raymond Grew, ed., *Crises of Political Development.*

7. This was especially true in Calabria, where, on the eve of the 1848 events, the government was so alarmed that it established a commission to compensate peasants who had been deprived of customary rights. On this episode, see John Davis, *Conflict and Control: Law and Order in Nineteenth Century Italy,* pp. 47–9.

8. But the rest of the Hapsburg Empire was much less serene. On the agitations in the

empire, particularly in Bohemia and Hungary, see Price's *The Revolutions of 1848,* pp. 28–9.

9. Here we must be cautious, since Godechot's term *manifestation* may lack the specificity of the form of collective action that we now call by that term; what Pierre Favre, in *La Manifestation,* defines as "a collective movement organized in public space with the goal of producing a political outcome by the peaceful expression of an opinion or a demand" (p. 15 [Author's translation]).

10. For a useful case study of the factory occupation at the key Renault plant at Boulogne-Billancourt, see Bernard Badie's *Strategie de la grève,* ch. 3.

11. On the French "events," the most detached recent treatment is by Jacques Capdevielle and René Mouriaux, *May 68: L'entre-deux de la modernité.* For a recent compendium of reflections, see Mouriaux, et al., *1968: Exploration du Mai français.* On the Italian *sessantotto,* see Peppino Ortoleva, *Saggio sui movimenti del 1968 in Europa e in America* and Sidney Tarrow, *Democracy and Disorder,* ch. 6. For the United States, the most pungent reflections on this period are found in Todd Gitlin's *The Sixties,* and James Miller's *Democracy Is in the Streets.*

12. For almost instant—and highly politicized—responses to the phenomenon of Solidarity, both reflecting something of the "privileged witness" syndrome, see Timothy Garton Ash's *The Polish Revolution,* Jadwiga Staniszkis' *Poland's Self-Limiting Revolution.* For the most reflective analyses in English, see Roman Laba's *The Roots of Solidarity,* and David Ost's *Solidarity and the Politics of Anti-Politics.*

REFERENCES

Aminzade, Ronald (1994). "Between Movement and Party: The Transformation of Mid-Nineteenth Century French Republicanism," in J. Craig Jenkins and Bert Klandermans, eds., *The Politics of Social Protest: Comparative Perspectives on States and Social Movements, in press.*

Anderson, Eugene N., and Pauline R. Anderson (1967). *Political Institutions and Social Change in Continental Europe in the Nineteenth Century.*
Berkeley and Los Angeles: University of California Press.

Brand, Karl-Werner (1990). "Cyclical Aspects of New Social Movements: Waves of Cultural Criticism and Mobilization Cycles of New Middle-class Radicalism," in Russell Dalton and Manfred Kuechler, eds., *Challenging the Political Order.* Oxford and New York: Oxford University Press, pp. 23–42.

Bunce, Valerie (1991). "Democracy, Stalinism and the Management of Uncertainty," in Gyorgy Szoboszlai, ed., *Democracy and Political Transformation.* Budapest: Hungarian Political Science Association, pp. 138–64.

Godechot, Jacques (1971). *Les Révolutions de 1848.* Paris: Albin Michel.

Hirschman, Albert (1982). *Shifting Involvements: Private Interest and Public Action.* Princeton: Princeton University Press.

Koopmans, Ruud (1993). "The Dynamics of Protest Waves: Germany, 1965 to 1989," *American Sociological Review* 58:637–58.

McAdam, Doug and Dieter Rucht (1993). "The Cross-National Diffusion of Movement Ideas," *Annals of the American Academy of Political and Social Science* 528:56–74.

Oliver, Pam (1989). "Bringing the Crowd Back In: The Nonorganizational Elements of Social Movements," in L. Kriesberg, ed., *Research in Social Movements, Conflict, and Change,* Vol. 11. Greenwich, Conn.: JAI, pp. 1–30.

Piven, Frances F. and Richard Cloward (1979). *Poor People's Movements: Why They Succeed, How They Fail.* New York: Vintage Books.

Postgate, Raymond (1955). *The Story of a Year: 1848.* London: Cassell.

Schlesinger, Arthur M., Jr. (1986). *The Cycles of American History.* Boston: Houghton Mifflin.

Sigmann, Jean (1973). *1848. The Romantic and Democratic Revolutions in Europe.* New York: Harper and Row.

Soldani, Simonetta (1973). "Cantandini operai e 'popolo' nella rivoluzione del 1848 in Italia," *Studi storici* 14:557–613.

Swidler, Ann (1986). "Culture in Action: Symbols and Strategies" *American Sociological Review* 51:273–86.

Tilly, Charles (1984). "Social Movements and National Politics," in C. Bright and S. Harding, eds., *Statemaking and Social Movements: Essays in History and Theory.* Ann Arbor: University of Michigan Press, pp. 297–317.

———. (1993b). *European Revolutions, 1492–1992.* Oxford: Blackwell's.

Tilly, Charles, Louise Tilly, and Richard Tilly, (1975). *The Rebellious Century, 1830–1930.* Cambridge: Harvard University Press.

Toqueville, Alexis de (1987). *Recollections. The French Revolution of 1848.* New Brunswick, N.J.: Transaction Books.

Traugott, Marc. "Use of Barricades in the French Revolution of 1848." Unpublished paper, University of California, Santa Cruz, California.

————. (1993). "Barricades as Repertoire: Continuities and Discontinuities in the History of French Contention," *Social Science History* 17:309–23.

Wejnert, Barbara (1994). "Prerequisites for Diffusion of Collective Protests: Student Movements in the Sixties," in L. Kriesberg, ed., *Research in Social Movements, Conflict, and Change.* Vol. 16. Greenwich, Conn.: JAI, in press.

Zolberg, Aristide R. (1972). "Moments of Madness," *Politics and Society* 2:183–207.

————. (1989). *Escape From Violence: Conflicts and the Refugee Crisis in the Developing World.* Oxford and New York: Oxford University Press.

28

MASTER FRAMES AND CYCLES OF PROTEST

DAVID A. SNOW • ROBERT D. BENFORD

The notion that social movements hang together or cluster in some fashion is a relatively old one in the literature. The concept of general social movement, initially coined by Blumer (1951; cf. Turner and Killian 1987), suggests that specific movements within any historical era are tributaries of a more general stream of agitation. Klapp similarly points to this clustering tendency in his aptly titled *Currents of Unrest* (1972) in which he suggests the applicability of the general systems concept of "oscillation" to the analysis of collective behavior. More recently, McCarthy and Zald's (1977) concepts of "social movement organizations, industries, and sectors" provide a conceptual basis for the temporal and spatial clustering of movement activity. And the concept of "cycles of protest," elaborated by Tarrow (1983), underscores even more concretely the clustering and sequencing of collective action. Taken together these concepts and ideas bear a striking "family resemblance" (Wittgenstein 1967) in that they all direct attention, first, to the ecological and cyclical aggregation of social movements and, second, to the embeddedness of social movement organizations (SMOS) in a particular cycle or sector of movement activity.

That movement organizations and activities do indeed cluster temporally in a cyclical fashion not only is a topic of theoretical speculation but is also well documented, as evidenced by several recent empirical investigations of collective action in Western Europe (della Porta and Tarrow 1986; Shorter and Tilly 1974; Tarrow 1983; Tilly et al. 1975; Tilly 1978). Similarly, the rise and decline of collective violence in American cities during the 1960s and early 1970s, the sudden flowering and subsequent wilting of religious cults in the late l960s and 1970s, and the recent eruption of collective action throughout much of Eastern Europe illustrate this cyclical pattern.

But what accounts for this clustering and apparent connection among movements within a cycle seems to be less well understood. Early collective behavior theory suggested contagion and convergence processes as possible explanatory mechanisms, but research during the past fifteen years has found that such processes tend to shroud rather than illuminate the dynamics of collective action. The more recent resource mobilization perspective focuses attention on changes in various structural factors such as social networks (Snow et al. 1980), indigenous organizational strength (McAdam 1982; Morris 1984), the structure of political opportunities (Eisinger 1973; Jenkins and Perrow 1977; Lipsky 1970), and resource pools (McCarthy and Zald 1977) as the key explanatory mechanisms that affect the waxing and waning of social movements. Although such variables are no doubt crucial to understanding the clustering of collective action, the factors that account for those changes are not unambiguously specified. Nor do purely structural explanations suffice in accounting for periodic shifts in the level of social movement activity. Why, for example, do citizens sometimes fail to act collectively on their shared grievances when the structural conditions appear otherwise ripe?

Thus, from our vantage point, two central questions are particularly problematic: first, what accounts for the temporal clustering of SMOS and activities, and second, what accounts for the cyclicity of social movement activity? We seek to advance understanding of these issues by examining theoretically the relation between cycles of protest and what we refer to as master

frames. More specifically, we will elaborate and explore a number of sensitizing propositions regarding this hypothesized linkage.

We see this exercise as essentially theoretic. Our aim is not to demonstrate empirically or to verify the propositions we elaborate but to develop a framework for conceptualizing and discussing the relation between master frames and cycles of protest. This endeavor builds on and extends our earlier work on frame alignment (Snow et al. 1986) and frame resonance (Snow and Benford 1988) in two ways: it provides conceptual clarification, and it extends our analyses from the microlevel to the macrolevel. Whereas we focused before on the framing activity of individual movement organizations, here we turn to an examination of how frames function in a larger context.[1]

Since our inquiry places a premium on ideational factors, we begin with a brief overview of their treatment in the literature. Next, we elaborate the characteristic features of collective action frames and then discuss master frames and cycles of protest, the two key concepts that are the focus of our inquiry. And finally, we discuss a number of sensitizing propositions regarding the relation among master frames, cycles of protest, and specific movements within these cycles.

Theoretical Issues and Concepts

Ideology, Signification, and Framing

References to ideology and its elements—values, beliefs, meanings—are commonplace in the social movement literature. The treatment of ideological factors in relation to the course and character of movements has been far from satisfactory, however. A survey of discussions of ideology in the literature suggests that the concept has been dealt with in essentially two ways. Before the emergence of the resource mobilization perspective, writers (with the exception of Turner and Killian 1987; Turner 1969) treated ideology primarily descriptively rather than analytically, and statically rather than dynamically. Some recognized its role in the social movement process, but their discussion of it seldom went beyond enumerating its functions and content, treating the latter as if it flowed almost naturally or magically from the movement's underlying strains. Description of movement ideology was seen as prefatory to the more important analytic task of ferreting out the relation between movement emergence and "structural strain" (e.g., see Smelser 1963).

Since the displacement of strain theory by resource mobilization perspectives in the mid-1970s, ideological factors have figured even less prominently in movement analyses. Indeed, the tendency has been to ignore or gloss over mobilizing beliefs and ideas, in large part because of their presumed ubiquity and constancy, which make them, in turn, relatively nonproblematic and uninteresting factors in the movement equation (Oberschall 1973, 133–34, 194–95; McCarthy and Zald 1977, 1214–15; Jenkins and Perrow 1977, 250–51; Jenkins 1983, 528). A number of critics have recently noted this oversight and have called for a broadening of resource mobilization theory to include ideational factors (Ferree and Miller 1985; Gamson et al. 1982; Zurcher and Snow 1981).

Whether mobilizing ideas and meanings are treated merely descriptively or as nonproblematic constants, both tendencies strike us as misguided on two accounts. First, meanings and ideas are treated as given, as if they spring almost imminently from the events and objects with which they are associated, rather than as social productions that arise during the course of interactive processes. And second, they ignore the

extent to which movements are engaged in "meaning-work"—that is, in the struggle over the production of ideas of meanings.

In the course of our fieldwork experiences with a variety of social movements (e.g., Nichiren Shoshu, Hare Krishna, the peace movement, and several urban neighborhood movements), we came to see this neglected aspect of movements as particularly interesting and also as problematic. From our vantage point, then, we do not view social movements merely as carriers of extant ideas and meanings that stand in isomorphic relationship to structural arrangements or unanticipated events. Rather, we see movement organizations and actors as actively engaged in the production and maintenance of meaning for constituents, antagonists, and bystanders or observers. This productive work may involve the amplification and extension of extant meanings, the transformation of old meanings, and the generation of new meanings (Snow et al. 1986). We thus view movements as functioning in part as signifying agents that often are deeply embroiled, along with the media, local governments, and the state, in what has been referred to aptly as the "politics of signification" (Hall 1982).

It is this signifying work that is the heart of this chapter. Consistent with our earlier work, we conceptualize this signifying work with the verb *framing*, which denotes an active, process-derived phenomenon that implies agency and contention at the level of reality construction. We refer to the products of this framing activity as collective action frames.

Characteristic Features of Collective Action Frames

The concept of frame has meaning in both everyday and academic discourse. Regarding the latter, its usage is neither discipline-specific nor particularly novel. It not only has found its way into sociology, primarily through the work of Goffman (1974), but has also been used in psychiatry (Bateson 1972), the humanities (Cone 1968), and cognitive psychology (Minsky 1975; Piaget 1954). In addition, the kindred concept of schema has been used widely and has generated considerable research in cognitive psychology (Hastie 1981; Kelley 1972; Marcus and Zajonc 1985; Neisser 1976). Throughout these works the basic referent for the concept of frame is essentially the same: it refers to an interpretive schemata that simplifies and condenses the "world out there" by selectively punctuating and encoding objects, situations, events, experiences, and sequences of actions within one's present or past environment. In Goffman's words, frames allow individuals "to locate, perceive, identify, and label" events within their life space or the world at large (1974, 21). The recent spate of research on the media and newsmaking both documents and highlights this characteristic function of frames (Gans 1979; Gitlin 1980; Tuchman 1978). Collective action frames not only perform this focusing and punctuating role; they also function simultaneously as modes of attribution and articulation.

To consider first the punctuating function, collective action frames serve as accenting devices that either underscore and embellish the seriousness and injustice of a social condition or redefine as unjust and immoral what was previously seen as unfortunate but perhaps tolerable. In either case, activists employ collective action frames to punctuate or single out some existing social condition or aspect of life and define it as unjust, intolerable, and deserving of corrective action (Gamson et al. 1982; Klandermans 1984; McAdam 1982; Moore 1978; Piven and Cloward 1977; Snow et al. 1986; Turner and Killian 1987). But the framing of a condition, happening, or sequence of events as unjust, inexcusable, or immoral is not sufficient to predict the direction and nature of collective action. Some sense of blame or causality must be specified as well as a corresponding sense of responsibility for corrective action.

This, then, takes us to the second characteristic of collective action frames: they function as modes of attribution by making diagnostic and prognostic attributions.[2] In the case of the former, movement activists attribute blame for some problematic condition by identifying culpable agents, be they individuals or collective processes or structures. And in the case of prognostic attribution, the Leninesque question is addressed by suggesting both a general line of action for ameliorating the problem and the assignment of responsibility for carrying out that action. Thus, diagnostic attribution is concerned with problem identification, whereas prognostic attribution addresses problem resolution.

In addition to their punctuational and attributional functions, collective action frames enable activists to articulate and align a vast array of events and experiences so that they hang together in a relatively unified and meaningful fashion. They are signaling and collating devices that decode and "package," in Gamson's terms (1988), slices of observed and experienced reality so that subsequent experiences or events need not be interpreted anew. The punctuated and encoded threads of information may be diverse and even incongruous, but they are woven together in such a way that what was previously inconceivable, or at least not clearly articulated, is now meaningfully interconnected. Thus, what gives a collective action frame its novelty is not so much its innovative ideational elements as the manner in which activists articulate or tie them together.

Master Frames and Their Variable Features

What we call master frames perform the same functions as movement-specific collective action frames, but they do so on a larger scale. In other words, they are also modes of punctuation, attribution, and articulation, but their punctuations, attributions, articulations may color and constrain those of any number of movement organizations. Master frames are to movement-specific collective action frames as paradigms are to finely tuned theories. Master frames are generic; specific collective action frames are derivative. So conceived, master frames can be construed as functioning in a manner analogous to linguistic codes in that they provide a grammar that punctuates and syntactically connects patterns or happenings in the world. Although all master frames function in this fashion, they can also differ in a number of respects. Three of these variable features warrant attention.

The first stems from the attributional function of master frames. As suggested above, a central feature of the framing process in relation to collective action is the generation of diagnostic attributions, which involve the identification of a problem and the attribution of blame or causality. All collective action frames perform this diagnostic function, but they can vary considerably in terms of the actual specification of blame. A central finding of attribution theory is that the causes of most behavior are attributed to internal or external factors. We assume that this tendency is also operative in the case of collective action, such that its nature will vary significantly depending on whether blame or responsibility for the problem at hand is internalized.

A central issue in attribution theory has concerned the factors that account for variation in the direction of causal attributions. Among the various factors identified as affecting this process, Kelley's (1972) concept of causal schemata is particularly relevant to our concerns. He argues that causal attributions are circumscribed in part by the general conceptions people have "about how certain kinds of causes interact to produce a specific kind of effect." In some respects, this argument is similar to Mills's (1940) contention that causal attributions are derived from "vocabularies of motive." Thus, whether using the language of "causal schemata" or "vocabularies of motive," both conceptualizations suggest that causal attributions are not made in a social void but are "framed" instead by attributional algorithms of sorts that can vary situationally and temporally.

Master frames perform a similar function, albeit on a larger scale, in that they provide the interpretive medium through which collective actors associated with different movements within a cycle assign blame for the problem they are attempting to ameliorate. Thus, in the case of SMOS associated with what might be termed the "psychosalvational" frame, such as TM, Scientology, and est, the source of personal suffering and unhappiness is seen as residing within the individual rather than within the larger sociocultural context.[3] That context may be seen as suffocating and decadent, but personal rather than societal transformation is regarded as the key to change. In contrast, from the standpoint of what might be thought of as the civil rights frame, blame is externalized in that unjust differences in life circumstances are attributed to encrusted, discriminatory structural arrangements rather than to the victims' imperfections.

The second variable feature of master frames is rooted in Bernstein's (1970; 1971) idea that there are two basic linguistic codes that yield different patterns of speech and orientation. One is referred to as "the restricted code" and the other as "the elaborated code." In the case of the restricted code, speech is rigidly organized in terms of a narrow range of syntactic alternatives; it is highly particularistic with respect to meaning and social structure, and as a consequence it is more predictable and reflective of the immediate social structure. In contrast, the elaborated code gives rise to speech that is more flexibly organized in terms of a wide range of syntactic alternatives, is more universalistic with respect to meaning and social structure, and thus is less predictable and reflective of immediate structures.

Bernstein's scheme is especially relevant to the articulation function of master frames. We have noted how they function in part as modes of articulation. But not all master frames perform this function in the same fashion. Some are rigid, whereas others are more flexible and elastic. Thus it is useful to distinguish between restricted and elaborated master frames. In idea terms, the former tend to be "closed" or exclusive ideational systems that do not so readily lend themselves to amplification or extension. As modes of articulation, they tend to organize a narrow band of ideas in a tightly interconnected fashion; as modes of interpretation, they provide a constricted range of definitions, thus allowing for little interpretive discretion. Stated more parsimoniously, restricted master frames are syntactically rigid and lexically particularistic. The nuclear freeze master frame, as we suggest below, is illustrative of a restricted one.

Elaborated master frames, on the other hand, are organized in terms of a wide range of ideas. They are more flexible modes of interpretation, and as a consequence, they are more inclusive systems that allow for extensive ideational amplification and extension. Being more syntactically flexible and lexically universalistic than the restricted frame, the elaborated master frame allows for numerous aggrieved groups to tap it and elaborate their grievances in terms of its basic problem-solving schema. The civil rights master frame, as we will discuss briefly, is clearly illustrative of an elaborative frame.

The third variable feature of master frames concerns their mobilizing potency. Potency is affected by two factors: where a master frame falls on the restricted/elaborative continuum and the extent of the frame's resonance. Regarding the first factor, we suspect that the more elaborated a master frame, the greater its appeal and influence and the more potent the frame. But potency is not assured by a highly elaborated frame. A master frame may lend itself to elaboration by various aggrieved groups across society, but such extensive elaboration may not be intensive in the sense of striking a deep responsive chord. In other words, its appeal may be only superficial or skin-deep. It follows that the potency of a master frame will also vary with the extent to which it is relevant to or resonates with the life world of adherents and constituents as well as bystanders. Hypothetically, the greater the resonance, the more potent the master frame.

Drawing on our earlier work (Snow and Benford 1988), we suggest three interrelated factors that affect the resonance dimension of potency: empirical credibility, experiential commensurability, and ideational centrality or narrative fidelity. By empirical credibility we refer to the apparent evidential basis for a master frame's diagnostic claims. Do its problem designations and attributions appear to be empirically credible from the vantage point of the targets of mobilization? To the extent that there are events that can be interpreted as documentary evidence for diagnostic and prognostic claims, a master frame has empirical credibility.[4]

Substantiation of designated problems does not mean that all potential constituents have firsthand experience with these problems. Some individuals may be keenly aware of social arrangements or occurrences punctuated as problematic and unjust, but those problems may be removed from their everyday life situation. For others, the problem may have already intruded into their everyday lives such that they have experienced it directly. When this is the case, the training has experiential commensurability and, presumably, greater potency.

The final variable affecting a master frame's resonance is its ideational centrality or narrative fidelity. Following Gramsci's (1971) distinction between "organic" and "nonorganic" ideology and Rude's parallel distinction between "inherent" and "derived" ideologies, as well as previous work on belief systems (Borhek and Curtis 1975; Converse 1964), we assume that the more central the ideas and meanings of a proffered framing to the ideology of the targets of mobilization, the greater its hierarchical salience within that larger belief system and the greater its "narrative fidelity" (Fisher 1984). In other words, the frame strikes a responsive chord in that it rings true with extant beliefs, myths, folktales, and the like. When that is the case, we suspect the frame is also considerably more potent.

To summarize, we have suggested that master frames vary in terms of their attributional orientation, their articulational scope, and their potency. Regarding the issue of potency, we postulate that it is a function of a master frame's elaborative potential and its resonance, which, in turn, is affected by the frame's empirical credibility, experiential commensurability, and narrative fidelity. We suspect that at least one of these resonance variables must be operative if a master frame is to exhibit much potency and treat the existence of all three translates into considerable potency.

Cycles of Protest

We now turn to the final key theoretical element: cycles of protest. Tarrow originally defined cycles of protest as sequences of escalating collective action that are of greater frequency and intensity than normal, that spread throughout various sectors and regions of society, and that involve both new techniques of protest and new forms of organization that, in combination with traditional organizational infrastructures, "determine the spread and dynamics of the cycle" (1983, 36–39). Although we accept the general thrust of this conceptualization, we think it would be theoretically and empirically fruitful to modify it in several respects. First, we would extend its scope so that it could be applied to temporal variation in collective action not only at the national or sector level but also at the level of communities, regions, and the world at large. In addition, we suspect that it would be interesting to examine empirically cyclical patterns of movement industries within a larger sector or cycle, in part to assess the extent to which movement industries within the same temporal frame are affected by each other as well as similar structural factors. Finally, we think the concept of protest should be used generically, in the fashion suggested by Lofland (1985), rather than limited to noninstitutional political challenges.

The Concepts Applied: Illustrative Propositions

With these conceptual and theoretical considerations in mind, we turn to an elaboration of sensitizing propositions that bear on the relation between master frames and cycles of protest. The first set of illustrative propositions pertains to the relation between master frames and the emergence of cycles of protest.[5] The second set concerns master frames and specific movements within a particular cycle. The third set deals with the relation between anchoring master frames and a cycle's tactical repertoire. Propositions pertaining to the relation between master frames and the shape of cycles of protest constitute a fourth set. Finally, we offer propositions associated with the relation between master frames and the decline of cycles of protest.

Master Frames and the Emergence of Cycles of Protest

Our fundamental argument is that framing activity and the resultant ideational webs that some movements spin or that emerge from the coalescence of collective action can also be crucial to the emergence and course of a cycle of protest. Since people do not act collectively without "good reason," to assert a linkage between master frames and cycles of protest may seem almost true by definition. Yet, just as the function of ideational elements and framing activity has not been given sufficient analytic attention by much SMO research, so it has been neglected at the macrolevel of cycles of protest. In his initial discussion of the characteristics of cycles of protest, for example, Tarrow (1983) makes only passing references to the role of mobilizing ideas and meanings in relation to the rise and decline of cycles.[6] Here we are not asserting such a linkage, but suggesting that master frames constitute an additional defining feature of cycles of protest. Thus, our orienting proposition, *Proposition 1: Associated with the emergence of a cycle of protest is the development or construction of an innovative master frame.*

The peace movement, as a movement industry, provides concrete illustration of this linkage. Randall Forsberg's proposal for a freeze on the development, testing, and deployment of nuclear weapons emerged, in 1980, as an innovative master frame that stimulated a dramatic upswing in peace movement activity throughout the first half of the decade. Previous attempts to revive the dormant peace movement had failed to generate mass mobilization. By 1963, the grim specter of nuclear holocaust had faded from the public spotlight, spawning only sporadic protests for the ensuing seventeen years (Boyer 1984), despite the fact that global strategic nuclear arsenals increased by more than eightfold during the period (Sivard 1982, 11).

Capitalizing on the bellicose rhetoric of the newly installed Reagan administration and NATO plans to deploy a new generation of nuclear weapons in Western Europe, the freeze movement amplified the severity and urgency of the nuclear threat. But it was the development of an innovative master frame that went beyond a diagnosis to include an original prognosis and a clear call to action that accounts in part for the reemergence of peace movement activity in the eighties. A bilateral, verifiable freeze provided what many felt had been *the* missing ingredient: a simple but concrete solution to the nuclear predicament (Benford 1988, 252). Hundreds of thousands of previously passive citizens were mobilized. They took to the streets in record numbers, organized lobbying campaigns, held community referenda, revived old peace organizations, and established hundreds of new ones.

These observations not only underscore the linkage between a master frame and the clustering of collective action but also suggest that in the absence of such a frame, all other things being equal, mass mobilization is unlikely. Thus, *Proposition 2: The failure of mass mobilization when structural conditions seem otherwise ripe may be accounted for in part by the absence of a resonant master frame.*

We noted above that the peace movement failed to generate mass mobilization throughout the 1970s, despite the fact that conditions appeared to be conducive. More specifically, the objective conditions—such as global militarism, wars, and relatively unabated increases in nuclear weapons stockpiles, as well as structural conditions including society's resource base, political opportunity structures, and organizational infrastructures—do not appear to have been any less facilitative of peace movement activity in 1975 than they were in 1980. What was lacking in the 1970s, however, was a resonant master frame that was subsequently provided by the nuclear weapons freeze campaign.

Master Frames and Specific Movements within a Cycle

If the foregoing set of propositions holds, it logically follows that at what point a specific SMO emerges within a cycle of protest affects the substance and latitude of its training efforts. Thus, *Proposition 3: Movements that surface early in a cycle of protest are likely to function as progenitors of master frames that provide the ideational and interpretive anchoring for subsequent movements within the cycle.* Let us return to the cycle of activity associated with the peace movement in the 1980s to illustrate this proposition.

Any number of problematic events or issues could have provided the impetus for a revival of peace movement action. International confrontations, border disputes, interventionism, militarism, chemical and biological weapons developments, apartheid, and institutional and structural violence—any could have rekindled the peace movement. Yet the reemergence of peace activity in the 1980s was associated almost solely with the nuclear threat. As already suggested, this is attributable in part to the development of the freeze concept as a master frame.

The freeze campaign framed war and peace issues in a narrow and highly compart-

mentalized fashion. Rather than addressing the structural roots of international conflict— superpower relations, the weaknesses of international peacekeeping institutions, and the lack of nonviolent alternatives to resolving disputes between sovereign states—the freeze defined the problem in technical terms. The ever-increasing size and destructive capacities of the United States' and the Soviet Union's nuclear arsenals constituted a threat to be controlled; the idea of a nuclear freeze offered a technological solution. Most peace movement organizations followed the freeze campaign's lead and focused attention almost exclusively on "stopping hardware" (Solo 1985, 10)—on preventing the testing, production, and development of particular weapon systems that the movement considered to be the most dangerous, the most likely to increase the probability of a nuclear war.

In light of such observations, the obverse proposition is suggested. *Proposition 4: Movements that emerge later in the cycle will typically find their framing efforts constrained by the previously elaborated master frame.* Returning to the foregoing illustration, not all peace groups went along with the freeze campaign's narrow focus. National peace coalitions and traditional pacifist organizations sought to expand the boundaries of the freeze frame to encompass other peace issues and social problems. But these frame extension efforts failed to elicit popular support and were often met by staunch resistance from freeze campaign activists. Rancorous frame disputes ensued between single-issue and multi-issue groups (Benford 1989).

The foregoing set of propositions can be further illustrated with reference to the civil rights movement. Its master frame, as initially espoused by Martin Luther King, Jr., and his associates, accented the principle of equal rights and opportunities regardless of ascribed characteristics and articulated it with the goal of integration through nonviolent means. Although there was always some tension among the movement's "big four" organizations (CORE, NAACP, SCLC, and SNCC), each initially proffered frames that were consistent with integrationist goals and nonviolent philosophy. By the mid-1960s, however, CORE and SNCC shifted their framings from the integrationist and equal rights goals of the movement's master frame to a more radical black power framing. Subsequently, both organizations suffered declines in contributions and support from both external sources and constituents, in large part because of their deviation from the movement's master frame (McAdam 1982, 181–229).

Such observations suggest that though master frames do not necessarily determine the framings of SMOS that emerge later in a cycle, they do exercise considerable constraint on the content of these framings. In addition, these observations and corollary propositions point to a central reason for conflict and factionalization among SMOS within a cycle of protest. Once a movement's collective action frame has become established as the master frame, efforts to extend its ideational scope may encounter resistance from its progenitors and guardians, as well as from external supporters. In turn, deviations from the master frame may be labeled as heresy and evoke social control responses from the movement's core supporters.

Master Frames and Tactical Repertoires within a Cycle of Protest

We noted earlier that master frames not only punctuate and encode reality but also function as modes of attribution and articulation. In light of these observations, it is reasonable to suggest that the tactical derivations and choices within a cycle of protest are affected in part by the movement's master frame. A master frame implies both new ways of interpreting a situation as well as novel means of dealing with or confronting it. Hence, *Proposition 5: Tactical innovation is spawned in part by the emergence of new master frames.*

A brief examination of the emergent tactical repertoire of the civil rights movement illustrates this proposition. As already noted, the movement's leaders fashioned a master frame that articulated the ideal of equal rights and opportunities regardless of ascribed characteristics. Jim Crow laws and segregationist practices prevalent throughout the South were targeted as blatant symbolic representations of prejudice and discrimination. Tactics such as the bus boycotts and lunch counter sit-ins were developed and deployed as a means of directly challenging Jim Crow, in part by creating within specific communities a "crisis definition of the situation" (McAdam 1983, 743). Although these tactics were not the invention of the civil rights movement, this was the first time they had been applied in those settings for that cause. The freedom rides, however, were the movement's own tactical creation. Like the boycotts and sit-ins, the freedom rides created a "crisis situation" by dramatizing for the entire nation the substance of the claims articulated by the civil rights movement's master frame (McAdam 1983, 745).

Each of these tactical innovations was congruent with the master frame espoused by King and other civil rights leaders and thus flowed directly from the movement's nonviolent philosophy. Other tactical choices, such as riots, robbery, sabotage, and violence, were eschewed by nearly all the movement's organizations and participants until the mid-1960s.

These observations further underscore the relation between master frames and tactical repertoires within a cycle of protest.

Hence, *Proposition 6: Movement tactics are not solely a function of environmental constraints and adaptations, but are also constrained by anchoring master frames.* In his research on "the pace of black insurgency," McAdam (1983) concludes that the civil rights movement's internal organizational and external political opportunity structures contributed to the development of innovative protest tactics and their diffusion. Moreover, he found that as rapidly as the movement devised new tactics that were effective, its opponents developed counter measures that neutralized the tactical inventions, prompting movement leaders to devise additional novel methods of protest. We do not take exception with these conclusions, but we do suggest that movement tactics are facilitated or constrained not only by the political environment and opponents' adaptation but also by master frames.

Master frames can exercise constraining influence on the development of tactics in two ways. First, the development or use of tactics that are inconsistent with the diagnostic and prognostic components of a movement's master frame as well as with constituency values is unlikely. If movement action is inconsistent with the values it espouses or with its constituents' values, it renders its framing efforts vulnerable to dismissal.

As we indicated above, the development of nonviolent philosophy and strategy by the civil rights movement precluded the use of violent tactics. A similar observation can be made with respect to the peace movement and its nonviolent philosophy. A stark example of the movement's sensitivity to such constraints occurred in the summer of 1985. Just prior to the movement's annual pilgrimage to Pantex (a facility near Amarillo, Texas, where all U.S. nuclear weapons are assembled), a disarmament activist removed several feet of track from the railway artery serving the facil-

ity. His actions and subsequent arrest were widely publicized. Although organizers of the peace pilgrimage publicly condemned the protester's tactics, their coalition's reputation and credibility were damaged. The fact that his actions had jeopardized lives contradicted the movement's most frequently amplified value and indeed its master frame. Few outside the movement, including most media representatives, differentiated the actions of the lone protester from the peace coalition (Benford 1987).

The second way in which a movement's master frame can constrain tactical evolution depends on the extent to which the frame is restricted or elaborated. The more restricted the movement's master frame the narrower the range of tactical options. In contrast, movements associated with highly elaborated master frames are likely to have greater discretion regarding tactical choices.

Again, the peace movement serves to illustrate this corollary proposition. We previously suggested that the freeze constituted a highly restricted master frame. Its prognosis, a mutual, verifiable agreement between the United States and the Soviet Union, implied the use of traditional political tactics, including lobbying members of Congress to encourage them to vote for the freeze resolution and against specific weapons bills, voting in local freeze referenda, and casting votes for and contributing to pro-freeze candidates. Other tactical choices, particularly acts of civil disobedience targeting defense contractors, were initially ruled out by the movement's mainstream activists and supporters.

Master Frames and the Shape of Cycles of Protest

Thus far we have discussed the relations among master frames and the emergence of cycles of protest, specific movements within those cycles, and their tactical repertoires. We now turn to the relation between master frames and the shape of protest cycles once they have emerged. Shape can be conceptualized in terms of two dimensional axes in which the vertical axis represents the cycle's ecological scope and the horizontal indicates its temporal span. By ecological scope, we refer to the diffusion of movement activity across different population and organizational sectors of society. Temporal span simply refers to the duration of a cycle of protest.

We have noted that one way in which master frames vary is in terms of their relative potency, and we conceptualized potency in terms of its elaborative potential and resonant capacity. We now integrate these observations with the conceptualization of shape by offering two additional propositions. The first concerns the general relation between potency and shape. Thus, *Proposition 7: The shape of a cycle of protest is in part a function of the mobilizing potency of the anchoring frame.*

The civil rights movement provides concrete illustration of this proposition. Because of its considerable elaborative and resonant qualities, it is a national movement that, conceptualized broadly, has spanned several decades. More specifically, its punctuation and accentuation of the idea of equal rights and opportunities amplified a fundamental American value that resonated with diverse elements of American society and thus lent itself to extensive elaboration. Movements championing women, the disabled, the aged, and American Indians, among others, were empowered in part by the civil rights master frame. Thus, though the civil rights cycle may have peaked at the height of black insurgency in the mid- to late-1960s, the cycle's ecological scope and temporal span have extended well beyond the 1960s and the plight of black Americans.

The peace movement provides further illustrative material bearing on the relation between a cycle's shape and its underlying master frame. It is our sense that the shape of the most recent cycle of peace activity in the United States is considerably different front that of the civil rights movement. The reasons are twofold. First, as we have argued elsewhere (Snow and Benford 1988), the freeze master frame lacked the same degree of empirical credibility, experiential commensurability, and narrative fidelity, thus limiting its ecological scope in comparison to the civil rights movement. And second, the highly restrictive nature of the freeze master frame limited its potential for elaboration. We suspect that the cycle's eventual decline was attributable, in part, to proponents' failure to amplify the freeze frame in more resonant and innovative ways.

In light of this observation, it follows that the shape of a cycle is not only a function of a master frame's potency; it can also be affected by the framing work of SMOS within a cycle. Hence, *Proposition 8: The shape of a cycle of protest is in part a function of the capacity of incipient movements within the cycle to amplify and extend the master frame in imaginative and yet resonant ways.*

This proposition alerts us to the fact that, whatever the elaborative potential of a master frame, it does not necessarily follow that it will be amplified and extended in ways that broaden the cycle's scope. Thus, the flowering of movements such as those associated with women, Chicanos, American Indians, the aged, and the disabled on the heels of the black movement was precipitated in part by the extension of the principle of equal rights and opportunities from the domain of black America to the situation of the other groups. The obvious implication of this extension of the early civil rights master frame has been the expansion of the cycle's ecological scope and temporal span.

Master Frames and the Decline of Cycles of Protest

In our first set of propositions we suggested that a crucial factor contributing to the emergence of a cycle of protest or, conversely, the failure of mass mobilization when structural conditions appear otherwise conducive is the presence or absence of a resonant master frame. If master frames are as useful as we suggest in facilitating the emergence of protest cycles, it stands to reason that they should also contribute to understanding the decline of cycles of protest. Hence, *Proposition 9: The decline or withering of an extant cycle of protest is due in part to changes in the prevailing cultural climate that render the anchoring master frame impotent.* Here we are suggesting that events can sometimes begin to pass by or overwhelm a master frame and thus erode its empirical credibility or its experiential relevance.

The decline of earlier cycles of peace movement activity is illustrative. Prior to both world wars, peace movement membership, organization, support, and activity swelled to unprecedented levels (Chatfield 1971, 1973; DeBenedetti 1980; Marchand 1972; Wittner 1969). Between 1901 and 1914, forty-five new peace organizations were established in the United States (DeBenedetti 1980, 70). Its traditional pacifist ranks expanded to include "an impressive number of the nation's political, business, religious, and academic leaders" (Marchand 1972, ix). Similarly, during the decade preceding World War II, peace activism and campaigns achieved new heights. By the mid-1930s, antiwar strikes and other demonstrations on campuses became commonplace (Wittner 1969).

In each instance, the outbreak of war reduced the movement to its pacifist core. World War I undercut peace adherents' "faith in human reason, progress, Christianity, Great Power harmony, and the need for a working peacekeeping mechanism" (DeBenedetti 1980, 79). Likewise, the rise of fascism, the onset of the Holocaust, and Pearl Harbor provided most peace adherents and sympathizers with a seemingly insurmountable challenge to the credibility of the movement's master frame. Consequently, by 1941 Americans "renounced pacifism with the same fervor with which they had previously renounced war" (Wittner 1969, 16).

Although the foregoing discussion illustrates that cycles can decline owing to changes in the cultural or political environment, their demise can also be explained in part by the emergence of frames that challenge or compete with the movement's master frame. The debates that ensue and the very existence of competing frames can chip away at the mobilizing potency of the original master frame. In light of such contingencies, we offer a final proposition. *Proposition 10: The emergence of competing frames can suggest the vulnerabilities and irrelevance of the anchoring master frame, thus challenging its resonance and rendering it increasingly impotent.*

The cycle of peace movement activity that emerged in the aftermath of World War II provides an illustration of this proposition. The gruesome effects of the war and the development of the atomic bomb led many pacifists and peace adherents to the conclusion that world government offered the only hope for the survival of our species. Although the notion of world government had been a persistent theme of earlier cycles of peace movement activity, it had constituted only one of many planks in the peace movement's platform. Following the war, however, world government emerged as a potent master frame, one that engendered widespread popular support (DeBenedetti 1980; Wittner 1969).

Its potency was short-lived, however. World government soon elicited competing frames from within the peace movement.

"What the world needed," countered some traditional pacifists, "was not more authority at the top, but rather greater cooperation of peoples at the bottom in solving their mutual problems" (Wittner 1969, 179). This and other competing frames underscored for many the weaknesses of world government as a panacea for problems pertaining to war and peace. Many peace activists subsequently defected from the world government movement.

If the internal attacks on world government diminished its potency as a master frame, external attacks dealt it a deathblow. By the early 1950s, counterframing efforts led by Senator Joseph McCarthy successfully equated world government with communism (DeBenedetti 1980; Wittner 1969). In the face of such resonant frames, individuals and peace organizations could no longer afford to be associated with world government advocacy. The movement subsequently dissociated itself from the master frame, and thereafter world government remained, at best, marginal to the peace movement. Lacking a potent master frame, the peace movement suffered a period of decline.

The fifth set of propositions could just as easily have been illustrated with reference to any number of other movements. But the foregoing discussion suffices to show that extant master frames can either lose their interpretive salience owing to the profusion of events and the proliferation of alternative framings or be neutralized by the repressive tactics of more powerful groups, or both. Hence, the mobilizing potency of the master frame begins to dissipate, and the cycle with which it has been associated begins to decline.

Conclusion

In the preceding pages we have explored the relation between master frames and cycles of protest by enumerating ten intercon-

nected propositions. Basing our argument on our contention that SMOS function as, among other things, signifying or framing agents actively engaged in the production of meaning and ideas, we have suggested that the products of this framing activity, which we refer to as collective action frames, can sometimes come to function as master algorithms that color and constrain the orientations and activities of other movements associated with it ecologically and temporally. Simply put, we have argued that master frames affect the cyclicity and clustering of social movement activity.

Although we realize that some scholars may take issue with the illustrative case materials employed, we reiterate that our objective here has been primarily theoretical, and, as such, we view this exercise as a springboard for systematic empirical investigation. Assessment of the analytic utility of this essay is contingent on future investigations.

Empirical reservations notwithstanding, we think several important implications flow from our conceptual framework. First, our scheme provides the conceptual tools for systematically examining the relation between existing ideologies and challenges to them and their dialectical relationship in a fashion consistent with Gramsci (1971) and Rude (1980), who, among others, regard ideational factors as important variables in the collective action equation.

A second implication pertains to ongoing sociological concern with the relation between micro- and macrostructural phenomena. Specifically, we have detailed theoretically how framing activity at the level of social movement organizations and actors can have significant implications for macrostructural phenomena such as cycles of protest.

Finally, our theoretical formulation complements and supplements resource mobilization and other structuralist perspectives in at least three ways. For one thing, the framing process and the concepts of collective action frames and master frames provide a basis for understanding the process through which collective action is inspired and legitimated. Second, these conceptual tools enable us to examine empirically rather than take for granted the process through which events and actions come to be regarded as desirable or undesirable, more or less costly, and more or less risky. And last, the analysis suggests that framing issues and processes can play an important role in affecting political opportunities, changes in the larger political environment, and the availability of resources.

ACKNOWLEDGMENTS

We are indebted to Bill Gamson, Aldon Morris, Carol Mueller, William Sewell, Jr., and Sydney Tarrow for their insightful comments and suggestions. An expanded version of this chapter was translated into Italian and published in *Polis: Ricerche Estudisn Societa E Politica in Italia* 3 (April 1989): 5–40.

NOTES

1. In attempting to illuminate the relation between master frames and cycles of protest, we focus almost exclusively on interpretive factors to the neglect of other variables such as social structure. This does not mean that we regard the latter as unimportant, nor do we seek to supplant structural explanations with an ideational framework. Rather, our purpose is to augment structuralist perspectives by calling attention to a set of heretofore neglected factors we see as crucial to developing a more thoroughgoing understanding of the ecological and temporal clustering of social movement activity.

2. Our discussion is informed by the extensive literature in social psychology on attribution theory (Crittenden 1983; Hastie 1984; Heider 1958; Jones et al. 1972; Jones and Nisbet 1971; Kelley 1967, 1971, 1972; Kelley and Michela 1980; Stryker and Gottlieb 1981) as well as by the application of attribution theory to social movement conversion processes and experiences (Snow and Machalek 1983, 1984).

3. The term *psychosalvational* was initially used by Wallis (1979) as a cover term for the array of religious and secular movements promising "individual or psycho-spiritual development and self-realization."

4. The issue here is not whether diagnostic and prognostic claims are actually factual or valid, but whether their empirical referents lend themselves to being read as "real" indicators of the claims. When they are, then the claims have empirical credibility. Although this is obviously an interpretive issue, we suspect that it is easier to construct an evidential base for some claims than for others.

5. We have designated our preliminary statements regarding the relation between master frames and cycles of protest as "illustrative" or "sensitizing" propositions so as to differentiate our assertions from more formal propositions. Although each proposition is empirically grounded in our various fieldwork experiences and observations, we do not consider them immutable components of a unified theory. Rather, we offer them as sensitizing propositions, analogous to Blumer's (1969) notion of "sensitizing concepts," to suggest and inspire questions researchers might pursue.

6. He has since incorporated ideational and framing considerations into his discussion of protest cycles (see Tarrow 1989).

REFERENCES

Bateson, Gregory. 1972. *Steps to an Ecology of the Mind.* San Francisco: Chandler.

Benford, Robert D. 1987. "Framing Activity, Meaning, and Social Movement Participation: The Nuclear Disarmament Movement." Ph.D. diss., University of Texas–Austin.

———. 1988. "The Nuclear Disarmament Movement." In *The Nuclear Cage: A Sociology of the Arms Race,* ed. Lester R. Kurtz. Englewood Cliffs, N.J.: Prentice-Hall, 237–65.

———. 1989. "Framing Disputes within the Nuclear Disarmament Movement." Paper presented at the annual meetings of the Midwest Sociological Society, St. Louis.

Bernstein, Basil. 1970. "A Socio-Linguistic Approach to Socialization." In *Directions in Socio-Linguistics,* ed. J. Gumperz and D. Hymes. New York: Holt, Rinehart, and Winston.

———. 1971. *Class, Codes and Control.* London: Routledge and Kegan Paul.

Blumer, Herbert. 1951. "Collective Behavior." In *Principles of Sociology,* ed. A. M. Lee. New York: Barnes and Noble, 99–121.

———. 1969. *Symbolic Interactionism.* Englewood Cliffs, N.J.: Transaction.

Borhek, James T., and Richard F. Curtis. 1975. *A Sociology of Belief.* New York: Wiley.

Boyer, Paul. 1984. "From Activism to Apathy: The American People and Nuclear Weapons, 1963–1980." *Journal of American History* 70, no. 4:821–44.

Chatfield, Charles. 1971. *For Peace and Justice: Pacifism in America, 1914–1941.* Knoxville: University of Tennessee Press.

———, ed. 1973. *Peace Movements in America.* New York: Schocken.

Cone, Edward T. 1968. *Musical Form and Performance.* New York: Norton.

Converse, Philip E. 1964. "The Nature of Belief Systems in Mass Publics." In *Ideology and Discontent,* ed. David Apter. New York: Free Press, 206–61.

Crittenden, Kathleen S. 1983. "Sociological Aspects of Attribution." *Annual Review of Sociology* 9:425–46.

DeBenedetti, Charles. 1980. *The Peace Reform in American History.* Bloomington: Indiana University Press.

Della Porta, Donatella, and Sidney Tarrow. 1986. "Unwanted Children: Political Violence and the Cycle of Protest in Italy, 1966–1973." *European Journal of Political Research* 14:607–32.

Eisinger, Peter K. 1973. "The Conditions of Protest Behavior in American Cities." *American Political Science Review* 67:11–28.

Ferree, Myra Marx, and Frederick D. Miller. 1985. "Mobilization and Meaning: Toward an Integration of Social Psychological and Resource Mobilization Perspectives on Social Movements." *Sociological Inquiry* 55:38–51.

Fisher, Walter R. 1984. "Narration as a Human Communication Paradigm: The Case of Public Moral Argument." *Communication Monographs* 51:1–23.

Gamson, William A. 1988. "Political Discourse and Collective Action." *International Social Movement Research* 1:219–44.

Gamson, William A., Bruce Fireman, and Steven Rytina. 1982. *Encounters with Unjust Authority.* Homewood, Ill.: Dorsey Press.

Gans, Herbert J. 1979. *Deciding What's News: A Study of CBS Evening News, NBC Nightly News, Newsweek and Time.* New York: Pantheon.

Gitlin, Todd. 1980. *The Whole World Is Watching.* Berkeley: University of California Press.

Goffman, Erving. 1974. *Frame Analysis: An Essay on the Organization of Experience.* New York: Harper.

Gramsci, Antonio. 1971. *Selections from the Prison Notebooks of Antonio Gramsci,* ed. A. Hoare and G. N. Smith. New York: International Publishers.

Hall, Stuart. 1982. "The Rediscovery of Ideology: Return of the Repressed in Media Studies." In *Culture, Society and the Media,* ed. Michael Gurevitch, Tony Bennett, James Curran, and Janet Woollacott. New York: Methuen, 56–90.

Hastie, Reid. 1981. "Schematic Principles in Human Memory." In *Social Cognition: The Ontario Symposium on Personality and Social Psychology,* ed. E. Tory Higgins, C. Peter Herman, and Mark P. Zanna. Hillsdale, N.J.: Erlbaum, 39–88.

———. 1984. "Causes and Effects of Causal Attribution." *Journal of Personality and Social Psychology* 46:788–98.

Heider, Fritz. 1958. *The Psychology of Interpersonal Relations.* New York: Wiley.

Jenkins, J. Craig. 1983. "Resource Mobilization Theory and the Study of Social Movements." *Annual Review of Sociology* 9:527–53.

Jenkins, J. Craig, and Charles Perrow. 1977. "Insurgency of the Powerless: Farm Worker Movements." *American Sociological Review* 42:249–68.

Jones, Edward E., D. E. Kanouse, Harold H. Kelley, Richard E. Nisbet, S. Valins, and B. Weiner, eds. 1972. *Attribution: Perceiving the Causes of Behavior.* Morristown, N.J.: General Learning Press.

Jones, Edward E., and Richard Nisbet. 1971. *The Actor and the Observer: Divergent Perspectives on the Causes of Behavior.* Morristown, N.J.: General Learning Press.

Kelley, Harold H. 1967. "Attribution Theory in Social Psychology." *Nebraska Symposium on Motivation* 15:192–238.

———. 1971. *Attribution in Social Interaction.* Morristown, N.J.: General Learning Press.

———. 1972. *Causal Schemata and the Attribution Process.* Morristown, N.J.: General Learning Press.

Kelley, Harold H., and John L. Michela. 1980. "Attribution Theory and Research." *Annual Review of Psychology* 31:457–501.

Klandermans, Bert. 1984. "Mobilization and Participation: Social-Psychological Expansions of Resource Mobilization Theory." *American Sociological Review* 49:583–600.

Klapp, Orrin E. 1972. *Currents of Unrest: An Introduction to Collective Behavior.* New York: Holt, Rinehart and Winston.

Lipsky, Michael. 1970. *Protest in City Politics.* Chicago: Rand McNally.

Lofland, John. 1985. *Protest: Studies of Collective Behavior and Social Movements.* New Brunswick, N.J.: Transaction Books.

Marchand, C. Roland. 1972. *The American Peace Movement and Social Reform, 1898–1918.* Princeton: Princeton University Press.

Marcus, Hazel, and Robert B. Zajonc. 1985. "The Cognitive Perspective in Social Psychology." In *The Handbook of Social Psychology,* ed. Gardner Lindzey and Elliot Aronson. New York: Random House, 127–230.

McAdam, Doug. 1982. *Political Process and the Development of Black Insurgency, 1930–1970.* Chicago: University of Chicago Press.

———. 1983. "Tactical Innovation and the Pace of Insurgency." *American Sociological Review* 48:735–54.

McCarthy, John D., and Mayer N. Zald. 1977. "Resource Mobilization and Social Movements: A Partial Theory." *American Journal of Sociology* 82:1212–41.

Mills, C. Wright. 1940. "Situated Actions and Vocabularies of Motive." *American Sociological Review* 5:404–13.

Minsky, M. 1975. "A Framework for Presenting Knowledge." In *The Psychology of Computer Vision,* ed. P. A. Winston. New York: McGraw-Hill.

Moore, Barrington. 1978. *Injustice: The Social Bases of Obedience and Revolt.* White Plains, N.Y.: Sharpe.

Morris, Aldon D. 1984. *The Origins of the Civil Rights Movement.* New York: Free Press.

Neisser, U. 1976. *Cognition and Reality: Principles and Implications of Cognitive Psychology.* San Francisco: Freeman.

Oberschall, Anthony. 1973. *Social Conflict and Social Movements.* Englewood Cliffs, N.J.: Prentice-Hall.

Piaget, J. 1954. *The Construction of Reality in the Child.* New York: Basic Books.

Piven, Frances Fox, and Richard Cloward. 1977. *Poor People's Movements.* New York: Pantheon.

Rude, George. 1980. *Ideology and Popular Protest.* New York: Knopf.

Shorter, Edward, and Charles Tilly. 1974. *Strikes in France, 1830–1968.* Cambridge: Cambridge University Press.

Sivard, Ruth Leger. 1982. *World Military and Social Expenditures, 1982.* Leesburg, Va.: World Priorities.

Smelser, Neil. 1963. *Theory of Collective Behavior.* New York: Free Press.

Snow, David A., and Robert D. Benford. 1988. "Ideology, Frame Resonance, and Participant Mobilization." *International Social Movement Research* 1:197–217.

Snow, David A., and Richard Machalek. 1984. "The Sociology of Conversion." *Annual Review of Sociology* 10:367–80.

Snow, David A., E. Burke Rochford, Jr., Steven K. Worden, and Robert D. Benford. 1986. "Frame Alignment Process, Micromobilization, and Movement Participation." *American Sociological Review* 51:464–81.

Snow, David A., Louis A. Zurcher, and Sheldon Ekland-Olson. 1980. "Social Networks and Social Movements: A Microstructural Approach to Differential Recruitment." *American Sociological Review* 45:787–801.

Solo, Pam. 1985. "A New Atlantic Alliance: European and American Peace Movement Participation." *Disarmament Campaigns* 49 (November):10.

Stryker, Sheldon, and Avi Gottlieb. 1981. "Attribution Theory and Symbolic Interactionism: A Comparison." In *New Directions in Attribution Research,* vol. 3, ed. J. H. Harvey, W. Ickes, and R. F. Kidd. Hillsdale, N. J.: Erlbaum, 25–58.

Tarrow, Sidney. 1983. *Struggling to Reform: Social Movements and Policy Change during Cycles of Protest.* Ithaca, N.Y.: Western Societies Program, Cornell University.

———. 1989. *Struggle, Politics, and Reform: Collective Action, Social Movements, and Cycles of Protest.* Ithaca, N.Y.: Western Societies Program, Cornell University.

Tilly, Charles. 1978. *From Mobilization to Revolution.* Reading, Mass.: Addison-Wesley.

Tilly, Charles, Louise Tilly, and Richard Tilly. 1975. *The Rebellious Century, 1830–1930.* Cambridge, Mass.: Harvard University Press.

Tuchman, Gaye. 1978. *Making News: A Study in the Construction of Reality.* New York: Free Press.

Turner, Ralph H. 1969. "The Theme of Contemporary Social Movements." *British Journal of Sociology* 20:390–405.

Turner, Ralph H., and Lewis M. Killian. 1987. *Collective Behavior.* 3d ed. Englewood Cliffs, N.J.: Prentice-Hall.

Wallis, Roy. 1979. "Varieties of Psychosalvation." *New Society* 20:649–51.

Wittgenstein, Ludwig. 1967 [1953]. *Philosophical Investigations,* trans. G. Anscombe. Oxford: Blackwell.

Wittner, Lawrence S. 1969. *Rebels against War: The American Peace Movement, 1941–1960.* New York: Columbia University Press.

Zurcher, Louis A., and David A. Snow. 1981. "Collective Behavior: Social Movements." In *Social Psychology: Sociological Perspectives,* ed. Morris Rosenberg and Ralph H. Turner. New York: Basic Books, 447–82.

29

CULTURE AND SOCIAL MOVEMENTS

DOUG MCADAM

Over the past two decades, the study of social movements has been among the most productive and intellectually lively subfields within sociology. But, as with all emergent paradigms, the recent renaissance in social movement studies has highlighted certain aspects of the phenomenon while ignoring others. Specifically, the dominance, within the United States, of the "resource mobilization" and "political process" perspectives has privileged the political, organizational, and network/structural aspects of social movements while giving the more cultural or ideational dimensions of collective action short shrift.

From a sociology of knowledge perspective, the recent ignorance of the more cultural aspects of social movements is the result of the rejection of the classical collective behavior paradigm, which emphasized the role of shared beliefs and identities but whose hints of irrationality and pathology (Klapp 1969; Lang and Lang 1961; Smelser 1962) made it unattractive to a new generation of scholars whose own experiences led them to view social movements as a form of rational political action. Whatever the reason, the absence of any real emphasis on ideas, ideology, or identity has created, within the United States, a strong "rationalist" and "structural" bias in the current literature on social movements. At the most macro level of analysis, social movements are seen to emerge in response to the

From *New Social Movements,* edited by E. Laraña, Hank Johnston, and Joseph R. Gusfield. Reprinted by permission of Temple University Press.

"expansion in political opportunities" that grant formal social movement organizations (SMOs) and movement entrepreneurs the opportunity to engage in successful "resource mobilization." At the micro level, individuals are drawn into participation not by the force of the ideas or even individual attitudes but as the result of their embeddedness in associational networks that render them "structurally available" for protest activity. Until recently, "culture," in all of its manifestations, was rarely invoked by American scholars as a force in the emergence and development of social movements. The renewed interest in the topic has been spurred, in part, by the European "new social movement" perspective, which has made cultural and cognitive factors central to the study of social movements (Brand 1990; Eyerman and Jamison 1991; Melucci 1985, 1989).

This chapter broadens the discourse among movement scholars by focusing on some of the links between culture and social movements. Specifically, I address three broad topics: the cultural roots of social movements, the emergence and development of distinctive "movement cultures," and the cultural consequences of social movements.

The Cultural Roots of Social Movements

The "structural bias" in movement studies is most evident in recent American work on the emergence of social movements and revolutions. With but a few exceptions, recent theorizing on the question has located the roots of social movements in some set of political, economic, or organizational factors. While acknowledging the importance of such factors, I add cultural factors and processes to this list as important constraints or facilitators of collective action. There are three distinct ways in which culture can be said to facilitate movement emergence.

Framing as an Act of Cultural Appropriation

Drawing on the work of Erving Goffman (1974), David Snow and various of his colleagues (Snow et al. 1986; Snow and Benford 1988) have developed the concept of "frame alignment processes" to describe the efforts by which organizers seek to join the cognitive orientations of individuals with those of social movement organizations. The task is to propound a view of the world that both legitimates and motivates protest activity. The success of such efforts is determined, in part, by the *cultural resonance* of the frames advanced by organizers. In this sense, framing efforts can be thought of as acts of cultural appropriation, with movement leaders seeking to tap highly resonant ideational strains in mainstream society (or in a particular target subculture) as a way of galvanizing activism.

Much has been made of Martin Luther King, Jr.'s use of Gandhian nonviolence as an ideological cornerstone of the civil rights movement. In fact, King's interest in and advocacy of Gandhi's philosophy was largely irrelevant to the rapid emergence and spread of the civil rights struggle. Far more significant was King's appropriation and powerful evocation of highly resonant cultural themes, not only in the southern black Baptist tradition, but in American political culture more generally.

Consider King's "I have a Dream" speech. Juxtaposing the poetry of the scriptural prophets—"I have a dream that every valley shall be exalted, every hill and mountain shall be made low"—with the lyrics of patriotic anthems—"This will be the day when all of God's children will be able to sing with new meaning, 'My country 'tis of thee, sweet land of liberty, of thee I sing'"—King's oration reappropriated that classic strand of the American tradition that understands the true meaning of freedom to lie in the affirmation of responsibility for uniting all of the diverse members of society into a just social order. (Bellah et al. 1985, 249)

Indeed, this was King's unique genius: to frame civil rights activity in a way that resonated not only with the culture of the oppressed but with the culture of the oppressor as well. King successfully mobilized Southern blacks while he generated considerable sympathy and support for the movement among whites as well.

The student democracy movement in Beijing in the spring of 1989 also drew on deeply resonant cultural themes and traditions in the early days of the struggle. The initial march on April 27 that stimulated the movement was ostensibly organized to mark and mourn the death of former premier Hu Yaobang. Such public displays of respect and veneration for departed leaders (and the dead more generally) have deep roots in Chinese political culture. By framing the march as an act of public mourning, movement organizers appropriated long-standing cultural symbols in the service of the movement. This helps explain both the large size of the initial march and the surprising restraint exercised by Communist party leaders in dealing with the students. The cultural legitimacy that attached to the march encouraged participation while constraining official efforts at social control.

Expanding Cultural Opportunities as a Stimulus to Action

Scholars such as Charles Tilly (1978), Sidney Tarrow (1994), Doug McAdam (1982), Theda Skocpol (1979), Jack Goldstone (1991), Hanspeter Kriesi (1990), and Herbert Kitschelt (1986), among others, have established the notion that social movements/ revolutions often emerge in response to an expansion in the "political opportunities" available to a particular challenging group. The argument is that movements are less the product of meso level mobilization efforts than they are the beneficiaries of the increasing political vulnerability or receptivity of their opponents or of the political and economic system as a whole.

Although I generally concur with this view, I think it betrays a "structural" or "objectivist" bias in many of its specific formulations. It is extremely hard to separate these objective shifts in political opportunities from the subjective processes of social construction and collective attribution that render them meaningful. In other words, "expanding political opportunities . . . do not, in any simple sense, produce a social movement. . . . [Instead] they only offer insurgents a certain objective 'structural potential' for collective political action. Mediating between opportunity and action are people and the subjective meanings they attach to their situations" (McAdam 1982, 48).

The causal importance of expanding political opportunities, then, is inseparable from the collective definitional processes by which the meaning of these shifts is assigned and disseminated. Given this linkage, the movement analyst has two tasks: accounting for the structural factors that have objectively strengthened the challenger's hand, and analyzing the processes by which the meaning and attributed significance of shifting political conditions is assessed. This latter task prompts speculation about the existence and significance of expanding cultural opportunities in the emergence of collective action. By "expanding cultural opportunities" we have in mind specific events or processes that are likely to stimulate the kind of collective framing efforts mentioned above. A close reading of the historical literature on social movements suggests that framing efforts may be set in motion by at least four distinct types of expanding cultural opportunities.

Ideological or Cultural Contradictions

The first type of cultural opportunity involves any event or set of events that dramatize a glaring contradiction between a highly resonant cultural value and conventional social practices. Many such examples can be found in the social movement literature. For example, the contrast between the egalitarian rhetoric and the sexist practices of the early American abolitionist movement have long been regarded as an important impetus in the development of the nineteenth-century women's rights movement. As Sara Evans (1980) and others have argued, much the same thing happened in regard to the women's liberation movement of the 1960s and 1970s. In this case, it was the egalitarian rhetoric and forms of sexual discrimination evident within the civil rights movement and the white student Left that fueled the development of a radical feminist "frame" legitimating protest activity.

One final example of the facilitating effect of this kind of ideological or cultural contradiction can be seen in regard to the threatened 1940 march on Washington. A. Philip Randolph, the president of the American Association of Sleeping Car Porters, organized a mass march on Washington to protest discriminatory labor practices in the defense industries. The apparent spur to action in this case was the glaring contradiction between President Franklin D. Roosevelt's growing anti-Nazi rhetoric—especially its "master race" philosophy—and his own tacit acceptance of racial discrimination at home (Fishel and Quarles 1970; Sitkoff 1978).

Suddenly Imposed Grievances Another cognitive stimulus to framing processes comes from what Edward Walsh (1981) has called "suddenly imposed grievances." The term describes those dramatic, highly publicized, and generally unexpected events—human-made disasters, major court decisions, official violence—that increase public awareness of and opposition to previously accepted societal conditions. As an example of this process, Walsh (1981) cites and analyzes the generation of anti-nuclear power activity in the area of Three Mile Island following a 1979 accident there. Bert Useem's (1980) analysis of a movement in Boston during the mid 1970s aimed at stopping the busing of school children to achieve school desegregation leaves little doubt that the resistance was set in motion by a highly publicized court order mandating busing. Harvey Molotch (1970) documents a similar rise in protest activity among residents of Santa Barbara, California, in the wake of a major oil spill that took place in 1969. The initial verdict in the Rodney King beating case (Los Angeles, California, April 1992) is another example of a highly dramatic event spurring protest activity.

Dramatizations of System Vulnerability Another "cultural" or "cognitive opportunity" that may stimulate increased framing and other mobilization efforts are those events or processes that highlight the vulnerability of one's political opponents. For example, the unanimous 1954 U.S. Supreme Court decision in *Brown v. Board of Education* declaring racially segregated schools un-

constitutional convinced many in the black community of the political and legal vulnerability of the southern system of segregation and, in turn, accelerated the pace of civil rights organizing nationwide (Gerber 1962; McAdam 1982).

The collapse of Communist party rule in Poland and the unwillingness of Mikhail Gorbachev to use military force to suppress the Solidarity movement was widely interpreted throughout Eastern Europe as a sign that all Communist regimes in the region were in trouble. This is not to deny the deep structural roots of the crisis in the Soviet Union (see Tarrow 1991), but a crisis needs to be transparent if it is to serve as a cue for collective action. The end of communist rule in Poland served as just such a cue. This pivotal event led, in turn, to increased framing and other mobilization activities by reformers in all of the Warsaw Pact countries.

Finally, the ineffectual 1991 coup attempt by Soviet hard-liners made it clear just how weak and out of touch the once formidable Communist party bosses had become, thus emboldening citizens from across the USSR to step up demands for political independence and economic reform.

The Availability of Master Frames Finally, one other cultural opportunity has the potential to set in motion framing efforts and mobilization more generally. This is the availability of what David Snow and Robert Benford (1988) term "master protest frames" legitimating collective action. Movement scholars continue to err in viewing social movements as discrete social phenomena. Instead, movements tend to cluster in time and space precisely because they are not independent of one another (McAdam and Rucht 1993). To illustrate, the major movements of the 1960s in the United States were not so much independent entities as offshoots of a single broad activist community with its roots squarely in the civil rights movement (McAdam 1988). One of the things that clearly linked the various struggles during this period was the existence of a "master protest frame" that was appropriated by each succeeding insurgent group. The source of this frame was the civil rights movement, but in short order the other major movements of the period used the ideological understandings and cultural symbols of the black struggle as the ideational basis for their efforts as well. Evans (1980) has documented the idealogical/cultural links between the women's liberation and civil rights movements, while Doug McAdam (1988) has done the same for the black struggle and the antiwar and student movements. The ideological imprint of the civil rights movement is also clear in regard to the gay rights, American Indian, farmworkers, and other leftist movements of the period. All of these groups, drawing heavily upon the "civil rights master frame," came to define themselves as victims of discrimination and, as such, deserving of expanded rights and protection under the law. They mapped their understandings of their own situations on the general framework first put forward by civil rights activists.

The same point applies with equal force to other periods of heightened movement activity. The rash of student movements that flourished around the globe (for example, in Spain, Mexico, Japan, France, Italy, Germany, and the United States) in 1968 were clearly attuned to and influenced by one another, resulting in the development and diffusion of a "student left master frame" (Caute 1988; Katsiaficas 1987).

In similar fashion, the success of Solidarity in finally breaking the Communist party's forty-four-year monopoly on power in Poland encouraged other Eastern European dissidents to adopt prodemocracy frames in their own countries. The same

process can be seen in the former Soviet Union, with the success of independence movements in the Baltic states encouraging the rise of ideologically similar ethnic nationalist movements in many of the other former Soviet republics.

The more general theoretical point is that successful framing efforts are almost certain to inspire other groups to reinterpret their situation in light of the available master frame and to mobilize based on their new understanding of themselves and the world around them. Thus, the presence of such a frame constitutes yet another cultural or ideological resource that facilitates movement emergence.

The Role of Long-Standing Activist Subcultures in Movement Emergence

Movement scholars have focused a great deal of attention on the role of existing organizations or associational networks in the emergence of protest activity (Freeman 1973; Gould 1991; McAdam 1982, 1986; Morris 1984; Oberschall 1973; Rosenthal et al. 1985). This literature betrays the "structural bias" of the field as a whole. Virtually all of these authors attribute the importance of prior organization to the concrete organizational resources, that is, leaders, communication networks, and meeting places, that such groups provide. Established organizations, however, are the source of cultural resources as well.

In other words, what is too often overlooked in structural accounts of movement emergence is the extent to which these established organizations/networks are themselves embedded in long-standing activist subcultures capable of sustaining the ideational traditions needed to revitalize activism following a period of movement dormancy. These enduring activist subcultures function as repositories of cultural materials into which succeeding generations of activists can dip to fashion ideologically similar, but chronologically separate, movements. To use Ann Swidler's (1986) term, these subcultures represent the specialized "tool kits" of enduring activist traditions. The presence of these enduring cultural repertoires frees new generations of would-be activists from the necessity of constructing new movement frames from whole cloth. Instead, most new movements rest on the ideational and broader cultural base of ideologically similar past struggles. To assert such continuity is to take issue with certain new social movement theorists (Melucci 1989) who hold that the movements of the 1960s and 1970s represented a total break with past activism. That these movements extended and modified existing activist traditions is undeniable. At the same time, it seems clear that they were initially rooted in the very traditions they subsequently transcended. Examples of these kinds of cross-generational continuities in movement activity are numerous.

In all western industrial nations, for example, the tradition of labor activism has served as a broad cultural template available to succeeding generations of workers as a resource supporting mobilization. In similar fashion, several generations of American peace movements have drawn on a rich pacifist tradition, as nurtured and sustained by a combination of religious denominations (for example, Quakers and Unitarians) and secular-humanist organizations (for example, American Friends Service Committee and Fellowship of Reconciliation). At the other end of the political spectrum, an enduring tradition of anti-immigrant and white Supremacist activism has served as a broad "tool kit" encouraging American right-wing movements over many generations. Finally, in Spain, long-standing separatist traditions in both Catalonia and the Basque region have served as

the wellspring from which several cycles of nationalist movements have flowed (see Johnston, Chapter 11).

Although the role of such long-standing activist subcultures has received little attention in studies of movement emergence, their imprint seems apparent. In his definitive study of the structural origins of the American civil rights movement, Aldon Morris (1984) documents the critical contribution made by what he terms "movement halfway houses." These were such established organizations as the Highlander Folk School and the Fellowship of Reconciliation that, despite intense repression, sustained earlier traditions of civil rights activism. They were available to play the role of organizational and cultural "midwives" in the "birth" of the new movement.

Leila Rupp and Verta Taylor (1987) provide a rich, detailed portrait of the survival of another enduring activist subculture—that of American feminism—during the long hiatus between the decline of the suffrage movement and the emergence of the contemporary women's movement. Like Morris, Rupp and Taylor focus on the crucial role of organizations and specific individuals in nurturing and sustaining an activist subculture during a period of movement dormancy. The result was the survival of a set of ideas, organizational practices, and activist traditions that served as one of the important "tool kits" shaping the cultural contours of modern American feminism.

Enrique Laraña offers another example of cultural continuity in activist traditions. He documents the historical persistence of Marxist discourse and images of struggle in one of the two wings of the Spanish student movement. Howard Kimmeldorf's (1989) comparative study of unionism among East and West Coast dockworkers has continued to shape the ideology and practices of the union to the present. Finally, the imprint of long standing traditions of student activism are evident on a number of American college or university campuses. For example, one of the best predictors of which colleges and universities contributed student volunteers to the 1964 Mississippi Freedom Summer project was the presence of an active socialist or communist student organization on campus during the 1930s. It should come as no surprise that Berkeley and other colleges such as Antioch and Oberlin sent large contingents of volunteers to Mississippi in 1964. In doing so they were merely drawing on and perpetuating the localized activist subcultures that have long existed on and around those campuses.

Movement emergence, then, is never simply the result of some fortuitous combination of macropolitical opportunities and meso level organizational structures. While important, these factors only afford insurgents a certain structural potential for successful protest activity. Mediating between opportunities and concrete mobilization efforts are the shared meanings people bring to their lives. These meanings, in turn, are expected to be shaped by the cultural resources and opportunities mentioned above.

The Emergence and Development of a Movement Culture

An interest in the relationship between social movements and culture clearly transcends the emergent phase of collective action. Indeed, that relationship becomes more complicated and potentially more interesting as the movement develops because the direction of causal influence in the relationship can run both ways. Not only will the movement bear the imprint of the broader cultural context(s) in which it is embedded but insurgents are also likely to develop a distinctive movement culture capable of reshaping the broader cultural contours of mainstream society.

That such cultures do exist is intuitively clear to anyone who has participated in any but the most ephemeral of movements. Social movements tend to become worlds unto themselves that are characterized by distinctive ideologies, collective identities, behavioral routines, and material cultures. The more thoroughgoing the goals of the movement are, the more likely it is that a movement culture will develop. This is not surprising. Having dared to challenge a particular aspect of mainstream society, there is implicit pressure on insurgents to engage in a kind of social engineering to suggest remedies to the problem. The challenge is to actualize within the movement the kind of social arrangements deemed preferable to those the group is opposing. Again, the more thoroughgoing the changes proposed, the more the tendency to conceive of the movement as an oppositional subculture—a kind of idealized community embodying the movement's alternative vision of social life.

Movement cultures are not static over time. Having opened up the question of the restructuring of social arrangements, there is no guarantee that insurgents will confine their attention to the specific issues or institutions originally targeted. When this happens, movements can take on the character of hothouses of cultural innovation. Anything and everything is open to critical scrutiny. Change becomes the order of the day.

At the moment, we lack any real theoretical or empirical understanding of the processes that shape the ongoing development of distinctive movement cultures, and such an understanding is beyond the scope of this chapter. We can begin to move in that direction by calling attention to two factors that would seem to influence the shifting character of a movement's culture.

Shifts in the Social Locus of the Movement

Social movements typically develop within particular social and generational strata or geographic locations. The expectation is that the culture of the movement will, at least initially, reflect these social, generational, and geographic origins. Movements are hardly the property of those population segments who gave them life in the first place. On the contrary, it is not uncommon for the locus of protest activity to shift over the life of a movement. As such shifts occur, we should see a shift in the ideational and material culture of the movement that reflects the new class, regional, generational, or other social loci of the movement.

One example of this process comes from Lynn Hunt's (1984) definitive study, *Politics, Culture, and Class in the French Revolution.* Hunt's work documents the dramatic shift in the dominant ideology and material symbols of the Revolution that accompanied the change in the class composition of the movement between 1789 and 1795. Dominated at the outset by the emerging bourgeoisie, intellectuals, and even elements of the aristocracy, by 1794–1795 control of the Revolution had passed to artisans, shopkeepers, lawyers, and other less class-privileged elements of French society.

An equally dramatic shift in the cultural content of a movement occurred in the American civil rights movement during the decade of the 1960s as a result of a fundamental shift in the class and geographic loci of protest activity. While the movement initially developed within the churches and other institutions of the Southern, urban, black middle class, by the late 1960s its "home" had shifted to the urban ghettos of a poorer and more secular Northern black community. Partly in response to this shift, the ideational and material culture of

the movement became less religious in nature, more explicitly political, and more aggressively focused on the assertion of a shared and distinctive "cultural nationalism" among black Americans. This is not to say that these shifts were solely the product of the geographic and social changes, but they clearly played a part in the broader cultural transformation that occurred during these years.

Nancy Whittier (1993) provides a final example of the shifting cultural content of a movement in her analysis of generational replacement in the contemporary women's movement. Whittier argues persuasively that the very real differences in the cultural content and "tone" of the current movement have come about not because the pioneering feminists of the 1960s and 1970s have changed their collective identities but because new "activist cohorts" have entered the movement and brought distinctive cultural styles and identities to the struggle.

Perceived Effectiveness of the Movement's Dominant Core

Successful movements tend to be fairly heterogeneous, drawing adherents from a variety of subgroups within the population. These subgroups will vie for cultural as well as strategic political influence over the movement. At any one time, however, it is usually possible to identify a particular segment within the movement as dominant. To the extent that this segment is widely perceived as substantively effective, its cultural "package" will likely be privileged as well. To the extent it is seen as ineffective, strategic and organizational control of the movement will likely shift (often following a period of conflict) to some other contender, thereby enhancing the importance of its cultural package.

The contemporary women's movement in the United States affords a prime example of this phenomenon. Initially, the movement coalesced around radical feminists with roots in both the American "New Left" and the "counterculture" of the 1960s. Eschewing formal organization and leadership, this wing of the movement pioneered the use of consciousness-raising groups as a form of activism. As effective as these groups were in drawing new recruits into the movement, they came to be seen by many as ineffective vehicles for pursuing political and economic change (Freeman 1973). Partly as a result of this critique, influence over the movement gradually shifted to an older, more politically and organizationally conventional group of women who were affiliated with the National Organization for Women (NOW). The results of this shift were cultural as much as political and organizational, with the countercultural affinities of the radical wing gradually giving way to the more conventional, professionalized ethos of NOW loyalists.

The Cultural Consequences of Movements

In assessing the impact of social movements, scholars have tended to focus their attention narrowly on political or economic consequences. Given the central importance attached to political or economic change by most social movements, this is certainly an important topic for systematic investigation. At the same time, resistance to significant political or economic change is likely to be sufficiently intense as to mute the material effects of all but the most successful movements. As many commentators have noted, even a movement as broad based and widely supported as the American civil rights movement failed to effect the fundamental redistribution in political and economic power that it ultimately sought. The opposition of the political and economic

establishment to such a redistribution was simply too strong and too united to permit its occurrence.

Given the entrenched political and economic opposition movements are likely to encounter, it is often true that their biggest impact is more cultural than narrowly political and economic. Although the topic has never been systematically studied, the examples of movement-based cultural change would seem to be numerous and extraordinarily diverse. What follows is an impressionistic survey of some of these many changes. It is not exhaustive; it merely reflects the richness and diversity of the forms of cultural innovation that may be the result of movement dynamics.

As Ralph Turner reminds us, social movements have been the source of some of the most transformative ideologies or belief systems the world has ever known. We would do well to remember that Christianity, Islam, the Protestant Reformation, and subsequent sectarianism began life as the organizing frames for specific social movements. In many other cases, movements served as the principal vehicles by which belief systems, derived elsewhere, were modified and extended. So, for example, Marxist thought was profoundly shaped and deepened by figures associated with both the Russian (Lenin, Trotsky), Chinese (Mao Zedong, Jou Enlai, Lin Biao), and Cuban (Castro, Che Guevara) Revolutions. Through such figures as Voltaire and Rousseau in France and Thomas Paine and Thomas Jefferson in the American colonies, the French and American Revolutions had a similar impact on Enlightenment thinking.

Specific social movements can also give rise to what Snow and his colleagues (1986) call "master protest frames"; that is, ideological accounts legitimating protest activity that come to be shared by a variety of social movements. So, as noted earlier, the civil rights movement advanced a "civil rights" master frame that was, in turn, adopted by other movements as the ideological grounding for their efforts. These movements include the women's, gay rights, handicapped rights, and animal rights movements. The various revolutions in Eastern Europe have appropriated the "democracy frame" first advanced by the Solidarity movement in Poland.

Social movements have also served historically as the source for new collective identities within society. For example, the identities Christian and Muslim emerged in the context of social movements. So, too, did that of the "working class" via the labor movement. In a more contemporary vein, the identity of "feminist" grew out of the modern women's movement. Indeed, many proponents of the new social movements perspective (Inglehart 1981, 1990; Melucci 1980, 1989; Offe 1985; Touraine 1981) argue that what is "new" about the new social movements—including the women's movement—is the central importance they attach to the creation of new collective identities as a fundamental goal of the movement. In fact, social movements have always served this function, whether it was an explicit goal of the movement or an unintended consequence of struggle.

Social movements have also been a force for innovation in strategic action forms. What began as emergent and often illegal tactics in yesterday's movements often become legitimate, institutionalized forms of politics in later years. The strike and the sit-in are two examples. Both tactics were pioneered in the labor movement, but later came to be recognized as legitimate forms of action by various groups. Elisabeth Clemens (1993) argues that the contemporary importance of lobbying owes historically to its successful and legitimating use by women activists in the period from 1880 to 1920.

Throughout history, social movements have also functioned as a source of new material cultural items. Hunt's (1984) cultural analysis of the French Revolution makes clear the extent to which popular symbols and the material culture of France were transformed during the Revolution. Virtually all political revolutions usher in cultural revolutions as well. The Chinese Revolution, for example, set in motion a thoroughgoing state effort to fashion a popular culture compatible with the ideals of the movement. The same thing has occurred more recently in Iran, with the Islamic Revolution ushering in a period of intense anti-Western feeling leading to the wholesale rejection of Western-style consumer goods and other cultural items. Ironically, the reverse process is currently underway in the Soviet Union, with the popular rejection of the Communist party encouraging a simultaneous process of Western-style cultural liberalization and experimentation.

Revolutions are not the only force that exert a powerful transformative effect on the material culture of a society. For example, the 1964 Mississippi Freedom Summer Project gave early expression to a number of specific cultural items that came to be associated with the 1960s counterculture (McAdam 1988). In general, as authors such as Morris Dickstein (1989) have shown, the counterculture and the movements of the 1960s had a profound effect on American popular culture. Dress and hairstyles, popular music, movies, dance, and theater were powerfully affected by the political turbulence of the era. The roots of the "drug culture" can also be found in the political and cultural movements of the 1960s. Language was affected; "black English" made inroads into popular English, and the feminist critique of the traditional vernacular prompted efforts to fashion more gender-neutral modes of expression.

Similar linguistic "insurgencies" are currently under way elsewhere. In the Canadian province of Quebec, French-speaking separatists affiliated with the Parti québécois have succeeded in making French the official provincial language. In Catalonia, separatists continue to press for the same designation for Catalan, underscoring their resolve by painting over street signs in Castilian with the equivalent word or phrase in Catalan.

To round out this survey, mention should be made of the effect of social movements on the culture and practices of mainstream institutions in society. In his thorough study of the impact of liberation theology on the Latin American Catholic church, Christian Smith (1991) provides a fascinating example of this process. Inspired in part by the spread of communist movements in the region, the liberation theology movement spawned a kind of revolution within the church that is still being waged today. In the United States, the movements of the 1960s have had a dramatic effect on the structure and curricular content of higher education in the United States. Structurally, the political turbulence of the era led to the establishment of African American, Native American, Hispanic, and women's studies programs on many college and university campuses. In addition, the heightened awareness of minorities spawned by the movements has resulted in far more curricular attention to minority groups in social science and humanities courses.

The forms of cultural change that flow from social movements are many and varied, and we know little about which factors or characteristics of movements account for the extent of their cultural impact. As a first approach to the question, I would emphasize the role of four factors in mediating the cultural consequences of social movements. These factors are: the extensiveness of the movement's goals, the movement's success in attaining those goals, the extent to which the movement results in prolonged and meaningful contact between two previously segregated groups, and the extent of the movement's access to existing cultural elites in society.

Breadth of the Movement's Goals

All other things being equal, the more extensive its goals, the more likely that a movement will be a force for cultural change. Given this understanding, it is not surprising that all of the examples of cultural change mentioned in the previous section are the products of movements whose goals were very broad. Revolutionary movements have the broadest goals; they seek nothing less than the replacement of an existing political, economic, and social order. Accordingly, of all types of movements, revolutions typically have the greatest potential for stimulating significant cultural change. Given their fundamental interest in replacing the old regime, insurgents will almost invariably seek to destroy the cultural expressions of the old order and substitute a new revolutionary culture in its place (Gramsci 1971). At the other end of the revolution to reform continuum, movements of the narrow reform variety typically exert little cultural force. For example, the current anti-drunk driving movement has but a few if any cultural, as opposed to legal or political, implications. Its goals are simply so narrow and so specific as to rule out any broader cultural critique of American society.

The Degree of Success Achieved by the Movement

History, as the old saying goes, is written by the winners. The same is true for all major forms of cultural expression. A second determinant, therefore, of the cultural impact of a movement is the degree to which the movement is successful politically. Following Marx (1977), it would seem to be the case that cultural dominance rests, to a large extent, on a firm political and economic base. Accordingly, I hypothesize that the cultural impact of a movement will be commensurate with the substantive political and economic success it achieves. Again, this is most evident in the case of successful revolutions, wherein the victors move to eradicate the cultural, as well as political, vestiges of the old regime and to popularize cultural forms expressive of the new revolutionary order. At the other extreme, movements that fail to achieve any political leverage typically leave few cultural traces behind.

Contact between Previously Segregated Groups

Those movements that have been especially important as sources of cultural innovation would seem to be those that resulted in meaningful, that is, egalitarian, contact between previously segregated social strata. The significance of this kind of contact—the interaction between what Harrison White (1991) calls two "value streams"—is its potential to produce a new cultural hybrid based on the two subcultures present in the movement. Movements of this type have been among the most important in human history.

The early Christian movement represented a unique cultural hybrid based on a merger of a rural ascetic Jewish tradition with that of urban Hellenized Jews and Romans throughout the eastern Mediterranean. The Indian independence movement facilitated unprecedented contact between the untouchables and the most privileged Indian castes. The result was not simply political success but a period of unusual cultural ferment as well. Finally, for a brief period of time, the American civil rights movement encouraged egalitarian contact between black civil rights activists and the white student left. In large measure, the roots of the 1960s counterculture are found in the distinctive cultural hybrid that grew out of this contact (McAdam 1988).

Ties to Established Cultural Elites

The final factor that can be expected to shape the broader cultural impact of a movement is the extent to which it is linked to established cultural elites in society. One of the commonplace observations concerning the cultural ferment of the 1960s was that it represented "culture from the bottom up." Instead of cultural innovation flowing, as it normally does, from an established cultural elite downward through society, it seemed to emanate from groups whose impact on mainstream culture is ordinarily quite small. What this observation misses is the fact that the groups in question had unusually strong ties to established cultural elites, thus granting them more access to the means of cultural production than they ordinarily would have had. The ties forged in the early days of the movement between civil rights activists and segments of the Northern intellectual and cultural elite afforded blacks increased opportunities for cultural influence. The white student left, dominated as it was by middle- and upper-middle-class youth, enjoyed considerable access to the means of cultural expression via their parents and other influential adults to whom they were directly or indirectly linked. Generally, those movements that are either rooted in culturally privileged classes or that are able to forge such links are likely to have a greater impact on the cultural contours of mainstream society than those movements that remain fundamentally isolated from the established means of cultural production.

Conclusion

What I offer here is the most preliminary statement of the relationship between culture and social movements. The topic is complex and multifaceted. These are the beginnings of what I hope will be an ongoing discourse on the subject by both movement scholars and cultural analysts. Only by encouraging such a discourse can we hope to move toward a fuller understanding of this relationship and move beyond the current structural and rationalist biases evident in the contemporary movement literature.

Acknowledgments

This chapter was completed while I was a Fellow at the Center for Advanced Study in the Behavioral Sciences. Partial support for the year at the Center was provided by the National Science Foundation (BNS-8700864). I would also like to thank Dick Flacks, Hank Johnston, Enrique Laraña, Dieter Rucht, David Snow, and Sidney Tarrow for their extremely helpful comments on various drafts.

REFERENCES

Bellah, Robert N., Richard Madsen, William M. Sullivan, Ann Swidler, and Steven M. Tipton. 1985. *Habits of the Heart.* New York: Harper and Row.

Brand, Karl-Werner. 1990. "Cyclical Aspects of New Social Movements: Waves of Cultural Criticism and Mobilization Cycles of New Middle-Class Radicalism." In *Challenging the Political Order: New Social and Political Movements in Western Democracies,* edited by Russell J. Dalton and Manfred Kuechler, pp. 23–42. New York: Oxford University Press.

Caute, David. 1988. *The Year of the Barricades.* New York: Harper and Row.

Clemens, Elisabeth. 1993. "Organizational Repertoires of Institutional Change: Women's Groups and the Transformation of U.S. Politics, 1890–1920." *American Journal of Sociology* 98:755–98.

Dickstein, Morris. 1989. *Gates of Eden.* New York: Penguin Books.

Evans, Sara. 1980. *Personal Politics.* New York: Vintage Books.

Eyerman, Ron, and Andrew Jamison. 1991. *Social Movements: A Cognitive Approach.* University Park: Pennsylvania State University Press.

Fishel, Leslie H., Jr., and Benjamin Quarles. 1970. "In the New Deal's Wake." In *The Segregation Era, 1863–1954,* edited by Allen Weinstein and Frank F. Otto Gatell, pp. 218–32. New York: Oxford University Press.

Freeman, Jo. 1973. "The Origins of the Women's Liberation Movement." *American Journal of Sociology* 78:792-811.

Gerber, Irwin. 1962. "The Effects of the Supreme Court's Desegregation Decision on the Group Cohesion of New York City's Negroes." *Journal of Social Psychology* 58:295–303.

Gitlin, Todd. 1987. *The Sixties: Years of Hope, Days of Rage.* New York: Bantam Books.

Goffman, Erving. 1974. *Frame Analysis: An Essay on the Organization of Experience.* New York: Harper.

Goldstone, Jack. 1982. "The Comparative and Historical Study of Revolutions." *Annual Review of Sociology* 8:187–207.

———. 1991. *Revolution and Rebellion in the Early Modern World.* Berkeley: University of California Press.

Gould, Roger. 1991. "Multiple Networks and Mobilization in the Paris Commune, 1871." *American Sociological Review* 56:716–29.

Gramsci, Antonio. 1971. *Selection from the Prison Notebooks of Antonio Gramsci.* Edited by Q. Hoare and G. N. Smith. New York: International Publishers.

Hunt, Lynn. 1984. *Politics, Culture, and Class in the French Revolution.* Berkeley: University of California Press.

Inglehart, Ronald. 1981. "Post-Materialism in an Environment of Insecurity." *American Political Science Review* 75:880–900.

———. 1990. *Culture Shift in Advanced Industrial Society.* Princeton: Princeton University Press.

Katsiaficas, George. 1987. *The Imagination of the New Left.* Boston: South End Press.

Kimmeldorf, Howard. 1989. *From Reds to Rackets.* Berkeley: University of California Press.

Kitschelt, Herbert P. 1986. "Political Opportunity Structures and Political Protest." *British Journal of Political Science* 16:57–85.

Klapp, Orrin. 1969. *Collective Search for Identity.* New York: Holt, Rinehart, and Winston.

Kriesi, Hanspeter. 1989. "The Political Opportunity Structure of the Dutch Peace Movement." *West European Politics* 12:295–312.

———. 1990. "The Political Opportunity Structure of New Social Movements: Its Impact on Their Mobilization," Paper presented at "Social Movements, Framing Processes, and Opportunity Structures," a conference held at Wissenschaftszentrum, Berlin, July.

Lang, Kurt, and Gladys Lang. 1961. *Collective Dynamics.* New York: Crowell.

Laraña, Enrique. 1975. "A Study of Student Political Activism at the University of California, Berkeley." Master's thesis, University of California, Santa Barbara.

McAdam, Doug. 1982. *Political Process and the Development of Black Insurgency, 1930–1970.* Chicago: University of Chicago Press.

———. 1986. "Recruitment to High-Risk Activism: The Case of Freedom Summer." *American Sociological Review* 92:64–90.

———. 1988. *Freedom Summer.* New York: Oxford University Press.

McAdam, Doug, and Dieter Rucht. 1993. "The Cross-National Diffusion of Movement Ideas." *Annals of the American Academy of Political and Social Science* 527 (May):56–74.

Marx, Karl. 1977. *Selected Writings.* Edited by David McLelland. Oxford: Oxford University Press.

———. 1979. *The Essential Marx: The Non-Economic Writings.* Edited and Translated by Saul K. Padover. New York: New American Library.

Melucci, Alberto. 1980. "The New Social Movements: A Theoretical Approach." *Social Science Information* 19:199–226.

———. 1985. "The Symbolic Challenge of Contemporary Movements." *Social Research* 52:789–816.

———. 1989. *Nomads of the Present: Social Movements and Individual Needs in Contemporary Society.* Philadelphia: Temple University Press.

Molotch, Harvey. 1970. "Oil in Santa Barbara and Power in America." *Sociological Inquiry* 40:131–41.

Morris, Aldon. 1984. *The Origins of the Civil Rights Movement.* New York: Free Press.

Oberschall, Anthony. 1973. *Social Conflict and Social Movements.* Englewood Cliffs, N.J.: Prentice-Hall.

Offe, Claus. 1985. "New Social Movements: Challenging the Boundaries of Institutional Politics." *Social Research* 52:817–68.

Rosenthal, Naomi, Maryl Fingrutd, Michele Ethier, Roberta Karant, and David McDonald. 1985. "Social Movements and Network Analysis: A Case Study of Nineteenth-Century Women's Reform in New York State." *American Journal of Sociology* 90:1022–55.

Rucht, Dieter. 1990. "The Strategies and Action Repertoires of New Movements." In *Challenging the Political Order: New Social and Political Movements in Western Democracies,* edited by Russell J. Dalton and Manfred Kuechler, pp. 156–75. New York: Oxford University Press.

Rupp, Leila, and Verta Taylor. 1987. *Survival in the Doldrums: The American Women's Rights Movement, 1945 to the 1960s.* New York: Oxford University Press.

Sale, Kirkpatrick. 1973. *SDS.* New York: Random House.

Sitkoff, Harvard. 1978. *A New Deal for Blacks.* New York: Oxford University Press.

Skocpol, Theda. 1979. *States and Social Revolutions.* New York: Cambridge University Press.

Smelser, Neil. 1962. *Theory of Collective Behavior.* New York: Free Press.

Smith, Christian. 1991. *The Emergence of Liberation Theology: Radical Religion and Social Movement Theory.* Chicago: University of Chicago Press.

Snow, David A., and Robert D. Benford. 1988. "Ideology, Frame Resonance, and Participant Mobilization." In *From Structure to Action: Comparing Social Movement Research across Cultures,* edited by Bert Klandermans, Hanspeter Kriesi, and Sidney Tarrow, pp. 197–217. Vol. 1 of *International Social Movement Research.* Greenwich, Conn.: JAI Press.

Snow, David A., E. Burke Rochford, Jr., Steven K. Worden, and Robert D. Benford. 1986. "Frame Alignment Processes, Micromobilization, and Movement Participation." *American Sociological Review* 51:464–81.

Swidler, Ann. 1986. "Culture in Action: Symbols and Strategies." *American Sociological Review* 51:273–86.

Tarrow, Sidney. 1989. *Democracy and Disorder: Protest and Politics in Italy, 1965–1975.* Oxford: Clarendon Press.

———. 1991. "'Aiming at a Moving Target': Social Science and the Recent Rebellions in Eastern Europe." *Political Science and Politics* 29:12–20.

Tarrow, Sidney. 1994. *Power in Movement: Social Movements, Collective Action, and Mass Politics in the Modern State.* New York: Cambridge University Press.

Tilly, Charles. 1978. *From Mobilization to Revolution.* Reading, Mass.: Addison Wesley.

Touraine, Alain. 1981. *The Voice and the Eye: An Analysis of Social Movements.* New York: Cambridge University Press.

Useem, Bert. 1980. "Solidarity Model, Breakdown Model, and the Boston Anti-Busing Movement." *American Sociological Review* 45:357–69.

Walsh, Edward J. 1981. "Resource Mobilization and Citizen Protest in Communities around Three Mile Island." *Social Problems* 29:1–21.

White, Harrison. 1991. "Values Come in Styles, Which Mate to Change." Paper presented at the interdisciplinary conference "Toward a Scientific Analysis of Values," Tucson, Arizona, February 1–4, 1989.

Whittier, Nancy. 1993. "Feminists in the 'Post-Feminist' Age: Collective Identity and the Persistence of the Women's Movement." Unpublished paper. Cornell University.

30

THE SOCIAL PSYCHOLOGY OF COLLECTIVE ACTION

WILLIAM A. GAMSON

Social psychology bashing among students of social movements is over. It had its day, and with good reason. Movement participants saw social psychology used to disparage their motives and their good sense. In some hands it seemed naive and reductionist, diverting attention from underlying structural conditions of conflict and oppression. Many American social scientists, reacting especially to that part of the collective behavior tradition flowing from Gustave Le Bon and other antidemocratic theorists of the nineteenth and early twentieth centuries, seemed ready to reject the entire social psychological project. One writer, for example, called the collective behavior tradition "stultifying" and a "straightjacket" for the study of social protest.[1]

In the United States, the 1970s were the decade of organizational theory and utilitarian economic models in the study of social movements. Problems of ideology and the emergence of shared beliefs of injustice were given short shrift. "Ideas and beliefs that have a revolutionary potential are usually present and are available for use by protest leadership. Sentiments of opposition, of being wronged, are also frequently present in the lower orders and can be easily linked with the more elaborate ideologies and world views," wrote Oberschall (1973, 133–34). Similarly, McCarthy and Zald argued that a focus on discontent is misplaced since there is always enough "to supply the grass roots support for a movement," and "grievances and discontent may be defined, created, and manipulated by issue entrepreneurs and organizations" (1977, 1215).

But as social movement theory continued to encounter the movements of the 1970s and 1980s, social psychology emerged again with such vigor that it has now become a major frontier. By the mid-1980s, Klandermans was asserting that "resource mobilization theory went too far in nearly abandoning the social-psychological analysis

From *Frontiers in Social Movement Theory*, Aldon D. Morris and Carol McClurg Mueller, eds. Copyright © 1992 by Yale University. Reprinted by permission of Yale University Press.

of social movements" (1984, 583–84), and Cohen was asking "Hasn't the critique of the collective behavior tradition thrown out the baby with the bathwater by excluding the analysis of values, norms, ideologies, projects, culture, and identity in other than instrumental terms?" (1985, 688).

This distrust of social psychology was largely limited to the emerging resource mobilization approach in the United States. New social movement theorists in Europe had no need to exorcise the long-departed ghost of Le Bon and his ilk. Their dialectic was not with heavily social psychological mass society and collective behavior theory but with various strains of Marxist theory whose social psychology was primitive and undeveloped. Nor did theorists of third world liberation movements need to escape from any social psychological straightjackets.

The resurgent social psychology has jettisoned the old baggage of irrationality and social pathology. Even the American collective behavior tradition has been cleansed of the idea that social movements are the destructive outbursts of "people going crazy together" (Martin 1920). In the "emergent norm" approach of Turner and Killian (1987), the process by which mobilization for collective action occurs becomes the central problem. The authors repudiate the idea that such action is more emotional or irrational than institutionalized forms. Emotion and reason are not irreconcilables, they argue. "To attempt to divide the actions of individuals into 'rational' versus 'emotional' or 'irrational' types is to deny the complexity of human behavior" (14).

None of this social psychology denies the importance of organization, social location, and the calculation of costs and benefits by movement actors. But there is an increasing recognition that an exclusive focus on such components leaves some of the most critical and difficult questions unanswered. As Ferree and Miller write, "Costs

and benefits play a role in generating movement support, but the translation of objective social relationships into subjectively experienced group interests is also critical in building movements, as in political activity generally" (1985, 39).

Many of the major questions animating contemporary work on social movements are intrinsically social psychological. Cohen (1985) has suggested three central problematics—collective identity, solidarity, and consciousness—to which we can add a fourth that cross-cuts all of them: micromobilization. This chapter will attempt to show, for each of these topics, its roots in a more generic social psychological literature that is not focused on social movements, how the ideas have manifested themselves in recent social movement writings, and the unresolved questions and major puzzles that need our attention.

Of course, there is not one social psychological tradition but several. In addressing questions on social movements, both psychological and sociological traditions have something to say at different points and we need awareness of both. My own tradition is an interdisciplinary one that is concerned with the interaction between different levels of analysis. This tradition begins with the distinctions among personality, social, and cultural systems: social psychological questions are those involving the mesh between self and society.

Each of the central problematics—collective identity, solidarity, consciousness, and micromobilization—concerns this mesh. In practice, the processes are thoroughly interwoven, but the distinction is useful analytically. Collective identity concerns the mesh between the individual and cultural systems. More specifically, the question is how individuals' sense of who they are becomes engaged with a definition shared by coparticipants in some effort at social change—that is, with who "we" are.

Solidarity, as defined here, concerns the mesh between individual and social system. More specifically, the question is how individuals develop and maintain loyalty and commitment to collective actors—that is, to groups or organizations who act as carriers of social movements. Consciousness also involves a mesh between individual and cultural levels. The question here is how the meaning that individuals give to a social situation becomes a shared definition implying collective action.

Micromobilization examines the micro-events that operate in linking individual and sociocultural levels in the operation of identity, solidarity, and consciousness processes. It is social psychological in its attempt to understand the social interaction and group processes involved in collective actions.

Much of the social movement work discussed below is by those who have no disciplinary identification with social psychology, but this is irrelevant to my argument. The questions, not the answers, are social psychological, and one must look to many different disciplines and traditions to understand how individual and social processes mesh.

Collective Identity

Social psychologists have always emphasized the centrality of social relationships and social location in the development of personal identity. Indeed, in the old pathological tradition in the study of social movements, identity theory provided the crucial link between social system breakdown and collective action. It is expressed most clearly in such classics as Fromm's *Escape from Freedom* (1941).

In cruder hands, such as Hoffer's *The True Believer* (1951), movements were seen in general as providing a substitute for a spoiled identity. "The frustrated follow a leader," Hoffer writes, "less because of their faith that he is leading them to a promised land than because of the immediate feeling that he is leading them away from their unwanted selves. Surrender to a leader is not a means to an end but a fulfillment" (116).

Cleansed of its assumptions about a spoiled or ersatz identity, there is a central insight that remains. Participation in social movements frequently involves an enlargement of personal identity for participants and offers fulfillment and realization of self. Participation in the civil rights movement, women's movement, and New Left, for example, was frequently a transformative experience, central to the self-definition of many participants in their later lives.

Work in the American resource mobilization tradition has been slow to recognize and address issues of personal and collective identity. But the opposite has been true for European writers who emphasize the centrality of identity issues in such "new" social movements as the environmental, antinuclear, and peace movements.[2] Their central message is only a paraphrase away from the Hoffer quotation above: "Participation in a social movement is not only a means to an end but a fulfillment."

For my purposes here, Melucci (1989) is the best exemplar of those writing in this tradition. He not only has an especially rich discussion of identity issues but also is most explicit in his social psychological orientation. He describes his arguments as deliberately cutting "a circuitous path between collective social and political processes and the subjective personal experiences of everyday life." Furthermore, Melucci's arguments are the most successful in combining elements of what Cohen (1985) calls "identity-oriented" and "strategically-oriented" paradigms.

Melucci suggests that the construction of a collective identity is the most central task of "new" social movements. This is a negotiated process in which the "we" involved in collective action is elaborated and given meaning. New social movement theorists emphasize the reflexivity of these movements—that is, their tendency to ask themselves explicit questions about "who we are." They argue that, since the participants do not define themselves in terms of their common social location in a class or ethnic group, the question is intrinsically problematic.

Some nascent movement groups will fail to produce any collective identity that engages the participants' self-definition, but others are quite successful. "This on-going process of construction of a sense of 'we' can succeed for various reasons," Melucci writes, "for instance, because of effective leadership, workable organizational forms or strong reserves of expressive action. But it can also fail, in which case collective action disintegrates" (1989, 218).

Melucci's central point is not simply the strategic one that a strong sense of collective identity is instrumental to the success of collective action but that it is a goal in its own right requiring us to rethink the concept of success. He argues against "an exclusively political view centered on the 'instrumental' dimension of action" because it treats "as 'expressive' or residual the self-reflective investments of the movements" (1989, 73–74). The creation of an ongoing collective identity that maintains the loyalty and commitment of participants is a cultural achievement in its own right, regardless of its contribution to the achievement of political and organizational goals.

The "we" that these movements construct is adversarial but not necessarily "political" because they "challenge the logic of complex systems on cultural grounds. . . . Linking personal change with external action, collective action functions as a new medium which illuminates the silent and arbitrary elements of the dominant codes as well as publicizes new alternatives" (Melucci, 1989, 23 and 63).

Nothing in this argument denies that social movement actors make strategic judgments based on their expectations about costs and benefits. The point is, rather, that any strategic paradigm necessarily presupposes a theory of identity. Assumptions about social identity are implicit. In individual utilitarian models such as Olson's (1965), the absence of a collective identity is assumed. This assumption ignores much of what we know about the social definition of identity and its impact on individual preference structures. When people bind their fate to the fate of a group, they feel personally threatened when the group is threatened. Solidarity and collective identity operate to blur the distinction between individual and group interest, undermining the premises on which such utilitarian models operate.

But even in more sophisticated rational actor models that postulate a *collective* actor making strategic judgments of cost and benefit about collective action, the existence of an *established* collective identity is assumed. As Melucci observes, "Only if individual actors can recognize their coherence and continuity as actors will they be able to write their own script of social reality and compare expectations and outcomes." Expectations are socially constructed and outcomes can be evaluated only by actors "who are capable of defining themselves and the field of their action. The process of constructing, maintaining, and altering a collective identity provides the basis for actors to shape their expectations and calculate the costs and benefits of their action" (1989, 32 and 34).

Blind Spots in New Social Movement Theory

Having granted the helpfulness of this paradigm in highlighting important issues of meshing personal and collective identities, let me turn to its own blind spots, crystallized in the term *new social movements*. The term is objectionable on several fundamental grounds.

First, it privileges one particular, albeit interesting, subset of social movements that happen to be predominantly white, middle class, and located in Western Europe and North America. These movements are well worth studying. But when they become a reified category of analysis—*the* new social movements—many of the most important social movements of the past two decades are rendered invisible. In a world larger than Western Europe and North America, one might notice such "new" social movements as Solidarity in Poland, the movement against the apartheid regime in South Africa, the *communidades de base* movement in Latin America, and the intifada in the Middle East, for starters.

I do not claim that the meshing of personal and collective identity is any less important for these movements than for the subset privileged by new social movement theorists. On the contrary, I accept it as a fundamental issue for all movements, past and present, in Western industrialized countries and elsewhere. But as the context changes, so does the status of such claims as: collective identity is especially problematic because participants do not define themselves in terms of their social location in a class or ethnic group. It seems reasonable to suppose that the problem of meshing individual and collective identity will take a different form in different types of movements.

Changing language from "new" social movements to "contemporary" social movements, as Cohen (1985) does, is clearly inadequate in overcoming the ethnocentrism of privileging a particular type. If recency is the relevant criterion, the Eastern European and third world movements referred to above are every bit as contemporary as the Greens in West Germany.

Reifying newness as a category of analysis also diverts attention from the collective identity processes involved in past movements and blurs what may be instructive continuities. Simultaneously, it obscures important differences in the collective identity problems of movements that are only superficially similar. In his study of ACT UP, an AIDS activist group, J. Gamson shows the insufficiency of lumping together movements "simply because of a shared cultural and identity focus. . . . Identity assertions in ACT UP point up boundaries, using the fear of the abnormal against the fearful" (1989, 364). The specific operations involved may be shared by movements that are subject to stigmatization and, hence, are in a similar position to "shock." But these operations may be inappropriate and irrelevant for other, equally culturally oriented movements. Hence, the category of "newness" can serve as a substitute for a concrete analysis of how collective identity processes operate in movements facing quite different sets of problems.

Expanding the Strategic Paradigm

Can such lessons about the centrality of identity processes be incorporated in strategically oriented paradigms such as resource mobilization? Cohen thinks not. "One cannot simply add a consideration of solidarity, collective identity, consciousness, or ideology to the resource mobilization perspective without bursting its framework," she argues (1985, 687).

She is right, of course, in the sense that a strategic focus will not highlight all aspects of the process of constructing a collective identity. But it does not even strain the paradigm let alone burst it to integrate many of the central insights. Strategy does not apply only to political or economic change as objectives. The first step is to recognize that people may mobilize resources and pursue various forms of collective action in the pursuit of cultural change. Change in the cultural definition of the "normal" serves as an excellent example.

Once one gives changes at the cultural level the same status as institutional changes, a further broadening of the resource mobilization paradigm is required. Political and economic changes involve more easily defined targets of influence—some set of authorities whose decisions affect the goals of challengers. But in the pursuit of cultural change, the target is often diffused through the whole civil society. State institutions continue to play a role, but in the twentieth century they have increasingly withdrawn from becoming directly involved in what Foucault (1979) calls the "normalization" process. The mass media frequently become a central target as the most visible purveyor of the broader cultural definitions they both reproduce and reflect.

Construction of a collective identity is one step in challenging cultural domination. The content must necessarily be adversarial in some way to smoke out the invisible and arbitrary elements of the dominant cultural codes. No matter how personally important it becomes for participants, it is never merely a fulfillment but a strategic step in achieving cultural changes that are mediated by the movement's external targets.

If the concept of collective identity sometimes seems excessively vague and difficult to operationalize, this may be in part because of the tendency to blur individual and cultural levels in some discussions of the concept. The locus of collective identity is cultural; it is manifested through the language and symbols by which it is publicly expressed. We know a collective identity through the cultural icons and artifacts displayed by those who embrace it. It is manifested in styles of dress, language, and demeanor. Collective identity need not be

treated as some mysterious intangible but can be as empirically observable as a T-shirt or haircut. To measure it, one would ask people about the meaning of labels and other cultural symbols, not about their own personal identity.

Social psychology helps us recognize that it is a task of all social movements to bridge individual and cultural levels. One does this by enlarging the personal identities of a constituency to include the relevant collective identity of their definition of self. New social movement theory suggests that this bridging process is especially critical in movements that (1) emphasize changes at the cultural level, (2) have the civil society rather than state or economic institutions as a primary target of influence, and (3) have a constituency that chooses whether or not to make visible their connection with the relevant group. But it is not particularly helpful when the construction of a collective identity is made *the* task of social movements at the inevitable expense of slighting other, equally critical components.

Resource mobilization theory suggests that the bridging of personal and collective identity can be viewed strategically, as one part of the mobilization process. Even when we regard the construction of a collective identity as an achievement in its own right, it has instrumental consequences for the rest of the process. It is central in understanding people's willingness to invest emotionally in the fate of some emergent collective entity and to take personal risks on its behalf. It has consequences for how people understand the sociocultural system they are attempting to change and which strategies and organizational forms they will see as appropriate. Groups that have achieved a successful integration of personal and collective identity will have an easier time doing what it takes to launch many kinds of collective actions.

But this depends in part on the type of collective action and its target. Many of the unanswered questions about identity processes concern the strategic consequences emphasized by resource mobilization theory. We still need to ask how and under what conditions the strength of a collective identity and its specific content make a difference for achieving movement goals.

Solidarity

There is both a social and a cultural level involved in loyalty and commitment to a social movement. Solidarity processes focus on how people relate to social movement carriers—that is, to the various collective actors who claim to represent the movement. These carriers need not be formal organizations but can include entities as varied as an advocacy network grouped around a journal or a grass-roots Christian community in El Salvador.

In practice, of course, collective identity and solidarity are closely intertwined, but it is possible to have one aspect of commitment without the other. A person may embrace the collective identity offered by a movement and feel alienated from its major organizational carriers. Conversely, there may be organizational loyalists whose personal lives are thoroughly intertwined with the fate of the carrier but feel little identification with any broader "we" that includes movement constituents.

What characteristics of movement carriers promote solidarity? Recent social movement literature has attempted to answer this in two ways: one focusing on the use of preexisting social relationships, the other on organizational forms that support and sustain the personal needs of participants and embody the movement's collective identity.

The argument that recruitment to a movement follows lines of preexisting social relationships and that recruitment networks are a critical part of the mobilization process has become part of our shared knowledge.[3] Strong, preexisting friendship ties seem especially important where the risk is high. McAdam (1986) examined the high-risk activism involved in participating in the 1964 Mississippi Freedom Summer project, comparing those who signed up and later withdrew with those who actually went to Mississippi. Those with strong ties to other participants had a drop-out rate of only 12 percent (compared to a 25 percent rate for the group as a whole).

Certainly any social psychologist reviewing the extensive literature on social support networks would have predicted this. Study after study has emphasized their importance in sustaining people through life's existential crises of illness, death, and separation.[4] High-risk activism is high-stress activity. Preexisting friendships are helpful in recruitment, no doubt, but unless the *continuing* relationships among activists have some of the qualities of a primary social support network, it seems hard to imagine that participants will develop organizational solidarity.

Insights about the centrality of social support processes have entered the social movement literature through discussions of cultural "free spaces," "prefigurative politics," and "affinity groups." Movements that practice high-risk activism operate in an adversarial environment and have a special need to create a protected subenvironment. As Evans and Boyte develop their concept of free spaces, "they are defined by their roots in community, the dense, rich networks of daily life; by their autonomy; and by their public or quasi-public character as participatory environments which nurture values associated with citizenship and a vision of the common good" (1986, 20).

Rather than creating such spaces de novo, movements try, when possible, to transform existing communal institutions into such protected environments. Morris (1984) shows the multifaceted role of the black church in providing such space for the civil rights movement as well as "movement halfway houses" such as the Highlander Folk School. He quotes its director, Myles Horton: "We never spent any time stating what we believed, and how we felt, or anything like that. . . . We just went ahead and ran our program and everybody was accepted as an equal and treated as an equal and they got the message" (148).

Highlander embodied in its practice Breines's concept of "prefigurative politics." The central task of such politics, she argues, is "to create and sustain within the lived practice of the movement relationships and political forms that 'prefigured' and embodied the desired society" (1982, 6). In the New Left movement she studied, it was intimately connected with the vision of a community that united public and private spheres. "By community," she writes, "I mean a network of relationships more direct, more total and more personal than the formal, abstract and instrumental relationships characterizing state and society" (6).

The organizational form that seems most clearly to reflect the needs for a sustaining social support system is that of "affinity groups." The movements against the Vietnam War, nuclear power, and intervention in Central America all spawned challengers that made use of this form of organization. Ideally, an affinity group, which is small (perhaps ten to twenty people), takes responsibility for activating its own members and participates as a unit in collective action. In addition to providing members with emotional support, these groups are typically expected to provide many of their instrumental needs for transportation, food, and shelter.

Affinity groups may employ an internal division of labor. The Pledge of Resistance, a challenger in the Central American anti-intervention movement, sometimes used site occupations as a tactic. Members of its affinity groups would decide in advance which ones would risk arrest and jail and which ones would act as partners for those detained, helping them meet the continuing demands of everyday life, of family and work.

All movements, of course, have informal friendship networks that help sustain the members. Affinity groups are innovative in formalizing the system of social support, making explicit who is affiliated with which subgroups and endowing them with decision-making and governance functions. Unlike the cells in more hierarchical organizations, affinity groups reflect a commitment to decentralization.

Free spaces, prefigurative politics, and affinity groups reflect sound social psychological insights on building commitment and solidarity, but they frequently exist in tension with the strategic imperatives of social movement organizations. The reconciliation or trade-offs involved remains one of the unsolved problems on the frontiers of social movement theory.

Breines's (1982) interpretation of the New Left movement highlights the conflict between prefigurative and strategic politics. The practice suggested by prefigurative politics has many implications for organization: direct participation rather than representation, decentralization rather than centralization, and holistic personal relationships rather than bureaucratic and segmented role relationships.

All well and good for building commitment, solidarity, and a collective identity, but social movement organizations frequently face the challenge of responding rapidly and skillfully to unexpected events or the actions of their adversaries. In the fall of 1965, for example, Students for a Democratic Society (SDS) was in the media spotlight and under attack for "sabotaging the war effort." Sale (1973) and Gitlin (1980) describe how SDS officers, in an effort "to take the heat off," held a press conference and issued a statement offering "to build, not to burn; to teach, not to torture; to help, not to kill."

The statement received widespread coverage and apparently achieved its immediate tactical purpose in reframing the discourse to center on the immorality of the war rather than on draft resistance. It proved helpful in recruiting on a number of campuses. In addition, it temporarily reduced the pressure on SDS while bolstering its allies and supporters.

This apparent success, however, produced mostly harsh internal criticism from SDS chapters around the country. It was not only the content that dismayed some members; as Gitlin (1980) put its, "There was much feeling that [SDS officers] had usurped the right to make any policy statement at all." The national secretary was not entitled to set policy in SDS. One critic suggested that reporters "should have simply been referred to local chapters which would tell them what was going on in any particular area" (Sale 1973).

Similarly, Barkan (1979) describes some of the problems that the Clamshell Alliance experienced in using affinity groups in the attempted occupation of the Seabrook, New Hampshire, nuclear site. The Clam had a coordinating committee of affinity group representatives, but this body had no established legitimacy among the rank and file, and representatives were required to return to their affinity groups for consent for proposed actions. When decisions were inevitably made by the coordinating committee under time pressure, members challenged the results and charged that the Clam was "controlled by a few 'heavyweights'" (Barkan, 1979).

The trick, of course, is to find a way to combine prefigurative and strategic politics,

to reconcile organizational forms that sustain commitment with those that can meet situational demands for rapid and skillful action. Can one mix decentralization for social support with more centralized decision making? Or does this reduction of participation in decision making inevitably undermine the importance of affinity groups and render them ineffective in building solidarity and commitment? Does formalizing and making explicit the social support system really add anything to what can be achieved through warm and supportive informal social relationships? The social support tradition in social psychology helps us understand the dilemma, but it doesn't provide the solution.

Finally, there is another tradition in social psychology that suggests that, notwithstanding the virtues described above, social support can have a distinctly negative side. An extensive literature on conformity, going back to the classical experimental studies by Sherif (1936) and Asch (1952), emphasizes the potential tyranny of groups. Participants in some social movements find an oppressive and stifling side to close-knit personal relationships.

So-called cultural free spaces sometimes become prisons from which some participants would like to escape but cannot because they lack the courage to defy the group censure and ostracism that would follow. At some point, social support can become social pressure. Students of social movements need to understand the conditions under which this occurs and how challengers can keep their social relationships liberating rather than having them become a new and more subtle form of oppression.

Consciousness

Consciousness concerns the mesh between cognition and culture—between individual beliefs about the social world and cultural belief systems and ideologies. We can learn something of value from work that focuses on a single level, but neither is adequate by itself if we want to understand the kind of political consciousness that affects people's willingness to be quiescent or to engage in collective action.

At the cognitive level, the most useful literature concerns the operation of "schemata" and "scripts."[5] These ideas are especially relevant for students of social movements because they assume an active processor who is constructing meaning rather than a passive recipient. They imply agency, providing a natural fit with strategically oriented social movement paradigms.

Schema theory does little to call our attention to the nature of the world that people encounter with their cognitive structures. It is simply there, a received world whose process of social construction is not itself treated as problematic. It is helpful to start with the assumption that people are active processors of meaning but not if this leads us to forget that, in the political world we encounter, meaning is already organized. Information and facts are always ordered into interpretive frames, and we must understand this process as well.

The cultural side of political consciousness is represented by traditions that focus on ideology and discourse. Most of this work is critical, emphasizing the shaping of political consciousness as part of a process of class or elite domination. Any change in consciousness involves an uphill symbolic struggle since every regime has some legitimating frame that provides the citizenry with a reason to be quiescent—except in the pursuit of their civic duty. It is a formidable task to cut what Freire (1970) calls the "umbilical cord of magic and myth which binds [the oppressed] to the world of oppression."

It is not through force or coercion that a regime maintains itself but through its ability to shape our worldview. As Edelman puts it, "Government affects behavior chiefly by shaping the cognitions of large numbers of people in ambiguous situations. It helps create the beliefs about what is proper; their perceptions of what is fact; and their expectations of what is to be done" (1971, 7).

At the center of this process of "manufacturing consent," to use Herman and Chomsky's (1988) phrase, are the mass media. Edelman (1988) calls the social construction constituted by news reporting a "political spectacle." It is an apt term for his argument since he emphasizes the institutionalized power at the root of the production process and the passivity and helplessness of the spectators. It is a great circus for the minority of news junkies who follow it, providing them with "weekly, daily, sometimes hourly triumphs and defeats" (6). Meanwhile, the masses go on with their daily lives, largely oblivious to the spectacle except intermittently.

Edelman is enormously impressed with the powerful social control that is exercised, largely unconsciously, through the manipulation of symbolism used in constructing the spectacle. The actors themselves get caught up in it and are avidly taken in by it even as they have a hand in its creation. The fetishes they create—for example, "world communism"—end up dominating and mystifying their creators. Problems, enemies, crises, and leaders are constantly being constructed and reconstructed to create a series of threats and reassurances. In Edelman's gloomy world, obliviousness may be the only faint protection from this pervasive form of social control; to take it in is to be taken in by it.

Work rooted in Gramsci's concept of ideological hegemony has a similar thrust. Gramsci recognized that there is no automatic passage from economic to political dominance. Consent must be created and actively maintained. He calls our attention not only to explicit beliefs but also to how the routine, taken-for-granted structures of everyday thinking contribute to a structure of dominance. Gramsci urges us to expand our notion of ideology to include the world of common sense. Creating alternative consciousness requires a struggle to forge a "new common sense and with it a new culture and new philosophy which will be rooted in the popular consciousness with the same solidity and imperative quality as traditional beliefs" (1971, 424).

The unraveling of such processes is an intellectual agenda, not an answer. As long as the mechanisms are left vague and unspecified, the analysis remains excessively abstract. Hegemony becomes a label that substitutes for explanation rather than providing it. In many discussions, as Gitlin puts it, hegemony appears as "a sort of immutable fog that has settled over the whole public life of capitalist societies to confound the truth of the proletarian telos. Thus to the question, 'Why are radical ideas suppressed in the schools?' 'Why do workers oppose socialism?' and so on, comes the single Delphic answer: hegemony. 'Hegemony' becomes the magical explanation of last resort. And as such it is useful neither as explanation nor as guide to action. If 'hegemony' explains everything in the sphere of culture, it explains nothing" (1979, 252).

There are undeniable truths and insights in the critical literature that attempts to explain how such institutions as the state and mass media collaborate to produce a quiescent political consciousness. But the active agent of schema theory seems to disappear. In the face of such deep-rooted institutional and cultural power, the possibilities of changing political consciousness seem remote.

Taken alone, both psychological and sociocultural approaches seem incomplete.

Students of social movements need a social psychology that treats consciousness as the interplay between two levels—between individuals who operate actively in the construction of meaning and sociocultural processes that offer meanings that are frequently contested. The concept of "framing" offers the most useful way of bridging these levels of analysis. As Goffman (1974) uses the term, it contains what Crook and Taylor call a fundamental "ambiguity": "between the passive and structured on the one hand, and the active and structuring on the other. Experiences are framed, but I frame my experiences" (1980, 246). Goffman warns us that "organizational premises are involved, and those are something cognition somehow arrives at, not something cognition creates or generates" (1974, 247). At the same time, he calls attention to the fragility of frames in use and their vulnerability to tampering.

This is no ambiguity but a necessary and desirable antinomy. It underlines the usefulness of framing as a bridging concept between cognition and culture. A cultural-level analysis tells us that our political world is framed, that reported events are preorganized and do not come to us in raw form. But we are active processors and however encoded our received reality, we may decode it in different ways. The very vulnerability of the framing process makes it a locus of potential struggle, not a leaden reality to which we all inevitably must yield. On most political issues, there are competing interpretations, ways of framing information and facts in alternative ways. Indeed, one can view social movement actors as engaged in a symbolic contest over which meaning will prevail. Particular frames ebb and flow in prominence and require constant updating to accommodate new events.

Students of social movements have applied this social psychological analysis through the concept of what Snow and

Benford, in this volume, call "collective action frames." They define them as "emergent action-oriented sets of beliefs and meanings that inspire and legitimate social movement activities and campaigns." *Emergent* calls attention to their formative character and the importance of understanding the process of what Turner and Killian (1987) call "emergent norms." *Action-oriented* calls attention to the mobilizing character of collective action frames—that is, their call that those who share the frame can and should do something about the situation.

There is a striking amount of convergence on another aspect of the content: collective action frames are *injustice* frames (e.g., see Turner and Killian 1987, 242; Piven and Cloward 1977, 12; Moore 1978, 88; McAdam 1982, 51). They face a field of combat that is already occupied by a competing legitimating frame that is established and quiescent rather than emergent and action-oriented. When truly hegemonic, the legitimating frame is taken for granted. Would-be challengers face the problem of overcoming a definition of the situation that they themselves may take as part of the natural order.

It is an achievement, then, for a challenger to force the sponsors of a legitimating frame to defend its underlying assumptions. The sheer existence of a symbolic contest is evidence of the breakdown of hegemony and a major accomplishment for a challenger.

To claim that collective action frames are emergent, action-oriented, injustice frames stilll leaves a number of ambiguities and questions. What is it about them that is emergent? Quiescence should not be confused with acceptance of a legitimating frame. For many groups, the injustice component may be of long standing and can hardly be said to be "emergent" at the time of collective action. Quiescence can be produced, even when injustice is taken for granted by a dominiated gorup, through the belief that the resistance is hopeless and fraught with peril.

For many social movements, the important emergent component may have much less to do with legitimacy than it does with mutability. Splits among authorities and the successes of the movement itself may make a social order that once seemed unassailable look increasingly vulnerable. The idea of "emergence" is useful in focusing attention on a reframing process, but the specific component that is changing may be different for different movements.

There are also unresolved issues concerning the "collective" component in mobilizing frames. Various authors have suggested that the content must define a collective cause and solution for the problem being addressed and specify antagonists—an "us" and a "them" (e.g., see Donati 1988; Ryan 1991). The collective identity defined by the frame must necessarily be oppositional or adversarial. But this is precisely what some social movements—McCarthy and Wolfson (1992) call them "consensus movements"—seem to lack.

Some environmental groups, for example, emphasize the thoughtless actions of individuals and see the solution to be large numbers of us changing our life-styles. This frame suggests neither a collective solution nor an us and them. Donati (1988), in his study of the Italian ecology movement, shows how the advertising industry used many symbolic elements from the movement's frame to suggest solutions through individual consumer behavior.

Can one mobilize for collective action on the basis of a frame that suggests no clear antagonist or target and, although action-oriented, sees change occurring through the aggregation of individual behaviors? Do some social movement actors challenge the legitimating frame without offering a collective action frame? And, if so, how does one characterize the alternative they offer? Do such alternatives help collective action frames by weakening the dominance of the legitimating frame or hurt them by undercutting the call for collective solutions?

The model of political consciousness offered here also raises difficult epistemological questions. The dilemma is especially well illustrated by Snow and his colleagues who have made the most sustained attempt to integrate into social movement theory a well-specified model of signifying work or framing (see Snow and Benford 1988 and 1992; Snow et al. 1986). In trying to explain the mobilizing potency of different frames, they suggest that one major factor is the "empirical credibility" of a frame. "By 'empirical credibility,'" they write, "we refer to the evidential basis for a master frame's diagnostic claims." Following this, they speak of its claims being "empirically verified" and conclude that "to the extent that there are events or occurrences that can be pointed to as documentary evidence, . . . then a master frame has empirical credibility" (Snow and Benford, 1992).

The authors have their feet planted solidly in a conventional positivist epistemology while their heads are in the clouds of a post-positivist, constructionist world. The very term "empirical credibility" suggests the unresolved conflict. They might have called it "empirical validity," making clear their commitment to positivist assumptions about frame-free methods of determining this. But the "credibility" term contains a subtle hedge; it is not that some frames can be proven true but that they have the *appearance* of truth. And they acknowledge, "Of course, what is constitutive of evidence for any particular claim is itself subject to debate" (1988, 208). This at least hints at the idea that whether a master frame seems plausible to the observer is itself an accomplishment of successful signifying work.

A successful theory of framing must be based on an epistemology that recognizes facts as social constructions and evidence as

taking on its meaning from the master frames in which it is embedded. The essence of frame contests is competition about what evidence is seen as relevant and what gets ignored. Bootlegging in assumptions that some master frames are more empirically verifiable than others by an objective, frame-free observer simply blurs this essential point.

The same problem arises when Snow and Benford discuss master frames being overwhelmed by events, likening it to a scientific theory being disproven. Kuhn's (1962) point about scientific "paradigms"—a close relative if not a synonym for frames—is that they are overthrown not by negative evidence but by rival paradigms that win the allegiance of a new generation. To extend the point here, it is not events that overcome frames but rival frames that do better at getting their interpretations to stick.

Does such a position lead us, as some would have it, to an "epistemological chasm" (Charles Tilly, private conversation, March 1989)? Are we inevitably led to what Goodman (1978) calls a "flabby relativism" in which all frames have an equal claim in interpreting the world and it is all a matter of whose marketing techniques are the most effective? Does the social construction model force us to abandon all attempts to evaluate the implications of empirical evidence for the claims of competing interpretations?

Clearly, there is an important and complicated relationship between the characteristics of events and the success of certain frames. To take an example from the nuclear power issue, the accidents at Three Mile Island and Chernobyl have not made life easy for those who frame nuclear power development as technological progress. But neither did they provide empirical refutation of this frame. As its advocates will point out, Three Mile Island "proved" that the "defense in depth" safety system works; even in this most serious of nuclear accidents, no one was killed and no significant amounts of radiation were released. And Chernobyl "proved" the wisdom of the American nuclear industry in building reactors with the reinforced concrete containment structures the Chernobyl plant lacked.

If "empirical credibility" illustrates the wrong epistemology, Snow and Benford's concept of "narrative fidelity" (or what other authors have called "narrative fit") has no such untenable assumptions. They define narrative fidelity as "the degree to which proffered framings resonate with cultural narrations, that is, with the stories, myths, and folk tales that are part and parcel of one's cultural heritage and thus function to inform events and experiences in the immediate present" (1988, 210). Like empirical credibility, this concept also deals with the relationship between frames and events, but here it is recognized that events take on their meaning from the story line contained in a master frame. Some events fit the scenario well, but others do not, even when they can be worked in by a creative rendering.

Frames, like metaphors, are ways of organizing thinking about political issues. One should ask not whether they are true or false—that is, their empirical validity—but about their usefulness in increasing understanding and their economy and inclusiveness in providing a coherent explanation of a diverse set of facts. But there is no need to abandon empirical claims about the relative success of a given frame in political discourse and in what accounts for its rise and fall.

Finally, there are unresolved issues concerning the role of public discourse in general, and mass media discourse in particular, in shaping people's willingness to adopt collective action frames. Much of what adherents of a movement see, hear, and read is beyond the control of any movement organization and is likely to overwhelm in sheer volume anything that movement sources try to communicate. Because media discourse is

so central in framing issues for the attentive public, it becomes, to quote Gurevitch and Levy, "a site on which various social groups, institutions, and ideologies struggle over the definition and construction of social reality" (1985, 19).

Acknowledging the importance of media discourse doesn't tell us how and in what ways it operates on the consciousness of different parts of the audience. Notwithstanding the powerful arguments showing the tendency of media discourse to produce quiescence, social movements do occur. Media practices both help and hurt social movement efforts in complex ways that differ from issue to issue.[6]

It is a reasonable working hypothesis that the importance of media discourse in shaping political consciousness is heavily dependent on the type of issue involved. The precise nature of this dependence has yet to be adequately developed. I suspect that we will understand consciousness more fully when we can explain how media discourse interacts with what Giddens (1984) calls "practical consciousness"—the complex tacit knowledge that people develop about the conditions and consequences of what they do in their daily lives.

Micromobilization

Micromobilization concerns the interaction mechanisms by which individual and sociocultural levels are brought together. It draws especially on those long-standing social psychological traditions that illuminate the operation of face-to-face encounters and group dynamics. The key concept is the *mobilizing act*: words or deeds that further the mobilization process among some set of potential challengers.

There has been only one attempt to develop a full-fledged theory of micromobilization—presented in a book that I co-authored: *Encounters with Unjust Authority* (Gamson, Fireman, and Rytina 1982). Norms against self-promotion make it a bit awkward, but I will cast them aside here and argue unabashedly that the theory presented in *Encounters* offers a large part of what we need for the systematic study of micromobilization.

Different micromobilization processes are highlighted by different kinds of encounters: recruitment meetings, internal meetings, mass media encounters, encounters with allies, encounters with counter-movement groups, and encounters with authorities. In the course of these encounters, potential challengers say or do things that help (or hinder) the development of a collective identity, solidarity, and a collective action frame. If one defines a successful mobilization career as one that culminates in collective action, then a mobilizing act is one that increases the probability of such action occurring.

Encounters unpacks the overall process into three simultaneous subprocesses: working together, breaking out, and adopting an injustice frame. Each process is advanced by different types of mobilizing acts, called respectively organizing, divesting, and reframing acts.

An *organizing act* is one that increases the capacity of the potential challengers to act as a unit. Encounters with authorities are not the best venue for studying the process since the bulk of such development takes place in encounters and informal interactions among members and sympathizers, away from the public arena of confrontations with authorities. Encounters with authorities, however, are frequently proving grounds, testing the degree to which various organizational problems have been solved.

Divesting acts, another type of mobilizing act, are necessary to break the bonds of authority that keep people quiescent. In ad-

dition to reification and other processes that make the legitimating frame seem part of the natural order, there are considerations of face-work in social interaction that help keep people in line. Goffman (1959) reminds us that every social interaction is built upon a working consensus among the participants, and its disruption has the character of moral transgression. Open conflict about the definition of the situation is incompatible with polite exchange.

Agents of authority, projecting a legitimating frame, benefit from these face-work considerations. Since the norms of polite interaction prohibit discrediting the claims of others, potential challengers run the risk of making asses of themselves in challenging the compliance demands of authorities. Apart from any consideration of sanctions, they may appear boorish and rude.

Finally, the process of adopting an injustice frame involves specific *reframing acts*. It is insufficient if individuals privately adopt a different interpretation of what is happening. For collective adoption of an injustice frame, it must be shared by the potential challengers in a public way. This allows the participants to realize not only that they share the injustice frame but that everyone is aware that it is shared. This process takes time and is rarely compressed into a single encounter.

Heirich (1971) suggests a useful distinction between two types of reframing acts. *Attention-calling* acts are words or deeds that point to something questionable in what the authority is doing or about to do. They say to other participants: "Look at what is happening here. Something that is not normal and unexceptionable is occurring." *Context-setting* acts identify or define what is wrong by applying an injustice frame to the encounter in an explicit and public way.

This theory offers a beginning but leaves many issues unresolved. As the context, type of encounter, and stage of the process change, different mobilizing acts may become appropriate. Those that work in one context may be inappropriate or counterproductive in another. Take humor, for example. In some contexts, one can see how it might help in the formation of a collective identity, but it is not hard to imagine circumstances under which joking seems to defuse or deflect collective action. Humor can be a substitute for action, expressing a fatalism or resignation that countermands a collective action frame. Even when it expresses hostility toward an antagonist, the subtext may be "grin and bear it." We are still a long way from specifying the conditions under which any alleged mobilizing act furthers the process.

The theory developed in *Encounters* is inevitably influenced by its focus on encounters with authority. For example, it differentiates the closely related processes of divesting and reframing but includes quite different kinds of acts under the general rubric of organizing. Hence, acts such as "speaking for the group" that contribute to the construction of a collective identity are thrown together with "apparatus-building" acts that work on the logistics and infrastructure of collective action. A theory focused on a broader range of internal movement encounters is likely to differentiate the varied processes of producing collective identity, managing internal conflicts, and building an infrastructure for supporting collective action.

Conclusion

To explain how identity, solidarity, and consciousness operate in mobilization for collective action, we must link individual and sociocultural levels of analysis. Collective identity is a concept at the cultural level, but to operate in mobilization, individuals must make it part of their personal identity. Solidarity centers on the ways in which individuals commit themselves and the resources they control to some kind of collective actor—an organization or advocacy network. Adopting a collective action frame involves incorporating a product of the cultural system—a particular shared understanding of the world—into the political consciousness of individuals. Individual and sociocultural levels are linked through mobilizing acts in face-to-face encounters.

These frontiers of social movement theory are in social psychological territory. The processes that European new social movement theorists, American resource mobilization theorists, and some third world theorists are attempting to unravel require an analysis that brings together individual and sociocultural levels. All four of the processes discussed here—collective identity, solidarity, consciousness, and micromobilization—have roots in long-standing social psychological traditions that are much broader than the study of social movements.

The authors who illuminate these processes vary in the explicitness of their identification with the social psychological project, but, regardless, their work reflects a renewal of this focus. If it is necessary to call attention to it, as this essay does, it is only because of a past in which social psychology seemed wedded to the disparagement of social movements and their participants. But this, it turns out, was mere historical accident, not the immutable character of the field.

Acknowledgments

I am indebted to David Croteau, Josh Gamson, Hanna Herzog, William Hoynes, Bert Klandermans, Sharon Kurtz, Aldon Morris,

Mary Murphy, Charlotte Ryan, Ted Sasson, Cassie Schwerner, David Stuart, and Ralph Turner for helpful comments and criticisms on earlier drafts of this chapter.

NOTES

1. See Gamson (1990, 130), the first edition of which appeared in 1975.
2. For good reviews of the new social movement literature, see especially Cohen (1985) and Klandermans and Tarrow (1988).
3. For evidence and elaboration of this point, see Bolton (1972), Orum (1974), Wilson and Orum (1976), Snow, Zurcher, and Eckland-Olson (1980), Klandermans (1986), McAdam (1986), and Klandermans and Oegama (1987).
4. For good reviews of the centrality of a social support network in health and its buffering effects in coping with stress, see House, Umberson, and Landis (1988) and House, Landis, and Umberson (1988).
5. For especially useful discussions, see Neisser (1976) and Abelson (1981).
6. For insightful discussions of the complex relationship between movements and media in the United States, see Ryan (1991) and Gitlin (1980), and, for Israel, Wolfsfeld (1988).

REFERENCES

Abelson, Robert A. 1981. "Psychological Status of the Script Concept." *American Psychologist* 36 (July):715–29.

Asch, Solomon E. 1952. *Social Psychology*. Englewood Cliffs, N.J.: Prentice-Hall.

Barkan, Steven E. 1979. "Strategic, Tactical, and Organizational Dilemmas of the Protest Movements against Nuclear Power." *Social Problems* 27:19–37.

Bolton, Charles D. 1972. "Alienation and Action: A Study of Peace Group Members." *American Journal of Sociology* 78:537–61.

Breines, Wini. 1982. *Community and Organization in the New Left, 1962–1968: The Great Refusal*. New York: Praeger.

Cohen, Jean L. 1985. "Strategy or Identity: New Theoretical Paradigms and Contemporary Social Movements." *Social Research* 52, no. 4:663–716.

Crook, Steve, and Laurie Taylor. 1980. "Goffman's Version of Reality." In Jason Ditton, ed., *The View from Goffman*. New York: St. Martin's Press.

Donti, Paulo. 1988. "Citizens and Consumers: The Ecology Issue and the 1970s Movements in Italy." Master's thesis, Sociology Department, Boston College.

Edelman, Murray. 1971. *Politics as Symbolic Action*. Chicago: Markham.

———. 1988. *Constructing the Political Spectacle*. Chicago: University of Chicago Press.

Evans, Sara M., and Harry C. Boyte. 1986. *Free Spaces*. New York: Harper and Row.

Ferree, Myra Marx, and Frederick D. Miller. 1985. "Mobilization and Meaning: Toward an Integration of Social Psychological and Resource Perspectives on Social Movements." *Sociological Inquiry* 55, no. 1:38–61.

Foucault, Michel. 1979. *Discipline and Punish*. New York: Vintage.

Freire, Paulo. 1970. *Pedagogy of the Oppressed*. New York: Herder and Herder.

Fromm, Erich. 1941. *Escape from Freedom*. New York: Farrar and Rinehart.

Gamson, Josh. 1989. "Silence, Death, and the Invisible Enemy: AIDS Activism and Social Movement 'Newness.'" *Social Problems* 36:351–67.

Gamson, William A. 1990. *The Strategy of Social Protest*. 2d ed. Belmont, Calif.: Wadsworth.

Gamson, William A., Bruce Fireman, and Steven Rytina. 1982. *Encounters with Unjust Authority*. Homewood, Ill.: Dorsey.

Giddens, Anthony. 1984. *The Constitution of Society*. Berkeley: University of California Press.

Gitlin, Todd. 1979. "Prime Time Ideology: The Hegemonic Process in Television Entertainment." *Social Problems* 26 (February): 251–66.

———. 1980. *The Whole World Is Watching*. Berkeley: University of California Press.

Goffman, Erving. 1959. *The Presentation of Self in Everyday Life*. New York: Doubleday Anchor.

———. 1974. *Frame Analysis*. Cambridge, Mass.: Harvard University Press.

Goodman, Nelson. 1978. *Ways of Worldmaking*. Indianapolis: Hackett.

Gramsci, Antonio. 1971. *Selections from the Prison Notebooks*, ed. Quintin Hoare and Geoffrey Nowell Smith. New York: International Publishers.

Gurevitch, Michael, and Mark R. Levy. 1985. *Mass Communication Review Yearbook*, no. 5. Beverly Hills, Calif.: Sage.

Heirich, Max. 1971. *The Spiral of Conflict: Berkeley, 1964*. New York: Columbia University Press.

Herman, Edward S., and Noam Chomsky. 1988. *Manufacturing Consent*. New York: Pantheon.

Hoffer, Eric. 1951. *The True Believer.* New York: Harper and Row.

House, James S., Karl R. Landis, and Debra Umberson. 1988. "Social Relationships and Health." *Science* 241:540–45.

House, James S., Debra Umberson, and Karl R. Landis. 1988. "Structures and Processes of Social Support." *Annual Review of Sociology* 14:293–318.

Klandermans, Bert. 1984. "Social Psychological Expansions of Resource Mobilization Theory." *American Sociological Review* 49 (October): 583–600.

———. 1986. "New Social Movements and Resource Mobilization: The European and the American Approach." *International Journal of Mass Emergencies and Disasters* 4:13–37.

Klandermans, Bert, and Dirk Oegama. 1987. "Potentials, Networks, Motivations and Barriers." *American Sociological Review* 52:519–31.

Klandermans, Bert, and Sidney Tarrow. 1988. "Mobilization into Social Movements: Synthe-sizing European and American Approaches." In Bert Klandermans, Hanspeter Kriesi, and Sidney Tarrow, eds. *From Structure to Action: Comparing Social Movement Research across Cultures.* International Social Movement Research, vol. 1. Greenwich, Conn.: JAI Press.

Kuhn, Thomas S. 1962. *The Structure of Scientific Revolutions.* Chicago: University of Chicago Press.

Martin, Everett D. 1920. *The Behavior of Crowds.* New York: Harper.

McAdam, Doug. 1982. *Political Process and the Development of Black Insurgency.* Chicago: University of Chicago Press.

———. 1986. "Recruitment to High-Risk Activism: The Case of Freedom Summer." *American Journal of Sociology* 82 (May):64–90.

McCarthy, John D., and Mark Wolfson. 1992. "Consensus Movements, Conflict Movements, and the Cooptation of Civic and State Infrastructures." In Aldon D. Morris and Carol McClurg Mueller, eds., *Frontiers in Social Movement Theory.* New Haven, Conn.: Yale University Press.

McCarthy, John D., and Mayer N. Zald. 1977. "Resource Mobilization in Social Movements: A Partial Theory." *American Journal of Sociology* 82 (May): 1212–34.

Melucci, Alberto. 1989. *Nomads of the Present: Social Movements and Individual Needs in Contemporary Society.* Philadelphia: Temple University Press.

Moore, Barrington, Jr. 1978. *Injustice: The Social Bases of Obedience and Revolt.* White Plains, N.Y.: M. E. Sharpe.

Morris, Aldon D. 1984. *The Origins of the Civil Rights Movement.* New York: Free Press.

Neisser, Ulric. 1976. *Cognition and Reality.* San Francisco: W. H. Freeman.

Oberschall, Anthony. 1973. *Social Conflict and Social Movements.* Englewood Cliffs, N.J.: Prentice-Hall.

Olson, Mancur, Jr. 1965. *The Logic of Collective Action.* Cambridge, Mass.: Harvard University Press.

Orum, Anthony M. 1974. "On Participation in Political Protest Movements." *Journal of Applied Behavioral Science* 10: 181–207.

Piven, Frances Fox, and Richard A. Cloward. 1977. *Poor People's Movements.* New York: Vintage.

Ryan, Charlotte. 1991. *Prime Time Activism.* Boston: South End Press.

Sale, Kirkpatrick. 1973. *SDS.* New York: Random House.

Sherif, Muzafer. 1936. *The Psychology of Social Norms.* New York: Harper.

Snow, David A., and Robert D. Benford. 1988. "Ideology, Frame Resonance, and Participant Mobilization." In Bert Klandermans, Hanspeter Kriesi, and Sidney Tarrow, eds., *From Structure to Action: Comparing Social Movement Research across Cultures.* International Social Movement Research, vol. 1. Greenwich, Conn.: JAI Press.

———. 1992. "Master Frames and Cycles of Protest." In Aldon D. Morris and Carol McClurg Mueller, eds., *Frontiers in Social Movement Theory.* New Haven, Conn.: Yale University Press.

Snow, David A., E. Burke Rochford, Jr., Steven K. Worden, and Robert D. Benford. 1986. "Frame Alignment Processes, Micromobilization, and Movement Participation." *American Sociological Review* 51 (August):464–81.

Snow, David A., Louis A. Zurcher, Jr., and Sheldon Eckland-Olson. 1980. "Social Networks and Social Movements." *American Sociological Review* 45:787–801.

Turner, Ralph H., and Lewis M. Killian. 1987. *Collective Behavior.* 3d ed. Englewood Cliffs, N.J.: Prentice-Hall.

Wilson, K., and Anthony M. Orum. 1976. "Mobilizing People for Collective Political Action." *Journal of Political and Military Sociology* 4:187–202.

Wolfsfeld, Gadi. 1988. *The Politics of Provocation.* Albany, N.Y.: SUNY Press.

31

COLLECTIVE IDENTITY IN SOCIAL MOVEMENT COMMUNITIES
Lesbian Feminist Mobilization

VERTA TAYLOR • NANCY E. WHITTIER

Understanding the relationship between group consciousness and collective action has been a major focus of social science research (Morris 1990). The resource mobilization and political process perspectives, in contrast to earlier microlevel analyses, have shifted attention to the macrolevel, deemphasizing group grievances and focusing instead on the external political processes and internal organizational dynamics that influence the rise and course of movements (Rule and Tilly 1972; Oberschall 1973; McCarthy and Zald 1973, 1977; Gamson 1975; Jenkins and Perrow 1977; Schwartz 1976; Tilly 1978; McAdam 1982; Jenkins 1983; Morris 1984). But the resource mobilization and political process theories cannot explain how structural inequality gets translated into subjectively experienced discontent (Fireman and Gamson 1979; Ferree and Miller 1985; Snow et al. 1986; Klandermans 1984; Klandermans and Tarrow 1988; Ferree, 1992.). In a recent review of the field, McAdam, McCarthy, and Zald (1988) respond by offering the concept of the micro-mobilization context to characterize the link between the macrolevel and microlevel processes that generate collective action. Drawing from a wide range of research documenting the importance of preexisting group ties for movement formation, they view informal networks held together by strong bonds as the "basic building blocks" of social movements. Still missing, however, is an understanding of the way these networks transform their members into political actors.

European analyses of recent social movements, loosely grouped under the rubric "new social movement theory," suggest that a key concept that allows us to understand this process is collective identity (Pizzorno 1978; Boggs 1986; Cohen 1985; Melucci 1985, 1989; Touraine 1985; B. Epstein 1990). Collective identity is the shared definition of a group that derives from members' common interests, experiences, and solidarity. For new social movement theorists, political organizing around a common identity is what distinguishes recent social movements in Europe and the United States from the more class-based movements of the past (Kauffman 1990). It is our view, based on existing scholarship (Friedman and McAdam, 1992.; Fantasia 1988; Mueller 1990; Rupp and Taylor 1990; Whittier 1991), that identity construction processes are crucial to grievance interpretation in all forms of collective action, not just in the so-called new movements. Despite the centrality of collective identity to new social movement theory, no one has dissected the way that constituencies involved in defending their rights develop politicized group identities.

In this chapter, we present a framework for analyzing the construction of collective identity in social movements. The framework is grounded in exploratory research on the contemporary lesbian feminist movement in the United States. Drawing from Gerson and Peiss's (1985) model for analyzing gender relations, we offer a conceptual bridge linking theoretical approaches in the symbolic interactionist tradition with existing theory in social movements. Our aim is to provide a definition of collective identity that is broad enough to encompass mobilizations ranging from those based on race, gender, ethnicity, and sexuality to constituencies organized around more focused visions.

After discussing the data sources, we trace the evolution of lesbian feminism in the early 1970s out of the radical branch of the modern women's movement and analyze lesbian feminism as a social movement community. Substantively, our aim is to demonstrate that lesbian feminist communities sustain a collective identity that encourages women to engage in a wide range of social and political actions that challenge the dominant system. Theoretically, we use this case to present an analytical definition of the concept of collective identity. Finally, we conclude by arguing that the existence of lesbian feminist communities challenges the popular perception that feminists have withdrawn from the battle and the scholarly view that organizing around identity directs attention away from challenges to institutionalized power structures (B. Epstein 1990).

We have used two main sources of data: published primary materials and interviews with participants in lesbian feminist communities. The written sources include books, periodicals, and narratives by community members (Johnston 1973; Koedt et al. 1973; Daly 1978; Baetz 1980; Cruikshank 1980; Stanley and Wolfe 1980; Moraga and Anzaldua 1981; Beck 1980; Smith 1983; Daly and Caputi 1987; Frye 1983; Grahn 1984; Johnson 1987) and newsletters, position papers, and other documents from lesbian feminist organizations. We have also incorporated secondary data from histories of the women's movement and ethnographies of lesbian communities (Hole and Levine 1971; Barnhart 1975; Ponse 1978; Lewis 1979; Wolf 1979; Krieger 1983; Davis and Kennedy 1986; Lockard 1986; Lord, unpublished; Echols 1989).

In addition, we have conducted twenty-one interviews with lesbian feminists who served as informants about their communities, which included Boston, Provincetown, and the rural Berkshire region of Massachusetts; Portland, Maine; Washington, D.C.; New York City; Key West and St. Petersburg, Florida; Columbus, Yellow Springs, Cleveland, and Cincinnati, Ohio; Minneapolis; Chicago; Denver; Atlanta; and Charlotte, North Carolina. The informants range in age from twenty-one to sixty-eight; sixteen are white, four are black, and one is Hispanic; the majority are from middle-class backgrounds. They are employed as professionals or semiprofessionals, small-business owners, students, and blue-collar workers. Interviewees were recruited through snowballing procedures and announcements and notices posted at lesbian events. The in-depth interviews were open-ended and semistructured, lasting from one to three hours, and were tape-recorded and transcribed. The analysis also draws on our experiences as members of the larger community.

Since this work focuses primarily on lesbian feminist activism in the midwestern and eastern regions of the United States, we regard our conclusions as exploratory and generalizable primarily to this sector of the larger lesbian community. It is important to keep in mind that not all lesbians are associated with the communities described here.

The Lesbian Feminist Social Movement Community

Analyzing the historical evolution of organizational forms in the American women's movement, Buechler (1990) proposes the concept of a social movement community to expand our understanding of the variety of forms of collective action. Buechler's concept underscores the importance to mobilization of informal networks, decentralized structures, and alternative institutions. But, like most work in the resource mobilization tradition, it overlooks the values and symbolic understandings created by discontented groups in the course of struggling to achieve change (Lofland 1985).

Here it is useful to turn to recent literature on lesbian communities that emphasizes the cultural components of lesbian activism, specifically the development of counterinstitutions, a politicized group identity, shared norms, values, and symbolic forms of resistance (Wolf 1979; Krieger 1983; Lockard 1986; Davis and Kennedy 1986; Phelan 1989; Esterberg 1990). From this perspective, we expand on Buechler's model by defining a social movement community as a network of individuals and groups loosely linked through an institutional base, multiple goals and actions, and a collective identity that affirms members' common interests in opposition to dominant groups.

We describe lesbian feminism as a social movement community that operates at the national level through connections among local communities in the decentralized, segmented, and reticulated structure described by Gerlach and Hine (1970). Like other new social movements, the lesbian feminist movement does not mobilize

through formal social movement organizations. Rather, structurally the movement is composed of what Melucci (1989) terms "submerged networks" propelled by constantly shifting forms of resistance that include alternative symbolic systems as well as new forms of political struggle and participation (Emberley and Landry 1989). Although participants use different labels to describe the movement, we are interested here in the segment of the contemporary women's movement characterized as "cultural feminism" (Ferree and Hess 1985; Echols 1989) or "lesbian feminism" (Adam 1987; Phelan 1989). We prefer "lesbian feminism" for three reasons. It is the label most often used in movement writings, although participants also refer to the "women's community," "feminist community," and "lesbian community." Second, it locates the origins of this community in the contemporary women's movement. Finally, the term makes explicit the vital role of lesbians in the women's movement. The term "cultural feminism" erases the participation of lesbians and obscures the fact that a great deal of the current criticism leveled at cultural feminism is, in reality, directed at lesbian feminism.

Scholars have depicted the women's movement that blossomed in the 1960s and 1970s as having two segments, a women's rights or liberal branch and a women's liberation or radical branch (Freeman 1975). The liberal branch consisted primarily of national-level, hierarchically organized, formal organizations like the National Organization for Women (NOW) that used institutionalized legal tactics to pursue equal rights (Gelb and Palley 1982). The radical branch emerged in the late 1960s out of the civil rights and New Left movements and formed a decentralized network of primarily local, autonomous groups lacking formal organization and using flamboyant and disruptive tactics to pursue fundamental transformation of patriarchal structures and values (Hole and Levine 1971; Evans 1979). It is impossible to comprehend contemporary lesbian feminism without locating it in the radical feminist tradition.

Ideologically and strategically, radical feminism opposed liberalism, pursued social transformation through the creation of alternative nonhierarchical institutions and forms of organization intended to prefigure a utopian feminist society, held gender oppression to be primary and the model of all other forms of oppression, and emphasized women's commonality as a sex-class through consciousness raising. Although it coalesced around common issues such as rape, battering, and abortion, radical feminism was never monolithic (Jaggar and Struhl 1978; Ferree and Hess 1985). By the mid-1970s, radical feminism confronted an increasingly conservative and inhospitable social climate and was fraught with conflict over differences of sexuality, race, and class (Taylor 1989a). Recent scholarship argues that the most important disputes focused on the question of lesbianism (Echols 1989; Ryan 1989).

Conflict between lesbian and heterosexual feminists originated in the early 1970s. Although women who love other women have always been among those who participated in the feminist struggle, it was not until the emergence of the gay liberation movement that lesbians demanded recognition and support from the women's movement. Instead they encountered overt hostility in both the liberal and radical branches. The founder of NOW, Betty Friedan, for example, dismissed lesbianism as the "lavender herring" of the movement. Since charges of lesbianism have often been used to discredit women who challenge traditional roles (Rupp 1989; Schneider 1986), feminists sought to avoid public admission that there were, in fact, lesbians in their ranks.

Echols (1989) traces the beginning of lesbian feminism to 1971 with the founding of the Furies in Washington, D.C. This was the first separate lesbian feminist group, and others formed shortly after in New York, Boston, Chicago, San Francisco, and other urban localities around the country. The Furies is significant because it included women such as Charlotte Bunch, Rita Mae Brown, and Colletta Reid who, along with Ti-Grace Atkinson, ex-president of the New York Chapter of NOW and founder of the Feminists, articulated the position that would lay the foundation for lesbian feminism (Hole and Levine 1971; Atkinson 1974; Bunch 1986). They advocated lesbian separatism and recast lesbianism as a political strategy that was the logical outcome of feminism, the quintessential expression of the "personal as political." As a result, heterosexual feminists found themselves increasingly on the defensive.

If early radical feminism was driven by the belief that women are more alike than different, then the fissures that beset radical feminism in the mid-1970s were about clarifying the differences—on the basis of race, class, and ethnicity as well as sexual identity—among the "group called women" (Cassell 1977). Recent scholarship argues that such conflict ultimately led to the demise of radical feminism and the rise of what its critics have called "cultural feminism," leaving liberal feminism in control of the women's movement (Echols 1989; Ryan 1989).

We agree with the dominant view that disputes over sexuality, class, and race contributed to the decline of the radical feminist branch of the movement. We do not, however, agree that radical feminism was replaced by a cultural haven for women who have withdrawn from the battle (Snitow, Stansell, and Thompson 1983; Vance 1984; Echols 1989). Rather, we hold that radical feminism gave way to a new cycle of feminist activism sustained by lesbian feminist communities. These communities socialize members into a collective oppositional consciousness that channels women into a variety of actions geared toward personal, social, and political change.

Although no research has been undertaken to document the extent of lesbian communities across the nation, existing work has focused on a number of different localities (e.g., Barnhart's [1975] ethnography of Portland, Wolf's [1979] study of San Francisco, Krieger's [1983] ethnography of a midwestern community, Lockard's [1986] description of a southwestern community). White (1980) describes the major trend-setting centers of the gay and lesbian movement as Boston, Washington, San Francisco, and New York. Although our analysis is exploratory and based on only seventeen communities, our data suggest that developments in the major cities are reflected throughout the United States in urban areas as well as in smaller communities with major colleges and universities.

Collective Identity: Boundaries, Consciousness, and Negotiation

The study of identity in sociology has been approached at the individual and systemic levels as well as in both structural and more dynamic social constructionist terms (Weigert et al. 1986). New social movement theorists, in particular Pizzorno (1978), Boggs (1986), Melucci (1985, 1989), Offe (1985), and Touraine (1985), take the politics of personal transformation as one of their central theoretical problematics, which is why these approaches are sometimes referred to as "identity-oriented paradigms" (Cohen 1985). Sometimes labeled postmodernist, new social movement perspectives are social constructionist paradigms (B. Ep-

stein 1990). From this standpoint, collective political actors do not exist de facto by virtue of individuals sharing a common structural location; they are created in the course of social movement activity. To understand any politicized identity community, it is necessary to analyze the social and political struggle that created the identity.

In some ways, the most apparent feature of the new movements has been a vision of power as operating at different levels so that collective self-transformation is itself a major strategy of political change. Reviewing work in the new social movement tradition suggests three elements of collective identity. First, individuals see themselves as part of a group when some shared characteristic becomes salient and is defined as important. For Touraine (1985) and Melucci (1989), this sense of "we" is evidence of an increasingly fragmented and pluralistic social reality that is, in part, a result of the new movements. A crucial characteristic of the movements of the seventies and eighties has been the advocacy of new group understandings, self-conceptions, ways of thinking, and cultural categories. In Touraine's model, it is an awareness of how the group's interests conflict with the interests of its adversaries, the adoption of a critical picture of the culture as a whole, and the recognition of the broad stakes of the conflict that differentiate contemporary movements from classical ones. Thus, the second component of collective identity is what Cohen (1985) terms "consciousness." Consistent with the vision of the movements themselves, Melucci defines a movement's "cognitive frameworks" broadly to include not only political consciousness and relational networks but its "goals, means, and environment of action" (1989, 35). Finally, for new social movement theorists, the concept of collective identity implies direct opposition to the dominant order. Melucci holds that social movements build "submerged networks" of political culture that are interwoven with everyday life and provide new expressions of identity that challenge dominant representations (1989, 35). In essence, as Pizzorno (1978) suggests, the purposeful and expressive disclosure to others of one's subjective feelings, desires, and experiences—or social identity—for the purpose of gaining recognition and influence is collective action.

Our framework draws from feminist theoretical approaches in the symbolic interactionist tradition (Gerson and Peiss 1985; Margolis 1985; West and Zimmerman 1987; Chafetz 1988). These formulations differ from structural and other social psychological approaches that tend to reify gender as a role category or trait of individuals. Instead, they view gender hierarchy as constantly created through displays and interactions governed by gender-normative behavior that comes to be perceived as natural and normal. Gerson and Peiss (1985) offer a model for understanding how gender inequality is reproduced and maintained through social interaction. Although they recognize the social change potential of the model, they do not address this aspect systematically.

Building on their work, we propose three factors as analytical tools for understanding the construction of collective identity in social movements. The concept of *boundaries* refers to the social, psychological, and physical structures that establish differences between a challenging group and dominant groups. *Consciousness* consists of the interpretive frameworks that emerge out of a challenging group's struggle to define and realize its interests. *Negotiation* encompasses the symbols and everyday actions subordinate groups use to resist and restructure existing systems of domination. We offer this scheme as a way of analyzing the creation of collective identity as an ongoing process in all social movements struggling to overturn existing systems of domination.

Boundaries

Boundaries mark the social territories of group relations by highlighting differences between activists and the web of others in the contested social world. Of course, it is usually the dominant group that erects social, political, economic, and cultural boundaries to accentuate the differences between itself and minority populations. Paradoxically, however, for groups organizing to pursue collective ends, the process of asserting "who we are" often involves a kind of reverse affirmation of the characteristics attributed to it by the larger society. Boundary markers are, therefore, central to the formation of collective identity because they promote a heightened awareness of a group's commonalities and frame interaction between members of the in-group and the out-group.

For any subordinate group, the construction of positive identity requires both a withdrawal from the values and structures of the dominant, oppressive society and the creation of new self-affirming values and structures. Newer approaches to the study of ethnic mobilization define ethnicity not in essentialist terms but in relation to socially and politically constructed boundaries that differentiate ethnic populations (Barth 1969; Olzak 1983). This is a useful way of understanding the commonalities that develop among members of any socially recognized group or category organized around a shared characteristic. It underscores the extent to which differentiation and devaluation is a fundamental process in all hierarchical systems and has two advantages over other approaches (Reskin 1988).

First, the concept of boundaries avoids the reification of ascriptive and other differentiating characteristics that are the basis for dominance systems (Reskin 1988); second, it transcends the assumption of group sameness implied by single-factor stratification systems because it allows us to analyze the impact of multiple systems of domination based on race, sex, class, ethnicity, age, sexuality, and other factors (Morris 1990). These distinct hierarchies not only produce differentiation within subordinate groups but affect the permeability of boundaries between the subordinate and dominant groups (Collins 1989; Morris 1990; Zinn 1990).

Boundary markers can vary from geographical, racial, and religious characteristics to more symbolically constructed differences such as social institutions and cultural systems. Our analysis focuses on two types of boundary strategies adopted by lesbian feminists as a means of countering male domination: the creation of separate institutions and the development of a distinct women's culture guided by "female" values.

Alternative institutions were originally conceived by radical feminists both as islands of resistance against patriarchy and as a means to gain power by improving women's lives and enhancing their resources (Taylor 1989a; Echols 1989). Beginning in the early 1970s, radical feminists established separate health centers, rape crisis centers, battered women's shelters, bookstores, publishing and record companies, newspapers, credit unions, and poetry and writing groups. Through the 1980s, feminist institutions proliferated to include recovery groups, business guilds, martial arts groups, restaurants, AIDS projects, spirituality groups, artists' colonies, and groups for women of color, Jewish feminists, disabled women, lesbian mothers, and older women. Some lesbian feminist groups were not entirely autonomous but functioned as separate units or caucuses in existing organizations, such as women's centers and women's studies programs in universities.

As the mass women's movement receded in the 1980s, the liberal branch abandoned protest and unruly tactics in favor of actions geared toward gaining access in the political arena (Rupp and Taylor 1986; Mueller 1987; Echols 1989). An elaborate network of feminist counterinstitutions remained, however, and increasingly were driven by the commitment of lesbian feminists. This is not to say that they were the sole preserve of lesbians. Rather, it is our view that what is described generally as "women's culture" to emphasize its availability to all women has become a predominately lesbian feminist culture.

A number of national events link local lesbian feminist communities, including the annual five-day Michigan Womyn's Music Festival attended by four thousand to ten thousand women, the National Women's Writers' Conference, and the National Women's Studies Association Conference. In addition, local and regional events and conferences on the arts, literature, and, in the academic professions, feminist issues proliferated through the 1980s. National newspapers such as *Off Our Backs*, national magazines such as *Outlook*, publishing companies such as Naiad, Persephone, and Kitchen Table Women of Color presses, and a variety of journals and newsletters continue to publicize feminist ideas and activities. In short, throughout the 1980s, as neoconservatism was winning political and intellectual victories, lesbian feminists struggled to build a world apart from male domination.

The second boundary that is central to lesbian feminist identity is the creation of a symbolic system that affirms the culture's idealization of the female and, as a challenge to the misogyny of the dominant society, vilifies the male. Perhaps the strongest thread running through the tapestry of lesbian feminist culture is the belief that women's nature and modes of relating differ fundamentally from men's. For those who hold this position, the set of traits generally perceived as female are egalitarianism, collectivism, an ethic of care, a respect for knowledge derived from experience, pacifism, and cooperation. In contrast, male characteristics are thought to include an emphasis on hierarchy, oppressive individualism, an ethic of individual rights, abstraction, violence, and competition. These gender boundaries are confirmed by a formal body of feminist scholarship (see, e.g., Rich 1976, 1980; Chodorow 1978; Gilligan 1982; Rubin 1984; Collins 1989) as well as in popular writings (see, e.g., Walker 1974; Daly 1978, 1984; Cavin 1985; Dworkin 1981; Johnson 1987). Johnson, for example, characterizes the differences between women and men as based on the contrast between "masculine life-hating values" and "women's life-loving culture" (1987, 226).

Our interviews suggest that the belief that there are fundamental differences between women and men is widely held by individual activists. One lesbian feminist explains that "we've been acculturated into two cultures, the male culture and the female culture. And luckily we've been able to preserve the ways of nurturing by being in this alternative culture."

Because women's standards are deemed superior, it is not surprising that men, including older male children, are often excluded from community events and business establishments. At the Michigan Womyn's Music Festival, for example, male children over the age of three are not permitted in the festival area, but must stay at a separate camp. Reversing the common cultural practice of referring to adult women as "girls," it is not unusual for lesbian feminists to refer to men, including gay men, as "boys."

Maintaining an oppositional identity depends upon creating a world apart from the dominant society. The boundaries that are drawn around a group are not entirely a matter of choice. The process of reshaping one's collective world, however, involves the investiture of meaning that goes beyond the objective conditions out of which a group is created. Seen in this way, it is easy to understand how identity politics promotes a kind of cultural endogamy that, paradoxically, erects boundaries within the challenging group, dividing it on the basis of race, class, age, religion, ethnicity, and other factors. When asked to define the lesbian feminist community, one participant highlights this process by stating that " if there is such a thing as a lesboworld, then there are just as many diversities of communities in that world as there are in the heteroworld."

Consciousness

Boundaries locate persons as members of a group, but it is group consciousness that imparts a larger significance to a collectivity. We use the concept of consciousness to refer to the interpretive frameworks that emerge from a group's struggle to define and realize members' common interests in opposition to the dominant order. Although sociologists have focused primarily on class consciousness, Morris (1990) argues that the term *political consciousness* is more useful because it emphasizes that all systems of human domination create opposing interests capable of generating oppositional consciousness. Whatever the term, the important point is that collective actors must attribute their discontent to structural, cultural, or systemic causes rather than to personal failings or individual deviance (Ferree and Miller 1985; Touraine 1985).

Our notion of consciousness builds on the idea of cognitive liberation (McAdam 1982), frames (Snow et al. 1986), cognitive frameworks (Melucci 1989), and collective consciousness (Mueller 1987). We see the development of consciousness as an ongoing process in which groups reevaluate themselves, their subjective experiences, their opportunities, and their shared interests. Consciousness is imparted through a formal body of writings, speeches, and documents. More important, when a movement is successful at creating a collective identity, its interpretive orientations are interwoven with the fabric of everyday life. Consciousness not only provides socially and politically marginalized groups with an understanding of their structural position but establishes new expectations regarding treatment appropriate to their category. Of course, groups can mobilize around a collective consciousness that supports the status quo. Thus, it is only when a group develops an account that challenges dominant understandings that we can use the term *oppositional consciousness* (Morris 1990).

Contemporary lesbian feminist consciousness is not monolithic. But its mainspring is the view that heterosexuality is an institution of patriarchal control and that lesbian relationships are a means of subverting male domination. The relationship between feminism and lesbianism is well summarized by the classic slogan "feminism is the theory and lesbianism is the practice," mentioned by a number of our informants. Arguing that sexism and heterosexism are inextricably intertwined, lesbian feminists in the early 1970s characterized lesbianism as "the rage of all women condensed to the point of explosion" (Radicalesbians 1973, 240) and held that women who choose lesbianism are the vanguard of the women's movement (Birkby et al. 1973; Myron and Bunch 1975; Daly 1978, 1984; Frye 1983; Hoagland 1988). The classic rationale for this position, frequently reprinted in newsletters and other lesbian publications,

is Ti-Grace Atkinson's analogy: "Can you imagine a Frenchman, serving in the French army from 9 A.M. to 5 P.M., then trotting 'home' to Germany for supper overnight?" (1974, 11).

Despite the common thread running through lesbian feminist consciousness that sexual relationships between women are to be understood in reference to the political structure of male supremacy and male domination, there are two distinct strands of thought about lesbian identity. One position holds that lesbianism is not an essential or biological characteristic but is socially constructed. In a recent analysis of the history of lesbian political consciousness, Phelan (1989) argues that lesbian feminist consciousness emerged and has been driven by a rejection of the liberal view that sexuality is a private or individual matter. A classic exposition of the social constructionist position can be found in Rich's "Compulsory Heterosexuality and Lesbian Existence" (1980), which defines lesbian identity not as sexual but as political. Rich introduces the concept of the "lesbian continuum" to include all women who are woman-identified and who resist patriarchy. By locating lesbianism squarely within the new scholarship on the female world, Rich, like other social constructionists, suggests that sexuality is a matter of choice.

If it is not sexual experience but an emotional and political orientation toward women that defines one as lesbian, then, as the song by Alix Dobkin puts it, "any woman can be a lesbian." Lesbian feminist communities in fact contain women who are oriented toward women emotionally and politically but not sexually. These women are sometimes referred to as "political dykes" or "heterodykes" (Clausen 1990; Smeller, unpublished), and community members think of them as women who "haven't come out yet." Some women who have had both male and female lovers resist being labeled bisexual and cling to a lesbian identity. For example, well-known singer and songwriter Holly Near explains: "I am too closely linked to the political perspective of lesbian feminism. . . . it is part of my world view, part of my passion for women and central in my objection to male domination" (1990). The significance of lesbian identity for feminist activists is well summarized by the name of a feminist support group at a major university, Lesbians Who Just Happen to Be Dating Politically-Correct Men.

The second strand of lesbian feminist thought aims to bring sex back into the definition of lesbianism (Treblecot 1979; Califia 1982; Ferguson 1982; Zita 1982; Hollibaugh and Moraga 1983; Rubin 1984; Nestle 1987; Penelope 1990). Criticizing the asexuality of lesbian feminism, Echols suggests that, in contemporary women's communities, "women's sexuality is assumed to be more spiritual than sexual, and considerably less central to their lives than is sexuality to men's" (1984, 60). Putting it more bluntly, sadomasochism advocate Pat Califia characterizes contemporary lesbian feminism as "anti-sex," using the term "vanilla feminism" to dismiss what she charges is a traditionally feminine passive attitude toward sex (1980). These "pro-sex" or "sex radical" writers tend to view sexuality less as a matter of choice and more as an essential characteristic. So, too, do some lesbian separatists, who have little else in common with the sex radicals. Arguing against social constructionism, Penelope (1990) places lesbianism squarely in the sexual arena. She points to the historical presence of women who loved other women sexually and emotionally prior to the nineteenth-century invention of the term *lesbian* and emphasizes that currently there are a variety of ways that women come to call themselves lesbian. In our interviews with lesbian activists, it was not uncommon for women who embraced essentialist notions to engage in biographical reconstruction, reinterpreting all of their prelesbian experiences as evidence of lesbian sexuality.

The emphasis on sexuality calls attention to the unknown numbers of women engaged in same-sex behavior who do not designate themselves lesbian and the enclaves of women who identify as lesbian but have not adopted lesbian feminist ideology and practice. These include lesbians who organize their social lives around gay bars (Nestle 1987), women who remain in the closet, pretending to be heterosexual but having sexual relationships with other women, and women who marry men and have relationships with women on the side. Describing the variousness of the contemporary lesbian experience and the multiple ways women come to call themselves lesbian, one of our interviewees discussed "pc [politically correct] dykes," "heterodykes," "maybelline dykes," "earth crunchy lesbians," "bar dykes," "phys ed dykes," "professional dykes," and "fluffy dykes."

For a large number of women, locating lesbianism in the feminist arena precludes forming meaningful political alliances with gay men. In part, this is because issues of sexual freedom that many feminists have viewed as exploiting women, including pornography, sexual contact between the young and old, and consensual sadomasochism, have been central to the predominantly male gay liberation movement (Adam 1987). Adam, however, suggests that, despite some conflicting interests, the latter part of the 1980s saw growing coalitions between lesbian feminists and gay liberationists surrounding the issue of AIDS. Our data confirm this hypothesis. Yet it is perhaps not coincidental that at a time when lesbian feminist communities serve increasingly as mobilization contexts for the larger lesbian and gay movement, lesbian activists describe a resurgence of lesbian separatism. Calls for more "women only space" pervaded gay and lesbian newsletters by the end of the 1980s (Japenga 1990).

Thus, our analysis suggests that an important element of lesbian feminist consciousness is the reevaluation of lesbianism as feminism. A number of recent studies, though admittedly based on small samples, confirm that the majority of women who openly embrace a lesbian identity interpret lesbianism within the framework of radical feminist ideology (Kitzinger 1987; Devor 1989; Phelan 1989). Removing lesbian behavior from the deviant clinical realm and placing it in the somewhat more acceptable feminist arena establishes lesbian identity as distinct from gay identity. Yet an increasingly vocal segment of lesbian feminists endorses a more essentialist, or what Steven Epstein (1987) terms "modified social constructionist," explanation of lesbianism. They have undoubtedly been influenced by the identity politics of the liberal branch of the gay liberation movement that has, in recent years, advocated that sexuality is less a matter of choice and more a matter of biology and early socialization.

Highlighting the significance of a dominated group's own explanation of its position for political action, Kitzinger (1987) uses the term *identity accounts* to distinguish the range of group understandings that emerge among oppressed groups to make sense of themselves and their situation. Our findings confirm that these self-understandings not only influence mobilization possibilities and directions but determine the types of individual and collective actions groups pursue to challenge dominant arrangements. In the next section, we examine lesbian feminist practice, emphasizing that it is comprehensible only because it pre-

supposes the existence of a theory of lesbian identity.

Negotiation

Viewing collective identity as the result of repeatedly activated shared definitions, as new social movement theorists do, makes it difficult to distinguish between "doing" and "being," or between social movement organizations and their strategies. Although recent social movement analyses tend to emphasize primarily the political and structural aims of challenging groups, personal transformation and expressive action have been central to most movements (Morris 1984; Fantasia 1988; McNall 1988). The insistence that the construction and expression of a collective vision is politics, or the politicalization of the self and daily life, is nevertheless the core of what is "new" about the new social movements (Breines 1982; Melucci 1988; Kauffman 1990). Thus, we propose a framework that recognizes that identity can be a fundamental focus of political work.

Margolis (1985) suggests the concept of negotiation, drawn from the symbolic interactionist tradition, as a way of analyzing the process by which social movements work to change symbolic meanings. Most interactions between dominant and opposing groups reinforce established definitions. Individuals differentiated on the basis of devalued characteristics are continuously responded to in ways that perpetuate their disadvantaged status (Reskin 1988). West and Zimmerman (1987) use the term *identificatory displays* to emphasize, for example, that gender inequality is embedded and reproduced in even the most routine interactions. Similar analyses might be undertaken with regard to class, ethnicity, sexuality, and other sources of stratification. From a social movement standpoint, the concept of negotiations points to the myriad of ways that activists work to resist negative social definitions and demand that others value and treat oppositional groups differently (Goffman 1959).

The analysis of social movement negotiations forces us to recognize that, if not sociologically, then in reality, "doing" and "being" overlap (West and Zimmerman 1987). Yet we need a way to distinguish analytically between the politics of the public sphere, or world transformation directed primarily at the traditional political arena of the state, and the politics of identity, or self-transformation aimed primarily at the individual. We think that the concept of negotiations calls attention to forms of political activism embedded in everyday life that are distinct from those generally analyzed as tactics and strategies in the literature on social movements.

Building on Margolis's (1985) work on gender identity, we suggest two types of negotiation central to the construction of politicized collective identities. First, groups negotiate new ways of thinking and acting in *private* settings with other members of the collectivity, as well as in *public* settings before a larger audience. Second, identity negotiations can be *explicit*, involving open and direct attempts to free the group from dominant representations, or *implicit*, consisting of what Margolis terms a "condensed symbol or display" that undermines the status quo (1985, 340). In this section, we identify actions that lesbian feminist communities engage in to renegotiate the meaning of "woman." Opposition to male domination and the societal devaluation of women is directed both at the rules of daily life and at the institutions that perpetuate them.

In many respects, the phrase "the personal is political," coined by radical feminist Carol Hanisch and elaborated in Kate Millet's *Sexual Politics* (1969), is the hallmark of radical feminism (Echols 1989). Influenced by the civil rights and New Left movements, feminists began in the late 1960s to form consciousness-raising groups designed to reinterpret personal experiences in political terms. Analyzing virtually every aspect of individual and social experience as male-dominated, the groups encouraged participants to challenge prevailing representations of women in every sphere of life as a means of transforming the institutions that produced and disseminated them (Cassell 1977). The politicization of everyday life extended beyond the black power and feminist movements into other movements of the 1960s. In contemporary lesbian feminist communities the valorization of personal experience continues to have a profound impact.

Community members see lesbianism as a strategy for feminist social change that represents what one respondent describes as "an attempt . . . to stop doing what you were taught—hating women." Other women speak of the importance of learning to "value women," becoming "woman-centered," and "giving women energy." Being woman-centered is viewed as challenging conventional expectations that women orient themselves psychologically and socially toward men, compete with other women for male attention, and devalue other women. To make a more complete break with patriarchal identities and ways of life, some women exchange their male-given surnames for woman-centered ones, such as "Sarachild" or "Blackwomyn." Loving and valuing women becomes a means to resist a culture that hates and belittles women. Invoking Alice Walker's (1974) concept of "womanist," one black woman we interviewed explained, "My lesbianism has nothing to do with men. It's not about not choosing men, but about choosing women."

At the group level, lesbian feminists structure organizations collectively (Rothschild-Whitt 1979) and attempt to eliminate hierarchy, make decisions by consensus, and form coalitions only with groups that are not, as one activist said, "giving energy to the patriarchy." Demands for societal change seek to replace existing organizational forms and values with ones similar to those implemented in the community (Breines 1982). A worker at a women's festival illustrated the importance of community structure as a model for social change by commenting to women as they left the festival, "You've seen the way the real world can be, and now it's up to you to go out there and change it."

Because a traditionally feminine appearance, demeanor, self-concept, and style of personal relations are thought to be among the mainsprings of women's oppression, lesbian feminist communities have adopted different standards of gender behavior. For example, one of the visions of feminism has been to reconstitute the experience of victimization. Thus, women who have been battered or raped or have experienced incest and other forms of abuse are termed "survivors" to redefine their experiences as resistance to male violence. New recruits to the community are resocialized through participating in a variety of organizations—women's twelve-step programs, battered women's shelters, martial arts groups, incest survivors' groups—that provide not only self-help but also a means for women to renegotiate a lesbian feminist identity. The very name of one such organization in New York City, Identity House, is illustrative. Lesbian mothers organize support groups called "momazonians" or "dykes with tykes" to emphasize that motherhood is a crucial locus of contestation. "Take Back the Night" marches against violence, prochoice demonstrations, participation in spontaneous protests, and feminist music, theater, and dramatic presentations are other examples of public arenas for negotiating new standards of gender behavior.

Essential to contemporary lesbian feminist identity is a distinction between the lesbian who is a staunch feminist activist and the lesbian who is not of the vanguard. Thus, commitment to the politics of direct action distinguishes members of the lesbian feminist community from the larger population of lesbians. One participant illustrates the importance of this distinction, stating that women "who say that they are lesbians and maybe have sexual relationships with women, but don't have the feminist politics" compose a category who "could have been in the community, but they've opted out." Women even choose partners based on political commitment, noting that "sleeping with a woman who is not a feminist just doesn't work for me; there's too much political conflict." The tendency to choose life partners and form other close personal relationships based on shared political assumptions is not, however, unique to lesbian feminism, but has been reported in relation to other movements as well (Rupp and Taylor 1987; McAdam 1988). In short, negotiating new gender definitions is central to lesbian feminist collective identity.

Challenging further the notion of femininity as frailty, passivity, and preoccupation with reigning standards of beauty, many women wear clothing that enables freedom of movement, adopt short or simple haircuts, walk with firm self-assured strides, and choose not to shave their legs or wear heavy makeup. Devor (1989) terms this mode of self-presentation "gender blending," arguing that it represents an explicit rejection of the norms of femininity and, by extension, of women's subjugation. By reversing reigning cultural standards of femininity, beauty, and respectability, lesbian feminists strike a blow against female objectification. How central this is to lesbian feminist identity is illustrated by a lesbian support group at a major university with the name Women in Comfortable Shoes.

Because appearance and demeanor are an implicit means of expressing one's opposition, community members' presentation of self is subject to close scrutiny or, to use the vernacular of the activists themselves, is monitored by the "pc police." Women who dress in stereotypically "feminine" ways are often criticized and admit to feeling "politically incorrect." As one respondent commented, "I've always had a lot of guilt feelings about, why don't I just buckle down and put on some blue jeans, and clip my hair short, and not wear makeup, and go aggressively through the world." Some of our interviewees report a return to gendered fashion in contemporary lesbian communities. Women who identify as sex radicals, in particular, have adopted styles of dress traditionally associated with the "sex trade," or prostitution, such as miniskirts, low-cut tops, and fishnet stockings, sometimes combined with more traditionally masculine styles in what is known as a "gender fuck" style of dressing. Suggesting that "the most profound and potentially the most radical politics come directly out of our own identity" (Combahee River Collective 1982), African-American feminists criticize the tendency of many white lesbian feminists to dictate a politics based on hegemonic cultural standards. Some women who are identifiably butch and dress in studded leather clothing and punk and neon haircuts offer class-based motivations for their demeanor, and African-American, Asian-American, and Latina lesbians embrace different cultural styles. In short, the changes in appearance and behavior women undergo as they come out cannot be fully understood as individually chosen but are often the ultimatum of identity communities (Krieger 1982).

We have presented three dimensions for analyzing collective identity in social movements: the concepts of boundaries, consciousness, and negotiation. Although we have treated each as if it were independent, in reality the three interact. Using these factors to analyze lesbian feminist identity suggests three elements that shape the social construction of lesbian feminism. First, lesbian feminist communities draw boundaries that affirm femaleness and separate them from a larger world perceived as hostile. Second, to undermine the dominant view of lesbianism as perversion, lesbian feminists offer identity accounts that politicize sexuality. Finally, by defining lesbians as the vanguard of the women's movement, lesbian feminists valorize personal experience, which, paradoxically, further reifies the boundaries between lesbians and nonlesbians and creates the impression that the differences between women and men and between lesbian and heterosexual feminists are essential.

Conclusion

In this chapter, we argue that lesbian feminist consciousness is rooted in a social movement community with ties to but distinguishable from both the gay liberation and the liberal feminist movements. In effect, we are suggesting that with the absorption of the liberal feminist agenda into the liberal mainstream, the legacy of radical feminism continues in the lesbian feminist community. It is difficult to imagine an argument that would be more controversial in feminist circles, for it confirms the premise that, at least in the contemporary context, lesbianism and feminism are intertwined. This leads to the question posed in a recent speech by feminist philosopher Marilyn Frye (1990), "Do you have to be a lesbian to be a feminist?" It is our view that lesbian communities are a type of social movement abeyance structure that absorbs highly committed feminists whose radical politics have grown increasingly marginal since the mass women's movement has receded (Taylor and Whittier 1992). However insulated, they function to sustain the feminist challenge in a less receptive political climate (Taylor 1989b). Our findings are controversial in another respect. By calling attention to the centrality of feminism for lesbian activism, our study paints a picture of the tenuousness of the coalition between gay men and lesbians in the larger gay and lesbian movement.

Drawing from new data and recent scholarship on lesbian communities, we use this case to illustrate the significance of collective identity for mobilization and to present a framework for analyzing identity processes in social movements. Adapting Gerson and Peises's (1985) framework, we identify as factors that contribute to the formation of collective identity: (1) the creation of boundaries that insulate and differentiate a category of persons from the dominant society; (2) the development of consciousness that presumes the existence of socially constituted criteria that account for a group's structural position; and (3) the valorization of a group's "essential differences" through the politicization of everyday life.

The concept of collective identity is associated primarily with the social movements of the 1970s and 1980s because of their distinctive cultural appearance. It is our hypothesis, however, that collective identity is a significant variable in all social movements, even among the so-called traditional nineteenth-century movements. Thus, we frame our approach broadly to apply to oppositional identities based on class, race, ethnicity, gender, sexuality, and other persistent social cleavages. Certainly any theory derived from a single case is open to criticism. But recent research in the resource mobilization tradition points to the impact that changes in consciousness have on mobilization (Klein 1984; Downey 1986; Mueller 1987; McAdam 1988).

There is a growing realization among scholars of social movements that the theoretical pendulum between classical and contemporary approaches to social movements has swung too far. Social psychological factors that were central to collective behavior theory (Blumer 1946; Smelser 1962; Killian 1964; Turner and Killian 1972) have become the theoretical blind spots of resource mobilization theory. Ignoring the grievances or injustices that mobilize protest movements has, as Klandermans (1986) suggests, stripped social movements of their political significance. In contrast to the structural and organizational emphases of resource mobilization theory, new social movement theory attends to the social psychological and cultural discontent that propels movements. But it provides little understanding of how the injustices that are at the heart of most movements are translated into the everyday lives of collective actors. Our analysis suggests that the study of collective identity, because it highlights the role of meaning and ideology in the mobilization and maintenance of collective action, is an important key to understanding this process.

Acknowledgments

We thank Myra Marx Ferree, Susan Hartmann, Joan Huber, Craig Jenkins, Laurel Richardson, Leila J. Rupp, Beth Schneider, Kate Wiegand, and the editors of this volume for helpful comments on earlier drafts.

REFERENCES

Adam, Barry D. 1987. *The Rise of a Gay and Lesbian Movement*. Boston: Twayne.

Atkinson, Ti-Grace. 1974. *Amazon Odyssey*. New York: Link Books.

Baetz, Ruth. 1980. *Lesbian Crossroads*. New York: Morrow.

Barnhart, Elizabeth. 1975. "Friends and Lovers in a Lesbian Counterculture Community." In *Old Family, New Family,* ed. N. Glazer-Malbin. New York: Van Nostrand, 90–115.

Barth, F. 1969. "Introduction." In *Ethnic Groups and Boundaries,* ed. F. Barth. Boston: Little, Brown, 1–38.

Beck, E. T. 1980. *Nice Jewish Girls: A Lesbian Anthology.* Watertown, Mass.: Persephone.

Birkby, Phyllis, Bertha Harris, Jill Johnston, Esther Newton, and Jane O'Wyatt. 1973. *Amazon Expedition: A Lesbian Feminist Anthology.* New York: Times Change Press.

Blumer, Herbert. 1946. "Collective Behavior." In *New Outline of the Principles of Sociology,* ed. A. M. Lee. New York: Barnes and Noble, 170–222.

Boggs, Carl. 1986. *Social Movements and Political Power.* Philadelphia: Temple University Press.

Breines, Wini. 1982. *Community and Organization in the New Left, 1962–68.* New York: Praeger.

Buechler, Steven M. 1990. *Women's Movements in the United States.* New Brunswick, N.J.: Rutgers.

Bunch, Charlotte. 1986. "Not for Lesbians Only." In *Feminist Frontiers II,* ed. Laurel Richardson and Verta Taylor. New York: Random House, 452–54.

Califia, Pat. 1980. "Feminism vs. Sex: A New Conservative Wave." *Advocate,* February 21.

———. 1982. "Public Sex." *Advocate,* September 30.

Cassell, Joan. 1977. *A Group Called Women: Sisterhood and Symbolism in the Feminist Movement.* New York: David McKay.

Cavin, Susan. 1985. *Lesbian Origins.* San Francisco: Ism Press.

Chafetz, Janet Saltzman. 1988. *Feminist Sociology.* Itasca, Ill.: F. E. Peacock.

Chodorow, Nancy. 1978. *The Reproduction of Mothering: Psychoanalysis and the Sociology of Gender.* Berkeley: University of California Press.

Clausen, Jan. 1990. "My Interesting Condition." *Outlook* 2:11–21.

Cohen, Jean L. 1985. "Strategy or Identity: New Theoretical Paradigms and Contemporary Social Movements." *Social Research* 52:663–716.

Collins, Patricia Hill. 1989. "The Social Construction of Black Feminist Thought." *Signs* 14, no. 4:745–73.

Combahee River Collective. 1982. "A Black Feminist Statement." In *But Some of Us Are Brave: Black Women's Studies,* ed. Gloria T. Hull, Patricia Bell Scott, and Barbara Smith. Old Westbury, N.Y.: Feminist Press, 13–22.

Cruikshank, Margaret. 1980. *The Lesbian Path.* Monterey, Calif.: Angel Press.

Daly, Mary. 1978. *Gyn/Ecology: The Metaethics of Radical Feminism.* Boston: Beacon Press.

———. 1984. *Pure Lust: Elemental Feminist Philosophy.* Boston: Beacon Press.

Daly, Mary, and Jane Caputi. 1987. *Websters' First New Intergalactic Wickedary of the English Language.* Boston: Beacon Press.

Davis, Madeleine, and Elizabeth Laprovsky Kennedy. 1986. "Oral History and the Study of Sexuality in the Lesbian Community." *Feminist Studies* 12:6–26.

Devor, Holly. 1989. *Gender Blending.* Bloomington: Indiana University Press.

Downey, Gary L. 1986. "Ideology and the Clamshell Identity: Organizational Dilemmas in the Anti–Nuclear Power Movement." *Social Problems* 33:357–73.

Dworkin, Andrea. 1981. *Pornography and Silence: Culture's Revenge against Nature.* New York: Harper and Row.

Echols, Alice. 1984. "The Taming of the Id: Feminist Sexual Politics, 1968–83." In *Pleasure and Danger: Exploring Female Sexuality,* ed. Carole S. Vance. Boston: Routledge and Kegan Paul, 50–72.

———. 1989. *Daring to Be Bad: Radical Feminism in America, 1967–1975.* Minneapolis: University of Minnesota Press.

Emberley, Julia, and Donna Landry. 1989. "Coverage of Greenham and Greenham as 'Coverage.'" *Feminist Studies* 15:485–98.

Epstein, Barbara. 1990. "Rethinking Social Movement Theory." *Socialist Review* 20:35–66.

Epstein, Steven. 1987. "Gay Politics, Ethnic Identity: The Limits of Social Constructionism." *Socialist Review* 17:9–54.

Esterberg, Kristin Gay. 1990. "Salience and Solidarity: Identity, Correctness, and Conformity in a Lesbian Community." Paper presented at the annual meeting of the American Sociological Association, August 11–15, Washington, D.C.

Evans, Sarah. 1979. *Personal Politics.* New York: Vintage.

Fantasia, Rick. 1988. *Cultures of Solidarity.* Berkeley: University of California Press.

Ferguson, Ann. 1982. "Patriarchy, Sexual Identity, and the Sexual Revolution." In *Feminist Theory: A Critique of Ideology,* ed. Nannerl O. Keohane, Michelle Z. Rosaldo, and Barbara L. Gelpi. Chicago: University of Chicago Press, 147–61.

Ferree, Myra Marx. 1992. "The Political Context of Rationality: Rational Choice Theory and Resource Mobilization." In Aldon D. Morris and Carol McClurg Mueller, eds., *Frontiers in Social Movement Theory.* New Haven, Conn.: Yale University Press.

Ferree, Myra Marx, and Beth B. Hess. 1985. *Controversy and Coalition: The New Feminist Movement.* Boston: Twayne.

Ferree, Myra Marx, and Frederick D. Miller. 1985. "Mobilization and Meaning: Some Social-Psychological Contributions to the Resource Mobilization Perspective on Social Movements." *Sociological Inquiry* 55:38–61.

Fireman, Bruce, and William Gamson. 1979. "Utilitarian Logic in the Resource Mobilization Perspective." In *The Dynamics of Social Movements,* ed. Mayer N. Zald and John D. McCarthy. Cambridge, Mass.: Winthrop, 8–44.

Freeman, Jo. 1975. *The Politics of Women's Liberation.* New York: David McKay.

Friedman, Debra and Doug McAdam. 1992. "Collective Identity and Activism: Networks, Choices, and the Life of a Social Movement." In Aldon D. Morris and Carol McClurg Mueller, eds., *Frontiers in Social Movement Theory.* New Haven, Conn.: Yale University Press.

Frye, Marilyn. 1983. *The Politics of Reality: Essays in Feminist Theory.* Trumansburg, N.Y.: Crossing Press.

———. 1990. "Do You Have to Be Lesbian to Be a Feminist?" *Off Our Backs* 20:21–23.

Gamson, William A. 1975. *The Strategy of Social Protest.* Homewood, Ill.: Dorsey Press.

Gelb, Joyce, and Marian Lief Palley. 1982. *Women and Public Policy.* Princeton: Princeton University Press.

Gerlach, Luther P., and Virginia H. Hine. 1970. *People, Power, Change: Movements of Social Transformation.* Indianapolis: Bobbs-Merrill.

Gerson, Judith M., and Kathy Peiss. 1985. "Boundaries, Negotiation, Consciousness: Reconceptualizing Gender Relations." *Social Problems* 32:317–31.

Gilligan, Carol. 1982. *In a Different Voice.* Cambridge, Mass.: Harvard University Press.

Goffman, Erving. 1959. *The Presentation of Self in Everyday Life.* Englewood Cliffs, N.J.: Prentice-Hall.

Grahn, Judy. 1984. *Another Mother Tongue: Gay Words, Gay Worlds.* Boston: Beacon Press.

Hoagland, Sarah Lucia. 1988. *Lesbian Ethics: Toward New Value.* Palo Alto, Calif.: Institute of Lesbian Studies.

Hole, Judith, and Ellen Levine. 1971. *Rebirth of Feminism.* New York: Quadrangle.

Hollibaugh, Amber, and Cherrie Moraga. 1983. "What We're Rollin' Around in Bed With: Sexual Silences in Feminism." In *Powers of Desire,* ed. Ann Snitow, Christine Stansell, and Sharon Thompson. New York: Monthly Review Press, 394–405.

Jaggar, Alison M., and Paula Rothenberg Struhl. 1978. *Feminist Frameworks.* New York: McGraw-Hill.

Japenga, Ann. 1990. "The Separatist Revival." *Outlook* 2:78–83.

Jenkins, J. Craig. 1983. "Resource Mobilization Theory and the Study of Social Movements." *Annual Review of Sociology* 9:527–53.

Jenkins, J. Craig, and Charles Perrow. 1977. "Insurgency of the Powerless: Farm Workers Movement (1946–72)." *American Sociological Review* 42:249–68.

Johnson, Sonia. 1987. *Going Out of Our Minds: The Metaphysics of Liberation.* Freedom, Calif.: Crossing Press.

Johnston, Jill. 1973. *Lesbian Nation: The Feminist Solution.* New York: Simon and Schuster.

Kauffman, L. A. 1990. "The Anti-Politics of Identity." *Socialist Review* 20:67–80.

Killian, Lewis M. 1964. "Social Movements." In *Handbook of Modern Sociology,* ed. R. E. L. Faris. Chicago: Rand McNally, 426–55.

Kitzinger, Celia. 1987. *The Social Construction of Lesbianism.* London: Sage.

Klandermans, Bert. 1984. "Mobilization and Participation: Social-Psychological Expansions of Resource Mobilization Theory." *American Sociological Review* 49:583–600.

———. 1986. "New Social Movements and Resource Mobilization: The European and American Approach." *Journal of Mass Emergencies and Disasters* 4:13–37.

Klandermans, Bert, and Sidney Tarrow. 1988. "Mobilization into Social Movements: Synthesizing European and American Approaches." In *From Structure to Action: Comparing Move-ment Participation across Cultures.* International Social Movement Research, vol. 1, ed. Bert Klandermans, Hanspeter Kriesi, and Sidney Tarrow. Greenwich, Conn.: JAI Press. 1–38.

Klein, Ethel. 1984. *Gender Politics.* Cambridge, Mass.: Harvard University Press.

Koedt, Anne, Ellen Levine, and Anita Rapone. 1973. *Radical Feminism.* New York: Quadrangle.

Krieger, Susan. 1982. "Lesbian Identity and Community: Recent Social Science Literature." *Signs* 8:91–108.

Krieger, Susan. 1983. *The Mirror Dance: Identity in a Women's Community.* Philadelphia: Temple University Press.

Lewis, Sasha Gregory. 1979. *Sunday's Women.* Boston: Beacon Press.

Lockard, Denyse. 1986. "The Lesbian Community: An Anthropological Approach." In *The Many Faces of Homosexuality,* ed. Evelyn Blackwood. New York: Harrington Park Press, 83–95.

Lofland, John, 1979. "White-Hot Mobilization: Strategies of a Millenarian Movement." In *Dynamics of Social Movements,* ed. Mayer N. Zald and John D. McCarthy. Cambridge, Mass.: Winthrop, 157–66.

———. 1985. "Social Movement Culture." In *Protest,* ed. John Lofland. New Brunswick, N.J.: Transaction Books, 219–39.

Lord, Eleanor. Unpublished. "Lesbian Lives and the Lesbian Community in Berkshire County." Mimeograph.

Margolis, Diane Rothbard. 1985. "Redefining the Situation: Negotiations on the Meaning of Woman." *Social Problems* 32:332–47.

McAdam, Doug. 1982. *Political Process and the Development of Black Insurgency, 1930–70.* Chicago: University of Chicago Press.

———. 1988. *Freedom Summer.* New York: Oxford University Press.

McAdam, Doug, John D. McCarthy, and Mayer N. Zald. 1988. "Social Movements." In *Handbook of Sociology,* ed. Neil Smelser. Newbury Park, Calif.: Sage, 695–737.

McCarthy, John D., and Mayer N. Zald. 1973. *The Trend of Social Movements in America.* Morristown, N.J.: General Learning Press.

———. 1977. "Resource Mobilization and Social Movements: A Partial Theory." *American Journal of Sociology* 82:1212–41.

McNall, Scott G. 1988. *The Road to Rebellion: Class Formation and Populism, 1865–1900.* Chicago: University of Chicago Press.

Melucci, Alberto. 1985. "The Symbolic Challenge of Contemporary Movements." *Social Research* 52:781–816.

———. 1988. "Getting Involved: Identity and Mobilization in Social Movements." In *From Structure to Action: Comparing Movement Participation across Cultures.* International Social Movement Research, vol. 1, ed. Bert Klandermans, Hanspeter Kriesi, and Sidney Tarrow. Greenwich, Conn.: JAI Press, 329–48.

———. 1989. *Nomads of the Present: Social Movements and Individual Needs in Contemporary Society.* Philadelphia: Temple University Press.

Millett, Kate. 1969. *Sexual Politics.* New York: Ballantine.

Moraga, Cherrie, and Gloria Anzaldua. 1981. *This Bridge Called My Back: Writings by Radical Women of Color.* Watertown, Mass.: Persephone.

Morris, Aldon D. 1984. *The Origins of the Civil Rights Movement.* New York: Free Press.

———. 1990. "Consciousness and Collective Action: Towards a Sociology of Consciousness and Domination." Paper presented at the annual meeting of the American Sociological Association, August 9–13, San Francisco.

Mueller, Carol McClurg. 1987. "Collective Consciousness, Identity Transformation, and the Rise of Women in Public Office in the United States." In *The Women's Movement of the United States and Western Europe,* ed. M. F. Katzenstein and C. M. Mueller. Philadelphia: Temple University Press, 89–108.

———. 1990. "Collective Identities and the Mobilization of Women: The American Case, 1960–1970." Paper presented at the colloquium on New Social Movements and the End of Ideology, July 16–20, Universidad Internacional Menendez Pelayo.

Myron, Nancy, and Charlotte Bunch. 1975. *Lesbianism and the Women's Movement.* Baltimore: Diana Press.

Near, Holly. 1990. *Fire in the Rain, Singer in the Storm.* New York: Morrow.

Nestle, Joan. 1987. *A Restricted Country.* Ithaca, N.Y.: Firebrand Books.

Oberschall, Anthony. 1973. *Social Conflict and Social Movements.* Englewood Cliffs, N.J.: Prentice-Hall.

Offe, Claus. 1985. "New Social Movements: Challenging the Boundaries of Institutional Politics." *Social Research* 52:817–68.

Olzak, Susan. 1983. "Contemporary Ethnic Mobilization." *Annual Review of Sociology* 9:355–74.

Penelope, Julia. 1990. "A Case of Mistaken Identity." *Women's Review of Books* 8:11–12.

Phelan, Shane. 1989. *Identity Politics: Lesbian Feminism and the Limits of Community.* Philadelphia: Temple University Press.

Pizzorno, Alessandro. 1978. "Political Science and Collective Identity in Industrial Conflict." In *The Resurgence of Class Conflict in Western Europe since 1968,* ed. C. Crouch and A. Pizzorno. New York: Holmes and Meier, 277–98.

Ponse, Barbara. 1978. *Identities in the Lesbian World: The Social Construction of Self.* Westport, Conn.: Greenwood Press.

Radicalesbians. 1973. "The Woman Identified Woman." In *Radical Feminism,* ed. Anne Koedt, Ellen Levine, and Anita Rapone. New York: Quadrangle. 240–45.

Reskin, Barbara. 1988. "Bringing the Men Back In: Sex Differentiation and the Devaluation of Women's Work." *Gender and Society* 2:58–81.

Rich, Adrienne. 1976. *Of Woman Born.* New York: Norton.

———. 1980. "Compulsory Heterosexuality and Lesbian Existence." *Signs* 5:631–60.

Rothschild-Whitt, Joyce. 1979. "The Collectivist Organization: An Alternative to Rational-Bureaucratic Models." *American Sociological Review* 44:509–27.

Rubin, Gayle. 1984. "Thinking Sex: Notes for a Radical Theory of the Politics of Sexuality." In *Pleasure and Danger,* ed. Carol S. Vance. Boston: Routledge and Kegan Paul, 267–319.

Rule, James, and Charles Tilly. 1972. "1830 and the Unnatural History of Revolution." *Journal of Social Issues* 28:49–76.

Rupp, Leila J. 1989. "Feminism and the Sexual Revolution in the Early Twentieth Century: The Case of Doris Stevens." *Feminist Studies* 51:289–309.

Rupp, Leila J., and Verta Taylor. 1986. "The Women's Movement since 1960: Structure, Strategies, and New Directions." In *American Choices: Social Dilemma and Public Policy since 1960,* ed. Robert H. Bremner, Richard Hopkins, and Gary W. Reichard. Columbus: Ohio State University Press, 75–104.

———. 1990. "Women's Culture and the Persisting Women's Movement." Paper presented at the annual meeting of the American Sociological Association, Washington. D.C., August 12.

Ryan, Barbara. 1989. "Ideological Purity and Feminism: The U.S. Women's Movement from 1966 to 1975." *Gender and Society* 3:239–57.

Schneider. Beth. 1986. "I Am Not a Feminist But . . ." Paper presented at the annual meeting of the American Sociological Association, New York, September 2.

Schwartz, Michael. 1976. *Radical Protest and Social Structure: The Southern Farmer's Alliance and the One-Crop Tenancy System.* New York: Academic Press.

Smeller, Michelle M. Unpublished. "From Dyke to Doll: The Processual Formation of Sexual Identity." Ohio State University.

Smelser, Neil. 1962. *Theory of Collective Behavior.* New York: Free Press.

Smith, Barbara. 1983. *Home Girls: A Black Feminist Anthology.* New York: Kitchen Table Women of Color Press.

Snitow, Ann, Christine Stansell, and Sharon Thompson. 1983. *Powers of Desire: The Politics of Sexuality.* New York: Monthly Review Press.

Snow, David A., E. Burke Rochford Jr., Steven K. Worden, and Robert D. Benford. 1986. "Frame Alignment Processes, Micromobilization, and Movement Participation." *American Sociological Review* 51:464–81.

Stanley, Julia Penelope, and Susan J. Wolfe. 1980. *The Coming Out Stories.* Watertown, Mass.: Persephone.

Taylor, Verta. 1989a. "The Future of Feminism." In *Feminist Frontiers,* ed. Laurel Richardson and Verta Taylor. New York: Random House, 434–51.

———. 1989b. "Social Movement Continuity: The Women's Movement in Abeyance." *American Sociological Review* 54:761–75.

Taylor, Verta, and Nancy Whittier. 1992. "The New Feminist Movement." In *Feminist Frontiers: Rethinking Sex, Gender, and Society,* ed. Laurel Richardson and Verta Taylor. New York: McGraw-Hill.

Tilly, Charles. 1978. *From Mobilization to Revolution.* Reading, Mass.: Addison-Wesley.

Touraine, Alain. 1985. "An Introduction to the Study of Social Movements." *Social Research* 52:749–87.

Treblecot, Joyce. 1979. "Conceiving Women: Notes on the Logic of Feminism." *Sinister Wisdom* 11:3–50.

Turner, Ralph H., and Lewis M. Killian. 1972. *Collective Behavior.* 2d ed. Englewood Cliffs, N.J.: Prentice-Hall.

Vance, Carole S. 1984. *Pleasure and Danger.* Boston: Routledge and Kegan Paul.

Walker, Alice. 1974. *In Search of Our Mothers' Garden.* New York: Harcourt Brace Jovanovich.

Weigert, Andrew J., J. Smith Teitge, and Dennis W. Teitge. 1986. *Society and Identity.* New York: Cambridge University Press.

West, Candace, and Don H. Zimmerman. 1987. "Doing Gender." *Gender and Society* 1:125–51.

White, Edmund. 1980. *States of Desire.* New York: E. P. Dutton.

Whittier, Nancy. 1991. "Feminists in the Post-Feminist Age: Collective Identity and the Persistence of the Women's Movement." Ph.D. diss., Ohio State University.

Wolf, Deborah Goleman. 1979. *The Lesbian Community.* Berkeley: University of California Press.

Zinn, Maxine Baca. 1990. "Family, Feminism, and Race in America." *Gender and Society* 4:68–82.

Zita, Jacquelyn. 1982. "Historical Amnesia and the Lesbian Continuum." In *Feminist Theory: A Critique of Ideology,* ed. Nannerl O. Keohane, Michelle Z. Rosaldo, and Barbara L. Gelpi. Chicago: University of Chicago Press, 161–76.

32

THE TRAJECTORY OF SOCIAL MOVEMENTS IN AMERICA

MAYER N. ZALD

In our preoccupation with the social movements of the day, or of a particular movement, it is easy to miss the grand, sweeping changes in the organization, tactics, and goals of social-movementlike phenomena. Indeed, except for the writings of Charles Tilly (1978) concerning the historical transformation of forms of collective action and, in a different vein, Garner and Zald (1985), the topic is rarely discussed. Instead, analysts usually focus on a single movement or on an epoch of social ferment, noting casually how the tactics or goals of the movement are shaped by changes in the social movement being discussed.

Understanding the trajectory and future of social movements is aided not only by systematic attention to the historical transformation of a single society but by some explicit comparison and contrast of the societal context. Social movements are intimately tied to the national and international context in which they exist.

The trajectory of movements in America can be illuminated by contrasting the space for and shape of social movements in other societies with those of the United States. If, for instance, convergence theory is correct, we would expect an increasing similarity of movements in all late-industrial nations. On the other hand, if there are large and impor-

tant differences in the organization of political life and the structure of nations, the shape of the social-movement sector and of specific movements will differ greatly between them. Even as late-industrial or postindustrial societies face similar problems, they may have large differences in the operation of their political systems.

In the next section we briefly sketch the historical transformation of movements in America. We then contrast the social-movement sector in the United States with those found in Western and Eastern Europe. The historical transformation and the comparative contrast are used to project the future of social-movement organizations (SMOs), tactics, orientation, and sites. Our general theme is that in an organizational society, the shape of social movements is closely tied to the technologies, forms, opportunities, and targets created by that society.

Historical and Comparative Contrasts

How to describe the transformation of movements? Think for a moment about the parallel transformation of large-scale organizations, both the profit-making firm and public bureaucracy. Some fairly clear lines of development can be sketched. Organizations have gotten larger in size and they have developed new modes of internal

From *Research in Social Movements, Conflicts and Change* 10: 1988:19–41. Reprinted by permission of JAI Press Inc., Greenwich, CT.

management, moving from patrimonial and personal modes of control to bureaucratic systems with well-developed rule systems (Edwards, 1979). Firms have changed their formal structures from those based on functional principles of delegation to divisional—profit-center—structures (Chandler, 1962, 1977). Moreover, corporations have become increasingly multinational—although capital has always found ways to cross national borders, the growth of multinational firms that manage the combination of capital, labor, and facilities in many nations is a phenomenon of the last half century.

How would we sketch a parallel history of the transformation of social movements? One major trend in social-movement transformation is represented by the growth of limited-purpose associations as formal organizations that are carriers of social movements. In the early part of American history, most social movements articulated with the major cleavages of society. Either loose networks of local notables (as in the Committees of Correspondence) interlinked to discuss grievances and to petition the authorities or pamphleteers communicated with their constituencies. Of course, leaders emerged from their local communities, as in Shay's and Bacon's rebellions, to generate substantial collective actions.

In the early nineteenth century, social-movement activity linked directly to party politics. Although the abolitionist movement was tied to associations stemming from an evangelical tradition, it also penetrated party debate. The two-party system was not as well institutionalized then, and new parties and splinter parties, especially at the local level, had a greater chance of success (Hesseltine, 1962). By way of contrast, modern SMOs and leaders maintain an independence from the established parties and find the third-party alternative risky. Although modern movement constituencies participate in politics, their re-

lated SMOs maintain a fair amount of institutional separation. Stated somewhat differently, sentiments for change are mobilized to support a social-movement sector of many industries; at the same time, the sentiments for change penetrate ongoing political parties and structures.

It would be a mistake to argue that there was a sudden change in the associational capacity of the United States. After all, de Tocqueville early on had seen the United States as the associational society. And Rosenthal et al. (1985) have recently documented the complexity of the associational field in which women reform leaders participated from 1840 to 1914. Yet, as urbanization and industrialization proceeded, the ability of social-movement entrepreneurs to capture resources for social-movement purposes stands out. And, by the turn of the century, the associational possibility had become a flood. Any examination of the organizational infrastructure in the progressive movement quickly reveals the growth of limited-purpose, middle-class-based SMOs (Wiebe, 1967).

I suspect that the progressive movement also ushers in another aspect of organizational change that is a hallmark of later developments—full-time reformers, professionals of social change if you will, make their appearance. There were two main threads of the progressive movement: the reform of urban government and the alleviation of the negative effects of poverty—child labor, housing, and health and safety codes. The reform of urban government led to civil service, urban planning, and the use of expertise in assessing urban needs. The last, aimed at alleviating the effects of poverty, led to the growth of social work as a reform agent—the settlement-house movement, legislative lobbying, and the mobilization around specific legislative targets.

It is worth noting that two major types of social movements that are theoretically important can already be distinguished in the nineteenth century. On the one hand, those based on a **beneficiary** constituency can be seen in such actions as the early feminist movement and the labor movement. On the other hand, abolitionism, the temperance movement, and the set of organizations and actions aimed at poverty alleviation in the first part of the nineteenth century represent movements largely based on **conscience** constituencies.

Not only do we see the growth of middle-class-based "professional" movement organizations in the first part of this century, we also see an enlarged role for the press, the growth of journalistic moral entrepreneurs. Such muckrakers as Lincoln Steffens and Ida Tarbell become key figures in defining issues. Their position is dependent on the expansion of the mass-circulation newspapers and weeklies and the growth of a national audience.

There is one other aspect of the long-range transformation that deserves comment. The aims of some of the early movements were to gain access to the polity, to gain standing (e.g., to secure voting rights and achieve standing as legitimate members of the polity).[1] But it was already the case for movements based in the middle class that the issue was not polity membership but policy influence and preferences. That is, individuals and groups have standing as citizens and right of access even when the issues with which they are concerned have little credibility or legitimacy. Later I shall argue that for modern social movements, the early issues of membership in the polity have largely receded. The extension of the franchise to women and the elimination of racial barriers to citizenship eliminate some of the historic issues of social-movement mobilization. Moreover, the existence of discretionary resources and the growth of technologies that aid in their aggregation mean that diverse interests are easily and continuously represented. As more groups are represented in the polity on the

one hand, and as groups that are well represented in the polity increase their tactical repertoire to include mobilizing the grass roots on the other hand, the line between social-movement analysis and pressure-group analysis becomes increasingly blurred.

These phenomena—the growth of a relatively continuous social-movement sector, the development of SMOs as enduring features of the society, the professionalization of movement leadership, and the transition from a search for membership in the polity to the search for specific policy outcomes—are broad historical trends that shape the way in which social movements manifest themselves in modern society. What will be the specific and short-range trends of the next several decades? There appear to be changes in the orientation of the social-movement sector as the issues of an industrializing society are transformed into those of a postindustrial society.

How has the social-movement sector and its evolution in America contrasted with the transformation of the same sector in Western Europe and Eastern Europe? This is a large topic, which can only be treated in passing here. We draw upon a recent publication of Garner and Zald (1985) that explicitly contrasts the structural features constraining the social-movement sector in Western Europe and the United States.

First, the central state apparatus grew more slowly in the United States than in Europe. For a variety of reasons (e.g., the absence of threatening neighbors, constitutional limitations, citizen distrust of central government), the United States was slow to develop national administrative capacities, including a coordinated national police apparatus. As Skowronek (1982) observes, the United States in the early nineteenth century was ruled by legislatures and courts. The national administration had neither the means nor the overreach to confront and contain dissent.

Second, and fundamentally, the commitment to freedom of association, to local voluntary associations, provides a template for the voluntarism of social-movement organizations. The associational tradition, which can be traced back to the antimonarchical and Protestant congregational traditions, created a space for organizational mobilization with minimum state controls.

Third, in contrast to those of many Western European countries, politics in America did not evolve along a neat left-right dimension. In many ways, the labelling of the Democratic party as the left and the Republican party as the right was a fortuitous conjunction of the Great Depression and regime succession, not a function of the long-range orientation of the parties. In Western Europe for almost a century, parties have been oriented around a conservative/social–democratic/socialist divide, with labor closely aligned—indeed, organizationally intertwined—with socialist and communist parties. The dominant political issues of social-movement change were pressed into a clear left-right political space. In America the parties have been more diffuse, and political issues were not as compressed into a left-right debate.

The combination of an associational tradition and a more fluid party system raises the potential benefits of pursuing political change through nonaligned or loosely aligned social movements and social-movement organizations. Political options are not preempted by left-right party mobilization.

How does the social-movement sector in the United States contrast with those found in Eastern Europe? Most obviously, monoparty authoritarian regimes in the modern age combine repressive means and the organization of political life in such a way as to force underground or defuse high levels of social-movement mobilization. Although "actually practiced" socialist states

vary in the amount of space they allow to be preserved for public discourse, they all sharply constrain the mobilization of dissent. The existence of a strong church, as in Poland, or the explicit recognition of ethnic pluralism, as in Yugoslavia, may encourage a looser arena for public debate than those found in Russia or Rumania. Given the constraints on public debate in Eastern Europe, currents of reform there depend on bureaucratic and professional movements to a greater extent than in the United States. (However, we argue below that increasingly in the United States movements occur within organizations and professions.)

Of course, the overriding feature of the contrast of the social-movement sectors in the United States and Western Europe with social movements in Eastern Europe is that in the former the orientation of the sector has become reformist, while in the latter the social-movement mobilization transforms itself into regime challenges. Because the party has, and insists upon, a monopoly of power, mobilization, even for limited goals, quickly becomes perceived as a threat to the monopoly. By way of contrast, mobilization and challenge for power are institutionally expected in the West.

Now that we have set the social-movement sector in America in its historical and comparative context, we can turn to the short-term trajectory of the sector.

Social-Movement Orientation and Targets in a Postindustrial Society

What will be the specific and short-range trends of the next several decades? There will probably be changes in the orientation of the social-movement sector as the issues of an industrializing society are transformed into those of a postindustrial society. There will also be changes in the technology of mobilization and representation. Finally, the organizational society creates the potential for social-movementlike phenomena *within* organizations and professions. Over the decades, the orientation of the social-movement sector has changed, either as society changed, eliminating the social base and problems of the movement, or as the social movement and political process achieved changed, reducing the demands for potential social movements. The abolitionist movement, including the Civil War, led to the end of slavery. The labor unrest of the thirties and the rest of the first half of the century has given way to a somewhat institutionalized labor-management bargaining system. In both cases, although the social movements led to a transformation of the challenged institutions, underlying racial and class structures and antagonisms were by no means fully transformed. Class and racial balances were changed, "progress" was made, surely the new institutions eliminated the gross injustices of the prior scene. Yet underlying class and racial antagonisms remained and surfaced in new forms.

To predict the orientation of the social-movement sector, the major goals of social movements, requires a juxtaposition of emerging social cleavage lines of class, race, religion, age, sex, and culture as they relate to the definition of actionable issues in the political system. Here I highlight the set of social-movement potentials created by the changing nature of industrial society and the changing demographic patterns that we are likely to see in the decades ahead.

Postindustrial Movements

We have already seen the growth of a cluster of movements that are reactive to the negative externalities of economic growth and the industrial production system. The environmental movement, the antinuclear-power movement, local movements to control toxic wastes, movements to regulate truck weights—all are aspects of a set of reactions to the spin-offs of the complexities and conflicts over technical decisions (Nelkin, 1984). They are likely to be with us for a long time.

One might argue that the government has already responded to the threat through the creation of regulatory mechanisms at federal and state levels, such as the Environmental Protection Agency, the Occupational Safety and Health Administration. Haven't we institutionalized mechanisms for assessing risk and limiting dangers?

Two features of the underlying set of problems suggest that new out-croppings of the negative externalities of industrial society, and new groups and movements that no longer accept the costs, will be part of the social-movement landscape. First, negative externalities are created in the form of unknown by-products of industrial processes and products (Mitchell, 1979). Only by preemptive and prohibitive research can the effects of all industrial processes and products be known before the damage occurs (Douglas and Wildavsky, 1982). At what point could the effects of acid rain have been known? How does one control for long-term negative side effects of new drugs? Thus the creation of issues for action is inevitable, though some risks can be avoided.

Second, the burden of the cost of different negative externalities falls on different groups at different times. Catastrophes occur in specific instances as concatenations of normal processes that were designed to avoid catastrophe. Systems are not foolproof (Perrow, 1984). There is no way that the residents of the Love Canal area or of Three Mile Island could have taken steps beforehand to minimize the risk. Mobilization and community organization to cope with the fallout from these failures represent a movement entrepreneurial opportunity that will come often (see Walsh, 1981; Walsh and Warland, 1983). As new problems emerge, affecting new groups and communities, local movements, linked to circles of experts and professions, are likely to result.

One feature of these postindustrial or late-industrial movements is that their definition and resolution call for a heavy dose of expert opinion. Analysis of the interplay of causes, costs, consequences, and options requires extensive knowledge of esoteric subjects, unavailable to even relatively well-educated laypeople. In modern society, experts play a role in defining facts and issues for many movements—from issues of tax redistribution to the impact of pornography on behavior. Yet issues of technological fallout are peculiarly vulnerable to battles over technical definitions and complex but often ill-defined systems of causation and long-term effects. In this situation movements become battles over expert definitions, and the ability of parties to command expertise becomes an important part of the power equation (Molotch, 1970).

Many of the postindustrial social movements are "consumer" movements. They stem not just from the impact of specific products but from the intersection of government policy, regulations, and law as they bear on specific client-age-category groups. As the purview of the state has enlarged and penetrated a greater range of activities, the implications of state policy for discrete categories of users and producers carve up the political space. Each arena of state action—the labelling and testing of specific products (e.g., tobacco) and the provision of specific services (e.g., remedial education)—create the opportunity for political mobilization.

Client-consumer movements are likely to be a continuing feature of the landscape for two reasons. On the one hand, the penetration of state action into many areas of life seems to be ineluctable. (A regime may attempt to cut back its overreach, but in the United States at least, citizens, politicians, and organizations will search out new arenas in the decentralized system.) On the other hand, client-consumer movements are likely to be a continuing part of the social-movement scene because of the transformation of social-movement technology. Many, if not most, client-consumer groups are made up of individuals affected by state action who are not members of solidary communities, usually a weak condition for mobilization. However, given that institutions often have a stake in creating groups for co-optation and support, and given the possibility of contingency fees in class-action suits, the linkage of consumer issues to professional careers, and the rise of SMOs, client-consumer groups no longer have a large deficit of mobilization potential (McFarland, 1976).

Sociodemographic Bases

Changes in the structure of the labor force and families, and in the categorization and life opportunities of segments of the population, do not automatically translate into social-movement goals. Nevertheless, the existence of "at-risk" populations, those which, because of changing social relations and structures, experience major value deficits vis-à-vis other parts of the population, becomes grist for the social-movement mill. Moreover, the mere growth in the number of people in a social category at risk represents a target of opportunity for movements.

There are at least three major changes in sociodemographics of the American population that may have a bearing on the development of political social movements: the growing proportion of the population that is aged, the changing racial-ethnic composition of the population, and the growth in the number of female heads of households combined with the high level of female participation in the labor force. These changes in sociodemographics and in social relations will vary in their impact on politics and social movements.

The growth of the aged population poses continuing problems that might be grist for social movements. Yet these problems are on the continuing political agenda. The aged do vote; there is a well-developed set of institutional programs and legislative committees to cope with the changing needs of the elderly; and more sets of programs have been implemented to deal with facets of the concerns of the elderly. Writers on the welfare state (such as Harold Wilensky, 1975) suggest a set of backlash political movements that attack the welfare state. And these are clearly in place. But in fact these backlash movements are more likely to be aimed at taxation policies, not at the aged per se. It is, however, entirely possible that a prolonged economic decline might be accompanied by a set of antitax, antiwelfare social movements. Since our legislative process encourages the enactment of benefits more than the cutting off, or cutting back, of old programs, and since the center of political gravity has maintained programs, extreme reactions to the welfare state may well develop among the fringe elements of the Republican party and outside of it. But the main point is that the effects of a changing age distribution of the population are, I believe, well encapsulated in normal politics. Indeed, Samuel Preston (1984) has argued that the aged's income situation has been well protected, compared with that of children in the period 1970–1982. He attributes this income protection to the extensive political participation and influence of the aged. While there will be significant opportunities for policy change as medical technology, mortality rates, and institutions create and cope with changes in the situation of the aged, the policy changes will work themselves out through normal politics.

The second aspect of demographic changes that might relate to social movements is the changing pattern of ethnicity and race in America. Demographic projections indicate a growth of the Hispanic population and a continuing enlargement of the Asian-origin population. These changes in ethnic composition are already affecting the politics of Florida, New York, California, and Texas. They affect the politics of Chicago and Detroit as well. In this area of demographics, too, citizenship rights are well established, the normal processes of political incorporation are already at work, and local and national party structures have begun to reflect the new constituencies.

The changing ethnic composition appears to me to have implications for social movements through two mechanisms: the creation of new coalitions and the redefinition of ethnicity and ethnicity at risk. The possibility of a "rainbow coalition"—the bringing together of different ethnic groups that are all defined as "have-nots"—as a distinct entity might presage a significant shift in the control of party policy. It does not, I believe, portend a new-left social movement, since its advocates tend to operate largely in the arena of electoral politics. But it might press the Democratic party to the left and might also press white supporters of the Democratic party to the right (Petrocik, 1981). Social-movement action will depend, I think, on the linkage of social democratic-populist ideology to the rainbow coalition (i.e., a hookup between Jesse Jackson and Tom Hayden outside of the party).

Here again, the actionable issues and the potential for mobilization emerge from the intersection of state policy and the situation of groups in society. Ethnicity is to some extent created by state policy. The disparate indigenous groups that make up the category Native Americans and that are impelled to act as a coalition and respond to similar policies would have no inherent unity without state policy. Similarly, Asian-Americans had (and have) little in common in their individual identities as Chinese, Japanese, Korean, or Vietnamese, for example. But state policy may transform the utility of coalition and transform identity (Nagel, 1982; Nielsen, 1985).

Although I am skeptical that trends in aging or in ethnicity will presage a new set of social movements, the prospects for social movements related to the feminist movement and the feminization of poverty are greater. First, the women's movement is in place and has not been incorporated into party alliances. The movement may lean slightly toward the Democrats, but there has been a systematic attempt on the part of SMOs and their leaders to maintain some distance. Second, there is a unique constellation of issues related to the movement and to the feminization of poverty that challenges the social system on fundamental issues. The established political parties have trouble coping with these issues. Finally, the structure of the movement lends itself to permanence.

The three issues around which the women's movement may generate a more active movement program are the government's defense policy and the antinuclear movement, the issue of equal pay, and the potential issue of child support and child-care policy for middle-class women. It is very clear that women are more likely to support the antinuclear power movement and to resist defense policies that create the threat of war (Brody, 1984). Second, the issue of equal pay for equal work, which has great moral impact and ideological resonance, is a direct threat to a fundamental ideological assumption of a capitalist system—the notion of a market price for labor. Third, the changing structure of the family and the feminization of poverty represent a potential policy agenda that goes far beyond the point to which our current welfare-state policies have already led us.

It is not the case that this set of issues is unsolvable in our usual muddling-through,

incrementalist manner, but each issue represents a significant policy that can be combined with the others into a women's-movement agenda with far-reaching potential. None of these issues is easily accepted by major political parties. Each is costly. And the first two, the issue of equal pay and the government's defense policy, represent direct threats to central postulates of entrenched elites.

Of the social movements on the current scene, a radicalized feminist movement represents the most likely candidate for domination of the movement sector. Since the movement has a number of single-issue items on its agenda because of its specialized organizations and constituencies (e.g., battered wives), the feminist movement appears to have the best chance for continued high levels of mobilization and activity.

Cultural Movements: The Transformation of Class and Status

Aside from the sociodemographic trends discussed above, there are other changes in the distribution of the population by region, by class and occupation, and by religion that have implications for the social-movement scene. The purported growth of "Yuppies" as a significant group; the growth of a new class of professionals and highly educated people who are critical of established values; the great shift of population to, and the economic growth of, the Sunbelt; the emergence of a large and relatively prosperous fundamentalist Protestant population—all have implications for the social-movement sector and the politics of the next several decades.

Part of the problem in assessing the implications of these trends for future social movements stems from definitional ambiguity. What, for instance, do we mean by "new class"? B. Bruce-Briggs (1979) has published a useful collection of essays whose authors present alternative definitions of the term and the implications of their alternatives for politics. Is the new class represented by the growth of people with college degrees? With advanced degrees? With professional degrees? With occupations in the media and human services? With degrees in the arts and social sciences? Moreover, occupation, or occupational training, does not make a social class. Steven Brint (1984) has attempted a systematic comparison of the definitions of the new class and an empirical test of differences in political attitudes of the groups identified under each definition. For the time period he studied (data sets collected from 1974 to 1980), there was a slight tendency for new entrants to the occupational and educational groups studied to be more critical of society than older members. More significantly for new-class theory, only people with arts related and social-science educational backgrounds tend to be consistently critical of business when compared with other groups. Brint concludes that the strength and permanence of the new class has been exaggerated.

A somewhat different part of the problem in assessing the implications of these trends is that these groups do not represent classes or corporate groups with clear interests and organizational bases. For instance, the population of Houston, Texas, is diverse. In the period when the oil industry was booming, its population had some interests in common with those of the growing Sunbelt population. But in the period of economic retrenchment that occurred with the decline in oil prices in 1983 and 1984, the economic interests of the people of Houston no longer coincided with those of the growing population of the Sunbelt. Moreover, Kevin Phillips (1982) argues convincingly that the purported conservative drift of the Sunbelt population is exaggerated in its permanence and unity. The migration of people

to the Sunbelt and its subsequent growth contribute to instability and change, but change without clear direction. Phillips does show that some of the newly emerging communities whose residents share a common occupational lifestyle have a distinctive political commitment. For instance, the high-tech/libertarian communities of Marin County, Palo Alto, Denver, or suburban Boston all share a distinctive political style. In 1980, these areas were major centers of support for John Anderson for president.

But in general, because the new class is amorphous, and because Yuppies are distinguished more by age and family income pattern than by anything else, it is hard to believe that they represent a base for any substantial social movement. Rather, they are likely to be a base for expressive styles, not for a systematic policy and ideological program. Physical fitness centers and aerobic dance classes are not a basis for organizational mobilization.

On the other hand, the growth of the fundamentalist Protestant churches, with their strong communal base married to modern social-movement technology, does represent a trend that is likely to have deep social-movement implications. Movements such as the Moral Majority represent a political expression of a deep cultural split, a reaction to the trends of modernism, to secularism, to sexual and social libertarianism. Fundamentalism is not new. What is new is the size and wealth of its participants and the readiness of its denominational and church leaders to participate in political action (Harding, 1983, 1985).

The **orientation** of the social-movement sector responds to underlying trends in the social structure as they relate to political process and actionable issues. We have located the future orientation of the sector in the demographic trends and emerging issues of postindustrial society. But the **volume** or size of the sector is also influenced by the organizational and mobilizational technologies available to the society. So the future of social movements in America is partly an organizational and technological question.

Organizational Changes and Resource Mobilization

We have described in some detail the factors that eased the creation of social-movement organizations. Briefly, affluence creates discretionary resources that can be allocated for social-movement causes, even when discretionary time is in short supply. Moreover, large numbers of people, especially college students, have discretionary time to allocate. The existence of marginal resources, gathered from many middle-class suppliers, or larger amounts of resources gathered through churches, philanthropic organizations, government agencies, and labor unions, permits movement entrepreneurs to find an organizational niche even when a mass base of activists or mobilized marchers is difficult to find. Every cause can find an organizational vehicle—concern about air safety is quickly translated into the Aviation Consumer Action Project—a Ralph Nader spin-off. The Children's Defense League, directed by Marian Wright Edelman, employs sixty people and has a yearly budget of $3 million.

Fund-raising and Organizational Development

There have been great strides in the techniques of mass fund-raising. Social-movement organizations share with political parties and televangelism the advantages of the computer revolution and mass mail-marketing techniques. These methods include computer-personalized letters, carefully cleaned and targeted mailing lists, and the ability to reshape letters and appeals to suit a variety of audiences. Hadden and Swann (1981) describe how evangelical ministers meld television mailing lists, viewers, and letters into a TV-network-based community. Compared with the methods of the leaders of evangelical religion, social movements are at a disadvantage in this particular game, because they are less able to utilize television on a routine basis. Their audience is smaller and more episodic in its attention span.

On the other hand, social movements do have access to foundation and government agencies in a way that religious organizations do not. Craig Jenkins (forthcoming) traces the growth and shifts in philanthropic foundation support for social-movement activity. Social movements are also aided by the general growth of voluntary association—community organization skills. The skills of networking, of notification of meetings, of developing newsletters, have spread quite remarkably in our society. Networking, fund-raising, and organizational techniques for utilizing the media are all translated from techniques learned on the job into formally transmitted skills. Professional fund-raisers—pollsters and campaign managers, for example—are guns for hire, and it is extremely easy to learn the formal skills necessary for organizational development. Larry Sabato (1981:340–343) lists more than fifty political consultants who provide polling, fund-raising, and campaign management skills to political candidates. Some of these consultants restrict their services to candidates of only one party and to social issues they find are ideologically compatible. Richard Viguerie (1981), a key figure in fund-raising for the right, is unique in his role as an ideologue as well as a fund-raiser.

The Representation of Groups

Earlier I asserted that the modern system of mobilization now permits most groups to be easily represented. In a sense, this is an assertion that basic access to the policy of societal members is easily achieved. Such an observation does not square with the obvious fact that groups may have access to, but not be on, the public agenda. Groups without resources or moral claims that appeal to a large segment of the population continue to be isolated from political action. Our earlier arguments about the professionalization of movement mobilization can be used to shed light on these problems.

There are two major routes to gaining access to the policy agenda. First, beneficiary-based movements can draw upon the infrastructure of support in a large interest category. While their mobilization process may depend in part on a wider moral discourse, perceived grievances within the group and a broader agenda of communal action may sustain the mobilization of such social movements, regardless of their support in the larger society. Second, groups whose members do not have citizenship status or have weak citizenship status (e.g., children, animals, prisoners), or that have few resources (e.g., welfare mothers), can draw upon the moral discourse of the larger society.

Modern society makes it possible for weak groups to be represented because of two major characteristics. The existence of multiple subcultures in modern society, created and sustained by the enormous institutionalization of professions and associations, maintains a continuous dialogue about the core values of those differentiated institutions. Most weak and underrepresented groups are represented by conscience constituents tied to institutions and associations. Children, whales, and dogs are objects of concern to foundations, voluntary associations, professional groups, and professional schools. These groups carry on a continuous dialogue and debate about the state and potential improvement of the lot of

their objects of concern. For instance, one of the more vigorous movements of 1984 and 1985 involved the attempt to stop or limit the use of animals for medical research. The movement and its followers used a wide variety of tactics (e.g., rallies, lobbying, and the bombing of medical laboratories) to attempt to achieve their ends. It was not merely a movement of pet lovers; it developed a full-blown ideology about the relation of *Homo sapiens* to other species.

That such representation occurs should not be taken to imply a strong representation. Professional Movement Organizations (PMOs) representing weak groups may be peculiarly dependent on attaching their causes to broad social movements or to exploring windows of opportunity that open in the policy arena. As long as they are isolated from the broader movements or from opportunities created by larger political events, coalitions, and processes, they may represent groups with little effect. But under the right conditions, PMOs can be major components of social change. Ronald Troyer and Gerald Markle (1983), for instance, have documented the extraordinary role of a PMO in changing American laws and regulations related to smoking tobacco. A PMO called ASH acted as fulcrum and manager in the antismoking campaign as the evidence of the negative effects of smoking mounted.

Tactical Transformation

The organizational revolution represented by the growing ease of mobilization has also been accompanied by a tactical transformation. Over a decade ago, Michael Lipsky (1968) taught us that movement tactics must be seen as multivalent. Such tactics may impose economic and political costs on authorities; they have an effect on the sympathies or antagonisms of the local "bystander" public and referent elites and, through the media, on bystander groups and referent elites who are not in immediate contact; finally, they have an impact on the sympathies, readiness to act, and enthusiasm of adherents and constituents.

The tactical repertoire of any movement is dependent in the first instance on the cultural-technological stock available to its cadre and adherents. Boycotts, petitions, guerilla theater, sit-ins, mass mailings to members of legislatures, class-action suits, voter-registration drives, hijackings, assassinations, car bombings, marches, truck blockades, computer referenda, telethons, and political action committees are social inventions. They are mixtures of hard technology, legal constraints on behavior, and organizational resources. Each tactic is learned and can be transmitted. Each requires a particular combination of skills, personnel, and tools that may or may not be available to the cadre. You cannot have a march with only five supporters. There is a *production function* for tactics.

Moreover, tactics occur in the stream of history. They take on meaning in specific situations and in relation to what has occurred before. Terrorism, for instance, is quite effective if the authorities are ambivalent about the legitimacy of their participation in a given setting, or if referent elites and mass publics are pressing for the withdrawal of authorities and their agents. Terrorism has the opposite effect, in the short run at least, if authorities and referent elites are unified in opposition to the terrorists and their cause. Indeed, terrorist attacks on a unified authority and referent elite may only lead to the strengthening of authority response. Especially in the early stages of a movement, terrorism may signify to sympathizers the vitality and potential of suppressed movements. To bystanders it signifies the potential costs of recognizing the legitimacy of the

movement. Over time, however, the repeated use of terror loses its shock-signifying value and is assimilated into the flow of events.

When new tactics are introduced, cadre and adherents must gain experience in their use so that the efficiency of deployment may increase over time. But tactics may decline in effectiveness as authorities and countermovements develop skills in responding or controlling them (see McAdam, 1983). If tactics are not followed by success, constituents may grow weary and despondent.

It is difficult to discuss trends in tactics without discussing the components of specific movements. The legitimation of tactics is not only a function of technological availability but also of the basic commitments of adherents. The more a movement rejects the fundamental social order as embodied in the state, the more likely it is to use terror and violence. On the other hand, even if the movement has narrower goals, if the enemy is seen as evil incarnate, more extreme measures are justified to some members of the movement. Prolife supporters have bombed the premises of a Planned Parenthood group, but so far retirees have not bombed any Social Security Administration offices. More abstractly stated, tactical choice is part of a moral economy—what seems legitimate and appropriate to constituents and what seems legitimate to external audiences may vary.

Two tactical trends are apparent. First, participants of social movements in the United States quickly learn how to link local and national venues. An organization such as Common Cause, which began as a national PMO, with only a mail membership, quickly learned the value of establishing local chapters and undertaking activity as means of building constituencies and developing a source for local pressure on legislators and authorities (McFarland,

1984). Conversely, the existence of local groups concerned with local problems creates an opportunity for entrepreneurs to coordinate their actions and represent their local interests on the national scene (e.g., the Civil Rights Leadership Conference, and the Federation of Neighborhood Organizations). Note that I am using as "tactical" the very structure of organizations; that is, organizational structure is chosen as a technique to achieve social movement ends.

Parenthetically, it should be noted that established pressure groups and even corporations with local branches have adopted similar strategies. Thus the coordinating associations for the electricity utilities developed local branches in order to support nuclear power. Firms like McDonald's and ARCO have also mobilized constituents to bring pressure on legislators. But our major point should be clear. In modern society, local groups can quickly develop a national presence, and groups that start at the national level can develop local arms.

A second tactical trend in the United States seems to be a decrease in the use of violent methods over long periods of time. I assume that large-scale conflict is prohibited in part, both by the strength of the state and the ability of the state to repress conflict *and* by the extent to which society has developed techniques for co-opting and for incorporating groups and movements into the procedures. Writing on conflict and social movements from the perspective of a world system, Edward Kick (1980:184) summarizes the matter nicely:

> In the core, several factors combine to reduce conflict intensity. Strong states more effectively institutionalize conflict among internal parties (e.g., labor and management) by initiating and, if necessary, enforcing rules of the game. The state itself is unlikely to become a party to intensely violent mass conflict because its very strength and capacity for repression when necessary inhibit efforts to seize the government. Moreover, that capacity rarely needs to be fully activated since politics in the core is not a zero-sum game. The polyarchic political system, coupled with an increasing pool of resources, generates a fairly high probability that groups seeking recognition and/or material benefits will actually acquire them. Also, the economic ability to institute broad social welfare programs may constitute a general, rather than group specific, mechanism for reducing conflict. This type of opportunity, or cost structure, greatly encourages the formation of conflict groups with limited goals. . . . That is even more true from the perspective of the population at risk for recruitment into such groups. Given the class structure of core countries, there is a relatively large pool of persons who are unwilling to risk involvement in unlimited political conflict or in the governmental changes that such conflict may initiate.

What are the implications of these tactical and organizational trends for the future of social movements in the United States? First, that movements easily develop national-local linkages implies that pure grassroots movements or national lobbying organizations can easily switch their forms. The availability of networks and organizations means that SMOs are not restricted by their constituency bases. Although we may find pure grassroots movements or pure national lobbying organizations—neither of which, for **tactical** reasons develops into the other—increasingly it is a tactical choice.

Second, since groups easily gain legitimate status, and since the political structures of the United States are tied to legal and ideological roots prescribing openness and consultation, movements are easily brought into a participatory mode—the combination of an open electoral system and bureaucratic representation co-opts movements. Indeed, violent tactics are as likely to be used between movements and countermovements or between branches of sects as they are between movements and authorities. It is striking that the two movements most likely to use violence in recent times have been the anti-abortion groups and the groups opposed to experimentation on animals.

Third, we can expect a continued evolution and refinement of the computer-television-personalized solicitation-lobbying interface. This technological organizational approach to fund-raising and mobilization is an American invention, now spreading to Western Europe. Leaders in the employment of this technology, such as Richard Viguerie, now have a European clientele, and political consultants such as Joseph Napolitan have clients in Latin America (Sabato, 1981).

Finally, the reformist character of modern American movements, coupled with the ease of organizing SMOs and the stability of the two-party system, implies the continuing pervasiveness of single-issue politics. In this electoral system, SMOs focus on marginal influence, rather than on the seizure of power.

By no means does this analysis imply an end to large-scale conflict in which social movements mount major challenges to established institutions. Nor does it imply an end to the destruction of lives and property as part of the interaction of movements and authorities. It is possible to develop a scenario of systemic economic decline that leads in this direction. Our analysis **does** imply that, short of a major change in the direction of the social system, reformist and

melioristic movements and contained tactics are more likely to be the mode.

The Situs of Social Movements

Our analysis has largely focused on movements that express themselves through demands on the central political system. But in modern society much social-movement activity in fact takes place in bureaucratic institutions and in the professions. For several decades, sociologists studying professions and organizations have recognized that social-movementlike phenomena do occur in organizations and professions (Bucher and Strauss, 1961; Weinstein, 1979; Zald and Berger, 1978). The growth of complex bureaucratic institutions, intersecting with professions as special-interest groups, suggests that much of social change and social-movement phenomena occur not through political legislation but as reform and innovation movements connected to established agencies. It is impossible to evaluate the sheer quantity of such social-movementlike activity, but let us give a few illustrations.

Over the last twenty years the hospice movement has spread rapidly (Paradis, 1985). It has been a social movement at the edge of the medical complex, led largely by medically related professionals. A prominent role has been taken by nurses and ministers related to medical settings. Although the institutionalization of the hospice movement has required changes in legislation and funding, a good part of the action has involved mobilizing local institutions. Another professional movement can be seen in the development of family therapy. It developed on the periphery of psychology, psychiatry, and clinical social work. It was at first frowned upon by the orthodox professionals, but it has had charismatic leaders and separate training institutions, and the family-therapy phenomenon spread like wildfire before it became well institutionalized.

Other movements in professional settings include the transformation of city planning in the 1960s. The emphasis changed from formal physical planning to community development and organization. It developed a new recruitment base and led to conflict within agencies (Needleman and Needleman, 1974; Ross, 1975).

Our tools for the analysis of movements within professions and bureaucracies are much weaker than are our tools for the analysis of political movements. These movements often resemble "idea currents" carried by new generations of professionals. The events of the movements are less dramatic than police–demonstrator confrontations or marches on Washington. And except in the case of organizational coups d'état, the media are unlikely to pay much attention to them. But in some cases these movements massively transform the territory of institutional operation. They occur at the intersection of technological change, professional and normative challenges to established practices, and organizational change. They are likely to become a dominant part of social change in an increasingly bureaucratized and professionalized society.

Conclusion

I have sketched the trends in the organization of SMOs, the transformation of tactics, the orientation of the social-movement sector, and situs. This is a risky business. Who knows? Tomorrow some new movement may emerge, totally unrelated to the current scene. "Speciism" as a social move-

ment may dominate the headlines. On the other hand, short of a major depression, war, or ecological catastrophe, I doubt that we will see a major reconstitution of the social-movement sector in our advanced industrial society. Aside from the potential movements and countermovements around the feminist issues and the movements around fundamentalism that I have discussed, no other movements on the current scene have much potential for social-movement action.

But it should be clear that a large-scale economic depression is possible; that ecological catastrophe in regions or in nations may occur. Such large-scale events would clearly reshape the social-movement sector. Adam Przeworski and Michael Wallerstein (1982) have tried to sketch the mix of short-term and long-run considerations shaping working-class mobilization that might be affected by a large-scale downward change in the economy. It is clear that a prolonged depression could change the mobilization of the working class, upset the well-institutionalized balance of management-labor conflict and bargaining, and transform allegiances to political parties and the ongoing system.

With these statements in mind, it is important to note that our analysis largely has been restricted to the United States. But just as the diverse economies of the world are increasingly interdependent, so too are the social movements of the world. Movements in one country create demonstration effects for citizens of other countries. Feminist, peace, and ecological movements are modeled on similar movements in other countries. The **shape** of the specific issues and of organization and tactics vary from country to country as adherents and authorities respond to provide the local context for action.

The social-movement sector is part of the larger sector of political action. It is possible that in postindustrial societies, the political sectors are also converging. Certainly, Western European politics in the late twentieth century is not as dominated by the left-right party space as it was in the earlier part of the century. Not only do social movements in one country provide a demonstration for adherents in another country, but increasingly they may operate in similar structural contexts. Lifestyle, class, and institutions of civic participation may converge, creating similar grievances and similar social-political opportunities for movement forms. On the other hand, however, regimes may restrict the diffusion of social movements by controlling the media and their citizens' opportunity to travel, as well as through the use of repression. New social movements will vary widely in their penetration of political debate.

Finally, social movements and nations exist in a larger context of global polarization and superpower conflict. Social movements in Poland, Afghanistan, South Africa, and Nicaragua cannot be separated from their larger international context.

NOTE

1. It may be that in T. H. Marshall's (1965) terms, issues of political rights have receded, but a range of economic and civil rights denied to specific groups continues to be a source of social-movement attack. The issue of political rights, however, has been central to a perspective on social movements that sees them as arising, in a sense, through societal members **outside** the polity. I believe this perspective on social movements is misguided. It starts the analysis of movements from below. Political social movements involve contests for power in which partisans believe their routine access and legitimate place on the agenda are inadequate. People of the right and the left, above and below, may believe the directions of the polity to be inadequate. They may believe that authorities do not represent their interests.

REFERENCES

Brint, S. 1984. "'New class' and cumulative trend explanations of the liberal political attitudes of professionals," American Journal of Sociology, 90(1):30–71.

Brody, C.J. 1984. "Differences by sex in support for nuclear power," Social Forces 63(1):209–28.

Bruce-Briggs, B. (ed.) 1979. The New Class? New Brunswick, N.J.: Transaction.

Bucher, R. and A. Strauss 1961. "Professions in Process," American Journal of Sociology. 66(December):325–34.

Chandler, A.D., Jr. 1962. Strategy and Structure: Chapters in the History of the Industrial Enterprise. Cambridge, Mass.: MIT Press.

———. 1977. The Visible Hand: The Managerial Revolution in American Business. Cambridge, Mass.: Harvard University Press.

Douglas, M., and A. Wildavsky 1982. Risk & Culture: An Essay on the Selection of Technological and Environmental Dangers. Berkeley: University of California Press.

Edsall, T. B. 1984. The New Politics of Inequality. New York: W.W. Norton.

Edwards, R. 1979. Contested Terrain: The Transformation of the Workplace in the Twentieth Century. New York: Basic Books.

Garner, R., and M.N. Zald 1985. "The political economy of social movement sectors." Pp. 119–145 in G.D. Suttles and M.N. Zald (eds.), The Challenge of Social Control: Citizenship and Institution Building in Modern Society. Norwood, N.J.: ABLEX.

Gitlin, T. 1980. The Whole World Is Watching: Mass Media in the Making and Unmaking of the New Left. Berkeley: University of California Press.

Hadden, J. K., and C. E. Swann 1981. Prime Time Preachers: The Rising Power of Televangelism. Reading, Mass.: Addison-Wesley.

Harding, S. 1985. "World consuming rhetoric: The movement behind the moral majority." unpublished paper, Ann Arbor: University of Michigan.

———. 1983. "Reverend Jerry Falwell and the Moral Majority: Origins of a movement." University of Michigan.

Hesseltine, W.B. 1962. Third-Party Movements in the United States. Princeton, N.J.: Van Nostrand.

Jenkins, C. (forthcoming) Patrons of Social Reform: Private Foundations and the Social Movements of the 1960s and '70s. New York: Russel Sage.

Kick, E.L. 1980. "World system properties and mass political conflict within nations: Theoretical framework." Journal of Political and Military Sociology. 8(2):175–90.

Lipsky, M. 1968. "Protest as a Political Resource." American Political Science Review. 62:1144–58.

Marshall, T.H. 1965. Class, Citizenship and Social Development. Garden City, N.Y.: Doubleday.

McAdam, D. 1983. "Tactical innovation and the pace of insurgency." American Sociological Review. 48(December):735–53.

McFarland, A. 1976. Public Interest Lobbies: Decision Making on Energy. Washington, D.C.: American Enterprise Institute.

———. 1984. Common Cause: Lobbying in the Public Interest. Chatham, N.J.: Chatham House.

Mitchell, R.C. 1979. "National environmental lobbies and the apparent illogic of collective action." In C. Russel (ed.), Collective Decision Making. Baltimore: Resources for the Future.

Molotch, H. 1970. "Oil in Santa Barbara and power in America." Sociological Inquiry 40:131–44.

Nagel, J. 1982. "Collective action and public policy: American Indian mobilization." Social Science Journal 19(January):37–45.

Needleman, M. and C. Needleman 1974. Guerillas in the Bureaucracy: The Community Planning Experiment in the United States. New York: Wiley.

Nelkin, D. 1984. Controversy: The Politics of Technical Decisions, ed. 2. Beverly Hills, Calif.: Sage Publications.

Nielsen, F. 1985. "Toward a theory of ethnic solidarity in modern societies." American Sociological Review 5(2):133–49.

Paradis, L.F. 1985. "The American hospice movement: A resource mobilization perspective." Unpublished paper presented at the annual meetings of the Southern Sociological Society, Charlotte, N.C.

Perrow, C. 1984. Normal Accidents: Living with High Risk Technologies. New York: Basic Books.

Petrocik, J.R. 1981. Party Coalitions: Realignments and the Decline of the New Deal Party System. Chicago: University of Chicago Press.

Phillips, K.S. 1982. Post-Conservative America: People, Politics and Ideologies in a Time of Crisis. New York: Random House.

Preston, S.H. 1984. "Children and the elderly: Divergent paths for America's dependents." Demography 2(4):435–56.

Przeworski, A., and M. Wallerstein 1982. "The structure of class conflict in democratic capitalist societies." American Political Science Review 76(June):215–38.

Rosenthal, N., et al. 1985. "Social movements and networks analysis: A case study of nineteenth-century women's reform in New York State." American Journal of Sociology 90(5):1022–54.

Ross, R.J.A. 1975. Advocate Planners and Urban Reform. Unpublished Ph.d. Dissertation. Chicago: University of Chicago.

Sabato, L.J. 1981. The Rise of Political Consultants: New Ways of Winning Elections. New York: Basic Books.

———. 1984. PAC Power: Inside the World of Political Action Committees. New York: W.W. Norton.

Skowronek, S. 1982. Building a New American State: The Expansion of National Administrative Capacities 1877–1920. Cambridge, England: Cambridge University Press.

Tilly, C. H. 1978. From Mobilization to Revolution. Reading, Mass.: Addison-Wesley.

Troyer, R.J., and G.E. Markle 1983. Cigarettes: The Battle Over Smoking. New Brunswick, N.J.: Rutgers University Press.

Viguerie, R.A. 1981. The New Right: We're Ready to Lead. Falls Church, Va.: Caroline House Publisher.

Walker, J.L. 1983. "The origins and maintenance of interest groups in America." American Political Science Review 77(June):390–406.

Walsh, E.H. 1981. "Resource mobilization and citizen protest in communities around Three Mile Island." Social Problems 29(October): 1–21.

Walsh, E.J., and R.H. Warland 1983. "Social movement involvement in the wake of a nuclear accident." American Sociological Review 48(December):764–80.

Weinstein, D. 1979. Bureaucratic Opposition: Challenging Abuses at the Workplace. Elmsford, N.Y.: Pergamon Press.

Wiebe, R.H. 1967. The Search for Order. New York: Hill and Wang.

Wilensky, H. 1975. The Welfare State and Equality: Structural and Ideological Roots of Public Expenditures. Berkeley: University of California Press.

Zald, M.N., and M.A. Berger 1978. "Social movements in organizations: Coup d'etat, insurgency and mass movement." American Journal of Sociology. 83(January):823–61.

33

TRANSNATIONAL POLITICAL PROCESSES AND THE HUMAN RIGHTS MOVEMENT

JACKIE SMITH

Introduction

The recent establishment of a United Nations High Commissioner for Human Rights marks the achievement of a major goal of the human rights movement of the past several decades. Indeed, human rights activists might be at least partially credited with many of the international advances in human rights protections (Donnelly 1993; Alston 1994, p. 389). Nevertheless, the movement's struggle to advance human rights can also be viewed as an uphill battle with few unambiguous victories (cf. Shestack 1978). Analysts of social movements might attribute these various movement successes and failures to changes in the "structures of political opportunities" for movement advances (McAdam 1982; Tilly 1978; Eisinger 1973), noting that political systems are dynamic and offer variable possibilities for movement mobilization and strategy.

The human rights issue has attracted the vast majority of organized transnational movement activity (Smith 1996). The predominance of human rights organizations among transnational social movement organizations (TSMOs) and the extent of TSMO activity around global human rights activities raise the question of whether the area of human rights promotion provides unique

opportunities for transnational social movement action that other issue areas may not exhibit.[1] This paper begins to examine this question using the concept of political opportunity structure, which has been important for explaining the emergence and outcomes of national and local social movements (Tarrow 1989; McAdam 1982; Tilly 1978; Eisinger 1973). Building on existing concepts of political opportunities, I outline the various transnational opportunities and constraints faced by human rights proponents over the past several decades and how human rights TSMOs have worked within this changing context in their efforts to affect global human rights policy.[2]

I define the human rights movement here as the collection of formal (national and transnational) social movement organizations designed specifically to further human rights aims; religious and professional organizations, temporary human rights committees within organizations, and less formal networks of individuals that engage in activities to further human rights. Often, elements of the movement work closely with local, state, and intergovernmental officials whose work relates to the area of human rights.[3] The efforts of the human rights movement are shaped—perhaps more than other movements are—by the transnational political context. Whether or not they are actually followed in practice, international legal agreements document states' acknowledgment of the existence of human rights

From *Research in Social Movements, Conflicts and Change* 18: 1995. Reprinted by permission of JAI Press Inc., Greenwich, CT.

and are treated as customary international law in some national courts (Buergenthal 1988, pp. 245–246; Donnelly 1986, p. 608). Many states have formally submitted to international enforcement of the International Covenants on Civil and Political Liberties and on Social and Economic Rights or of regional human rights agreements. These agreements can provide opportunities for local activists to circumvent national politics and bring their grievances to the attention of the international political community (cf. Pagnucco and McCarthy 1992; Thomas 1994; Pagnucco 1996).

The Globalization of Social Movements

In *From Mobilization to Revolution,* Charles Tilly (1978) traces the gradual emergence of what he calls "national social movements." He found that the growth of the nation-state had a tremendous impact on the ways in which people organized and participated in politics. Parties, unions, and other associations "specializing in the struggle for power" grew in importance with the development of electoral politics, as did "parallel streams of people" who organized to raise "sustained, self-conscious challenge[s] to existing [national] authorities" (Tilly 1984, p. 304) and who "overflowed the narrow channels of elections or labor-management negotiations which were being dug at the same time" (Tilly 1984, p. 310). Tilly sees "national social movements" as growing from these "parallel streams of people" which were deliberate formations of "new groups for the offensive pursuit of new rights and advantages" against those who ran national states (Tilly 1984, p. 304). In other words, the organization, strategies, and tactics of citizens acting collectively evolved in tandem with the growth of national political and eco-

nomic power. As political decisions of importance to citizens became the domain of increasingly remote political structures, tactics had to be developed to influence those structures. Tarrow further observed that the consolidated state provided common policy or structural targets for mobilization, standardized procedures for relating to political authorities, and cognitive frameworks that facilitated alliance-building among challengers (Tarrow 1995). The growth of TSMOs in the twentieth century might be seen as the result of the continuation of the processes of political centralization. If social movements "grew up with national politics," (Tilly 1984, p. 313) then the formation of TSMOs might be seen as a consistent response to the increasing institutionalization of international politics.

The emergence of more centralized political structures significantly alters the nature of political processes. Tilly observed that:

> The distinctive contribution of the national state was to shift the political advantage to contenders who could mount a challenge on a very large scale . . . in a way that demonstrated, or even used, their ability to intervene seriously in regular national politics (1984, p. 310).

As the size of political jurisdictions increased, therefore, any challenger to this broader political unit had to grow comparably in its political resources if it was to effectively influence national politics (cf. Young 1989; Oliver and Furman 1989). Thus, for a challenger to engage successfully in transnational politics, we should expect to find a need for an even broader resource base—including a membership that consists of persons from more than one nation-state.[4] Transnational challengers also need to adopt political strategies that are appropriate to the global political arena. These strategies are likely to vary from those used in national arenas, since—although their ultimate target is still the state—they seek to mobilize bystander publics beyond national boundaries (cf. Lipsky 1968) and to bring transnational political processes to bear on particular conflicts. For example, in describing the work of the Service for Peace and Justice in Argentina, Pagnucco and Mc-Carthy (1992) show how human rights advocates used transnational movement networks to mobilize a transnational constituency against the Argentine junta's abuses. These transnational networks were important for bringing diplomatic pressure on that regime from the U.S. administration and others. At the same time, human rights organizations used the formal United Nations mechanisms in an attempt to bring further international pressure on Argentina (Guest 1990; Pagnucco 1996). Thus, while the tactics may be similar to those used in national conflicts, transnational social movement strategies must account for an expanded political environment with its own set of informal and institutionalized political dynamics.

Global Politics: A Three-Level Strategy

While some conflicts are played out in the transnational "arena" (see Rucht 1990), many remain in national arenas which may or may not be influenced by outcomes of the transnational conflict.[5] Indeed, once key battles are won in the transnational arena, if the real goals of social movements are to be achieved, TSMOs must take the spoils of that victory back into national struggles. Once decisions are made at the transnational level, the task of reforming national and local institutions so that they conform with these decisions remains. Furthermore, even as transnational political institutions gain authority, states remain the strongest political units in the global arena. Thus, as TSMOs engage in transnational politics, states—the strongest political actors as well

as the fundamental components of intergovernmental organizations (IGOs)—usually remain their ultimate targets.[6] Leatherman, Pagnucco, and Smith (1994) describe TSMOs' strategies for influencing state policies in terms of three levels: the people-to-people, national or state, and transnational levels. The people-to-people level involves educational campaigns, citizen exchanges, information sharing, or services that increase public awareness of issues and their global dimensions, foster transnational solidarity networks, monitor local-level implementation or effects of international agreements, or satisfy humanitarian needs which states violate or ignore. National-level strategies seek to bring individual states' policies more in line with international standards, to influence foreign aid or diplomatic policies in order to put pressure on other states (or nonstate actors such as the World Bank or transnational corporations) that violate certain international norms, or to influence states' positions within multilateral decision-making fora. Finally, transnational level strategies involve attempts to influence multilateral decision making and policy implementation. A transnational strategy can involve lobbying delegates at international meetings, providing delegates or IGO bureaucrats with information on global problems and draft proposals for action, or monitoring states' compliance with international agreements. TSMOs may be involved in one or more of these levels, and there are frequent attempts to coordinate TSMOs' activities by forming global coalitions. Consequently, while not determining state behavior, TSMOs may constrain the range of choices available to states or force states to address issues they might otherwise avoid.

These three levels or strategies are related, and in some cases it is clear that TSMOs' relationships with IGOs are more often complementary than contentious. Their attempts to influence IGOs, moreover, may be seen as actually part of an indirect strategy whose ultimate aim is to influence states' behavior. This strategy is possible because states may sign international agreements for symbolic rather than instrumental reasons: some of the world's worst human rights violators signed international human rights agreements in order to appear more legitimate as formal adherents to an increasingly evident global consensus (Donnelly 1986). The unintended consequences of these political actions were that dissidents within these countries then had access to international fora that were charged with investigating human rights complaints (Pagnucco 1996; Thomas 1994). TSMO efforts to establish human rights protections as part of a system of global legal norms and later to develop effective mechanisms for the enforcement of those norms has limited the ability of states to employ coercive force against its subjects (Tolley 1987). As states' interests are increasingly dependent upon the behavior of other states, their freedom to make independent policy choices is constrained. The growth of interdependence in the modern international system means that a failure to cooperate with internationally accepted standards or norms brings greater costs to states (Keohane and Nye 1971, 1977).

Through their intervention in global politics, TSMOs seek to exploit the vulnerabilities of states that are created by interdependencies. They do this by working to affect (directly or indirectly) the range of policy choices available to national and transnational level decision makers, usually by expanding the "audience" of the national conflict arena to incorporate third parties that lie outside the national polity (cf. Rucht 1990, p. 216). As Jenkins and Perrow observed in their national level analysis, "powerlessness may be overridden if the national political elite is neutralized and members of the polity contribute resources and attack insurgent targets" (1977, p. 249). With a transna-

tional strategy, movements might mobilize representatives of other states or international agencies in order to pressure domestic targets. By bringing an essentially domestic conflict into the international political arena, TSMOs raise the stakes in the conflict, bringing greater international costs for a national elite that remains unyielding. Moreover, by globalizing the conflict, TSMOs mobilize other members of the international polity, including diplomats from other states and nationally-based constituencies that can bring pressure to affect their own states' position on a particular conflict as well as mobilize more concrete resources for the movement. For example, Amnesty International mobilizes an international base of human rights advocates who question individual states (of which they are not citizens) about their human rights practices, while it also provides material resources and legal services for victims of human rights abuse and their families (Ennals 1982; Mahant 1989).

Political Opportunity Structures

The social and political contexts in which social movements operate affect movement structures and strategies as well as their prospects for influencing policy. Social movements are most likely to emerge under political and economic conditions that support (or at least which do not completely suppress) mobilization and where their capacity for political influence vis-à-vis established political actors is favorable (McAdam 1982; Piven and Cloward 1979; Eisinger 1973). Moreover, the form that collective action takes is shaped largely by the character of targeted political institutions (Tilly 1978, 1984). While a favorable environment is vital to social movement emergence, social movement actors do not merely passively await new political opportunities: they actively attempt to shape these opportunities and "convert" them into expanded movement actions (McAdam 1990). This might be especially true of international political opportunity structures, as the institutions that both define and support international norms and standards are rather fluid when compared with more firmly established (and defended) state structures.[7]

The concept of political opportunity structure refers to the set of environmental constraints and opportunities that "encourage or discourage [collective action] and lead it toward certain forms rather than others" (Tarrow 1988, p. 429). Rucht (1995) disaggregates the concept of political opportunity structure, which he calls "context structure," into the cultural, social, and political contexts. The social and cultural contexts are closely related, and they help define the possibilities for mobilization of people and resources, while the political context delimits the possibilities for political action. Rucht's distinction is important for sorting out the specific ways in which various types of opportunities shape movements. Different environmental factors will have different effects and will be more or less significant across different movements and times. I refer to the social and cultural facets of movement opportunity structures as the *mobilizing opportunities*. The political context, on the other hand, defines movements' strategic opportunities. Subsequently, I describe some transnational dimensions of mobilizing opportunities and their relationships to movements' *strategic opportunities*. This is followed by a description of forms of strategic opportunity and a detailed analysis of the transnational strategic opportunities faced by the human rights movement.

Mobilizing Opportunities

Social and cultural contexts directly affect the possibilities for the aggregation of interests, or the forming of associations, organizations, and alliances that might influence individuals' political views and mobilize collective political action. The social context consists of the structural and spacial organization of the population the movement seeks to affect, or what McCarthy (1995) calls "mobilizing structures." Because people with social ties who share similar interests or identities are the most likely segment of the population to be mobilized (Tilly 1978), the scope and structures of work and school organizations, salience of class or status hierarchies, amount of political and nonpolitical association, and the density of these social networks in a given community affect movements' mobilizing possibilities in that community. The cultural context, on the other hand, refers to the attitudes and behaviors of the population which a movement seeks to influence. The cultural context is important for movements' attempts to mobilize individual and organizational adherents, active supporters, sympathetic media coverage, and material resources for its political struggle. As Snow and Benford (1988) argued, social movement organizations must frame their struggle in such a way that it is consistent with the values, experiences, and beliefs that are typical among a population. A movement's success in capitalizing on mobilizing opportunities to recruit adherents will impact its strategic possibilities: who and how many are part of a movement are important questions asked by policymakers and by potential movement allies.

Social Contexts

A number of mobilizing structures may lend themselves to transnational organizing and mobilization. Churches, unions, professional, and other associations are often transnational in structure, and at times these organizations become involved in movement activities. In recent decades, global social contexts have changed to expand even further the possibilities for transnational mobilization. Perhaps the most important shift has been the proliferation of democratic institutions. Despite continued uncertainties about democratic prospects in many areas, it is clear that the international community is committed to encouraging—with words if not deeds—democratic participation. While the protection of democratic rights and principles is a major goal of the human rights movement, the movement's success in defending these rights contributes to its subsequent mobilization of adherents. Freedom of association and speech are crucial for any movement's survival, and the expansion of these particular rights can lead to the expansion of human rights organizing and action as new human rights groups form where they were once banned or as other organizations, whose survival is dependent upon the continued respect for democratic freedoms, develop.[8]

Another important factor affecting the social context of mobilization is the proliferation of technology that facilitates the movement of information and people across national boundaries. Telephones, faxes, and computers as well as the expansion of mass media make it far more difficult for governments to maintain control of the information flowing across their borders. Governments that try to limit such information flows undermine the countries' economic development and thereby reduce their regime's possibilities for survival. Consequently, even resource-poor challengers in many countries can gain regular access to some form of telecommunications. These technological changes significantly alter the conditions under which challengers work to build effective political influence. They make it increasingly possible to mobilize material resources and to organize a protest constituency that transcends state boundaries.

Another, less obvious element of the social context, namely, the society's economic and power relations, affects the possibilities for human rights mobilization. This has been heatedly debated as part of a "cultural relativity" argument, and has pitted governments like China against human rights groups and any government delegate pressuring it to respect human rights. It is also part of the struggle over women's rights, which have been interpreted (even by movement sympathizers) as a form of Western imperialism. A major source of this tension is that human rights mobilizing frames may criticize or seek to reform cultural practices without addressing the underlying power relationships that allow such practices to flourish. Abolishing slavery without providing former slaves with other means of economic advancement and survival will result in de facto slavery. The practice of female genital mutilation is viewed by many Western rights activists as a clear violation of human rights, while for many young women who are subject to such treatment, at stake are self-esteem as well as their prospects for future marriage and survival. A broader rights frame that first seeks to alter women's social status by means of economic and educational advancement before attacking long-standing cultural practices that grew from male-dominated social relations, will be more appealing in such a context (see Muzigo 1994).

Cultural Contexts

In the human rights case, the cultural context consists, in part, of popular awareness (and acceptance) of international human rights norms. The movement's mobilizing prospects are affected by the cultural context because at the core of the human rights movement strategy is an effort to hold states accountable to an internationally accepted body of human rights norms. Therefore, the definition and expansion of these norms as well as broadening public awareness of them has been an essential part of the movement's strategy. Thomas describes the establishment of international human rights norms as "[a]ltering the symbolic contest and distribution of legitimacy in society, [and thus] shifting the opportunity structure faced by societal actors" (Thomas 1991, p. 1). They do this by introducing an alternative normative framework that may provide a transnational source of legitimacy for organizations that are considered illegitimate in their home countries and which may be subjected to government attempts to demobilize or to publicly discredit and humiliate them (Thomas 1991, p. 3). In other words, TSMOs can identify international frames of interpretation in order to show the appropriateness of their claims in terms of global rather than national standards. Gamson states that "[e]very regime has a legitimating frame that provides the citizenry with a reason to be quiescent" (1988, p. 219). Challengers within a state face huge difficulties in confronting these well-defended, regime-legitimating frames. However, international institutions and norms provide a vital resource for TSMOs by furnishing alternative frames backed by international legitimacy. This may contribute significantly to the processes of "cognitive liberation" (McAdam 1982) whereby citizens come to assign blame for their grievances to state institutions rather than to individual or other causes. The significance of the UN Truth Commission's public disclosure of the names of El Salvador's human rights violators for victims attests to the importance of these normative frames for challengers.

These expanded norms backed with the legitimacy of their international character can provide an important resource for movements faced with domestic repression. Around these norms, TSMOs may mobilize both domestic and international consensus that can facilitate their political challenges. Where no avenues for domestic action are available for human rights activists, going beyond state boundaries through international nongovernmental organizations and through IGOs to appeal to an international "conscience constituency" (McCarthy and Zald 1977) committed to the promotion of human rights standards may be the only means of protesting a state's abuses (Pagnucco and McCarthy 1992; Pagnucco 1996; Brysk 1994; Thomas 1994). This appeal to international norms, however, is only likely to be a movement resource in a cultural context where the state is widely seen as abusing its authority or as illegitimate. In contexts where the state is generally seen as a legitimate authority that uses its power appropriately, a movement that appeals to international standards is likely to be viewed as treasonous. Mobilization efforts that frame that state as a violator of international norms are not likely to be successful mobilizing tools.

The predominant world views and the extent to which a population can be described as "globally aware" or "cosmopolitan" is another important aspect of a movement's cultural context. TSMOs must confront the challenge of developing mobilizing "frames" that are consistent with potential constituents' understandings of their own routine experiences (Snow and Benford 1988, p. 205). Societies that are more isolated and less informed about events outside their locality will be less readily mobilized around frames appealing to international norms and a logic of global interdependence. Also, in communities where basic nutritional and health needs are not met, appeals to political rights may appear extraneous.[9] In short, some human rights frames may compete at times with widely held views of the world. The Cold War era, for example, encouraged the view (at least in the West) of a bipolar world where conflicts around the world were viewed in terms of the overarching East-West struggle. The perception that human rights were used as a political tool of anti-communists prevented many in the U.S. peace movement (who were generally supportive of human rights) from actively embracing human rights frames (Cortright 1993; Kleidman 1993).[10]

Strategic Opportunities

The opportunities for political action by existing challengers within a given political system are shaped to a large degree by political institutions and influential elites. Specifically, movement strategies are affected by: (1) access to formal policy-making processes; (2) policy implementation capacities of international institutions; (3) movement alliance structures; and (4) movement conflict structures (Rucht 1995). I focus specifically on these dimensions as they affected the development of a human rights agenda and supportive institutions in the United Nations, because it is here that TSMOs have been most active in working to influence human rights policy. The UN is not, however, the only or the most relevant institution for some human rights activities, and TSMOs often work simultaneously (through their international offices and national sections or affiliates) within the UN, regional IGOs, and national and local institutions.[11] My purpose here is not to provide an exhaustive description of the international political opportunity structures of social movement actors, but rather to begin to elaborate a framework, drawing from existing literatures on social movements and on international relations, for the further analysis of the significance of political opportunities for transnational social movements.

Access to Global Institutions

A central factor that shapes collective political action is institutionalized access to the political system, or institutional opportunity structures (Kitschelt 1986). Challengers hoping to influence policy may have a number of formal as well as routine, informal mechanisms for influence which they might use in conjunction with extra-institutional strategies. They might also be systematically constrained from having influence by existing structures (cf. McCarthy, Britt, and Wolfson 1991; Pagnucco and Smith 1993). Therefore, in order to assess the possibilities for transnational social movements, it is important that we identify their points of access to international institutions. An interesting variation exists between the national and transnational movements here. As international institutions only emerged in the late nineteenth century, there already existed an active social movement sector (Tilly 1978) characterized by a range of formal SMOs. Thus, activists with national organizing experience and organized constituencies were able to claim a role even as the United Nations was being designed. The process involved struggle, nevertheless, but there were clear successes as international negotiations on the UN showed that TSMOs were accepted as actors in a global polity (cf. Gamson 1990, pp. 31–32). Social movement organizations were central to laying the foundations for nongovernmental actors' access to the United Nations. Article 71 of the United Nations Charter allows nongovernmental organizations (NGOs)[12] to apply for consultative status with its Economic and Social Council (ECOSOC). TSMOs, in consultative status with ECOSOC are permitted to send an observer to those sessions of ECOSOC which are pertinent to their respective area of expertise and to receive selected documents. Those with first or second level status are permitted to submit written statements to the Council members and to address selected assemblies of members.[13]

Article 71 was by no means an aspect of the UN Charter to which its founding members freely consented: here movements had to create opportunities (cf. Gamson and Meyer 1995). It was the result of heavy lobbying on the part of the U.S. delegation at the San Francisco Conference in 1945. Nor was the United States particularly interested in allowing nongovernmental actors a voice in the newly forming United Nations Organization. The presence of Article 71 in the Charter is the result of national and transnational SMOs' pressure on a uniquely susceptible U.S. delegation (Woods 1993, p. 10; Archer 1983, p. 306; Robbins 1971).

The U.S. State Department embarked on plans for a new, postwar international organization in the early forties, with the memory of the dismal failure of Wilson's efforts in the League of Nations fresh in their minds. Their efforts to draft a proposal for a postwar organization began around 1943 and included the involvement of SMOs whose participation was viewed as vital to the eventual acceptance of an international treaty by the U.S. public and, ultimately, Congress (Tolley 1987, p. 4). The State Department also appointed a committee of national, as well as TSMO, "consultants" to accompany its delegation to the San Francisco Conference (Tolley 1987, p. 4). This arrangement proved essential to TSMO influence in the Charter process, and has been traced to the key Charter provisions on TSMO access and on human rights, which resulted from the U.S. delegation's pressures. Other nongovernmental actors were present in San Francisco as well—perhaps as many as 1,200—hoping to lobby various national delegations as they built consensus around a Charter for a United Nations Organization

(Willetts 1982, p. 11). TSMO participation in international organizations originated with the League of Nations, which eventually granted informal consultative status for TSMOs and later allowed TSMOs to speak and circulate documents (Woods 1993, p. 10). Thus, some of the TSMOs attending the San Francisco meetings were somewhat experienced as transnational policy advocates (see Chatfield 1996).

Besides establishing access to formal intergovernmental structures, TSMOs also worked for a human rights dimension of the UN mandate. Their lobbying efforts resulted in Article 55, which calls on the United Nations Organization to "promote . . . universal respect for and observance of human rights and fundamental freedoms for all . . ." (Tolley 1987, p. 5). This language serves as the legal basis for the subsequent establishment of more specific human rights standards by the UN (Forsythe 1985, p. 251). But the establishment of a formal, legal commitment to vaguely defined human rights was insufficient in the eyes of TSMO representatives in San Francisco, who pressured for the establishment of formal mechanisms through which the United Nations Organization could attempt to enforce members' compliance with this commitment. The result was Article 68 of the UN Charter, which allowed the Economic and Social Council to establish commissions, as necessary, to carry out its explicit missions (Tolley 1987, p. 6). It is here, then, that TSMOs helped to establish formal mechanisms for their subsequent input into UN human rights work.

The Human Rights Commission

As the UN organ charged with reviewing human rights complaints, as well as with drafting universal standards for human rights, the Human Rights Commission attracted much attention from TSMOs.[14] The simple existence of a Human Rights

Commission, however, was not enough to ensure official action on behalf of human rights claims. After all, the members of the United Nations are states, and these members have little interest in voluntarily relinquishing their sovereignty. As Scoble and Wiseberg have found, historically, "[i]n the human rights arena, [TSMOs] have played an initiating role and governments the ratifying one" (Scoble and Wiseberg 1976, p. 616). Thus, for nearly two decades after its founding, the UN Human Rights Commission denied itself the power to act in response to the abundant human rights complaints it received, and it denied TSMOs substantial influence in the Commission. In 1949 John Humphrey, a Canadian serving as the Director of the Secretariat's Division of Human Rights, called the resulting procedures of the Commission "the most elaborate wastepaper basket invented" (quoted in Tolley 1987, p. 18).

It was not until 1967 that ECOSOC Resolution 1235 was passed, and the Commission was allowed to "examine information" and "thoroughly study" situations that "reveal a consistent pattern of violations of human rights" (ECOSOC Res. 1235 (XLIV), 1967). This Resolution, however, did not grant the Commission power to actively investigate human rights complaints against a member state. Nor did it allow wide powers of review, as it limited the Commission's jurisdictions to those complaints that were "relevant to gross violations of human rights and fundamental freedoms, as exemplified by the policy of apartheid as practiced in the Republic of South Africa and to racial discrimination practiced notably in Southern Rhodesia . . ." (ECOSOC Res. 1235 (XLIV), 1967). This was interpreted narrowly by Commission members who effectively limited the Commission's discussion of human rights complaints to those against these explicitly mentioned countries as well as against Israel.

TSMOs were, nevertheless, able to use the opening created by Resolution 1235 to push for the gradual expansion of the Commission's jurisdiction beyond South Africa and Israel. Their efforts also aimed at increasing the ability of the Commission to receive and investigate complaints of human rights abuses (Forsythe 1985, pp. 261–262). It was not until 1970, with ECOSOC Resolution 1503, that the Commission began to formally accept individuals' written statements and to hear witnesses on human rights complaints. This resolution, then, marks a key opportunity shift, as it explicitly opened a point of access to the UN for human rights TSMOs. Once provided with this access to human rights mechanisms, TSMOs were in a position to facilitate the more effective functioning of UN human rights mechanisms. It is therefore not surprising that we find significant growth of the human rights movement in the 1970s (Wiseberg 1991, p. 528).[15]

Other UN Agencies

While the Human Rights Commission has historically been the major focus of human rights TSMO activity, it is not the only UN human rights organization that allows access to TSMOs. As international human rights treaties and institutions develop, so too does movement access to relevant decision processes. Examples of more recently gained access are the Human Rights Committee and the High Commissioner for Human Rights. The Human Rights Committee, charged with overseeing compliance with the International Covenant on Civil and Political Rights, may hear individuals' complaints against any of the (currently sixty-six) parties to that Convention's first Optional Protocol (Donnelly 1993, p. 65). The newly established UN High Commissioner for Human Rights will undoubtedly provide new avenues for TSMO input into the global politics of human rights. Because the mandate for this office is vague, TSMOs' contributions will depend partly on the openness of the individual serving as High Commissioner as well as on the assertiveness, cooperation, and creativity of the human rights movement.

UN Conferences

UN-sponsored international conferences on various issues of global concern serve as another point of access for TSMOs into the international political process. These conferences resemble more local or national government efforts to legitimate an agency's existence by creating or supporting organized collective action (McCarthy and Wolfson 1992, p. 290), as they were designed to disseminate information widely, to attract public attention to UN programs, and to deliberately cultivate wide participation from TSMOs (Archer 1983, p. 312). World Food conferences of 1963 and 1970 cultivated TSMO involvement and served as "training grounds for [TSMOs]" (Archer 1983, p. 312). TSMOs have since learned to use this point of access increasingly effectively: they have sought greater impact on pre-conference planning and agenda-setting; organized parallel "unofficial" conferences of TSMOs; and published daily NGO newspapers that help to coordinate lobbying strategies and to raise issues of concern that are not addressed in official forums (Atwood 1982, 1996; Archer 1983; Willetts 1982; Rowlands 1992). These international gatherings also provide useful sites for protest demonstrations that target global actors and institutions, as was especially evident in TSMOs' use of this forum at the UN Conference on Environment and Development in 1992. The World Conference on Human Rights held in June of 1993 provided human rights TSMOs with an important opportunity to shape international debate on human rights protections and to attract greater pub-

lic attention to these issues. It also pushed these organizations to develop more formal international structures to coordinate their human rights activity.[16]

Enforcement Capacities of International Institutions

Global institutions typically lack many of the resources essential for enforcing policy decisions. While member states are often willing to sign international accords that formally recognize and extol universal values such as human dignity, they are far more reluctant to devote the resources necessary to monitor and enforce international agreements. While politicians may sign international resolutions so they can show their constituencies that they are taking action on pressing global issues, these same individuals are not ready to endow international institutions with the means to effectively address these issues (Donnelly 1986). This reality creates a paradoxical dual opportunity for TSMOs: the absence of effective enforcement mechanisms makes states more willing to sign agreements that are politically attractive, and it forces intergovernmental bureaucrats to rely on TSMO expertise in order to carry out their official mandates.

In the absence of sufficient state contributions to the executive aspects of institution-building, TSMOs are often able to offer some of these resources (in however modest amounts), thus making them important actors, at least in the eyes of IGO politicians, managers, and bureaucrats (Ness and Brechin 1988; Rowlands 1992, p. 214). TSMOs further the interests of IGO politicians and bureaucrats by helping to provide information on states' compliance with international agreements. This function is most evidenced in the human rights arena, and is indispensable to enforcement efforts.[17] In essence, the information that TSMOs provide makes it feasible for international institutions to devise enforcement mechanisms. TSMOs help to channel human rights complaints from individuals to the appropriate agencies of regional and global institutions. When possible, TSMOs, like Amnesty International, send fact-finding missions into states suspected of abuses in order to supplement their other sources of data (Ennals 1982). This monitoring function provides the evidence that is necessary for the enforcement of human rights norms, and that is not likely—because of costs as well as political constraints—to be gathered by the UN itself. Moreover, such information requires decentralized mechanisms for its collection and is difficult and costly to gather (Lopez 1992). TSMOs' closer contact with grassroots memberships facilitates this data collection which would be impossible for international institutions to assemble on their own.

The possibility for TSMOs to contribute to the operations of international institutions varies across issue arenas. For example, TSMOs make major contributions to human rights monitoring, and many are uniquely equipped to do so. In contrast, areas such as nuclear weapons nonproliferation or arms trade require different kinds of specialization that few TSMOs possess. The costs of monitoring the latter kinds of agreements are typically much higher than for monitoring human rights. Moreover, states are often less willing to allow TSMOs significant access to international decision-making fora which address security concerns, making it more difficult for TSMOs to have an impact in this area (Atwood 1982).

Movement Alliance Structures

A third dimension of variability of strategic opportunity structures is the configuration of allies that a movement may rely on for symbolic, material, and/or political support (Rucht 1995).[18] Symbolic support consists of formal, public endorsements by leaders of social groups of human rights goals and can help to demonstrate public support, legitimate movement efforts in the eyes of key political elites, or otherwise draw wider attention to movement goals. Material support from strategic allies may come in the form of office space, staff or services, money, and volunteers. Political support—perhaps the most crucial—comes from allies who are in positions which allow them to directly influence political processes. For example, a labor union ally might use its influence on politicians in a particular country to influence that country's position in a particular multilateral policy decision. At times, movements have key allies within government delegations to multilateral fora, and these allies will consult with movement leaders on policy decisions, advise them on strategy, and use their positions to further movement goals. These official allies are occasionally appointed to their posts from the ranks of the movement itself.

Broader geopolitical factors influence the opportunities for mobilizing particular allies from the ranks of governmental and intergovernmental officials. The national level parallel to this opportunity structure is the electoral alliance structure (Piven and Cloward 1979; McAdam 1982). At the international system level, we find strategic alliances among blocs of states which share similar interests. For example, the Cold War period was marked primarily by an East-West alliance structure, while the post–Cold War period has witnessed the predominance of North-South divisions. Alliance blocs also tend to form around more localized regions or interests. In any case, these structures determine to some degree the possibilities for finding movement allies among government and IGO officials.

By the late 1950s and early 1960s, a new majority was emerging in the United Nations as the process of decolonialization led to the emergence of newly independent states in the less developed world. These new member states brought new sets of priorities to international decision-making bodies and emphasized themes of anticolonialism and antiracism in the Human Rights Commission. One significant result of this was that delegates from less developed countries (LDCs) were able to raise a strong voice in a struggle to reverse the Commission's "policy of self-denial" and to force it to act in opposition to colonialism, racism, and other forms of discrimination (Tolley 1987, p. 51). In 1958, TSMOs responded to this theme and sponsored a conference whose aim it was to pressure the Commission to help eradicate prejudice and discrimination (Tolley 1987, p. 51).

As was noted earlier, the recent thaw of the Cold War has brought a realignment in the international system. Brody and Weissbrodt noted a slight decrease in ideological polarization of the Commission during its 1989 session (1989, p. 587), which they saw as a possible signal for the advancement of some human rights issues. However, only a year later the Commission session was marked by a growing North-South division (Brody, Parker, and Weissbrodt 1990, p. 587). This division might escalate as the Commission's membership is restructured to make it more representative of LDCs, although the experiences of the 1992 meeting of the Commission suggests that "protective bloc voting" by new LDC members may not be inevitable (Pitts and Weissbrodt 1993, pp. 128–129).[19] As was evidenced during much of the Cold War period, the presence of strong regional blocs makes it difficult (but not impossible) for TSMOs to effectively raise human rights issues and to build coalitions of states to support international action to protect human rights victims.

Within these structural, geopolitical confines, state delegates or whole delegations may become some of the most crucial

movement allies.[20] Depending upon their level of commitment to movement goals and their relationship with movement organizations and leaders, they may serve as persistent advocates of movement goals, and may use their influence in UN decision-making forums to raise particular TSMO-drafted proposals, to protect TSMO rights and privileges in IGO forums, or to draft and/or support legislative initiatives favored by TSMOs. Since TSMOs are nonvoting observers of IGO meetings, and since they often lack access to meetings where key decisions are taken, such allies are essential if TSMOs are to have any legislative impact. For example, the aforementioned effort surrounding the placing of Article 71 in the UN Charter was partially due to the support of other states, which saw the provision of NGO consultative status as "a way of curbing great power control of the UN and drawing more attention to economic, social and humanitarian issues" (Woods 1993, p. 10). The International Commission of Jurists also found an ally in the Costa Rican delegation, which agreed to formally raise (and claim credit for) its proposal for an independent Commissioner on Human Rights (Tolley 1987, p. 564). TSMOs must, however, be cautious that their cooperation with particular states is not misconstrued as partisanship, for such a criticism of a human rights TSMO can destroy its credibility as an objective advocate of human rights principles (Wiseberg 1991, p. 529). Moreover, the criticism of partisanship toward a particular state can lead to other states' action to revoke a group's consultative status.

IGO bureaucrats are another important type of ally for TSMOs. These bureaucrats may be particularly sympathetic to TSMOs, since TSMOs provide them with key resources (usually in the form of information gathering and processing). For example, TSMOs provide the Human Rights Commission with the necessary evidence of human rights abuses against which the Commission can check states' reports (Forsythe 1985, p. 262). TSMOs are uniquely capable in this area, since individual complaintants would have difficulty showing a "pattern" of abuse in their claims, whereas TSMOs can present the Commission with aggregated data showing patterns more clearly. Moreover, the Commission procedures prohibit the submission of anonymous complaints, but TSMOs like Amnesty International work to protect their informants and might thus help overcome the understandable inhibitions of potential complaintants. TSMOs also facilitate the work of the Sub-Commission[21] by identifying which international "instruments," or formal standards apply to these cases, by submitting multiple copies of their work for dissemination to all Sub-Commission members, and by preparing summaries appropriate for use by the larger Commission (Tolley 1987, p. 72). Also, when the Human Rights Commission drafted international standards on torture and detention, both Amnesty International and the International Commission of Jurists (ICJ) provided legal expertise which the Division otherwise lacked, a service "which in national lawmaking would come from executive departments" (Tolley 1987, p. 582; on AI and the Convention on Torture, see Leary 1979). These skills are also likely to be provided by TSMOs in other situations where the drafting of legal standards is necessary. McCarthy and Wolfson (1992) describe similar bureaucratic dynamics as essential to the cooptation of state infrastructures for the pursuit of movement goals. While national elites might oppose the employment of state resources in this way, lower level agencies may find it to their direct benefit to facilitate certain movements, as this is likely to generate legitimacy and perhaps new resources for that unit of government which may be essential to fulfilling its assigned function (cf. McCarthy and Wolfson 1992).[22]

Another key ally for TSMOs is the broader community of nongovernmental actors. To be effective actors in transnational politics, TSMOs must build coalitions that help to streamline efforts on particular policy issues. They must coordinate their strategies at intergovernmental meetings and appear united in their demands in order to be most effective (Atwood 1982; Brody and Weissbrodt 1989, p. 611). Indeed, international political opportunity structures in many ways create pressures for greater cooperative efforts among TSMOs. States are particularly united in defense of their sovereignty, and UN mechanisms are designed to preserve states' power. Therefore, TSMOs must cooperate if they are to wage an effective transnational political movement. The ICJ played a leading role in coordinating human rights TSMO strategies by sponsoring TSMO conferences to devise proposals for action and coordinate lobbying strategies (Tolley 1987). Various human rights TSMOs also cooperate in the gathering of information on human rights abuses (Smith, Pagnucco, and Romeril 1994). TSMOs may collaborate by authoring joint statements in order to use their increasingly limited speaking time in IGO sessions more efficiently (Pitts and Weissbrodt 1993; Parker and Weissbrodt 1991). One major result of the 1993 World Conference on Human Rights was greater efforts on the part of activists to coordinate their national and international efforts (Brody, Sullivan, and Guest 1993, p. 3). Despite this evidence of cooperation, there are still forces that foster competition among TSMOs similar to that found among national SMOs, as groups compete for similar constituencies and resource bases (Zald and McCarthy 1980).

Movement Conflict Structures

Movement conflict structures consist of the configuration of opponents that seek to limit, undermine, or repress social movement mobilization and activity. At the national level, conflict structures typically consist of repressive governments or their agents as well as nongovernmental actors ("countermovements") that use terror or other tactics to restrict movement mobilization.[23] To the extent that conflict structures restrict national mobilization, TSMO efforts can be hindered. But we can also identify conflict structures at the transnational level that more directly affect the possibilities for effective TSMO political strategies.

The actors with the greatest ability to block TSMO transnational strategies are states. A constant tension exists between the UN Charter's call for the establishment of a Human Rights Commission that is capable of ensuring the promotion of human rights protections and the limits placed upon the Commission by the primacy of the principle of noninterference in members' internal affairs. From the San Francisco Conference to the present, many states have vigorously resisted attempts by IGOs to constrain their behavior. The kind of cooperation between TSMOs and IGO agencies described earlier is what many states have worked hard to prevent and which they continue to try to obstruct. States have at their disposal numerous procedures that they can use to restrict TSMO access to UN decision-making bodies. I describe some of the most significant of these as follows.

A major weapon for states is the removal of a TSMO's consultative status or the refusal to grant such status. This weapon has been used numerous times by states with clearly political motives. For example, in 1952 the United States proposed the withdrawal of consultative status from three human rights organizations that were critical of its Korean operation on the grounds that these organizations "failed to meet the requirement that the organization [in consultative status] shall undertake to support the work of the United Nations" (Tolley 1987, p. 30). Other targets of TSMO censure, including the Soviet Union, Argentina, Chile, Brazil, and Iran, sought to similarly "discipline" their critics (Tolley 1987, p. 62). In 1967, with the entrance of nonaligned movement (NAM) states, a review of NGO status was undertaken, in which states resolved to: require NGO budget statements showing all external—for example, governmental—sources of funding; review TSMO activity to determine whether they have engaged in "politically motivated acts" against states; and require a quadrennial report from every NGO in consultative status summarizing its contributions to the work of ECOSOC (Tolley 1987, p. 62). In 1977 the ECOSOC Committee on NGOs[24] dealt a blow to TSMOs by requiring a consensus in the committee for the approval of new applications for consultative status. The makeup of this Committee ensures great difficulty for TSMOs in this process, since it includes (as of 1987) nineteen voting members from geographically dispersed regions of the world. This procedure allowed the applications of "several highly respected human rights groups" to be deferred for two years at the 1987 session (Tolley 1987). More recently, in the UN preparatory meetings a few states managed to exclude TSMOs from participation in key official sessions of the 1993 World Conference on Human Rights in Vienna. Such exclusion prevented governments from being accountable for the positions they took on the final Conference document and meant that "[t]he real work of the conference [. . .] took place behind closed doors. Shielded from the direct scrutiny of rights advocates, repressive governments found it easier to water down key proposals to strengthen the UN's human rights program" (Brody, Sullivan, and Guest 1993, p. 3). These examples show how tenuous TSMO access to international institutions may be, and how TSMOs must be engaged in a fairly constant effort to maintain their limited access to significant decision-making bodies.

As world economic competition heightens and as human rights advocates expand their efforts in the realm of economic rights, the right to development and for protection against impoverishing structural adjustment policies (Skogly 1994), the human rights movement is likely to face a far more unified and stronger conflict structure than it might have in the past. Indeed, in some ways the Cold War may have aided human rights groups by allowing for an unlikely coalition of the left and anticommunist right for the cause of human rights. Business leaders found common ground with peace activists and churches protesting Soviet human rights abuses in Eastern Europe. The anticommunist aims of the United States and its allies in the Helsinki Accords were the rationale for strong human rights language (Thomas 1994). With the end of the Cold War, this common ground is gone, and business interests have no obvious financial incentives for supporting human rights. Instead, their efforts—at least in the United States—have focused on limiting government constraints on trade policies based on human rights conditions.

Discussion and Conclusions

This reading works to expand existing thinking on social movements to account for their increasingly transnational nature. It builds upon Rucht's (1990, 1995) critiques of the concept of political opportunity structures as it has been used to examine social movement emergence and development. The concept of political opportunity has been too confined to national levels of opportunity, whereas opportunities exist "both beyond and below the national level"

(Rucht 1990, p. 216). Moreover, opportunities vary throughout the course of the conflict and are influenced by interactive conflict processes, and that nonpolitical opportunities are important for explaining movement development (Rucht 1990). This analysis furthers the case that we need to think about transnational political opportunities as important factors that shape social movement development and action. The ability of social movement actors in some cases to go outside state institutions to carry out their struggles alters the strategic possibilities for movements. It is also clear that the static notion of structures must be abandoned: a "constant" structure cannot explain variation in movement activity (Rucht 1990, p. 216). As this analysis shows, in the actual course of a struggle, institutional structures channel the conflict and define the arena of interaction, but they can also be transformed or new ones developed, thereby altering the nature of the system and the course of future struggles. The major strategy of TSMOs has been to create and strengthen new structures—including the body of international law and organizational mechanisms designed to enforce these laws—aimed at altering relationships between governments and the people they govern. For reasons independent of the changes in political elites or strategic alliances, the political arena faced by human rights groups of the 1990s looks dramatically different from that of the early 1950s.

I have drawn from Rucht's work to propose two major dimensions of international political opportunity structures: mobilizing and strategic opportunities. Mobilizing opportunities define the conditions under which a movement is most likely to recruit and attract adherents and build a social base for political action. The key dimensions of variation here are the social and cultural contexts. Movements can flourish best in social contexts where they can build upon pre-existing organizational bases and interpersonal networks. But successful human rights mobilization also demands that the underlying power relations within a society be addressed. Where social infrastructures are built upon the structurally reinforced[25] dominance of a particular class, race, and/or gender, human rights frames may have to be expanded to address inequitable structural relations as a fundamental aspect of individual and group rights. The cultural context, or the attitudes and beliefs of a population whose behavior a movement seeks to influence are also important to the success of movement efforts. A key question here for analysts and activists is how well do movement frames resonate with the widely held beliefs or experiences of a target population.

Strategic opportunities, on the other hand, are defined largely by political institutions. The mobilization of popular support and other resources helps to get the movement's issue on the agenda, but from there a variety of political realities condition its possibilities for policy impact. The locations of authoritative decision making and the rules that structure decision-making processes determine the possibilities for a player's (or potential player's) engagement in struggles over political decisions. Specifically, formal and informal access to decision-making processes, policy-making capacities of IGOs, and the configurations of actual and potential allies and antagonists define the major strategic opportunities for transnational challengers. Key questions for strategists and analysts here are: How are decisions made and where are the possibilities for influencing choices? Are existing political institutions capable of carrying out the changes the movement seeks? If so, which institutions are most relevant? If not, might institutions be adapted in some way to meet these needs? Who are likely allies in this struggle, and what motivates

their interest in this issue? What opposition might we face, and are there ways to avoid it or use it to our advantage?

Future Prospects

The human rights movement of the 1990s faces a dramatically changed structure of political opportunities due to the demise of the Cold War and subsequent transformation of global political institutions. As the United Nations takes a more prominent role in attempting to resolve various regional crises, the relationship of human rights to broader security concerns is becoming more apparent (Human Rights Watch 1993). General concern about the human costs of escalating conflicts as well as uncertainties about appropriate political action may create favorable mobilizing opportunities for the movement in the form of broader public awareness and support as well as more open mobilizing infrastructures within national contexts. Should human rights monitoring and protection become a more consistent and integral part of future United Nations peace-keeping efforts, this may open new strategic opportunities for the movement as more formal mechanisms for UN-TSMO cooperation and policy implementation are developed and as powerful elites who depend on this cooperation to further their political aims cultivate stronger alliances with TSMOs.

The establishment of the UN High Commissioner for Human Rights should help to centralize and rationalize the now disparate human rights activities of UN agencies. This creates important new inroads for TSMOs' roles in human rights protection, and it significantly strengthens the United Nations human rights enforcement capacities. These positive developments may help to temper the negative developments that could hinder human rights progress such as the consolidation of a conflict structure consisting of those promoting unconstrained trade policies, a decline in international humanitarian activism caused by a stagnating global economy, and the rise of forces that threaten states' capacities for effectively guaranteeing human rights such as those now seen in Rwanda, Yugoslavia, and Somalia.

Acknowledgment

This is a revised version of a paper that received the 1993 student paper award from the American Sociological Association's Section on Collective Behavior and Social Movements. I am grateful to Ron Pagnucco for his helpful suggestions on the paper in its various stages; to the participants in the Workshop on International Institutions and Transnational Social Movement Organizations, co-sponsored by the Kroc Institute for International Peace Studies and the Social Science Research Council and to an anonymous reviewer.

NOTES

1. The term "TSMO" was introduced by Pagnucco and McCarthy (1992) and it refers to social movement organizations which have members in two or more nation-states and which have an international office or secretariat charged with coordinating and/or facilitating transnational activities, communication, and/or strategies.

2. While I focus my analysis on the transnational dimensions of political opportunity structures, it is clear that domestic or national and local contexts continue to affect mobilizing efforts as well. There are a number of ways in which these different levels of opportunity might interact: transnational political context might, at times, provide new opportunities where domestic ones are closed (cf. Thomas 1994; Pagnucco 1996); the extent to which a state is involved in international agreements may affect the relevance of transnational politics for domestic groups (cf. Risse-Kappen 1995); and favorable opportunities within influential states can strongly affect the global opportunities.

3. Sikkink (1993) and Keck and Sikkink (1994) emphasize the importance of relationships between national and transnational movement actors, public officials, the media, and foundations by calling the collection of actors working in a particular issue arena the "international issue network." I prefer to maintain a distinction between movement and other actors because of the many dimensions of variation that can exist in a "network" (e.g., degree of centralization and formalization, scope of mobilization, extent of cooperation or conflict, etc.).

4. UN decision-making arrangements are such that the statements of organizations with more globally representative constituencies are most likely to demand officials' attention. Moreover, international membership is a requirement if a TSMO is to earn Consultative Status with the United Nations Economic and Social Council (ECOSOC). This is presumably true for consultative status of or recognition with other IGOs as well. Consultative Status allows TSMOs to send representatives to relevant official ECOSOC meetings, submit written communications to ECOSOC meetings, and to propose agenda items.

5. The U.S. civil rights movement could have adopted the language of "human rights" which were recognized internationally in the Universal Declaration of Human Rights, and some early leaders pushed in this direction (Layton 1993). But the struggle was deliberately defined within the national, Constitutional context. However, unlike what was the case for the Eastern European movements (Thomas 1994), such language might have—in the context of the Cold War—delegitimized the movement by allowing its opponents to label the movement anti-American or Communist.

6. TSMOs can also, however, have non-state targets, including transnational corporations or multinational financial institutions.

7. Although as Rucht (1990) argues, even national structures are subject to change during the course of interactions between movements and authorities.

8. Over the past decade, TSMOs have expanded their membership base in all the world's regions (see Smith 1996). The subset of TSMOs

working on human rights bear out similar patterns of growth in all parts of the world, with the strongest growth being in the former Soviet Union. There was also impressive expansion in Latin American and in African memberships in human rights TSMOs.

9. Steiner (1991) describes tensions among human rights frames as groups from developing countries espoused social, economic, and cultural rights more than civil and political ones, while groups from developed countries focused on civil and political rights.

10. A survey of U.S. groups and organizations working for peace in 1988 and in 1992 showed a significant increase in the proportion of groups working in human rights issues after the Cold War (see Colwell and Bond 1994; Marullo, Pagnucco, and Smith 1996).

11. Transnational organizations may also be less necessary in regional political contexts that often do not require transnational memberships as a prerequisite for formal access. (On regional IGOs and human rights, see Donnelly 1986, 1993; Thomas 1994).

12. NGOs is the term used commonly by governmental and intergovernmental agents as well as political scientists to refer to nongovernmental organizations. Therefore, direct quotes and references to these materials might employ this term when referring to what are called here TSMOs. Since this term can be used to refer to national and international organizations that range from professional associations to Olympic committees to cultural associations, it is necessary to further disaggregate the term. Thus, we should view that subset of NGOs that includes transnational organizations *acting to further social and political change goals* as "TSMOs."

13. The ECOSOC categories for NGO consultative status are "Category I," the highest category reserved for those organizations determined to be the broadest representatives of the population. Most TSMOs are given "Category II" or "Roster" status, since they are viewed as having more delimited constituencies. Those NGOs on the "Roster" have the most restricted access.

14. TSMOs in Consultative Status with the Economic and Social Council are able to circulate documents and/or address meetings of its sub-bodies, including the Human Rights

Commission. National groups may have access to these institutions through organizations in Consultative Status. Ad hoc committees and investigative missions may also grant direct access to nongovernmental organizations that lack formal status within the UN system. Outside the formal provisions for TSMO access to international decision-making processes, many forms of informal access also persist. TSMO representatives lobby in the corridors near official meetings, distribute information to key delegations, cultivate working relationships with key delegates, and so forth.

15. This growth may be related to the opening created by Resolution 1503 or to other factors such as the broadened international discussions of human rights issues in the newly forming Conference on Security and Cooperation in Europe (CSCE) (Thomas 1991, 1994) and other intergovernmental forums, increased funding (beginning in 1975) for human rights by the Ford and Rockefeller foundations (Weissbrodt 1984; Sikkink 1993), or some combination of these. More systematic research is needed to clarify these relationships.

16. Based on a personal communication with human rights organizer, Bernard Hamilton of Minority Rights Group International—Washington, D.C. office, August 1993. Also, see Brody, Sullivan, and Guest 1993.

17. The recent development of a UN Commission on Sustainable Development which is modeled on the Human Rights Commission and which explicitly calls for TSMO assistance in the enforcement of environmental agreements further attests to TSMOs' importance in global institutions (Rowlands 1992; Lewis 1992).

18. The collection of movement actors and allies may be comparable to what Sikkink (1993) and Keck and Sikkink (1994) call "issue networks." Nevertheless, there will be different constellations of these actors even within a single issue area: the collection of TSMOs and their allies that work for refugee rights will look quite different from those focusing on women's rights or prisoners' rights.

19. The 1992 session passed several resolutions providing criticisms or greater scrutiny of Asian LDCs, including Sri-Lanka, East Timor, Afghanistan, Burma, and Cambodia. Pitts and Weissbrodt see the end of the Cold War

and the increasing effectiveness of TSMO protection efforts as helping to preclude the emergence of strong Southern state bloc voting (Pitts and Weissbrodt 1993, p. 129).

20. While they are less likely to have much effect on structural, geopolitical factors, changes in national political elites often affect the supportiveness of national delegates. For example, in the early 1970s a human rights coalition emerged in the U.S. Congress and this was followed by the election of Jimmy Carter and his new emphasis on human rights within the U.S. administration. Carter's appointment of Andrew Young to the U.S. delegation at the UN brought key human rights advocates like Brady Tyson into important policy arenas (see Pagnucco 1996). Also, the fact that the UN High Commissioner for Human Rights came about within the first year of Bill Clinton's administration is probably coincidental: the U.S. delegation to the Vienna conference was headed by a prominent human rights activist, and that delegation pushed strongly for the High Commissioner throughout the conference (Brody, Sullivan, and Guest 1993; U.S. State Department 1993).

21. The Sub-Commission on Prevention of Discrimination and Protection of Minorities is the "*de facto* Sub-Commission on Human Rights," although it has created temporary subcommissions on other issues (Tolley 1987, p. 168). Sub-Commission members are not instructed governmental representatives but rather are independent "experts" serving in individual rather than governmental capacities. In practice there are varying degrees of independence and expertise among its members (Tolley 1987, pp. 163–164). This body carries out much of the ongoing work of the Commission by processing complaints, producing studies and reports.

22. The cooptation of state infrastructures, according to McCarthy and Wolfson, is more likely for "consensus" movements, which they define as movements with widespread public support and little organized opposition (1992, p. 273). The human rights movements at the transnational level might be seen as having some qualities of a "consensus movement" (although in many ways it faces strong, organized opposition at national and transnational levels) as it is backed by a series

of international agreements and norms to which many states have *formally* agreed. Few states will publicly deny the legitimacy of these norms, but they do resist international attempts to enforce them, claiming sovereignty over their domestic affairs. The potential constituency for the human rights movement is very broad, and the movement itself is based on the ideal of nonpartisanship (Wiseberg 1991, p. 529). The movement's success in mobilizing or "coopting" a variety of civic structures (including political parties and professional associations) to participate in "urgent action" and other campaigns demonstrates its broad appeal (Wiseberg 1991, p. 533).

23. Conflict structures often constrain movements, but they may in some cases serve as opportunities: third parties, which are initially indifferent (or perhaps hostile) to the movement aims, may enter the conflict in order to oppose countermovement forces.

24. The ECOSOC Committee on NGOs meets biannually to review applications for consultative status and to review the work of NGOs generally.

25. For example, through economic and political institutions and practices.

REFERENCES

Alston, P. 1994. "The UN's Human Rights Record: From San Francisco to Vienna and Beyond." *Human Rights Quarterly* 16: 375–390.

Archer, A. 1983. "Methods of Multilateral Management: the Interrelationship of International Organizations and NGOs." Pp. 303–325 in *The US, the UN and the Management of Global Change*, edited by T.T. Gati. New York: New York University Press.

Atwood, D. 1982. "Nongovernmental Organizations and the 1978 United Nations Special Session on Disarmament." Doctoral dissertation, University of North Carolina at Chapel Hill.

———. 1996. "Action for Disarmament: Public Involvement and the United Nations Special Sessions on Disarmament." In *Solidarity Beyond the State: The Dynamics of Transnational Social Movements*, edited by C. Chatfield, R. Pagnucco, and J. Smith. Syracuse, NY: Syracuse University Press.

Brody, R., P. Parker, and D. Weissbrodt. 1990. "Major Developments in 1990 at the UN Commission on Human Rights." *Human Rights Quarterly* 12: 559–588.

Brody, R. and D. Weissbrodt. 1989. "Major Developments at the 1989 Session of the UN Commission on Human Rights." *Human Rights Quarterly* 11: 586–611.

Brody, R., D. Sullivan, and I. Guest. 1993. *The 1993 World Conference on Human Rights: A Critical Analysis.* Washington, D.C.: International Human Rights Law Group.

Brysk, A. 1994. *The Politics of Human Rights in Argentina: Protest, Change and Democratization.* Stanford, CA: Stanford University Press.

Buergenthal, T. 1988. *International Human Rights in a Nutshell.* St. Paul, MN: West Publishing Co.

Chatfield, C. 1996. "The Interrelated World of TSMOs and IGOs to 1945." In *Solidarity Beyond the State: The Dynamics of Transnational Social Movements,* edited by C. Chatfield, R. Pagnucco, and J. Smith. Syracuse, NY: Syracuse University Press.

Colwell, M.A.C. and D. Bond. 1994. "American Peace Movement Organizations: The 1988 and 1992 Surveys." San Francisco: Institute for Nonprofit Organizations, University of San Francisco, Working Paper #21.

Cortright, D. 1993. *Peace Works: The Citizens' Role in Ending the Cold War.* Boulder, CO: Westview.

Donnelly, J. 1986. "International Human Rights: A Regime Analysis." *International Organization* 40: 599–642.

———. 1993. *International Human Rights.* Boulder, CO: Westview.

Eisinger, P. K. 1973. "The Conditions of Protest Behavior in American Cities." *American Political Science Review* 67: 11–28.

Ennals, M. 1982. "Amnesty International and Human Rights." Pp. 63–83 in *Pressure Groups in the International System,* edited by P. Willetts. New York: St. Martins Press.

Forsythe, D. 1985. "The United Nations and Human Rights." *Political Science Quarterly* 100: 249–269.

Gamson, W. 1988. "Political Discourse and Collective Action." Pp. 219–244 in *International Social Movement Research* (volume 1), edited by B. Klandermans, H. Kriesi, and S. Tarrow. Greenwich, CT: JAI Press.

———. 1990. *The Strategy of Social Protest* (2nd ed.). CA: Wadsworth.

Gamson, W. and D. Meyer 1995. "The Framing of Political Opportunity." In *Political Opportunities, Mobilizing Structures and Framing: Social Movement Dynamics in Cross-National Perspective,* edited by D. McAdam, J. McCarthy, and M. Zald. Cambridge, MA: Cambridge University Press.

Guest, I. 1990. *Behind the Disappearances: Argentina's Dirty War Against Human Rights and the United Nations.* Philadelphia: University of Pennsylvania Press.

Jenkins, C. and C. Perrow. 1977. "Insurgency of the Powerless: Farmworkers Movement (1946–1972)." *American Sociological Review* 42: 249–268.

Keck, M. and K. Sikkink. 1994. "International Issue Networks in the Environment and Human Rights." Paper prepared for Workshop on International Institutions and Transnational Social Movement Organizations: Kroc Institute for International Peace Studies, University of Notre Dame.

Keohane, R.O. and J. Nye. (eds.). 1971. *Transnational Relations and World Politics.* Cambridge, MA: Harvard University Press.

———. 1977. *Power and Interdependence: World Politics in Transition.* Scott, Foresman and Co.

Kitschelt, H.P. 1986. "Political Opportunity Structures and Political Protest." *British Journal of Political Science* 16: 57–85.

Kleidman, R. 1993. *Organizing for Peace: Neutrality, the Test Ban and the Freeze.* Syracuse, NY: Syracuse University Press.

Layton, A.S. 1993. "The International Context of the U.S. Civil Rights Movement: A Strategy Used by Civil Rights Leaders." Annual Meeting of the American Political Science Association: Washington, DC.

Leary, V. 1979. "A New Role for Non-Governmental Organizations in Human Rights: A Case Study of Non-Governmental Participation in the Development of International Norms on Torture." Pp. 197–210 in *UN Law/Fundamental Rights: Two Topics in International Law,* edited by A. Cases. The Netherlands: Sijthoff & Noordhoff.

Leatherman, J., R. Pagnucco, and J. Smith. 1994. "International Institutions and Transnational Social Movement Organizations: Challenging the State in a Three-Level Game of Global Transformation." Paper prepared for Social Science Research Council Sponsored Workshop on International Institutions and Transnational Social Movement Organizations: University of Notre Dame.

Lewis, P. 1992. "New Environmental Debate Expected as UN Convenes." *New York Times* September 15: A10.

Lipsky, M. 1968. "Protest as a Political Resource." *American Political Science Review* 62: 1144–58.

Lopez, G.A. 1992. "Data Sources and Data Needs In Human Rights Monitoring." Pp. 47–62 in *Monitoring Human Rights Violations. Paper #43,* edited by A.P. Schmid and A.J. Jongman. Leiden: Center for the Study of Social Conflicts.

Mahant, E. 1989. "Amnesty International and the International Human Rights Regime." Paper presented at the International Studies Association Meetings, London.

Marullo, S., R. Pagnucco, and J. Smith. 1996. "Frame Changes and Movement Contraction: U.S. Peace Movement Framing After the Cold War." *Sociological Inquiry* 66(l).

McAdam, D. 1990. "Political Opportunities and Framing Processes: Thoughts on Linkages." Paper prepared for Workshop on "Social Movements, Framing Processes and Opportunity Structures," Berlin.

———. 1982. *Political Process and the Development of Black Insurgency.* Chicago: University of Chicago Press.

McCarthy, J.D. 1995. "Mobilizing Structures: Constraints and Opportunities in Adopting, Adapting and Inventing." In *Political Opportunities, Mobilizing Structures and Framing: Social Movement Dynamics in Cross-National Perspective,* edited by D. McAdam, J. McCarthy, and Mayer Zald. Cambridge, MA: Cambridge University Press.

McCarthy, J.D. and M. Wolfson. 1992. "Consensus Movements, Conflict Movements and the Cooptation of Civil and State Infrastructures." Pp. 273–298 in *Frontiers in Social Movement Theory,* edited by A. Morris and C. McClurg Mueller. New Haven: Yale University Press.

McCarthy, J.D., D. Britt, and M. Wolfson. 1991. "The Institutional Channeling of Social Movements in the Modern State." Pp. 45–76 in *Research in Social Movements, Conflict and Change* (volume 13), edited by L. Kriesberg. Greenwich, CT: JAI Press.

McCarthy, J.D. and M. Zald. 1977. "Resource Mobilization and Social Movements: a Partial Theory." *American Journal of Sociology* 82: 1212–1241.

Muzigo, R.K. 1994. "Invoking International Human Rights Law for the Emancipation of Women in Uganda." Master of Laws Thesis, University of Notre Dame Law School.

Ness, G.D. and S.R. Brechin. 1988. "Bridging the Gap: International Organizations as Organizations." *International Organizations* 42: 245–273.

Oliver, P. and M. Furman. 1989. "Contradictions Between National and Local Organizational Strength: The Case of the John Birch Society." Pp. 155–177 in *International Social Movement Research.* Greenwich, CT: JAI Press.

Pagnucco, R. 1996. "Promoting Human Rights and Democracy: The Work of SERPAJ." In *Solidarity Beyond the State: The Dynamics of Transnational Social Movements,* edited by C. Chatfield, R. Pagnucco, and J. Smith. Syracuse, NY: Syracuse University Press.

Pagnucco, R. and J.D. McCarthy. 1992. "Advocating Non-Violent Direct Action in Latin America: The Emergence and Structure of SERPAJ." In *Religion and Politics in Comparative Perspective,* edited by B. Misztal and A. Shupe. New York: Praeger.

Pagnucco, R. and J. Smith. 1993. "The Peace Movement and the Formulation of U.S. Foreign Policy." *Peace and Change* 18: 157–181.

Parker, P. and D. Weissbrodt. 1991. "Major Developments at the UN Commission on Human Rights in 1991." *Human Rights Quarterly* 13: 573–613.

Pitts, J.W. and D. Weissbrodt. 1993. "Major Developments at the UN Commission on Human Rights." *Human Rights Quarterly* 15: 122–196.

Piven, F.F. and R. Cloward. 1979. *Poor People's Movements: Why They Succeed, How They Fail.* New York: Vintage.

Risse-Kappen, T. 1995. "Bringing Transnational Relations Back In: Introduction." In *Bringing Transnational Relations Back In: Non-state Actors, Domestic Structures, and International Institutions,* edited by T. Risse-Kappen. Cambridge, MA: Cambridge University Press.

Robbins, D.B. 1971. *Experiment in Democracy: The Story of U.S. Citizen Organizations in Forging the Charter of the United Nations.* New York: The Parkside Press.

Rowlands, I. H. 1992. "The International Politics of Environment and Development: The Post-UNCED Agenda." *Millennium: Journal of International Studies* 21: 209–24.

Rucht, D. 1990. "Campaigns, Skirmishes and Battles: Anti-Nuclear Movements in the USA, France and West Germany." *Industrial Crisis Quarterly* 4: 193–222.

———. 1995. "The Impact of National Contexts on Social Movement Structures: A Cross-Movement and Cross-National Comparison." In *Political Opportunities, Mobilizing Structures and Framing: Social Movement Dynamics in Cross-National Perspective,* edited by D. McAdam,

J.D. McCarthy, and M. Zald. Cambridge, MA: Cambridge University Press.

Scoble, H. and L. Wiseberg. 1976. "Human Rights NGOs: Notes Toward Comparative Analysis." *Revue des Droits de L'Homme*: 611–644.

Shestack, J.J. 1978. "Sisyphus Endures: The International Human Rights NGO." *New York Law School Law Review* 24: 89–123.

Sikkink, K. 1993. "Human Rights, Principled Issue-Networks, and Sovereignty in Latin America." *International Organization* 47: 411–441.

Skogly, S. 1994. "Social Costs of Structural Adjustment: Economic Inefficiency or Human Rights Problems?" Paper presented at International Studies Association Annual Meeting: Washington, DC.

Smith, J., R. Pagnucco, and W. Romeril. 1994. "Transnational Social Movement Organizations in the Global Political Arena." *Voluntas* (Summer).

Smith, J. 1996. "Movement and Organization: Change in the Post-1945 Transnational Social Movement Sector." In *Solidarity Beyond the State: The Dynamics of Transnational Social Movements,* edited by C. Chatfield, R. Pagnucco, and J. Smith. Syracuse, NY: Syracuse University Press.

Snow, D. and R. Benford. 1988. "Ideology, Frame Resonance, and Participant Mobilization." Pp. 197–217 in *From Structure to Action: Social Movement Participation Across Cultures: International Social Movement Research* (volume 1), edited by B. Klandermans, H. Kriesi, and S. Tarrow. Greenwich, CT: JAI Press.

Steiner, H.J. 1991. "Diverse Partners: Non-Governmental Organizations in the Human Rights Movement." Retreat of Human Rights Activists, Harvard Law School Human Rights Program and Human Rights Internet.

Tarrow, S. 1988. "National Politics and Collective Action." *Annual Review of Sociology* 14: 421–440.

———. 1995. "States and Opportunities: the Political Structuring of Social Movements." In *Political Opportunities, Mobilizing Structures and Framing: Social Movement Dynamics in Cross-National Perspective,* edited by D. McAdam, J.D. McCarthy, and M. Zald. Cambridge, MA: Cambridge University Press.

———. 1989. *Democracy and Disorder: Protest and Politics in Italy, 1965–1975.* New York: Oxford University Press.

Thomas, D. 1991. "Social Movements and International Institutions: A Preliminary Framework." Paper delivered at American Political Science Association Annual Meeting, Washington, DC.

———. 1994. "The Helsinki Movement: International Norms, Social Mobilization in Eastern Europe, and Policy Change in the United States." Paper prepared for Social Science Research Council Sponsored Workshop on International Institutions and Transnational Social Movement Organizations, Kroc Institute for International Peace Studies, University of Notre Dame.

Tilly, C. 1978. *From Mobilization to Revolution.* Reading, MA: Addison Wesley.

———. 1984. "Social Movements and National Politics." In *Statemaking and Social Movements: Essays in Theory and History,* edited by C. Bright and S. Harding. Ann Arbor: University of Michigan Press.

Tolley, H. 1987. *The U.N. Commission on Human Rights.* Boulder: Westview.

United States Department of State. 1993. "Intervention on Discussion of Vienna Declaration by John Shattuck, U.S. Representative to WCHR, July 25, 1993" Washington, DC.

———. 1989. "Popular Sovereignty and International Law: ICJ Strategies for Human Rights Standards." *Human Rights Quarterly* 11: 561–585.

Weissbrodt, D. 1984. "The Contribution of International Nongovernmental Organizations to the Protection of Human Rights." Pp.403–438 in *Human Rights in International Law* (volume 2), edited by T. Meron. Oxford: Clarendon Press.

Willetts, P. 1982. "Pressure Groups as Transnational Actors." Pp. 1–27 in *Pressure Groups in the International System,* edited by P. Willetts. New York: St. Martins Press.

Wiseberg, L. 1991. "Protecting Human Rights Activists and NGOS: What More Can Be Done?" *Human Rights Quarterly* 13: 525–544.

Woods, L.T. 1993. "Nongovernmental Organizations and the United Nations System: Reflecting Upon the Earth Summit Experience." *International Studies Notes of the International Studies Association* (Winter) 18: 9–15.

Young, D. 1989. "Local Autonomy in a Franchise Age: Structural Change in National Associations." *Nonprofit and Voluntary Sector Quarterly* 18: 101–117.

Zald, M.N. and J.D. McCarthy. 1980. "Social Movement Industries: Competition and Cooperation Among Movement Organizations." Pp. 1–20 in *Research in Social Movements, Conflict and Change* (volume 3), edited by L. Kriesberg. Greenwich, CT: JAI Press.

34

A MOVEMENT SOCIETY?

SIDNEY TARROW

In 1789, as word of France's revolution reached England, abolitionist Thomas Clarkson crossed the Channel to urge his French colleagues to join his country's antislavery agitation. Clarkson took the same route again in 1814, following a second wave of agitation in Britain. But "twice," writes the leading American student of antislavery, "he failed utterly." (Drescher 1994). Although the French abolished slavery in their colonies in 1794, this was no more than "a desperate response to wartime contingencies," writes Drescher (1991:712), and was reversed when Napoleon came to power. Only when it coincided with greater political earthquakes did antislavery cross the channel (pp. 719–20).

Two hundred years later, diffused by word of mouth, printed page, and television, collective action spread rapidly across the internal boundaries of the Soviet bloc. As the French were commemorating—and burying!—the bicentennial of their revolution,[1] a new wave of revolution swept over the Communist world. Centered on Eastern and Central Europe, enjoying a brief, tragic echo in China, the movement eventually gave way to savage confrontations in Romania, in the Caucasus and ultimately in Yugoslavia. Not only in semi-Stalinized Poland and in the restive Baltic states, but in iron-fisted East Germany and subjugated

Czechoslovakia, within a year communism was gone. By 1991, even the Soviet Union, heartland of proletarian internationalism, had collapsed, giving way to a galaxy of semi-democratic, semi-market, deeply conflicted societies.

When we compare the rapid diffusion of the movements of 1989 to Clarkson's inability to bring abolitionism across 30 miles of water, we can begin to understand the progress of the social movement over the past two hundred years. For not only did Eastern Europeans rebel *en masse* in 1989: They did so against similar targets, at virtually the same time and in the name of goals that varied only in their details. In 1789 antislavery advocates had difficulty crossing the English Channel. But in 1989 the democracy movement spread from Berlin to Beijing in a matter of weeks.

The significance of this change is still emerging, and its implications for democracy are mixed, to say the least. But its implications for the nature of social movements were profound. For not only did these changes close the door on the most important revolutionary movement of the twentieth century; by the end of 1989, not only in Eastern Europe, but all over the Communist bloc, the movement against state socialism had become general and its modalities modular. Even in Italy, so far from the periphery of world communism that its Communist Party was barely recognizable by 1989, party leaders rejected their historic identity and changed their flag (Ignazi 1992).

But the heart of the movement was in Eastern Europe. There, with little prior organization, people who had never met (or who knew each other in the apolitical networks of what Eastern Europeans were calling "civil society") were employing similar forms of organization and action, and in the name of similar frames of meaning, rose up against authorities. If the Communist Party elites gave in practically without a fight, it was not only because they had lost heart, but because they could see what forces were arrayed against them and knew what it would take to suppress them. Not only this movement, but *the* social movement triumphed in 1989.

The rapid spread and dramatic success of the movement of 1989 was a reflection of the powers of movement that I have described in this book. But it also raises some troubling questions for social movement theory and about the emerging world order; about the increase of violence, the recrudescence of ethnic conflicts, the possible transcendence of the national state and the internationalization of conflict. In this chapter, I will first review what I have argued here about the power in movement before turning to the questions raised by the cataclysm of 1989 and its violent aftermath.

Two Hundred Years of Movement

Since collective action is the common denominator of all kinds of social movements, we began with the theory of collective action. Twenty years ago, political scientists and sociologists interested in social movements began to look at their subject not from the standpoint of actions taken, but as a puzzle; based on the assumption that collective action is difficult to bring about. I have argued that this puzzle *is* only a puzzle (and not a sociological law), because in so many situations and against so many odds, collective action *does* occur, often instigated by people with few resources and little inherent power.

The "solution" to that puzzle was first sought by collective action theorists building on economist Mancur Olson's theory that "large groups" mobilize members through selective incentives and constraints. While the Olsonian theory worked well for interest groups, it was inadequate for social movements for the simple reason that they are multipolar actors in sustained conflict with opponents and have few incentives or constraints to deploy. Unlike voluntary associations, movements are not organizations, and those who try to lead them have little or no control over those they hope will follow them.

The central task for movement organizers is to resolve what I called the "social transaction costs of collective action"; creating focal points for people who have no sources of compulsory coordination, who often lack direct connections with one another and have few, if any, internal resources. While large firms and interest groups solve their transaction cost problem by internalizing their assets, movements seldom have this option. Indeed, organizers who try to turn their "base" into disciplined cadres squander much of their energy on achieving internal control. How movements become the focal points for collective action and sustain it against opponents and the state was the central question of the book.

I argued, in response to this question, that the main incentives for movement creation and diffusion are found in the structure of political opportunities. Increasing access to power, realignments in the political system, conflicts among elites, and the availability of allies give early challengers the incentives to assault the power structure and create opportunities for others. The diffusion of movements takes place by many mechanisms and draws on a variety of resources; but the major incentive for new groups to join a movement are the political opportunities that are exposed by the actions of "early risers" and exploited by others.

In response to political opportunities, movements use different forms of collective action singly and in combination to link people to one another and with opponents, supporters, and third parties. They take advantage of both the familiarity of these forms of action—by a kind of "contract by convention," in Russell Hardin's term (1982)—innovating around their edges to inspire the imagination of supporters and create fear and uncertainty among opponents. Collective action is best seen not as a simple cost, but as both a cost and a benefit for social movements.

The balance between the costs and benefits helps determine the dynamics of the movement. As the benefits of a particular form of collective action decline, organizers have incentives to develop new actions, increase the numbers of participants, or radicalize their interaction with opponents. The conflicts and defections within social movements, as well as their confrontations with the state, are, in part, the result of the attempt to maintain the movement's momentum through the use of new and more daring collective actions.

But in the formation of a social movement, there is more than a "pull" toward particular forms of action; there must also be a "push" from solidarity and collective identity. Solidarity has much to do with interest, but it produces a sustained movement only when consensus is built around common meanings and values. These meanings and values are partly inherited and partly constructed in the act of confronting opponents. They are also constituted by the interactions within movements. One of the main factors distinguishing successful movements from failures is their capacity to link inherited understandings to the imperative for activism.

Collective action is often led by movement organizations, but these are sometimes beneficiaries, sometimes inciters, and at other times destroyers of popular politics. The recurring controversy about whether organizations produce movements or suppress them can be resolved only if we examine the less formal structures that they draw upon—the social networks at the base of society, and the mobilizing structures that link them to the focal points of conflict. Sustaining a movement is the result of a delicate balance between suffocating the power in movement by providing too much organization and leaving it to spin off uselessly away through the tyranny of decentralization (J. Hellman 1987).

Opportunities, Cycles, and the Consumption of Movement

But collective action repertoires, cultural frames, and organization are only the potential sources of power; they can be employed just as easily for social control as for insurgency. Recurring protest cycles are the products of the diffusion of political opportunities that transform the potential for mobilization into action. In these crucibles of conflict and innovation, movements not only take advantage of available opportunities; they create them for others by producing new forms of action, hammering out new "master frames," activating social networks, and making coalitions that force the state to respond to the disorder around it.

That response is often repressive, but even repression is often mixed with reform. Particularly when counterelites within the system see the opportunity to aggrandize themselves in alliance with challengers, rulers are placed in a vulnerable position to which reform is a frequent response. As conflict collapses and militants retire to lick their wounds, many of their advances are reversed, but they leave behind incremental expansions in participation, changes in popular culture, and residual movement networks. Movement cycles are a season for sowing, but the reaping is often done during the periods of demobilization that follow, by latecomers to the cause.

If cycles of protest are opened up by expanding opportunities, how do they decline as they inevitably do? Is it simply because people tire of agitation, because enervating factional struggles develop within their movements, because organizations become oppressive, or because elites repress and placate challengers? All of these are contributory causes of cyclical decline, but there is a more systemic cause as well: Since the power in movement depends on the mobilization of external opportunities, when opportunities expand from challengers to other groups and shift to elites and authorities, movements lose their primary source of power. For brief periods of history the power in movement seems irresistible; but it disperses rapidly and passes inexorably into more institutional forms of politics. Let us turn to how the power in movement has changed.

1789/1989

If each new social movement had to create anew its forms of collective action, its frames of meaning, and its mobilizing structures, then the collective action problem would be insuperable and the world would be a much quieter place than it has become. If there is a central message, it is that the power in movement is cumulative. Social theorists are forever discovering waves of "new" social movements; but the claim of "the new" fades when we contemplate the larger historical picture. For new movements not only repeat many of the themes of

their predecessors, like identity, autonomy, and injustice (Calhoun 1993), but build on the practices and institutions of the past.

It was the consolidation of the national state in the eighteenth century that created the framework in which national social movements developed. They resulted both from statebuilders' penetration of society and from their creation of common frameworks for citizenship. Although expanding states sought to repress opposition and reduce the periphery to obedience, they also created national categories of identity, standard relationships, and offered a fulcrum on which people could fight out their social conflicts with others.

This creation of a central state target and fulcrum for conflict transformed how people made claims. Using the central state to seek a benefit or attack an opponent meant using the repertoire of collective action that state elites recognized. In democratic states, the mass, modular, and largely peaceful repertoire of the twentieth century was the result. The novelty of this new repertoire was not that it existed, but that it had the capacity to bring broad coalitions of challengers together in sustained interactions with national states, and to mount general claims against them.

Why did this capacity develop when it did in the West? It was the rise of modern states and an international capitalist economy that provided the targets and the resources that helped movements to flourish and that laid the bases for today's social movements. Movements began in the West because that was where the consolidated national state first appeared. When western states and expanding capitalism moved outward to colonize the rest of the world, they brought the preconditions and the practices of the social movement with them.

In the process of movement development, two major structural changes were critical: regular associations which provided legal and conventional forms that more contentious actors could employ; and new and expanded means of communication which diffused models of collective action and new cognitive frames from one sector or country to another. Though early analysts insisted on the importance of class in galvanizing these movements, it was through the interclass and translocal coalitions created through print and association that the first successful movements took shape. The nationalist movements that spread across Europe and America and throughout the world had the capacity to cross class lines and form such interclass coalitions.

These were not random processes. Repeated confrontations linked specific social actors with their antagonists through forms of collective action that became recurring routines: the strike between workers and employers; the demonstration between protesters and opponents; the insurrection between insurgents and the state. The national social movement developed as a sequence of sustained challenges to elites, authorities, or opponents by people with collective purposes and solidarity, or by those who claimed to represent them.

Once these opportunities, conventions, and resources became available to ordinary people, the problem of social transaction costs could be solved and movements could spread to entire societies, producing the periods of turbulence and realignment that I have called cycles of protest. Such periods had repercussions that sometimes resulted in repression, sometimes in reform, often in both. They were the major watersheds for the innovations in collective action we see today, for changes in political culture, for increased political involvements, and for the creation of future networks of militants and supporters.

The first major cycle of protest occurred in 1789, but its diffusion across the borders of France was carried mainly on the tips of French bayonets. The first major international cycle occurred during the 1848 Revolution. The most recent ones before 1989 were the anticolonial movements of the post-World War II period, and the 1960s movements in Europe and the United States. These latter movements were, in the main, nonviolent. While 1848 ended in armed strife and foreign intervention, both anticolonial nationalism and the movements of the 1960s brought the tools of nonviolent direct action to new heights of refinement and effectiveness.

The movements of Eastern Europe in 1989 were in many ways the culmination of these trends. Like these earlier movements, they were not class movements; they were, at first, remarkably nonviolent; and they spread rapidly across the region. Both new and old forms of collective action were employed; new frames of meaning like anticorruption and participation joined the themes of injustice and liberation; the organizations used were weak but collective action and consent spread through social networks at the base. As in the past, the major incentives that turned underlying discontents into movements were political opportunities.

Of these opportunities, the most important were transnational: the openings, the realignments, the splits between reform and orthodox Communists and the encouragement to dissidents produced by Gorbachev's domestic reforms and by his policies toward Eastern Europe. As each country in the region experienced the weakening of its elites and the crumbling of their resistance, newer and wider opportunities were created. The movement spread much as the 1848 Revolution had done, by a process of imitation, diffusion, reaction, and transformation of scattered movements, culminating in elite negotiations and the attempt to build new institutions out of struggle.

But like 1848, as the movement wound through Eastern Europe, the mood shifted from liberalism and representative government to ethnic particularism and national assertiveness. If crowds of Czechs and Slovaks turned out to demonstrate for freedom in Prague and Bratislava in 1989, by 1992 these cities had become the capitals of a country split in two; if thousands of Hungarians demonstrated at the tomb of Imre Najy in 1988, by the early 1990s, the parties that liberated their country from communism were having difficulty attracting a plurality of voters. If West and East Germans joined in an ode to freedom on the Berlin Wall in 1989, by 1991 "Ossies" and "Wessies" were watching each other with suspicion. In Poland, the Solidarity leaders who had started the process a decade earlier split into rival political parties. And in Russia the democratic movement of the late 1980s gave way to a range of semi-parties, some of them holdovers from the recent regime and others reviving forms of xenophobia from the Czarist past.

Immediately after the ebullience of 1989, some observers foresaw old elites being rapidly swept off the public scene, state-run economies rapidly privatized and a new democratic politics emerging in the image of the West. But by the early 1990s, not only were old elites still active in many parts of the former Communist world—some of them transformed from *apparachniks* into *entrepreneurniks*—but the privatization of their economies was making heavy weather. Under the strain, the opportunities and the uncertainties of the post-1989 years provided space for a variety of players, not all of whom had democracy or the market as their goals. Just as the Springtime of Freedom of 1848 was closed by Napoleon's coup of 1851, the Ode to Freedom at the Berlin Wall was the prelude to the ethnic conflicts of the 1990s and the carnage at Sarajevo.

A Movement Society: Transnational and Violent?

How representative was the movement of 1989? It certainly had peculiarities due to the nearly unique nature of the Soviet bloc. For example, it was the first movement in history to destroy a powerful multistate empire in one blow. It was also—at least at first—predominantly handled through peaceful negotiation, with the menace of mass violence held in abeyance in almost every country of the region until state socialism was gone. But despite its particularity, the 1989 cycle can help us to see some of the ways in which the national social movement has changed in its two-hundred-year history. If these changes are substantial and cumulative, then the world may be moving from a logic of alternation between periods of movement and periods of quiescence into a permanent movement society. At this stage, all we can do is guess at the possibilities and speculate about their implications.

Transnational Movements

When we return to the comparison between Clarkson's failure in 1789 and the success of 1989, we see one major difference; that movements spread far more rapidly now than they did in the past—even in the absence of formal organizations. This is, in part, an expression of the universality of the repertoire of collective action, in part, due to the rapidity of global communication, and, in part, because of the appearance of transnational movements. The contrast between antislavery in 1789 and the movements of 1989 will illustrate all three points.

In contrast to Clarkson's inability to bring abolitionism across a mere thirty miles of water in 1789, the knowledge of how to mount a social movement had become so general by 1989 that the liberation from state socialism took remarkably similar form across a continent and a half. For example, the human chain that protestors stretched across the Baltics in 1989 was the same tactic that had been used a few years earlier by the European peace movement. The "round table" that was used to outline the future division of power in Poland was adopted in many other countries of the region. "What is remarkable," write Valerie Bunce and Dennis Chong, "is the speed with which the masses in each country converged on particular strategies, coordinated its actions, and successfully executed its plans" (1990: 3).

Second, the appearance of global television had a great influence in the diffusion of the movement, and this is not limited to Eastern Europe in 1989. In the eighteenth century, movements were still diffused by word of mouth, by print and association, or by people like Clarkson who acted as missionaries of movement. But in 1989, the spread of the democratic movement in Eastern Europe—not to mention its tragic echo in China—left little doubt that collective action can spread by global communication. Not only do potential protestors learn about political opportunities through the mass media; when they see people not very different from themselves acting in contentious ways succeeding, it is easy for them to imagine themselves doing the same. And just as they learn *from* television, they have become skilled at using it to project word of their movements to international centers of power.

Third, because of the centrality of the national state, movements like antislavery spread slowly and took different forms in different parts of Europe (Drescher 1987: 199); so did the democratic movement of the late eighteenth century. In the nineteenth century, both radical democracy and socialism were diffused more quickly, but it still took fifty years for social democracy to reach Russia—and it arrived in very different form than in the West.

The most recent cycles of protest have been inherently—and perhaps increasingly—transnational and thus have diffused more rapidly. The decolonization movements in the former British and French empires; the European and American New Left of the 1960s; the peace movements of the 1980s; global environmental movements like Greenpeace: These are no longer cases of simple imitation and diffusion, but expressions of the same movement acting against similar targets. The movements of 1989 in Eastern Europe were extreme in this respect, but in their interdependence and mutual dependence on international trends, they were not so different than these other recent movements.

The archetypical case of a transnational movement in recent years has been militant, fundamentalist Islam. Its spread from Iran to Afghanistan, to the Bekaa Valley and the Gaza Strip, and more recently to North Africa bridges institutional religion and guerilla warfare. In between these extremes of violence and institutionalization, its organizers have employed an array of similar tactics everywhere: the mobilization of slum dwellers, the intimidation of women, the extortion of funds from small businessmen—even elections, when this has been convenient. One deeply rooted secular movement—the Palestinian Liberation Organization—has been severely challenged by Islamic competition; the Soviet army was forced out of Afghanistan by another; while the Sudanese government was overthrown by a third. The Algerian government was only saved from Islamic domination by a military takeover. And by 1992, even secular Egypt was under attack from internationally supported fundamentalists.

The spread of such transnational movements as militant Islam leads to a larger and more portentous question. Since we seem to be living in an increasingly interdependent world, are we becoming a single movement society? And if we are, will movements lose the cyclical and national rhythms of the past and take on the character of continual turbulence spreading across national boundaries out of the control of national states? A movement society may be an increasingly violent society. What is the evidence for such a claim?

Ex-prisoners of the State?[2]

In his book *Turbulence in World Politics*, James Rosenau argues that we are becoming a single, more turbulent world. Rosenau sees the entire period since the end of World War II as the beginning of a new era of "global turbulence." Among the factors that convince him that ours is an era of turbulence is "a marked increase in the number of spontaneous collective actions" and their rapid spread around the world (1990: 369). If Rosenau is right, then the implications for the future of civil politics is troubling.

The national social movement grew out of the efforts of states to consolidate power, integrate their peripheries, and standardize discourse among groups of citizens and between them and their rulers. Many of the characteristics of the social movements we have seen in this book grew out of that relationship—including the conventionalization of collective action, the channeling of movements into national opportunity structures, and the institution of citizenship itself. If movements are becoming transnational, they may be freeing themselves of state structures and thence of the constraining influence of state-mediated contention.

Three kinds of arguments can be made on behalf of this thesis. First, the dominant economic trends of the late twentieth century have been toward greater international interdependence. "The increasing fluidity of capital, labor, commodities, money, and cultural practices," argues Charles Tilly in a recent paper, "undermines the capacity of any

particular state to control events within its boundaries" (1991: 1). One result is that strikes that used to be mounted against domestic capitalists must now be risked against multinational corporations whose capital can be moved elsewhere. The interdependent global economy may be producing transnational collective action.[3]

Second, the economic growth of the 1970s and 1980s increased the imbalance of wealth and poverty between the North and West and the East and South, while bringing their citizens cognitively and physically closer to one another. This is not only the result of faster communication and cheaper transportation, but because, since the end of World War II, Third World countries have attempted to mimic the economic success of the West. The result is that the East and South have internalized elements of the social structure of the West and North but have not internalized their wealth" (Arrighi 1991: 40).

Interdependence and the international gap in income both contribute to a third factor: a continued stream of migration that takes different forms than in the past. In the nineteenth century, much of the international movement of population went from core to periphery, with migrants permanently leaving their homes behind. The current wave of migration overwhelmingly favors the industrial countries of the West and immigrants seldom lose touch with their country of origin. "The Filipino maid in Milan and the Tamil busdriver in Toronto," observes Benedict Anderson, "are only a few sky hours away" from their homeland and seconds away by satellite telephone communication (1992: 8).

While mass population movements have become one of the major sources of domestic conflict in the contemporary world (Zolberg 1989), citizenship—the expected outcome of immigration in the nineteenth century—has become an impossible dream for most immigrants. A major cultural cleavage pits immigrant groups with restricted citizenship rights against increasingly restive indigenous populations in states whose governments, from Paris to California, are under pressure to reduce the rights of resident immigrants and to cut them off from further entry. All over the West, from the eastern border of Germany to the southern border of the United States, doors are being shut to immigrants, and—just as important—earlier arrivals are being sealed off into immigrant ghettos.

One result—the rise of racist movements in Western Europe—we have already seen. But another is the rise of what Anderson calls "long-distance nationalism" (1992). For every nineteenth-century Mazzini and Garibaldi who fomented revolution at a great distance from their home country, there are thousands of Palestinians in New York, Punjabis in Toronto, Croats in Australia, Tamils in Britain, Irish in Massachusetts, Algerians in France, and Cubans in Miami whose ties to their countries of origin are kept alive through transnational social networks (Anderson 1992: 12).

Most of these meekly accept their subaltern status and hope for an affluent return to their homelands. But others use the ease of international communication and transportation to support movements at home. By more or less covert financial contributions, by fax and E-mail, by letter bombs and discrete arms purchases, these long-distance nationalists are disturbing the neat symmetry between national states and national social movements that the world has inherited from the last century.

Not only nationalist migrants, but transnational ecologists, developmentalists, and fighters for the rights of minorities increasingly aim their actions at other people's governments. We live in an age when rubber tappers in Brazil can enjoy the assistance of American nongovernmental organizations; when U.N.-supported technical teams teach Indian ecologists to use video cameras that they can employ to mobilize peasants; and when racist propaganda produced in the United States finds it way to the apartments of European skinheads. The modern state, which began its consolidation in opposition to its territorial enemies, is becoming increasingly permeable to nonterritorial movements. As a result, the social movement may be becoming an ex-prisoner of the state.

If this is true, what are the implications for the character of social movements and for social conflict in general? If nothing else, the characteristic pattern whereby political cycles result from the processing of challenges within national states may be extended over time and space by cross-national extension. Fundamentalist Islam is the most successful example: When the expansion of the Iranian revolution failed in the Iran–Iraq war, Afghanistan became the major field of action; when the Red Army left Kabul, fundamentalist militants moved on from Peshawar to Cairo, to Algiers, and eventually to New York.[4] Where movements respond to political opportunities across state boundaries, they can escape the mediation and control of any single state.

As long as these expressions of integral religious nationalism were bounded within the Third World, Western governments and their citizens remained relatively indifferent. But with the attack by Islamic militants on the World Trade Center in New York in 1993, long-distance nationalism moved to the West. The diffusion of militant fundamentalism to the heart of world capitalism showed that, in the interdependent contemporary world, modernization does not equal secularization and that international trends deeply affect the internal order of states.

This leads to an even more worrying concern. Over the past two hundred years, there has been a slow, ragged but inexorable civilizing trend in the nature of collective action and in the state's means of controlling it. As modular repertoires linked social movements to the state, violent and direct forms of attack were increasingly replaced by the power of numbers, by solidarity, and by an informal dialogue between states and movements. The cycle of the 1960s, with its remarkably low level of violence and employment of nonviolent direct action, was the apotheosis of this trend. But the guerilla wars, the hostage takings, and the ethnic conflicts of the past two decades must make us wonder whether the trend to a peaceful repertoire was no more than a historical parenthesis and is now being reversed.

The integralist beliefs—if not the violent methods—of militant Islam bear a striking resemblance to trends in Western culture: to politicized ministers who preach intolerance on Sunday morning television; to the "rescuers" of unborn fetuses who refuse to recognize women's rights to reproductive freedom; to orthodox attacks on secular values in education and personal life; and to xenophobic political parties that claim their nations' natural superiority. The methods are different, but how different are the French *Front National* or the Hungarian Way from the zealots of Gush Emunim or the fanatics of the Party of God?

Citizens of modern states have lived through such "moments of madness" before. It is enough to remember that severed heads were paraded around the streets of Paris on pikes during the great democratic French Revolution, or that Jews were attacked in France and Germany during the Springtime of Freedom in 1848, to find parallels for the violence and intolerance that have emerged in the West since the 1980s. The concern raised by these more recent outbreaks is that if, in fact, a "movement society" *is* developing out of the social, economic, and cultural changes of the late

twentieth century, it will have a different cultural valence than the movements that broke out in Boston in 1765, in Paris in 1848, and in the nonviolent movements of the 1960s.

Is the New World Order that was supposed to result from the liberation of 1989 turning instead into a permanent state of violence and disorder? Have the resources for violent collective action become so widely accessible, integralist identities so widespread, and militants so freed of the national state that a permanent and violent movement society is resulting? Or will the current plethora of ethnic and religious movements be partially outgrown, partially domesticated, and partially mediated by the political process, as in previous cycles of protest?

The violence and intolerance of the 1990s constitute a truly alarming trend. But this is not the first great wave of movement in history, nor will it be the last. If its dynamic comes to resemble the social movements that we have encountered in this book, then its power will at first be ferocious, uncontrolled, and widely diffused, but later ephemeral. If so, then like previous waves of movement, it will ultimately disperse "like a flood tide which loosens up much of the soil but leaves alluvial deposits in its wake. "[5]

NOTES

1. "No hint of subsequent radicalization, no echo of social conflict, no shadow of the Terror could mar this season of commemoration," observed historians Keith Baker and Steven Kaplan of the Bicentennial in their preface to Roger Chartier's *The Cultural Origins of the French Revolution*, p. xii. Even as they celebrated it, the French in 1989 were interring their Revolution. See Kaplan's *Adieu 1789*, which reads the Bicentennial as a celebratory rite for the funeral of the Revolution.

2. In a 1991 paper, Charles Tilly provocatively writes, "As Europeans unconsciously subvert the state in the very act of affirming its

desirability, comparative-historical sociologists are unwittingly peripheralizing the state while declaring its centrality." See his "Prisoners of the State," p. 1.

3. The most articulate advocates of this global view of industrial conflict are Giovanni Arrighi and Beverly Silver. See the former's "World Income Inequalities and the Future of Socialism," and the latter's "Class Struggle and Kondratieff Waves, 1870 to the Present," as well as her "Labor Unrest and Capital Accumulation on a World Scale."

4. See the account of the links between Afghan-trained Islamic militants and the attackers of the World Trade Center in the *New York Times,* August 11, 1993.

5. Aristide Zolberg, "Moments of Madness," p. 206.

REFERENCES

Anderson, Benedict (1992). "Long-Distance Nationalism. World Capitalism and the Rise of Identity Politics," Center for Asian Studies, Amsterdam, Netherlands.

Arrighi, Giovanni (1991). "World Income Inequalities and the Future of Socialism," *New Left Review* 189:39–65.

Bunce, Valerie and Dennis Chong (1990). "The Party's Over: Mass Protest and the End of Communist Rule in Eastern Europe," presented to the annual meeting of the American Political Science Association, San Francisco, Calif.

Calhoun, Craig (1993). "New Social Movements of the Early Nineteenth Century," *Social Science History* 17:385–427.

Drescher, Seymour (1987). Capitalism and Anti-slavery: British Mobilization in Comparative Perspective. Oxford: Oxford University Press.

Drescher, Seymour (1991). "British Way, French Way: Opinion Building and Revolution in the Second French Slave Emancipation," *American Historical Review* 96:709–34.

Drescher, Seymour (1994). "Whose Abolition? Popular Pressure and the Ending of the British Slave Trade," *Past and Present.*

Hardin, Russell (1982) *Collective Action.* Baltimore and London: Johns Hopkins University Press.

Hellman, Judith Adler (1987). *Journeys Among Women. Feminism in Five Italian Cities.* Oxford and New York: Oxford University Press.

Ignazi, Piero (1992). *Dal PCI al PDS.* Bologna: Il Mulino.

Rosenau, James (1990). *Turbulence in World Politics: A Theory of Change and Continuity.* Princeton: Princeton University Press.

Tilly, Charles (1991). "Prisoners of the State." Working Paper No. 129, the Center for Studies of Social Change, the New School for Social Research, New York.

Zolberg, Aristide R. (1989). Escape from Violence: Conflict and the Refugee Crisis in the Developing World. Oxford: Oxford University Press.

Conclusion
The Centrality of Social Movements

If I can't Dance . . . I don't want to be part of your revolution.

—EMMA GOLDMAN

Although collective action has a history as old as humanity itself, the social movement is a distinctly modern form of collective action. The modern world emerged with the rise of capitalism, rational-legal authority, industrialization, urbanization, and state-building. Social movements were intertwined with these processes as both cause and consequence of the changes associated with modernity. Since then, social movements have become increasingly central to the discipline of sociology and the production of society.

Within sociology social movements embody and illustrate many fundamental sociological concepts. Consider the process of institutionalization. The concept refers to a complex dynamic that begins when people act collectively to achieve a particular goal. If we assume that they meet with some success, their actions bring about social change that gradually becomes institutionalized as part of the social order and eventually becomes accepted as a routine part of life. Through this dynamic, social practices that may have been unthinkable for one generation of people may be taken for granted by another generation of people.

An example is provided by the woman suffrage movement's protracted efforts to win the right to vote for women. In the mid-nineteenth century when this movement began, the idea that women should vote was unthinkable to many people and was perceived as too radical even by many women's rights activists. Nevertheless, a seventy-year

movement unfolded, gradually changing social realities to a point where voting rights were granted to women in 1920. As this practice was institutionalized, it was taken for granted by subsequent generations. In our own time, even the most ardent anti-feminists have not proposed that the right to vote should be taken away from women. Thus, over several generations, this social movement saw its goals become a routine part of our social structure in a way that completely reversed cultural understandings of what was "unthinkable." Understanding how this dynamic operates in the case of social movements can help us to see other aspects of our "taken for granted" social structure as the social creations of prior generations of social actors.

This process is rich in other sociological lessons as well. Several different sociological theories agree that society is a social creation but that people often "forget" their role in creating their society. This process of forgetting is central to the concepts of alienation and reification. In the Marxist analysis of alienation, people do not just forget that they create the world; they do so (as workers) in ways that transfer power to others (capitalists) who use this power to further their own goals. In the social constructionist analysis of reification, people lose sight of their role in creating social reality and come to see their social environment as purely objective "social facts" that control them and provide no meaningful options for change. In both traditions, the price of forgetting the human authorship of the world is a denial of the ability to change the world, and hence a loss of potential control over one's own life. Of all the forms of action studied by sociologists, social movements are the most dramatic way that human beings periodically break through the illusions of an alienated and reified world view to reclaim their authorship of the world and their power to shape that world in keeping with their aspirations.

This analysis suggests a somewhat heroic view of social movements that must be tempered with an awareness of the limitations on such efforts. One of the most profound sociological insights is that purposive social action often results in unintended and unanticipated consequences. That is, people seeking to do one thing often end up doing other things that they never wanted or thought would happen. Once again, social movements provide rich illustrations of the unintended and unanticipated consequences of action. History is replete with examples of revolutionary movements in the name of liberty and freedom that ushered in new forms of tyranny and oppression. Contemporary movements often successfully agitate for government regulation of some social problem, only to realize that their efforts have contributed to another social problem in the form of centralized state power. Finally, it is not at all uncommon for successful movements to stimulate counter-movements that oppose them—and sometimes the counter-movements achieve more success than the initial movement. The lesson of these examples is not that such efforts should not be attempted (as conservatives have historically argued). The lesson is rather that social action is always more complex than our ability to predict or control it in the moment of its unfolding. Social movements provide some of our most poignant examples of this lesson.

Collective action also has great relevance for addressing two major debates in sociological theory concerning the relation between agency and structure and the connections between micro- and macro-levels of society. The agency-structure debate is about balancing the fact that people choose courses of action with the reality that social structure always limits their choices. Sociological theories have tended to favor either agency or structure at the expense of the other, producing theories that exaggerate the degree of freedom in social life or that present an overly deterministic view of social action. The micro-macro debate is about balancing social practices on the micro-level in which individuals play a prominent role with social structures on the macro-level dominated by groups and organizations. Once again sociological theories have tended to emphasize either micro-level interaction or macro-level structures, thus sidestepping the difficult question of how the two levels are interrelated.

Social movements have much to offer these debates. As a topic, movements offer concrete, accessible examples for exploring what are otherwise very abstract theoretical debates. By their very nature, social movements are vitally concerned with agency, that is, with finding ways of acting effectively in a given social situation. Such actions are always conditioned by social structures that limit possible actions and present a certain combination of opportunities and constraints. Thus, one way to clarify abstract speculations about agency and structure is to examine the specific cases provided by social movements and the lessons that such movements offer. In a parallel way, movements consist of a limited number of social actors on the micro-level seeking to bring about change in macro-level structures that they define as a problem. By studying the conditions under which social movements succeed or fail in their attempts to modify macro-level structures, we can shed light on the larger question of how these multiple levels of social reality are related.

Social movements are also relevant to these debates as a set of practices. That is, social activists confront their own versions of the agency-structure debate and the macro-micro dilemma as concrete practical problems they must overcome. These problems cast social movement activists into the role of everyday sociologists who must find effective ways to engage in collective action. Whereas social scientists test their hypotheses through research, social activists test their hypotheses through strategies and tactics designed to achieve movement goals. Social activists are thus amateur sociologists conducting ongoing experiments to overcome obstacles to collective action posed by macro-level structures. A close study of the theories-in-use developed by social activists, thereby, promises to enrich academic sociological theory.

In all these ways, social movements embody core insights of the sociological tradition and contain many lessons for that tradition. The increasing centrality of social movements within sociology is thus a welcome development that can help us understand some of the most complex issues in the construction and transformation of the social world. However, there is an even more important reason why social movements have become more central to the discipline of sociology. Simply stated, social movements have also become more central in society over the last two hundred years. We live in a world increasingly shaped by the purposive efforts of people acting collectively to bring about certain outcomes. Thus, the growing centrality of social movements in the discipline of sociology is an appropriate reflection of their increasing role in the production and transformation of our society.

This development is a logical extension of the fact that social movements were born with the modern age. For most of human history, social order was explained through complex mythical, cosmological, or religious beliefs that presumed that the world had divine or supernatural origins. Such views were challenged by the French Enlightenment of the eighteenth century, which substituted reason for faith as a means of evaluating social order. In this distinctly modern intellectual tradition, the social world came to be seen as a social construction that could be other than it was. If the current social order could not meet these new standards of rationality, then it was incumbent upon rational thinkers to transform it into a better one. The premise that society is a social construction that can be transformed through purposive collective action is the intellectual heritage that ties social movements to the modern age.

During the last two hundred years, this insight has grown in several ways. With the expansion of education, literacy, democracy, and opportunities for political participation, greater numbers of people have come to share the premise that society is a social construction subject to purposive reconstruction through collective action. And with the growing reach of modern technology, more aspects of social life have actually become subject to social reconstruction. Even aspects of our world that until recently have still seemed "natural" are increasingly coming under the sway of human intervention—for better or worse. Examples include new technologies that are transforming the planetary atmosphere and genetic engineering that is altering human reproduction. As the "natural" recedes in the face of increasing social intervention, more of our world becomes a socially constructed product reflecting the goals of those with the power to pursue their preferred outcomes. We have thus entered an age that the French social theorist Alain Touraine describes as the "self-production of society."

Although we may live in an increasingly self-produced society, clearly there is no consensus about who we are—about who comprises the "collective self" that is producing its own society. Such disagreements come as no surprise to those familiar with the sociology of conflict. As we have emphasized throughout this book, the roots of social conflict are built into social organization itself, because any social order will benefit some groups and not others. Among the benefits that modern social order provides (to some) is the potential to direct social change as we move into the twenty-first century. This potential is likely to become central in future conflicts over the shape of modern society. There is every reason to think that social movements will play an increasingly important role in these ongoing conflicts over the self-production of society.